Visions of Canada

The Alan B. Plaunt Memorial Lectures

1958–1992

EDITED BY BERNARD OSTRY
AND JANICE YALDEN

Published for Carleton University by
McGill-Queen's University Press
Montreal & Kingston · London · Ithaca

© McGill-Queen's University Press 2004
ISBN 0-7735-2638-2 (cloth)
ISBN 0-7735-2662-5 (paper)

Legal deposit second quarter 2004
Bibliothèque nationale du Québec

Printed in Canada on acid-free paper.

Publishing consultant: Malcolm Lester & Associates

McGill-Queen's University Press acknowledges the support of the Canada
Council for the Arts for our publishing program. We also acknowledge
the financial support of the Government of Canada through the Book
Publishing Industry Development Program (BPIDP) for our publishing
activities.

National Library of Canada Cataloguing in Publication

Visions of Canada: the Alan B. Plaunt memorial lectures/edited
by Bernard Ostry and Janice Yalden

Lectures given 1958–1992.
Includes bibliographical references.
ISBN 0-7735-2638-2 (bound)
ISBN 0-7735-2662-5 (pbk)

I. Canada. I. Ostry, Bernard, 1927– II. Yalden, Janice, 1931– III. Title:
Alan B. Plaunt memorial lectures.

FC60.V58 2004   971   C2003-907456-0

Typeset in Times 10/13
by Caractéra inc., Quebec City

VISIONS OF CANADA

Alan B. Plaunt

Contents

Preface
The Plaunt Lectures in the Intellectual Life of Carleton University

In 1956 Claude Bissell, then president of Carleton University, entered into negotiations with the Plaunt family, who wished to establish a lecture series in memory of Alan B. Plaunt, a pioneer of Canadian broadcasting. Plaunt's widow and his daughter, Frances, felt that it was appropriate the lectures be given at Carleton, situated in the Ottawa Valley where Plaunt was born and grew up.

The first lecture was delivered in 1958, and the series continued until 1992. The presentations, scheduled for the spring and signalling the end of the academic year, were a major intellectual and social event at Carleton for many years. Prepared under the aegis of the president's office, and later that of the dean of the faculty of arts, they were preceded by a dinner in honour of the current speaker, and a reception was always given at their conclusion. For a long time, guest speakers were asked to give two lectures on two consecutive days, but as other events increasingly came to compete with public lectures in the evenings, the presentations were shortened to a single lecture.

In his introduction both to the series and to Professor Jacob Viner's inaugural lecture, the Honourable Brooke Claxton (then a member of the Board of Governors of the university) noted that Alan Plaunt's life was cut short by illness in September 1941, when he was thirty-seven. Claxton stated that Plaunt, "for all his adult years ... devoted a large part of his talents, his energy, and his private means to his concept of what Canada was and his vision of what it might become. More than almost anyone else he had to do with the birth of the Canadian Broadcasting Corporation and the formation of its character as a great source of information and entertainment serving the Canadian people in the cause of national unity and understanding." The lectures were designed to celebrate Plaunt's interests and achievements, and their publication will continue in the same spirit, for the themes chosen by the lecturers have proven to be both important and persistent in public discourse in Canada. They are also themes that represent significant areas of research at Carleton, an institution with an outlook and opportunities specific to its location in the nation's capital.

Each lecture has been rendered as a paper in its own right. To this end, asides tangential to a lecture's topic but delivered during the course of the lecture have been eliminated.

Many individuals at Carleton University assisted me in the initial preparation of the manuscripts. In particular, Dr Stuart Adam, vice president Academic and provost of Carleton University, provided financial support for this stage of the project; Dr Roger Blockley, dean of Graduate Studies and Research, furnished invaluable advice throughout the process; Patti Harper, the Carleton archivist, and her staff were patient and helpful in locating the manuscripts – dispersed through many files; and Ross Mutton and his staff found the audio and video tapes needed to complete the collection. To all of these colleagues, I would like to express my gratitude for their support and encouragement.

JANICE YALDEN
Emeritus Professor and former dean of the Faculty of Arts
Carleton University
December 2003

Foreword

My involvement in the preparation and production of this splendid volume of elegant words and brilliant ideas began by accident. It came to fruition by luck.

In late 1991 I was asked whether I would be interested in delivering a lecture in the Plaunt series at Carleton University. I was as surprised as delighted: surprised because it had been more than a decade since I left Ottawa, and I had almost forgotten the wonderfully informative and inspiring lectures I'd enjoyed in the past; and delighted because I had been offered an opportunity to speak about public broadcasting, the subject area in which I had started and ended my days of formal employment. Also, it was the subject area of Plaunt's greatest contribution to his country but one that had never been touched upon in the series honouring his name! The "accident," however, was not so much my lecture as the fact that when I inquired in the mid-nineties as to why I had ceased being notified of the series, I was told that it had been terminated by Carleton and the Plaunt family. Mine had been not only the first lecture on Plaunt's subject, but alas also the last in the series.

Learning of the reasons for termination did not lessen my shock and consternation. What to do? While it seemed clear that restarting the series would prove impossible, I wondered whether the lectures themselves might, by being published (or republished in a few cases), prove of value and possibly encourage a similar new series. But my connections with Carleton had long ceased, except in the case of one distinguished scholar – to our great good fortune.

Janice Yalden, one of my dearest friends, had devoted her working life to Carleton and not only lived in Ottawa, but also still maintained her pre-retirement contacts there. She needed no convincing about the value of the proposed project

and immediately contacted her former colleague Dean Roger Blockley. In short
order, she was given every assistance in seeking out the files, correspondence,
and lectures themselves. Without her enthusiastic support and that of both her
former colleagues and the university itself, the project would have gone nowhere.

Although I had spent much of my working life in areas of public service
devoted to cultural policy – and was thus familiar with the issues affecting
subsidized publishing – I had long forgotten just how dependent publishers had
become on financial assistance. Once again I was able to turn to friends: first,
to Robert Rabinovitch, the new president of the CBC, who generously did not
hesitate both to advise and to seek financial ways to assist. Help was soon
forthcoming conditional on finding other parties. Another dear friend and former
colleague, Allan Gotlieb, directed me to the Donner Foundation, which he chairs,
and to sister institutions. So I am forever indebted to Janice and her Carleton
colleagues; to Allan, without whose friendship and the Donner Foundation's
financial help this work would not have seen the light of day; and, of course, to
Robert Rabinovitch and the CBC.

We have made every effort to include all the Plaunt lectures. In some cases,
this proved impossible. There is no text extant, for instance, of George Steiner's
lecture (and he doesn't recall even giving it!); Henry Steele Commager's lecture
is also lost (and a search by the archivist of Commager's papers at Amherst
College failed to turn it up); and only a portion of Jean Boggs's lecture is
audible.

It is not always clear why the Plaunt lecturers chose the topics they did, but
in most cases they offer their own reasons, locating their remarks in the context
of significant events of the time. Such is the case with F.R. Scott's 1959 discussion
of civil rights as the Canadian Bill of Rights was being drafted, Jane Jacob's
1970 lectures on Canada's newly urbanizing economy, Peter Lougheed's 1986
thoughts on the report of the Royal Commission on Economic Union and
Development Prospects for Canada in the midst of free-trade negotiations with
the United States, Mel Hurtig's 1988 response to the *fait accompli* – the 1987
Free Trade Agreement – and Lise Bissonnette's 1991 contemplation of the
viability of Canadian federalism following the release of the Bélanger-Campeau
report. In other cases, the choice of topic more specifically reflects the speaker's
own experience: Mordechai Richler's 1973 lectures on being a Canadian writer,
John Hirsch's 1975 description of his life in Canadian theatre, and Allan Gotlieb's
1989 reflections on Canadian foreign policy following the end of his tenure as
Canadian ambassador to the United States. Still, for a few of the lectures, we
can only hazard a guess as to what was in the speaker's mind. What, for example,
provided the impetus for economist Jacob Viner, in 1958, to focus his inaugural
lecture on Canada-US relations? Could it have been the landslide victory of Prime

Minister John Diefenbaker's government in the Canadian Parliament? Almost fifty years after the event, we are left to wonder.

Ultimately, the book speaks for itself; it needs neither my praise nor criticism. It should be read by everyone previously unlucky enough not to have been exposed to these lucid and imaginative minds. In its pages one will find both the famous and the forgotten. One will discover a freshness of thought that the years have not eclipsed as well as a challenging relevance particularly apt in today's "globilized" world. These lectures deserve to be read, studied, and discussed by policy makers, students, and the public at large. Enjoy!

BERNARD OSTRY
Chair and CEO, ImagiNationsUnlimited, Inc.
December 2003

Introduction

I am truly honoured to introduce this volume of Plaunt Memorial Lectures, which pays tribute to one of the great pioneers of modern day Canada: Alan B. Plaunt.

Plaunt saw national broadcasting as central to bridging the vast geographic, linguistic, and cultural divisions that made Canada an "improbable nation." He believed that Canada's very survival depended on tempering the growing cultural influence of our American neighbours, making him the first persistent voice on an issue that now resonates globally ... and a true visionary.

From 1958 to 1992 the Plaunt Memorial Lectures helped to further Plaunt's ambitions for Canada by providing a platform for discussion of our nation's most important and enduring issues. Plaunt lecturers were influential and innovative thinkers of their times. In 1959, for example, Frank Scott shared views about constitutional change that shaped the actions of Prime Minister Pierre Trudeau almost two decades later. In 1975 John Hirsch's personal and often amusing account of coming to Canada as a Hungarian refugee and finding a land of immense cultural opportunity was a poignant reminder that our nation was built by diverse peoples unified in their search for refuge and hope for their children. The Hon. Peter Loughheed's 1986 plea for support of free trade dealt with one of the most important – and divisive – issues ever to test Canadians' confidence in themselves and their nation.

It is the last of the Plaunt Lectures, Bernard Ostry's 1992 contribution, entitled *The Survival of Canada through Broadcasting*, that most directly addresses Plaunt's area of greatest achievement. Ostry recounts Plaunt's "brilliantly successful lobby and agitation" for national public broadcasting in Canada and equates it with the Canadian National Railway as a contribution on the path to nationhood. Speaking during hard fiscal times, when CBC/Radio-Canada's budget was under attack, Ostry reminded us that only a strong and vibrant public broadcaster can complement the activities of the private communications firms and deliver high quality, genuinely Canadian choices. In urging a return to the principles so hard fought for by Plaunt, Ostry realized a prediction made by Plaunt's cohort Graham Spry that "every generation will have to re-fight the battle for national broadcasting."

Fast forward to 2004. Globalization and technological change have fundamentally altered the world in which we live and how we function as individuals and citizens. The same forces have also changed broadcasting, yielding an interactive, multichannel, and specialized universe that offers a dazzling array of choice. As in Plaunt's day, however, Canadians continue to be bombarded by foreign programming. Market forces still make it more profitable to broadcast popular American programming than to produce indigenous choices. If we accept that shaping "made-in-Canada" solutions to modern-day challenges requires that Canadians understand one another and where they fit in the world, we must reach the same conclusion as Plaunt did so many years ago: Canada needs a public space for Canadian voices, perspectives, and discourse now more than ever.

For almost seventy years on radio, over fifty years on television, and about a decade on the internet, CBC/Radio-Canada has been connecting Canadians to one another and to Canada. We remain the only broadcaster offering services in English and French across the country and in eight Aboriginal languages in the North. Our award-winning news and information programming delivers an unmatched Canadian perspective on events across Canada and around the world. We showcase Canadian talent and nurture Canada's creative and production industries. We offer a space for sharing Canadian experiences across regions, languages, and cultures. We provide a safe and educational viewing experience for Canada's children and youth. We present Canadian drama, documentaries, public affairs, and arts programming produced in all parts of this country. Finally, like every other broadcaster in Canada and around the world, we continue to evolve and renew our programming and operations to ensure that we remain relevant in these rapidly changing times. Indeed, we continue to seek out ways to cooperate with our international counterparts to ensure that the most diverse and interesting product is available to our respective audiences.

Plaunt would be proud of today's CBC/Radio-Canada and delighted that 95 per cent of Canadians still consider their national public broadcaster to be an essential service. He would also be very pleased to see the Plaunt Memorial

Lectures published in this way so that new generations of Canadians can under-stand the hard-fought battles that have gone into making Canada the best place in the world to live.

ROBERT RABINOVITCH
President and CEO, CBC/Radio-Canada
January 2004

VISIONS OF CANADA

I

Canada and Its Giant Neighbour

JACOB VINER, 1958

PART ONE

When I had chosen as the topic of this paper the relations – cultural, political, and economic – of Canada with its giant neighbour, with the intent of giving special attention to the role played in these relations by the disparity of size between the two nations, Canadian friends, out of overflowing kindness for which I am duly grateful, wrote at once to warn me that the topic I had chosen was a provocative one, perhaps especially so for an ex-Canadian; that the time was inopportune since there was running in Canada a current of anti-American sentiment, which might only be a ripple but might possibly be a tidal wave; and that as sensitive toes abounded almost everywhere, about the only way to avoid stepping on at least some of them was to avoid doing any stepping.

Above all, they warned me – not, I hope, in the belief that I stood in very special need of such warning – that any lapse from dead seriousness, in tone or manner or matter, any attempt at irony or wit, by an American dealing at this time with almost any aspect of Canadian-American relations, would be exceedingly hazardous behaviour. In the prevailing climate of opinion and sentiment, they told me, Canadians were ill-disposed toward even innocent merriment in this field, and many of them would regard a joke – even a passably good one – as not at all a laughing matter.

This all took me aback, as well it might. It made me realize how much out of touch I was with current Canadian affairs and how ill-prepared I was to avoid fluttering any dovecotes, if such avoidance should have been a major objective of mine. But the warning came too late, I fear, for me to do much about it, even if I had known what to do. I have upon occasion tried to trim my words to the supposed sensibilities of an audience, but invariably the truth did out despite my best efforts to the contrary. Dullness I can easily achieve without half trying, but it somehow does not seem appropriate deliberately to impose it on an innocent audience. Resort to synthetic and contrived sweetness might constitute a barrier to genuine analysis of genuine or imagined problems. A sophisticated audience, moreover, should be expected to be easily surfeited with rhetorical honey, "whereof a little more than a little is by much too much." Moreover, though I have an abiding affection for my native land, I have affection also, and beyond the call of duty, for my adopted land. If the tug between rival sentiments were to become a tug between sentiment and obligation, I would feel compelled to follow the maxim that I once proposed for the mantelpiece above the fireplace of a projected Canadian Club in an American city – a proposal that was even more promptly rejected than the club-building project – *non ubi nascor, sed ubi pascor* (not where I was born, but where I feed).

I will therefore say my piece as I see it, with all the objectivity, but also with most of the frankness, I am capable of. A character in one of Shakespeare's plays is made to say that he was not in a mood for music, unless the orchestra could play music that could not be heard, which was the only kind he liked. I have not tried to compose silent music for this paper, but if I do perchance strike what seem to be jarring notes, I beg they be blamed on my delivery and not on my planned score.

The emphasis throughout will be on the disparity in size between the two neighbouring nations and its apparent consequences. The aspects of size I am concerned with are relative size of population, of aggregate wealth, of power, but not, of course, of area, with respect to which both countries are giants, and Canada is somewhat the more gigantic.

My first topic is the pattern of cultural relations between the two peoples and the impact thereon of the preponderance in numbers and in aggregate wealth of the American people. The aspects of culture I will deal with will be such matters as literature and music and art and learning, and not the differences in moral patterns or tribal rituals or dietary habits that engage the professional attention of the cultural anthropologists when they compare two peoples.

The phenomenon of cultural nationalism is a familiar one wherever a people believes that its native culture is in danger of erosion or of submergence by the impact of an external culture. I did not have to wait for warnings from my Canadian friends to be aware that there was widespread concern in Canada lest her indigenous culture be swamped out by an invasion of American culture. I could reasonably expect there to be in Canada a tendency to find in the preponderance in size of the American culture the chief explanation of any capacity it might be demonstrating to dislodge the native, or the inherited British, elements in Canada's pattern of intellectual and artistic life. It is this question that I propose to examine, but I do so with claims to purely amateur status that even college football, in your country and in mine, cannot rival.

The most effective single barrier to external subversion of a native culture is physical isolation, by which term I mean to cover not only distance from foreign neighbours, or intervening mountain barriers, swamps, jungles, but also contrived physical obstacles to communication, such as poison arrows or iron curtains.

As between Canada and the United States, there are no physical barriers of consequence to movement of people or ideas, and there were few even when such movement was more earth-bound than it is today. I suppose it is still true that as far as purely physical boundaries are concerned, long-range north-and-south movement across the Canadian-American boundary remains on the whole easier than long-range east-and-west movement within Canada. But the progress of highway and railroad facilities, and the development first of the telegraph and the telephone, later of the airplane, and still later of the radio and television, which are relatively free from the limitations of earthbound communication, have physically at least lessened the disparity in internal geographical unity as between Canada and the United States. The movement of the Canadian population northward has, I presume, operated to increase the average physical distance of Canadians from the contaminating American boundary. Nevertheless, I think I need not further labour the point that physical obstacles to communication are not a significant barrier either to the submergence of one of our two cultures by the other or to the blending of the two.

Next to physical isolation, the most effective protection to the autonomy of a national culture is difference in language from that prevailing in neighbouring countries and, still better, from that prevailing anywhere else. Striking evidence in support of the power of common language to produce common culture is the extent to which peoples with a common language inheritance, but politically independent of each other for many generations, without substantial contact with each other through business or tourist travel, and with completely different economic patterns, nevertheless retain close similarity in at least the most obvious elements of cultural patterns. A notable illustration is in the resemblance to each other of the cultural patterns of Spain and its former American colonies, or of India and the sectors of populations of East Indian origin in the West Indies and in South and East Africa, although in both these sets of cases religion is also operative as a powerful preservative of an old culture against either internally generated change or influence by a surrounding alien culture.

As between English-speaking Canada and the United States, there are no language differences less trivial than differences in the way in which honour and neighbour are spelt, or than differences in pronunciation that are not much more marked than those between different regions or social classes within Canada and within the United States.

The situation is of course different with respect to French-speaking Canada. But I will argue, perhaps unnecessarily, that in dealing with the question of Canadian-American cultural relations, I can reasonably give most of my attention to the cultural impact of the United States on English-speaking Canada. To French Canadians, I feel sure, what seems dangerous to their own culture is not specifically an American impact thereon, but the impact thereon of a potentially dominant English-language culture, of which the Canadian and the American variants are scarcely worth while distinguishing. If anything, I suspect, they fear the impact of Torontonian culture more than that of present-day Bostonian culture. I suspect, also, that at least with regard to those phases of a national culture with which I am primarily concerned, the "Canadian" culture English-speaking Canada is anxious to protect, to preserve, and to improve is the specific culture of English-speaking Canada.

Unless there have been major changes, as well there may have been without my becoming aware of it, since the time when I knew things Canadian at first hand, there are two distinct Canadian cultures, and not an Anglo-French blend in the sense, say, in which Mexican culture is a Spanish-Amerindian blend or the culture of present-day India, or of at least upper-class India, is an English-Hindu blend. Indeed, I know of few instances of so successful immunization against an adjoining, and in fact a surrounding, culture – made possible by differences in language, as well as differences in religion – as that shown by the English-speaking minority in Montreal when I knew Montreal well. I had fourteen years of schooling in Montreal, but to the best of my memory I was never required to read a French Canadian book, or learn a French Canadian song, or read a French Canadian newspaper. Let me add, however, that except for a few elementary school books, and except for one or two books assigned in my senior year at McGill University, I was never required to read an English Canadian book either! What we were really brought up in, as far as literary culture was concerned, was not an English Canadian culture but a British culture with many of the marks of a British provincial lag, as compared to London, of perhaps a generation. In any case, it would have taken great skill in literary chemistry to have found in it any trace of French Canadian culture.

Next to difference in language probably comes difference in religion as a factor generating new or preserving old differences in cultural patterns. As between English-speaking Canada and the United States, however, there are, I take it, no substantial differences in religion.

The only remaining factor visible to me that can operate strongly to generate or to preserve the differences between two national cultures is a wide divergence in national per capita income levels or in the patterns of distribution as between economic classes of the national wealth and income, or in both, for these can have important cultural consequences.

There have no doubt prevailed throughout the past two centuries significant differences in these respects between the Canadian and American peoples. Canadians have on the average been poorer than Americans. Canada also has had in smaller proportion, if it has had it at all, the support of cultural advancement in the intellectual sense and especially in the arts that can come from the existence of communities of families with wealth inherited through a large enough number of generations to establish – by example, by prestige, and by financial aid – a nucleus for an intellectually, and aesthetically, sophisticated culture. I am not aware that Canada has had any parallel to the "Brahmin" society of Boston and its environs, or to Rittenhouse Square in Philadelphia, from both of which have come lasting influence on the upper levels of American culture. The lower average level of income in Canada, as well as the somewhat lesser urbanization of Canada, must also have tended to make the Canadian a less malleable and less sophisticated, and therefore in these aspects at least a somewhat different, culture than the American.

These differences in social and economic structure between the two countries have, however, never been great in degree and, I feel confident, have in the past two generations been tending fairly rapidly to disappear. Whatever may have been true in the past, they cannot be relied upon in the future appreciably to contribute to the maintenance or enlargement of differences in cultural patterns between the Canadian and the American peoples.

If there is merit in my analysis so far, therefore, I have gone quite a way toward demonstrating that none of the powerful forces maintaining or generating differences in cultural patterns between peoples – not physical isolation, not differences in language, not differences in religion, not differences in per capita wealth or in class structure – is strongly operative in the cultural relations between English-speaking Canada and the American people. This, if true, would go far to explain the absence of marked differences between the existing cultural patterns in the two countries and to justify the forecast that what differences do exist are more likely to diminish than to increase. But it would still leave unanswered the question why, if the two cultures have come closer to each other or are coming closer to each other, it should be because the Canadian culture is becoming Americanized, as Canadians seem to be agreed it is, and not because the American culture is becoming Canadianized, or not because the two cultures are becoming, or have already become, to a significant extent, a Canadian-American blend.

If, in fact, Canadian culture is in the process of being Americanized, it might appear as an obvious and adequate explanation that relative size carries with it relative preponderance in capacity for cultural dominance. I am sure that there is a good deal in this, and I do not wish unduly to minimize its importance. It seems to me evident, however, from historical observation, that relative size is far from a complete explanation of the extent and even the net direction of cultural influence on each other of neighbouring peoples with a common language. I will choose my historical illustrations only from the modern age.

From about 1725 to somewhat beyond the end of the eighteenth century, there was a remarkable flowering of Lowland Scottish culture, whose impact not only on England, but also on English-speaking America and on the Continental Enlightenment, was great and long-lasting. Little Scotland was then teacher to the world: in matters economic, as witness David Hume, Sir James Stuart, and Adam Smith; in moral philosophy, as witness Francis Hutcheson, David Hume, Adam Smith, and Dugald Stewart; in metaphysics, as witness David Hume, Thomas Reid, and Thomas Brown; in historiography, as witness David Hume, William Robertson, James Dunbar, Sir David Dalrymple, and Adam Ferguson; in medicine, where Edinburgh provided great teaching and important discovery; in chemistry, where John Black, at Glasgow, was an outstanding figure. None of these illustrious persons was an isolated character, but each was associated with a sizeable group of less distinguished but nevertheless important and original thinkers, all of them Lowland Scots.

This cultural flowering was not fostered by size, as compared to England, nor by wealth, nor by differences in language, nor even by differences in religion, unless one wants to insist on the superiority for purposes of cultural development of, on the one hand, the Scottish eighteenth-century mixture of very moderate, very highly secularized, and very diluted Presbyterianism with skepticism, over, on the other hand, the English eighteenth-century mixture of very moderate, very highly secularized, and very latitudinarian Anglicanism with skepticism. There were at the end of the century perhaps a million and a half Lowland Scots as compared to about eight million Englishmen. Scotland was, per capita, much poorer than England. Nevertheless, I know of no qualified historian of British education who would deny that the level of teaching and the level of thought at the Universities of Edinburgh, Glasgow, and Aberdeen were markedly higher than at Oxford or Cambridge. And I know of no worker in the field of intellectual history who would dispute that, excluding the fine arts, in the cultural balance of payments of the latter half of the century as between Scotland and England, Scotland ran a persistent and substantial credit surplus on current account.

German Austria, chiefly Vienna, from say the 1870s to the 1920s, offers a somewhat similar picture vis-à-vis the much larger Imperial Germany. Here the intellectual currents flowed strongly in both directions, and I am not prepared to say that overall the impact of the culture of Germany on German Austria was not greater than that of German Austria on Germany. But the tendency seems to be nowadays to reappraise downward the intellectual achievements of Germany during this period, and to reappraise upwards the contribution that Vienna then made. In any case, the original contributions that Vienna was then making – in economics, in logic, in psychology, in medicine, in music, and in the theatre – contributions not only of a handful of great men but of a cultural community, had a conspicuous fame throughout the Western world.

I will take as my final example tiny Geneva, French-speaking, almost surrounded by French territory, and with religion as the only apparent barrier to its being, like the French provinces in the main, a mere cultural dependency of Paris. Yet this small canton, which even today has scarcely 200,000 inhabitants, has since the days of Calvin – who was, however, not himself Genevese – produced a steady stream of thinkers of international reputation, not only and indeed not notably theologians, but natural scientists, economists, psychologists, and so forth. With limited economic resources, it has maintained a community level of educational facilities, museums, learned societies, learned periodicals, and music that would be the pride of any American city five times its size, if there were any such American city that sought occasion and excuse for pride in this particular direction.

If these illustrations mean anything, they go to show, at the least, that the limited size of a people's population is not an insuperable barrier to the highest level of sustained intellectual and aesthetic productivity, permeated by distinctive cultural features, even when there are giant neighbours sharing the same language.

It is also true that population size is not a sufficient guarantee of cultural achievement or cultural autonomy even if it is associated with a high per capita income level. I will cite in illustration only the United States because it provides me with the most pertinent illustration I can think of. The United States began its independent existence in the glory of a magnificent display of political originality and creativeness. Its per capita level of real income, though not at all its level of accumulated wealth, was already probably superior to that of England. Well on in the nineteenth century, however, an English reviewer could still ask: "Who ever reads an American book?" This was already perhaps an unfair question, and when Hawthorne, Melville, Cooper, Emerson, Channing, Poe, Henry James, and others had done their work, it was an impossible question for any literate Englishman to ask. It remains true, however, that in proportion to its population and to its economic status, the American contribution to the higher culture fell far short of being impressive until there came that cultural "Coming of Age" that, whether it is to be dated at the turn of the century or later, was clearly slow in making its appearance.

The usual American explanation of this delay is that the American people were preoccupied with opening the West. One should not expect, it is true, frontiersmen to write great operas, or even good novels or poems, but the proportion of the American people that at any time was directly engaged in pioneering or was living in frontier communities could never have been very substantial after, say, 1850. The Eastern Seaboard, in any case, drew revenue from the westward movement almost at once, and did not have to wait for long-delayed returns from long-term investments before many could live there in ease and comfort. Much of the long-term investment in the West came, moreover, from Europe, and the American East drew middlemen's incomes and promoters' profits from the beginning of these investments even when for the European investors the returns were destined to be deferred to eternity. If for a long time the United States was on the whole a cultural backwater, living largely on borrowed and often pirated goods, and on inferior imitations, not the whole explanation, but a substantial part of it, was that it was not the higher learning or the finer arts to which Americans wanted to direct their energies or their spending. In the Bible Belt, which means over a wide range of settled American territory, there was an identification of higher learning, and especially of the finer arts, with sin in several of its allegedly most mortal shapes, and this persisted somewhat even after piety had ceased even there to be closely associated with poverty and semiliteracy.

It may be objected that in speaking only of the upper reaches of cultural creation and appreciation, I have been evading the essential issue that Canadian cultural nationalists have been raising. The manifestations of genius and of approaches to genius are notoriously of mysterious origin, and much that is at the time or later recognized as genius is by all appearances emancipated from all the local influences of customs, manners, topography, climate, and formal education. The cultural nationalist, on the other hand, is often concerned that thought and artistic creation shall *not* be emancipated from the local circumstances, and may even be willing to pay a heavy price in "quality," or totally to forswear "quality," if necessary to preserve local flavour, atmosphere, and values. It may therefore be that what many Canadians are really concerned about is not that Canadians shall write novels or paint pictures that Englishmen and Swedes and Frenchmen will enjoy reading or seeing, but that the novels Canadians read and the pictures Canadians look at shall not only be the products of Canadians, but shall be "Canadian" in the atmosphere they reflect, in the landscapes they evoke, in the folk memories they arouse, in the loyalties to region and to the past to which they respond and that in so doing they strengthen and invigorate.

I have respect for this point of view. But I am skeptical as to the practicability of planned furtherance of it, and skeptical also as to the probabilities that a country's supply of talent will realize its potentialities of artistic and intellectual achievement if it is under any kind or degree of pressure to find its raw material in the local folk dances or the local peculiarities of diction, household management, and family mores. Where, moreover, does this logically stop? Should Canadians aim also at acquiring a Peace River school of fiction and a Bluenose school of poetry? Not all good wines are exportable, but I wonder if even Scots would have remained as loyal to Robby Burns if his merits were substantially confined to his use of the vernacular and of local colour.

Perhaps I am still on the wrong track. It may be that when Canadians worry about an American cultural invasion, it is not an invasion either on the highest or on the middle cultural levels that they have in mind, but an invasion of the "popular arts," and especially by the often tawdry stuff that gets into American films, on television, and on radio, or into the mass-circulation periodicals.

It is a quite recent phenomenon, as history goes, for the American "popular arts" to have a substantial export market. This new phenomenon may in part be the result of American cultural developments or of a new receptiveness outside the United States to old ingredients of American culture. It is, however, certainly in part the result of technological change and of other economic factors that are of themselves neutral with respect to cultural factors, but that foster American predominance. The American economy has a comparative advantage, to use economists' jargon, in mass production. In so far as this is true, relative size of population becomes a significant factor, and superiority in size can bring the capacity to dominate markets, irrespective of "quality" as appraised by noncommercial standards.

The "popular arts" are in modern times a species of marketable commodity, susceptible to economies of large-scale manufacture and distribution, to artificial creation of a market for them by skilful promotion, and to profitable export at dumping prices if the home market is large-scale. This applies to the radio, to television, to popular music, to popular fiction, to picture magazines and popular journalism. The manufacturers and distributors of these commodities, whether they are Americans or not, are, I presume, not consciously hostile to quality, and may even have a yearning for it. But they often are operating in a semicompetitive framework, in an oligopolistic framework, if I may again resort to economists' jargon, and if they don't place their first emphasis on vendibility, they will go broke. In this field, certain kinds of deviation from quality, as for instance vulgarity, may contribute to vendibility. It may therefore be to the interest of a manufacturer whose personal taste is of the highest to search out vulgarians to design and style his or her product on the principle that it takes a vulgarian to appeal successfully to an existing or potential taste for the vulgar.

Even more serious is that in the "popular arts" what is consumed today contributes to determining what tomorrow's taste shall demand. It thus becomes possible to fashion and mould future demand, and it becomes conceivable that it is sometimes good business progressively to degrade and corrupt the public taste, so that it will cease to have independent criteria of appraisal and will accept a standardized product with relish provided its appreciation makes no demands on discriminating judgment and on refinement of taste. There could conceivably arise, therefore, through the association of low quality with mass production, and through the special affinity for American technology of the economies of large-scale production, a close correlation between American competitive superiority in the field of the popular arts and low quality, as judged by noncommercial standards, of the American product. Even if, in the absence of the American imports, the resulting vacuum were filled by a domestic product no higher in quality, there would be many, I am sure, who would be gratified by the reflection that if Canada's culture were being degraded it was Canadians who were doing it and that at least they were doing it without denationalizing it.

Let me now drop for a few moments my discussion of "quality" and confine myself to the supposition that, quality for quality, the American producer will still have a competitive advantage because of the larger scale of his or her operations. The American product, whether it is a popular song, or a popular novel, or a play, or a magazine, will have been produced in the United States primarily for the American market, primarily by American craftsmen. It will therefore inevitably, even if surely unintentionally, be introducing into Canada American social patterns, American moral attitudes, American political ideas. On the assumption that Canadians are moulded by the movies they see, the music they dance to, the periodicals and comics they read, the radio they listen to, the Canadian mind may be undergoing a subliminal brainwashing. If I were a Canadian and believed this was happening, I would be concerned, and I would look into the problem to see whether there was anything that should be done about it.

I would, however – I hope – look objectively. It is arguable, for instance, that despite their admitted and glaring faults, the American popular arts bear also gifts of the gods, that in the net they are elevating tastes, not lowering them, that they bring supreme artistry to the meanest hearth, skilfully presented so that it shall be welcomed there, and that in the net they far exceed in quality what would take their place if it were possible to exclude them from the Canadian market. If it were only a selective elimination that was contemplated, who would be the authorities who would decide what the public should be permitted to see or hear or read or dance to, and who would appraise *their* taste? And how would the Canadian public be protected from the conceivably real danger that any restrictive measures against imports of the popular arts from the United States would be utilized rather to protect Canadian producers of even more inferior products than to protect the Canadian consumer from mental or moral or artistic corruption, or from Americanization?

I think it is worth mentioning also that the American mass producers of popular articles of culture are not in intent culture-nationalists, still less culture-imperialists, deliberate Kultur-spreaders. They are, in their pursuit of profit, in a constant and worldwide hunt for talent, and especially for glamourous talent, and they determine the input-mix of their products in response to estimates of prospective vendibility and of cost, without patriotic observance of any minima of national input. I am confident that as Canada develops dramatists, novelists, song-writers, composers, with the requisite potential mass vendibility, these American dispensers of culture will spy them out early, and will without qualms of conscience expose their American customers to them – with accentuation rather than minimization of any Canadian local colour they may bring with them. But I am open to the retort that because of the difference in the relative strength of the cultural impacts, the fact that Americans could look upon this if it occurred with perfect equanimity would not imply that Canadians can with equal safety and good sense behave likewise.

I am skeptical, however, as to whether, with the increased international mobility in modern times of people, ideas, and tunes, with the development of the radio, television, and tourist and business travel, cultural autonomy is any longer possible in any substantial degree anywhere this side of the Iron Curtain. In my earlier discussion of the effective barriers to international acculturation, I perhaps should have included illiteracy, but this also is now an unattainable instrument of defence against cultural alienation.

I have been treating English Canadian culture as if it recently were or still is substantially different from American culture and therefore had substantial differences to preserve. I am not at all sure that this is correct, but the only objective judges would be neither Canadians nor Americans themselves, for these would tend to take the resemblances for granted and to notice only the differences. The two countries have inherited from the British Isles a common language, common religions, a common literature, common legal institutions, and a common tendency toward the elimination of legalized class privilege and toward a democratic way of life. Their cultures have both been moulded by the presence of the family farm, by bush and prairie frontiers, by the preponderance during their formative periods of rural and small-town rather than metropolitan populations, and by the absence of a land-owning aristocracy.

If there nevertheless do exist substantial differences in the cultures of the two peoples, they are, I suspect, largely attributable to one fact: the greater impact on American than on Canadian society of traits, skills, and values brought in on the tide of immigration from Continental Europe. This tide of Continental immigration was for the United States greater in proportion to population than for Canada, was earlier, and perhaps also found a more open society, so that it was able more quickly to attain status and prestige and thus to bestow as well as to receive cultural influence.

This would suggest that the American culture is to a larger degree a cosmopolitan culture than the Canadian one, which I think it is. It may then be that if a process of Americanization of English Canadian culture is under way, it is not so much that specifically Canadian elements in that culture are being eroded by specifically American influences as that more or less Continental influences are tending, via the United States, to reduce the relative importance of British-inherited ingredients in the Canadian culture. But that is also happening in London, and happening without American mediation, and I am not at all sure that if Kansas City or Halifax or Victoria could impose their present-day cultures on London, they would not make it culturally more British – but also culturally less up-to-date – than it actually is.

I am not wholly convinced that it would ever be desirable, assuming the practicability under modern conditions, to protect the details of a national culture from alienation through the impact of external cultural influences not dangerous to the national language, to morals, or to religion. I am even less convinced that it is practicable, except at great risk of involving "thought-control" and of impeding healthy progress. I do think, however, that the intellectual and aesthetic quality of a national culture may need protection against deterioration and stimulus to improvement, that deliberate effort to this end, in which government has a large potential role to play, is justified and often even urgent, and that if you can maintain or restore or improve the quality of a national culture, you have the best defence available against its erosion by unworthy influences, whether these come from abroad or originate at home.

The quality of a country's intellectual and aesthetic culture is in the first instance a consequence of social inheritance through the home and to that extent largely beyond the possible realm of social control. In the area of possible deliberate action to improve – or preserve – culture, the general educational system is by far the most powerful of the available instruments. In this connection, "the importance of not underestimating the importance of education cannot be overestimated."

It must be recognized, nevertheless, that a given culture acts on the educational system as well as being acted upon by it. If educational matters are left to "natural forces," or to the spontaneous initiative of individuals, or even to the initiative of the existing supply of educational administrators, confidence that the level of quality of a country's culture can be lifted or can even be preserved despite the operation of powerful counterforces, by pulling on the country's existing stock of educational bootstraps, may be totally misplaced confidence.

Education costs money, how much depending both on the quantity supplied and on the quality of what is supplied, although it is possible, and it has been achieved, to supply a limited and inferior education at high cost. There are dangers, moreover, in economy in education that are largely peculiar to it. If there is undue economizing, with respect either to quantity or quality, in the construction of bridges, or in protection against fire or flood, or in subsidies to organized groups of voters, a day of political reckoning is almost certain to come. It is not so in the field of education. Here, the best way to keep citizens from knowing that their children are getting an inferior education is to have avoided giving them a good one. Here, the easiest path to economy is the underpayment of teachers, and there is no real danger that this will result in an undersupply of teachers if there is, on the part of the educational administrators, even a moderate degree of capacity for efficiency and speed in lowering to the extent needed the minimum standards of acceptability of teachers.

As compared to Western Europe, the outstanding characteristic of the American educational system is the virtual absence – at all stages of the system, in many cases for an individual school or college, in most cases for a local educational system, in all cases for a state system, and above all for a church-controlled system – of effective external minimum standards for curriculum, quality of instruction, or physical facilities. The average annual pay of school teachers in the United States is far below the average annual pay of plumbers. Since the pay of plumbers suffices to give them a quite tolerable level of living, the statement I have just made does not of itself constitute a statement of a "problem." The real problem arises out of the fact that – whereas American plumbers, being highly paid even on American standards, are on the basis of international comparisons probably superb plumbers – American school-teachers, in comparison with the teachers of England, or Scotland, or France, or Sweden, or Switzerland, are on the average decidedly not superb.

I know more about American higher education than about the American schools. Even the passing tourist on the American highways can see that there are colleges and universities, many of them, with the highest of standards of physical facilities for their gladiators and also for the extra-curricular needs of their students, but with miserable physical facilities for the scholarship of either their teaching staff or their students. The educational buildings, it is true, may be more attractive to look at than the athletic and recreational buildings, for the former may be old and consequently quaint and covered with ivy, while the latter may have only the glitter and gloss of acres of stainless steel and glass. But the chief function of ivy on American college campuses is to give honour to past educational effort by making its obsolete and decayed relics picturesque. When

I see a university flaunting on its campus a huge stadium, a huge athletic field house, and luxurious dormitories, while in the shadows cast by these expensive votive offerings to higher learning there stands a wretched little library, down-at-the-heels externally despite the ivy, and with a pitifully small array of books inside, and even these of low quality in their respective categories, and when I hear its students chant with feeling and conviction their local, but not different, Hail Alma Mater, I feel that they are thereby demonstrating, beyond serious chance of error, that they are not being successfully educated to discriminate between glory and dross.

"American" is a notoriously ambiguous term, and its ambiguity may at this point be involving me, though in all innocence, in that hazard of stepping on sensitive toes to which I referred at the beginning of this paper. Let me, therefore, be as explicit as I can. It is only US education at which I have been directing my jeremiad. And lest I leave an unfair impression of US education, let me in all honesty make the boast on its behalf that, while it abounds in miasmic swamps and cultural slums, while in places it sinks to depths for which mediocrity would be a term of undeserved praise, it rises also, in quite a few places, to the very highest peaks of achievement. This absence of minimum standards associated with capacity and resources for attaining the highest standards is, I believe, peculiar to American education.

What the Canadian overall situation is, I am not sufficiently informed to justify my venturing comparisons. But this I can say with conviction: If Canadians are really concerned lest their culture undergo deterioration because of contamination by inferior American cultural importations, let them look anxiously to their educational institutions. With respect to these institutions of themselves, there is much, I am sure, that they can borrow from American models and experiments with profit to all concerned, but there is also much in American education as it is today that Canada should avoid like poison. With respect to the protection of Canadian culture against contamination by meretricious American, or Canadian, or even British novelties, the best of all possible defences is through a superior Canadian education, one that will endow Canadians with the capacity to distinguish the true, the good, and the beautiful from "rock 'n' roll" and the horror comics, which will foster the will to make the proper choice between them and which will cultivate the skills whereby to add to the world stock of truth, virtue, and beauty. This will cost money, a lot of it. But Canada now has a lot of money and has recently been given official assurance that its manifest destiny is to acquire a great deal more in the not-too-distant future. If Canada truly wants good education, it will not therefore be lack of money that will prevent it from having it. But other things than money are often also essential, especially wisdom, and determination, and dedication, and this may well be true for Canada also.

I come at last to the state of the political relations between Canada and the United States. The Government of Canada has in recent months made it abundantly evident to the American Government, though not yet, I regret to say, to the American people at large, that it is lacking in enthusiasm for certain phases of American economic foreign policy. According to the newspaper reports that I have seen, recent official notes from Ottawa to Washington have been, depending upon the two reports that have come my way, either sharp or blunt. Even if both reports are correct, I see nothing to find fault with in this, provided, of course, that the severity of the criticism is not out of proportion to the occasion for making it, for frankness between friends where they have differences of manageable proportions has never injured the workings of diplomacy.

I see also by the newspapers that the distinguished and able American ambassador to Canada has defended American economic foreign policy before a Canadian audience, against Canadian criticisms of it. This also seems proper and in accordance with the rules of the game. An eighteenth-century Frenchman condemned the behaviour of the rhinoceros as unpardonable: "Cet animal est très méchant; Quand on l'attaque, il se défend." It is not reasonable, however, to expect the American official hide to be as thick as that of the rhinoceros. But as I will deal with American economic foreign policy in part two of this paper, I defer my defence of it – or possibly my attack on it – until then.

Canada and the United States have since the Ogdensburg Agreement – that is, since prior to American entrance into World War Two as an open belligerent – been military allies, first against Hitler and later against the Soviet menace. As far as I know, the military cooperation has been close, mutually friendly, and mutually satisfactory. The agreement on the major principles and on the details of the grand policy that must govern military strategy has no doubt not been perfect, but it has easily been sufficient to enable the military cooperation to proceed smoothly and harmoniously. And it must continue to be so, for in the security field we *must* walk together, and "Shall two walk together, except they have agreed?"

American foreign policy, however, is now very much on the anvil, and the hammer blows are coming from every direction, from at home as well as abroad. There is especially sharp criticism of its recent mode of formulation and execution, and there are many Americans who would agree with the opinion of innumerable non-Americans that the quality of the day-to-day formulation of American foreign policy, to be admired, must be seen from a particular point of view whose location has not yet been satisfactorily determined. Of late, however, there has been increasing and increasingly sharp criticism of what I take to be the fundamental principles on which American foreign policy has rested since the end of World War Two, and especially since Korea. Some of this criticism has come from distinguished Canadians. I am one of the comparatively few who is not an expert on high diplomacy and Great Power politics, and I will confine myself to a layman's comments on the possible implications for Canadian-American political relations of the special role with which the United States is saddled in the East-West crisis.

As I see American foreign policy, it rests on a series of vital assumptions believed to be in accordance with the facts or believed at least to have, in the light of all available present knowledge, undeniably high probability. The overriding, the supreme, objective of American foreign policy is peace, but not at the expense of surrender, actual or imminently potential, of American freedom from external domination, and not at the price of delivery of any now free and not hostile country to the mercies of Russian domination. There is one conceivable opponent in major war, and that is Russia and her satellites. The Communist bloc has great military power, possibly great enough to give victory for Russia in case of war, in Russian judgment, a high degree of probability. Russia has a cluster of present objectives, capable of indefinite expansion, for which she would be prepared to risk war if a cheaper alternative for gaining them were not available and if there were a good chance that she could wage war successfully without involving herself in intolerable costs. Some of these objectives are of a kind that involve unacceptable impairments of the security of the free world. The sole effective deterrents to Russia's immediate pursuit of some of these objectives by military or diplomatic pressure are the potential damage that could be inflicted on her by Allied nuclear attack and the possibility that in full-scale war she would not emerge the victor. If there were assurance on the part of Russia that nuclear weapons would not be used against her, she would, today, without need of use of anything but diplomatic pressure, subversion, and conventional weapons, have the Continent of Europe completely at her mercy. The appraisal of Russian objectives must always be contingent and should be continually re-examined in the light of internal developments in Russia, of changes in the world pattern of alignment, and of changes in military technology. Policy must be flexible enough to adjust appropriately to any such changes. It must not be so flexible, however, that neither the American people, nor the Allies of the United States, nor Russia herself shall be without doubt as to the firmness of American policy and of American determination not to permit weakening of the defences of the free world by concessions to taxpayer fatigue, to domestic political objectives of a lower order of importance, or to the universal preference for butter over guns or bombs as more conducive, at least in the short run, to the easy life. The United States needs and wants allies and friends if she is to maintain confidence that the Russian threat can be withstood, and the rest of the free world, without exception, must place major reliance on American strength and American resources for their continual freedom. To maintain leadership of a strong alliance, the United States must so conduct her relations with them as to retain their goodwill and their confidence in the propriety of her objectives and in the wisdom and efficiency of her pursuit of them. To maintain a strong morale at home, in support of these objectives, those in charge of American foreign policy must also keep the American people convinced that these are the objectives truly being followed and that those in charge are competent to pursue them with reasonable efficiency.

This summary of American foreign policy covers all its really fundamental aspects as I see them, although not, of course, in concrete detail. It is in this general setting, a crisis setting if ever there was one, that specific American measures and acts need to be appraised and that Canadians must appraise the political relations of Canada with the United States.

The past year has been a bad year for American foreign policy. No one, I think, will seriously dispute that Russian prestige stands higher and American – and with it Western – prestige lower than it did a year ago. It now also seems apparent to the lay public that Soviet military and economic power are much greater than was supposed a year ago. There is room for difference of opinion as to the extent to which the present troubles of American foreign policy have resulted from American mistakes in timing and execution and from unwarranted American complacency. But the skilful and unemphasized use of hindsight by a critic can easily be the sole factor that makes his or her criticism appear weighty and penetrating. It is not reasonable, moreover, to hold the United States to standards of perfection in the formulation and execution of foreign policy.

If the fundamental structure of American foreign policy is substantially as I have ventured to outline it, it involves the American government in an unintermittent task of deciding the proportions in which finite diplomatic, military, and economic resources shall be allotted to: building-up deterrent military power; preserving the strength of the American economy as the major arsenal for support of the security of the West; granting economic aid to allies in need, to friendly neutrals, to neutral neutrals, and to Yugoslavia, Poland, Egypt, India, Burma, Spain, Jordan, Morocco, Tunisia, the Argentine, Ceylon, and Indonesia; endeavouring to conciliate Russia by concessions that do not undermine security or weaken or betray alliances; seeking an escape from the dilemma of either supporting anticolonialism, and thus arousing the resentment of important and valued allies, or not supporting anticolonialism, and thus provoking the Asiatic, African, and Latin American countries; and so forth.

Everyone has a right to find fault with the proportions in which the United States has mixed these ingredients in its foreign policy brew. As long as the United States bears the responsibility for leadership in the resistance to the

Communist menace, it will be urgent that it shall be patient, understanding, and responsive with regard to even unfriendly criticisms, provided they come from basically friendly or potentially friendly sources. The United States must also be as cautious and restrained as is humanly possible in criticizing, in turn, errors of policy or shortcomings in contribution to the common burdens of alliance of such of its allies as are also capable of falling short of perfection.

But the critics also bear some responsibility. Everyone is entitled to his or her own judgment as to the optimum proportions in which military deterrence, conciliatory diplomacy, and economic aid should play their roles in the Cold War, and every country not in the Soviet bloc except the United States has some species of right to remain wholly or partially aloof from the Cold War. But there is one right that no one has, whether American or non-American, whether a statesman or just an ordinary human being, and that is the right to the strong conviction that he or she possesses, or has means of acquiring, the one best formula for resolving the crisis in which the world finds itself.

What seems to be needed is a modern equivalent in the foreign policy field of a Dover's powder, a remedy for most human ailments that was popular in England in the eighteenth century and remained, I understand, in the British pharmacopoeia until not long ago. The remedy contained opium, which is an effective painkiller, but is also habit-forming and a poison if taken in too large doses. It also contained ipecac, an emetic, in such exact proportion to the opium that it would make the user vomit as soon as he or she took more opium than was safe. That American foreign policy could put to good use a Dover's powder if one were available, I willingly concede. But I stand amazed at the number of scholars and statesmen, as well as persons with lesser pretensions, who speak or write as if they have up their sleeves, or in their dispatch cases, the precisely right formula. Pronouncements on foreign policy today tend to make grim and dull reading. We must nevertheless continue to read them and to study them closely, for it is the freedom of the world that they are helping to make or break. I suggest that one will find it a source of some lightening of the burden of reading such pronouncements, as well as a real aid to their proper evaluation, if, as one reads, one notes mentally whether the writer is explicitly or implicitly claiming to have in his or her possession the recipe for an effective Dover's powder for what ails the world in the field of international politics.

Little if anything of what I have been saying with respect to high foreign policy may have any special application to Canada, except as it is an important partner in the general Western coalition to maintain security for freedom. Much of what I have said is as applicable to Americans as to non-Americans. The only special Canadian-American problems in this area that I can identify are, first, the danger that frictions in the economic field may make continued collaboration of the two countries on the higher levels of security politics more difficult and, second, that failure of American diplomacy to keep Canadian interests and sentiments sufficiently in mind may make it, for Canadian politicians, and even for Canadian statesmen, harder psychologically, less profitable or more unprofitable in terms of domestic politics, and less rewarding emotionally to keep in mind the heavy responsibilities for the security of the free world that the United States carries.

The great danger here is that American government and the American press will take Canada too much for granted. I find, for instance, that of 5,883 Department of State personnel in 1957 stationed outside the United States, only 120, or a fraction over 2 per cent, were stationed in Canada. In the same source, I find that 577 American missionaries are stationed in Canada, and that they constitute appreciably more than 2 per cent of the total number of American missionaries operating outside the United States.

One should not, of course, attach too much significance to these statistics. The proximity of Ottawa to Washington; the lack of occasion for American officials to function in Canada as dispensers of American economic aid; the American belief that Canadians already have adequate appreciation of the virtues of the American way of life, and especially of its exportable ingredients; the notorious competence of American businessmen to find for themselves the opportunities in Canada for profit and for sales that still remain ungrasped; the absence of need for translators and interpreters: These no doubt go a long way toward explaining why the American diplomatic personnel stationed in Canada are so small in number. I presume also that it is mainly to serve the Aboriginals and the Inuit that American missionaries are sent to Canada, so that their number as compared to the number of diplomatic officers sent there is not to be relied on as a good index of the American judgment as to the comparative need of the Canadian people for spiritual salvation and diplomatic appeasement.

I nevertheless think that there is a problem here, one of long standing, which is how to bring the concerns and the interests of Canada more prominently to the attention of the American government, of Congress, and of the American people at large. I feel all the more that there is a genuine problem here since, although the American stock of goodwill toward Canada is very great, it is almost wholly without focus on specific matters where it might operate to bring concrete benefits to Canada and to Canadian-American relations.

With a few notable exceptions, the American press does not help very much. Its foreign reporting, which I am sure in volume and quality exceeds that of any other country, nevertheless tends to concentrate on problem areas. The recent Canadian criticisms of things American have not yet penetrated deeply enough into the American consciousness to make the American public or press conscious that a new "problem area" may be developing for the United States sufficient in importance, or in potential reader interest, to justify systematic and large-scale journalistic exploitation. Such exploitation of course would not necessarily be productive of good consequences. When one starts a rock rolling down a hill, one may get some fun out of it, at least if one enjoys rolling rocks down hill. It is also a useful activity if there is more use for the rock elsewhere than at the top of the hill. But once the rock has been started rolling, it is the lay of the land, and not the wishes of the person who started it on its course, that will decide how far and how fast it will travel, and with what results to the landscape. I am convinced, however, that the more the American public learns about the prevailing trend of Canadian sentiment, provided it gets an accurate and balanced account, the better it will be for the future of Canadian-American relations. There is here, I believe, an important task for American government and for the American press, and one that they are, on the whole, failing to perform.

A partial solution may lie in Canadians finding or making the opportunity to do more complaining in the United States – and, perhaps, less of it at home. Of this I feel certain: that they would receive a fair and sympathetic hearing and that, in so far as they convinced their audiences that there was merit in their complaints, it would help to make correction of whatever shortcomings there are on the American side of Canadian–American relations politically more feasible.

PART TWO

In what follows I will deal with the economic relations of Canada and the United States, but once again with special reference to the significance for Canada of the disparity in economic size between the two countries. A few figures will suffice to indicate how close is the integration of the Canadian economy with that of the United States. About 60 per cent of Canadian total commodity exports go to the United States and about 75 per cent of total Canadian commodity imports come from the United States. In 1956 Canada's net import of capital, mainly from the United States, amounted to about one-third of her total annual net capital formation, and her gross import of capital amounted to about 40 per cent of her total annual net capital formation.

These are all exceptionally high ratios for economic relations of one country to another. They cannot be matched, taken together, I feel certain, for any other two countries in the free world. These high rates cannot be accounted for solely by the relative size of the two countries or even by relative size plus proximity. An additional factor operative to tie the Canadian into the American economy is the complementary character of the two economies: Canada has surpluses of raw materials of which the United States has deficiencies; standard American capital goods are well adapted to Canadian production techniques; the consumption standards and tastes of the two countries are almost identical, so that American consumers' goods find a ready market in Canada. But relative size has a great deal to do with it.

Also largely, though not solely, because of the disparity in size, the Canadian economy, while important to the United States as an export market and source of supply, is not nearly as important to the United States as the latter is to Canada. Out of this disparity in importance there arise for Canada some problems, some fertile sources for justified, for doubtful, and for gratuitous misgivings, and some great economic blessings.

Prominent also in the economic relations of the two countries is the heavy investment of American capital in Canada. Here disparity in size is once more important but not crucial. Small but relatively rich countries have often been substantial exporters of capital to much larger countries in which capital was relatively scarce; the capital investments in the United States of Holland and Switzerland before 1900 are notable illustrations. Disparity in size does play its part, however, in Canadian-American capital relations; perhaps the most striking way of illustrating this is that while American capital investment in Canada is many times as great as Canadian capital investment in the United States, Canadians, per capita, have invested at least twice as much in the United States as Americans, per capita, have invested in Canada. Once more, the United States is very much more important economically to Canada than is Canada to the United States.

I will deal first with the impact on Canada of American trade policy. Given the importance of Canadian-American trade to Canada, and given the nature of American commercial policy, it would not be surprising if Canadians were somewhat critical of American commercial policy. Before I proceed to discuss the Canadian criticisms of American protectionism that I have encountered, I feel it advisable to say something about my general attitude toward protectionism, which is such, perhaps, as to make my own critical approach to American commercial policy different from that of a Canadian who is prepared to condemn the American tariff almost as severely as I would but regards the Canadian tariff as a horse of an entirely different colour.

The trade of Canada with the United States consists largely of the exchange of metals, minerals, forest products, and agricultural commodities for industrial, highly processed products, such as machinery, machine tools, special steels, chemicals, and durable consumers' goods. It is this aspect of Canadian-American trade that seems most to disturb Canadians because they think it imposes on them an undistinguished and inherently unremunerative role of being "hewers of wood and drawers of water." I suspect that many Canadians who use this phrasing forget

that, if it was originally employed to indicate humble status, it was not because
hewing wood and drawing water were obviously low forms of manual work, but
because labour of any kind was held in low esteem. For it seems to me a strange
sentiment that on grounds of dignity and honour leads to a strong preference for,
say, spinning yarn or puddling iron or casting-up accounts, to hewing wood and
drawing water with the aid of the most massive of modern machinery.

   In modern times the distinction between rural and urban is accepted as a crucial
distinction in the national allocation of resources, with the urbanized countries
yearning for recovery of a sturdy peasantry and the predominantly agrarian countries hoping for rapid urbanization. It would not be fruitful for me to enter into
a discussion of the relative merits of urban and rural life per se. Such discussions
rarely get much beyond affirmation of subjective preferences unaccompanied by
an explanation of why practice has not conformed to the expressed preference.
Whatever the preferences, however, any country that attains a moderately high
per capita level of income will, under modern conditions, have a majority of its
population living in urban areas and engaged in urban occupations. This will be
true whether the country is industrialized or not, in the sense of having large
factories and an extensive manufacturing industry. As per capita incomes rise, an
increasing proportion of these incomes universally is spent on the products of
so-called "tertiary industry" – that is, on services (other than domestic service)
such as distribution and marketing, entertainment, education, transportation,
publishing and printing, repair, maintenance, and cleaning of producers' and of
consumers' goods and of buildings, and above all on government. All of these
tend overwhelmingly to be urban- and suburban-centred.

   Aside from the influence of changes in per capita income, changes in technology are on the whole moving production from the countryside to the city.
Agriculture itself has to a considerable extent undergone this type of transformation. If it were possible to compare a representative farm budget of today with
one of say fifty years ago, it would become apparent that the modern farmer's
outlay on production consists to a much smaller extent of payments for labour
on the farm and for farm-produced input-items and to a much larger extent of
payments for tools, machinery, fuel, implements, power, and services produced
in the cities. Similarly, the modern farmer's consumption consists much more
today than was the case fifty years ago of commodities and services provided
by the cities and much less of commodities and services produced on his or her
own or on neighbouring farms. The most striking illustration in the United States
and Canada of this effect of technological change in conjunction with rising
incomes is the substitution, on the farm and in supplying the farm, of the internal-
combustion engine for horsepower and manpower. This means a substitution, for
the horse and its food and housing and for the hired labourer and his or her food

and housing, of electrical power, of machinery, of motor-vehicles, and of petro-leum products, as well as the substitution of synthetic fertilizers for animal manure. In other words, much of modern agriculture is carried on in the cities.

Economists and others also speak freely of the desirability for a country of a proper "balance" between urban and rural population and between agriculture and manufacturing, but often they advisedly refrain from any attempt to define "balance" in meaningful terms and are content if by the use of the term they have persuaded you that a change in the existing proportions between rural and urban workers, and between agricultural workers and factory workers, in the direction they prefer, would be a movement in the direction of "balance." Others mean by balance variety of occupations. A prosperous country, as I have argued, always has a wide range of urban occupations, many of them "tertiary." A poor country may have a large urban population, especially if it has high tariffs, but this urban population will consist more largely of factory workers than will be the case for the cities of the richer countries. It is not at all necessarily the case that a high tariff or even complete suppression of imports – and consequently also of exports – will increase the variety of occupations. If the country is poor, whether or not it is predominantly urban or rural, whether or not it has a restrictive trade policy, its tertiary industries will be of minor importance and therefore will make limited contribution to the range of occupations available to the population. In any case, prosperity brings the variety rather than the other way around.

If a country has efficient and smoothly operating market institutions, if monop-oly and organized restrictions on movement of persons into or out of occupations are not important, and if the population is at least moderately intelligent, alert, and economically motivated, the presumption would be strong that the productive resources of the country would find (approximately) their optimum location, as between town and country and as between the available occupations, without need of extensive government guidance, regulation, subsidization, or restriction.

In countries with as yet little urbanization and little industrialization, the fact that money wages are typically substantially lower in the country than in the city is commonly used as an argument to show that in those countries at least people do not spontaneously abandon a low-pay for a high-pay occupation. From this it is concluded that it is good economic policy to stimulate the migration of labour from the farm to the city by providing to urban industries, through tariffs and other forms of subsidy, inducement to furnish employment for greater numbers of workers.

The technological changes I have already referred to are almost everywhere working to make nationally profitable a relative increase in urban population. The natural rate of increase of population is generally, though, as we now know,

not universally greater for the rural than for the urban population. The combination of these factors means that, at least in the absence of large immigration
from abroad to the cities, a substantial migration from the farms to the cities is
economically a healthy phenomenon. American experience, as well as, I am sure,
that of many other countries, is that, if left to take its own course, this migration
will fall short of the optimum rate, whether because of lack of knowledge, inertia,
lack of preparedness for city jobs of the farm boy or girl, urban trade-union
restrictions on entry into the unions, or what not. Granting this, I would argue
that the most appropriate remedy is to provide to the surplus rural youngsters
the information as to opportunities in the town, the education, and the vocational
training, which will make it possible for them to find urban employment and to
adjust more easily to the urban mode of life.

But lower money earnings on the farm do not themselves suffice to show that
even on strictly economic considerations the farm boy should go to the city.
There are nonpecuniary forms of income that are relatively more important on
the farm, and especially on the old-fashioned farm, than in the city, as, for
example, food and shelter in part produced on the farm and services provided
within the household that in the city have to be bought for cash. There are also
deductions from nominal money earnings that need to be made in the city but
not, or not in the same proportion, in the country, in order to ascertain true
income. Such are, for instance, the cost in the city of getting to and from work,
the cost of clothes needed on the job to conform to the urban pattern, union
dues, taxes for water, for police protection, and for sanitary services, and no
doubt others. In the United States and Canada, moreover, a good deal of farming
is a part-time occupation, with the consequence that data as to income per farm
give too pessimistic a picture of income per farmer.

It is reasoning like this, plus the argument from the international-friction-
breeding character of trade restrictions, that makes me almost a free-trader, even
without the aid of resort to a cosmopolitan point of view. I say "almost" rather
than "wholly" because I do not deny that there can be special circumstances, and
especially considerations arising out of imperfections in market processes, out of
monopoly and immobilities, that would justify a moderate resort to protection.
It may also be possible, although not in my opinion ordinarily probable, that
governments may be able to identify opportunities for profitable employment of
resources that businessmen would not discover for themselves, and that the hazards of new ventures result in general in their being delayed longer than the
prospects of long-run profit if rationally appraised would justify. Where such is
highly likely to be the situation, there is valid scope for the grant of protection
on the "infant-industry" principle. In any case, what I will say from now on is
likely to reflect the near-free-trade character of my personal convictions. I have

therefore both given fair warning as to my assumptions and preconceptions and rendered it possible, I hope, to make reasonably clear how I reach my specific conclusions without needing to spell it out in detail in each instance.

I have concocted a list of criticisms made in recent months by Canadians of American official commercial policy. It is perhaps a grossly incomplete list, since my search has been far from exhaustive. I nevertheless have some confidence in its adequacy since I have been unable to think up possible additions to it of real consequence. The list of criticisms by Canadians of American commercial policy that I have found is as follows:

(1) American import duties and quota limitations on Canadian agricultural products, minerals, forest products, and fisheries products are excessive.

(2) Given the levels of these duties, it is unfair, or unkind, or both, of the United States to impose still higher rates of duty on processed than on unprocessed or less-processed products.

(3) American commercial policy is unreasonably unstable.

(4) The United States buys too little from third countries, which lessens their capacity to buy Canadian exports.

(5) The American agricultural policy, and especially its price-support and export-subsidy policy for wheat, is unfairly and seriously injurious to Canada.

(6) American customs procedure is unreasonably and unnecessarily burdensome, inequitable, and restrictive of trade.

(7) The United States buys less from Canada than it sells to Canada.

(8) The United States is not giving strong enough leadership to the promotion of a more liberal trading pattern in the Western world.

In my discussion of friction points in Canadian-American commercial relations, I will follow a one-sided procedure. I will confine myself almost wholly to the Canadian complaints about American behaviour that I have just listed. Except perhaps for a few occasional lapses, I will ignore the a priori probability that there is also some basis for American complaints about Canadian tariff behaviour. My main reason for doing so is that I am much better acquainted with the defects of American commercial policy than with either the merits or the defects of Canadian commercial policy. I do know that American students of Canadian commercial policy are less ready than I am to assume that Canada conducts its own commercial policy primarily with the interest either of demonstrating to the United States how neighbourly a good neighbour can be if it tries hard enough or of making manifest to the world at large the dedication of Canada to the free-trade species of universal fellowship. I will on the whole disregard this, however, in partial acceptance of what I presume is the Canadian belief that the disparity in economic size of the two economies justifies at least a moderate disparity in the commercial policies of the two countries. In the standard account of the famous debate between the kettle and the stove on the colour question, the outcome was a draw. I would neither be much surprised, nor very disapproving, if I were to discover that it was part of the Canadian cultural pattern for parents to teach their children a special Canadian version in which the kettle emerges from the debate triumphant by resort to the clinching argument that after all it was a small kettle while the stove was a very, very large stove.

I have neither the disposition, nor the slightest sense of obligation, to defend American commercial policy. As a near-free-trader from the point of view both of my interpretation of the United States' national economic interest and of my interpretation of what are the international obligations of the United States both in terms of international equity and in terms of higher foreign policy in a critical stage of world history, I accept substantially, as having substantial validity, all but one of the criticisms of American policy that I have enumerated, and I do not reject even that one outright. I will therefore not mount a defence of American commercial policy, except in a very qualified sense of the word defence. I will defend present American commercial policy as compared to what it has been in the past, and, I regret to say, threatens somewhat to become again in the future. I will offer also some comments in explanation of American commercial policy, but these will not be intended as defence except perhaps as my explanation points to the conclusion that no phase of American commercial policy is the result of American malice directed against Canada or against the outside world.

To take up, first, the American duties and quotas, past, actual, and prospective, on imports from Canada of lead, zinc, cattle, petroleum, rye, and so forth. The United States is well into a recession at the moment. Signs of recession came early in the field of the nonferrous metals, of petroleum production, and of agriculture before it became at all evident that the recession was to be widespread and possibly severe. Much of the American nonferrous-metal mining industry is in genuine distress. The American oil industry has to operate under severe official restrictions of its domestic output. It is normal practice for governments that import substantial fractions of their consumption of particular commodities to come to the assistance at such times of their depressed domestic industries by imposing additional restrictions on imports. This is not to me the right way to deal with the problem. I am sure that it can hurt Canada more than it can help the depressed American industries and that it will not help the American economy as a whole sufficiently to warrant the injury to Canada. I assume that the American action is within the letter and the spirit of American treaty obligations, but I do not think that the United States should be content so to conduct its international relations as to make adherence to treaty obligations the only obligation of real weight. I believe, in particular, that one of the worst offences to international comity is to resort as a remedy for internal distress to measures which export that distress in aggravated degree.

When the United States levies higher import duties on imports of processed articles than on imports of the raw materials they contain as, except through Congressional inadvertence, it always does, it of course is thereby endeavouring to assure that the processing of raw materials produced abroad for the American market shall be carried out in the United States and not elsewhere. I regard this as uneconomic and unneighbourly policy. But criticism of it comes, I think, with better grace, or without as much need for explanation, from a near-free-trader like myself than from, say, a Canadian who approves of his or her own country's tariff, of which the duties on imported processing – as measured by the ratio to processing margin of the excess of total duty over duty, if any, on raw materials – are often much heavier than most of the American ones.

There has long been a mild tendency in Canada to seek to countervail the effect of the American import duties on processing by restricting in one way or another the export from Canada of unprocessed materials. Export restrictions seem to me in principle to be on a parity with import restrictions, no worse and no better. If used successfully as bargaining instruments to obtain the removal or moderation of another country's import restrictions, a positive case can be made for them. If applied only to offset the effect of another country's import restrictions on the location of processing, they can also be defended even from a free-trade point of view. As applied to the Canadian situation, however, they face some special difficulties and hazards.

First, the producers in Canada of these raw materials, whether they be Canadians or non-Canadians, have presumably been encouraged to invest their skills, if they are employees, and their capital, if they are entrepreneurs, in the development of the facilities in question; export restrictions would operate to depress the prices at the point of production of these commodities; export restrictions would therefore be injurious to them and would be in violation of what had been their reasonable expectations. Second, such action could result in the loss of export markets for the product in either processed or unprocessed form, so that the remedy would be incomparably more damaging to Canada than the disease it was intended to cure. Third, any such action would create a new barrier to rapid development of the natural resources of Canada, whether by Canadians or non-Canadians.

It is reasonable for the commercial partners of the United States to complain against instability in American commercial policy since this can be a costly and disturbing burden to them. With the exception of a small number of commodities, however, the actual range of instability in an upward or more restrictive direction in American import barriers has been since 1934 not only less than ever before in the United States, but less than has been normal in recent years in most countries of the free world. The American record has been less good with respect to *potential* instability, to apparent risk of impending increases of restrictions, although even here the record to date is not really a bad one, as such things go. It is true, however, that the adverse impact of such instability, actual and potential, as has prevailed, has been mainly on a few countries, notably Canada and Switzerland, but this has been fortuitous and not by design.

The complaint that because of its restrictions on imports the United States buys less from third countries than it otherwise would and thus impairs their capacity to buy Canadian products is merely another form of the general complaint that American trade barriers are too high. I agree. Unlike the case in some other countries, the *effective* American tariff is much lower than it seems, but it is not nearly as much lower than it was in the days before 1934, as official American propaganda for external consumption claims. The effective American system of import barriers is a heavily restrictive one on my standards, but not so on the prevailing standards of probably at least 80 per cent of the free world. I learned long ago not to expect the rest of the world to stay with me in the age of Cobden and Bright.

The complaint that by its price-support program the United States has unduly encouraged the production of agricultural staples and by its direct and indirect export subsidies has disturbed world markets and created for other exporting countries serious and in some cases probably unmanageable burdens, I accept as fully valid. American agricultural policy is in my belief unjustifiable even in terms of American national economic interest. From a broader and more international point of view, it is inexcusable and irresponsible.

I feel reasonably confident that a referendum of the American people would condemn the agricultural price-support policy, though probably in milder terms than I have used. That the American administration is unhappy about it is no secret, especially now that it is proposing to Congress revision of the program and especially authorization of support price minima of only 60 per cent of parity, which if accepted and enthusiastically administered would within a few years eliminate the worst sting of the program for other countries exporting the commodities involved.

As contributing further to explanation, though not to defence, I want to draw attention to the sharp distinction between "administration" and "legislature" in the American system of government, to the great power of the legislature as compared to the administration, and to the limited resources available to the administration to influence or coerce a Congress that has views differing from its own. I would add to this that the political parties as such are also, as compared to many and probably most other countries in the free world, relatively powerless in dealing with individual congressmen and senators and that through resort to log-rolling and other cooperative devices individual American legislators can and freely do magnify their inherent power to resist coercion by party leaders or party organization, by the administration, by national public opinion, and by world opinion. Add to this that the farmers, as the result of historical and geographical accident and of deliberate contrivance, are grossly overrepresented in both the House of Representatives and the Senate and that American legislators do not systematically govern their behaviour by what national referenda show, or could be expected to show, as to the state of national public opinion on particular issues. It seems, in consequence, to be the prevailing judgment that there is not the slightest chance of the administration's proposals as they now stand being accepted this year, an election year, and that if the administration seriously presses its proposals it will manifest a degree of courage in a good cause that is magnificent but not politic. But I advise not selling the American Congress too short. As in the case of American education, it also can rise to supreme peaks. One should exercise restraint in charging with disregard of international obligations a legislative body that has since 1945 voted, even if reluctantly at times, over $58 billion in economic foreign aid.

For Canada, the major concern is wheat. The whole wheat situation in the world at large is a manifestation of a loss of faith in the recent past in the adequacy of free-market processes as regulators of production and of patterns of sale, with consequent substitution of government agencies, of price-fixing, of official gambling on the trends of world prices and of production. Wheat is much more important for Canada than for the United States and for this reason, as well as because the United States is a richer country, the United States can afford to give its wheat away on a more lavish scale than can Canada. Aside from this, the two countries seem to me to be, as far as wheat is concerned, very much in the same leaky boat, uncertain as to where they came from and why, and where they are now, and where they are going. It was less American misdeeds, and more Canadian official misjudgment as to the future trend of wheat prices, that was the major cause for the present huge surplus of unsold and unsaleable Canadian wheat. Both countries are in trouble because they have meddled overmuch with free-market prices and because they have failed to solve for democracy the problem of how to cope with organized producer-groups who have mistaken views of what is good for themselves in the long run, who have the conviction that what is good for themselves is good for the country, and who have irresistible, or at least unresisted, political power. I do not ask that the American administration or Congress not be condemned harshly for failure to solve the agricultural surplus problem. All that I would suggest is that in drawing upon available resources of reproof and blame for this purpose, Canadians keep enough in reserve to take care of urgent domestic needs.

There is one line of solution of the American surplus-stock problem that would not injure, or would keep within moderate limits the injury to, wheat-exporting countries like Canada and Australia, that would bring gratitude to the United States rather than blame from the rest of the world, that the United States can afford, and that may conceivably be politically possible, which is for the United States to lower moderately its support prices and to give away the bulk of its surplus stocks of wheat to very poor countries where undernourishment is chronic but, because of poverty, imports of food of any kind are normally small, the wheat to be used for current consumption and as reserves against famine, but with strict avoidance of re-export. In the absence of such a program, I see no substantial relief in sight for Canada's wheat-surplus problem except such as may come from a succession of bad harvests in the United States or in Europe.

The complaint that American customs administration is unnecessarily burdensome and inequitable is justified and in fact is made most strongly by American importers. There have been significant administrative and legislative improvements in recent years, however, and more are in prospect.

The complaint recurs in Canada that the United States sells to Canada more than it buys from Canada. In 1956, for example, Canada's import surplus in its commodity trade with the United States exceeded one and three-quarter billion dollars and exceeded the overall Canadian import surplus. I am not sure that the complaint does not rest on the notion that import surpluses are bad per se. The Canadian import surplus, as of recent years, is of course primarily the natural and inevitable consequence of the Canadian import of capital. Unless the latter is bad, the former is not bad. That the import surplus is concentrated in trade with the United States may be valid ground for complaint in so far as this is the consequence of American barriers on imports from Canada and in so far as these barriers can reasonably be held to be unreasonable by persons or countries themselves protectionists and who regard their own trade barriers as part of the providential order of nature. Except, however, on the assumption, which I am not prepared to concede, that in past tariff bargaining between Canada and the United States the Canadian negotiators were tricked or bullied into reducing Canadian import duties to lower rates than were in the circumstances in Canada's best interest, the fact that Canadian importers choose, at equal or higher rates of duty, to buy American products rather than those of third countries seems to me a legitimate ground for moderate pride to American manufacturers but not a legitimate ground for Canadian complaint against either the American government or the American people.

The last in my list of Canadian grievances against American commercial policy is the alleged failure in recent years of the United States to give adequately strong and effective leadership to the movement toward a more liberal pattern of international trade in the free world, and especially the failure of Congress so far to approve American participation in the General Agreement on Tariffs and Trade (GATT) on a firm statutory basis. This criticism also I accept as valid. Once more, therefore, my comments will be in the nature of explanation, rather than of defence.

The American movement toward more liberal commercial policy that started in 1933 was at no time the response to an upsurge of American popular sentiment. It was the product primarily of dedicated, some would say fanatical, leadership on the part of a small group of high officials in the Department of State, and especially of Cordell Hull.

Since then there has been a change in party control of the administration in Washington. The Republican Party is traditionally enamoured of exports and hostile to imports and inherently suspicious on principle of international economic cooperation. Even Democratic Congressmen, moreover, would naturally give more whole-hearted support to a liberal economic foreign policy when it was the policy of a Democratic administration than when it is, as at present, the policy of a Republican administration. Added to this is the fact that the South, the traditional stronghold both of Democratic Party allegiance and of liberal commercial policy, in consequence of its industrialization and the changed status of its agriculture, has ceased to be a reliable supporter of programs of trade liberalization.

President Eisenhower is personally a firm believer in liberal commercial policy, both on economic and on higher foreign-policy grounds. In the nature of things, however, the demand on his time and attention is always heavy, and at the critical moments trade policy has in the past tended to slide downward on his list of priorities. The burden of getting the required legislation through Congress has fallen therefore in larger part than was expedient on his Cabinet and administrative staff. In the light of the professed economic foreign policy of the administration, the high officials with major responsibility for carrying American official policy into practice are an odd lot, indeed. The present secretary of state, when he was a senator, voted against renewal of the Trade Agreement Act, the only statutory barrier to a relapse to the tariff levels of the Hoover age. The secretary of commerce, before he came to Washington, was a high officer of the Boston Home-Market Club, an organization that has for generations been an outstanding practitioner of cultural lag, with its interest in uplift confined strictly to tariff rates. The Tariff Commission has been packed with unreconstructed protectionists. The official in charge until very recently of the administration of economic foreign aid was notoriously and openly hostile to economic foreign aid. Such are the men who have to persuade Congress that it should act vigorously and promptly in support of the GATT and of further lowering trade barriers. The only comforting idea that has come my way with reference to this seemingly desperate conjuncture is that if responsible officials with such a past press upon Congress the necessity to move in the direction of freer trade, Congress will be persuaded that the urgency on grounds of higher foreign policy of such movement must indeed be great.

An additional factor that has operated unfavourably for the success of the administration's economic foreign policy is the downgrading of the status of the egghead in the processes of Washingtonian policy formulation. This began under the Truman administration and has progressed much further under the Eisenhower administration. In consequence, the former role of the trained economist has been in large part taken over by the businessman and the lawyer. It is only the recognition that I cannot expect any audience to credit me with full and unalloyed objectivity in this matter that restrains me from revealing how unfortunate a development I think this has on the whole been, above all in the field of economic foreign policy. I do not claim, however, that even in this field there operates a law such that the trained economist necessarily makes a superior civil servant in the American pattern as compared, say, to the successful businessmen. The record of Will Clayton, one of Cordell Hull's aides, for one, provides clear evidence to the contrary.

Despite these unfavourable factors, I would not advise Canadians to be more than moderately gloomy about the prospects for American commercial policy in the near future and about the consequences for Canada. American commercial policy is not nearly as important as the level of American economic activity in determining the volume in which and the prices at which the United States makes its Canadian purchases. It is clear that 1958 will not be a good year. But since the coming of the statistical age, there has been only one period longer than fifteen months in which the American economy ceased to expand, the one exception being the aberration of 1929 to 1932. The National Archives Building in Washington has carved on its front the inscription "The Past is Prologue." A Washington taxi driver makes it his practice to interpret it to sightseeing visitors as meaning: "Mister, you ain't seen nuthin' yet." That is also my opinion as to the future of the American economy and as to the long-run prospects that the American market offers to Canadian exports, even if American import barriers remain very much as they are and even if they should undergo a moderate rise.

Canadians express concern about the extent to which Canada's national prosperity is dependent on exports to the United States. In the past two decades the American market has been for Canada, on the whole and on realistic standards, a fairly dependable one. It has been a market profitable to Canada beyond all previous expectations and beyond all comparison with what has been available to Canada elsewhere or to other countries anywhere. If Canadians nevertheless are not happy with it, they would be even less happy without it. A young lady, upon being told that it was St Paul's opinion that those who married did well, and those who remained unmarried did better, replied that she had no ambition to do better than well. Canada's power of choice is even more restricted than was hers. Canada has no visible alternatives, even inferior ones. The movement in Europe for a Common Market and a Free Trade Area; the movement in Latin America for regional preferential arrangements; the large proportion of the world's population that is Communist: These facts seem to point decisively against any major decline in the early future in the relative proportions in which Canada's exports must seek an American market. It will also not be soon, although I feel sure there will be a time, when Canada will be able to have declining exports and increasing prosperity simultaneously.

None of this is intended to discourage Canada from pressing, and from pressing hard, for ameliorations in the American trade-restriction pattern. It seems easily predictable, however, that such pressure is more likely to bring concrete results if it is not permitted to rest too openly on a conviction that in commercial negotiations with the United States the reciprocity should be all on one side. I would advise, moreover, that any Canadian bill of complaints should concentrate on the more important and more substantial grievances and that argument be confined to what can be argued with reason and with force in the general setting of Canadian-American relations and of American political and other obligations to third countries.

It is the custom of American lawyers when they prepare a brief, even when they have a very strong case, to multiply their arguments as much as possible, mixing good and bad ones promiscuously, in the hope, I suppose, that they can catch the judge and opposing counsel off guard. I don't suppose this has any ill effects in litigation since there is universal recognition that such procedure is a cherished prerogative of the American legal profession. In diplomacy, where the appeal is to governments, to legislatures, and to public opinion, not to trained and impartial judges, such practice can well lead to the failure of the negotiations. Rebuttal or rejection of the arguments that are weak, captious, or fanciful can readily provide an effective pretext for neglect or minimization of the strong ones. There is in diplomacy no judge with the authority and the will to separate out the good from the bad arguments in order to adjudicate solely on the basis of the good ones. The press, and special-interest groups, may indeed find it in their interest to do exactly the reverse and to destroy the effectiveness of what is on the whole a strong case by stressing the weaknesses in its mode of presentation. In the field of commercial policy, it is especially important that the planning and the conduct of negotiations be guided by professionally qualified personnel, for they alone will know, or will be equipped quickly to find out, what it is permissible and sensible to ask for, in the light of historical precedent, of treaty obligations to third countries, of possible conflict with other national interests, and of the standard rituals and practices of successful diplomacy.

In negotiations with the United States, it should be borne in mind that Congress is the key agency and that it will take combined pressure from the administration and from American public opinion to induce Congress to take action of a liberalizing kind in trade matters. The goodwill toward Canada of the American public, as I have said before, is genuine and strong. It will not be possible, however, to bring it heavily to bear in favour of Canada on commercial-policy matters if the American public should acquire the conviction, or perhaps even a strong suspicion, that the complaints against American policy are delivered not so much to promote the improvement of Canadian-American relations as to serve partisan domestic political objections. There may even be American politicians who, out of a sense of professional fraternity with their Canadian counterparts, may help them to preserve their political ammunition for repeated use on future occasions by refraining from doing anything themselves that would contribute to the resolution of Canadian-American controversies. I have noticed that the Chateau Laurier regularly offers bear steak on its grill-room menu. This may be ideal diet for domestic politics; it will not serve conciliatory diplomacy well.

On the last of the topics I will deal with, the complaints Canadians are making about the consequences for the Canadian economy of the American capital invasion, I will have to be brief. I will the more contentedly keep my comments short because, try as best I can, I can either find little merit in the Canadian complaints against American business operating in Canada, or find them of minor economic significance, or find myself unable to appraise them because they never seem to be supported by careful, competent, and reasonably objective collection and analysis of what confirmatory evidence there may be. It seems also to my perhaps prejudiced view that much of the complaint suffers from lack of historical perspective and of due sense of proportion, and that some of it displays at least slight traces of either genuine or contrived hysteria. If I had regard only for American interests, I could also without much feeling of restraint be brief: because in this area American official policy is not seriously involved; because it lies easily within the power of Canada to check and even to reverse the inflow of American capital very much as it pleases; and because while this would no doubt involve American business in disappointment with respect to realization of prospective profit, American business would not have entered Canada unless it had supposed it was welcome and will sadly but determinedly depart if it becomes convinced that it has outworn its welcome. In all sincerity, however, I do feel that Canada here has a very great deal at stake, whereas (except for the overriding interest of retaining Canadian goodwill) the American economic stakes in Canada, though substantial, are (relative to the total scale of the American economy) not such as will determine in one direction or the other the main trend of American prosperity. American business has in good faith sought partnership with the Canadian economy and in good faith has believed that it had won it to the mutual satisfaction and profit of both parties. It has believed that in such partnership there had been generated a rise of Canadian prosperity to hitherto nonexistent and even unanticipated levels; that continuance of this partnership would very nearly guarantee continuance of this Canadian upsurge; and that from it American business could derive legitimate profit for itself. Canada should not, in its own interest, deliberately do anything to end or even to reduce the proportions of this partnership except after careful and judicious consideration of the possible consequences for itself. My own opinion is that for some time into the future the most promising prospect for Canadian growth in wealth, in strength, in population, and in wellbeing in general for Canada is to maintain unimpaired its links with the secular upward trend in American prosperity, in full confidence that Canada knows where the American economy is going, and that Canada has nothing to fear and much to hope for from going along with it.

An English, eighteenth-century, country parson, Philip Henry, sought in marriage the only daughter and heiress of a Mr Matthews, a rich and aristocratic-minded squire. When his daughter pleaded with him that he should not reject the parson's suit, Mr Matthews demurred. He allowed that Mr Henry was a gentleman, a scholar, and an excellent preacher, but he was poor, his manners and bearing were not always quite *comme il faut,* and they did not even know where he came from. "True," said Miss Matthews, "but I know where he is going, and I should like to go with him." My own personal opinion, for what it is worth, is that Canadians, including Canadian businessmen, would do well for themselves if they responded in the spirit of this Miss Matthews to the opportunities for partnership with American business.

Until I have been confronted with more and more persuasive evidence, I will be skeptical that American business operating in Canada, even when it almost preempts certain fields by virtue of its longer experience, its greater financial resources, and its greater scale of operations, reduces instead of increasing in the net the scope for enterprise, investment, and profit open to Canadian business. In contributing as it has to the growth in size and in profitability of the Canadian economy, American business has created for Canadians many more opportunities for successful careers than it has provided for Americans. The complaint has been repeatedly launched in Canada that American business operating in Canada offers inadequate openings to Canadian talent. Here, fortunately, I do have some statistical data. American firms operating in Canada had in 1956 a total of over 114,000 persons on their Canadian payrolls, of whom 2,058 were American citizens. No doubt, not all of these 2,058 were presidents of subsidiaries, branch managers, and so forth. Canadians protest that American business operating in Canada does not sufficiently provide facilities for Canadian financial participation in the Canadian operations and for Canadian membership on the boards of directors of their Canadian subsidiaries. I do not believe that this is of much economic consequence, but I have become convinced that American business in the interest of friendly relations should move as fast as is consistent with its needs and practicabilities to establish Canadian equity securities for its Canadian subsidiaries and to appoint Canadians to its Canadian-company boards of directors. Except for public relations, no great benefits should be expected to flow from this. Canadian directors will be chosen and retained, as long as majority control rests with the head companies, on the basis of their loyalty to the companies' interests, and no matter how patriotically Canadian they may be, these directors will continue to expect Canadian diplomacy and Canadian commercial policy to be determined in Ottawa and not in Canadian boardrooms. As to Canadian financial participation, an outstanding New York security analyst tells me that over the years those who have invested in the securities of American mother companies have done very much better for themselves than those who have invested in the securities of their foreign subsidiaries.

The complaint is made that American business operating in Canada does not contribute as generously to local charities and to Canadian universities and colleges as does Canadian business. I have seen statements by two high officers of Canadian universities citing specific instances where the absorption by an American company of a local Canadian company has meant that the local university has lost a valuable and valued contributor. I have no first-hand information in this regard, but it does seem to me that there may here be a genuine difference in the mode of operation of American and of Canadian business with respect to charitable and educational contributions. I remember that when I first came to the United States and observed fund campaigns by great American universities, I was surprised to find that, unlike the flow of gifts to McGill University from important Canadian companies with head offices in Montreal, American companies in the United States made no or only quite minor gifts to universities. This has changed somewhat in recent years, but I think that it is still predominantly true that American business makes its contribution to chari- table and educational purposes through personal gifts by individual businessmen or through gifts by family foundations established by businessmen in their personal capacity, and not through appropriations from company funds by the companies that they may dominate. Whatever the merits of this pattern of behaviour for the American scene, it may well be an inappropriate pattern for Canada. I am certain, however, in the light of the way in which American business operates today in general, and also in the light of the special adaptations to local cultural patterns that American business cheerfully and readily makes in its non-Canadian foreign operations, that it would not at all be difficult to secure a prompt adaptation by American companies operating in Canada to this special, and no doubt admirable, Canadian cultural pattern. All that would be necessary, I think, would be for some appropriate Canadian organization to prepare a dignified and informative brochure, giving well-authenticated data as to the differences in behaviour in this respect between Canadian-owned and American- owned corporations operating in Canada, and to distribute it to an appropriate American mailing list, such as all Canadian companies selling uranium stocks on the American market know where to purchase.

    When I read the Canadian complaints against the wrongs committed by American business in Canada, I feel a good deal of sympathy with the prisoner at the dock who objected because the judge had taken the word of one man who saw him commit the crime, when he, the prisoner, could readily bring hundreds of people who could honestly testify that they had not seen him commit the crime. But I do not know the facts at first hand, and I am especially ignorant of what reply, if any, American businessmen operating in Canada make, or could make, to these complaints. I have neither the time, nor the required skills, nor the facilities, to conduct such a study on my own, and my regular pattern of university activity, even if it would be libelous to describe it as a mutually profitable partnership between teacher and students, whereby the teacher supplies ideas, good and bad, and the students supply the facts, true and false, to support them, does make me in such matters wholly dependent on the studies of others. Such studies, alas, seem to be totally lacking. I do know something, however, more or less at first hand, about American businesses operating in Latin America, and what I know indicates that it is the first order of American businesses to adapt their mode of operation as far as at all practicable to local wishes and local needs. I feel confident that American businesses will do likewise in Canada as soon as they discover the apparent strength of Canadian dissatisfaction with their present ways of doing things. Once more, however, I must express my conviction that the consequent gain to Canada will be more sentimental than economic.

Finally, a few words applied to the attempt to set the American capital inflow into Canada in a historical perspective that will support the view I hold that however serious at the moment may be the problem posed for Canada by this inflow, whether in its contribution to rising emotional temperatures or in its more tangible economic and political significance, it is probably a transitory problem destined to shrink greatly if not to vanish entirely through obsolescence before long.

The scale on which American capital has come into Canada since the end of World War Two and the specific forms that the invasion has taken have been both cause and consequence of the rapid economic expansion that has occurred in Canada and that has excited the admiration and aroused the envy of other countries still in an immature stage of economic development. The basic factors responsible for this upsurge – if I may take for granted the supreme capacity of the Canadian people for hard work, for enterprise, and for recognizing the main chance when it makes itself conspicuously apparent – have been the series of magnificent discoveries of rich natural resources; the availability of a great American market for the products of the newly discovered resources; the willingness of the Canadian people to save an appreciable fraction of their rising incomes for use in development of the Canadian economy; the support to this development that has come from the increase in the Canadian labour force as a consequence of the fertility of Canadian mothers as well as of the inflow of additional workers from Europe; and, finally, the aid and initiative provided, at market prices, by American capital, enterprise, technical skills, and experience.

The Canadian expansion has been of a type that is specially capital-intensive, if I may, for the last time, resort to my professional jargon. I have seen quoted a Canadian estimate that it now takes $5 of additional capital investment to add $1 per year to the Canadian gross national product. This is a very high capital ratio as compared to other expanding economies, and unless the discoveries of new and rich natural resources continue at their recent pace – which would seem to me to be too good to be probable – it is almost bound to decrease. Much more than half of the necessary capital already comes from internal Canadian savings. As Canadian incomes rise, the Canadian ratio of savings to income will also tend to rise, while the more advanced forms of economic development, and especially the tertiary industries, will call for less capital relative to labour and relative to the value of annual product than has been the case for mines, oil wells, hydroelectric plants, and steel-processing factories. As American companies operating in Canada complete their pioneering, they will expand less rapidly and in less capital-using ways. They may even find elsewhere greener fields, or fields more saturated with oil, to which to apply their special talents. In consequence of these and other factors, it is a reasonable prospect for Canada that it will increasingly rely on its own generation of capital resources and will increasingly reduce its dependence on American capital, enterprise, and skill in its pursuit for its people of a richer and larger national economy. Meanwhile, Canada should accept in good grace the cooperation of American business in full confidence that this in large measure meets a passing but urgent need and that it does not endanger but on the contrary serves to promote the objectives that wise, patriotic, and informed Canadians should strive for: namely, a greater, a richer, and an eternally Canadian Canada.

JACOB VINER became the third Walker Professor of Economics and International Finance at Princeton University in 1946 after teaching at the University of Chicago for thirty years. He was editor of the *Journal of Political Economy* for eighteen years. Dr Viner retired from Princeton in 1960 and then spent a year at Harvard as Taussig Research Professor. He also served as an advisor to the US government during World War One and as an advisor to the Treasury Department, where he participated in the planning of the Social Security Program in the 1930s. He was later a consultant to the board of governors of the Federal Reserve System.

Dr Viner was a member of the Princeton Institute for Advanced Study, an honorary fellow of the London School of Economics, and a fellow or member of honorary academies in the United States, Great Britain, Sweden, and Italy. He was awarded the American Economic Association Francis A. Walker Medal and honorary degrees from thirteen universities. Dr Viner died in 1970.

2

Civil Liberties and Canadian Federalism

F.R. SCOTT, 1959

PART ONE

In this paper I will discuss the relationship between civil liberties and the Canadian constitution in the light of the steps now being taken to write a bill of rights into the law. But I want to enter upon this discussion from a much wider point of view than that suggested by present political alternatives or by the necessity of taking sides when it comes to a vote on a particular bill. I doubt whether anything I have to say will help any member of Parliament to make up his or her mind on Mr Diefenbaker's Bill C–60[1] – assuming, of course, that our party system permits any such daring assertion of the individual will. What I am primarily concerned with is the growth of the constitution and with our current interest in civil liberties and human rights as evidence of that growth. I shall talk about civil liberties, but civil liberties as part of a never ceasing constitutional evolution.

We sometimes forget that Canada has one of the oldest constitutions in existence. So rapidly is the whole world moving forward into new relationships, so swiftly does technological change compel readjustments in the internal structures of contemporary societies, that nations are few that have been able to adapt themselves peacefully and gradually to constitutional inevitabilities. Revolution has been the order of our day. Peaslee's *Constitutions of Nations* lists seventy-two countries with constitutions younger than our own. England is, of course,

---

[1] An Act for the Recognition and Protection of Human Rights and Fundamental Freedoms.

the prime example of a major power that has maintained an unbroken rule of law over the centuries – nearly three centuries now, dating from the glorious revolution of 1688 – while undergoing changes in social and political structure that may properly be called revolutionary. At crucial times that have strained and might have broken her legal order – 1832, the first Reform Bill; 1911, the first Parliament Act; 1931, the Statute of Westminster; 1945, the first socialist government – major shifts of political power have been accomplished within and under the constitutional framework, which continues after the great events to look remarkably like what it was before them though in fact nothing can ever be quite the same again. Truly it has been said that the English change everything but the name, whereas in many other countries revolutions change nothing but the name. Canada has now enjoyed close on a century of unbroken constitutional evolution with a constitution that in outward appearance has altered remarkably little despite the transformation from the agricultural to the industrial base, from colony to nation, from horse-and-buggy to aeroplane, and from four provinces to ten. Since 1867 we have steadily developed our processes of government under this constitution, strengthening some parts of the state machinery, allowing others to sink into virtual disuse, and generally putting Canadian flesh on the dry bones of the legal skeleton.

Looking back on our history with the eye of the constitutional lawyer, I would single out four main lines of constitutional growth as being the chief measure of our achievement. The first was the consolidation of the vast British North American territories into a single state. Confederation at first included only Ontario, Quebec, Nova Scotia, and New Brunswick, and of these Nova Scotia was a very reluctant partner. There was as yet no Dominion stretching from sea to sea. Negotiations with the British government resulted in the passing of the Rupert's Land Act in 1868 and the purchase of the rights of the Hudson's Bay Company. Canada then had title to enormous tracts of empty land in which the forms and processes of federal government had to be introduced. Manitoba, a federal creation, became the first post-Confederation province. British Columbia joined in 1871, and Prince Edward Island was brought in, or more accurately, bought in, by 1873. Sir John Macdonald had then achieved the first great part of his nation-building task, and the writ of the Canadian government ran across the continent. The northern frontier was still formless and vague, but in a simple one-page document called the Order-in-Council of 31st July 1880, the significance of which we can appreciate more fully today, the Imperial government transferred to us "all British Territories and Possessions in North America, and the Islands adjacent to such Territories and Possessions which are not already included in the Dominion of Canada," with the exception of the Colony of Newfoundland. Thus we had claim to Arctic regions at whose extent and value we could only guess. When, in 1949, Newfoundland was at last added to the Canadian family, the dream of 1867 had become a reality, for we must not forget that delegates from Newfoundland attended the Quebec Conference in 1864 and voted in favour of the proposed federation.

The second marked evidence of our constitutional growth since 1867 lies in the definition of the status of provinces within the federal structure. Here opinions may well differ as to whether what happened was what was intended to happen by the Fathers, but the end result is clear. In the two leading cases of *Hodge v. The Queen* and *The Liquidators of the Maritime Bank v. The Receiver General of New Brunswick,* a legal basis was laid for the notion of provincial autonomy that has come to be accepted as an inherent part of our federalism. *Hodge's* case held that sovereignty existed in the provincial legislatures as fully as the Imperial Parliament possessed and could bestow it. Not only did this mean that provinces could therefore delegate their legislative powers to subordinate administrative bodies (and without such a rule it is difficult to see how government could have been carried on), but it also means (and this is relevant to any discussion of civil liberties) that provincial legislatures acting within their spheres of jurisdiction may enlarge or contract civil liberties and human rights as much as they please. They are curtailed only by what may be found in the British North America Act, and as we shall see, such restrictions are few. The *Liquidators* case held that the royal prerogative flowed into provinces for all purposes of provincial government, thus ending forever any notion that they were nothing more than glorified municipalities. When we add to these two cases the many others that greatly enlarged the content of specific words in section 92 of the BNA Act listing provincial powers, the resulting growth in status of provincial governments is obvious.

Apart from judicial interpretation, we now perceive that section 109 of the constitution, which declares that the provinces should continue to have jurisdiction over their lands and minerals, was one of the most important powers that they possessed, for this has given provincial governments a major responsibility for the development of our natural resources. I doubt if the results were contemplated by the framers of the constitution. The main economic activities of Canadians in 1867 were agriculture, fishing, and trade and commerce, and these were all named as exclusive or concurrent federal heads of jurisdiction; all three have received so restrictive an interpretation in the courts as to discourage attempts at economic regulation in times of peace. This has fitted in remarkably well with our dominant philosophy of individualism, for it has meant that any government planning must operate within a relatively restricted area, the provinces being too small and the federal government too circumscribed (at least outside the Northwest Territories) to control, even if they wished to, the vast aggregations of capital that still operate under the label of free enterprise. It is surely obvious today that there are some corporations within the country more powerful than several of the provinces. The prairie provinces have not even the power to tax the Canadian Pacific Railway; the sovereignty of three Canadian governments, representing nearly three million people, is subordinated to the interest of one private corporation.

The growth in the status and power of provinces has had a special significance for Canada in the evolution of our concept of dual cultures. For while provincial autonomy and minority rights are by no means the same thing, as the whole history of our separate school cases dearly shows, it is a fact that most French Canadians live in Quebec and that over wide areas of the social life of the province, though by no means over all, the legislature has exclusive jurisdiction, so that provincial autonomy and cultural particularism become largely synonymous. I do not propose to elaborate on a theme so familiar. Like so many other aspects of our national life, the heart of the matter is social rather than constitutional; with the important exception of the use of two languages in provincial courts and laws, and the inability of the Quebec Legislature to delegate its powers to Parliament under section 94 of the BNA Act (which no other province has ever used anyway), there is no difference between the constitutional position, or power, of Quebec and that of the other original federating provinces. While the Quebec Royal Commission of Inquiry on Constitutional Problems, commonly known as the Tremblay Commission, evolved in its Report of 1956 some novel, not to say revolutionary, concepts of Canadian federalism, so far these ideas have had no effect on the evolution of our constitutional law.

A third striking growth in our constitution is evidenced by the development of Canada since 1867 from the position of colony to that of an independent nation state within the Commonwealth. This change, with its concomitants of the definition of Canadian citizenship in 1946 and the abolition of appeals to the Privy Council in 1949, seen in the long perspective of history, is but the completion of the struggle for responsible government that was perhaps the greatest single constitutional development prior to Confederation. So gradual and prolonged was the process that we are left at the end not knowing exactly when the magical transformation took place; indeed, I still meet Canadians who feel it is not quite nice to say that we are an independent country. Yet as one who took some part in the movement for various constitutional reforms prior to World War Two, I cannot help finding satisfaction in the statement in the third edition of Halsbury's *Laws of England* that "With the decline of the concept of common allegiance, manifested by the creation of separate citizenship's and the increasing evidence of the divisibility of the Crown afforded by the new form of the royal styles and titles, the theory of automatic belligerency can be regarded as outmoded."

Shades of our great debate in the 1930s! Similarly satisfactory to me is the further statement in the same volume that "By this time [1947] the terms 'Dominion' and 'Dominion status' had come to be thought to convey a misleading impression of the constitutional and international status of the countries concerned, if not to imply subordination to the United Kingdom. The terms have therefore ceased to be used for official purposes, and the designation of the Secretary of State for the Dominions has been changed to Secretary of State for Commonwealth Relations." This radical transformation of colony into nation state, it should be noted, has occurred without so much as the change of a comma in the BNA Act. It was climaxed by the new Letters Patent constituting the office of Governor General of Canada, effective 1 October 1947, which transferred "all powers and authorities" lawfully belonging to the Crown in England in respect of Canada to our governor general. I emphasize that little word "all." If I had to choose our Independence Day, it would be this date. Incidentally, 1 October is a good time of the year at which to have a holiday.

Last in this list of striking changes since 1867, I would mention the enormous growth of governmental activity on all levels: federal, provincial, and municipal. Collectivism is creeping upon us with every increase of population and automation, and its coming is reflected in the almost total covering of our society by group activity, be it public or private. We are all civil servants or organization men today. The farmer, last stronghold of individualism, is steadily being brought into the system through integration, floor prices, bulk sales, and other devices. Most noticeable among the enlarged federal activities are defence, social welfare, and fiscal policy, using that term to include all measures intended to maintain economic stability. These new responsibilities of Parliament have produced the only two changes in the distribution of legislative powers that have been made since 1867: namely, the unemployment insurance amendment of 1940 and the old age pensions amendment of 1951. Consequent upon the growth of state power has come the necessity of finding new financial relations between federal and provincial governments, for the original concept of provincial powers and functions, needing only direct taxation and subsidies to finance them, has broken down before the increasing demands of the welfare state and the requirements of fiscal policy. The courts have also developed in the law of the constitution the theory of emergency powers to enable Ottawa to deal in an unhampered way with the heavy responsibilities of wartime. This last power, the emergency power, raises technical legal problems I will not go into here, but we must keep it in mind when thinking of civil liberties and their protection since it is commonly, and in my view erroneously, assumed that there is no place for the assertion of fundamental freedoms in wartime. Mr Diefenbaker's Bill of Rights specifically provides that nothing done under the War Measures Act shall be deemed to be an infringement of the liberties proclaimed in the statute, thus giving a dangerous parliamentary approval, if the bill passes in this form, to the notion that in a war fought for democracy there are no limits to what the state may do to the citizen in an effort to achieve victory. There is need, I suggest, for a greater clarification of the limits of emergency powers and of the conditions under which, if at all, traditional protections for the individual, such as habeas corpus, may be suspended. Surely our behaviour during the spy scare of 1945 is a warning that we may easily exceed the measures reasonably necessary for our internal security.

It is against this background of a stable, well-tested, and maturing constitution that I want to discuss the question of civil liberties and human rights. Only in recent years have we begun to concern ourselves with the place of civil liberties in our system of government; it was minority rights that first received attention. We have had many cases involving rights of citizens brought into the courts from time to time, but we have dealt with them as they arose and have not generalized from them any broad principles of freedom. It has been traditionally said among us that we were like the British in this, as in so many other ways, and that any declaration of rights was incompatible with our kind of constitution. Does not the preamble of the BNA Act say that we are to have a constitution similar in principle to that of Great Britain? And does not this mean that we leave the protection of our freedoms to the ordinary courts of law?

Most of us in the law schools are reared in the Diceyan gospel that with us,

every official from the Prime Minister down to a constable or a collector of taxes, is under the same responsibility for every act done without legal justification as any other citizen. The Reports abound with cases in which officials have been brought before the courts, and made, in their personal capacity, liable to punishment, or to the payment of damages, for acts done in their official character but in excess of their lawful authority. A colonial governor, a secretary of state, a military officer, and all subordinates, though carrying out the commands of their official superiors, are as responsible for any act which the law does not authorize as is any private and unofficial person.

These are noble words and express the legal content of what we call the rule of law. The statement about the liability of a prime minister, incidentally, has no footnote reference to any authority in Dicey, such as is given for the colonial governor, the secretary of state, and the military officer; I am happy to note that our Supreme Court in *Roncarelli v. Duplessis* has recently supplied such an authority, the first in the history of the Commonwealth. With Magna Carta in the background, and Dicey's rule of law in the foreground, we have not seemed to need any further safeguard for civil liberties. And in truth when we look at other constitutions with bills of rights in their written texts, not excepting the

American constitution, and compare the rights of citizens under them with what has commonly prevailed in Canada, we have not felt that we were under any particular disadvantage.

Unfortunately we are missing several weaknesses in this idyllic picture. So simple a method of protecting human rights as the English use depends upon basic assumptions on which we cannot wholly rely in Canada. It depends upon three things: parliamentary restraint in legislation, bureaucratic restraint in administration, and a strong and live tradition of personal freedom among the citizens generally. We have some of all these factors, but not in any permanent or reliable degree. We have eleven legislatures to watch, not just one, and the eleven possess almost unlimited sovereignty within their spheres. We have enormously expanded the administrative authority of the state, for reasons I have just explained, and this means we have delegated state authority to thousands of officials not all of whom can be expected to be models of deference in the exercise of their multitudinous powers. Even in England this administrative growth has raised fears of a "New Despotism," or "administrative lawlessness," and other supposedly un-British characteristics. And we have in Canada a very mixed population, drawn from many different European and Asiatic societies, that has not yet been brought to a common understanding of the processes of parliamentary democracy by centuries of shared struggle and lively history. We are, moreover, embarked upon a governmental task that the English have never had to face: that of working out the terms and conditions of the coexistence of two cultures with very different concepts of the relationship of the individual and the church to the state. All these factors make the Canadian experiment in democracy unlike the British in easily discernible ways. We are now realizing that magnificent though our legal and constitutional inheritance may be, it may not suffice for our present purposes. We would do well to take stock of our position and to devise more precise methods for the strengthening of those principles of democratic government without which the creation of modem Canada would hardly seem justified.

Moreover when we stop to think of our own history we realize that we have in fact not relied upon tradition as sufficient. If we go back to our constitutional roots in English history, we find several notable formulations of rights and liberties, from Magna Carta in 1215 down to the Bill of Rights of 1689, and on to the Balfour Declaration of 1926 and the Statute of Westminster of 1931. The theoretical sovereignty of the British Parliament has tended to blind us to the reality of the limitations upon that sovereignty residing in the theory of government these documents proclaim. The kings and queens of England knew they ruled on the terms of a contract with their subjects, a contract to observe the laws and customs of the realm and to safeguard the rights and liberties of the people. When James II fled he was said to have broken this contract. We know that the United Kingdom Parliament has the theoretical power to repeal the Statute of Westminster, but we also know, to use the words of Lord Sankey in the *British Coal Corporation* case, that "that is theory and has no relation to realities." The realities are that Parliament is restrained in England by certain principles of government almost as effectively as if they were written into a binding constitution.

If we look into our own Canadian history, we can find similar examples of the outstanding constitutional document. From the earliest days of British rule in Canada, we have found it necessary to formulate, with increasing clarity, certain declarations of particular rights. The first of these had to do with those rights that pressed most early upon us. The Treaty of Utrecht of 1713, the Treaty of Paris of 1763, and the Quebec Act of 1774 laid the basis for the bicultural character of Canada by legalizing the practice of the Roman Catholic religion in Nova Scotia and Quebec respectively; the Quebec Act also restored the French civil law on all matters of property and civil rights and altered the oath of allegiance so that Catholics might with good conscience hold public office. No future constitution could ignore these basic Canadian facts. Habeas corpus was introduced into Quebec by special ordinance in 1785; religious and civic equality for the Jews was provided in a Lower Canada statute of 1831. Jews sat in Parliament in this country before they could take a seat at Westminster. Then in 1851 the old Province of Canada adopted the Freedom of Worship Act, which proclaimed in section 2:

2. The free exercise and enjoyment of religious profession and worship, without discrimination, or preference, provided the same be not made an excuse for acts of licentiousness, or a justification of practices inconsistent with the peace and safety of the Province, are by the constitution and laws of this Province allowed to all his Majesty's subjects living within the same.

This statute has continued in Quebec, appearing today as chapter 307 of the Revised Statutes, 1941. Ontario, however, ceased to reprint it after 1897 though it has never been repealed in that province. It is my view that this pre-Confederation statute not only is in force today throughout Quebec and Ontario, but cannot be repealed or amended by the provincial legislatures since the subject matter of section 2 falls within federal jurisdiction under the criminal law power. If this be the true view, it means that Mr Duplessis's recent amendments to the statute, designed to curb the activities of the Jehovah's Witnesses, are ultra vires (a matter now before the courts of Quebec) and that our two largest provinces are under a religious bill of rights. They cannot change it, and the Parliament of Canada,

while able to, is certainly unlikely to change it. Hence we seem to find ourselves
endowed by history with a peculiarly untouchable statute.

Our pre-Confederation history thus provides us with indications of the need
to formulate civil liberties in Canada not as a comprehensive and broad declaration of rights, but as specific solutions to practical problems. The growth of
the concepts was cumulative: positions gained at one stage lasted through any
constitutional changes that came after. Take the question of the two official
languages: Neither the Treaty of Paris of 1763 nor the Quebec Act of 1774 nor
the Constitutional Act of 1792 protected the use of French, yet from the moment
the first legislature in Lower Canada met, it published its statutes in the two
languages, side by side in the same volume. Durham's rather naive faith that
French Canada would gradually become British in language and institutions, and
the strong feelings aroused by the rebellions of 1837–38, led to the prohibition
of the publication of the laws in French in the Act of Union of 1841, but by
1848 an amendment reintroduced French as an official language. This settled the
matter for Quebec, and the language provision in the BNA Act, section 133, was
the result. Carrying the story forward, we know that the federal Parliament wrote
the two languages into the Manitoba constitution and into the Northwest Territories law, only to have both these extensions of bilingualism later removed by
local action and pressure. The French network of the Canadian Broadcasting
Corporation has produced a practical extension of French over large sections of
the West in a manner more meaningful than a simple printing of statutes would
achieve, but the situation from Quebec's point of view is still unequal and
unsatisfactory. Yet what an enormous national asset it is to possess as our two
official languages the two working languages of the United Nations! It is probably too much to expect that we shall all be bilingual, but it is not too much to
hope that bilingualism may be increased in English Canada where it is least
developed. This would have international as well as national advantages. In the
summer of 1959 at the International Congress of Comparative Law in Brussels,
delegates from thirty-four countries, including some from behind the Iron Curtain,
used French as the language of communication; those who could speak only
English had to have everything they said translated into French.

The pre-Confederation era saw other ideas, vital to civil liberties, emerge into
constitutional form. Responsible government is an obvious example; its winning
marked the first great Canadian achievement of the principle contained in article 21
of the Universal Declaration of Human Rights, which states: "Everyone has the
right to take part in the government of his country, directly or through freely
chosen representatives." Briefly, responsible government meant that, for all
domestic purposes, we had nationalized the Crown. At the same time the establishment of an independent judiciary, excluded from the executive and legislative

branches of government, came about slowly through statutory changes; it was not something we inherited from England at the start but had to be fought for all over again in the colonies despite the well-known rule in the Act of Succession of 1701. So, too, the extension of the franchise, the payment of members of Parliament, and the completing of parliamentary processes generally represented a steady growth in the democratic idea and the placing of self-government on a firm basis of law and convention.

In the light of this historical survey, we can appreciate better the degree to which the text of the BNA Act of 1867 formulated or took for granted certain principles of civil liberty and human rights. It is true the act did not contain a bill of rights of the type found in the American and other constitutions, but it is certainly not true that it contained no such rights at all. The reference in the preamble to the United Kingdom constitution as the model to be followed is itself indicative of the intentions of the framers: The United Kingdom at that time was a parliamentary democracy headed by a constitutional monarch who reigned but did not govern; it had a long tradition of civil liberties, and the rule of law was firmly established. True, the doctrine of parliamentary sovereignty was a basic principle of English law, and to be "similar" to this concept our legislatures, even though limited in the area of their jurisdiction, had to possess the same kind of sovereignty within their spheres. This seems to argue us away from any notion of superior law restraining legislative action, but there is a counter-argument, first enunciated by Chief Justice Duff in the Alberta Press case in 1938, where he said, Davis J. concurring:

The statute [BNA Act] contemplates a parliament working under the influence of public opinion and public discussion. There can be no controversy that such institutions derive their efficacy from the free public discussion of affairs, from criticism and answer and counter-criticism, from attack upon policy and administration and defence and counter-attack from the freest and fullest analysis and examination from every point of view of political proposals. This is signally true in respect of the discharge by Ministers of the Crown of their responsibility to Parliament, by members of Parliament of their duty to the electors, and by the electors themselves of their responsibilities in the election of their representatives.

Mr Justice Cannon expressed similar views. Not unnaturally this new line of argument opened a wide door to the discovery within the text of the act of an inherent limitation on Canadian legislatures, both federal and provincial, deducible from the meaning the courts must give to words like "Parliament" and "Legislature." "There shall be one Parliament for Canada," says section 17; does not this mean, in the light of the preamble, that there shall be one freely elected

Parliament for Canada, chosen after a free discussion of the party programs in the press and on the hustings? The Alberta Press case went no further than to suggest that provincial legislatures could not take away basic freedoms. Mr Justice Abbot has extended the principle; he said in an *obiter dictum* in the Padlock Act case: "Although it is not necessary, of course, to determine this question for the purpose of the present appeal, the Canadian constitution being declared to be similar in principle to that of the United Kingdom, I am also of the opinion that as our constitutional Act now stands, Parliament itself could not abrogate this right of discussion and debate."

There was also a remark of Chief Justice Rinfret in the case of the *Alliance des Professeurs catholiques* suggesting a similar restriction on provincial legislatures: He said that a legislature, even if it wished, could not enact the absurdity that a court acting without jurisdiction could be protected from writs of prohibition. And in the *Chabot* case, which upheld the right of a parent, a Witness of Jehovah, to require exemption for his children at school from Catholic religious instruction, Mr Justice Casey went so far as to suggest that Canadian legislatures might be restrained by natural law. He quotes: "But for natural law there would probably have been no American and no French revolution; nor would the great ideals of freedom and equality have found their way into the law-books after having found it into the hearts of men." And then adds: "On this point there can be no doubt for if these rights find their source in positive law they can be taken away. But if, as they do, they find their existence in the very nature of man, then they cannot be taken away and they must prevail should they conflict with the provisions of positive law." While I personally think this statement goes beyond the limits of possible interpretation of the BNA Act – for it is not related, as was Chief Justice Duff's approach, to the specific word "Parliament" in the text of the act – it is indicative of a tendency to find limits to the notion of parliamentary sovereignty and limits precisely designed to protect human rights and fundamental freedoms. This all goes to show the creative role the courts can and, I suggest, should play in the growth of the constitution.

More important than the preamble to the act, because they comprise part of its enacting clauses, are certain provisions that are intended to guarantee liberties. Section 11 provides for a Privy Council to aid and advise the governor general; this gives a statutory basis for responsible government. Responsible government was stipulated in the terms of admission of British Columbia. Section 20 states that there must be a session of Parliament once at least in every year, and section 50 says that every House of Commons shall last for five years and no longer; while this last term may be postponed by special vote in time of emergency under the 1949 amending power, the annual session cannot. These two provisions are a kind of bill of rights against prolonged government without popular consent, though we must remember that Mr King showed us in 1940 that an annual session of Parliament might last only a few hours. We have lost the guaranteed right of provinces to representation in proportion to population that existed in the original constitution since this matter is now subject to amendment by federal statute, but no one doubts that the principle is firmly fixed among us. There is even in the BNA Act a special protection intended for the English-speaking minority in the Eastern Townships of Quebec; section 80 provides that no bill altering the electoral districts of that area can be passed unless a majority of their members have voted for it. This is, however, one of the several parts of the act that have been repealed, without any Canadian consultation or request, by the odd process used by the British for their statute law revision. Section 80 should never have been removed since it contains a minority right, something the law officers responsible for the revision presumably knew nothing about. It was bad enough to have our constitution amended in Britain without our consent before the Statute of Westminster, but it becomes absurd to find the process going on as late as 1950, when section 118, dealing with provincial subsidies, was removed secretly and silently; though it had been superseded by the 1907 amendment, it was still a formal part of the statute, reminding us of the old Nova Scotian complaint that their people were sold to Canada for eighty cents a head.

Minority rights to separate schools and the two languages are set our in sections 93 and 133; these operate as limitations upon the sovereignty of provincial and federal legislatures. Minority rights were matters peculiar to Canada and not part of our British inheritance. We saw how they formed a basic part of the pre-Confederation arrangements, so it is not surprising to see them entrenched in the fundamental law. What is perhaps strange is that no guarantee of religious freedom accompanied them into the BNA Act; apart from the reference to separate and dissentient schools for Protestants and Roman Catholics that existed at the time of the Union or might be established afterwards, the act is silent upon the subject of religious toleration. This is a matter we should do well to remember when we come to write our own Canadian constitution since it may well be that laws affecting religious observance, and presumably therefore laws prohibiting or restricting any religion, fall within the federal criminal law power, over which Parliament may be found to possess dangerously wide if not unlimited sovereignty. Such at least would seem to be a conclusion that follows from the *Birks* case, about which more will be said in part two of this paper.

An essential part of the 1867 arrangement was the federal power of disallowance of provincial laws. This was intended to be used to prevent interference with minority rights or discriminatory legislation injurious to Dominion interests. In the Confederation Debates, Georges Etienne Cartier, in reply to a question from Hon. John Rose of Montreal as to what would happen if the French majority

in Quebec tried to gerrymander the electoral districts so that no English-speaking
member could be returned to the Legislature, replied that the veto power might
be used. Hon. Mr Holborn asked, "Would you advise it?" and Cartier answered,
"Yes, I would recommend it myself in case of injustice." Disallowance, as we
know, is an uncertain weapon, easier to use against small provinces than large
ones, and was not resorted to in such striking examples of interference with
minority rights and civil liberties as the Manitoba Acts of 1890 abolishing the
separate school system and the use of the French language, or the Quebec
Padlock Act of 1937. Yet the threat of it may have induced Prince Edward Island
to repeal the worst features of its violently antilabour Trade Union Act of 1948;
and Mr Smallwood's even more extreme interference with freedom of association
as expressed in his recent legislation against the International Woodworkers
Association and the Teamsters Union has again confronted the federal government with the necessity of deciding whether or not to use the power. Surely if
disallowance can be used to save us from Social Credit legislation, as it was, it
can be used to protect us from laws striking at fundamental freedoms. Are not
trade unions a "minority" that needs protection? At the Constitutional Conference
in 1950, every provincial premier expressed himself as opposed to the veto
power, but I suggest that we should be chary of removing it, until we have at
least a bill of rights written into the constitution itself and binding on provincial
legislatures as well as on Parliament.

There is an important provision in the act of 1867 that has caused and still
causes much confusion with respect to the all-important problem of which of
the two levels of government, federal or provincial, has the principal jurisdiction
over civil liberties. This is the well-known head 13 of section 92 giving to
provincial legislatures jurisdiction over "Property and Civil Rights in the Province." The phrase "civil rights" is the one currently used in the United States to
cover the basic freedoms of religion, of speech, of the press, and so on, which
we tend to describe as civil liberties or fundamental freedoms. Several judicial
pronouncements have indicated that the words include the same freedoms in
section 92, which would mean that the provinces would become the chief
guardians of our traditional liberties. The alternative view, however, has been
receiving strong support in some of the recent cases in our Supreme Court,
notably the *Saumur,* the *Birks*, and the Padlock Act cases. I have no doubt myself
that this view is correct and that the words "civil rights" were intended to refer
only to private law rights between individuals, and not to those public rights,
such as freedom of religion, of speech, of the press, of association, and of the
person, that are really attributes of citizenship and the limits of which are set in
the criminal law. The late Mr Justice Mignault has made the distinction between
civil rights, political rights, and public rights very clearly in a passage of the
first volume of his treatise that Mr Justice Kellock, I think, was the first to read

into a Supreme Court judgment in the *Saumur* case in 1953. There is, however, a difficulty of interpretation here that will require more Supreme Court decisions before it can be fully resolved, for there are undoubtedly some aspects of our civil liberties that fall within provincial jurisdiction if we include in the term such matters as defamation, trade union certification in provincial employments, voting rights in provincial elections, the status of married women, and so on.

The BNA Act provided us with a written constitution of strict law, embedded in a context of constitutional convention and tradition. From that moment the growth of our ideas about civil liberties and human rights took place inside and under that constitution. The formative influences were the courts, in their interpretations, and the legislatures, in their enactment of laws. The courts in theory can protect only those rights, like the right to separate schools and to the use of the two languages, that are entrenched in the law. For the rest, they are confined to saying whether a particular law is or is not within the jurisdiction of the legislature that enacted it. With the justice of the law, with its policy and philosophy, once it has been found valid, they are not supposed to be concerned. The sovereignty of Parliament must be allowed to operate. As Mr Justice Riddell once put it, "The prohibition 'Thou shalt not steal' has no legal force upon the sovereign body." Hence the role of the courts in the development of our constitutional freedoms operates within defined limits. It is their duty to declare the law as it is, and the legislatures make the law.

In fact, however, even under a written constitution without a bill of rights of a comprehensive sort, the judicial role is extremely important. The discretion of the judge, particularly in constitutional cases, is very wide. There are two ways in which judges may in their interpretations lean to the side of liberty.

First, there is the established rule that all statutes should be strictly interpreted if they limit or reduce the rights of the citizen. Parliament must always be presumed to have intended the least interference with our freedom, not the most. Hence if two views of what a statute means are possible, the one will be preferred that leaves the larger freedom to the individual. Since words are clumsy things at best, and seldom convey a precise, invariable meaning, it is seldom that a statute does not allow of some alternative reading. This explains how in the same case a judge may be found to declare that there is only one possible view of what the law means and a court of appeal will equally firmly, and more authoritatively, declare that it means something else. A strong tradition of freedom in the judiciary thus acts as a corrective to illiberal tendencies that may exist in the legislature, whether it is that of a province or Parliament itself.

Second, the courts must say of any challenged statute whether or not it is within the powers of the enacting legislature. This judgment is a very complicated and difficult one, requiring a nice balance of legal skill, respect for established rules, and plain common sense. It is not and never can be an exact

science. Law and statesmanship are inextricably intermingled in the interpretation of constitutions. When the Privy Council first had to decide whether a
province in Canada could tax the banks, which are federal creatures, the argument was used that if they could they might abuse the power and make banking
impossible. Their lordships said that the fact a power might be abused was no
proof it did not exist, and the tax was upheld. Later when the Privy Council was
met with the precise situation of a tax on banks, imposed by the Social Credit
government of Alberta, which was so severe as to put the banks out of business
if upheld, their lordships found that the tax was not a true tax at all but an
invasion of the field of banking legislation. The abuse was checked. There are
so many ways of drawing the line between what is and what is not constitutional
that it is not difficult to find some reason why a particular piece of legislation
is invalid if the judges are so inclined. Thus even without a bill of rights there
is a certain degree of freedom in the courts to protect us against legislative
tyranny. For, by saying that a particular statute exceeds the jurisdiction of
Parliament or legislature, the courts remove the statute from the books, and the
liberties it destroyed are restored. For the time being at least our rights are saved.
The great value of constitutional guarantees is that the courts can use them to
check tides of opinion that can easily produce statutory infringements of our
freedoms. In so far as we can achieve it, we place the courts above the political
ferments of the day. I do not say that they always exhibit an Olympian detachment or that they are not themselves moved by the same feelings and emotions
as other people in the society about them. What I do say is that it is their function
and duty to act as guardians of our rights whether we have a bill of rights or
not and that the more we understand and respect this role the more adequately
will they fulfil it. Let me cite a definition given by Percy Corbett, formerly dean
of the McGill Faculty of Law: "Law is our collective name for what is perhaps
the most important set of institutions by which man has sought to reinforce his
reason against his passions."

PART TWO

I concluded part one with an analysis of the role of the judges in the protection
of our basic rights against legislative or bureaucratic infringement. This judicial
function is so important that I intend to continue with an examination of some
typical cases that have arisen in the past in order to show just what attitude the
courts have taken in the face of concrete situations. We shall be in a far better
position to judge of the necessity and nature of a bill of rights if we have some
knowledge of these facts of our constitutional history. We need particularly to
know about the leading civil liberties cases that have come before the Supreme

Court of Canada in the past decade. In no other period of our history have so many important questions of this kind arisen. I shall not confine myself, however, to recent history but shall include a selection of older cases that illustrate both the nature of our constitution and the kinds of behaviour of Canadians in different provinces that give rise to court battles over civil liberties.

Before explaining these cases I must be a little more specific as to what I mean by civil liberties and human rights. It seems to me that in Canada we must think of human rights and fundamental freedoms as comprising at least four main types of rights. I think we must include our minority rights among them. The United Nations Declaration does not contain minority or group rights, but in our history they have been of the first importance, and I would say without question that they rank ahead of nearly all other rights in the minds of most people in Quebec. I think that if the English were an equally surrounded minority, they would feel the same way. At any rate the notion of minority rights guaranteed in the constitution is so fundamental to us and so closely related to the idea of a bill of rights that we should include them in our thinking on human rights. This does not mean, however, that they must be rewritten in the new Bill of Rights, if it is adopted; their place in the present constitution is fully entrenched and need not be changed.

A second group of rights are more usually called civil liberties or fundamental freedoms. They include freedom of religion, of the press, of speech, and of association. With these I would put freedom of the person: the right to move about unmolested, to be free from arbitrary arrest or unlawful detention, and the right to live where one chooses. Here, too, I would put the right to participate in one's government: the right to vote and to stand as candidate for legislative bodies. And I think academic freedom belongs among the civil liberties as one aspect of freedom of speech and of conscience. A third kind of right is concerned with protecting the equality of status of citizens against discrimination due to race or religion: I would include here the types of statute we call Fair Employment Practices Acts and Fair Accommodation Practices Acts, and the Equal Pay for Equal Work Acts. These categories of rights I mention can never be exact; somewhere in this second or third group we should have to place not only the right to a fair trial in criminal cases, but also a right to a fair hearing and to be treated in accordance with the principles of natural justice before all administrative boards and tribunals. Fourth, there is a vaguely defined group of economic and cultural rights. The right to own property and not to be deprived of it without compensation is well recognized, but we must think today of many other and even more basic rights such as the right to work and to protection against unemployment, the right to health and education and social security, and so on. These are spelled out more fully in articles 22 to 27 of the Universal Declaration of Human Rights. While these rights may not lend themselves so readily to legal protection in constitutions, they are as vital a part of a free society today as the older civil liberties. We have learned from bitter experience that the satisfaction of basic human needs is essential for the survival of any form of orderly government, and in a highly industrialized society the state cannot leave this task to unregulated private enterprise.

Taking this wide area of law and rights as our field of enquiry, let us look then at some of the judicial decisions that have illuminated this part of the law of our constitution. I must be highly selective, but I shall choose some examples from the earlier days before coming to the important cases that have crowded upon us in the last few years. The interpretation of the minority rights clauses in the BNA Act was the first problem to be judicially resolved in the field of human rights after Confederation. In 1871 the Privy Council held that, whatever separate schools may have existed in practice at the Union in New Brunswick, none existed by law, and therefore the Common Schools Act adopted by the province in 1871 was constitutional. At the creation of Manitoba, the rights to separate schools existing either by law or by practice were guaranteed, and in consequence our Supreme Court held ultra vires the 1890 legislation that destroyed the separate school system set up in 1871; by a unanimous judgment our judges felt that rights enjoyed in practice at the Union were prejudicially affected. The Privy Council overruled and added fuel to the great fire that died down, but was not extinguished, by the election of Laurier in 1896. Provincial autonomy had won over minority rights.

The same autonomy prevailed in the Ontario language dispute occasioned by Regulation 17 of the year 1913; it was found that the class of persons whose rights were protected under section 93 of the BNA Act was a class formed by religion and not by language, and hence the province was not prevented by the constitution from requiring instruction to be carried on in the schools in the language of its regulations. We can see the Privy Council in these cases showing the same favourable view of provincial legislative authority as their lordships disclosed in other questions involving provincial jurisdiction. The right to appeal to the federal government for remedial legislation was upheld, and Ontario was checked in certain measures taken to enforce Regulation 17, but I think we can say that the result of judicial interpretation was to confine the school rights of the BNA Act within sharply defined limits. Other separate school cases since then have turned more on the interpretation of provincial laws than the BNA Act itself and so do not directly concern our topic, but I would refer again to the very interesting judgment of the Quebec Court of Appeal in the *Chabot* case in 1957, where the right of the parent to choose the kind of religious instruction to be given to the children was firmly upheld. This is a right spelled out in article 26 of the United Nations Declaration.

Turning to the language provisions of the BNA Act, and dealing only with the legal questions that have arisen, I have already noted how it was held that the right to use a particular language in the schools was not protected in the constitution. Strangely enough the validity of Manitoba's statute of 1890 abolishing French as an official language in that province was never tested in the courts; had it been, I personally do not see how it could be upheld. It has always seemed to me that Manitoba was placed on the same footing as Quebec and that, if the Manitoba law of 1890 establishing English as the sole official language was valid, then there is no security for the English language in my province. The abolition of the use of French in the Territories was on a different footing since it occurred before the creation of provincial governments in Saskatchewan and Alberta.

An interesting language question arose on the interpretation of a federal statute in 1935 when it was found that there was a difference between the English and French texts of the law; our Supreme Court held that since both texts were equally authoritative, that version was to be preferred that best expressed the intention of the legislature, which in that instance was clearest in the French. It was held, partly because of the French text, that a government car on a road could not be a "public work." I like to point out to English-speaking practitioners in provinces other than Quebec that in order to practise law with the utmost skill, they must always compare the two texts of the federal statutes if they want to make sure that they are giving their clients the full protection of the law. Appropriately enough, the cause of action in this case arose in a locality called Britannia. It was on the same principle of equal authority of the two languages that Mr Duplessis was induced to repeal a statute that the Legislature of Quebec had passed in 1937 which purported to make the French text of the Civil Code prevail over the English in all cases of conflict.

Questions of racial discrimination, both in employment and in exercising the right to vote, gave rise to a number of cases from the turn of the century onward, particularly in the province of British Columbia. The power of disallowance was also used to set aside several of the provincial statutes aimed at the Asians on the ground that they affected Imperial relations with Japan. Among these cases I would single out *Cunningham v. Tomey Homma* in 1903 as having established a very important principle. It held that a British Columbia law barring Chinese, Japanese, and Aboriginals, whether naturalized or not, from the provincial franchise was a valid exercise of the province's power to amend its own constitution. British Columbia has of course removed these discriminations since then, but the case remains as a reminder that the possession of Canadian citizenship is no guarantee of the equal protection of the right to vote. Once again provincial autonomy stands as a potential threat to equal status before the law. This case did much to overrule the earlier case of *Union Colliery v. Bryden,* which had held that a British Columbia statute that prohibited Chinamen from working underground in coal mines was an invasion of the federal power over "natural-ization and aliens." There are still some aspects of the law of citizenship that have not been fully worked out, and it may be that the status of Canadian citizen may come to mean more than it seems to now, but we have to take the cases as we find them, and racial discrimination in electoral laws seems clearly within provincial powers. No purely federal bill of rights could change this fact. With regard to employment, we have a Supreme Court of Canada decision of 1914 holding that a Saskatchewan law prohibiting white girls from working in Chinese restaurants and places of business was valid. Fair Employment Practices Acts are now taking care of this situation; we now have a federal statute and six provincial statutes of this type. Something else we can see looming on the judicial horizon is the question of the validity of the Alberta legislation limiting the right of the Hutterites to purchase land near the existing brotherhoods. Are we to make forms of Christian communism a legal offence? Is the right to own property to be restricted to those who use it in a capitalistic manner?

Two other examples of discrimination will illustrate the wide area of provincial law covering this aspect of human rights. The problem of the restrictive covenant in leases and sales has received attention in the well-known cases of *In re Drummond Wren* and *Noble v. Wolf.* The question is whether a vendor or landlord can attach a condition to the premises excluding their purchase or lease by persons of a particular race or religion. Here we see the right of private contract, and the right of a man to do what he likes with his own property, coming in conflict with the notion that no person should be discriminated against on grounds of race, religion, or colour. Mr Justice Mackay's courageous judgment in the *Drummond Wren* case invoking the Universal Declaration of Human Rights as evidence that such a condition was contrary to public policy will be perhaps more remembered outside than inside the law courts, for the decision in the *Noble v. Wolf* case went on less humane grounds. Here is part of what his Lordship said:

In my opinion, nothing could be more calculated to create or deepen divisions between existing religious and ethnic groups in this province, or in this country, than the sanction of a method of land transfer which would permit the segregation and confinement of particular groups to particular business or residential areas …

Ontario and Canada, too, may well be termed a province, and a country, of minorities in regard to the religious and ethnic groups which live therein. It appears to me to be a moral duty, at least, to lend aid to all forces of cohesion, and similarly to repel all fissiparous tendencies which would imperil national unity. The common law courts have, by their actions over the years, obviated the need for rigid constitutional guarantees in our policy by their wide use of the doctrine of public policy as an active agent in the promotion of the public weal.

... If the common law of treason encompasses the stirring up of hatred between different classes of His Majesty's subjects, the common law of public policy is surely adequate to void the restrictive covenant which is here attacked.

As Mr Smout said in commenting on these cases in the *Canadian Bar Review:* "The courts did not wait for education to convince the gamblers of the moral impropriety of gambling, but meanwhile held the gambling contract unenforceable. There would seem to be no reason why the courts should wait for the intolerant to become tolerant before holding the discrimination covenant to be also unenforceable." Unfortunately we have not arrived at that point either, it seems, in the law of Quebec or in the common law provinces. The courts have it in their power to come to the aid of racial equality, but unless the proposed Bill of Rights be taken by future judges as having clearly defined Canadian public policy more surely than has the Universal Declaration, it will not affect provincial law.

Besides restrictive covenants, we have had cases of racial discrimination in the refusal of restaurant keepers and others to serve customers on grounds of race and colour. The Fair Accommodation Practices Acts are designed to make this an offence. It is indeed encouraging that Ontario and Saskatchewan have adopted such bills and that one is being contemplated in Nova Scotia. In Quebec the law seems to be fixed by the *Christie* case, which went to the Supreme Court of Canada in 1941; there, damages were denied to a Negro who had been refused a glass of beer because of his colour, in the York Tavern, though tavern keepers can only operate under provincial licence and might reasonably be considered as acting under public authority. Freedom of commerce prevailed over racial equality, the tavern not being held to be a restaurant or hotel, which by Quebec law are obliged to serve all comers. In choosing the particular result in this case, the majority of the judges exercised a discretion that could as well have gone the other way; once again we see the important role the judges must play in selecting which of two alternative views they will adopt.

I do not propose to go into the special problem of civil liberties in wartime or to recount the various forms of censorship imposed under the Defence of Canada Regulations. It was said by Mr Justice Stuart in a sedition case in 1916: "There have been more prosecutions for seditious words in Alberta in the past two years than in all the history of England for over 100 years, and England has had numerous and critical wars in that time." We can hardly expect normal rules to apply in times of such stress, yet we must I think be as vigilant in wartime as we should be in peacetime to see that the bounds of reasonable limitation are not exceeded. Because the freedoms may have to be less does not mean that they should cease to exist. In particular, we are left with a legacy from World War Two that I think should be discarded. The Privy Council, going a little further than our Supreme Court, upheld in full the Orders-in-Council of 1945 providing for deportation of the Canadian Japanese. Surely this interpretation of our constitution is as frightening as the policy of deportation was reprehensible. For it means that even Canadian-born citizens can be deported by Order-in-Council under the War Measures Act – assuming, of course, that a country can be found willing to receive them. I fail to see on what conceivable ground such a power can be felt to be necessary in the hands of our federal government. As citizens, have we not the right to pay whatever penalty the law may require of us for breach of the law and then to return to our own community after release from prison? In the case of the Japanese, of course, they had committed no crime whatsoever. I notice that the proposed Bill of Rights does not save us from this power in any future emergency. I suggest that the War Measures Act should be amended at least to prevent the federal executive from possessing this authority. To take it away from Parliament itself would seem to require an amendment to the BNA Act.

Now I wish to look at the cases that have recently come before our Supreme Court and that have so sharply focussed our attention upon questions of fundamental freedoms. The first I wish to mention is that of *Boucher v. The King,* decided in 1951. This was a charge of seditious libel taken against Boucher, a Witness of Jehovah, for having distributed the pamphlet known as "Quebec's Burning Hate" to several persons in the district of Beauce, Quebec. The pamphlet was written in protest against the numerous arrests of members of the sect that had been going on in Quebec for some years and against what was alleged to be the mob violence used on various occasions. It undoubtedly contained strong language directed to the conduct of officials in church and state; the question was: Was it seditious? This involved the court in defining closely the Canadian law of sedition, particularly in the light of certain recent amendments to the Criminal Code. The lower courts agreed that the pamphlet was seditious, but the Supreme Court by a majority found otherwise. The decision is of the greatest importance to the law on freedom of speech, in my view, since it removed a rather vague idea that merely saying or writing something that might stir up feelings of ill-will between different classes of subjects constituted sedition in itself, whether or not there was an intention to incite to violence. Such an intention to promote violence or resistance or defiance for the purpose of disturbing constituted authority is now essential to the crime. As Mr Justice Rand observed:

There is no modern authority which holds that mere effect of tending to create discontent or disaffection among His Majesty's subjects or ill-will or hostility between groups of them, but not tending to issue in illegal conduct, constitutes the crime, and this for obvious reasons. Freedom in thought and speech and disagreement in ideas and beliefs, on every conceivable subject, are of the essence of our life. The clash of critical discussion on political, social and religious subjects has too deeply become the stuff of daily experience to suggest that mere ill-will as a product of controversy can strike down the latter with illegality. A superficial examination of the word shows its insufficiency: what is the degree necessary to criminality? Can it ever, as mere subjective condition, be so? Controversial fury is aroused constantly by differences in abstract conceptions; heresy in some fields is again a mortal sin; there can be fanatical puritanism in ideas as well as in morals; but our compact of free society accepts and absorbs these differences and they are exercised at large within the framework of freedom and order on broader and deeper uniformities as bases of social stability. Similarly in discontent, affection and hostility: as subjective incidents of controversy, they and the ideas which arouse them are part of our living which ultimately serve us in stimulation, in the clarification of thought and, as we believe, in the search for the constitution and truth of things generally.

This case provides an excellent example of how in the definition of terms the area of freedom can be broadened or restricted. But I would point out that this was simply an interpretation of the present criminal law; if Parliament chose to tighten the law, it could do so by amending the code, and no Bill of Rights short of an amendment to the BNA Act would save us.

I take next the case of the *Alliance des Professeurs catholiques*, decided in 1953. The alliance was an association of Catholic school teachers that had been certified as a bargaining agent for the Catholic schools of Montreal by the Quebec Labour Relations Board. The alliance was never popular with the School Commission, to say the least, and a request for decertification was made to the board. The request came from Montreal, but it was accorded on the same day by the board sitting in Quebec, and the alliance was notified by telegram immediately without having been summoned for a hearing and before even the written document containing the request had reached the board. As Chief Justice Rinfret aptly remarked: "Voila une justice expeditive." The decertification was held invalid on the ground that one of the principles of natural justice, *audi alterarn partem,* had not been followed. The case fully supports this great principle of administrative law; unfortunately, in the outcome, the alliance lost its suit because by the time it reached the Privy Council, the Quebec Legislature had amended the Labour Relations Act retroactively. Provincial autonomy won over the power of judicial interpretation, and this will ever be the case in all matters falling within provincial jurisdiction if we do not have a true bill of rights in the constitution.

In the same year as the *Alliance* case came a somewhat similar trade union case from Nova Scotia, and again our Supreme Court, this time upholding the

courts below, took a liberal view of the law. The Nova Scotia Labour Relations
Board had refused to certify a union because it found that its secretary-treasurer
was a Communist. No justification for this refusal was found in the law. Again
quoting Mr Justice Rand: "There is no law in this country against holding such
[i.e. communist] views. This man is eligible for election or appointment to the
highest political offices in the province: on what ground can it be said that the
legislature of which he might be a member has empowered the Board, in effect,
to exclude him from a labour union?" Here, the court drew the distinction, so
necessary for us to maintain in times of strong controversy, between unpopularity
and illegality. How much more fair and reasonable this approach is than that of
the British Columbia Court of Appeal, which upheld the Bar of the province in
refusing permission to practice law to a law graduate believed to be a Communist. It is not difficult to make out an argument that no one with a loyalty outside
Canada should hold public office, but in that case why bar only Communists?
Why not Catholics and others who may conscientiously place religious obligation above their duty to the state?

I pass now to a case that is not easy to analyze because of the variety of
judicial opinion it contains but that raises a question of the utmost importance
to civil liberties: the *Saumur* case. Saumur was a Witness of Jehovah in Quebec
who attacked the validity of a city by-law forbidding the distribution in the streets
of the city of any book, pamphlet, circular, or tract whatever without permission
of the Chief of Police. Let us pause a moment to reflect upon the thoroughly
menacing nature of this type of bylaw, which any Quebec municipalities may
adopt under a special statute enacted in 1947 by the Legislature. It means that
freedom of the press is placed under the censorship of the police. In Montreal
at one time even federal election literature could not be distributed from door to
door without the approval of the city executive, so that the operation of the
Federal Election Act was subject to municipal control. A man walking down the
street would commit an offence if he pulled a pamphlet out of his pocket and
gave it to his friend beside him. One zealous Quebec municipality went so far
as to prohibit the distribution of literature inside private houses. This form of
violation of civil liberties is not peculiar to Quebec; similar bylaws have been
enacted in the United States and have been held unconstitutional by the American
Supreme Court, though I know of no other province of Canada that has adopted
them. Aimed at the Witnesses, Communists, and, very probably, trade unions,
such bylaws take away the rights of all of us.

Now the holding in the *Saumur* case was satisfactory in that the Quebec City
bylaw was found not to prohibit the Witnesses from distributing in the streets,
principally because of the Quebec Freedom of Worship Act. But the bylaw itself
was not held invalid, and it would seem that a majority of the Supreme Court
at that time considered that a city might properly exercise such control over

literature distributed in the streets. If this decision stands, a more damaging blow at our traditional electoral practices and at freedom of the press and of speech and of association can hardly be imagined. For a circular announcing a public meeting would require police approval, so that the ability of the citizens to meet together and to hear public speakers discuss the issues of the day is struck at by the simple process of controlling this means of communication. While there are other ways of announcing meetings, for those who can afford to pay for them, these too are liable to be under other forms of censorship and control from private persons. There was a time when the *Montreal Star* would not take a paid advertisement calling a Cooperative Commonwealth Federation (CCF) meeting. The City of Montreal bylaw dealing with distribution of literature has been held unconstitutional by the Superior Court, but we are left in a somewhat uncertain state as to the general right of municipalities to affect fundamental freedoms under their authority to regulate what goes on in the streets.

I shall refer now to two cases that illustrate the danger to civil liberties from illegal police behaviour. These are the *Chaput* and the *Lamb* cases, derided in the Supreme Court in 1955 and 1959. Both involved Jehovah's Witnesses; in both the police were condemned to pay personal damages to the persons whose rights were violated. In the *Chaput* case the police, on orders from a superior officer, broke up an admittedly orderly religious meeting being conducted in a private house. Religious books and pamphlets were seized, and the officiating minister was forced to leave the premises. No charge of any kind was laid against anybody. In a unanimous judgment, overruling the Quebec courts, Chaput was awarded damages. The case brings out several important rules of our constitutional and administrative law. On the constitutional side, Mr Justice Taschereau enunciated with great clarity the doctrine that in Canada there is complete equality among the various religious beliefs. He said:

Dans notre pays, il n'exist pas de religion d'Etat. Personne n'est tenu d'adhérer à une croyance quelconque. Toutes les religions sont sur un pied d'égalité, et tous les catholiques comme d'ailleurs tous les protestants, les juifs, ou les autres adhérents des diverses dénominations religieuses, ont la plus entière liberté de penser comme ils le désirent. La conscience de chacun est une affaire personnelle, et l'affaire de nul autre. Il serait désolant de penser qu'une majorité puisse imposer ses vues religieuses à une minorité. Ce serait une erreur fâcheuse de croire qu'on sert son pays ou sa religion, en refusant dans une province, à une minorité, les mêmes droits que l'on revendique soi-même avec raison, dans une autre province.

On the administrative law side, the case illustrates the well-known rule that orders from a superior officer are no defence. The lesser official in the governmental hierarchy is not protected in wrongdoing because the superior officer tells him or her to do something; the illegal order merely makes the superior officer liable too. This rule is essential to the preservation of the rule of law as we have inherited it; it makes each and every public officer personally responsible for right behaviour and unable to hide behind some cloak of authority. In this case the police were actually committing a crime: that of disturbing a religious ceremony. How can orders to commit a crime make the crime lawful? This is the expression in our domestic law of the rule we wish to write firmly into international law, so that those who commit crimes against humanity may be brought to book, as at Nuremberg, without being able to plead superior orders.

Another aspect of this, as of some similar cases, deserves comment. Sociologists may explain how it is that even in our supposedly civilized societies we seem capable of developing the concept of the outlaw. The outlaw is: outside the law; he or she has no rights of any kind, and therefore no one can do wrong in attacking, defaming, arresting, or assaulting an outlaw, or even in destroying his or her property. It seems that the Witnesses of Jehovah were placed in that category in some parts of Quebec. Because one of their pamphlets was once held to be seditious, it was assumed by some officials that not only were all their other pamphlets seditious but that every member of the sect belonged to a seditious conspiracy though no court had ever held this and no such charge was ever laid. Roncarelli, for instance, was accused of fomenting sedition and had his private business deliberately destroyed when all he had ever done, besides being a member of the Witnesses, was give lawful bail in a lawful court with the lawful approval of the presiding judge. So, too, it seemed at one time as though every person called a Communist was immediately outlawed. The outlawry of certain trade unions in Newfoundland has been attempted by more formal means, but the intention is the same. There is no more dangerous concept than this to the cause of civil liberties. Civil liberties are always needed most by unpopular people. Even the worst criminals after conviction have rights, and of course before conviction they are presumed innocent. It is the function of the law, and of the independent judges who apply it as well as of the independent barristers who practise it on behalf of all clients who need their help, to uphold the notion of legality against the pressures of angry opinion. Should the lawyers be afraid to take unpopular clients, and the judges afraid to give unpopular decisions, all the principles of the law would be worthless.

The *Lamb* case is merely another example of police illegality, but it is part of the dismal picture that has too often been exposed in Quebec in recent years. Miss Lamb, another Jehovah's Witness, was illegally arrested, held over the weekend in the cells without any charge being laid against her, not allowed to telephone a lawyer, and then offered her freedom on condition she sign a document releasing the police from all responsibility for the way they had treated her. When reading such a story one wonders how many other innocent victims have been similarly treated by the police but have not had the courage and the backing to pursue the matter through to final victory – in this instance twelve and a half years after the arrest had taken place. We should be grateful that we have in this country some victims of state oppression who stand up for their rights. Their victory is the victory of all of us.

It will be noted that both these police cases from Quebec involve a defence of civil liberties by the normal process of the action in damages against the officials who have violated them. We see here the civil law of Quebec being brought into operation exactly as is the common law in similar cases. The rule of law of Dicey, whether based on civil law or common law, operates in very much the same way. It is probable, however, that the protection afforded by the civil law is somewhat wider than that given by the common law, for the reason that the civil law of delict is more fully evolved than the common law of tort. There is a universal principle of delict and quasi-delict, whereas there are only specific torts. Hence it is easier to bring a new situation under the law of delictual responsibility than it is to bring it under the ancient torts. This is theory, however; all will depend upon judicial willingness in interpretation, and unfortunately in almost every case coming from Quebec recently the provincial courts have not seen their way to protect civil liberties, whereas the Supreme Court of Canada has. Technicalities seem to loom more largely in the minds of the Quebec judges, whereas the Supreme Court appears to find more ways of securing that substantial justice shall be done.

Let me refer now to two cases that involved interpretations of the BNA Act: namely, the *Birks* case and the Padlock Act case. In the *Birks* case a Montreal bylaw, passed in virtue of a provincial statute, required that storekeepers should close their stores on the six Catholic holy days. Question: Is this a law providing more holidays for employees, or is it a law for compulsory observance of the religious practices of one religion upon all people whether belonging to that religion or not? By a unanimous judgment the Supreme Court, overruling the Quebec Court of Appeal, found that religious observance was the pith and substance of the law since, among other reasons, no additional holiday was provided for the employees of the stores if one of these holy days happened to fall on a Sunday. But, in so holding, the wider rule was laid down that laws affecting religious observance belonged within the field of criminal law and hence were exclusively within federal jurisdiction. This is therefore a leading case on the meaning of the BNA Act and will have future consequences much more important than those decisions that, like the *Chaput* and *Lamb* cases, turned primarily upon provincial law that the Legislature could amend if it wished.

The same results follow from the Padlock Act case. This was a statute that purported to make illegal the preaching of communism or bolshevism in houses

in Quebec and the printing and distribution of literature propagating or tending
to propagate these ideologies anywhere in the province. The attorney general of
Quebec, upon any evidence that seemed to himself adequate, could order the
padlocking of houses where the offence was committed and the seizure of all
such literature, without trial or conviction of any sort. Outside of the Defence
of Canada Regulations in wartime, I know of no other equivalent attempt at
thought control in the history of Canada. The act had been upheld in earlier
judgments in the Quebec courts, the late Chief Justice Greenshields having once
remarked from the bench: "I fail to find in the statute any interference with
freedom of speech." Fortunately this judicial blindness did not affect the Supreme
Court, which held that the subject matter of the act fell under the criminal law
power. Had the opposite view prevailed, we would have had the extraordinary
situation in Canada that while the federal Elections Act would decide who could
be a candidate for Parliament, a province might have barred the use of any public
hall or building to members of any particular party. We would have been left
with what I call the "open-field" theory of democracy; freedom of speech would
have existed only in the open air. As Mr Justice Rand said: "Parliamentary
government postulates a capacity in men, acting freely and under self-restraints,
to govern themselves; and that advance is best served in the degree achieved of
individual liberation from subjective as well as objective shackles. Under that
government, the freedom of discussion in Canada, as a subject-matter of legislation, has a unity of interest and significance extending equally to every part of
the Dominion." And he added: "Legislatures and Parliament are permanent
features of our constitutional structure, and the body of discussion is indivisible."

I come now to the last of the recent cases I wish to refer to: that of *Roncarelli
v. Duplessis*. This case has many angles and lends itself to a variety of interpretations but, I think, can be reduced to a very simple and reasonable
proposition. When public officers exceed their authority, and thereby cause
damage, they must pay for it personally. This is a basic rule of English constitutional and administrative law that Quebec inherited along with all other
Canadian provinces. It is really what we mean when we say, as we can say with
pride, that in our polity the state is under the law. For the state is nothing but
the people who compose it, arranged in various groupings called legislatures and
courts and senates and crowns-in-council. Constitutional law prescribes the
groupings and their functions; administrative law tells us what authority each
official possesses and how he or she may exercise it. No public officer has any
power beyond what the law confers upon him of her, and the courts say what
the law is. Thus the law puts a definite boundary around each official beyond
which one acts at his or her peril. I say this, in Ottawa, with all the emphasis at
my command. Any citizen – and this is a crucial corollary to which there are

few exceptions – can sue any official in the ordinary courts if that official has damaged him or her in a manner not permitted by law. No one is immune, not even a prime minister.

Now I am happy to note that no judge in any court in the *Roncarelli* case disagreed with this fundamental proposition. Where the disagreement came was on the facts of the case (for instance, did the prime minister actually cause the licence to be cancelled, or did he merely give advice that it could be cancelled?) and on the legal question as to whether the powers of an attorney general included that of ordering a cancellation under the circumstances of the case, or whether or not notice of action should have been given. No judge said a prime minister could not be sued. None said that he was free to exceed his powers.

I do not think there is any new law in this holding; it is really the same rule as was applied to the policemen in *Chaput* and *Lamb*. But it is always a triumph for the law to show that it is applied equally to all without fear or favour. This is what we mean when we say that all are equal before the law. The statement is by no means as true as it should be; Anatole France's quip that the law is the same for the rich as for the poor, since both are allowed to sleep under bridges, has its counterpart in the statement that it is the same for both rich and poor since both are allowed to pay what it costs to carry their case to the Supreme Court of Canada. Yet the truth in the statement is, I suggest, even more important than the element of untruth, and woe betide any nation that loses sight of it.

Another reflection is appropriate upon the *Roncarelli* case. Our administrative services in Canada are carried on, in the main, by two methods: either through a government department, headed by a Cabinet minister, or through some public board or commission, like the Canadian Broadcasting Corporation or the Quebec Liquor Commission. Some of these boards must be under close supervision of a minister or even of the Cabinet, but some should be and are intended to be independent. Where they are independent, politicians have no right to interfere or to tell boards how to behave. If they do, they exceed their powers. This rule is essential for our protection against a too powerful state machine. When we distribute our powers, we want them to stay distributed, and here the courts can help as they did in *Roncarelli's* case. Politicians must learn that political power is not the same as legal authority.

Finally, the case is important in upholding the citizen's right to give bail. Bail is a great protection for civil liberties; it prevents the innocent from being punished by being held in prison pending trial, and every case starts with a presumption of innocence. To punish a person for giving bail is like punishing jurors for their verdicts or witnesses for their testimony. It is, or should be, in my view, a crime and not just an excess of authority. For it is interfering with a judicial process.

These are some of the civil liberties cases that have come into the courts. Now let us see what we may hope from a bill of rights. We must begin our thinking here by making some elementary distinctions.

The first is the distinction between a declaration of rights, which states principles but does not make law, and a bill, which is law in the strict sense and is provided with sanctions. It is the difference between the Universal Declaration of Human Rights, on the one hand, and the American Bill of Rights, on the other. Mr Diefenbaker's Bill C–60 as drafted belongs in the category of declaration since the legal consequences that would flow from its enactment are at best extremely few if any. Opinions may differ about the value of a declaration of rights; in my thinking the educational effect of such bills is far greater than might be supposed. The importance of Magna Carta in the history of England is not diminished by the fact that it could be set aside at any time by any later act of Parliament. The United Nations has taken few steps more influential than the adoption of its declaration; to measure its effect upon only ourselves, we have merely to note the very important changes we have made in our electoral and other laws since its proclamation ten years ago, most of which were undoubtedly stimulated by its provisions and our adherence to them. I understand that the celebration of the tenth anniversary of the declaration in Halifax in December 1958 has already given rise to a Bill for Fair Accommodation Practices in that province. Two special committees of Parliament have already reviewed the Canadian situation in the light of the United Nations principles and prepared the ground for the step we are now contemplating with our own federal Bill of Rights. If eternal vigilance be the price of liberty, then a declaration of rights helps to keep vigilance vigilant.

A second distinction we must make is that between a bill that confines itself to enunciating the traditional civil liberties and freedoms and one that is comprehensive enough to include modern concepts of economic and cultural rights. Shall the bill speak only the language of the past, or shall it have a forward look and enunciate principles for the guidance of public policy into the future? Here I feel the answer may depend upon whether the bill is merely declaratory or whether it makes strict law. If we are only going to state objectives of national policy, why not state more rather than fewer objectives? To raise living standards, to give equal opportunity to all to develop their talents to the best of their abilities, to recognize the duty of the state in safeguarding employment and social security are surely in keeping with our modern view of a democratic society. These are the driving forces of our age, and I think a declaratory bill should express them. Then all Canadians can find something in the bill that relates to their needs and aspirations. But if the bill is to be a true bill of rights in the sense that it limits the sovereignty of legislatures in order to guarantee individual freedoms, then it may well be confined to civil liberties of the traditional type. Even this true bill of rights, however, can contain an enunciation of social objectives, as is common enough in the more recently drafted constitutions of new states.

Other distinctions impose themselves. We have the choice of amending the BNA Act and putting our desired freedoms alongside the entrenched minority rights or doing what has already been done in Saskatchewan and is now proposed for the federal Parliament: passing a statute that only purports to cover the particular area of provincial or federal jurisdiction. It will be remembered that Senator Roebuck's Committee of the Senate in 1950 preferred an amendment to the BNA Act, though it did recommend a declaration of rights by the Canadian Parliament as an interim measure. This is pretty well the course the present government has followed. Mr Diefenbaker has himself described his bill as a first step. But I feel we should be very cautious about this first step.

It seems to be assumed that a first step is always a good thing. Presumably a first step is a good thing if it is taking us closer to a desired goal and will be followed by a second step. But if the taking of the first step confuses the issue and discourages people from any further effort, then it may not be a good thing. I am frankly afraid that this is the position we may be facing.

The reason for the hesitancy to attempt to amend the BNA Act is said to be the need to consult the provinces and the improbability of their agreeing to the change. And it is true that attempts to secure other amendments, notably that made in 1950 to achieve an amending clause, have dismally failed. But does it follow that a proposal to adopt a bill of rights would also be rejected? Not all previous attempts to secure amendments have been opposed: The 1951 amendment for old age pensions was unanimously agreed upon, and the 1940 amendment on unemployment insurance received some kind of approval from all provincial governments or leaders. A bill of rights in theory should win acceptance more easily since it does not disturb the balance of power between Ottawa and the provinces. No centralization of power takes place; the authority of both federal and provincial legislatures over certain matters now within their jurisdiction would be equally reduced. Might not a conference to discuss the proposal be worth the effort? If it succeeded, even over a modest bill containing only the recognized civil liberties, a major victory would have been achieved; if it failed, the way would still be open for a purely federal statute. The educational value of such a conference would surely be great.

Other possibilities present themselves. The federal Parliament might itself seek an amendment guaranteeing certain rights against future federal legislation. This would amount to a retransfer of jurisdiction from Ottawa back to the United Kingdom Parliament, there to await the process of amendment by joint address

in the future should it be desired. If Ottawa gave the lead, then provinces might
be invited to adhere individually to the amendment so as to secure the rights
against their own legislation as well. If it be pointed out that this might leave us
with some provinces who might not agree being in possession of more power
than others who did agree, then I point to the inability of the western provinces
to tax the Canadian Pacific Railway as proof that we already have a difference
between the provincial autonomies. Minority rights are not the same in all
provinces. Political pressures would mount inside provinces that had not adopted
the bill to make them join the others. It would not be necessary on this method
to have identical bills of rights in each province, though for purposes of uniformity of interpretation this would be desirable. There have always been and there
probably always will be some differences in the rights of Canadians living in
different regions. The voting ages are not the same in all provinces; racial
discrimination is more prohibited in some than in others; the rights of trade
unions vary considerably. On the basic civil liberties such as freedom of religion
and of speech there can scarcely exist a wide diversity of laws: "The body of
discussion is indivisible," as Mr Justice Rand has said. But there is room for
some diversity in many aspects of human rights viewed in their larger sense.
Hence it does not matter if some provinces have a bill of rights and some do not.

If we are not prepared to amend the BNA Act, all we can have are separate
bills of rights for Parliament and for the provincial legislatures of a more or less
declaratory type. Mr Diefenbaker's proposed bill is of this sort. Let me describe
its main provisions. First of all it declares that in Canada there have existed and
shall continue to exist the following rights and fundamental freedoms:

(a) the right of the individual to life, liberty, security of the person, and enjoyment of
    property, and the right not to be deprived thereof except by due process of law;
(b) the right of the individual to protection of the law without discrimination by reason
    of race, national origin, colour, religion, or sex;
(c) freedom of religion;
(d) freedom of speech;
(e) freedom of assembly and association; and
(f) freedom of the press.

It then goes on to require that all past and future laws within federal competence
shall be so construed and applied as not to abrogate or infringe any of these
freedoms. In addition, it declares that no federal statute or regulation shall be
construed so as to impose any cruel, inhuman, or degrading punishment; or to
deprive a person who is arrested of his or her right to know the reason for the
arrest, to retain counsel without delay, and to the remedy of habeas corpus; or

to deprive a person of a fair hearing in accordance with the principles of fundamental justice for the determination of his or her rights and obligations.

This is the essence of the bill, and one will note that in so far as it commands anything, it is merely an instruction to judges; it tells them to interpret all federal laws in a certain liberal way. This sounds impressive, but in fact the courts have already a duty to interpret statutes in a liberal way, and the bill adds little to their present powers. There are no sanctions of any kind in it; it does not attempt to create any new crimes. An individual whose freedoms are interfered with by another will stand in much the same position after this bill is enacted as he or she did before; that is, one will have to rely upon his or her action in damages against the offending party or upon habeas corpus, injunction, or other appropriate writ. No new machinery is created for the enforcement of rights, such as the Americans have set up with their Civil Rights Section of the Justice Department and such as we are experimenting with under the Fair Employment Practices Act. Our minister of justice, it is true, is required by section 4 to examine all future laws to see that they fulfil the purposes of the bill, but presumably he reports to Parliament only and does not investigate any violations of rights in the country at large.

There are further limitations in the bill. Because of the notion of parliamentary sovereignty I noted earlier, this bill in my view cannot bind future Parliaments. The instruction to the judges to interpret all future laws in favour of these freedoms would have to give way before any later law that in fact clearly took away the freedoms. I think this is true whether the future law says it is amending the Bill of Rights or not. Hence the bill does not put our liberties on a secure foundation. Doubtless no future Parliament would lightly contravene these principles; but then, even without the bill, it would not lightly do so. Provincial legislatures can abrogate human rights exactly as much after the bill becomes law as they may have done in the past, and Canadian history shows that provincial legislatures are more likely than the federal Parliament to violate minority rights and individual freedoms. Provinces are more easily swept by new doctrines that might endanger our traditional liberties.

I conclude therefore that this bill has perhaps educational value; it will stand as a solemn affirmation of democratic beliefs; it spells out a number of specific rights in a detailed way. It is a bill of rights for all Canadians, yes, because all Canadians come under some federal law. But it is a very partial bill, applicable only in peacetime, no stronger than the self-restraint of our federal members of Parliament at any given moment and inapplicable to provincial legislatures. Moreover, it is confined to political and personal freedoms; it makes no attempt to protect other human rights, like the right to nondiscrimination in employment. Cultural and economic rights are also omitted. It is moreover drafted in technical legal jargon. If this is the best we can do, we are admitting that we are not really deeply concerned about civil liberties.

Let's not forget that quite apart from this bill there is another great constitutional change coming some day in Canada. We like to think that our nationhood is complete, but from the point of view of constitutional law, it is not complete. We are still in a partly colonial relationship to Britain, for we still have to return to the British source of our constitution for its major amendments. We failed in 1950, during the federal provincial conference, to agree upon a satisfactory method of amending the BNA Act. This must some day be done. A new attempt will have to be made to complete Canada's legal sovereignty. We must eventually nationalize the constitution, as we have nationalized the Crown. We must get rid of one anomaly called the British North America Act, replacing that obsolete title by the Constitution of Canada, and another anomaly called the Joint Address of the Senate and House of Commons, which, on adoption at Ottawa, goes for approval to a distant legislature (in which no Canadian sits) every time we need an amendment. At the same time, we must clear away a lot of dead wood in the text of the act. When we have reached this final point of maturity, when at last we shall take our fate in our hands, and the United Kingdom Parliament has renounced all authority over Canada, as it has done over other nations of the Commonwealth, then at last we shall be a truly independent people, dual in culture but single in democratic statehood. That will be the proper time at which to entrench in the constitution those further fundamental freedoms and human rights that are inadequately protected by purely Canadian declarations.

F.R. SCOTT was a Rhodes scholar, poet, social activist, and dean of law at McGill University. As a member of the Montreal Group of poets in the 1920s, he helped to found the *Canadian Mercury* literary journal. He served as a UN technical advisor in Burma; as a member of the Royal Commission on Bilingualism and Biculturalism; and as national chairman of the Cooperative Commonwealth Federation (CCF), where he was involved in the transition of the CCF to the New Democratic Party. F.R. Scott retired from McGill in 1968; he died in Montreal in 1985.

Dr Scott was a Companion of the Order of Canada and a member of the Royal Society of Canada. He was awarded the society's 1962 Lorne Pierce Medal for literature; the 1967 Molson Prize for outstanding achievements in the arts, humanities, and social sciences; the 1977 Canada Council Translation Prize for *Poems of French Canada*; and two Governor General's Awards: in 1977 for *Essays on the Constitution: Aspects of Canadian Law and Politics* and in 1981 for *The Collected Poems of F.R. Scott*.

3

Roots and Values in Canadian Lives

JEAN-CHARLES FALARDEAU, 1960

PART ONE

One aspect of Canadian life that strikes us first when we look at it – and it is commonplace to repeat it – is the extent to which it looks like American life. The first phase in describing our own visage is to ascertain how much it is like that of our neighbour, how much we are a mirror of it. And, indeed, we are. The manner in which our houses are built, the ways in which people dress, eat, and take their leisure, from Halifax to Vancouver, including Quebec City and Montreal, do not differ greatly from those that are observed in Vermont, in Michigan, or on the Pacific seaboard. Restaurants, movie houses, office buildings are inter-changeable between Toronto and Rochester, and so too could be, in many instances, their occupants. Our daily routine of life, our domestic habits, as well as our personality types are largely modelled according to the stereotypes pat-terned by the brave new world of our Ford. The heroes of the youth and the myths of their parents have been transmitted to us by the "verbivocovisual" media of mass communication. "Suburbia" circumscribes our living space and our mental landscape. Our economic institutions – administrative, civic, and religious – are run by "organization men." For a great proportion, perhaps for the majority of the families in our country, the ownership of a house, of two cars, and of a TV set represents the fulfillment of life's ambition.

One peculiar paradox of the North American civilization – at least of a form of modern civilization that has found its ultimate expression in America – is that in this highly productive society, individuals (as Eric Fromm has pointed out) have been reduced, or have consented to be reduced, to the role of consumers. They are consumers not only of material goods that are offered and imposed on them in greater and greater quantity, from soap suds to monstrous cars, but also of all that was formerly called the "finer things of life": how to spend one's leisure time, how to behave with friends, how to think, how to pray. Individuals in our society are no more active, but passive, beings. They are lived more than they live. And this, I imagine, is one of the fundamental features that is meant, or at least implied, by David Reisman when he describes people as "other directed." Social conformism has become the secular gospel of behaviour. The statistical average has been raised to the dignity of a moral norm. One values what is valued by his or her peers of the socio-economic stratum where he or she belongs or where he or she has the ambitions to belong.

Of course, this sketchy summary oversimplifies reality. Fortunately, there are hundreds and thousands of individuals in our country, and in the country south of the border as well, who still prefer and will always prefer to drink Chianti instead of Coca-Cola and who would rather save money to buy a picture, or even paint one, than go to a movie. But I will not have discovered America by reminding us, after hundreds of others, that, as people living on the North American continent in the age of automation and conformism, our own lives have been taken away from us. Rather, our lives have slipped off from us, absorbed by the solicitations of a continent of plenty that, in many ways, is a moral vacuum.

The Two Canadian Cultures: English and French

Such traits often leave the outside observer, and even ourselves, under the impression, after a first glance, that Canadian society is not dissimilar from that of our overpowering neighbour to the south. But we know that deeper in us there are feelings, attitudes, and identifications that are closer to our real selves. I would now like to turn to these. The first evidence that one has to note is that the Canadian society is not one but two. The nation is made of two peoples: the English- and the French-speaking. Even though both have shared common experiences, even if they give allegiance to a few identical symbols and are held together by the same political structure, each has its own sense of identity, its characteristic norm and motivations – in a word, its own culture.

Literature. One of the most startling ways of ascertaining some of the deep differences between the two Canadian cultures and societies is to look at them through their respective literatures. If one compares the English and the French literatures in Canada, one is impressed by the fact that the former expresses itself along an axis that I would call horizontal and the latter along a vertical axis.

Most critics of English Canadian literature recognize that one of its essential themes is the tension between individuals and their milieus: first, their geographical environments; second, their social milieus. The main characteristic of contemporary novels, since Grove and Callaghan, has been what Claude Bissell calls "contemplative realism." The novel as an art form must "strive to present a tragic vision of man in a realistic social environment." The English Canadian novel dramatizes as significant the human situations where there exists a gap between collective norms and individual behaviour. When the novel is not strictly descriptive, it is implicitly or explicitly moralizing. Or it entwines political "theses" or the defence of a conventional ideal with the frustrations of a human adventure, as in Hugh MacLennan. Or it depicts the tensions created, in the course of a happy human life, by the blind forces of nature, as in Grove. Or, finally, it depicts the tensions and conflicts between ethnic groups, as in Gwethalyn Graham's *Earth and High Heaven* or John Marlyn's *Under the Ribs of Death*. For most English Canadian novelists, the novel as artistic expression is more the description of a social situation than a plunging into the depths of an individual soul. Similarly, the most notable works written for the theatre, for the last fifteen or twenty years, have almost naturally perpetuated, with a new verve and a new gusto, the great tradition of nineteenth-century, English Canadian theatre-satire. Whether in the plays of Lister Sinclair, or Robertson Davies, or half a dozen highly talented playwrights, the dominating objective is to uncover and ridicule conformisms, inferiority complexes, and pharisaisms.

What accounts for such a preoccupation in the novel and in the theatre? Must it be related to the geographical scattering of the population? To regional particularism? To a puritanical tradition? To a religious mentality that is more social or political than supernatural? The beginning of an answer seems (to me at least) to be indicated by the fact that the only two English Canadian novelists whose works have a vertical dimension, A.M. Klein (*The Second Scroll*) and Adele Wiseman (*The Sacrifice*), are of Jewish origin. Of all the English-speaking Canadians, those of Jewish ancestry are the ones whose immediate cultural environment is the most dense. They are deeply rooted in it, both here and abroad. Whether they accept it or not, they feel bound to a fate, the beginning and the end of which are given from above, against which they must, like Jacob against the Anger, fight alone. The novels of Mordecai Richler could have been written by contemporary young French Canadian novelists.

In the latter's writings, as in those of their immediate predecessors, one finds the vertical dimension. In the French Canadian novel, either with Langevin, Elie, or Charbonneau, the characteristic tension is one between individuals and themselves – or more exactly, between individuals and their destinies – or with an absolute. Of course, the central characters of these novels have to fight against their social environment. They are generally introspective young men, modelled by a close society that chokes them with verbalized moral imperatives and that obnubilates the sources of essential thirst of which they nonetheless feel the imperious needs. They painfully live in solitude, tortured by a quasi-metaphysical anguish, in quest of a liberating truth. They are torn between the wish to abdicate and the wish to escape. They are not far from resembling the heroes of James Joyce's *Dubliners,* baffled and entrapped.

The typical drama of the hero of the French Canadian novel is beyond mere moralizing; it involves a basic protest, indeed, but its main drive is toward an absolute, which the hero knows he cannot, in the end, escape. The avenues toward this absolute are hope, purity of life, holiness (*sainteté*). He can discard his society. He knows that he cannot discard the tragical freedom of asking who is God and how to reach Him. This is equally true of the most vivid plays of the recent French Canadian theatre, as in the works of Marcel Dubé and Gratien Gélinas. Although the satirical vein is strong in Gélinas's theatre, it is ambiguously carried by an undercurrent of sadness, frustration, and remorse. The plays of more recent playwrights for the theatre of television, while they dramatize and transpose the contradictions and evils of the local society, also drive toward the same basic interrogations of the individual concerning human fate and human hope. The institutional stereotypes of the church and of conventional family life have determined strong impulses toward protest and anger. The ultimate essential truths on which these stereotypes were based and that they have distorted are deeply ingrained in the individual whose earthly predicament it is to rediscover them and to understand them for himself.

Personal Experience   Let us now turn to reality and try to establish the extent to which similarities and differences counterbalance one another in the two cultural universes. The path in which I want first to venture is somewhat delicate for I am intending to recapitulate my personal experience of contact and relationship with people on the other side of the cultural barrier. Presumptuous as this may be, it may throw an unexpected light on the predicaments involved in being a Canadian for a man of my generation and of my milieu.

I had discovered my country through books, but I had my first actual contacts with English-speaking Canadians when I was a university student, shortly after the mid-1930s. I was an adolescent in the Depression years, and I discovered that this experience had left the same imprint on those students from McGill, Toronto, and Winnipeg whom I first met around 1936–37. They were of rural or urban middle-class families, as I was. They were all, or most of them, members of the Student Christian Movement (SCM) – and many were later (or so did I hear) to join the Cooperative Commonwealth Federation (CCF) or to sympathize with farther left-of-centre political movements or fancies. I was a member of no movement. Very much to the contrary. Having been a boarder for seven years in a Jesuit college and being solicited by innumerable church-inspired or "apostolic action" groups, my only, but very strong, wish was to be left free, outside the bondage and the directives of zealous leaders who were the sonorous prophets of the status quo. Yet I was interested in national students' organizations, and it is there that I discovered new friends whose country I had heard of from the books of André Siegfried and royal commission reports. I discovered also, through them, that the SCM, of which they were members, grouped people who were social or political reformists. Some were radicals. Others pretended to be bohemians. They all looked animated by a contagious zeal. And they were – so did it seem to me – at war with, or being emancipated from, the middle-class values of their still-puritanical society. Some of my French Canadian friends and I looked exotic to them. They had read Horace Miner's *Saint-Denis,* and they would question us on the family system and the operations of the clergy in Quebec. We discovered that some of the authors we had read and who had influenced us were the same: Ignazio Silone, Maritain, Malraux. We took the same, republican, side in the Spanish War, and the great preoccupations that crystallized our conversations and our options were of non-Canadian origin. They were all of an international, at least European, character, and they all more or less centred around the struggle between freedom and the various forms of fascism. But our discussions always remained exclusively political and social; never was religion a topic of conversation, nor did we even venture as far as to refer to spiritual values. There existed between us a feeling of parallelism without real, deep communication.

It was only later in 1948, when reading *The Pickersgill Letters*, that I discovered, through the intimate correspondence of at least a young English Canadian of my generation, that some of the philosophical and moral questions that were almost the obsession of my French Canadian friends had also tormented – without our knowing it – our English-speaking compatriots of the same generation. Why had they not known our periodical, *La Relevé*, which had voiced in aesthetic, yet anguished, terms the perplexities of a youth who deeply felt that its predicament resulted from something more than the straitjackets of a conformist society, than the temporary erratic determinism of economic forces, but had spiritual, metaphysical dimensions? Why had *we* not known the Frank Pickersgills? Perhaps we crossed and encountered dozens, hundreds of them. But such was the thickness of silence between us, such was the psychological distance, that we never knew – on either side.

Later, at the beginning of my academic career – we were then in the immediate post-war years – I participated resolutely and enthusiastically in the undertakings of such national organizations as the Canadian Youth Commission, the Canadian

Citizenship Council, and in adult-education experiments. Again, I met people from all across the country, many of whom my elders, some my contemporaries, who were animated with an undaunted zeal for civic and welfare causes. We were a few French-speaking participants not only in the gatherings but also in the sharing of the workload. We knew that what we were doing was far beyond the conventional gestures of emotional *bonne-entente*. There was equal dedication and critical exchange of opinions. The cooperative purpose now was not political but educational. There was, on each side, the assumption and the evidence of moral motivation, but the foundations of cooperation were implicit rather than explicit. Never were the postulates from which each side derived its impulses formulated, nor were the respective patterns of action questioned. Yet how strange it seemed to our nucleus of French Canadian participants in these undertakings not so much to hear our English-speaking colleagues refer to such concepts as "democratic spirit," or "the sense of citizenship," or "social welfare," but to see their joyful conviction that, by the mere evangelical use of these concepts, they would magically mobilize hundreds, thousands, of their compatriots throughout the country. Such assurance resting on the manipulation of such symbols was utterly alien to our mentality and to our own experience. We knew how hard it was, in our milieu, to mobilize people already so strongly integrated in traditional religious or professional units of social life, and how complex it would be to transpose the concepts of citizenship and democratic drive into easily understandable and meaningful terms. Similarly, while our English adult-educator colleagues would centre their discussions and efforts on techniques and methods of group work, we would be preoccupied with objectives and the philosophy of group action. Not a few times have we had the feeling that whereas there was formal agreement in our discussions, what went on was a dialogue between deaf interlocutors and that the big stone that the English-speaking Sisyphuses were magnanimously rolling up on one side of the mountain would soon after run down the other, French slope of it.

My main association, of course, has been with colleagues in the academic world. There, as could be expected, is the area where one finds the least number of barriers to communication. Either at the annual meetings of the "learned societies" or through participation in national committees or councils, I have experienced the directness of mature relationships. The assumption of frankness is at its maximum, and there is, on each side, an expectation of similar scientific objectivity, the reassuring feeling of sharing identical intellectual perspectives that would help interpret the broader philosophy of life and understand its recent reformulations. The interest is global but remains intentional. There are, of course, outstanding exceptions who, because they know French for reasons of geography, vocation, or avocation, can be said to participate truly in the two cultures. But it is only recently, in my experience, that conversations with English-speaking friends have reached below the surface, down to the deeper layers, where lie the questions that one asks one's self concerning the meaning of one's relations with the rest of the world and with what is beyond it.

English-French Differential Systems of Values and Identification What are then, in fact, the ingredients of the value system and of the sense of identification characterizing each of the two cultural universes constituting the Canadian nation? That inventory has been tried, more than once, from one angle or another, but never extensively, and I shall try only to summarize what seems to me its main features.

I shall turn first to the French-Canadian culture, which I know best. Actually, I feel less and less that I know it, for it is increasingly hard to generalize about the French-Canadian society. At the recent fiftieth-anniversary celebration of *Le Devoir*, one speaker, Gérard Pelletier, aptly remarked that instead of talking about the present face of French Canadian society, one should use the plural and refer to its numerous, contrasting faces. Not only are new socio-economic classes emerging – such as the working class, a bourgeois class of businessmen and entrepreneurs, and an intellectual elite more and more aloof from the local society – but each of these is adapting a particular outlook, a specific symbolism, and new attitudes.

Yet, whatever may be the importance of the internal differentiations, there remains such a cultural entity as a French Canadian "in group." To be French Canadian not only means to claim a French origin, or to speak the French language, to be Catholic, or to share certain traditions; it means essentially to identify oneself with the French community in Canada, in any of its geographical areas but chiefly in Quebec. This identification itself is made through a reference to a same Canadian history, which is the history of the French in North America. The sense of history shared by the French Canadian is retrospective and nostalgic. One must not forget that the motto of the province of Quebec is "Je me souviens": I remember. What the French Canadian chiefly remembers is a French paradise lost as well as the political struggles that, after the British conquest up to the last third of the nineteenth century, conditioned and strengthened his or her survival. Survival has been the key concept of French Canadian history writing, and it remains the chief psychological preoccupation of a society surrounded by a culturally and linguistically different continent.

Correspondingly, although "French Canada" refers to all the geographical areas in the country where there are numerically important and socially visible groups of French-speaking people, it refers chiefly to the province of Quebec. That province, for the French Canadians, is not interchangeable with others. They strongly feel that it is theirs. It is, in a way, what they still hold of the former estate of their ancestors (who were charter-members of the country). It is altogether the framework and the political incarnation of their survival as a cultural group. Canada, for the French Canadian, is, first of all, Quebec. This historical attitude of self-centeredness remains politically dominant, although it has been considerably altered by the professional contacts and allegiances of many groups or classes with their counterparts in the rest of the country. One of the present dilemmas of French Canadian society is to reconcile its political imperatives, which are centripetal to Quebec, with the dynamic imperatives of its culture, which lead to creation and to communication over any boundaries. Such cultural communication, of course, is primarily oriented toward France, but modern France has long ceased to be referred to as a mother country. The chief sources of inspiration of contemporary French Canadian art and literature are truly indigenous. Academic research work and teaching do not follow any particular European pattern. They are spontaneous and try to be authentic. There is an increasing consciousness among those who perform such activities that French Canada is at a cultural crossroads – a stimulating incentive to redefine its traditional values and to create new channels of relationships with the broader world.

Because of their long association with, and permeation by the church, French Canadians still show a relatively acute sense of authority, which has been emphasized by the traditional family system and by the educational structure. There remains also a strong, unchangeable identification made between religion and language, and the humanistic education of the classical colleges have perpetuated an intellectual tradition that gives priority to ideas over techniques and to moral obligations over empirical experience. It is a truism to repeat that French Canadians do not think of democracy in the same way as their English-speaking compatriots. Traditionally encouraged by a paternalistic church to submit to political rulers and to accept any established social order, they do not have the feeling that the government is *their* government. It may be less true today than it was fifty years ago to say that they are faithful parishioners more than active citizens. Yet they remain more electoral than truly political beings.

Turning now to the non-French cultural part of Canada, I realize how naive it may be to refer to it as though it were a homogeneous whole. Yet, in the eyes of many observers from outside – from André Siegfried to Mason Wade – and, indeed, in the eyes of French-speaking Canadians, notwithstanding the regional and provincial differences, notwithstanding the outlook and the habits of numerous ethnic groups constituting the Canadian mosaic, notwithstanding the manifold social and linguistic diversity within the English-speaking world, there are traits in it that make it a coherent cultural entity. What I may have to say about it though will be mostly from vicarious or bookish knowledge and may only reveal the reality of the thick wall of silence and ignorance that I mentioned earlier.

Judging from what we read by Canadian authors, we have the feeling that there can hardly be in this country any vivid allegiance except to one's local community or to one's region – at the most, to one's province – the country being so big and so empty, or as Northrop Frye puts it, "a country divided by ... great stretches of wilderness, so that its frontier is a circumference rather than a boundary; a country with huge rivers and islands that most of its natives have never seen; a country that has made a nation out of the stops on two of the world's largest railway lines." "The ninety years of [Canada's] nationhood," writes C.B. Macpherson, "have been dominated by two endeavours: ... expansion and survival." It may be that one main motivation of one's identification with, or pride in, Canada would be the feeling of participation in this expansion and benefit from this survival. Another may be an increasingly vivid sense of differentiation from the United States as well as a deep satisfaction of having attained full political autonomy within the British Commonwealth. "There is," as Malcolm Ross writes, "a North Americanism which is Canadian and not 'American.'"

Thus, so does it seem to me, English-speaking Canadians are in general emotionally attached to a relatively recent Canada that has emancipated itself from colonialism. Although there exists a "latent loyalty" to the British throne and to the Crown symbolism, the strongest allegiance to the country may have been crystallized by the participation in two world wars for the defence of it. Often, it has been when they were abroad, away from their country, either in war or in peace, that many Canadians have discovered their country as a whole, for the first time, and also discovered, almost with surprise, how proud they were of it.

This pride and this interest, historically, have been chiefly economic and political. At the core of this pride lies a quasi-religious belief in democratic government and, more precisely, in British parliamentary institutions. Democracy is the overall concept, which comprises not only a political credo in individual freedom, a transcendental faith in the individual, but a whole way of life. This way of life incites to cooperation with one's neighbours, and it is tolerant. Tolerance is also a religious attitude, and it involves the recognition of any variety of religion. Religion is left to the individual's choice, but it may lend itself, in situations of collective frustration or crisis, to movements of social protest and to reformist political action.

This oversimplification may not correspond to the experience of what it is to be an English Canadian – but again, this is the view of it that one has from outside. Fortunately, there have been, in recent years, more and more English- and French-speaking Canadians who have had a common experience of cooperation and of closer acquaintance with one another – in public administration and political life, in academic and scientific circles, in professional associations, in business and labour organizations, in artistic or welfare national councils of various sorts. Alan B. Plaunt was one of those who deliberately and imaginatively created the occasions of such cross-fertilization. Yet the process still seems hesitant. It is only recently that an English Canadian writer, Hugh MacLennan, in his *Two Solitudes*, has become aware of the dramatic dimensions of Canadian coexistence. And also it is a French Canadian novelist, Jean Simard, who is chronologically the first (to my knowledge) among Canadian writers to have had either enough intuition, or knowledge, or audacity to create a character belonging to the "other" cultural world.

Common Intellectual Heritage

One of the most comforting signs of rapprochement and understanding between the two cultural solitudes, at present, is that more and more individuals in either universe, in academic life and elsewhere, are becoming aware of the basic elements of our respective spiritual heritages. They are becoming aware not only of the content of these traditions, of their similarities, but of the fact that they are both in strong continuity with their origin, and that this origin is historically rooted in the same Western European intellectual tradition. Setting aside the spiritual values that our respective religions or systems of ethics owe to Christianity, I want to consider briefly some elements of the humanistic tradition, which, on either side, is what we cherish most, talking so much about it because we feel it is endangered. Each of our intellectual traditions has flowered out of classical humanism. To recapture the meaning of the spiritual community from which humanism developed and to ascertain some of its significant subsequent acquisitions may be one of the best ways of ascertaining a lasting common denominator between us as well as of identifying one primary duty offered to our good will.

Classical humanism – and I use the term closer to the French terminology as including the broad field of humanities as they have been so admirably exposed, defended, and illustrated in our country by such authentic scholars as A.S.P. Woodhouse, Northrop Frye, and Malcolm Ross, to mention only a few – is the expression of a type of human excellence formulated by antiquity, then recaptured and reformulated successively by three restorations: the Carolingian reform; the mediaeval, golden thirteenth century; and the Renaissance. It has been stated as an ideal of intellectual and moral achievement on the basis of norms formulated by the Greek and the Roman civilizations. Two typical intellectual trends, in contrast and often in opposition to each other, had characterized ancient thought. One, isocratic or sophistic, aimed at the education of the ideal "man of action" and emphasized the priorities of the language arts. It culminated in rhetorics, and it found its most complete expression in Cicero's *De Orators*. The other trend, Platonician and Aristotelian, favoured science and speculation. Both trends remained harmoniously interwoven in the Middle Ages, but the Renaissance accentuated a divorce that Western thought has perpetuated, often painfully, down to the present time: that between "humanities" and the "sciences."

The humanists of the Renaissance emphasized the Greek and the Roman ideal types of individual as permanently exemplary ideas, yet they somewhat forgot the concurrent Greek and Roman traditions of scientific inquiries. They were curious about the literary, aesthetic, and philosophical achievements of antiquity but less curious about its social and political institutions, as indeed about their own. Classical humanism remained chiefly literary and philosophical, dissociated from scientific inquiry into the nature of the physical world and of the social world. Yet the other intellectual current to spring from antiquity, that of systematic curiosity and experimentation, developed brilliantly out of its own momentum, thanks to men like Bacon and Da Vinci, later Descartes and Pascal, but was concentrated on the physical world. Scientific investigation was concerned with what was nonhuman and outside of the self, not with what people were as individuals and as social beings. Consequently, when the teaching of humanities in the eighteenth century partly annexed the teaching of sciences, these were still only "natural" or "physical" sciences.

It is only much later that – capitalizing on the wealth of ethnographical material accumulated by the world discoverers and historians, as well as on the new vistas opened by the Enlightenment philosophers and the French encyclo-pedists – the social sciences developed, at the beginning of the nineteenth century. Thanks chiefly to the influence of Comte and Spencer, they first prolif-erated in many directions: jurisprudence, history, ethnography, folk psychology, political economy, and human geography. The history of their eventual differen-tiation one from each other and of the elucidation of their methodology is a colourful, often painful history up till after the beginning of the present century. That history can be best described by Paul Valery's observation: "In the past, almost all the (novelties) which had successively appeared were solutions or answers to very old, almost immemorial problems and questions. The novelty which confronts us, modern men, consists in this that the questions themselves are unheard of, and not the solutions; it is the problems which are new and not the answers."

The social sciences have formulated these new problems posed to modern individuals by the industrial age and changing societies. They are both the expression of a social challenge and the response to that challenge. Each in its own fashion – economics, political science, sociology, or any other of them – has enabled us to decipher the network of social determinisms within which human fate is being lived. They help us to ascertain the objective reality of individuals as social beings. In so doing, they have widened our conception of human experience, and they oblige us to widen also the traditional concept of humanism. Sociology and social anthropology, in particular, by uncovering the multiplicity of human cultures, have pushed back the frontiers within which one formerly looked after a stable, unidirectional definition of human nature. The social sciences have brought about a de-Westernization of the concept of culture and of civilization. Henceforth, "to the concept of the privileged individual in a dominating culture, has succeeded a global scheme within which all cultures and all men assume an equal importance, involved in identical historical processes, and interacting on one another with the same privileges and the same dignity."

Thus, to the traditional meaning of culture understood as the intellectual development of the individual apt to appreciate "the finer things of life" in the Western society, has been added a wider sociological concept according to which culture defines "the total way of life of any society." Insofar as the social sciences endeavour, each pursuing its particular query, to identify and to comprehend, from society to society, the constancy and recurrence of such cultural conditions that fashion the personality and the life-orientation of individuals, they constitute a vast problematical investigation of human beings.

Such is, or should be, the perspective of modern humanism. Without discarding the sense of a hierarchy of values in human beings nor the sense of the excellence of those spiritual achievements that characterized the traditional humanism, it adds to it the sense of pluralism that forms of human excellence can take. Such a widened humanism is never definitely given. It consists in a long, patient, and systematic investigation – an investigation corresponding to the need that modern individuals have of becoming conscious of themselves.

The New Humanism: A Challenge

The main point toward which this whole paper is oriented is that it is through our universities and in our universities that the latent values dominating Canadian life should be reevaluated and incarnated. Canada will achieve sooner and more powerfully the fusion of its dual cultural heritages by spiritual avenues rather than politically. And such an achievement can be attained in our institutions of higher learning if we bring forth, with imagination and conviction, the creative potentialities of the classical humanism, rejuvenated by the broad perspectives of the social sciences.

This is a great challenge, as I see it, to which we must respond if we are to become true to our deep, real selves and if we are to make a contribution to the world in which we live. It is in its institutions of higher learning that the guiding light of a nation must originate. This light, in our country, will, to a great extent, result from the integration of the permanent and lasting acquisitions of the old world with the discoveries of the modern one. The North American world around us is a Pandora's box of titanic proportions. What it has to offer and what we have already borrowed from it is far from all evil. It has latent ideal ambitions and nostalgias, and it is animated by an adventurous spirit. It has made fascinating explorations into the nature of the human mind and of our behaviour as social animals. We must make ours a similar, bold spirit with a view to assuming a positive responsibility, even a leadership, as a ferment of Western civilization.

If we are to do this, our universities must rehabilitate the notion that they are, essentially and above all, *republics of learning*. They should rediscover the true meaning of "university," an institution shaped by the Middle Ages as the pedagogical embodiment of their own intellectual integration. I am not advocating here a mere return to the past, as past, but suggesting an example of innovation through recourse to a dynamic model. In order to create our own model, we must resist the forces that would make our universities mere factories for the production of technicians or large-scale cafeterias catering to the whims and fancies of a versatile public. We must rehabilitate the notion that education and learning are valuable ends in themselves. We should rehabilitate the ancient concept of the *magister* who was a seeker of truth and a lover of wisdom. Education, as it has been said, is an act of self-discovery and a judgment upon the self thus discovered – an act whereby a man rediscovers the past, grasps the present in its most profound and hidden currents, and thereby comes to know himself in depth as well as breadth.

If the university wants to become again a true republic of learning, it must not only make possible but stimulate what, according to Plato, is the true form of human thought: the dialogue. First, the dialogue between masters of varied humanistic and scientific disciplines. Also, the widened dialogue between masters and students. This means that those who teach will have to remain, as were "scholars" in the old sense of the term, *inner-directed* or *tradition-directed* individuals. What they must communicate is the superabundance of their own, personal research. In order to do this, they must be allowed all the possible chances – financial, administrative, and academic – to be dedicated to their subjects and to their students – that is, to contemplation and communication.

If Canadian universities can achieve this in a more explicit and a more original way than ever, I am convinced that all the other important things that we are looking for shall be added unto us. We shall, as Jacques Barzun said, "Keep the men who run our national educational plant from being run by it." Running it with their minds set on a rediscovery of what gives meaning and consistency to the lives of human beings, they will provide the community with its more powerful anchor – an anchor set above it and that pulls it upward, toward the better part of itself.

PART TWO

I want to return now to our discussion of the social sciences. I do this not only to submit to a professional bent, but because the social sciences provide us with this most adequate perspective for observing and analyzing some fundamentals of Canadian life.

Thus far I have tried to illustrate how the social sciences had broadened the traditional humanism and how, consequently, they were a challenge to higher education in our country insofar as they enabled and stimulated us to reconcile the acquisitions of the classical tradition with the values of the new world. I would like to analyze this challenge further – more exactly, to consider how the social sciences offer us a tool for a better definition of Canada as a nation as well as for a better definition of our international relations in a smaller and smaller and more and more complex world.

Canada and the Social Sciences

It is appropriate to recall that the establishment of the social sciences in Canada has been a fairly recent development. They are not older than forty years or so, and, as Professor C.B. Macpherson has shown, their development has reproduced the two main endeavours that have dominated Canada's accession to nationhood: "The patterns of social and historical thought in Canada, their rates and directions of growth, have been shaped in various ways by the two impulses of expansion and survival, which in a sense, caution each other. As the economic, political, and social problems created by Canada's expansion broke out with sufficient magnitude, particularly at the turn of the century, they had to be settled by the politicians." But, as Macpherson also notes, "It gradually became realized, perhaps from the fact that the politicians could never get the problems settled, that the cultivation of some specifically Canadian social sciences would be advantageous." Individual scholars and groups of scholars in the fields of economics, history, and political science appeared in Canadian universities and were "the main authors of the social and historical writing of our time."

The social sciences in Canada have appeared as a response to the challenge of the environment, both physical and social, and they have, in their turn, brought about changes in this environment. This process of counter-play could be illustrated in the fields of geography, demography, ethnology, and anthropology, as well as, of course, economics, politics, science, and anthropology. One has only to recall such monumental studies as W.A. Mackintosh's *Canadian Frontiers of Settlement* series; C.A. Dawson's *Peace River Settlement* series; the late H.A. Innis's classical economics monographs on the fish, lumber, fur, and railroad industries; and the late MacGregor Dawson's *Canadian Government* series – not to mention the equally imposing works of the historians and of the anthropologists.

The development of social sciences in French Canada, more recent chrono-logically but synchronic methodologically, has similarly reflected the basic processes of the milieu in which they were born – about twenty-five years ago. The impact there was accelerated by industrialization and by the destructuration of a formerly homogeneous society. Social sciences were the tool for describing the changes in values and their social implications and repercussions. They were also a tool for a redefinition of the community's objectives and of the new forms of its communication with others.

As they progressed along different paths, often on intersecting or diverging avenues, the social scientists felt the need for a rationalization of their efforts, which itself might help focus their respective objectives and even coordinate them. This need was fulfilled with the creation, in 1940, of a Social Science Research Council that has been, ever since, an invaluable superstructure of Canadian academic life. Not only has it fostered interest in and encouragement to the social sciences inside and outside the universities; it has made possible a cooperation between the social scientists and the humanists, through an intimate relationship with a Humanities Research Council that had also been created in 1945. Thanks to this alliance, many collective social research projects were undertaken by the council on problems that had vital significance in contempo-rary Canadian social life. Thanks to such research, we have acquired a truer and more objective portrait of ourselves.

It is through the experience gained by personal association with such a project that I want to submit some further thoughts on the nature of the Canadian nation. This project was chiefly sociological in scope, and its purpose was to study the nature of biculturalism in Canada. Many individuals and groups collaborated on it, and the result of their observations and efforts will become manifest next fall in the form of a book of *Essays on Canadian Dualism*. What I shall have to say does not involve the opinion of any of our contributors. I merely want to formulate the outline of a sort of sociological model in the perspective of which I have tried to give meaning to the work of my colleagues and to give my own perception of Canada. Our country has always been in quest of its identity. My present effort is added to countless others that have been made in the past to reach a clearer view of what we are and why we are what we are.

A Model for the Understanding of Canada

The model that I intend to suggest is empirical, and it takes first into account the elementary fact that Canada is a single federative political structure superimposed transcontinentally, almost in contradiction to north-south geographical forces. Our country combines the diversities of at least five natural economic areas, but these, in their turn, are carved out into ten provincial political units, each with its Confederation-old tradition of bargaining against the central power, each constituting a strategic framework for the definition of local interests and self-cultured allegiance.

Inside this geographical and provincial diversity there is the population mosaic of numerous groups of various ethnic origins – Ukrainian, German, Polish, Italian, etc. – who constitute over one-fifth of the country's population and to whom have been added, since the end of World War Two, the stimulating flow of immigrants who have sought in our country either a haven or a secure democratic place to live. Many of these groups have kept cherished customs, or the use of their languages, or deep allegiances to the memories of their countries of more or less ancient origin. They constitute the lively elements of the Canadian social pluralism.

But, notwithstanding this political unity cementing social diversity, the dominant fact of Canada as a nation is that it is composed of two major linguistic universes, the English- and the French-speaking universes, each of which has its own culture, which is itself embodied in the fabric and the structures of a characteristic type of society. These two linguistic and cultural groups have historically constituted the essential partners of national life – almost two nations within the nation. The history of contemporary Canada is the history of the contacts, oppositions, tensions, conflicts, and gradual rapprochement between the two. As one of Canada's most brilliant essayists, Malcolm Ross, has written: "We are inescapably, and almost from the first, the bi-focal people." Canada as a political entity is largely the result of adjustment between these cultural universes, between two people whose association has often been referred to as a *mariage de raison*.

The leading postulate in the perspective of which the interaction and the relationships between these two partners should be perceived is not that of "assimilation" but that of duality. Too often in the past, the mistake has been made of considering the fate of the French in Canada in the light of the history of minority groups in the United States as though the two situations were comparable. Now, modern North America has been settled by immigrants from Europe, Africa, and Asia. As each new group came in, there set in, with varying rapidity, a process known as "Americanization." It was assumed generally the end result would be the same: the almost complete disappearance of the marks of the country from which the immigrants came. Not a few studies on Canada have adopted a similar scheme of interpretation. They have assumed that French Canadians would be gradually assimilated. The French Canadian people as an entity would be or should disappear by being absorbed into the large universe of the English-speaking people. This view implies that French Canadians do not differ from any other "minority" group in the United States or in Canada. French Canada is only one among the variety of groups of non-English-speaking origin. But such a view is contrary to history and sociologically erroneous.

Minorities are of many kinds. There can be distinguished at least four specifically different varieties: the status minority; the Diaspora; the immigrant minority; and a fourth category, which Everett Hughes has called the "charter-member" minority. French Canadians constitute in Canada a minority of this kind. They have become a minority by virtue of invasion, of conquest. They have a deep consciousness of having been in the country first. They are "charter-members" of Canada. Hence their determination to be recognized as having a special claim on it. Hence their conviction, emphasized by a feeling of deep-rootedness, of being different from other minority groups.

This definition of themselves by the French Canadians is also accentuated by their conception of the constitution of the country. In the eyes of the French Canadians, the BNA Act, which created the Canadian Confederation, is not only a juridical act of the Imperial government creating Canadian provinces and binding them into a federal unit. It is a covenant between the English-speaking majority and the French-speaking cultural minority of the Canadian nation. It is a pact according to which French-speaking Canadians obtained the recognition of a status of partners in the government and in the life of the whole nation.

Already, I have briefly recapitulated some specific features of the French and English societies in Canada. Each of the two societies is heterogeneous, but each has definite traits that are irreducible to those of the other. The boundaries between them are not geographical but linguistic and cultural. Reference to history and to the contemporary situations shows that each one has its own sense of identification, its own conception of history, and its conception of its role in the nation. Each has its philosophy of life, its notion of religion, as well as its notion of the responsibility of the citizen toward the state. Each preserves its own educational system. Each has even its conception of Canada; each has its preferred national symbolism, its favourite heroes, its holidays.

But if each of these two individualized elements must be seen and understood in itself and for itself, it is sociologically as important that each should be seen and understood in its relationship with the other. The understanding of intergroup relations must be focused, first of all, on the *relation*. As Everett Hughes again expresses it, ethnic relations can be no more understood by studying only one or the other, or one *and* the other of the groups involved, than can a chemical combination by the study of a discrete analysis of each element, or a boxing bout by successive observation of the two fighters. No matter how different from each other are the two Canadian cultural groups, each has been part of an interacting system with the other, and each one must be seen as participant to this play and counter-play as well as *a result of it*. The act of living together and acting upon one another, either in a negative or in an affirmative fashion, does transform the very nature of each participant. The English and the French societies in Canada are not a product of isolation. Each is a product of interaction with the other.

It has been one objective of the Social Sciences Research Council's *Essays on Canadian Dualism*, which I mentioned earlier, to undertake such an analysis. The contributors to these essays have endeavoured to establish the extent to which the social institutions, the ideologies, the attitudes of one group had influenced those of the other. How deeply, for example, have the patterns of the life-ambition of the young French Canadian been influenced, in one way or another, by the English Canadian models? What does the Quebec French, originally "Catholic," labour movement owe to its relationship with national "English" labour organizations? To what extent has not only the French language been transformed due to exposure to English, but also the very style of thought and the ideologies? Reciprocally, what has been the impact, if any, in English-speaking Canada of French Canadians' educational system, of their enthusiasm for liberal arts, of their enjoyment of the good life as something not necessarily sinful? Unfortunately, we know very little about all this. The most interesting questions often remain without an answer – although many contributors to the *Essays* bring out fascinating observations in the fields of economics, politics, and even religion. One of the least expected areas where reciprocal influence and cross-fertilization has occurred is that of law. Professor Louis Beaudoin of McGill University meticulously details the ways in which French civil law, in the province of Quebec, has been gradually transformed by the influence of common law, not only in its interpretation but, in many cases, in its conceptualization. Reciprocally, there seems to have been a counter-influence, in Canadian jurisprudence, of the French philosophy of law and/or its need for clarity of definition. Such have been the processes of our symbolic situation, and to scrutinize them with more precision would improve our knowledge of ourselves.

Psychological and Political Consequences

From a fuller realization of these data of Canadian national life, there would proceed a certain number of important consequences, and first is the very nature of identification with our country. We would grasp with a new evidence that to accept Canada in its wholeness is not as much a spontaneous emotional attitude as an act of reason. Canada is not a starting point but a goal. It is not a datum but a construct. It is a becoming, and there is no definitely set pattern to follow for becoming it. Patterns and objectives have to be constantly redefined and improvised. A well-tempered yet positive national life will consist always, as it has in the past, in such a motion. But in a motion that, as Malcolm Ross so vividly described it, will remain founded on tension. "A motion which takes its energy in tension, a motion which is visible in unfolding spirals of irony, a motion in which nothing is left behind or lost."

One such spiral of irony at the moment lies in the fact that English-speaking Canadians are undergoing an experience that is not dissimilar to an earlier experience of the French Canadians and that may help them to understand the latter better. More and more among them are alarmed at seeing what they cherish in their Canadian way of life submitted to certain sterilizing influences of the American culture. Seeing their own culture endangered makes it dearer and worth preserving and defending. This produces a feeling of self-identification and cultural assertion that may not be nationalism, as such, but that reflects a determined effort for survival. Now, such an effort and such a struggle toward self-recognition has been a long story for the French Canadians, and it has been the root of what was often misleadingly called French Canadian "nationalism." The French Canadian has had the experience of seeing his or her culture endangered or compromised by alien forces. For the English Canadian, to meditate over this experience and to relate it to his or her own, might be a fruitful way of discovering an area of psychological rapprochement with, and perhaps of forming an attitude of renewed interest toward, the French Canadian.

But whatever the rapprochement may become, it will have to rest; it will be all the stronger if it rests on the recognition of duality. This cultural duality has been, in recent years, stated in eloquent terms in many public documents and, in particular, in the reports of the Massey Commission and of the Fowler Commission. The official definition that our country has given of itself, on many occasions, even in speeches or statements by the queen, has asserted, even emphasized, this duality. *Unhyphenated* Canadianism is a fiction. But this asser-tion should not be merely verbal or official. It should be recognized with conviction. Its practical consequences must be carried over earnestly on all levels of daily life, in Ottawa as in Quebec; in many other places in Canada as in Quebec; on airlines as on railways – by which I mean having wine available as well as the French language.

It goes without saying that I am not advocating here anything resembling a separatist attitude or any policy that would, on the part of the provincial government of Quebec, mean an exclusively defensive or aggressive attitude toward the central Canadian government, as though the capital of the country were the capital of a foreign country. Nor am I subscribing to the thesis that has been obsessively orchestrated for the last few years by one of my very vocal compatriots, the historian Michel Brunet, of the University of Montreal. According to this thesis, Canadian dualism is not only a dualism, but a dichotomy. It is not only cultural, but political. There are in Canada two irreducible social species, those that Brunet, after his own domestic concoction, calls the "Canadians" and the "Canadiens." There is between both an insuperable Chinese wall. Actually, Canada is made of two Canadas. The nation state – so says the gospel according to Brunet – which has developed in Canada since 1760, especially since 1867, is "a realm created by the British Americans ... This nation-state is monarchic, Britannic, Protestant ... The government of Ottawa has become and will remain exclusively the national government of an English Canada." Its main and only responsibility is "to safeguard and to stimulate the flowering of the 'Canadian' culture." This is, indeed, not only verbal excess, but a most damaging and essentially erroneous definition of the Canadian situation and all the more strange since it comes from a historian (but we have been used to realizing that among Canadian historians, and historians in general, there is more than one mansion in the house of Macaulay, Creighton, and Lower). I should add that this view is not held by a great number of followers. In any case, it is widely removed from the simpler and more realistic thought to which I am trying to draw attention: that if a bicultural country is going to make any headway it has to take its twinship into account.

Other consequences of the twinship will follow, on the level of internal national policy. I have already referred to the well-known fact that Canada, as we know it, is politically the result of constant compromises. It is the result of round-table discussions. Our constitution was elaborated in this way. Our national policy has been shaped and remodelled at the cost of innumerable, often endless, royal commissions. We can either deplore this or rejoice in it, but we have actually not much other choice. Such a style of national policy making is inevitable in a country that came into being under economic and geographical forces from outside rather than under a collective wish from inside. Is it necessary to recall once more that there never was here a collective national revolution as there has occurred in most modern nations. We never had a collective act of political emancipation out of which, as it happened for other nations, we would have spontaneously created the symbols identifying and perpetuating our rise to adulthood: a flag, a national anthem, a national holiday. We may regret to have missed, or to have been bypassed by, such an occasion. It is too late now. Our nation has become adult through patience and without colour. It has had the

sober beginning of a *mariage de raison* between two partners who had not chosen
to live together. Consequently, it is my opinion that we should not make too
much effort to create artificially the symbols of national life that history has
refused to us. We should refrain from imposing on ourselves a meaningless
national symbolism. A national flag cannot properly be born out of round-table
discussions or parliamentary committees. The result, as we already have more
than one indication, might too easily look like an abstract hooked rug designed
and woven by blind artists of conflicting schools of painting. If we regret not
having that expression of nationhood, we may discover that – in another, higher
perspective – it is a blessing. Perhaps, in a not too distant future, in a world
where national boundaries will have become meaningless and national arro-
gances catastrophic, we may be envied by many other nations as "the country
without a flag."

Our International Responsibility

The fact of having been bypassed not only by the extreme forms of nationalism,
but by nationalism itself, if it seems an apparent weakness domestically, is an
element of our strength in our international policy and attitude; in world affairs
we have shown many distinctive characteristics that draw the attention, often the
admiration, of an increasing number of nations. Some of these distinctive traits
are prudence, understanding, tolerance, and an unflinching zeal for peace. These
qualities on the international scene reflect and derive from the necessities of our
behaviour on the domestic scene. Prudence and understanding have been the
conditions of relative peace in a country that had to live on compromise. And that
prudence, as Malcolm Ross again puts it, "is not a negative virtue ... If it seems
to suggest immobility, let us think of the immobility at the centre of a moving
wheel." It is prudence that sets us in motion, and in international affairs, that
motion has been around a central act of faith in other people's goodwill and reason
and in their ability to use these qualities for salvation rather than destruction.

   I am far from being a specialist in international affairs, but I have a strong
feeling that one of the reasons accounting for Canada's growing international
prestige is our relative lack of biases and prejudices in our dealings with others
and, consequently, our attitude of attention to others and of understanding of
their problems. Indeed, we have preferences, within the Western world, that are
not exclusively determined by economic or strategic interests. It is normal and
immensely valuable, for example, that the texture of our bonds with the countries
of the Commonwealth be as strong as they are flexible. But I consider it as
profoundly significant that we should have been so alive to the ambitions of the
countries of Asia and Africa, which have lately, out of their choice, attained

the status of independence; that we should have been so discreet in recognizing the form of government that they wanted for themselves; and that we should have been so spontaneously ready to help those among them who were in need of economic or technical aid. But I am not the only one to wish that our presence in international affairs and our role in determining global policy should be more positive, even more dynamic. Qualities other than mere prudence will be more and more needed, for prudence often degenerates into, or simply conceals, hesitation or uncertainty.

As an optimistic friend of Canada, Professor Denis William Brogan, recently expressed it, "It will be one of the problems of Canadian leadership in the next few years to think out Canadian policies that the great powers do not, for whatever reason, think out or propose. But it will not be enough to propose a policy, it will be necessary to put behind it the weight of an enlightened country." I am concerned here, of course, with our relationship with the world of the hydrogen bomb as well as with our stand in the alignment of the two great blocks of forces now confronting each other. But this struggle, as we know, is most likely to stop short of global destructive war, and it has already been reduced to a level of competition that is economic and cultural. It is in this perspective that I see our country's positive role and also see it, realistically enough, I think, with a particular reference to the Asiatic and African countries – those countries of which most are economically underdeveloped and culturally developed differ- ently from ours and that, according to French terminology, are now called *le Tiers Monde* (the Third World).

Our country's positive role and responsibility will then have, to a great extent, a cultural dimension. We must enter into communication with countries and nations of different civilizations, and in order to communicate with them, we must understand them, comprehend their civilizations – and indeed, we must comprehend fully what we are and what we have to offer to them: the values of our own, Western civilization. Are we ready to answer such a challenge? For, before entering into a dialogue with others, we must have a clear view of who we are and who they are. I must, at this point, refer to one or two observations made earlier and also widen the scope of the challenge that I have ascribed to institutions of higher learning in our country.

I have suggested that one datum of the social sciences, particularly of social anthropology and of sociology, is the equal importance of the culture of each society and of any type of civilization. Not only must we agree with this perspective, but we must make it the framework of our own outlook. We must de-Westernize our concept of civilization since we have been raised to confuse our own civilization with CIVILIZATION itself. We must become aware of the fact that there have been forms of wisdom, ideals of good life, and patterns of social structures or of government, such as those of India or China, that are much more ancient than the ideal norms that we value in our civilization and that these not only have documentary interest, but are still the meaningful models of life for millions of people. Actually, we have no choice in doing this or not, for, in the words of the great scholar Sardepali Radakrishnan, the vice-president of India: "The days of cultural tribalism, of separate cultural universes, are over. We belong to the same world. Our tribe is mankind and nothing that is human is alien to us ... The new world environment requires a tradition which is neither Eastern or Western but universal and based on the conception of man, on the recognition of his uniqueness, the freedom and creativity of the individual person, the demand for personal dignity and autonomy."

Such a responsibility does not mean that we have to alter, still less to forget, our Western values. On the contrary, for we shall be in a position to enter into fruitful dialogue with other civilizations only insofar as we shall have a full grasp of all the values of our civilization, of their intellectual, moral, and political implications. As I have tried to point out, the rejuvenation of our Canadian intellectual life, as well as a better polarization of our general way of life, depends on a return to the sources of the Western civilization, which we have inherited from Rome, Greece, and also Israel. In an address delivered at the Annual Summer School for Teachers at Oxford in the summer of 1959 on "The Essential Values of Western Civilization," the Hon. Lester B. Pearson summarized these values so vividly that I cannot resist quoting him:

From the Greeks, we have received the ideal of quality before quantity, of honour before wealth, balance before bigness, principles before practice, and in law, politics and military service, the superiority of the dedicated amateur over the professional.

From Rome we have received a tradition of order and organization, of one law for all citizens, of the essential personal responsibility of every citizen to do his duty to the state.

From Israel came the spiritual heritage of one God, and the worth and value and equal rights of every person under that God.

To this richness have been added the treasures of the humanistic tradition, of a democratic ideal, of a scientific method applied to the physical as well as the social world, and of new goals of life ambition created by stupendous technological inventions. We have to reconcile the youth of our human experience and the use to be made of our too rapidly acquired wealth with ancient notions concerning the immediate and ultimate good of human life. To this challenge, which is confronting, above all, our institutions of higher learning, is added the challenge of making our values known to peoples of other civilizations. Our communication with them must be a two-way process, for we may have much to borrow and to learn from them. How fruitfully, for example, we could refresh our concepts of human rights and of human freedoms by exposing them to the candid vigour of Oriental wisdoms that, many centuries before Plato and Aristotle, had formulated an ideal of human peace and deference. How much we might benefit from rediscovering both the sense of harmony and the noble prescriptions of such ethics as those of Confucius, Achoka, or Buddha, which, more than many Western ethical systems, have insisted on the demands of human dignity.

One timely incentive toward this urgent task is provided to us by the ten-year "major project" of the United Nations Educational, Scientific, and Cultural Organization (UNESCO) on "the mutual appreciation of Eastern and Western values." Already Canada is alertly cooperating in this project through its National Commission for UNESCO and through some universities. This is only a beginning, and it points out the right direction. Canada has, on the Pacific, a wide-open window on Asia. In three Canadian universities, McGill, Toronto, and British Columbia, there are research institutes on Asia. These and similar institutes should develop and should become, along with institutes of medieval studies, with faculties of philosophy and letters, and with humanities departments, the most highly treasured laboratories of Canadian universities. We have made fairly satisfactory headway in the other technical or professional departments of human learning in the natural and the social sciences. We should now give to ourselves, and to others, the image of a people whose ambition is not so much to reach the moon, as to transcend our psychological space in order to reach the moon, as to transcend our psychological space in order to reach the closer at hand, but better worth loving, nations around us.

JEAN-CHARLES FALARDEAU occupies a central place in the history of sociology in Quebec. He was a professor – innovative teacher and scholar – and then head of the Department of Sociology at the University of Laval from 1943 to 1981, a period of unparalleled social and cultural, as well as academic, transition in Quebec. He was a founder of the journal *Recherches sociologques* and author of groundbreaking articles and books on the social sciences, culture, and language in French and English Canada.

Dr Falardeau received the Innis-Gérin Medal from the Royal Society of Canada in 1973 and became a member of the society ten years later. He was also a member of l'Académie canadienne-française and received the 1981 Prix Esdras-Minville de la Société Saint-Jean Baptiste and, in 1984, the prestigious Prix Léon Gérin. He received a number of honorary degrees and, following his death in 1989, was recognized by the magazine *L'Actualité* as one of the hundred greatest Québecois in the previous hundred years.

4

Canada in a Changing World Economy

HARRY G. JOHNSON, 1962

INTRODUCTION

As a Canadian I am sensitive to the fact that some of the things I shall say here on the matter of the changing world economy and Canada's place in it will be unpopular, and perhaps offensive, to some members of my audience. Probably the most irritating aspects of my discourse to some will lie not in any specific remarks I make, but in the implications of the general way I approach my subject. I shall place in the forefront of my argument the changing nature of the international economy, and only after I have discussed that will I turn to considering Canada's place in it specifically. This approach carries the implication that, contrary to the contentions of Mr Bruce Hutchison and other Canadian patriots, Canada is not "a giant among nations" but in many relevant respects a small country of limited power and influence. Appreciation of this fact permeates Jacob Viner's inaugural Plaunt lectures and informs most of his wise remarks; but he was able to sugar the pill by emphasizing the giant size of Canada's neighbour, whereas I shall have to dwell explicitly on Canada's limitations. While this is likely to be wounding to Canadian self-esteem, I consider it part of my duty not to shrink from delivering salutary shocks of this kind. In my considered opinion one of the chief obstacles to intelligent discussion of Canadian problems, in both the political and the economic fields, is the traditional tendency of Canadians to hanker after an unobtainable greatness and to seek to attain it by methods contrary to Canada's true self-interest.

To start with, I shall be concerned with describing and commenting on the changing world economy. That phrase no doubt suggests the dramatic and widely publicized changes in the foreign-trade policies of various countries that have been announced in the past year: Britain's decision to apply for membership in the Common Market, the successful negotiation of the second stage of the Common Market, and President Kennedy's application to Congress for sweeping new powers of tariff reduction. I shall deal with these matters in due course; but they are surface reflections of more fundamental changes that have been going on, and will continue to go on, in the world economy, and I shall begin with these more fundamental changes.

THE CHANGING BALANCE OF POWER IN THE WORLD ECONOMY

By far the most fundamental economic development of recent years has been the dramatic shift in what might loosely be called the balance of power in the world economy, a shift marked especially by an increase in the relative importance of Europe in world economic affairs and a decline in the relative importance of North America, but also by some increase in the importance of the Communist bloc and of the underdeveloped countries. This shift has been associated with the relatively rapid industrial growth of Europe, Japan, and the Communist bloc, as compared with North America, and with the beginnings of industrialization in the underdeveloped countries. The shift, I need not point out, has been paralleled by a shift in the balance of world political power away from North America.

I have used the term "North America" to include both Canada and the United States not merely because the shift of economic power to which I am referring has affected them both, but also because in the postwar period it has increasingly made sense to think of the economies of the two countries as one closely integrated and highly industrialized economic region.

The two North American economies emerged from the war as the one industrial region that had not been damaged, and indeed had been greatly strengthened, during the war. Partly for that reason, the region enjoyed a prolonged growth boom in the dozen or so years after the war. Canadian participation in this boom was largely based on the development and exploitation of Canadian resources for the growing United States market, the prosperity of Canada's staple export industries supporting her industrial development. And the joint processes of American investment in Canadian resource industries and manufacturing and of Canadian export to the American market linked the Canadian economy – and Canadian prosperity – ever more closely to the American economy. The combination of prosperity and growing interdependence with the United States was a new historical experience for Canada and raised the question of "Canadian independence" in a new and acute form. In the past, Canada had been able to pursue the political goal of independence and the economic goal of prosperous economic development simultaneously because prosperity and development depended on the growth of exports to European – primarily British – markets and could be financed by British sources. Thus development in the past had meant increasing economic independence from the United States, whereas in the postwar period it meant increasing interdependence with the United States. In short, for the first time, there appeared to be a serious conflict between the economic and political goals of the Canadian nation – and whether this was or is a real conflict is a question to which I shall return. For the moment, let me note merely that the more rapid growth of Canada than of the United States, together with the expansion of Canadian secondary manufacturing in this period, also fostered the hope that Canada was shedding its dependence for growth on exporting extractive industry products and becoming capable of self-generating industrial growth.

For its part, the United States was impelled by its industrial predominance and the outbreak of the Cold War to commit a growing quantity of resources from its growing, national income to finance the responsibilities it assumed as undisputed leader of the non-Communist world – first for the Marshall Plan and military aid, then for economic aid to underdeveloped countries. The United States also took the lead in the negotiation of mutual reduction of barriers to international trade through the General Agreement on Tariffs and Trade. In addition, without the United States consciously planning or intending it, the dollar gradually became an international reserve currency – a currency held by other countries in lieu of holdings of gold – and the United States assumed the responsibilities of a world banker. These commitments, as will appear later, have become an important source of difficulty for the United States in the face of the changing balance of power in the world economy.

The result of the prolonged North American boom was that, five years or so ago, the United States and Canada seemed well established on the path of steady economic growth at an adequately rapid rate. (The Gordon Commission, one may recall, predicted that Canada would continue to grow at a rate more rapid than that predicted for the United States.) Since then, the North American economic situation has changed sharply for the worse and has remained so, at least in Canada: The growth boom has tailed off into a period of noticeably slower growth and high average unemployment. Explanations of the change differ in the weight they attach to different factors, but most economists would I believe agree that part of the explanation, for both the United States and Canada, is to be found in two factors: the growth of effective competition in manufacturing from Europe and Japan, and the tight money policies that have been followed by the central banks of the two countries. I would myself attach considerable weight to the effects of restrictive monetary policy aimed at the prevention of inflation, a policy that I think was seriously mistaken – especially in Canada, where the existence of a floating exchange rate relieved the monetary authorities of the need to worry about balance-of-payments deficits. I think that the policy was seriously mistaken, incidentally, because I think that the policy makers both vastly exaggerated the evil consequences of a moderately rising price index and paid quite insufficient attention to the economic and social loss entailed by slow growth and unemployment.

Be that as it may, the slackening of economic activity and growth in North America has been one factor in the relative decline in the importance of the region in the world economy. A far more important factor has been the economic recovery of Continental Europe and the sustained rapid economic growth of that region since 1950. The fact of European growth, and its implications, was for a long time disguised by the persistence of the dollar problem and the investment of European surpluses in dollar balances, and recognition of them was further postponed by the effects of the Suez invasion. But the formation of the Common Market and the emergence after 1957 of a chronic United States balance-of-payments problem have dramatically called attention to Europe's rapid growth and competitive power. I shall not try to explain this growth in terms of fundamental causes: Some of my economist colleagues, looking at Western Germany, have attributed it to the virtues of free enterprise and competition; Canadian businessmen, looking at the same evidence, seem to find the explanation in the freedom of European business to form cartels unrestricted by a Trade Practices Commission; other observers, looking at France, have found the explanation in the virtues of long-range economic planning. Whatever the fundamental explanation – and I suspect that the psychology of military defeat and political impotence, on the one hand, and the flexibility of skilled and intelligent people, on the other, have a lot to do with it – the rapid growth of Europe has been based on the accumulation of capital and the application and development of modern technology and mass production. The same features characterize the continued rapid growth of the countries of the Communist bloc and of Japan, while the emergence of various underdeveloped countries as industrial producers also rests on the use of capital and the acquisition of technology and human skill.

On a broad interpretation of recent economic history, one can say that relative decline in the economic power of North America has been intimately associated with the spread of industrialization to other parts of the world. On the one hand, the second industrial revolution – the oil, electricity, mass production, chemicals, and technology revolution – has spread from North America to the industrially advanced countries of Europe and Japan; on the other hand, industrial production has begun to develop in countries and regions formerly predominantly agricultural. The spread of industrialization around the world has meant both that North America has been losing its leadership over Europe and that Europe and North America have begun to lose the virtual monopoly of industrial production they enjoyed up to the beginning of World War Two.

These trends are certain to continue, and they have conflicting implications for the future prosperity and growth of North America. On the one hand, the spread of industrialization implies rising real incomes in the rest of the world, a factor that should contribute to the growth of real income in North America through the familiar mechanism of rising demand for North American products. On the other hand, the spread of industrialization implies increasing foreign competition with North American industry and the possibility of a relative (not necessarily an absolute) decline in American living standards – a narrowing or closure of the gap between incomes per head here and in the rest of the world. In economic jargon, industrialization elsewhere has both an income and a substitution effect on foreign demand for North American products.

Before I continue with this part of the argument, let me digress for a moment to develop the proposition that the spread of industrialization represents the dynamic working out of the classical law of comparative costs. Economists customarily state this law in static terms, in some such formulation as this: Given the opportunity to engage in international trade, a country will tend to specialize in the production of those commodities in which its natural, human, and capital resources give it a comparative advantage and exchange them in foreign trade for commodities in which it has a comparative disadvantage; by so doing the country will maximize the income it can obtain from its resources. This formulation takes for granted not only the supply of human and natural resources, but also the supply of capital and, what is more important, the technology with which the factors of production are combined in the production process. A dynamic version of the law of comparative costs would take account of the fact that all of these "givens" can in fact be altered by investment – in capital goods and human skills, on the one hand, and in research on improved methods of production, on the other – and that such investment will tend to occur whenever and wherever it promises to be exceptionally profitable.

The implication in the present context is that there is a natural and persistent tendency for capital and advanced technology to be applied wherever labour is cheap relative to its skill and educability and thus to undermine the competitive position of countries enjoying a high standard of living derived from the possession of superior skills and technology; similarly, there is a tendency for technology to undermine high incomes accruing solely from monopolies of natural resources. The process, of course, works slowly and imperfectly and is counterbalanced by the tendency of superior technology to be maintained by further technical progress. But it does work, and its workings have been reinforced in the present age by two developments: the prevalence in one form or another of governmental planning for economic growth, and the rise of the great international corporation producing and marketing on a world scale. It has two important implications for an internationally trading country, both of which have tended to be neglected in modern theorizing about international trade. The first is that a country's standard of living depends primarily on its level of technology and resources of capital and human skill, the gains from trade – and particularly changes in the gains from trade resulting from changes in other countries' commercial policies – playing a relatively very secondary role. The second implication is that continuing comparative advantage in a technologically advanced world may rest on superior capacity in developing the technology of a particular line of production or on – which is often associated with this – exploitation of the economies of large-scale production, rather than on any innate advantage of overall resource endowment.

To return to the question of the effects of the spread of industrialization in the world economy on the future prosperity and growth of the North American economy, it is I think obvious from what I have just said about the dynamics of comparative costs that these effects will depend very much on how effectively the North American economy is able to adjust to the competition resulting from the application of capital and advanced technology in other countries by progressively raising the quality of its own technology and human skills and shifting from industries in which it is losing comparative advantage to those in which it is acquiring new comparative advantage. A large part of the answer depends on the flexibility and resiliency of the private enterprise system itself, a matter about which one may I think entertain a fair degree of confidence. But much of it depends on the wisdom of governmental policy and especially on how far governmental policy facilitates or hinders the functioning of the free-enterprise system, a matter about which recent experience gives much less ground for confidence. I shall return to these matters later.

THE CHANGING INTERNATIONAL ECONOMIC SYSTEM

Let me now turn from the underlying change that has been going on in the world economy to its more immediate manifestations in the evolution of international economic relations and institutional arrangements. To begin with, it is useful to gain perspective by recalling the chief features of the international economic system that wartime planning for postwar reconstruction sought to establish for the postwar world. Postwar reconstruction planning was strongly influenced by the breakdown of the interwar gold exchange standard in the 1930s under the impact of international, short-term capital flights ("hot money" movements) and the resulting constriction and disorganization of international trade by competitive currency depreciation, quota and exchange control restriction of imports, and bilateral trading; it was also strongly influenced by certain American prejudices in favour of conservative banking practices and the principle of nondiscrimination in international trade. The reconstruction planners sought to establish an institutional framework for a multilateral, nondiscriminatory trading system that would secure the advantages of the gold exchange standard system of fixed exchange rates without its rigidity and vulnerability to short-term capital movements. The framework was to be embodied in three new international institutions, two of which were actually established and the third of which has been provided by a less formal substitute. The first was the International Monetary Fund (IMF), whose purpose was to provide a stronger international monetary system by providing a pool of international reserves on which members could draw to supplement their gold reserves; by accepting the right of members to control short-term capital movements; by establishing a mechanism by which members could alter their exchange rates in case of "fundamental disequilibrium"; and by adopting a "scarce-currency clause" by which persistent creditor countries could be disciplined. The second institution was the International Bank for Reconstruction and Development, whose purpose was to provide a flow of internationally guaranteed loans to countries in need of capital. The third, whose function was assumed by the General Agreement on Tariffs and Trade (GATT), was to embody and police a code of fair trade restriction practices, nondiscrimination being the fundamental principle, and to provide an agency for the negotiation of nondiscriminatory tariff reductions. But, while new preferential trading arrangements were excluded, exception was made for completely discriminatory trade arrangements in the form of customs unions and free-trade areas.

It is an ironical reflection on the powers of official foresight, as well as a vindication of the analytical ability of some of the contemporary critics of these arrangements, that while these institutions can justly be said to have performed useful functions in postwar economic affairs, the limitations of the principles on which they were constructed can equally be held to blame for the strains that have developed in the non-Communist world economy in the past few years and particularly for the difficulties now facing the United States. The preservation of the monetary role of gold inherent in the structure of the International Monetary Fund, the development of the use of the dollar as a reserve currency prompted by the limited resources of the fund, and the increasing unwillingness of members to contemplate changes in their par values have brought the world back to something very like the interwar gold exchange standard. And the fact that it has proved impossible to control short-term capital flights and impolitic to discipline creditors has meant that the new gold exchange standard is as vulnerable as the old to hot money movements and, like the old, has had to rely increasingly on the willingness of central banks receiving hot money – or their governments – to lend it back to the country losing it. The conservative principles of the International Bank have made it, quite appropriately, an unsuitable instrument for raising and administering the vast sums of money it is now thought obligatory for the advanced nations to contribute to the development of the underdeveloped nations, so that this burden has increasingly been assumed by the United States government. Finally, the exception of customs unions and free-trade areas from the general principle of nondiscrimination has legitimized the formation of the European Common Market and other projected customs unions and the resulting prospective division of the world economy into regional trading blocs, quite contrary to the intentions of the GATT system. Moreover, the nondiscrimination principle is likely to make it difficult for the United States to persuade the Common Market to negotiate mutual reduction of tariffs.

These reflections, however, take me to a story whose end I have yet to tell: the story of why the postwar international economic system has turned out so differently from what was expected and particularly of why the non-Communist world economy is in the process of being divided between two rival, giant, protected trading areas: Europe and the United States. The key developments leading up to the present situation have been, on the one hand, the emergence after the war of the United States as the preeminent leader of the free world – and its assumption of the corresponding, economic responsibilities to the non-Communist countries – and, on the other hand, the subsequent emergence of the European Common Market as a potentially more powerful influence on international economic relations than the United States. The primary sources of both developments are to be found in the economic and political developments of the immediate postwar period: economically, in the unexpected difficulty and protracted delay in the restoration of the European countries to full currency convertibility and in the focusing of Europe's difficulties on a shortage of dollars; politically, in the outbreak of the Cold War.

Europe's dollar problem prompted the United States to the boldly imaginative suggestion of the Marshall Plan; the outbreak of the Cold War provided a political motivation for the commitment of American resources to the support of European reconstruction and, thereafter, the motivation for increasing commitment of American resources to military and economic assistance to the underdeveloped countries. The dominance of the United States in world trade and its increasingly large foreign lending and transfer operations, together with the inconvertibility of European currencies and the unprofitability of holding international reserves in the form of gold, led to the increasing use of dollar balances as international reserves by other countries. Finally, the United States (together with Canada) took the lead in negotiating tariff reductions through GATT. In these various ways, the United States rapidly assumed the responsibility of centre country in the world economy – supplier of capital for other countries' development, reserve currency country, practitioner of a liberal trading policy – which Britain had carried in the nineteenth century (and has struggled so onerously and unprofitably to carry in the twentieth).

THE EUROPEAN ECONOMIC COMMUNITY

To turn to European developments, the Common Market is fundamentally a political creation, the economic manifestation of the ambition to build a United States of Europe, or European Federation, a project that a number of influential Europeans adopted at the end of the war as the only feasible means both of containing the disastrous rivalry of France and Germany and of rebuilding the political influence of Europe in the face of the dominating power of the United States and Russia. The Cold War both fanned this ambition in Europe and led the United States to support it strongly as a means of building up the political stability and economic strength of Europe against the Communist menace. The long period of dollar shortage and dependence on Marshall Plan aid laid the foundations for the successful achievement of European economic integration by accustoming the European governments to collaborating in economic affairs and considering each other's economic interests; an important factor here was that the aid was initially allocated according to the individual countries' dollar requirements and had to be redistributed among them according to overall resource needs, the Organization for European Economic Cooperation being set up for that purpose. The OEEC, however, was primarily concerned with cooperation in the reduction of quota and exchange control barriers to trade, rather than with European economic integration in the positive sense, and the development of the Common Market took place outside it and indeed in rivalry to it.

The most important factor in the successful achievement of the Common Market was the rapid economic growth that the Continental countries of Europe enjoyed after 1950, a growth that occurred in spite of (or perhaps because of) the balance-of-payments difficulties most of them continued to experience. This rapid economic growth ensured the success of their first experiment with the common market idea (the European Coal and Steel Community, formed in 1952 by France, Germany, Italy, Belgium, Luxembourg, and the Netherlands, "the Six" as they soon came to be called) and gave the participating countries the confidence to carry the experiment forward into the formation of a comprehensive common market. It is significant, in the light of later developments, that Britain was invited to participate in the Coal and Steel Community but refused to do so.

The proposal for the formation of a Common Market among the six members of the European Coal and Steel Community was first advanced early in 1955; the treaty that gave effect to the scheme was signed in March 1957, and the European Economic Community, as it is called, came into existence on 1 January 1959. Much happened in the intervening period, but before I describe those events I should describe the economic philosophy and central features of the Common Market since an understanding of these is essential to both appreciation of Britain's relations with it and evaluation of possible changes in its relations with the rest of the world.

As I have mentioned, the Common Market has been motivated primarily by the desire to form a political union in Europe; this motivation is strongly stamped on the economic philosophy of the Common Market Treaty, which bears a much closer resemblance to the protectionist theories of Hamilton and List than to the free-trade theories of the English classical economists. That philosophy is difficult to summarize – much of it has been written by Frenchmen and displays the combination of rhetorical flair and logical imprecision so characteristic of the rational French mind – but it can I think be reduced to three central propositions.

The first proposition is that countries can only overcome the economic disadvantages of small national markets by eliminating trade barriers among themselves so as to create a large common market; the advantages of a large market are envisaged partly in terms of the classical gains of specialization and division of labour but much more in terms of exploitation of the economies of large-scale production, long production runs, and up-to-date technology, and it is stressed – a point Canadians should note – that only in a large market will there be sufficient competition to ensure that the advantages of large-scale production are in fact realized and passed on to the consumer in the form of lower prices. It should also be noticed that this proposition implicitly assumes that the countries concerned are employing tariffs and trade restrictions to protect their domestic industries and that the proposition neglects the economic loss entailed in any diversion of purchases from nonparticipating to participating country producers that may follow the elimination of trade barriers among participating countries and the erection of a common tariff around the market area – what Jacob Viner has labelled the loss from trade diversion.

The second proposition is that elimination of barriers to trade – tariffs, quotas, and exchange controls – is not enough: To reap the full potential advantages of a common market it is necessary to make the market genuinely a common one by eliminating distortions and inequalities in conditions of competition. This is a far-reaching proposition: It includes not only the elimination of impediments to the free movement of goods other than those imposed by governments – the elimination of discriminatory transport charges, for example – but also the elimination of impediments to the free movement of labour, capital, and enterprise within the market area, the "harmonization" of tax systems and social legislation, and the establishment of codes enforcing competition – though Europeans are more ready than North Americans to believe that agreements between businesses may have beneficial effects for the consumer. Most of these stipulations, it may be remarked, are unnecessary according to the pure theory of international trade though some of them have turned out on more sophisticated analysis to be quite sensible.

The third proposition is that free competition in the market between countries widely different in their social and economic characteristics or stages of economic development is likely to have adverse effects on the economic development of some of them and particularly of the less developed countries or regions. Consequently, it is argued, a common market is feasible only between countries with common geographical, historical, social, and economic characteristics, which characteristics will enable them to understand each other's problems and cooperate in ensuring that the benefits of economic development achieved through the common market are fairly distributed among the members. This third proposition, I need hardly point out, departs most widely from the classical argument for free trade, both in its assertion that free trade benefits the more developed at the expense of the less developed – a standard protectionist argument, which is also used to justify protection of European producers against American competition – and in its emphasis on the need for close governmental collaboration among the members of the common market. The belief that free trade is unfair to the underdeveloped is of course very widely held in the modern world; in Canada it is one of the few beliefs that the Ontario manufacturer and the Maritimer have in common.

The economic philosophy I have just outlined is embodied in the Treaty of Rome. Again, I shall confine myself to describing the central points. First and foremost, the treaty provides for the establishment of a customs union – that is, the elimination of tariffs and other restrictions on trade between members and the adoption of a common tariff schedule on their imports from nonmembers – to be brought into effect in three stages; the first of these has since been accelerated and was completed early this year. Second, the treaty provides for free movement of labour and capital and the elimination of a variety of distortions of competitive conditions; these latter provisions include the adoption of a common agricultural policy (the Europeans employ minimum prices and import restrictions to protect their agriculture) and a common transport policy. Third,

the treaty provides certain institutions to facilitate adjustment of participating
countries to the Common Market, notably a European Social Fund to finance
the retraining of labour and a European Investment Bank to assist the financing
of investment in underdeveloped parts of the European Economic Community.
Fourth, the treaty provides a set of supranational institutions to direct the transition to and operation of the community, of which the most important are an
independent commission to do the work, and a Council of Ministers of the
member countries to make the final decisions; from the beginning of the second
(present) stage of the establishment of the European Economic Community, these
decisions are to be arrived at by a qualified majority vote, so that a member may
be obliged to act against its own preference.

The Common Market scheme, as I have mentioned, was first proposed in 1955;
its prospective fruition threatened to split the European countries, which hitherto
had been cooperating in the reduction of trade barriers in the OEEC, into two
rival groups. This prospect seriously alarmed the British government on grounds
both of altruism (the threat to the restoration of a liberal world trading order)
and of economic self-interest (the threat to Britain's exports to the Six). Not only
did exports to the Six account for about one-eighth of Britain's total exports, but
their demand for imports of manufactured goods was growing far faster than the
demand from any of Britain's other markets. On the other hand, Britain did not
feel that she could join the Common Market for three main reasons: aversion to
the surrender of sovereignty to supranational institutions and to the grander
ultimate project of political unification of Europe; unwillingness to switch from
her own system of protecting agriculture by subsidies to the Continental system
of protecting agriculture by price supports and import restrictions; and unwillingness to sacrifice Commonwealth trading relations, a consideration that bulks
larger in British thinking than some Canadians seem to believe.

With characteristic ingenuity, the British government devised a scheme to
resolve the dilemma: It proposed the formation of a European Free Trade Area
in industrial products, in which both the Common Market countries and the other
members of the OEEC would participate and that would be administered by the
regular OEEC procedures. In a free-trade area, each member eliminates tariffs on
imports from other members but retains control of its own tariffs; and this feature,
combined with the exclusion of agriculture, would have enabled Britain to secure
the free access to the European market for her manufactures that she desired
while leaving the competitive position of something like 90 per cent of Commonwealth exports to Britain unaffected.

The cleverness of this scheme and its concentration on economics to the
exclusion of political considerations were its undoing. The supporters of the
European Economic Community, particularly the French, realized that the Free

Trade Area would offer participants the economic benefits of free trade in industrial products without obliging them to accept the other forms of economic integration and the political commitments involved in the Common Market; they proceeded to block the scheme, first by using delaying tactics and finally by breaking off negotiations. In this strategy they relied on United States support for the idea of European integration and antipathy to the weaker Free Trade Area scheme. The British went on to negotiate a Free Trade Association with six other countries of "outer Europe," an association that came into effect in July 1960. But even at the time this association appeared to be more of a temporary bargaining tactic than a permanent alternative to a British accommodation with the Six, and Britain's decision to apply for membership in the Common Market, announced at the end of July 1961, has confirmed this impression.

Britain had already drifted a long way toward willingness to accept the terms of membership in the Common Market during the negotiations over the Free Trade Area. For one thing, the shock of the failure of Suez, and the Commonwealth reaction to Britain's action, had forced the British to revise drastically downward their opinion of their own importance in world political and military affairs and to turn their attention toward Europe rather than the Commonwealth as an area for the exercise of the British talent for leadership. For another thing, the dramatic contrast between their own slow growth rate and the rapid growth of Continental Europe fostered the hope that by associating their economy with Europe's they could accelerate economically. I would stress that this is a hope, not a valid deduction from economic theory or economic history, but it now has a powerful hold on the British imagination, as does the whole philosophy of competition in a large market. Finally, the contrast between the high rate of growth of European manufactured imports and the relatively much lower rate of growth of Commonwealth imports suggested that in foreign-trade policy they were backing the wrong horse, that "the Commonwealth is a wasting asset." These ideas have continued to germinate in British public discussion and have been stimulated by observation of the continued rapid growth of the Six and the starkly contrasting relative stagnation of Britain, a stagnation associated with the chronic weakness of the British balance of payments and the policies required to deal with it. The decision to apply for membership was obviously prompted by the 1961 balance-of-payments crisis though it was probably also influenced by continued American pressure on Britain to join.

An application for membership in the Common Market, however, is an engagement and not a wedding. Whether Britain actually joins will depend on whether the terms she can negotiate are acceptable to British public opinion – which would probably be tested by an election – and this will depend in part on whether these terms conform to British conceptions of Britain's responsibilities to the Commonwealth – which is not exactly the same thing as conformity to the leading Commonwealth countries' conceptions of Britain's responsibilities to them. I am not prepared to venture a guess as to the probable outcome.

STRAINS ON THE AMERICAN DOLLAR

In discussing the development of the Common Market, I have stressed the strong formative influence of the rapid postwar economic growth of Continental Europe. That rapid growth, and the increasingly strong, competitive position of Europe in world markets associated with it, eventually permitted the restoration of full convertibility of European currencies, which was effected at the end of 1958 just prior to the initiation of the Common Market, and the virtual termination of balance-of-payments discrimination against dollar imports into Europe, effected subsequently. The achievement of these goals of postwar planning and prolonged North American endeavour has, however, been more than slightly soured by the simultaneous emergence of the Common Market as a discriminatory, regional trading bloc. It has been further soured by the fact that the recovery of Europe has been accompanied by a weakening of the balance-of-payments position of the United States, which has become a chronic deficit country on a serious scale. The balance-of-payments difficulties the United States has experienced over the past four years have made the American administration acutely aware of the burdensomeness of the responsibilities of the centre country in the world economy that the United States assumed in the immediate postwar period and have led the United States authorities to attempt to induce the European countries to assume a larger share of these responsibilities, commensurate with Europe's growing international economic and political status. But the weakness of the United States balance-of-payments position has made it increasingly difficult for the United States to give strong leadership in making further progress toward a liberal trading world, and it is therefore doubtful whether the free world economy will evolve in this direction rather than – as at present seems more likely – in the direction of regional trading arrangements.

The balance-of-payments difficulties the United States has experienced since 1958 have had two aspects: On the one hand, the United States has had a chronic deficit, which averaged $3.7 billion a year between 1958 and 1960; on the other, it has suffered from short-term capital outflows prompted by higher interest rates in Europe or by loss of confidence in the dollar. On the surface, these difficulties can be attributed to a relative loss of American competitiveness in world markets, associated with a rise in American money costs relative to European. Fundamentally, however, they reflect the postwar evolution of the international monetary system into a rigid and potentially dangerously unstable system.

The International Monetary Fund, it will be recalled, was intended to provide a more flexible international monetary system than the interwar gold exchange standard: first, by providing for agreed changes in exchange rates in cases of "fundamental disequilibrium"; second, by enabling creditors to be disciplined by the use of the scarce currency clause; and third, by providing additional reserves and enabling countries to reduce reserve losses by controlling short-term capital movements. In fact, the major countries have proved extremely unwilling to change their exchange rates, especially to appreciate them, and the scarce currency clause has never been used for the simple reason that no one is willing to try to discipline a creditor who can be persuaded to put up more money. In consequence, the burden of correcting balance-of-payments disequilibrium has been transferred largely to the domestic policies of deficit countries. This implies a larger need for international reserves, but the postwar inflation has reduced the real value both of gold stocks and IMF resources and of the annual contribution to reserves from new gold production.

The gap has been filled by increasing use of the dollar as an international reserve currency, but the consequence of this has been a steady growth in United States short-term dollar liabilities relative to gold reserves – to the point where the former exceed the latter. This in turn has meant both an obligation on the United States to keep faith with its creditors by maintaining the gold value of the dollar and increased difficulty in doing so because any loss of gold due to balance-of-payments deficits or interest-induced capital outflows may inspire speculation against the dollar and rapid withdrawal of deposits in the form of gold. In short, the postwar monetary system has redressed toward the interwar system, with the United States instead of Britain as reserve currency country, and while exchange rates are not quite so immutably rigid as they were under the earlier system, this is probably more than compensated by the much reduced willingness of countries to balance their international accounts by severe internal deflation.

Along with other measures it has taken to overcome its deficits, the United States has sought to persuade the European countries to assume a larger share of the responsibilities of centre country – responsibilities that, as I have explained, include the international monetary system, development aid, and trade policy. In the money field, the United States has sought for the provision of additional international reserves in the form in which experience has shown them to be needed most: additional IMF resources of the European currencies into which short-term capital is most likely to fly, resources on which the United States can draw to offset such capital flights. In this quest it has been successful; the required resources have been provided by the recently announced agreement of ten leading industrial countries (including Canada) to provide $6 billion of standby credit to the International Monetary Fund. But the details of the agreement leave some doubt as to how effective the arrangement will prove in bolstering the modern gold exchange standard since the agreement leaves the creditors a great deal of discretion concerning the amounts of credit they will actually provide in particular cases.

In the aid and trade fields, the effort to persuade Europe to share responsibilities has made no comparable visible progress. The effort has been based, ideologically, on the discovery by the United States of the "Atlantic Community" of Western Europe, the United States, and Canada – a concept originated by Mr Lester Pearson – as the natural unit of leadership in the free world. To give effect to this concept, the United States has taken the lead in reconstituting the OEEC as the Organization for Economic Cooperation and Development, with Canada and the United States as full members, and will seek to turn the new organization into an agency for extracting more capital for the underdeveloped from Europe. The United States also evidently hopes that the "Atlantic Community" concept will help to persuade the Common Market to negotiate mutual tariff reductions. Some success in that direction has already been achieved with the agreement on mutual reduction of the Common Market and American tariffs in the present round of GATT negotiations – negotiations that were preceded by a conditional 20 per cent reduction of the Common Market tariff that was obviously offered in response to United States pressure. But it is extremely unlikely that the Europeans will be sufficiently impressed by the ideal of strengthening the North Atlantic Community – a concept that has a certain aroma of sucker-bait about it – to take the lead from the United States in the march toward freer trade. It is even doubtful how far they would go in negotiating mutual tariff reductions with the United States given the political purpose and economic philosophy of the Common Market and the fact that any reductions would have to be generalized in accordance with the most-favoured-nations clause – and remembering the fate of the European Free Trade Area. It is possible, however, that the Germans – and the British if they join – would be sufficiently attracted by the idea of freer access to the American market to carry the more protectionist-minded French and Italians along with them.

The crucial question, however, is whether the United States Congress will give the administration the new tariff-bargaining authority that the president has requested and that is necessary if the United States is to initiate a new drive for lower tariff barriers. The president has asked for general authority to reduce tariffs in reciprocal negotiations by 50 per cent and special authority to negotiate elimination of tariffs on groups of products for which the United States and the European Economic Community between them account for more than 80 per cent or more of world trade in a representative period – the "dominant supplier" authority. Both the sweeping nature of these powers and the emphasis on bargaining on a product-group basis would be new departures in American legislation and are a response to the Common Market's procedures for moving toward

internal free trade. To cushion the impact of loss of protection on American industry, the proposed legislation contains important and novel provisions for adjustment
assistance to the industries and workers adversely affected, provisions that are
the American parallel of aspects of the Rome Treaty, which I have discussed.

In attempting to obtain power to initiate a new move toward freer trade at this
time, the administration faces considerable difficulty because the higher average
unemployment and the balance-of-payments deficits of the past four years have
strengthened the arguments of the advocates of protection, just as the same
phenomena have done in Canada. The proposed legislation attempts to meet
these arguments both by retaining escape clauses and procedures and by providing adjustment assistance, and the "dominant supplier" authority is artfully
framed to support the argument that the United States will gain from mutual
tariff reduction under it since the product groups included are those in which the
United States has demonstrated superior competitive efficiency and flexibility.
The case for the legislation is being presented to the American public not only
as a help to the balance-of-payments, but also as a challenge to the ability of
the American enterprise system to compete in a free market, and it is conceivable
that the Americans will rise to the challenge as the Europeans have done. It is
certainly too early to write the new legislation off as already doomed to failure
in Congress.

On the other hand, the continuance of the United States balance-of-payments
deficit offers some ground for more general anxiety about the capacity of the
United States to sustain leadership in the free world. The maintenance of a fixed
exchange rate requires a country to pursue appropriate domestic policies and
may involve it in a conflict between balance-of-payments equilibrium, on the
one hand, and domestic growth and full employment, on the other. This problem
has been plaguing the United States in recent years, and there has been some
tendency to sacrifice growth and employment (not to speak of the niceties of
liberal trade policy) to the balance of payments. So far the new administration
has not had to face this problem in an acute form – it was lucky enough to come
into office near the bottom of a recession – but as the recovery proceeds the
balance of payments may well deteriorate sharply and the administration be
forced to choose between internal and external stability. If so, it is greatly to be
hoped that it will choose to alter or abandon the present fixed rate of the dollar
on gold rather than retreat into economic isolationism or deflationary policies.

STAGNATION IN THE CANADIAN ECONOMY, 1958–61

I have already referred briefly to the growth boom that Canada and the United
States enjoyed in the dozen years after the war – a boom based on increasingly

close integration of the two economies through the process of investment of American capital in the production of Canadian resource products for export to the American market – and to the decline in the rate of growth and increase in average unemployment in the subsequent four years. The more rapid growth of the Canadian than the American economy in the boom supported the development of an ebullient national confidence and revived the sentiment that "the twentieth century belongs to Canada." At the same time, the increasing interdependence between Canada and the United States, especially the high proportions of American goods in Canadian imports and of American capital in Canadian enterprises, prompted growing fears of "American domination" of Canada, which expressed themselves in advocacy both of increased protections – a policy especially favoured by the representatives of Canadian subsidiaries of American firms – and of resort to Canada's traditional offset to the economic pull of the United States: a strengthening of Canada's traditional relations with Britain. The virtual stagnation of the Canadian economy in the past four years has, so far as one can judge, sadly damaged Canadian confidence in the future. Slow growth and unemployment have strengthened anti-American sentiment and provided new arguments for protection, to which the government has been giving legislative effect. European and Japanese competition in the Canadian market has increased the difficulties of Canadian manufacturers and added a new and poignant note to their pleas for increased protection. The formation of the Common Market has faced Canada with a threat to her exports to Europe, and, unkindest cut of all, Britain's decision to apply for membership in the Common Market has kicked the props out from under the vague – and completely unimplemented – promise of the present government to reduce Canada's economic dependence on the United States by diverting her trade toward the United Kingdom. Finally, President Kennedy's appeal to Congress for the new legislation required for a new American initiative toward freer trade has challenged Canada to declare her attitude on the future direction the system of international trade should take – a challenge to which the Canadian response has been characteristically conservative.

The changes in the world economy that I described earlier have in fact manifested themselves in two major problems: One has been the prolonged stagnation of the Canadian economy; the other, the direction Canadian trade policy should take in the face of increasing foreign competition and the emergence of the Common Market. Of these, the second has aroused the more public discussion. But the first is by far the more important, economically speaking; it is also a problem whose solution is fully within the competence of the Canadian government, unrestricted by dependence on the reactions of other countries' policies. I need scarcely point out that in its dealings with neither of these problems can the Canadian government boast a record of noticeably positive accomplishment.

When I speak of the virtual stagnation of the Canadian economy in the past four years, I am of course using a rather emotive term to describe some complex phenomena, and in saying that the remedy for stagnation is within the competence of the government, I do not wish to imply that all of these phenomena are equally tractable to government policy or that there are no limits to what the government can do. Nor do I mean to imply that these phenomena appeared suddenly on 1 January 1958 without having made their presence known beforehand. Economic history does not work that way. Nevertheless, there is a sharp enough difference between the economic condition of Canada in the past four years and in the preceding period to justify the descriptive term I have used, and the most important element of difference – unemployment – is well within the powers of government to handle.

I have already identified stagnation with slow growth and high average unemployment. As to unemployment, there can be no doubt of the difference between the past four years and the previous period, as the following statistics indicate: Unemployment in Canada averaged 3 per cent in the four years 1950–53 and 4.5 per cent in the four years 1954–57, an average of 3.6 per cent over the first eight years of the 1950s; in the four years 1958–61, unemployment has averaged 6.8 per cent, and in the past two years it has been over 7 per cent. As to growth, the statistics show a much less sharp change in the past four years as compared with previous experience, indicating instead a major change early in the 1950s: Real gross national product per head of population grew at the compound rate of 3.28 per cent from the fourth quarter of 1948 to the second quarter of 1953, at the much lower rate of 0.72 per cent from the second quarter of 1953 to the second quarter of 1957, and has actually declined since. Gross national product per head is a poor indicator of growth, however, since it absorbs the effects of changes in population structure, labour force participation rates, and unemployment. A better though still imperfect measure is gross national product per head of employed population: This grew at 4.02 per cent compounded and at 1.30 per cent compounded in the first two periods I mentioned and at the still lower rate of 0.93 per cent compounded between the second quarter of 1957 and the first quarter of 1960, the last period for which I have official statistics.

Both heavy unemployment and slow growth of productivity can be regarded as evidence of stagnation, but they represent stagnation of different types since they differ in their causation and amenability to governmental policy and in the appropriate remedy they call for. Let me consider them in turn.

THE UNEMPLOYMENT PROBLEM

Heavy unemployment, as Keynes taught (and some economists seem to have forgotten), is the consequence of inadequate demand for labour and can be remedied by governmental policies designed to expand effective demand. In an open economy – one engaging in international trade – expansion of effective demand affects the current account of the balance of payments adversely by increasing the demand for imports and possibly by reducing the supply of exports. In addition, and particularly if demand is expanded by reducing interest rates, the capital account of the balance of payments will be affected adversely by a tendency for people to borrow in the country and invest their savings elsewhere. In a country on a fixed exchange rate, the worsening of the balance of payments may result in a loss of reserves serious enough to threaten the stability of the exchange rate, and this consideration may force the government to stop expanding effective demand before unemployment is reduced to a satis-factorily low level – the problem that has plagued the United States in recent years. If, however, a country has a floating exchange, as Canada has had since 1950, the worsening of the balance of payments is automatically corrected by a depreciation of the exchange rate, and there is no external limit on the pursuit of a policy of maintaining high employment; the only limits are internal limits arising from the fact that a lower percentage of unemployment is likely to be accompanied by a faster rate of price increase and set by the relative weights the government policy makers place on the disadvantages of higher unemploy-ment as compared with a more rapid rate of price increase.

Now suppose a country with a floating exchange rate that has enjoyed a high level of employment accompanied by a noticeably rising trend of prices, and suppose that a variety of developments – a reduction in the rate of growth of demand for exports, increased competition from imports, a slackening of demand in the home market – reduces the level of demand for the country's output at the prevailing exchange rate and level of interest rates. The appropriate policy will obviously be an expansion of demand, and if sustained growth is one of the government's objectives, the most appropriate way to expand demand will be by increasing the quantity of money and reducing interest rates. But suppose that the central bank instead chooses to follow a tight money policy either because, being a central bank, it regards the preservation of the value of money as a moral issue or because it is influenced by the fact that the other central banks in the world, which unlike itself are on fixed exchange rates and are trying to operate a fixed exchange rate system with inadequate reserves, so that they have to be concerned with the influence of their domestic price levels on their international competitive position, have begun to lecture each other on the perils of inflation and the necessity of stopping it.

The result will be heavy unemployment in the country concerned, unemploy-ment created either directly by the effect of tight money on the willingness of industry to invest or indirectly by the effect of tight money on the exchange rate and the international competitive position of industry. The high exchange rate will lead industry to blame its difficulties on foreign competition and demand more protection; the more progressive business people will blame their troubles on low productivity, discover that to increase productivity costs more than it yields or requires concentration and rationalization of the country's industrial structure, and demand subsidies for new investment and research or relief from the restrictions the combines laws place on their freedom to divide up the market more profitably among them. The effect of high interest rates in inducing domestic enterprises and local governments to borrow abroad, and in making domestic assets cheap for foreigners to acquire, will make it plausible to blame the high exchange rate and the resulting unemployment on foreign investment in the country. The reduction in government revenue resulting from lower incomes will unbalance the budget – which will prevent income and employment from sagging as badly as they otherwise would – and the government's need to borrow on a large scale to meet its deficits will make it plausible to blame the finance minister and not the central bank for high interest rates. Since a decline in demand is never spread evenly over the different industries, and since recent investment will have been undertaken in the expectation that the economy would continue to grow at its accustomed rate, it will be plausible to argue that unemployment is due to structural maladjustments of the economy and the errors of past investment decisions. Since skilled and educated employees are both more worth retention on a standby basis to their employers and more adaptable to alternative occupations, unemployment will be concentrated on the unskilled and the illiterate, and it will be plausible to argue that unemployment is due to insufficient education of the population. Since firms are likely to hold on to labour made redundant by labour-saving improvements when the labour market is tight and to discharge it when the labour market is easy, it will be plausible to attribute unemployment to labour-saving inventions and automation. It will also appear plausible to argue, quite fallaciously, that because firms are employing excess labour for the reasons just given, an expansion of demand will not increase employment, when the correct inference is, of course, that demand needs to be expanded more than would appear necessary at first sight. Thus all sorts of explanations of unemployment will be advanced other than the fundamental one, the inappropriate monetary policy of the central bank, and memories being short and unemployment easy for the employed to get used to and rationalize, the central bank will even be congratulated for its firmness in resisting inflation. And it will become a matter of boastful pride whenever unemployment falls to a level considerably higher than used to prevail.

This theoretical analysis seems to me to fit fairly closely to what has been going on in the Canadian economy in recent years, at least until the change in fiscal policy and replacement of the governor of the Bank of Canada in mid-1961. Regardless of the details of the explanation, it is certain that the shift from a 4.25 per cent to a 6.8 per cent level of unemployment has cost Canada a great deal in foregone production and real income, not to speak of the social costs and misery of unemployment, which have fallen particularly hard on the young and the immigrant. Just how great the cost has been is a difficult matter to estimate, but it is considerably greater than the unemployment figures alone would indicate. This is because an increase in unemployment is accompanied by a reduction in the hours worked by those remaining employed and a decrease in their productivity and by a reduction in the numbers in the labour force. In the United States, the Council of Economic Advisers has calculated that a one-point reduction in the percentage of unemployment toward 4 per cent is accompanied by a 3 per cent increase in gross national product.[1] If this calculation were anywhere near applicable to Canada, it would indicate that the difference between the 7 per cent average unemployment of 1960 and 1961 and the 4.25 per cent average of 1954–57 corresponded to a loss of gross national product of between two and a half and three billion dollars in each of the last two years. It is that sort of order of magnitude, in comparison with other estimates of the cost to Canada of the new trading arrangements in Europe (to which I shall refer later), that underlies my judgment that the problem of stagnation is far more serious for Canada than the problem of trade policy.

As I pointed out at the start of my theoretical argument, there is no external restraint on the pursuit of a full employment policy in a country with a floating rate of exchange. The only restraint in principle is the economic cost of the inflationary trend of prices generally associated with levels of unemployment. A great deal has been written and said about the costs and dangers of inflation in North America in the past five years, but most of it has had no basis in fact whatsoever. Nor has any serious attempt been made to calculate the magnitude of the alleged economic cost of the kind of inflation in question and to compare it with the cost of unemployment. To begin with, there is good reason to question how much genuine inflation there has been: Consumer price indexes are well known to contain a significant upward bias, owing to the fact that new goods are not included until most of the reduction in their cost made possible by mass production has already occurred and that insufficient account is taken of improvements in the quality of goods, especially durable goods. A group of economists who studied the rise in the American consumer price index between 1953 and 1960 – which rise was roughly the same as the rise in the Canadian price index

---

1 *Economic Report of the President,* transmitted to Congess, January 1962, together with the *Annual Report of the Council of Economic Advisers* (Washington: US Government Printing Office, 1962), 49–53, especially page 50.

– concluded that the rise could be accounted for entirely by quality improvements and that the true index had not risen and might have fallen in the period.[2] Second, there is reason to doubt that the price index, especially in an open economy, is very sensitive to changes in unemployment; the Canadian consumer price index, for example, rose at the rate of 1.6 per cent per annum from 1953 to 1958 and at the rate of 1.1 per cent per annum from 1958 to 1961 – a reduction of 0.5 of a percentage point in the rate of increase associated with (not even necessarily caused by) the substantial change in average unemployment I have already described. Third, and most important, the evidence does not support the usual myths about inflation: that wages lag behind prices, that inflation causes massive redistributions of income, that inflation distorts and hinders the functioning of a competitive economy, that inflation reduces savings and economic growth, that inflation inevitably accelerates into hyperinflation, that inflation – even hyperinflation – inevitably leads to monetary collapse. The fundamental reason why all these allegations about inflation turn out to be myths is that income earners and investors quickly get used to continuing inflation, and their recognition of it is expressed in a compensating increase in money rates of interest; consequently, the main effect of inflation is the minor inefficiency resulting from the fact that higher rates of interest induce people to economize on the use of money at a cost in real resources. I should perhaps emphasize that I am speaking here of continuing inflation in a peace-time, free-enterprise economy, not of inflation suddenly imposed on an economy by the needs of wartime finance and accompanied by price and income controls – a much more demonstrably evil type of inflation, which the central banks of North America did nothing to prevent when it happened.

I have so far been arguing that the unemployment that has characterized the Canadian economy for the past four years has been a direct consequence of Canadian government policy (or lack of policy) and specifically of the policy of the central bank, and I have argued that the only reasonable justification for this policy – the necessity of stopping inflation – has been an extremely weak one when evaluated by its extremely tenuous economic benefits and serious economic consequences. I do not wish to imply that none of the factors to which others have pointed in explanation have played any part – obviously adjustment to the slowing down of growth in the United States and the emergence of Europe as an international competitor would have imposed strains on the Canadian industrial

---

2 The research on which the conclusion is based may be found in *Government Price Statistics,* Hearings before the Subcommittee on Economic Statistics of the Joint Economic Committee, Congress of the United States, 87th Cong., 1st sess., Part 1, 24 January 1961. The inclusion referred to was given to me as the consensus of the economists by Professor George J. Stigler, Chairman of the Research Committee.

structure under even the most favourable economic conditions – but I would argue strongly that these strains would have been far more easily absorbed by the normal processes of competitive adjustment in a mature industrial economy had activity and employment been maintained at high levels.

Before I leave this subject, let me make two brief observations on some more general aspects of the difficulties Canada has had with its central bank in the past four years. The first is that these difficulties amply demonstrate that, to ensure the efficient conduct of monetary policy, it is not enough to select intelligent, responsible, and well-trained people and put them in charge of the central bank's policy operations armed only with general instructions to aim at some vaguely described desirable general objectives. Without concrete specification of the objectives to be aimed at and a clear understanding of the procedures to be followed in achieving them, it is only too easy for the central bank to cover up its mistakes or disguise the fact that it is pursuing other objectives than those intended and only too difficult for outside observers to detect these mistakes or covert changes in objective. This problem has appeared at various times since the war in each of the three countries I know well; in the United States it has led a number of economists to propose a reform that I think deserves serious consideration: that the central bank should be bound to follow some simple rule of monetary management – for example, to increase the money supply at a constant rate corresponding to the long-run rate of growth of the need for money at a stable price level, this rule to be based on economic research into the relation of money to the functioning of the economy. Such a rule would not necessarily be absolutely binding or unchangeable, but it would provide a standard of reference by which to judge the performance of the central bank superior to the present practice of judging central banks largely by the persuasiveness of their own descriptions of what they are doing.

My second observation is that the recent fracas over monetary policy in Canada suggests that some of the traditions that Canada has taken over from Britain may be inappropriate to the efficient conduct of policy. One of these clearly is the tradition of central bank independence, transferred to Canada in the 1930s when it was thought that the achievement of dominion status required a country to establish its own imitation of the Bank of England; in my judgment, the traditional independence of the Bank of England has been a behind-the-scenes source of trouble for the economic policy of the United Kingdom itself. Another possibly inappropriate tradition is the tradition of the career civil service, at least as it affects the top echelons. A civil service, particularly when one party is in power for a long time, develops its own views of what policy should be, and this makes it difficult for a new government to take over with the assurance that the new policies it wants will be put into operation. Observation of the ferment of ideas now going on in Washington suggests that the freedom allowed by the flexibility of the American system to bring fresh minds to bear directly on policy problems has much to recommend it, as compared with the dependence on royal commissions that the Canadian system of government entails.

THE PROBLEM OF GROWTH

Let me now turn to the second aspect of stagnation, the slow growth of productivity. On this subject economic theory has much less to say because the central problem involves the determinants of the rates at which economic variables change, and economic theory has until very recently been mostly concerned with the determinants of the direction of change of economic variables rather than with the speed of change.

I have already mentioned one way by which the rate of growth of productivity could be increased: by raising the level of demand and reducing unemployment. This method hinges on the fact that when economic conditions are depressed, improvements in methods of production occur that are not fully reflected in increases in measured productivity because firms are operating below capacity but that will be exploited as the economy moves to a higher level of activity. The presence of such latent increases in productivity reflects the more fundamental principle that unless demand is increased sufficiently to absorb the additional output that technical progress and capital investment make possible, the fruits of such improvements in productive potential will appear in the form of productivity increases only to the extent that they also appear in the form of increased unemployment. Thus policies designed to increase productivity must be complemented by policies designed to increase effective demand correspondingly if they are to be effective in increasing output – a point frequently overlooked by those who stress increased productivity as the solution to depression and unemployment.

The increase in productivity that accompanies increased economic activity, however, can provide only a transient increase in the rates of growth of productivity – though it is not, of course, to be despised on that account. The more difficult problem for policy is how to increase the normal rate of increase of productivity – say, the rate of increase of productivity the economy would enjoy at a given percentage of unemployment constant over time. The difficulties of this problem are inherent in three subtleties that are generally overlooked by those with easy answers: first, mathematically a rate of increase has both a numerator and a denominator; second, by assumption the available resources of the economy at any one time are given; third, policy cannot operate directly on productivity itself but must operate on the factors that determine productivity.

One might suppose, for example, that full employment, as contrasted with high average unemployment, would stimulate the rate of productivity increase by providing a combination of buoyant demand and a tight labour market. But while such conditions will tend to increase the absolute amount of productivity-increasing investment and research, they will not necessarily have enough effect to make the larger income of a full-employment economy grow faster than the smaller income of a less fully employed economy. In fact, comparative evidence shows no close association between a country's rate of economic growth and its unemployment percentage. Similarly, a more sophisticated theoretical analysis might lead one to suppose that a country's rate of growth will be higher the higher the proportion of its income it saves and invests. This is in fact a basic proposition in the modern theory of economic growth, and it must be true provided that investment is as productive in high-saving as in low-saving countries. But there is nothing to prevent a high rate of saving from being offset by a low productivity-increasing effect of investment; and, in fact, historical and comparative evidence shows no close relation between saving ratios and growth rates. The same qualification applies to the proposition that a country's rate of growth will be higher the more, proportionally, it spends on research; and while I have no figures on the matter, I strongly suspect that this proposition would be as hard to verify as the corresponding proposition about investment. I must add, however, for purposes of later argument, that these remarks do not in any way deny the possibility, indeed probability, that by raising its proportionate expenditure on investment or research, a country can increase its growth rate temporarily. The question is rather how long it would be before the stimulus to growth from a higher savings ratio was offset by the need to resort to low productivity-increasing investment or research to dispose of the extra expenditure.

In spite of the theoretical difficulties I have outlined, the growth-accelerating potential of new investment and scientific research has so captured the imagination of influential opinion, including that of some economists, in Canada and elsewhere that it has been widely recommended that government should subsidize investment and research expenditure by tax concessions, and these recommendations have been or may be given legislative effect. Attractive as this device may seem at first sight, economic theory suggests that such subsidies are likely to reduce growth rather than increase it: There is no convincing reason for believing that the forms of expenditure chosen for such favour yield a return to the economy as a whole significantly in excess of the private return that the firms undertaking the expenditure would normally consider – the only theoretical justification for a subsidy on specific forms of investment expenditure – and the resulting insertion of consideration of possible tax advantages into the firm's calculations of the profitability of such expenditures is likely to distort the allocation of investment funds and reduce the average return on investment to the economy as a whole. It may be objected that these subsidies will increase total investment. But, barring the possibility of a high interest-elasticity of supply of saving, this could only occur either if there are unemployed resources that can become employed in the additional investment (a possibility I have ruled out by assuming a given percentage of unemployment) or if the government makes more resources available by increasing taxes or reducing expenditure; and in either case it is likely that the additional resources would be much more efficiently allocated among alternative productivity-increasing forms of expenditure by a general reduction in interest rates than by a system of tax concessions on specific items of productivity-increasing expenditure.

To put the same argument in a more positive form: If it is desired to increase the rate of growth of an economy operating at a normal level of unemployment, the first requirement is to increase the rate of saving by budgetary means. If that is done, there is a strong case for leaving the allocation of savings among alternative investment and research opportunities to the normal competitive processes of the market, rather than trying to direct this allocation by the crude and unreliable device of tax concessions. In choosing, say, research expenditure for special tax favour, the government has no way of knowing whether research expenditure increases productivity more than would, say, the availability of cheaper credit to unincorporated businesses; and it is quite possible that the tax favours will encourage research that has no effect in increasing productivity or even reduces it.

Whether an increase in savings squeezed out of the economy by fiscal means and passed back into it by lowering interest rates would produce a substantial and sustained increase in the growth rate is another question; there may be some significance in the fact that the period of most rapid North American economic growth – immediately after the war – was characterized by budget surpluses and low interest rates, while the subsequent period of slower growth has been characterized by budget deficits and higher interest rates.

In presenting the foregoing arguments, I have assumed the desirability of a more rapid rate of growth and have concerned myself with the question of how economic policy might set about achieving it. It has become customary in modern discussions of economic policy to attach considerable importance to the rate of economic growth and to identify virtuous and successful economic management with the achievement of a high rate of economic growth. Much of this emphasis on growth, however, is a by-product of the Cold War and the rivalry of the United States with Russia for the political support of the underdeveloped countries – and, in Canada, of rivalry with the United States. It can be argued that on strictly economic grounds there is little reason for a government in a mature industrial society based on free-enterprise principles to make economic growth for its own sake an object of policy and that – provided full employment is maintained – the rate of growth should be left to be determined by private decisions about saving and investment. This argument, however, ignores completely the large role that government plays in a modern economy and the fact that the presence of government as a taxer and spender and as a major debtor tends by itself to reduce the rate of economic growth below the socially optimal rate. The size of the government's budgetary operations inevitably makes it an influence on the rate of growth through the influence of the government's surplus or deficit on the supply of saving available for private investment. Further, the presence of a large public debt, by providing the public with a supply of assets to which there corresponds no equivalent stock of real capital, tends to reduce the desire to save. What is probably much more important, the financing of governmental activities by taxation of income makes the marginal private return to investment significantly lower than the marginal social return, thereby making the rate of saving and investment lower than it would be if savers received the full social return on their investment. There is, therefore, a prima facie case, on strictly economic grounds, for the government to stimulate economic growth by increasing the rate of saving in the economy by budgeting for a surplus and ensuring that the saving is translated into investment by pursuing an appropriately easy monetary policy.

THE PROBLEM OF FOREIGN TRADE POLICY

I have dwelt rather extensively on the domestic problem of economic stagnation because I consider it by far the more important of the two problems in which the changing nature of the world economy has manifested itself in Canada and also much more within the control of the Canadian government's economic policy. Let me now turn to the other problem, the problem of the direction Canadian trade policy should take in the face of the growth of international competition in manufacturing and the emergence of the Common Market. Public discussion of this problem in Canada has been mostly concerned with the implications of the emergence of the Common Market as the largest protected trading area in the world and has focused on the dilemma the Common Market poses – especially if Britain joins – for the two traditional bases of Canadian commercial policy: reliance on trade with Europe to offset the economic pull of the United States and reliance on protection of secondary manufacturing to promote Canadian industrial growth in rivalry with the United States. The dilemma is that the Common Market, especially if it includes Britain, threatens to restrict Canada's exports to Europe, while any effort to prevent or offset the threatened restriction of European imports from Canada by new trade arrangements will require a lowering or elimination of Canada's protective tariffs. Faced with this dilemma, the Canadian government has devoted its efforts to a vain – in both senses of the word – and undignified effort to deter the British from seeking or gaining membership in the Common Market, while denying the feasibility or desirability of any of the alternative trading arrangements that its critics have with more or less enthusiasm been recommending. The adoption of this posture inevitably calls to mind a cartoon by David Low that appeared sometime during the war. The cartoon depicts Colonel Blimp in the steam room of his club proclaiming with great emphasis, "By gad, sir, what we have we'll hold – if we can get it back!" The new developments in international relations obviously call for a more positive policy than this, and Canadians have not been backward in putting forward suggestions for new departures in Canadian commercial policy.

Before I discuss alternative possible policies, I must point out that the adverse effects on Canada's economic welfare and growth of the formation of the Common Market and Britain's impending adhesion to it have been greatly exaggerated in recent Canadian discussion and policy and that the problem is of far less economic significance than the domestic problem of stagnation. Popular discussion tends universally to exaggerate the influence of other countries' commercial policies on a country's economic welfare mainly because in assessing the effects of tariff changes, people – even trained economists who ought to know better – fall back on the weak analytical instrument of political imagination rather than the scientific tools of economic analysis. Thus it is commonly assumed that loss of a preference or an increase in the duty levied in a foreign market will wipe out all trade and leave the resources that produce the goods concerned entirely unemployed. This assumption may be valid for considering the immediate effect of a sudden and unexpected loss of preference or tariff increase on an inflexible economy that does not pursue a full employment policy and maintains a rigid exchange rate; but it is certainly invalid for considering the effect of a change in tariffs that is phased in over a period of years and well publicized in advance in an economy that is reasonably flexible and could be sensibly managed. In such an economy – and the Canadian economy is reasonably flexible and could be sensibly managed – one would expect the resources employed in producing the affected exports to shift to producing for other markets or, if they could not so shift, to accept the relative lowering of their real incomes necessary to enable them to continue to dispose of their products in their accustomed markets.

Also, one would expect that, once the adjustments to the higher trade barriers had been made, the affected country's exports to the tariff-raising country would tend to grow along with any expansion in that country's total income – contrary

to the popular notion that a tariff barrier around a market cuts the outside world
off from participation in the growth of that market. Thus the loss inflicted by
the raising of tariffs against a country's exports would be a once-over loss, whose
annual magnitude would be determined by the flexibility of the economy affected,
the extent to which tariffs were raised against it, and the amount of trade subject
to those tariffs. "The flexibility of the economy" is a portmanteau term for the
degree to which the economy can escape the necessity of accepting lower
incomes by shifting its resources to alternative uses and is extremely difficult if
not impossible to quantify. But the other two determinants of the annual loss are
quantifiable and permit one to estimate, at least roughly, the magnitude of the
maximum annual loss that a country may suffer from an increase in the tariffs
it faces. That maximum loss is the decrease in the average price of its exports
that would be necessary to offset the increase in the average tariff rate facing
them multiplied by the quantity of exports in question.

This method of estimation has been applied by Dr Grant Reuber to estimate
the maximum cost to Canada of the increases in tariffs on exports of Canadian
industrial materials to Europe – over half of Canada's total exports to Europe –
that would follow the establishment of a Common Market including Britain and
the Six on the extreme assumption that the price reductions required to offset
increased tariffs would have to be granted to all Canada's other customers.[3]
Dr Reuber arrives at a figure of $157 million (0.45 per cent of gross national
product) as the maximum cost estimate for 1959 trade; of this $157 million, $64
million represents the extra cost imposed by British membership in the Common
Market. No estimate has been made (or could yet be made) of the cost to Canada
of the Common Market's common agricultural protective policy and of Britain's
participation in it, but detailed studies of the competitive position of Canadian
agriculture in Europe and consideration of the likely development of European
agricultural policy do not suggest that the loss will be great. Dr S.F. Kaliski has
attempted a comprehensive estimate of the annual cost to Canada of the loss of
preferences in the British market and arrived at an outside limit of $55 million.[4]
Both Reuber's and Kaliski's estimates are rough and incomplete, but at least they
give some idea of the orders of magnitude of the loss to Canada involved in
the establishment of the Common Market and British membership in it. The
estimated maximum costs are not insubstantial, especially for the individual

3 G.L. Reuber, "Western Europe's Demand for Canadian Industrial Materials," *Canadian Journal of Economics and Political Science* 28, no. 1 (February 1962): 16–34, especially Table 5 at page 32.
4 S.F. Kaliski, "Canada, the United Kingdom and the Common Market," *International Journal* 17, no. 1 (winter, 1961–62): 17–24, especially page 21.

industries on which the tariff changes concerned would bear most heavily, but when placed alongside the estimated loss from unemployment of $2.5 to 3 billion that I mentioned earlier or Professor J.H. Young's well-known estimate of $1 billion as the cost of protection to the Canadian consumer,[5] they suggest very clearly that the alarm that has been generated by the Common Market, and especially by Britain's desire to join it, has not been justified by a corresponding importance of these new developments in Europe's trading relationships to the Canadian standard of living. I would emphasize that these estimates are maximum estimates, and that the real loss is likely to be much less than the figures I have given, and that the estimates take no account of the indirect benefits to Canada that would result if, as the British believe, membership in the Common Market assisted Britain to solve its chronic balance-of-payments problem and accelerate its rate of economic growth.

CHOICES IN CANADA'S COMMERCIAL POLICY

The analysis I have just presented is intended to place the adverse effects of the Common Market on Canadian trade in their proper economic perspective. I now turn to consider the chief proposals that have been made for change in Canada's commercial policy in the face of the new developments in international trading relationships. Given the character of the Common Market as a novel and exciting scheme for achieving reciprocal free trade in a large market on a regional basis, and the traditional concentration of Canadian trading interests on the two areas of Europe and the United States, it is natural that these proposals have taken the form of advocacy of a similar regional grouping in which Canada would be included. But most such proposals have shown little understanding either of the political motivation of the European Economic Community or of what is involved in the formation of a customs union or common market. I shall ignore the more far-fetched of these proposals and, in discussing the major ones, will draw summarily on various arguments and considerations that are implicit in my earlier account of the postwar evolution of the world economy.

The emergence of the Common Market as a rival trading bloc to the United States and the spectacle of Europe's rapid economic growth have prompted the proposal that Canada should join the European Economic Community or seek associate membership in it, a proposal that has the appeal of conformity with the traditional Canadian policy of relying on trade with Europe to offset the economic pull of the United States. This proposal, however, ignores both the

---

5 J.H. Young, *Canadian Commercial Policy* (Ottawa: Royal Commission on Canada's Economic Prospects, 1958), chapter 6 at 73.

ultimate political objective of political union of Europe that underlies the
Common Market, an objective that allows no place for Canada as a non-European
country, and the prerequisites for successful economic union specified in the
philosophy of the Common Market, prerequisites that past Canadian economic
relations with Europe do not fulfil. It is simply not open to Canada to join the
Common Market. Nor is it at all likely that Canada could obtain association with
the Common Market. While the article of the Rome Treaty pertaining to association of other countries with the Common Market technically would permit
some sort of Canadian association, it is clear that the article was included for
the benefit of other European countries and of colonies achieving nationhood,
not of countries like Canada. Quite apart from the fact that Canada does not
belong with Europe and would be unlikely to be welcome in it, it is extremely
doubtful that a mutually satisfactory form of association could be worked out
that would pass the GATT rules against discriminatory trading arrangements,
especially as the United States' willingness to support the Common Market in
the interests of strengthening Europe economically and politically would be
unlikely to extend to tolerance of such an arrangement. Finally, it is prima facie
likely that Canada would lose rather than gain economically from a trade
relationship with Europe that discriminated sharply against the United States.
The reason is that the elimination of Canadian tariffs on imports of manufactures
from Europe, while it would lead to replacement of high-cost Canadian manufactures by lower-cost European manufactures, would also divert Canadian
imports from lower-cost United States sources to higher-cost European sources,
and since the United States provides such a large share of Canadian imports, the
potential loss from trade diversion could easily be substantial.

Appreciation of the potential economic cost to Canada of an economic union
with Europe and unwillingness to sacrifice Canada's political and economic ties
with the United States have prompted the alternative suggestion of an Atlantic
Economic Community embracing Europe, the United States, and Canada. This
scheme has the appeal of protecting both of Canada's major trading interests
simultaneously, but it has two major drawbacks. One is that it is unlikely to attract
the Europeans, to whom the erection of a common tariff barrier is an economic
prerequisite of European unification; the other is that it would conflict with important United States commitments to and political interests in Latin America, Asia,
and Africa. The North Atlantic Economic Community would be a rich person's
club and a white person's club, and even if it devoted a larger proportion of its
riches to carrying the "white man's burden," its existence would be highly unpopular in the rest of the non-Communist world, especially if its major motivation
appeared to be to support an aggressively anti-Communist military alliance.
Attempts have been made to give it a broader cultural and political justification

by appealing to the notion of a "North Atlantic Community" of nations with common institutions, history, and ideals, but this notion has all the earmarks of a dangerous political fiction – dangerous because it usually comes into play as part of an endeavour to secure for the country in which it is advanced a position of political importance enjoyed in an earlier period but no longer consistent with economic and political facts. Thus in the United States the notion of the "Atlantic Community" is advanced in the hope of persuading the Europeans to assume without qualification the objectives of United States foreign policy; in Canada it is advanced in the hope of restoring Canada's war and postwar roles as mediator between the United States and the United Kingdom and spokesperson for the new nations; in England it is advanced in the hope of restoring the United Kingdom's "special relationship" among European countries with the United States – all of which ambitions have been rendered anachronistic by the shift in the balance of economic power toward Continental Europe, an area where the notion of Atlantic Community seems to generate little enthusiasm except among militant anti-Communists.

A third alternative is the proposal for a customs union, a free-trade area, or "selective" free trade between Canada and the United States, a proposal prompted by recognition of the extent to which the North American economics have become economically integrated in the postwar period and by the desire to increase the efficiency of the Canadian economy by exposing Canadian producers to the free play of competition and securing for them the ready access to a large market required for the exploitation of economics of mass production and modern technology. This proposal, in contrast with the others, contains all the ingredients usually thought necessary for successful economic integration – territorial contiguity; similarity of social, economic, and cultural characteristics; and a long history of close economic collaboration – as well as the potentiality of a substantial net gain in economic efficiency according to economic theory of customs unions. The main objection to this proposal is, as it always has been, political rather than economic, derived from the fear of political absorption of Canada by the United States. That fear seems to me completely irrational, an anachronism inherited from a historical era that has long since passed in the nineteenth century; when economic development in North America was based on the settlement and exploitation of new farming regions and when the United States was bent on territorial expansion, there was good reason for that fear. In the twentieth century, economic development is no longer based on land settlement – like most other advanced nations, Canada and the United States suffer from an embarrassing surplus of farmers – and the United States has long since ceased to seek expansion by the acquisition of new territory. In fact, a Canadian demand to join the United States would be acutely embarrassing to the United

States, as political union with Canada would wreck the delicate political balance
that the United States has worked out between the North and South and between
the industrial and farming groups.

But the occasion for a deliberate policy of seeking economic integration with
the United States is not available now and may never occur. Such an endeavour
would represent the acceptance by Canada and the United States of the trend
toward regionalization of world trade, and the American administration is instead
seeking to contain that trend in a new movement toward nondiscriminatory
multilateral free trade. I would strongly suggest that Canada's economic interests
lie in the same direction and that Canada should support to the full the new
American initiative by declaring her willingness to reduce or eliminate tariffs,
reserving the possibility of North American regional integration for subsequent
exploration in the event that the United States initiative should fail to win
acceptance by the United States Congress or – the other hurdle that has to be
crossed – by the European Economic Community.

My reasons for this recommendation follow from my earlier analysis of the
spread of industrialization around the world and the requirements of sustained
domestic economic progress in a changing world economy – flexibility in changing from activities in which comparative advantage is disappearing to activities
in which new comparative advantage is appearing. The more liberal the trading
policies pursued by other nations, the greater the opportunity for Canada to
exploit its comparative advantages by developing to the full the advantages of large-
scale production and technological leadership in specialized branches of economic activity. Much more important, the lower the level of Canadian tariffs,
the greater the freedom of Canadian producers to determine where Canadian
comparative advantage lies and to exploit it to the fullest possible extent.

Protection is generally advocated as a means of raising the standard of living
and promoting economic growth. In fact, the reverse is the truth, at least in an
advanced economy like Canada's. Protection promotes inefficient allocation of
resources; in place of industrial specialization and the economics of large-scale
production, it fosters fragmentation of the market, inefficiently small production
units, excessive diversification of product, and short production runs. I have
noticed, incidentally, that it has become fashionable to blame these phenomena
of inefficiency – like all the rest of Canada's economic problems – on American
investment in Canada; but the slightest observation of other small economies is
sufficient to demonstrate that resort to protectionism can produce these and other
examples of wasteful inefficiency without any American help whatsoever. By
fostering inefficiency, the tariff reduces the standard of living; the cost of
protection to the Canadian consumer, as I have mentioned, has been estimated
at about one billion dollars per year, a figure that accounts for about one fifth

of the difference between the Canadian standard of living and the American. What is more important in the long run, an established policy of protection promotes resistance to economic change, resistance that takes the form of demanding increased protection to avoid the need for adapting to change. But change – especially change in other countries – cannot be stopped by the tariff; all that increased protection can do is to waste resources in a futile effort to resist the irresistible.

But it is not sufficient, in the modern world, simply to rehearse the classical arguments for free trade. It is necessary to recognize and take account of the functions the tariff performs and to substitute more efficient methods of performing these functions. In the first place, the tariff has been used to encourage investment in particular lines of production, investment that has been undertaken in the expectation of profits guaranteed by the tariff; the substitution of private for governmental decisions about the most profitable lines of investment entailed in removing tariff protection should logically be accompanied by compensation to the industries concerned for the loss of their profit opportunities. Second, and of more lasting importance, it should be recognized that the tariff has become an instrument for cushioning the impact of adverse economic changes on particular industries and regions. As a form of social security for unfortunate businesses and their employees, the tariff has notorious defects; but failing alternative methods of assistance, there will inevitably be demands for tariff support. It is for this reason that the Treaty of Rome provides for a Social Fund and an Investment Bank and that President Kennedy's new tariff legislation provides for adjustment assistance. Adjustment assistance is a positive and constructive solution to the problem of helping industries adversely affected by foreign competition, far more so than tariff increases; I would suggest only that it should not be restricted to assisting adjustment to foreign competition, but should be designed to assist industries afflicted by the effects of rapid economic change whether that change is foreign or domestic. I would also point out that, with the international competition that low tariffs or free trade would encourage, it would no longer be necessary for the combines administration to keep a suspicious eye on cooperative efforts by Canadian industry to adjust to economic change.

I have been recommending the abandonment of Canada's traditional policy of promoting industrialization by tariff protection in favour of a liberal trading policy better designed to foster Canadian growth in a changing world economy. Acceptance of this recommendation requires a fundamental rethinking of accepted ideas on Canada's place in the world economy, a rethinking that the changing shape of the world economy has made long overdue. Canadian economic policy has historically been dominated by the ambition to create a country rival in power to the United States, and so to prove that the Americans were wrong to revolt from colonial rule in 1776. The ambition to outgrow the United States is a futile one; in spite of the boasting about Canada's faster growth in the postwar period, it is a fact that this growth was insufficient to raise the ratio of the Canadian to the American population to what it was in 1860. For the sake of interest, I calculated the date at which Canada's population would equal the population of the United States if both countries' populations continued to grow at the 1949–60 rate. That happy event is due to occur, as near as I can reckon it, at 9:36 P.M. on the 22nd of January 2212 A.D. – 212 years after the end of the twentieth century that Sir Wilfrid Laurier claimed for Canada.

The ambition to surpass the United States is not only hopeless, but pointless. It is quite clear that, if the twentieth century does not belong to Canada, it does not belong to the United States either; it belongs to all the nations of the world according to their capacities to make the best of the resources they have. In this endeavour Canada has a fortunate head start over most nations of comparable size in technology, capital, human skill, and natural resources, and she has every chance of continued prosperity and growth provided she has the courage and wisdom to manage her economic affairs intelligently.

HARRY G. JOHNSON was the Charles F. Grey Distinguished Service Professor of Economics at the University of Chicago. He taught at universities throughout the world, predominantly at the London School of Economics and the University of Chicago, where he remained until his death. As the author of countless books and articles, his contribution to economics is vast and varied. He was the editor of the *Journal of Political Economy* and a member of government commissions in Canada and the United States, including the 1962 Porter Royal Commission on Banking and Finance.

Harry Johnson was an Officer of the Order of Canada, a Fellow of the British Academy, and a member of the Royal Society of Canada and the Econometric Society. He was awarded the Bernhard Harms Prize by the University of Kiel and the Royal Society of Canada's Innis-Gérin Award. He received honorary degrees from seven universities and served on the executives of numerous professional organizations. Dr Johnson died in 1977.

5

The Changing Conditions of Politics

J.A. CORRY, 1963

PART ONE

It is being said nowadays, with some point, that this is a bad time for politicians. It is also a bad time for the students of affairs, sometimes called, without strict accuracy, political scientists. Some years ago, when I still rated myself in this category, I said that my subject, the study of politics, was being whittled away by theology at the one end and by sociology at the other. The remark was a pleasantry, and not an apt figure of speech.

I was not intending to say that others were poaching on our preserves. I really meant that political studies could no longer be confined to the frame many of us had thought adequate, that the field, as we had conceived it, did not bring nearly enough relevant matter under consideration. Further, I meant that we were not working in sufficient depth, either in the realm of theory or in our analysis of political institutions and political behaviour. I was admitting that sociologists and theologians and philosophers were more at home than we in some of the wider areas needing to be considered, and in some sections of the field had better tools for probing in depth.

In these admissions, I should take care not to speak for all political scientists but only for the majority, who staked the field more narrowly and took a restricted view of what was directly relevant for political analysis. There have always been others who did not accept such limitations and pioneered in breadth and depth. (I add that, with a few reservations conceded to a native skepticism, I belonged to the majority). Further, I should like to make clear that, in saying what I shall say in this paper, I am not proposing an assignment in bankruptcy but rather arguing that the old firm needs to be reorganized in the light of new political realities that cannot be ignored.

What I meant some years ago can be said now with greater particularity and emphasis. First, the elements of human nature that were generally thought relevant for politics were too few and too simple to be adequate for basing political ideas and theories in our present situation. The view of human nature to which I refer was an optimistic one derived from the eighteenth century. Human beings were believed to be essentially rational and respectful of the claims of their fellows, acting in "general honest thought and common good to all." They were moved also by self-interest, but the elements were so mixed in them as to ensure a basic nobility and goodness. Endowed with reason and a general disposition to the good, they could be trusted with a general freedom. Given the right conditions in which to exercise their reason and freedom, they could make of their lives and society something nearly as fair as their best dreams. Free them from superstition, and you give them knowledge; free them from outmoded custom, arbitrary government, and odious privilege, and you give them equality of opportunity. In such a setting, no limits should be placed on the possibilities of human progress.

These ideas were perhaps adequate enough for the purposes in hand in the age of individualism and of liberal optimism that first stirred in the sixteenth century and matured in the eighteenth century, when only a small part of life was politicized. They were only partial insights, and they diverted attention from aspects of human beings that now bear on politics in a collectivist society (some would say mass society) where government intervenes deeply in everything and so brings a far more complex human response. The political ideas and theories that were based on these insights and that formed the staple of political debate and shaped the pattern of political events and institutions for so long have lost much of their power to stir us. More than that, events in the world at large have taken an alarming turn in the last generation for which the rationalist theories had not prepared us and for which they provide no satisfying explanation.

This, of course, is where the theologians come in. For the most part, they have always held to a more pessimistic and, in some respects, a more penetrating estimate of human nature. From their vantage point of the necessary imperfections of the finite, they have always put emphasis on sides of human nature that liberal rationalism has discounted too heavily. Holding that human destiny is not entirely amenable to the rational faculties, they have stressed the distractions of self-interest and self-love that can prostitute reason. They have been keenly aware of the depths of human nature, where anxiety and fear generate malice and evil.

The clear-headed among the liberal rationalists have never denied the reality of egoism, malice, and evil. The very existence of superstition, privilege, and tyranny was proof of their pervasiveness and strength. In laying their bets on human goodness, they were really preferring to trust the generality of individuals rather than an oligarchy of entrenched and obscurantist authority. Nevertheless, having placed their money, they stressed the best qualities of their entry in the race and thus passed on to us an incomplete picture of human nature. The theologians have put stress on the other side; their estimates have clear relevance for the understanding of our times.

Since this is not an assignment in bankruptcy, I am not required to attribute failure to original sin or any other cosmic plight. In the perspective of time as distinct from eternity, other factors mould human behaviour, if not the deep essence of human nature, that may have bred the events for which we were unprepared and which our traditional political theories can no longer vitally engage.

This brings me to a second venture in particularizing: that occasioned by confining intensive study and analysis, as we have in the past, to the essentially political phenomena, to the organization and operation of governments, political parties, and so on. (Political scientists have not taken enough account of the immense influence that the social structure as a whole exerts on political behaviour and on the movement of politics.) In the age of individualism, perhaps this was justified. For a long time, political action through governments barely rippled the surface of the deeper reaches of society. Indeed, political laissez faire permitted the scientific and economic revolution of the past two centuries to work a profound revolution in the social structure, creating our collectivist society.

The collectivist society has generated new kinds of human behaviour, if indeed it has not created new kinds of human beings. Only when the social revolution was well advanced did government begin to intervene drastically in society. Government now penetrates and moulds almost every aspect of society, and it is inevitable that social forces should in turn react strongly on governments and politics. Students of politics and practising politicians have to cope with much more than the specifically political institutions, with much more than overt, specifically political behaviour. Politics now has to do with all aspects of the social structure, and that is where the sociologists come in.

Because of lack of competence, I cannot offer here the kind of analysis that the theologian and sociologist would give. I shall try not to "overreach my information" in a presumptuous way. I shall try to bring into relief some of the developments and current perplexities seen in one form or another in the United States and Britain as well as in Canada and fairly described as changing conditions of politics. I think our present perplexity is of the order described in an aphorism of Thurman Arnold: "Unhappy is the nation that has run out of words to explain what is going on." So in the rest of this part of my paper I shall consider the difficulties of understanding our present-day political world with the stock of political ideas and theories hitherto usually relied on for the purpose.

In the second part, I shall look at some aspects of the collectivist society and consider how far these may be producing new dimensions in political behaviour. It would be much better if I could say, with the cautious novelist hiding from the law of libel, that all parties and countries adverted to are entirely fictitious and that any resemblance to existing parties and countries is purely coincidental. Because I cannot do this, I shall proceed with as much detachment from the current scene as I can.

The age of individualism had revealed its main features by the seventeenth century. It matured, according to its nature, to form the liberal democratic age in the nineteenth century. Its constant aim was to tame the state. After the middle of the nineteenth century, it took up the supplementary purpose of making the state the sure instrument of the people. Irresponsible political power was taken to be the prime evil of the mundane world. It yielded little to law while it supported indefensible social privilege and so was the root of all injustice and oppression. The remedy was to replace the reign of monarchs with the reign of law and to make everyone equal under the law. This would secure freedom for all under laws that all must obey.

The main technique for getting this happy result was extension of the franchise and the enlargement of the powers of popularly elected bodies and persons. Universal franchise was demanded in the sanguine hope that thereafter all the laws would be for the good of all. Although there were always some who knew better, it was widely believed that in the regime of freedom under laws made in the name and under the authority of all, social and economic deficiencies and injustices would for the most part melt away.

Early in the twentieth century, formal freedom and formal equality under the law were achieved for all in Western Europe and North America. But formal freedom in itself did little to relieve basic poverty. Large sections of the population were still denied any effective meaningful freedom. The grossness of material inequality showed little sign of retreat. The continuing evils were now charged to laissez faire: the leeway that freedom gives to the unscrupulous and the ruthless as well as to the energetic, the single-minded, and the toughly disciplined. Assaults on laissez faire began early in the twentieth century, with the emphasis in political aim shifting from freedom to equality or, more correctly, to the substantial reduction of inequality through use of the power of the state. Effort moved from political reform to social reform through political action.

Laissez faire, in the sense of a dominant theory determining public policy, was finally routed in the 1930s. But the social reformers who thus triumphed in a succession of battles from 1900 on over those who cherished the past (whether from self-interest, fear, or scruple) split into socialists and liberal reformers, using the latter term (correctly I think) to cover both liberals and conservatives from 1930 on.

The socialists, in fiery revulsion against the indignity of mass unemployment and of poverty in the midst of plenty, were fortified in their long-standing conviction that meaningful freedom and social equality could only be gained by socializing the means of production and distribution. They had a passionate conviction of the essential goodness of man. They were sure that the capacity of man for generosity, compassion, cooperation, and high endeavour was being stifled by capitalism. They were sure that all these qualities would blossom in a socialist society.

Strongly influenced by liberal democracy, in which tradition they stand, they chose constitutional, parliamentary means to bring about the socialist society. They determined to capture the state through persuasion of the electorate and to make the government the official receiver of the entire estate of the bankrupt capitalist system. They confidently hoped to end injustice and inequality by nationalizing industry and adopting comprehensive measures of social security. They engaged to guarantee order, stability, and coherence by overall social and economic planning, which thus became the most majestic function of government. Somehow, this program was going to add economic democracy to political democracy, release all the generous and cooperative instincts, and realize the dream of effective freedom and social equality.

To the right of the socialists were ranged the older parties, whom I have labelled reformers because they acknowledged that capitalism needed some reforming. Despite the tribulations of the free economy, they were confident of its resilience. They counted on it to reach new high levels of productivity, which under proper contrivance would greatly narrow social inequalities. But where contrivance for equality seemed to threaten to submerge individual freedom, they were for freedom as the precious key to all social advance.

The great debate over these issues raged throughout the thirties. It was muted, if not suspended, by war and recovery from war in the forties. Modern war, of course, is a great socializer: The war of 1939–45 laid the foundations for a comprehensive system of social security by bringing into existence a steeply progressive tax structure. It extended the grip of government on economic life, a grip it has never really relinquished. In Britain a socialist government between 1945 and 1951 kept up the socializing momentum of war, nationalizing large sections of industry and completing a great structure of social security. Even in the United States and Canada, without aid of socialist governments, the welfare state came to be accepted. A mixed economy emerged, neither socialist nor capitalist, that was motored, if you like, by private enterprise but levered and controlled, if not directed, by government.

A goodly part of the democratic socialist objectives was reached by the early 1950s, although without nearly enough socialization of industry to satisfy doctrinaire prescriptions. One might have expected a redoubling of socialist energies to round out the program. In fact, however, socialists never recovered their old fire and conviction after the war. Of course, much that they had argued for had been accepted, but they could well have reviled it as being done in the wrong way and for wrong reasons.

Other factors also weakened the socialists. By lending their weight to reform and so lightening social injustice, they weakened their own fighting arm. Much of their popular support rested on discontent and near-despair, and it fell away as material conditions improved sharply. Substantial numbers of workers, seeing the way open to ascent in the social scale, became climbers, aspired to the middle class, and actually acquired something of a bourgeois style of life.

But there is more to it than all this. Many socialists have become uncertain where they really want to go. They are plagued by doubts rising from experience. In the Soviet Union, freedom did not broaden down from precedent to precedent as many had hoped. In fact, in every country where government became fully master and planned people's lives, frightful things were done. Socialists, genuinely concerned for the essential freedom of the human spirit, found themselves pondering more anxiously than before Lord Acton's dictum that all power corrupts.

There came to be more doubt, too, about the positive gains to be set against the dangers in the exercise of massive governmental power. The workers in the nationalized industries of Britain did not feel any freer and were scarcely more grateful to or more cooperative with the new socialist, than with the old capitalist, management. All idealism suffers in its exposure to hard reality. The dream is never realized in all its purity. After six years of socialist government in Britain, so many things remained unbettered if not unchanged. Disenchantment set in and spread to the faithful in Canada and the United States.

The doubts have loosened the grip on doctrine. Revisionism, the disease that has always threatened socialist unity, waters down programs until it appears that socialist parties are becoming middle-class parties just as the working class, under the softening effect of prosperity and the welfare state, is becoming middle class in habit and aspiration. The burning conviction that once fired both leaders and followers does not glow as before.

The ideas and theories that fed the convictions are either accepted and absorbed into the consensus or tried and found wanting or filed away as too dangerous to be put to the touch. Not sure any more how to make a new society, socialist parties incline to think the present society might be nearly all right if they could get a chance to run it and put in a few new features. As someone said recently in Britain, "to try to alter the structure of British society by means of the British Labour Party is to surf-ride on two inches of water at ebb tide." Whatever else may be found to rouse generous socialist passion against, one can be pretty sure it will not be the ideas and theories that served in the recent past.

If socialist parties are "fresh out" of ideas, the parties to the right of them are even worse off. Such of them as have marched under the banner of reform in the last half-century, have reached their objectives, seen their main program put into force. Such of them as have been reluctant or opposed to the dominant political trends of the twentieth century may be still doubtful of where we are going, but they cannot muster enough conviction to offer leadership in retreat from positions they fear to be untenable. The conservative reaction of the last decade, of which we have heard so much, has really been a movement of intellectuals. Its leaders have not been able to sell their doctrine to political parties on the democratic right. I suspect this is because their ideas do not appear to have any clear relevance to the political situation. No one can discern a line of retreat that is politically practicable.

So we seem almost to have reached the point where there is nothing to fight for and nothing to fight against. This is not literally true. In the vast range of affairs within the ambit of governmental action, there are hundreds of issues on which political parties can take up opposing positions: more for housing and less for hospitals, old-age pensions to be raised by $15.00 or $20.00, and so on almost endlessly. But arguments on such points are less than fascinating to the politically conscious members of the electorate and do not nourish solid political conviction. Tension has largely disappeared from politics, and we have gone slack.

In all this, there is nothing about which I should want to reproach the politicians or the political parties. We are not suffering from failure or bankruptcy but, it may well be, from the very magnitude of our success. It is worthwhile to pause and look at the scale of the achievement. In the countries under discussion, destitution has been ended, social inequalities greatly narrowed, and social security cushions provided against the major risks of an uncertain life. We have curbed economic exploitation and given dignity to labour insofar as mass production methods will allow. We have established economic equilibrium (still tenuous perhaps) in a mixed economy. Perhaps we have not abolished capitalism, but we have changed it into something that neither its enemies nor its supporters in the early years of the century would recognize. We have done all this without either the civil war or the revolution that we were told so confidently a generation ago would be inevitable. We have done it without damaging the underlying consensus on which all democratic institutions depend.

Indeed, we leave enlarged the consensus and brought firmly within it most of the things I have been enumerating. Considering the millions of persons involved and the complexity of their affairs, this must be one of the high political achievements of history. Perhaps we are just dizzy from success.

At least it is true that the wide scope and firmness of the consensus has narrowed the front of the political struggle and brought it down, for the time being at least, from the realms of high strategy to the muddy ground of minor tactics, where the fighting arm is not the flashing cavalry of ideas but the grubby sappers of inconsequential salients.

At any rate, we are disenchanted, and we are asking why. Is it that the threat of the nuclear holocaust that hangs over us has paralyzed initiative in our domestic affairs? Is it that the aims of conservatives, liberals, socialists, the lot, have been too much focused on material improvement to be satisfying to the human spirit fallen when immediate material needs are largely met? Does lurking puritanism in us give us an uneasy conscience as we come close to wallowing in abundance? Or is it, as Justice Holmes thought, that life needs to be a roar of bargain and battle, and not to have the roar is a bore? Does life get its savour from uncertainty and peril, which we might just barely overcome if we committed all our powers and faculties to the effort? Do we miss "the gaunt troops mustering in the grisly dawn"? In short, why do we lie in the doldrums, taking no pride in our political achievements?

I do not pretend to have answers to these questions. None of them can be asked seriously without acknowledging the possibility that human beings are something other, or more, than most of the rationalist liberal theories and ideas about politics have assumed them to be. Put more precisely, the question is whether elements of human nature that we thought could be left out of account in political circulation now have to be counted as engaged in the political process. This, by the way, should not be surprising. Politics now cuts deeply into everybody's life and social relationships and can be expected to evoke a fuller and much more varied response. It is even possible, as I shall suggest in part two of this paper, that drastic changes in the social structure are producing a new kind of individual, or at least bringing hitherto latent potentialities of the creature into overt expression.

Leaving all that aside for the moment, some suggestions may be ventured. The long struggle to reduce inequalities in the distribution of this world's goods was materialist enough in immediate aim and for good reasons. Chill poverty froze the genial currents of the soul. When the means to mend the situation came to hand, failure to press them to that purpose would have been a gross form of injustice. But all the while it was dreamed that, if the curse could be lifted, the spacious opportunities thus opened would lift spirits everywhere, and we would soar beyond the confines of the material. We have begun to fear that this may not happen. On the evidence, we seem to be settling down to enjoy ourselves in the lap of comfort. The advertisers give us soothing assurance that this is all we know or need to know. Indeed, we have come to fear that our children learn more about the good life from the advertisers than from their teachers.

It surely does not overstate the case to say that life needs more purpose than can be found in taking our ease among our gadgets. The shiftlessness of much of our enjoyment leads to disquiet and boredom. Everywhere, we reproach ourselves for lack of standards, for the dearth of commitments beyond ourselves. The boredom extends to politics because we are unable to see how we can act politically to remedy this dearth and lack. The enrichment of life, the finding of purposes on which to spend ourselves, are essentially matters of individual commitment and action. They cannot be achieved by collective action. Collective action can create liberating opportunities. This we have been doing. But it cannot command performance to the measure of the opportunity. Because politics does not seem to open way for what we most need, we become frustrated as well as bored with it. I know how risky it is to try to guess the minds of people, but I will hazard that this is a very widespread mood among them.

In Britain, in these days, there is much demand for a sense of national purpose to overcome admittedly widespread apathy. A recent Canadian book, in its title and its first two chapters, calls for a social purpose for Canada and documents our purposelessness. The bulk of the book, however, does not deal with purpose but only with the means of liberating opportunity through government policy. Getting a unified social purpose, collectively hitching ourselves to a star, is not an easy matter nor one to be taken up lightly.

As far as I know, democratic governments have not been able to gear them-selves to a unified social purpose except in times of war. In the aim of winning a war, government finds ready made an overriding purpose that is generally approved. As we know, this purpose or objective is used to submerge for the time being many of the diverse and conflicting purposes of individuals and groups. Government establishes firm priorities among the claims and demands that come up spontaneously from below. It goes further and brushes aside, if it does not crush, the reservations and resistances of minorities.

Of course, there are satisfactions in this sense of unity of aim that frees us from the distraction of cross-purposes. There is exhilaration in marching together when none is for the party and all are for the state. Who has not yearned to find in times of peace a moral equivalent for war? Yet in our reflective moments, we know that such moods of exaltation do not last – indeed are only maintained at heavy psychic cost. When release from the tension of the forced march comes, the zest for undisciplined expression is almost pathological and could only be checked by severe repression.

Except in times of extreme peril generally recognized as such, a free society cannot take things at this pitch. Genuine freedom bears its fruit in diversity of aim and interest. Individuals and groups will try to do what they find good, and the pursuit brings them into collision and struggle. Liberal democratic govern-ment exists to compromise these crashes without civil war and not to infuse us all with a sense of national purpose.

Why then are we yearning for such a sense of purpose? Clearly because we think we are not, as a people, doing anything like justice to the possibilities that near-affluence has suddenly opened up for us. Until yesterday, so to speak, large sections of the population found an all-absorbing purpose in keeping the wolf from the door. With the marked easing of the grim pressure of poverty, relatively few of them find quickly alternative forms of self-discipline to absorb them. This should not be taken as ground for condescension or puritanical criticism. Most of us have too much glass in our houses to risk throwing stones.

Elevating and edifying purpose has never been a universal characteristic of the comfortable classes. But as long as the numbers in the comfortable classes were few, the volume of frivolity in our society seemed small and could be looked at indulgently. It is the sudden multiplying by hundreds of times of those who seem not to be steadied by self-imposed purpose that makes the impression of aimlessness so oppressive and brings us as close to a sense of sin as a skeptical generation can come.

We want a sense of national purpose and are distressed not to be able to articulate it in our politics. We have come to expect governments to fix up whatever is wrong without recognizing that it is one thing for governments to remove barriers and obstructions to the good life and quite another to ensure that the good life will be lived at a high pitch. Some of the vitality of initiative in our social life has weakened in the last thirty years. I shall try to suggest reasons for this in part two of this paper.

It is time to worry about a society when initiative does not well up from below in a diversity of demands and aims that keep governments hard at work to reconcile. If we need to be set on fire – as I think we do – what is needed is a renewal of zest and dash all through our society, and not mandates to governments to find purposes and then bind us to them.

Another set of changes in our circumstances is of great significance. In the course of reaching consensus on the mixed economy and the welfare state, we have created an economic and political structure of great complexity. The steadily accelerating spread of large scale enterprise and organization has removed large sectors of the economy from the dictates of the market. As the self-regulating capacity of the economy declined, governmental regulation advanced to cover the deficiency. This in turn diminished still further that self-regulating capacity. Economic life is now governed by a mixture of private decisions made in the corporate sector of the economy and of public decisions made by the governments, with the latter constantly assuming greater importance. Whether or not the aim is confessed, the gropings of governments in relation to economic policy are designed now to get a good measure of integrated planning under government auspices. (The result is towering economic organization, massive governmental structure, and an extremely complex interlocking of relationships between them. We find all this extremely bewildering.)

We know our duty as citizens to understand the complexities. The liberal individualistic belief over three centuries has been that individuals, by taking thought, could control their destinies. We have plenty of examples around us showing what happens when massive power – economic, political, or whatever – gets out of control. Yet if we propose alteration of policy in a way that seems eminently sensible or strike out at action that seems outrageous to the fair-minded, we soon find we are tearing at a seamless web, and the thing we want to move will involve moving many other things as well, some of them, as like as not, things we cherish. We come to see that government policy as a whole finds an equilibrium not by applying the full logic of clear and lovely ideas, but by a series of compromises of a variety of groups, all mobilized to defend their interests.

We have little confidence that the infinitesimal weight of our vote in periodic elections will do much to modify the pattern of governmental action. Attempts to force a modification of the pattern in any other way require the pressure of highly organized groups brought to bear at precisely the right time and place. The existing equilibrium is defended against attack not so much because of its merits (although they will be loudly proclaimed) but because even minor shifts in adjustment in one sector of public policy are likely to have widespread and, to some extent, unforeseeable consequences in other sectors. It is indeed too delicate to be exposed to any tinkering that can be resisted, and patterns of governmental action and expenditure sometimes persist even when they are no longer defensible.

Citizens are tempted to conclude that as government action brings more and more aspects of their lives and affairs within its orbit, they are being progressively stripped of effective influence on its direction. Of course, they would be wrong so to conclude. Individuals, standing alone, have rarely had any significant political influence on central, as distinct from local, governments. But this is most beside the point. The waning of confidence in the political process does not rest on judgments about the facts but on a general feeling of remoteness from it all. Control over what government does seems to pass into fewer and fewer hands, those of a relatively small coterie of political leaders, higher civil servants, and spokespersons for tightly organized interests.

So we reach the concept of the establishment, a notion that has had much derisive elaboration in Britain and covers the insiders of one kind or another who seem to have taken our destiny out of our bands. Most significantly, the establishment is now often defined as including such political leaders now out of power and organized interests presently out of favour as are likely to come to power and favour at the next turn of the wheel. Even if they do not possess our birthright at the moment, it is thought that they soon will, and therefore they fall under the same odium. In this mood we flirt with movements that have not yet incurred the odium, imagining mistakenly that somehow it will be in their power and interest to restore to us something we feel we have lost. Short of destroying the consensus we have reached, the politico-economic structure calls for political power to be exercised much as it has been exercised in the past fifteen years.

Ironically, the mood of disenchantment and frustration that arises because politics has disappointed us endangers such recovery of control over our destiny as is open to us. Given the decisive influence of government policy on our economic and social arrangements, it is, of course, vital that government should be firm and resolute, yielding only the minimum to dispersive pressures. The only likely way to secure such government is to have a reasonably well-disciplined party system in command of Parliament.

The range of government action is so wide and affects us in so many diverse ways that a welter of issues confuses every election. Voters find themselves drawn to one party on one issue and repelled on another. The old simplicities like home rule for Ireland, free trade, Dominion status are gone, and none with such deceptive clarity has taken their place. The mood of irritation clouds the vision still further and takes as its object precisely the political parties that have pressed discipline on Parliament as well as limited our leverage on our representatives there. For these are the two faces of the coin.

In the world of big organization in which we, as individuals, are now bundled and jammed, the main hope for combining coherence and stability with responsible criticism and orderly adjustment of economic and social life is to submit to still other big organizations, the political parties that can be counted on to create majorities in Parliament at one time or another. In this country at least, the changing conditions of politics raise doubts about the ability of the party system to create such majorities.

I said earlier that the Anglo-American countries had made a great achievement in reaching a broad consensus on the mixed economy and the welfare state. Taken by itself, this tends to confirm the more optimistic views of human nature as it bears on politics. Individuals moved by "general honest thought and common good to all" would, of course, be likely to come to such a consensus.

Yet, to our surprise, hard on the heels of this achievement, new dimensions in our politics seem to open. Perhaps all we need is time to take our bearings, and then the circumstances and moods that puzzle us will pass. Not having foreseen that we would come to this point, perhaps we should not take too seriously the fact that we do not see how we are to get away from it. Periods of hesitation in the life of a society are not at all unusual. However, there is a view that we are confronted by much more than political ripples on the surface of society. It is held that profound social changes that have been going on for a long time are forcing their way into politics and contributing strongly to the hesitations, moods, and attitudes I have spoken about. This possibility will be considered below.

PART TWO

I shall now focus mainly on the relationship of the individual to society. Much of the debate on this subject assumes that individuals and society must always be in conflict. Actually, such talk is scarcely older than the seventeenth century. In the Middle Ages, human consciousness was always social. People thought of themselves as members of an organic group, be it a family, feudal manor, guild, corporation, or parish. Not until the Renaissance and Reformation did they think of themselves as detached entities, separate from society and so, potentially at least, in conflict with it.

The sixteenth century ushered in the age of individualism, in whose twilight we still live. For reasons we need not enter into here, some people became intoxicated with the possibilities of individual freedom and rebelled against the social restraints of immemorial custom, church, and government. From this impulse came by stages all the freedoms we have known and celebrated: freedom to think beyond the boundaries of the socially approved wisdom; economic freedom from the restraints of manor, guild, and government decree; political freedom from the rule of dynasties and monarchs.

The individual became the fundamental premise for political theory. Human beings, as individuals, are born free. They are the basic data of nature. Society and government are artifices designed to serve the individual, who is primary, all social arrangements being secondary and derived. All social bonds are open to criticism and to dissolution if they do not serve the aims and needs of the individual.

The sanguine liberal view of the eighteenth and nineteenth centuries regarded the individual as essentially good, depreciated social restraints, and urged an almost anarchic freedom. John Stuart Mill, in the essay *On Liberty,* argued that an individual's freedom should only be restricted when his or her actions threatened definite and assignable harm to others. Indeed, with laissez faire effectively keeping the hands of government off individuals in his day, Mill thought the most obnoxious restraints on freedom were those imposed by society through custom rather than by the state through law. The individual was set in opposition to society and thought to be in perennial conflict with it.

We got into this way of thinking because it took so long to emancipate the individual, to break the authority of long-standing social custom fortified by religious taboos, and to throw off the burden of mercantilism and other indefensible privileges maintained by the state. The enormous reservoirs of energy and initiative released at each stage of the freeing of individuals seemed to show that they were indeed the key to progress. They were the indestructible entities whose nobility consisted in standing for themselves by themselves. Free them from the social shackles that had bound them in the past, and the future was illimitable.

Of course, individuals have never been able to stand by themselves but have always had to be buoyed up by social supports. Individuals as persons always emerge with the stamp of a social matrix on them. The very structure of an individual's personality arises from the particular network of social relationships in which he or she is enmeshed. How else would we get the rich variety of identifiable types and styles of persons? The families from which people come and the communities in which they share contribute not only to their queerness but to their preferences, their demeanour in success and adversity, their stock of stability, integrity and fortitude, in fact their whole character. All this we know without access to the case studies of the psychiatrists.

Modern individualism is a product of Western Europe. The original inspiration for it came from people nurtured in medieval society, which itself was marked by a uniquely rich community life. The manorial village, the guild, the local corporation, the free city, the parish, the monastery, and religious orders gave status to their members, bound them together in protective association, and provided social supports of a remarkable, even if confining and restrictive, order. The revolutionary changes of the sixteenth century shattered some of these forms of community, transformed others, and sowed the seeds of some new ones. With the breaking of these moulds, individualism got its chance. But it got its chance in a society that still retained many vital forms of group and community life. At the least, there continued in vigour and good repair, from the sixteenth century on to the nineteenth, the family, the parish, the village, and a range of self-sufficient districts and small regions that produced identifiable types of people and gave them a sense of belonging as they tried, or were forced to try, to carry the role of the free self-directing individual. In North America, essentially similar patterns of community were created out of imitation or need, or both.

For the most part, these communities had a unity from which many, although by no means all, of their members drew strength. They were not as tightly knit as the medieval communities. There was more movement in and out of them and much less sense of the corporate responsibility of the group for the welfare of its members. As economic life broke free from the earlier social and religious restraints, the "weak and unfortunate" often went down into destitution as the strong went up. Individualism always had high costs, and these rose sharply as the Industrial Revolution got underway.

Nevertheless, the family, the village, town, district, were generally economic and social units, more or less self-sufficient, in which many individuals could see themselves as carrying significant functions and sharing significantly in a common life. The parish and the church not only ministered to spiritual needs, but also provided material succour and welfare. Most of the conditions of life were set within these boundaries, and so the members of the community understood them and could try to cope with them. Even when their members were divided into social classes, these communities were simple in structure, and face-to-face relationships eased the acerbities of class feeling. Individuals readily understood their places in them and got a sense of belonging to a vital functioning community. In family, church, and local community, the indispensable supports for individualism were found.

Venturesome individuals were always moving out of them and into the wider world, where they often appeared convincingly as free individuals standing alone and making their way without visible social supports. Whether they stayed at home or went afield, they had been formed and shaped and the structures of their personalities set by the local community. They often thought of themselves as being in revolt against the community that had shaped them. Yet they were, in the truest sense, its product, individuals formed in the matrix of their particular community.

From the beginning of the nineteenth century, this social structure began to break down, and it has gone on crumbling ever since at different rates for different countries and regions, but always at an accelerating pace. The primary causes, of course, were the unleashing of individual initiative from social restraints, the releasing of inventiveness, the development of transport and communications. Economic freedom led to expanding trade and a growing articulation of the free market for goods and labour. These, in turn, promoted division of labour and specialized production. Then came newer and still more effective machines, new forms of power, bigger units of production, the assembly line, giant corporations, vast industrial cities, all in breathtaking rapidity in some 150 years.

The economic outcome of this is the highly integrated industrial structure with concentration of control of the critical sectors of it in large, and often huge, corporations. To be able to match the corporations, trade unions must reach for size and power. Other participants in economic life try to organize, by one means or another, on a comparable scale. The free market that used to determine the movement of prices and allocate the factors of production no longer conducts the economic orchestra but takes a subordinate and supporting role. Instead, more and more of the basic critical decisions are made by, or at least in the name of, big organizations, corporations, trade unions, and trade associations with or without the stimulus, pressure, admonition, or direction of governments.

The social outcome is the massing of people in sprawling urban confusion. Few persons in these cities are their own masters in their own work. For the most part, they are employees working under direction at highly specialized tasks, more or less infected by dull mechanical routine. The daring and resourceful entrepreneur of an earlier day has been succeeded by the "organization man."

I said that the older social structure typical of the modern age until the late nineteenth century has been crumbling under the stress of these developments. To the eye, many of the elements of that structure are still visible, but the independent vitality they once exhibited has been greatly weakened. The family persists and still is central to the lives of many people, but speaking generally it has lost much of its tight unity and sense of corporate responsibility for its members, as they spend their day in occupations remote from it and merely come home to sleep. The local community, whether village, town, or countryside, with its focus in neighbourhood institutions of school and church, is still there in profusion, but its relative self-sufficiency and sense of close identity have largely gone. The basic reason for this has been the industrial and the technological revolution of the last 150 years.

Increasingly, and at different paces in different countries through the nineteenth century and into the twentieth century, the magnetic pull of distant markets drew more and more of the energies of these communities into specialized production for those markets. In time, they were nearly all drawn into deep dependence on a continued demand for their products in far-away places and so were exposed to events quite beyond their control and still further beyond their understanding. Finally caught up on a national and even international exchange of goods and services, they lost most of their self-sufficiency and independence, and the vitality of these social supports of individuals was sapped away.

In the great industrial cities, to which vast numbers have been drawn out of the small towns and countryside, generation after generation, the populations have never known any significant self-sufficiency or enjoyed any effective individual independence. Most of them are irretrievably committed to employment at specialized jobs and thus heavily dependent on economic events and decisions beyond their ken and control. Except for subsistence farmers on the fringes, we have all been enticed far out on the limbs of interdependence, where we may be sawed off anytime by whimsical chances of economic change.

When large sections of the nation got drawn into this order of interdependence and found themselves racked by economic change, or economic growth, or whatever one wants to call it, the vulnerable specialists of every kind were driven to beg for the intervention of the state. The government was implored by the victims of economic change, and by the comfortable people with social consciences, to regulate the economy, to compensate for its swings and shifts, and to cushion individuals against the misfortunes they were unable to ward off by their own actions. In a very short time, almost before we knew it, we were drawn into the mixed economy and the welfare state. The growth of big organization in the private sphere was matched by the growth of big government.

Perhaps big government can regulate, compensate, stabilize, and cushion. Given the economic and social structure we have, only two main ways are open. Government may dominate the private sphere completely by its edicts and plan our lives comprehensively. Or it may secure close cooperation between itself and a private sector composed of corporate, industrial, and financial power, trade unions, organized agriculture, and so on. But in either case, a relatively few persons and small groups will make the decisions, taking somewhat into account the pressures and influences that play upon them. The intense intellectual effort that used to go into trying to understand the economic mysteries of the market is being steadily diverted into the study of the logic, psychology, and sociology of decision making. We know that decisions made somewhere by others than ourselves will be fateful for us all.

Effective power is being gathered into relatively few hands, and face-to-face communities that might combat anonymity and restlessness have been enfeebled. If the individual personality is in large measure the product of the society in which it emerges, what kind of persons can this society be expected to produce? If stalwart individuality always has to be underpinned by social supports, what trusswork of the present social structure will serve? Where do people, for whom vital decisions are made without their sharing in them in any meaningful way, learn a sense of responsibility for themselves and their actions? Where people are always conscious of dependence on hidden events beyond their reach and control, how do they escape the pathological worries and anxieties that can only be kept at bay by assurances of security from the cradle to the grave. Will there be any enthusiasm for a widespread personal freedom in which the risks and responsibilities seem incommensurate with the foreseeable gains and advantages?

I do not ask these questions for rhetorical effect but because I do not think answers to them can be given with confidence. Of course, there is a very close relationship between the personality structure and the structure of society. Yet it would be rash to say that personality is merely a function of the social structure. For example, the decline in the firmness and intensity of religious belief weakens the obligation felt to resist social pressures and take the burden of individual freedom and responsibility. Certainly the conviction that one will have to answer at the judgment seat for one's witness in the world here below has, in the past, stiffened the demand for individual freedom because freedom was needed to get ready to face that awful responsibility. Yet a vital religion has to bind together the fragments of knowledge and experience in an interpretation that makes sense of that knowledge and experience. The great advance of knowledge and the changes in society in the last two centuries were certain to provoke the radical reassessment of religious beliefs and values that has been going on for a long time now. While it is going on, some of the older religious certainties are under suspended sentence, to say the least. So it is not clear to me that the weakening of specific religious conviction is any more cause than it is consequence in the complex relationships under discussion.

At any rate, the dominant patterns of our social life are no longer individualistic but collectivist in the sense that groups and closely knit organizations, instead of individuals, are the units of decision and action. Physically, a great part of the population is massed in urban areas. By occupation and material interest, they are massed as wage or salary employees or as members of trade unions or similar associations. Politically attempts are made, sometimes with success, to mass them for election purposes. The entertainment industry tries to mass them for its spectacles, which are cooked up for what are believed to be the mass tastes. There is much talk about mass society and about the mass individual who takes supinely the proffered standards of his or her society and responds predictably to stimuli that move the great bulk of his or her fellows.

We are being told, too, about the alienation of the mass individual. Marx first gave currency to the concept of alienation as the estrangement of the exploited worker from the satisfactions of creative work as he or she worked for a capitalist employer. The concept has now been extended to include estrangement of the individual from any satisfying form of identity with a community and even from him or herself as an effective human person. The social analysts of today, who are not studying decision making, are studying mass society, the mass individual, and alienation.

Even if I had the competence, it is beyond my scope here to spell out in longhand, as it were, the analysis for which these words are the shorthand. In the briefest terms, the weakening of older primary forms of community and the failure to replace them with enough and vital forms of association leave the individual insecure, unfulfilled, frustrated, and alone with a terrifying burden of consciousness. If this conclusion is right, our present time is more individualistic than any the modern world has known. But the atomized individuals of today, it is said, are not the confident, self-reliant people cherishing their freedom and distinctiveness that we have idealized for so long. They cannot find a focus for individual expression in mechanized work, whose dull routines have little meaning for them. Nor can they find it in impersonal consumption of standardized products. In their hunger to belong somewhere, they seek shared experience in standardized entertainments and mass spectacles. In their rootlessness, they become mass individuals.

At the same time, many vital decisions affecting average individuals' lives are removed from any forum in which they can take a direct and effective part. Economic and political centralization reduces the number of persons who set the main terms of existence and entangles the deliberations in expert and technical considerations that they cannot follow, even if they know where and by whom matters are being settled. "The area of individual action, decision and responsibility shrinks in favour of collective planning and decision." In this sense, society becomes collectivist and the collective institutions that have, to a marked degree, supplanted the older forms of community do not integrate individuals in them in a vital way.

Individuals, conscious of their vulnerability and dependence and aware of the need for authority somewhere to hold together the parts of the vast interdependent structure of present-day society, cease to feel any deep responsibility for what goes on. They acquiesce in, if they do not actively push for, extension of government action and direction. People listen resignedly to politicians who assure them that, given power, they will do what is needed to integrate the society and protect its members from the mischances of rapid economic and social changes. The power and scope of the state grow with great rapidity. The social forces that formerly acted as a check on the state decline in strength, and this decline raises sharply the question of how excessive concentration of power in the state is to be prevented. In this analysis, the vulnerable individual and the all-powerful state are two sides of the same coin.

It is very hard to say how far the emerging social realities prefigure the alarming features of the mass individual and the all-powerful state. Social causation is the most complex of all studies even when we are looking at clearly defined, fully shaped phenomena. We have not that advantage – or disadvantage – here. The most that the prophets of the mass individual say is that it is coming, the type is emerging, and that dangerously large numbers of persons in urban industrial areas exhibit more or fewer of its features. Equally it is not yet seriously urged that the state is really out of control but rather that it is moving rapidly in this direction.

Of course, there are substantial numbers of rootless people who feel that society does not provide them with enough opportunities for meaningful existence and who fail to establish any satisfying relationship with vital social groups. There have always been numbers of these, even when the older forms of primary community were going at their best. The issue really is the new strength of the tendencies, the proportion of the population seriously exposed to the tendencies, and how deeply disinherited peoples' situation makes them feel. Measuring the disintegrative forces at work on millions of people is a delicate task in which the margin of error may well invalidate the findings.

The summary account given here of the factors driving toward mass society overlooks or skimps on a number of important considerations. First, even in great industrial cities, neighbourhood institutions persist – or develop – giving many of the inhabitants some sense of mutuality and belonging. The fact that London can be described as a collection of villages illustrates the point. The massive national and international trade unions are among the large-scale organizations that dwarf the individual and help to form his or her impression of remoteness from significant decisions. This, however, is only part of the picture. Trade unions had their origins in friendly societies and mutual benefit societies in which industrial workers in the early nineteenth century tried to compensate for the loss of older forms of rural and village community. Trade union locals every-where provide today some of the texture of community for their members, aside altogether from the better-known function of collective bargaining. Cooperatives, both of producers and consumers, serve the same kind of ends.

Indeed, for at least two hundred years, as people have felt the loosening of the older social bonds, they have tried to compensate for the loss by a wide scatter of voluntary associations. The Masonic Order, for example, came to life late in the eighteenth century and provided, for a long time, a quality of cohesion that was often alarming to governments. Countless other similar orders and fraternities have risen and fallen. While their life histories do not suggest enduring vitality, they do testify to the continuing effort to find a social meaning for existence.

The effort has intensified in our own day, if the number and variety of the voluntary associations that rise and flourish is a reliable index. In a great many of them, the bond is occupational, and they become, if they do not begin as, political pressure groups. As such, their competition keeps up the tension of political life and contributes to an equilibrium that avoids extremes. However, being of the sappers rather than of the cavalry, they do little to elevate political discussion.

Moreover, the associations that aspire to weighty political influence need the weight of mass membership. As membership gets big, control of the higher activities of the association slips away from the rank and file and into the hands of a few. The association becomes an aggravation rather than a mitigation of bigness, remoteness, and anonymity.

Many of the groups formed on the basis of a common interest are devoid of political content. Membership in such as these may well constitute resignations from political involvement, thus releasing politicians from importunities. Unfortunately, a low level of political awareness cannot be a gain for liberal democracy because the unreflecting voter is the most vulnerable to demagogic appeal.

Nevertheless, all lively voluntary action in groups knits people into social textures. Where such groups flourish in abundance, they are checks on the emergence of the mass individual. Dictators always try to crush voluntary associations because they are potential centres of opposition to them. They want a mass society because they know that its members will need them and will rise to their appeals. Quite independent of this fact, the evidence is clear that political extremism is in inverse ratio to the number and vitality of voluntary associations. The Anglo-American societies still have marked powers of resistance to the deepening spread of the stain of alienation.

There are still other relevant considerations. Even within massive industry itself, which has long been a principal source of alienation, the numbers of jobs calling for a high degree of technical knowledge rise rapidly.

Here, as elsewhere, knowledge can be power. Individuals who have indispensable knowledge share in decisions. Thus both pride of competence and sense of responsibility are nurtured. The more their jobs call upon them to think, the more they will want to think for themselves. Automation will call for steadily rising proportions of the workforce to have and to exercise educated judgment. Also, automated industries, not needing to be planted alongside large pools of labour, offer new chances for physical deconcentration that would lessen the mass tendencies always at work in the great cities. But whether the net effect of automation will be beneficial depends on what is done about the redundant workers it displaces. The alienated mass individual at the extreme is the unemployed and unemployable derelict.

It needs also to be remembered that the responses of individuals to their environments is affected by their levels of education. As secondary education comes within the reach of most youngsters and as access to university education is greatly widened, we can talk, without wild inaccuracy, more about an educated society. An educated society will have more resources to resist alienation and the herdlike responses that characterize mass society.

Aside from all specific consolations, it must be kept in mind that these are times of rapid and dismembering change. Living by habit and custom as much as we can, we are most alert to the disintegrative, which disturbs what we have known. Recuperative forces may go unrecognized because they appear in the repellent garb of the new.

Yet, when all the reservations have been made and all the cautions put, there is little doubt that the grain of mechanized industrial society runs toward regimentation and standardization. The rationalizing of processes and of organization argues for larger and larger organizations so that more things will be calculable and manageable at the top. Freedom and diversity always seem, on the surface at any rate, to make trouble for those charged with getting the gears to mesh. Compensating for this bias calls for awareness, energy, ingenuity and vigilance.

There is plenty of evidence that all these are needed. We are baffled to see juvenile delinquency rise despite the general rise in the standard of living. We could find the clue in the fact that juvenile delinquency is found at its worst not in the countryside, not in the nonindustrial community, but precisely in the urban industrial city. Youth is responsive to the immediate in its environment. So it is tempting to conclude that family and neighbourhood ties are failing to satisfy the ache to belong somewhere. The most popular postwar philosophy for younger people is existentialism. Its basic appeal is the assertion that individuals are solitary and alone, alienated from the world. To save their dignity from abject complicity in the absurd, they must outface despair by acceptance and commitment to life without illusions. (Right or wrong, this calls for courage and so is hopeful.) For a philosophy to get attention, it has to make sense in the experience of those who embrace it. If there were genuine rapport with inherited values and satisfaction in social relationships, young people would be affirming with animal spirits, if nothing else, and leaving disillusion and despair to the older and wiser.

Whether deep in disillusion and despair or not, much of the working force of today finds little that is exciting and satisfying in its work. For those caught up in mechanized work processes over which they have no significant control, unrest is never far around the corner. The attempt to make such work interesting has almost been given up. Instead, hopes are fastened on shorter hours so that people can find themselves in extended leisure. Play, recreation, and amusement are heavy preoccupations today. Many of the offerings, however, are canned and packaged with little of spontaneous play or lively sharing in them. Do we conclude that, in the main, the tension of work is so wearing to the spirit that no mean between frenzy and passivity will serve? Anyway, at the best, the results so far are an indifferent return on the dreams about what release from unremitting toil would do.

Whether or not leisure so used restores individuals to face their work, it adds little to their stature as citizens. The counselling of mass advertising on the uses of leisure is no doubt thought to be fitted to its audience. If any of this advice suggests the raptures of study and reflection about public things, it has escaped me. Even after a heavy discount for the perennial puritan distaste for folk pleasures, the corrected judgment would still be bleak. The end of the urban workday releases a jaded spirit wanting to be steeped in forgetfulness rather than an eager citizen blasting to the library or the forum. The serious issue thus posed is whether the fault is irremediably in ourselves or in the social and work environment that closes us in.

The likely effects of these social trends on politics can now be sketched. Individual freedom will not be as highly prized by people who lack the zest and the genuine opportunity to use it in their social and economic relations. If government is not seen as a baleful threat to opportunities they want to seize and can see ways of using, they will not be so vigilant to keep it in check. On the contrary, as the autonomy of the face-to-face communities and groups in which they live is eroded by social and economic change, they are led to put their trust in government rather than in themselves because government has the long reach that is needed and that they lack. At the least, in their anxiety and dependence, they are open to persuasion to this effect. The rule of law, for example, is not maintained, in the long pull, by courts, constitutions, and bills of rights but by the citizen's passion for liberty. Bagehot made the point by saying that the citizens of Massachusetts could work any constitution. It is not likely that the mass society will produce this kind of citizen, even in Massachusetts.

It is said that people shirk responsibility. It is always a burden, and burdens are always irksome. In propitious times, they can be led to welcome responsibility because of compensating advantages seen to reside in freedom. But if effective power is denied one in one's own affairs, why play a game that one must always lose? Moreover, faculties rust if they do not shine steadily in use. If, in one's daily work, one does not think for one's self, weigh the pros and cons, decide on action, and abide the consequences, it is rather much to expect reasoned and responsible decision to be exercised intermittently in politics. Of course, there has never been a society in which the great bulk of the citizens was thus prepared for political participation. The essential point is that the fraction so habituated by their lifestyle and experience is declining sharply in our society. Most of us are employees of one kind or another.

At the very time when the attraction to, and the capacity for, participation in things public is diminishing, the sphere of things political moves to cover issues beyond our immediate experience. Because government has come to envelop a large part of our lives, the issues multiply and take on a forbidding perplexity. The clear-cut simple alternatives disappear. Instead of yes or no, the alternatives are often more or less. Deficit financing was wrong last year, but right this year, and so on. These are not the problems for jaded spirits to take up and judge.

In these circumstances, politicians will be driven to simplify and dramatize. How near to demagoguery they have to go to do this is open to dispute. At least, it is clear that, if the need of individuals to belong somewhere is not satisfied in the primary communities and in face-to-face relationships, they are all the readier to be taken, as crowds, into the emotionally charged fellowship of the nation. When moved in this way, they are not asserting their freedom and diversity as individuals but running for cover into the shelter of the state, which can become a prison.

For whatever tendencies there are in this direction, I shall not be the one to blame politicians. Like every other artist, they are, in large measure, subdued by their materials. If their materials are crowds rather than a multiplicity of diverse and opposing wills and interests, they have to work in that medium. As soon as the crowd element is decisive, they will cease to be the democratic politicians we know and become charismatic leaders.

Politicians in a free society always have to face a wide range of conflicting interests and wills. The interests are clearly articulated as expressions of the desire for freedom of action and the belief in its possibilities. For the same reason, the wills are stubborn and, left unmediated, would disrupt public order. The job of democratic politicians is to reconcile the conflicts by compromise in a policy that is tolerable to nearly all, even if congenial to few. To do this job, they need room for manœuvre. It must be open to them and their parties to propose, and to carry through, changes of policy that meet the prime and indispensable need for reconciliation of conflicting interests and wills.

Here we come upon another significant feature of the changing conditions of politics. As the scope of state action has widened enormously and government has superseded the market in fixing many of the terms of economic and social activity, the freedom of action of the politician has correspondingly narrowed. In the complex interlocking of economic life, adjustments in one sector affect many other sectors. Everything is related to everything else. If stability is to be maintained and the hopes for economic growth realized, government has to pursue a set of interrelated policies that cannot be reshuffled with impunity. More than this, in the setting of the policies in the first place, and in any responsible adjusting and modifying of them, the likely effects have to be calculated.

Expert judgment is needed at every turn. The higher civil servants have to be relied on for the *expertise,* and they thus come to play a big part in the policy making. To a degree, policy becomes bureaucratized and caught in the rigidities that always vex large-scale organization. So politicians are denied some of the flexibility they need for working out their reconciliations. Their room for manœuvre is narrowed. In a sense, they too are alienated from their proper work and subject to frustrations.

The logic of the argument can be carried one step further. When the market really ruled, its decrees were inexorable. People were compelled to adjust themselves to it at whatever cost. We decided a long time ago that the human cost was much too high. We have deposed the market and are putting government in its place. Government decree may not be as pitiless as was that of the market, but if we are to maintain economic stability and nourish economic growth, it must have its own inexorability. Public policy cannot be adjusted to every need for political compromise. Accordingly, instead of adjusting policy to the people, it will be necessary, in considerable measure, to adjust the people to the policy. This feat does not call for the arts of the democratic politician but rather for the magic of the leader whose art is not so much reconciliation as submergence of wills and interests.

Clearly enough, then, the mass tendencies in society and the transformed role of government work together to threaten drastic changes in our politics. They will continue so to work as long as large-scale organization and centralization of power seem to us the necessary conditions for ensuring rapid economic growth and for raising productivity. And we are all preoccupied with getting greater material means and distributing the benefits more widely for the relief of the human estate.

However, we do know from the events of the last thirty or so years the horrors of unlimited power. We are beginning somewhat belatedly to see the costs to individual freedom and richly diverse human personality that are inherent in the tendencies to mass society. This is one root of the present slackness in our politics. Few of us at present see any way out of a baffling dilemma. Bigness and concentration of power seem to be the prerequisite for material advance and for the extension of liberating opportunity and at the same time the enemy of other humane values. The dilemma is just as serious for socialists as for other liberal democrats.

Hesitations caused by the dilemma have brought us, for the time being at least, to what has been called "the end of ideology," to the slipping of ardent convictions on what can be achieved through politics. Both moderate individualists and socialists used to have assurance in their diverse prescriptions for setting the conditions of the good life. Both are now unsure of some of their assumptions and values. There is some doubt about how broadly based is the desire for a vital individual freedom, as also about the compatibility of meaningful freedom with some of our other objectives. Ironically it was easier to believe in the inherent dignity of the individual when we saw the gallantry of the struggle against heavy odds in poverty and privation than it is when we see the aimlessness of much of our consumption of leisure and other goods in the present day. When we watch the experts in applied psychology appeal to emotions and drive reason from the field, we sometimes wonder whether rational sequence is more than a freak form of mental activity. If rationality comes under suspicion, one of the props of the ardent faith in the people and in the coherence and sanity of the popular will begin to buckle. The people may not come to reasonable conclusions at all. In these circumstances, no confident political initiative springs from our tradition, and we are in the doldrums.

To get out of them, we need to decide whether the liberal faith in human beings in its chastened and skeptical, as distinct from its more optimistic, form is wrong, a gross misreading of our essential nature and of human possibilities. Or is it right with a vengeance? Is the proof now before us that human nature *is* malleable, that individuals *can* control their destinies in regressive as well as progressive ways? Is it that in running our affairs over the last two hundred years, we took a wrong turning and are creating forms of society that bias us to regress rather than progress? Is our trouble due to an earlier failure of intelligence to take full account of the problem rather than to any incurable defects of human nature?

In the end, we are unlikely to get utterly convincing answers to these questions, and we shall still have to go for a faith rather than a certainty. Having to conclude here without a certainty, I recall an important consideration bearing on a faith. The alternative to a generous faith in human beings is a craven faith in authority freed, it is true, from responsibility to our fickle selves but still wielded by fallible individuals. In our present disenchantment with ourselves and our fellows, we should remember that long ago we were thoroughly disillusioned with authority, whether of priests, kings, or oligarchs.

J.A. CORRY was a Rhodes Scholar, professor of law at the University of Saskatchewan, and Hardy Professor of Political Science at Queen's University. During his years at Queen's, he also served as vice-principal – helping to found the Queen's Faculty of Law – and then as principal. He wrote a number of influential books, including *Democratic Government and Politics*, and delivered the 1971 Massey Lecture, "The Power of the Law." Dr Corry remained active after his retirement from Queen's, teaching, writing, and, from 1968–70, acting as a consultant to the federal Department of Justice. In this latter capacity, he was responsible for an analysis of the proposed changes to Canada's Constitution.

Dr Corry was a Companion of the Order of Canada and a Fellow of the Royal Society of Canada. Among his many awards were the 1973 Royal Bank Award for his contributions to Canadian education and honorary degrees from fourteen universities. Dr J.A. Corry died in 1985.

6

Right and Wrong in Foreign Policy

JAMES EAYRS, 1965

"THE WAYS OF STATECRAFT"

It has been more than four hundred years since Machiavelli advised his prince in what ways he should keep faith and in what ways not. During this time, the scope for wrongdoing in foreign policy has greatly expanded, and of its expansion governments have not been reluctant to take advantage. In their dealings with other governments, and with other peoples, their behaviour is characteristically bad. It is deceitful. It is treacherous. It is cruel.

Deception is central to most of the techniques of statecraft. Consider negotiation. I am not concerned with the white lie, the half-truth, the repression of what one really thinks. Without such mild deceptions, there could be no diplomacy at all. No, I am thinking of the *grand guignol* of negotiations: of Japanese ministers smiling and bowing at their American colleagues even as the Imperial Fleet steamed toward Pearl Harbor; of Britain's refusal to disclose to its closest ally its plans for the imminent invasion of Egypt; of Andrei Gromyko's assurance to the president of the United States that no strategic missiles had been sent to Cuba, while locked in a safe ten feet from where they talked was indisputable evidence that Gromyko was lying; of the first minister of Kenya promising the British that once independent, Kenya would work for federation in East Africa – a promise, Jomo Kenyetta later gleefully told his countrymen, he had never intended to keep. The examples would fill a book. No one government, no type of government, has a corner on the market. Great powers do it. Small powers do it. Even middle powers do it.

Consider propaganda. Not all propaganda is deceptive –though much of it is. But all propaganda is tendentious. Governments do not wish to tell the world of their shortcomings. In decisions about what to tell the world – the truth as one sees it, part of that truth, what is known to be untrue – expedience prevails over ethics. What matters is not the truth of the message but the credibility of the message. And the estimate of the credibility of the message is determined by the estimate of the gullibility of the masses.

At one extreme is the assessment of fascism. The masses are craven and gullible. They lack the independence of mind and spirit to denounce as false anything bearing the hallmark of authority. The greater the falsehood, the more readily acceptable as fact, once stamped with the imprimatur of state. Propaganda to be credible should be a compound of monstrous untruths. And Hitler and Goebbels made it so.

At the other extreme is the assessment of liberal democracy. It thinks not of masses but of the man in the street – Bagehot's baldheaded gentleman at the back of the bus. Of his intellectual discrimination, it takes a lofty view. It believes he can distinguish not merely between truth and falsehood, but among shadings across the spectrum of veracity. Propaganda to be credible should be scrupulously fair and rigorously unbiased.

Some governments today cling to the technique of the Big Lie, practising without remorse a sort of psychic genocide. A few – a very few – try to be fair. Most fall in between. Their apparatus for persuasion, usually called ministries of information, might better be called ministries of mendacity. They accept with zeal the job of putting out versions of events they know to be untrue. Never before have so many statesmen with so little scruple been engaged in the deception of so many people.

Deceit is commonplace in foreign policy. Betrayal no less so.

Treachery, in private ethics, is a grave offence. You do not flatter a man by calling him Judas. Jean Genet, casting perversely about for ways of soiling the moral precepts of a society from which he is so spectacularly alienated, settles unerringly upon betrayal, which forms, with thievery and homosexuality, his satanic trinity of categorical imperatives.

Treachery, in foreign policy, is not such a grave offence. Consider three cases, in an ascending order of moral difficulty.

The betrayal of Abyssinia in 1935 was easily done. A remote country. A people alleged to be of inferior race. Benighted creatures, they were thought scarcely to be capable of knowing whether they were betrayed or not. "No interest in Ethiopia, of any nature whatever, is worth the life of a single Canadian citizen." So said Ernest Lapointe in Quebec City, with Mackenzie King nodding approval at his side. That was one judgment, and it happened to prevail. But it was not the only judgment. The next day, from the rostrum of the Palais des Nations at Geneva, the delegate of Haiti uttered another: "Great or small, strong or weak, near or far, white or coloured, let us never forget that one day we may be somebody's Ethiopia." But on this occasion, as on many others, it was not easy to apply to foreign policy even so diluted a version of the Golden Rule.

The betrayal of Czechoslovakia, in 1938, was less easily done. The operation was delicate and tricky. It involved the dismemberment of a state at once an ally and a friend. Here was a civilized country in the heart of Europe, free, white and – dating its independence to the Peace Treaties – almost twenty-one. Canada considered it remote: Lapointe cabled frantically from Geneva to insist that "immediate cause of war namely minority problems in Eastern Europe not of a nature to enthuse our people." Britain and France found it too close for comfort. Gratefully their governments fell upon the doctrine of national self-determination: Wasn't Sudetenland full of Germans? But that was dangerous doctrine: Wasn't Scotland full of Scotsmen, Algeria of Algerians? No, the justification for the betrayal of Czechoslovakia had to be found elsewhere.

We all know about Munich, so we all know what it was. The sacrifice of Czechoslovakia was said to be a small price for peace. (That it had brought not peace but time to prepare for war is an argument contrived after the event.) There was not more ecstatic endorsement of the deal than the Canadian. "On the very brink of chaos," Mackenzie King cabled to Chamberlain, "with passions flaming and armies marching, the voice of Reason has found a way." Again this judgment prevailed, though not for very long. But it was not the only judgment. Out in Winnipeg, one of the greatest of Dafoe's editorials asked rhetorically: "What's the Cheering For?" A free people had been handed over to a tyrant: that, said Dafoe, "is the situation; and those who think it is all right will cheer for it." Almost everybody did.

The betrayal of large numbers of Rumanians, Hungarians, and Bulgarians in 1944–45, consigned against their will to the kind of peoples' democracy favoured by Stalin, was assented to by the United States and the United Kingdom governments as the price to be paid for appeasing the Soviet Union. What was done at Moscow and at Yalta differed in degree of wrongdoing from what was done at Munich: What was betrayed on this occasion was not so much a people already under the yoke of the Red Army as the ideals for which the war had ostensibly been fought. The Atlantic Charter makes painful reading when set beside transcripts of Allied negotiations four years later. Of what then went on, Winston Churchill has left a dramatic account:

The moment was apt for business, so I said [to Stalin]: "Let us settle about our affairs in the Balkans. Your armies are in Rumania and Bulgaria. We have interests, missions, and agents there. Don't let us get at cross purposes in small ways. So far as Britain and Russia are concerned, how would it do for you to have ninety per cent predominance in Rumania, for us to have ninety per cent of the say in Greece, and go fifty-fifty about Yugoslavia?"

During the translation, Churchill wrote out the percentages on a piece of paper. His account continues:

I pushed this across to Stalin, who had by then heard the translation. There was a slight pause. Then he took his blue pencil and made a large tick upon it, and passed it back to us. It was all settled in no more time than it takes to set it down ...

After this there was a long silence. The penciled paper lay in the centre of the table. At length I said: "Might it not be thought rather cynical if it seemed we had disposed of those issues, so fateful to millions of people, in such an offhand manner? Let us burn the paper."

"No. You keep it," said Stalin.

The people of small states, with a faith more touching than reasoned, believe such inequities to be the failing of great powers only. This is not always true. A former American minister to Canada has recorded his shock on learning how cheaply the Department of External Affairs appeared to value the liberty of the Baltic countries in 1942. He was told by the permanent head of that department that nobody (in London or Ottawa) worried about Finland and that Estonia, Latvia, and Lithuania were a small price to pay to convince Russia of Britain's trust and earnestness. He remarked that "what the British Government was suggesting and what [the Canadian Government] was endorsing could certainly not be reconciled with the Atlantic Charter." But the Canadian government, or at any rate the Canadian prime minister, did not hold the Atlantic Charter in such high regard. "To me," wrote Mackenzie King in his diary, "it is the apotheosis of the craze for publicity and show."

I have spoken of deceit and of treachery; I shall speak now of cruelty in foreign policy.

Cruelty is not confined to the maiming and killing of innocent people – though we know only too well how often governments practise this kind of cruelty. Those who passed indifferently by that certain traveller between Jerusalem and Jericho were cruel in their behaviour – this is the point of the parable – even though they were not guilty of his wounds.

The ethic that it is wrong to be cruel is more widely accepted today than ever before. Few of the world's religions, few of its ideologies, remain unaffected by it. The injunction to love one's neighbour has been sent bounding across the world's communications systems. Only about half of its inhabitants have ever heard of Jesus; and of them maybe half have heard of Gandhi.

All the same, the scale and scope of cruelty in statecraft are greater today than ever before. Why is this so?

Twentieth-century war is increasingly an instrument of doctrinal conviction. Doctrinal war, more than war fought for gain, or to preempt attack, is likely to be total war and brutal war. Crusades are notorious for their cruelty. "I implore you," Martin Luther wrote to a friend, "if you rightly understand the Gospel, do not imagine that its cause can be furthered without tumult, distress, and uproar." Luther meant the gospel of the New Testament; but his words apply to other gospels and to other testaments, to Lenin's and Mao's, Wilson's and Johnson's – to all who dispose of great power linked to an idea. "Bismarck fought 'necessary' wars," a historian has noted, "and killed thousands. The idealists of the twentieth century fight 'just' wars and kill millions."

And on the occasion of the twentieth anniversary of the ordeal of Hiroshima and Nagasake: "Our world will be a safer place and healthier place when we can admit that every time we make an atomic bomb we corrupt the morals of a host of innocent neutrons below the age of consent."

As to safety, Auden is no authority: Strategists better than poets may determine whether we really would all be safer by unilaterally dismantling the apparatus of deterrence by which we believe ourselves preserved. But as to ethics, Auden is as good a guide as any strategist, possibly more reliable. Surely he is right to force our attention upon the plight of the innocent. Why do we punish a kidnapper more condignly than a robber, even sometimes a murderer? It is because we abhor, and properly abhor, the crime of holding innocent life as hostage. By what sort of reasoning, then, does our society not only condone but indulge in the holding as hostage the lives of millions of innocents?

The issue has been posed in this way: "Nuclear-missile weapons hold out the prospect of conflict which may be neither subject to restraint nor meaningfully described as defensive. Can such a war be justified? Can there be a moral sanction for threatening to take a measure which, if circumstances ever required carrying it out, could find no justification." On 22 October 1962, speaking on television with all the emphasis at his command, the president of the United States uttered the following words: "It shall be the policy of this nation to regard any nuclear missile launched from Cuba against any nation in the Western Hemisphere as an attack by the Soviet Union on the United States, requiring a full retaliatory response upon the Soviet Union." By what moral law, by what sacred text, by the precept or example of what saintly figure, in response to what promptings of his own conscience, could John Kennedy dare to serve a national interest by risking the mutilation of humankind?

If you put this question to a statesman, he will have an answer – of sorts. He will say that it is not a fair question.

If you put it to strategists, they will lecture you on the distinction between "action" policy and "declaratory" policy. Action policy, they will tell you, is what a government intends to do. Declaratory policy is what it says it intends to do, very likely without intending to do it. The president's statement, they will assure you, is declaratory policy, not action policy.

This answer is hardly more satisfactory than the statesman's answer. It does not explain how the distinction between action policy and declaratory policy, which the enemy is not supposed to understand, will be readily apparent to those who are not the enemy. Nor does it answer the question of the ethical right of any statesman in any circumstances to indulge for whatever reason in such dire and dreadful threats, action or declaratory as the case may be.

So what happens if you put the question to a moralist? Up to now, the moralists have asked to be excused. They have no answer to the question. They have not even considered the question. "I find myself profoundly in anguish," an American scientist has lamented, "over the fact that no ethical discourse of any weight or nobility has been addressed to the problem of nuclear weapons. What are we to think of such a civilization, which has not been able to talk about the prospect of killing almost everybody, except in prudential and game-theoretical terms?"

Not without reason have moral philosophers and theologians shied away from questions of this kind.

The predicaments thus posed are so macabre, so horrific, that to apply to them the traditional apparatus of ethical discussion results only in black humour and sick jokes. Our playwrights, frustrated because reality is so much more lurid than any plots they can devise, have created the theatre of the absurd. We are still waiting for our moral philosophers and theologians to create an ethics of the absurd.

The work may have already begun. At the meetings in 1964 of the Ecumenical Council of the Roman Church, the committee charged with formulating positions for the church in the modern world was faced with the task of contriving some ethical precepts for nuclear warfare. The committee could not reach agreement. One of the formulations causing its members to set the task to one side was the following: "Although, after all the aids for peaceful discussions have been exhausted, it may not be illicit, when one's rights have been unjustly hampered, to defend those rights against such unjust aggression by violence and force, nevertheless, the use of arms, especially nuclear weapons, whose effects are greater than can be imagined and therefore cannot reasonably be regulated by men, exceeds all just proportion and therefore must be judged before God and man as most wicked."

This may not seem an extreme position for those who profess devotion to the gentle carpenter of Galilee. But it was too extreme for some of the more worldly churchmen on the council. "It is important to make clear," one of the dissenters argued, "that there may well exist objects which, in a just war of defence, are legitimate targets for nuclear weapons, even of vast strength ... To attack a ballistic missile or a satellite missile in the outer atmosphere would be a legitimate act of defence, and with just proportion duly preserved might require the use of a weapon of vast power ... The Council should not condemn the possession and use of these weapons as essentially and necessarily evil." And it has not done so.

At the deliberations of these divines, solemnly debating the morality of a nuclear anti-missile missile system, one does not know whether to laugh or weep. They recall recondite discussion within the thirteenth-century church. They recall as well Oppenheimer's image of morality as a flying trapeze and Kierkegaard's comparison of the man of faith to an acrobat. But funambulism is not enough. If we keep our balance, if we keep our faith, if indeed we keep our sanity throughout the ethical inanities of the atomic age, it is not by acrobatics but by an operation on the inner ear of conscience that renders us impervious to height and to the depths below.

Suppose we assume, with Niebuhr, that within the immoral society that is the state system there dwells a moral humankind. How should we react? Should we accept its inequities with resignation or with indignation? Ought we to come to terms with it, or ought we to declare war on it? Is it a condition to be borne or a situation to be changed?

The literature of political theory provides two traditions in which to find an answer. They are usually described as the realist tradition and the idealist tradition. I will accept this terminology for convenience, but so as not to oversimplify I shall identify the principal strains that occur in each.

Plato's Thrasymachus, asked to define justice, replies that it conforms to the interests of the stronger. Here we have the first two strains of the realist tradition. I will call it brutal realism.

Brutal realists are realpolitikers of an extreme kind. Ethics, they insist, have no place in politics. Might makes right. What is good for the state is good. Characteristically, brutal realists take pleasure in their brutal realism. They pride themselves on their tough-mindedness. Their noses are hard. They enjoy the company of hawks.

Brutal realists are not so fashionable as they used to be, perhaps fortunately; specimens are hard to find. But not that hard, for there is at least one old State Department hand, still an important figure in the Washington policy community, who waves his brutal realism about like a bullfighter's cape. Some months ago Mr Dean Acheson recalled, with evident satisfaction, how lightly moral considerations weighed with those, among whom he was one, who in 1949 made the decision to produce the hydrogen bomb: "A respected colleague advised me that it would be better that our whole nation and people should perish rather than be a party to a course so evil as producing that weapon. I told him that on the day of Judgment his view might be confirmed and that he was free to go forth and preach the necessity for salvation. It was not, however, a view which I could entertain as a public servant." Here is the authentic voice of the brutal realist: rasping in tone, sardonic in debate, crushing in rejoinder, sure that he is right.

To belong in the realist tradition one does not have to be a brutal realist. There is another strain, which we may call skeptical realism. Skeptical realists are no disciples of Thrasymachus, proclaiming the mighty to be right and throwing the weak to the wolves. Still less are they disciples of Nietzsche, extolling an anti-ethic of force and violence. They are realistic not because they are sadistic, but because they are skeptical.

They are skeptical of the supposition that if their own government dealt impeccably with others, those others would deal impeccably with it. A unilateral declaration of morality would cause the rest to take advantage of such a curiosity as a government determined to make its foreign policy conform to what is right. Machiavelli, often thought to be a brutal realist, is for this reason a skeptical realist. He does advise his prince "not to keep faith when it would be against his interest," but this is counsel not of perfection but of necessity. "If men were all good," he immediately concedes, "this precept would not be a good one; but as they are bad, and would not observe their faith with you, so you are not bound to keep faith with them."

They are skeptical, as well, of the supposition that moral judgments may be made with confidence in such a welter of confusion. The skein of history is so tangled, the motives of statesmen so mixed, the cause of events so obscure, that rarely are they sure of what is right and what is wrong. If a gifted historian can trick out so obvious a villain as Hitler in such a way as to exonerate him from responsibility for the Second World War, with how much less assurance does one approach the more morally ambiguous figures of our times: Lenin, for example; or Neville Chamberlain; or Ayub Khan. (Or Gengis Khan, or Herman Kahn.)

Hard as it is to judge the statesmen, it is harder still to judge their statecraft. "There is no standard of right and wrong applicable to conflicts of political interests," wrote the permanent head of the British Foreign Office in 1912. "Was Alexander right or wrong in invading the Persian Empire and erecting on its ruins the foundations of a flourishing Greek civilization? Was William III right or wrong in putting an end to the reign of James II? Is Great Britain right or wrong in holding dominion over India?" There is no shortage of similar examples in our own day. The struggles for Kashmir, for Berlin, for Rhodesia, for Vietnam: In each case, each disputant is convinced of the justice of its cause and views the struggle as one between good and evil, right and wrong. The skeptical realist views the struggle as one between two conflicting conceptions of right.

It has been said that when John Kennedy was president, it was his habit to ask not whether a proposed course of action was good or bad, right or wrong; he asked instead: "Can it work? Can it help? Can it pass?" Such are the concerns of the skeptical strain in the realist tradition.

I now turn to the idealist tradition, where again two strains are found.

One is brightly hopeful, blithely optimistic. I will call it the strain of liberal idealism, for it carries within itself two of the tracers of liberal thought: belief in the sweet reasonableness of humankind; and belief in the certain improvement of humankind. Keynes has told of how he and his young friends at Cambridge at the turn of the century believed so passionately "in a continuing moral progress, by virtue of which the human race already consists of reliable, decent people, influenced by truth and objective standards," and Stephen Spender relates in his autobiography how he was taught at school of the

terrible things which had happened in the past: tortures, Court of the Star Chamber, Morton's Fork, Henry VIII's wives, the Stamp Tax, the Boston Tea Party, slavery, the Industrial Revolution, the French Revolution, Bismarck, the Boer War. Weighing in the scale of human happiness against these were the Reform Act, Wilberforce, Mr. Gladstone, Home Rule, Popular Education, the United States, Health Insurance, the League of Nations. If the history books were illustrated, they gave the impression that the world had been moving steadily forward in the past thousands of years, from the vague to the defined, the savage to the civilized, the crude to the scientific, the unfamiliar to the known. It was as though the nineteenth century had been a machine absorbing into itself at one end humanity dressed in fancy dress, unwashed, fierce and immoral, and emitting at the other modern men, in their hygienic houses, their zeal for reform, their air of having triumphed by mechanical, economic and scientific means over the passionate, superstitious, cruel, and poetic past.

For the future of international politics, such an outlook was heartening. Every day in every way international politics would get better and better. Its inequities stemmed from some mere malfunction of the system, not from some inherent defect or fatal flaw in human nature. In a speech to Congress on the eve of war in 1917, President Wilson forecast what the future surely held in store: "We are at the beginning of an age in which it will be insisted that the same standards of conduct and of responsibility for wrong shall be observed among nations and their governments that are observed among the individual citizens of civilized states." Only a liberal idealist could risk so reckless a prediction. Two decades later, nations and their governments stood silently by while Italian airman dropped mustard gas on Ethiopia, and Nazi troopers killed Jews on German streets. Much worse would follow.

The strain of liberal idealism accordingly has weakened in the West but elsewhere flows more strongly than ever. Leaders of newly independent states in Asia and in Africa do not accept realpolitik as real. Its characteristic deceptions, betrayals, cruelties, they construe not at all as characteristic but as a species of deformity. For the deformation of international society, they blame the shackles of colonialism. When these are cut away, the system will be transformed.

But what if the shackles are cut away and the system remains? What if nations are freed but keep on fighting? There is still no need to despair. Colonialism has given way to neocolonialism. Its shackles are less visible but no less deforming. And in time these, too, can be cut away. And then the day will dawn.

The second strain in the idealist tradition I will call Pharisean idealism. (Luke's Pharisee, one will remember, "prayed thus with himself: 'O God, I give thee thanks that I am not as the rest of man, extortioners, unjust, adulterers.'") Pharisean idealists, like liberal idealists, are optimistic. There are such things as right and wrong in foreign policy, for is not their foreign policy nearly always right?

Pharisean idealism in recent years has been practised most spectacularly by the United States government, and of all Americans, John Foster Dulles has the most celebrated reputation for Pharisean statements. But the Pharisean idealism of which his speeches are so perfect an epitome by no means ceased with his death. President Johnson's address in Baltimore in April of 1965 dealing with American policy in Vietnam provides an exquisite example:

For centuries nations have struggled among each other. But we dream of a world where disputes are settled by law and reason. And we will try to make it so.

For most of history men have hated and killed one another in battle. But we dream of an end to war. And we will try to make it so.

For all existence most men have lived in poverty ... But we dream of a world where all are fed and charged with hope. And we will help to make it so.

And a month later, explaining why he found it necessary to send troops into Santo Domingo, the president declared: "This is required of us by the values which bind us together." And he went on – or rather his speechwriter went on – to quote the great Bolivar: "'The veil has been torn asunder, we have already seen the light, and it is not our desire to be thrust back in darkness.'"

The Pharisee of whom Luke tells us may have been a hypocrite, and Pharisean idealism may be hypocritical. But it does not have to be, and in its American manifestations there is usually no hypocrisy at all. When Conor Cruise O'Brien writes that the face of Adlai Stevenson at the United Nations, "with its shiftily earnest advocate's expression," was "the ingratiating moral mask which a toughly acquisitive society wears before the world it robs," he gets it all wrong. The pious utterances that I have quoted are not at all a facade behind which a cluster of cynical manipulators go about their dirty business. Dirty business it may be, but it is not thought to be so, and it is characteristic of Pharisean idealism that it is thought not to be so. What caused the look of pain that from time to time crossed the features of Adlai Stevenson when defending the United States at the United Nations was not his hatred of hypocrisy; it was his distaste for the insensitivity of his political masters, whose voice he had allowed himself to become. When McGeorge Bundy remarks that "measured against the record of others ... the breakdown in the relation between what we do and what we believe seems less severe in the United States than in any other major nation," there is no reason to think him insincere. He really believes it. That may be the problem.

Between realism, on the one hand (whether brutal or skeptical), and idealism, on the other (whether liberal or Pharisean), lies no easy choice. We face not an embarrassment of riches, but an option of difficulties. Still, I would not be the good Canadian I like to think I am if I did not try to open up a middle way.

Let us call it practical idealism.

Practical idealists know the ways of statecraft well. They know its deceptions, its betrayals, its cruelties. They know how pitiless are its laws. They cannot hope to do away with it; they cannot accordingly share the outlook of the liberal idealist. They cannot hope to be exempt from it; they cannot accordingly share the outlook of the Pharisean idealist.

But practical idealists know just as well how much wrongdoing may be done by statesmen whose moral mandate is too permissive. They will on this account refuse to allow *raison d'etat* to be the statesman's guide. Statesmen are not to be trusted with so dangerous a doctrine. It leads straight to massacre and genocide, to total war with terrible weapons.

And so practical idealists, their idealism at once prompted and tempered by their realism, cling to a more stringent ethic in international life than may be warranted by the facts of international life. If international morality did not exist, they would find it necessary to invent it, for they know that if international morality did not exist, people might not exist.

Practical idealism may be found in the thought of Ernst Troeltsch, who, knowing full well how obvious are the philosophical difficulties of the concept of natural law, urged its acceptance in a last despairing effort to save Weimar democracy from fascism: "We cannot afford to neglect it ... While we recognize the obstacles which actually confront these moral postulates, we must nonetheless cling to them as our ideal. At the heart of all the current ideas about a League of Nations, the organization of the world, and the limitation of egoisms and forces of destruction, there is an indestructible moral core, which we cannot in its essence reject, even if we are painfully aware ... of the difficulties which it presents." Practical idealism may be found in Freud, to whom ethical systems are shock troops of the reinforcements called up by culture for battle against the aggressive instincts of humankind.

Imagine, then, a meeting of the Cabinet. A crucial foreign policy decision is to be made – whether or not to run the blockade of Berlin, send troops to Korea, send troops to Vietnam. Various divisions of labour take place. The prime minister worries about national unity. The finance minister is concerned about the cost. The defence minister is anxious about logistics. The secretary of state for external affairs frets about effects on friends and foes. But there is no secretary of state for conscience to speak up to ask two crucial questions: Is it good? Is it right?

Lacking a secretary of state for conscience in the organization of our government, we should, as practical idealists, insist that his or her function be performed by statesmen whose portfolios bear more prosaic titles. Otherwise we are in trouble.

"THE WAYS OF KEEPING FAITH"

"In every system of morality, which I have hitherto met with, I have always remark'd, that the author proceeds for some time in the ordinary way of reasoning ... when of a sudden I am surpriz'd to find, that instead of the usual copulations of propositions, *is* and *is not*, I meet with no proposition that is not connected with an *ought* or *ought not*. This change is imperceptible, but is, however, of the last importance." So David Hume complained two centuries ago. It is a fair complaint, and I am anxious not to invite the same reproach. Let me therefore announce that I am changing gears. Before, they were (more or less) in neutral; now, they are engaged. They are shifting from the *is* and *is not* to the *ought* and *ought not*. Thus far I have attempted to describe the ways of statecraft. In the following I am concerned with the ways of keeping faith. What ought we to expect of the moral individual caught in the coils of the iniquitous state system?

Part One

A critic of the policy of appeasement practised by the governments of the United Kingdom and the Dominions before the Second World War wrote of its practitioners: "One could not blame them, one could not admire them, one could not admire anybody." Why not blame them? Is it just because they did their best? Are statesmen to be excused their follies if they act in good faith? Are we to judge them for effort in a world that usually judges for result? What is so special about statesmen that when their plans miscarry and their statecraft goes awry, we are not to find them guilty?

A theological answer holds that statesmen, being instruments of God, are beyond reproach by lesser morals. Thus the professor of religion at Princeton University opens a discussion of the ethics of intervention – by which he means Suez, and the Bay of Pigs, and Santo Domingo, and Vietnam – by observing: "Religious communities need to stand in awe before people nowadays called political "decision-makers," or rather before the majesty of top-most political agency. Political decision and action is an image of the majesty of God."

A secular version of this doctrine requires not so much deference to the makers of policy as compassion for the makers of policy. It is not the divinity of their position but the poignancy of their position that entreats our indulgence. Those who ask this of us are usually those set in authority over us – naturally so, for they stand to profit by our forbearance, just as they stand to lose by our condemnation. And so they say to us, "Look, you do not know, you cannot know, how it is. You do not understand the agony of making decisions in an imperfect world. If you knew, if you were one of us, you would not judge so harshly." Or else they say, "Unless you have been one of us, you have no right to judge so harshly." They may even say, "Unless you have been one of us, you have no right to judge at all."

What are we to make of special pleading such as this? Is it simply self-pity? Is it, less simply, part of the defensive fortification by which statesmen seek to protect their niche in history? Or is it a genuine manifestation of the poignancy of power?

Much depends on circumstance, much depends on personality. Certainly, in reading those portions of Mackenzie King's diary where he compares his lot as prime minister of Canada to Christ's agony in Gethsemane, one's inclination (if not too offended by the blasphemy) is to recall Harry Truman's advice: "If you don't like the heat, get the hell out of the kitchen." But this is not really very helpful. Cooks are temperamental creatures; some of the best chefs give notice at the crucial stage of the preparation of a banquet. But a prime minister who quits in the middle of some grave international crisis just because he finds the awefulness of making decisions too heavy to be borne doesn't deserve our gratitude and doesn't get it either. But perhaps the advice is harsh as well as unhelpful. Power has its poignant aspects. Those who dispose of it can never do the perfect thing with it. Always the policy maker is robbing Peter to pay Paul, the poor to pay the veterans, the old to pay the young, the farm to pay the factory, the Maritimes to pay Ontario. (Or, of course, the other way around). Nor, it is said, can he do the generous thing with it. Behaviour admired in individuals – kindliness, compassion, benevolence – is not permitted to statesmen. An individual who gives everything to the poor, who lives his life by the Sermon on the Mount, may be as admired as he is hard to find. But statesmen who guide their statecraft by the Sermon on the Mount will bankrupt their country within a week, invite aggression within a month, accomplish the destruction of their country within a year.

If the profession of statecraft is unlike other professions, should we then not judge the statesman by more lenient standards? A physician whose patient dies through malpractice or neglect faces an inquest or a suit for damages; an engineer whose bridge collapses through faulty mathematics or through too much sand and too little cement faces a royal commission or a penitentiary sentence. But statesmen whose policies bring ruin to a nation do not even ask forgiveness. There is, they say, nothing to forgive.

Why this should be so I do not understand. No doubt the purely political leader cannot perform the purely perfect act. But there are no purely political leaders, just as there are no purely perfect acts. These exist as constructs and abstractions only; they are not found in this world. For analytical purposes we may separate the public figure and the private individual. But there is always a private individual in every public figure; and often he or she bursts through to tell the public figure what to do. Not even the most dedicated, the most ruthless, the most public-centred, the power-hungriest of statesmen can always keep their emotions from intruding upon, and giving final form to, their statecraft. Nor is it desirable that they should.

In 1946 the British government entered into negotiations with New Zealand. It needed food badly and had very little to pay for it. The minister involved has since recalled what happened:

I expected a bargaining session as difficult as any other. Instead, the leader of the New Zealand delegation opened the proceedings in words I shall never forget. "We have not come to ask you 'What can you give?' We have come to ask 'What do you need?' When you stood alone, you preserved our freedom for us. Now tell us what butter, what meat, what grains you need – and, whatever the sacrifice may be for the New Zealand people – we will supply it."

And they did. Some years later, the New Zealanders were the beneficiaries of magnanimity in statecraft. In 1962 the delegates to the Common Market discussed the probable effects of British entry upon New Zealand's economy. These were thought to be disastrous, but the foreign minister of France remained unmoved. "What obligations," asked M. Couve de Murville, "have we towards New Zealanders?" The foreign minister of Belgium answered, "The fact that twice in our lifetime their men have come over to be killed for freedom." M. Couve de Murville was unimpressed. "Why are we bound," he persisted, "to do anything for them?" "Because," M. Spaak replied, "because we are sitting around this table organizing their ruin."

For no good reason, then, theological or secular, are statesmen exempt from judgements. But how are they to be judged? What is the criterion of guilt?

Not, certainly, failure. The history of foreign policy is replete with failures, of which some are ignoble and others magnificent. Churchill's failure to prevent appeasement; Attlee's failure to prevent partition; Hammarskjold's failure to prevent war: These are magnificent failures. In each case the statesman concerned tried to do the right thing. He is not guilty just because he did not succeed.

Not the failure of their enterprises, but the pursuit of the wrong enterprises, ought to bring upon statesmen the wrath of others. And they pursue the wrong enterprises through asking the wrong questions. In the first part of this paper I spoke of the creed of the skeptical realist, of which I was critical, and of the creed of the practical idealist, of which I was not. The skeptical realist asks: "Will it work? Will it pass? Will it help?" To practical idealists, the last of these questions is of the first importance, and they ask it in an amended form: not just "Will it help?" but "Will it help to relieve human suffering, here and now?"

Statesmen who treat this question cynically, or to whom it seems irrelevant, or to whom it never occurs, have broken faith with the political community that is their trust. They do not deserve its admiration, and they should not escape its blame.

Part Two

Political obligation is for Machiavelli a problem for people at the pinnacle of power: He is concerned with the way princes keep faith. But what of people lower down? What of those who serve the prince and execute his commands? How may they keep faith?

"A diplomat is an honest man sent to lie abroad for his country." This weary pun, now more than three hundred years old, may not flatter the profession but conveys well enough its occupational hazard. It is striking how few of its members protest against the sort of things it requires them to do. This is not at all because what they are required to do is always clean and decent. Rather it is because the whole ethos of the profession is designed to quell the moral sensibilities of its members. It is as though foreign offices have built into their basements some sort of low temperature chamber where fledgling foreign service officers deposit their consciences on recruitment for redemption only on retirement. By then they are too deeply frozen to thaw out in time.

Satow's *Guide to Diplomatic Practice* tells how to write dispatches and warns against accepting bribes (though not against accepting gifts). But it offers no hints to junior diplomatists on how to go about expressing to their superiors their qualms about their country's policies. These are dangerous thoughts, which the seasoned diplomatist will long since have learned to suppress. For, as Satow cautions, "those in whose hands is placed the supreme direction of foreign relations are alone able to decide which should be the main object of state policy."

Diplomacy is not an art but a craft. Its practitioners take satisfaction not in creation but in workmanship, from their loving attention to detail. If the object of their labour turns out to be some hideous gargoyle, that is not their fault. They are executants of the designs of others. These may be squalid as well as grand.

The modern diplomatist is fortunate in having little time for brooding. If there were not so many cables to read and dispatches to draft and parties through which to whirl, he or she might go quickly to pieces. Even so the strain is great. Occasionally it shows.

The local equivalent of Satow's *Guide* is Cadieux's *The Canadian Diplomat*. This contribution to the literature by the present under secretary of state for external affairs alludes to "a certain tenseness, an uneasiness, which can be occasionally glimpsed beneath the unruffled exterior of the diplomat, whose profession consists in a curious blending of freedom and of restraint, of the changing and of the stable, of splendour and of simplicity, of crests and hollows, of coming and going." M. Cadieux is himself too much a diplomat to explain just what he is getting at in this mysterious passage, but what he really means is this: The diplomatist is a tragic figure. An artist compelled to be an artisan, a painter forbidden to paint, a poet who must spend his most creative hours grinding out the gibberish of state.

Not for a moment is any foreign service officer on this account entitled to our sympathy. "The tragedy of his position," Louis Halls has written, "is implicit only. Since the measure of tragedy is always the quality of the victim, the implicit tragedy is realized only to the extent that the diplomat represents intellectual and moral distinction. Most career diplomats, like most of us others, have no aim except to get on with their careers." But there are exceptions.

I spoke in the first part of this paper of Adlai Stevenson. As a politician his career is among the select company of magnificent failures. As a diplomatist it was a tragedy. "For six weeks I had to sit there in the United Nations," Adlai Stevenson told a friend soon before his death," and defend the policy of my country in Santo Domingo although it was a massive blunder from beginning to end … Those six weeks took several years off my life."

My other exception is a Canadian. In 1938 Loring Christie was the second ranking member of the Department of External Affairs. Like one or two others who have climbed to the top of that greasy pole, he was a man of profound and even passionate sensibility, which he went to great lengths to conceal. What happened at Munich was too much for him to bear in silence, and he poured out his feelings in a letter to a friend:

I have been reflecting on what I have to do to earn my keep. I am a member of one of these sovereign creatures – Canada. I am paid by the other members, the people of Canada, to help manage and express their creature in its relations with the others. The ultimate test on my desk is: "Will this 'save' the people of Canada? Will it advantage them?" The chain of responsibility allows no escape from this.

I am not at the moment recoiling from having to mess around in the filthy mug's game which is called "diplomacy" and "international relations." I am simply illustrating ... I have seen the inside of this creature; I have had to concoct and even mouth his gibberish; I *know* how lost these monsters are ... I do not yet know what the job of being one of their servants will eventually do to me.

Those who serve the state as warriors are largely spared these emotional stresses and strains. They are protected by their training and their ethic, which, more than in any other profession, cultivate the ideal of unquestioning obedience to higher command. They are protected as well by the nature of their mission. Diplomatists may well experience malaise when required to execute policies that seem to them likely to result in war, for the onset of war is to them a signification of their failure. But to the military the onset of war signifies opportunity, not failure. It enables the military to serve the state in the traditional way. The motto of the Strategic Air Command notwithstanding, war is its profession.

Even so, the military servant of the state is not wholly free of ethical dilemmas. The most disciplined warrior may confront the issue of conscientious objection.

It does not happen often. After all, soldiers are trained to kill. They are professionals at cruelty. They do not balk at bloodshed. To be sure there are exceptions. General de la Bollardiere resigned his command in Algeria because, as he said, he was a paratrooper, not a Gestapo torturer. But such individuals are rare. The bombers of Hiroshima and Nagasaki (leaving aside the curious case of Major Eatherley) seem marvellously untroubled. The airmen who daily scourge the villages of Vietnam have ready replies to those who exhibit concern on their behalf: This, they say, is war; and war, they say, is hell. There is a story that at the time of Suez, when the Soviet Union threatened the United Kingdom with nuclear bombardment if the Egyptian operation was not abandoned, President Eisenhower called his strategic air commander to order an attack alert. "Very good, Sir," came the instant reply, "Which side?" General LeMay was a real professional.

The amateur warrior, unused to the cruelties of war, is less able to rise to such heights – or to sink to such depths. And since much military power is today provided by amateur warriors — civilian soldiers conscripted by the state – their situation is worth attention.

Civilized society makes provision for conscientious objection. That might be more strongly put. Civilized society demands conscientious objection. It holds that when citizens find they have to disobey the state in order to obey their conscience, they are better citizens for obeying their conscience.

When conscientious objection becomes a virtue, so that the conscientious objector is in a sense the ideal citizen, it is because society holds as valid two basic assumptions: first, that the defection of a small number of conscientious objectors will not imperil the safety of the state; second, that the society, being civilized, will not act in such a way as to provoke conscientious objection on a large scale.

Neither of these assumptions can today be held with much assurance. The behaviour of states in the modern state system, characterized by deceit, by treachery, by cruelty, is precisely of a kind to provoke large-scale protest among any morally sensitive citizenry. And small-scale defection may have the gravest consequences. When a nuclear physicist goes over to the enemy, taking his secrets with him, the entire balance of power may be changed. When civilian soldiers refuse to embark for a theatre of war because the war to them seems evil, their refusal may touch the national nerve, causing it to fail; or touch the national conscience, causing it to stir.

Part Three

That publics are more morally fastidious than statesmen about foreign policy was the confident belief of those liberal idealists who survived the First World War. "Throughout this instrument," said Woodrow Wilson of the League of Nations, "we are dependent primarily and chiefly upon one great force, and that is the moral force of the public opinion of the world – the cleansing and clarifying and compelling influences of publicity." And Lord Robert Cecil: "The great weapon we rely on is public opinion ... and if we are wrong about that, then the whole thing is wrong."

It turned out they were wrong about that. Public opinion between two world wars was not cleansing; it was not clarifying; and if it compelled at all, it compelled as often as not in the wrong direction. Expected to exert a constructive influence upon the conduct of foreign policy, public opinion proved instead to be fitful and gullible, fickle and craven. When the need was to rearm, the public clamoured for disarmament. When the need was for belligerence, the public was pacifist. When the need was for defying the dictators, the public was for appeasing dictators.

Has it done much better since? This, I suppose, is a matter of opinion; my own is that it has not done much better since. There is as much gullibility about as ever, and there is something else: We seem to have developed an addiction to violence, a morbid fascination with crisis. Albert Camus has noted the reaction of people during the Hungarian Revolution: They spared "neither applause nor virtuous tears before returning to their slippers like football enthusiasts after a big game." The week must be crammed with catastrophe, so that at its close the hour may have seven days.

A new form of public protest has recently appeared among us. It operates in a twilight zone between violence and nonviolence. Its techniques are varied, sometimes very daring. The protestants paddle tiny boats where great powers prove their nuclear prowess. They cling to the hulls of atomic submarines. They march on missile bases and lie on tracks in front of troop trains. They withhold taxes. They burn draft cards. Norman Morrison has burned himself.

Of their effectiveness it may be too soon to speak. Their ranks, we know, are few. They consist of knaves, and fools, and heroes – in what proportion who can tell? They may give aid and comfort to the enemy. They may give the president sleepless nights. But will they change his mind?

Hey, Hey, LBJ!
How many kids did you kill today?

If this cruel rhyme is representative of their attitude, one would think not. They may mortify; they will not convert.

Nor will they reach, save as irritating noises off, the ears of the people in the street. They have neither taste nor temperament nor time for such shenanigans; they are preoccupied with second cars and second mortgages. They are likely to look upon the Protestants for Peace as shrill and sour and cranky, outside the mainstream of national life, offering nothing of relevance to the making up of their own minds.

Foreign policy, in societies like ours, is meant to be an expression of the contents of these minds: biased, addled, empty as they may variously be. Only when they are straightened out will foreign policy straighten out. But can we wait so long?

Part Four

If, as I have argued, neither the public service nor the public at large is specially equipped, and therefore specially obligated, to confront statesmen with their wrongdoing, can no one do the job? Some one can. The intellectual.

There may still be Canadians who smile or snigger at this suggestion. I suppose them to be in the same condition of arrested development as Canadians forty years ago who thought a professor was "a man who plays the piano in a house of meretricious entertainment." It is my conviction that the intellectual is uniquely a custodian of the national conscience. Thus I am more interested in discussing the difficulties the intellectual faces in carrying out this assignment than in an argument over whether or not it is properly his to carry out.

There are as many ways of defining intellectuals as there are intellectuals to define themselves. I like the definition Camus once jotted down in his notebook: "An intellectual is someone whose mind watches itself." An intellectual breaks faith when he allows his mind to give up the watch, to go off duty.

No kind of intellectual has more spectacularly broken faith than the scientific intellectual. The scientist has lugged Pandora's box into his laboratory and left the lid open for years on end. Only a fiend could knowingly do this; and it is fitting that the arch-fiend in one of Hochhuth's dramas is not a Nazi politician, not a storm trooper, not even Eichmann, but a doctor: "Brain tissue, from a pair of Jewish twins, two kids from Calais, preserved in formaldehyde. Rather interesting comparative sections. I brought the specimen with me for a girl who's taking a first course in histology." In the presence of such a monster, we are in the presence not of sin, but of absolute evil. It knows no guilt; it knows no shame.

But there is another kind of scientist who knows both guilt and shame. Typically he invents and produces weapons of mass destruction. Typically he is a physicist, a nuclear physicist.

It is not his intention to do wrong, and, at the beginning, he was not conscious of doing wrong. One is struck by the gusto, the enthusiasm, the almost school-boy exuberance, of the scientists of the Manhattan Project, working to perfect a product to kill 100,000 people. Only the deed itself shocked them into recognition. Then guilt fell on them like radioactive rain. Many of those who had cheerfully worked on the atomic bomb shrank from work on the hydrogen bomb. A majority on a scientific committee advised the president not to make the hydrogen bomb: Such restraint, they argued, might help to end the arms race. A minority flatly proclaimed that "this weapon is an evil thing ... We think it is wrong on fundamental ethical grounds to initiate development of such a weapon." But their protest was ignored. The work went forward. Thermonuclear weapons were designed, built, tested, mass-produced.

It could not have been done without scientists to do it. Enough came forward, their moral burden lightened by a minute division of labour. "Men work on gyromechanisms, on micro-miniaturized electronics, on plasma physics. It is easy to forget the monstrous machines of destruction to which their work is a contribution." Fragmentation is the mother of amnesia.

But in the subconscious, guilt remains, never to be driven out. "In some sort of crude sense which no vulgarity, no humour, no overstatement can quite extinguish," one of their number has written out of the depths of his torment, "the physicists have known sin; and this is a knowledge which they cannot lose." No wonder the dramatists have had a field day with physicists: Brecht, and Durrenmatt, and now a play based on the transcript of the proceedings in the case of J. Robert Oppenheimer, than which no stage drama could be more bizarre or poignant.

First cousins to the scientific intellectuals, often coming from their ranks, are the defence intellectuals – that group of scholar-strategist-consultants (not necessarily in that order) who, it has been said, prowl the corridors of the Pentagon like Jesuits moved through the Courts of Vienna and Madrid three centuries ago. Their profession is to think about the unthinkable – about the circumstances in which nuclear wars might be fought, about the consequences of nuclear wars being fought. It is not a pretty subject; it is not a pleasant profession. But can it fairly be charged with lacking moral scruple just for thinking of such things? Herman Kahn's lectures on thermonuclear war were treated as Hitler's *Mein Kampf* ought to have been treated (but, alas, was not). An "evil and tenebrous book," someone called it, "a tract on mass murder: how to plan it, how to commit it, how to get away with it, how to justify it." I add at once that no reading of the book undertaken with any intellectual discrimination could possibly sustain so perverse an interpretation of its thesis and its purpose.

All the same, preoccupation with the problems of nuclear war, while not itself morally reprehensible, tends to make those so preoccupied somewhat deficient in moral sensitivity. All too easily, all too frequently, they succumb to the sickness of brutal realism in its most sadistic and disagreeable form. Consider the sort of scenario on which the members of the Hudson Institute are wont to sharpen their wits: "The military balance of power has changed and US forces become so vulnerable that after a Soviet first strike at US forces the US no longer has a devastating second strike capability. At that point the Soviets warn that for every Soviet city we destroy, they will demolish five of its American counterparts. The ultimatum concludes: "You know better than we do what kind of country you want to have when the war is over. Pick whatever major cities you wish to be destroyed and we will destroy them." The exercise consists in figuring out what Washington does next. The game is called "Urban Renewal."

I recognize, of course, the need to allow the intellect the freest possible play and the widest possible latitude. But surely its prolonged attention to these sorts of problems is not very good for the human spirit. It may not be so very good for the human race either.

But what of the rank-and-file, run-of-the-mill intelligentsia – those who work well within the outer limits of science and strategy? Their moral dilemmas are less spectacular – but no less troublesome.

One temptation is to enter the service of the state. It is a temptation to be resisted.

I do not intend to demean in any way the public service or to diminish the importance of what it does. I am told that the life of the civil servant is deeply satisfying. Dean Acheson testifies that "to everyone who has ever experienced it the return from public life to private life leaves one feeling flat and empty." It may well be so. I take his word for it.

But the public service is no place for the intellectual. The intellectual cannot do it justice. The environment is alien. Particularly the environment in which foreign policy is made.

Intellectuals, displaced from their proper preoccupations to advise governments on foreign policy, tend characteristically to under- or overreact. They underreact if, as is likely, they are unduly deferential in the presence of power. Arthur Schlesinger tells in his memoirs of the Kennedy presidency of his failure to protest against the Bay of Pigs operation despite a strong premonition of disaster: "One's impulse to blow the whistle on this nonsense was simply undone by the circumstances of the occasion. It is one thing, for a special assistant like myself, to talk frankly in private to a president; and another for a college professor, fresh to government, to interpose his unassisted judgment in open meeting against such august figures as the Secretaries of State and Defense and the Joint Chiefs of Staff."

Or else, and just as likely, the intellectual is unduly scornful of events and circumstances, ignoring or belittling their capacity to frustrate his or her favourite project. "As he could mould the printed word to suit his ideas," Hans Morgenthau points out, "so he now expects the real world to respond to his actions. Hence his confidence in himself, his pride, his optimism" – his or her overreaction. Hence also his or her almost invariable record of failure. The history of recent international relations is strewn with the litter of the schemes of intellectuals-turned-policy-makers or of intellectuals-turned-policy-advisors, schemes contrived in haste, put forward in conceit, and abandoned, as soon as was decently possible, by the professionals in government who know from hard experience what policy making is all about.

But intellectuals as policy makers not only make a mess of policy; they largely destroy themselves as intellectuals. "It is only knowledge freely acquired that is disinterested," Walter Lippmann wisely remarked many years ago. "When those whose profession it is to teach and to investigate become the makers of policy, become politicians and leaders of causes, they are committed. Nothing they say can be relied on as disinterested. Nothing they teach can be trusted as scientific." It is a harsh verdict, but fair.

So if intellectuals are to remain useful critics of foreign policy, retaining their capacity for detached analysis and informed condemnation, they must stay out of government.

They must also stay out of the consulting business. A mind whose function it is to keep watch on itself cannot function properly when rented out to special pleaders. The practice is too common for comfort, too common for comment. A conspiracy of silence muffles the activities of what one authority has described as "a new kind of condottieri, mercenaries of silence and scholarship hooded with doctorates and ready for hire on studies to contract specification." Intellectuals should keep their distance from those who want to buy their thoughts. Keeping their distance will help them to keep their principles, and in keeping their principles, they keep faith.

If intellectuals experience the crudest kind of degradation when they deliver their minds to someone else's payroll or to someone else's charge, they are exposed to degradation at its deadliest when they are self-employed. Then it is that they may allow their capacity for moral protest to serve themselves more than community.

An article lavish in its praise for the first of the American teach-ins describes its origins in "an idea which permitted the concerned professional to envision himself as the conqueror, not of governments, but rather of his own sense of impotence." Motives are always mixed, and it is foolish to expect simon-purity. But when the motive of protest becomes primarily therapeutic, it places in jeopardy that sense of moral discrimination that it is the first duty of intellectuals to develop. They develop instead a craving for protest. The time comes when any cause will do. Unscrupulous parties flourish the appropriate symbols and imagery before them, sure of their response. Moral protest becomes moral pot. Such intellectuals, hooked by the needs of their addiction, no longer are able, no longer care, to distinguish right from wrong. Here is the ultimate in *trahison des clercs*.

Confronted in the first part of this paper with a dilemma of my own devising, I sought escape through the device, so typically Canadian, of the middle way. This time there is no such exit.

Before the intellectual are two lifestyles and two alone. One is the lifestyle of detachment. The other the lifestyle of commitment. One has to choose.

My late teacher, Harold Innis, knowing better than anyone how heavily mined and menaced are the slopes of commitment leading away from the ivory tower, begged the intellectual to remain within its precincts.

I used to think this good advice. Now I think otherwise. It is the intellect of commitment that, in spite of all my cautionary tales, I must finally recommend. Not just because it is in short supply – although in Canada, God knows, it is in short supply. But rather because it alone enables the intellectual to do his or her job. A detached mind may keep watch upon itself, but it watches over wasteland. Only a mind ethically anaesthetized, morally lobotomized, remains detached from what statesmen are doing to our world.

JAMES G. EAYRS is Professor Emeritus in the Department of Political Science at Dalhousie University. He taught at the University of Toronto before moving to Dalhousie as the Eric Dennis Memorial Professor of Political Science and Government. He also served as editor of the *International Journal* of the Canadian Institute of International Affairs from 1959 to 1984. James Eayrs is one of the pioneers in the study of twentieth-century Canadian foreign and defence policy, and his influential scholarly works include *The Art of the Possible: Government and Foreign Policy in Canada*, published in 1961, and the five-volume series, *In Defence of Canada: From the Great War to the Great Depression*, published between 1964 and 1983. He is also known for his many popular articles on Canadian and international affairs.

Dr Eayrs is an Officer of the Order of Canada and received the Canada Council for the Arts Molson Prize in 1984 for his work as a teacher, scholar, and writer.

7

On University Freedom
in the Canadian Context

KENNETH HARE, 1967

PART ONE

Introduction

What should be the relations between the provincial government and the universities? This problem is quite universal in the English-speaking world. University expansion is in progress everywhere, and so are the problems that it brings. One cannot hope to avoid the issue, in fact: In Ontario the provincial exchequer now meets over half the operating costs of universities and a higher proportion of the capital costs. The proportion in Britain is even higher, and it is worth reciting the facts because Ontario is heading in the same direction. Of the total British income for university education of $372 million in 1964–65 (spread over 174,434 students, or about $2,400 each), funds came from the following sources:

Endowments	1.9 per cent
Donations, etc.	0.6 per cent
Exchequer grants	71.7 per cent
Local authority grants	1.4 per cent
Tuition fees	8.1 per cent
Research grants, etc.	11.4 per cent

If one bears in mind that most of the tuition fees, research grants, and other income also come from public funds, the British dependence on the taxpayer is very evident.[1] It does not follow in a civilized state that he who pays the piper calls the tune, but it is still usually so. In Ontario the creation of eight new chartered universities since 1959, and the expansion of the rest, is a guarantee that a new relation with the provincial government must be worked out. Not only is this venture an extraordinary leap forward, an act of faith in the university world by the public at large; it is also a dive into deep financial waters for the provincial treasurer. Not only is university education getting more widespread; it is getting much more expensive. Particularly is this true of research and graduate studies. The Spinks Commission reckoned that there will be 23,000 graduate students in the Ontario universities by 1975–76, a more than threefold increase.[2]

Diagnosis: Threat from Within?

Academic freedom is part of the general freedom of liberal democratic societies, but it is also something special. A case has to be made for it even in the most enlightened countries. There is nothing self-evident about the right to teach whom, what, when, and how one wants. The proof that academic freedom is a desirable end is empirical. The best universities – those that pursue and disseminate learning most effectively – seem to be those that govern themselves. It is true that one can justify such freedom on other grounds. A democratic society must try to limit governmental regulation and control; the more its institutions are free and independent, the more effective is democracy itself, and the more true freedom remains to its citizens. A state that cherishes such free institutions will usually put the universities high among them, for universities are, or ought to be, not only the home of knowledge and wisdom, but also the intellectual conscience of the nation. Nevertheless, the practical case for freedom is that free universities are better than servile universities, and hence they serve the public interest.

Those, like Robbins and Ashby, who make this claim point to the unfree for their evidence, for we know what unfreedom is. In Robbins's words, "an academic institution is unfree if its members are forced to confine their teaching to modes and creeds in which they do not believe, if appointment depends, not on excellence of qualification and performance but on membership of a political

---

1 University Grants Committee, Returns from Universities and University Colleges in Receipt of Exchequer Grant, Academic Year 1964–65, London, H.M.S.O., Cmnd. 3106, 1966, Table 11.

2 J.W.Y. Spinks, chairman, Commission to Study the Development of Graduate Programmes in Ontario Universities, *Final Report,* Toronto, Department of University Affairs, 1966, Table 4.

party or of a church, and if the search for truth and values is subordinated to the exigencies of particular ideologies."[3] And of course we see this unfreedom about us in many places: in Nazi Germany yesterday; in the Soviet Union, Spain, and South Africa today. We recognize it closer to home in those few institutions that still apply a religious test at their gates. It has had its victims in Ontario, though miraculously the clouds have rolled away in the last few years. In such unfree environments greatness may still be achieved but in a narrow intellectual frame dictated by the state or church. Technical competence may be achieved, too, as in the Marxian universities. But I don't doubt that the free universities of the West, and especially of the English-speaking countries, are immensely stronger. Let me quote, not for the last time, some words of Eric Ashby delivered before an audience in the beleaguered University of the Witwatersrand: "To forbid the student to learn where and what he will, or the teacher to teach whom and how he will, is to put a curb on the hazardous adventure of thinking, and a nation where thinking is rationed simply cannot survive in today's world."[4] I'm forced to ask: Is this really true? The Soviet Union and South Africa have had a good run for their money while denying it; and General Franco seems quite unimpressed. But, true or false, it remains our liberal creed. We assume it here, and await the further proofs that we hope will appear. Academic freedom has two aspects, related but distinct. There is the freedom claimed by the individual scholar. And there is the autonomy of the university to which he or she belongs. I am tempted to say that the fight for individual freedom is about won in Canada, as it has long been in Britain. In the Ashby dictum I have just cited, one may recognize the Germanic twins of *lehrfreiheit* and *lernfreiheit*. We have been jealous of the teacher's *lehrfreiheit* – his right to teach as he wants – and have almost achieved it in the English-speaking world. The *lernfreiheit* of the student is not as healthy: We dragoon our young in all our middle-aged confidence that we know what is good for them. But at least we let them pick their own universities and main subjects; and there is far more *lernfreiheit* about Canadian degrees, with their high elective content, than there is about the martial discipline of a British honours school. Leaving aside this question of the student's rights, then – though I shall return to it – we can agree that in most places the freedom of the scholar from his or her university "administration," from society beyond the gates, and from the interference of the state, has been largely won.

---

3 Lord Robbins, *Of Academic Freedom* (London: Oxford University Press, for British Academy, 1966), 16.

4 Sir Eric Ashby, *Universities Under Siege* (Johannesburg: University of the Witwatersrand, 1962), 19.

But I am not so sure about the second aspect, that of the freedom of universities as institutions – their so-called autonomy. And herein lies the reason for these lectures. If autonomy is a good thing, we must try to preserve it. Doing so will depend on waking up to the dangers that face not only Ontario, but the whole of the English-speaking world, not least Britain. I shall argue later that these dangers – I will call them threats – are as much internal as external, as much due to our own unpreparedness as to any dragons in Queen's Park, Whitehall, or on Capitol Hill. In spite of incessant warnings, I believe that the university community, here and overseas, does not yet see this threat clearly. In Canada the professor's main concern has been with his own freedom and with his rights inside his institution: The enemy has been the governor or trustee, not the state. When I was myself the president of a branch of the Canadian Association of University Teachers eleven years ago, the internal government of universities was our main worry – together with our anxiety to increase federal financial support. And I'm sure that the average governor, nettled by this attitude, and habituated to the authoritarian atmosphere of upper management in Canadian industry, would probably have called the professor the university's chief liability. The representative document of this period was Willson Woodside's book *The University Question*,[5] significantly subtitled *Who Should Go? Who Should Pay?* It dealt with money, with what the universities ought to teach, with the level of student intake, with where to get professors, with relations with industry. The decision makers, in Woodside's eyes, were the governors and presidents; professors still emerged as employees. And he was right, as a good journalist usually is. In his book he did not suggest that university freedom was anything to lose any sleep over. These attitudes have coloured Canadian thinking to the present time, and the issues are not yet dead.

The great documents of the past two years have been the Duff-Berdahl report on internal university government[6] and the Bladen commission report on university finance.[7] The Duff-Berdahl report is a statement of the liberal position on internal government and of the extent to which Canadian practice falls short of it. The tenth chapter deals with the relations between universities and provincial

5 Willson Woodside, *The University Question: Who Should Go? Who Should Pay?* (Toronto: Ryerson Press, 1958).
6 Sir James Duff and R.O. Berdahl, *University Government in Canada*, report of a commission sponsored by the Canadian Association of University Teachers and the Association of the Universities and Colleges of Canada (Toronto: University of Toronto Press, 1966).
7 Vincent W. Bladen, chairman, *Financing Higher Education in Canada*, report of a commission established by the Association of Universities and Colleges of Canada (Toronto University Press and les Presses de l'Université Laval, Quebec, 1965).

governments, but this is secondary to the authors' real purpose, which is to accelerate the reform of internal government. Considering its joint sponsorship, we can think of the report as the culmination of the long struggle of the academic community to run its own internal affairs in order to ensure that academic policy flows upward from the faculty meeting, and not downward from the board room. Reforms along Duff-Berdahl lines have already penetrated the better Canadian universities, and where they have the change has produced much goodwill: The president tends to be as much the faculty's man or woman as the governors', and the suspicion between professor and governor is dwindling. May I repeat: This issue is not dead. There are Canadian universities that will have to be dragged, kicking and screaming, into Confederation's second century. Nevertheless, I am sure that the battle is nearly won and that the dinosaurs will soon be seeking their last bed of pitch.

The Bladen report, another crucial document, is the culmination of the other main issue of the decade: enough money. To quote Cyril James in the foreword to Woodside's book: "But if the people of Canada fail to provide *at once* [James was writing in 1957] the additional financial resources that are needed to enlarge teaching staffs and to construct additional buildings, the price of this expansion in student enrollment will be the standardization of university education in this country at a more mediocre level."[8] Conscious of the spanking new campuses in Ontario, one will agree that the people of Canada seem to have risen to James's challenge. When I revisit McGill these days I reflect that the mainly French Canadian provincial government, until very recently, seems to have treated my old academic home more generously than the British state does the University of London. Looking in from outside, I find the changed situation in Canada remarkable, and can only praise the response to the need. Bladen's commission made it clear that great efforts will be still needed to maintain progress; the next decade will be very difficult. But here again I feel the main battle has been won: The public admits that it has really got to pay for higher education. The argument is about how much and by what means.

I come now to my central point. "How much" is a figure so large that university expenditures are becoming one of the biggest items in the country's provincial budgets. In Saskatchewan (whose 1966–67 provincial budget for all purposes is smaller than that of the university of California) the university system gets nearly 10 per cent of the public kitty. The ratio is lower in the large provinces, but it is still high. Bladen's estimates for the next decade make stark reading:

---

8 F. Cyril James, "Foreword," in Willson Woodside, *The University Question: Who Should Go? Who Should Pay?* (Toronto: Ryerson Press, 1958), vii.

Estimated and projected total public expenditure
on universities and student aid[9]
(millions of 1965 dollars)

1964–65 (estimate)	1970–71 (projected)	1977–76 (projected)
355	1,112	1,704

Thus in eleven years the cost to the federal and provincial governments of the national university system is expected to rise five-fold. How in the face of this can we hope to ensure that the academic community retains its institutional autonomy? Can Canadian politicians, or indeed politicians anywhere, face expenditures on this scale without claiming detailed control over its use?

Obviously this is not simply an Ontario problem. In Canada it is nationwide; every province is seeking, ought to seek, or has sought, a proper solution for it. Outside Canada it is literally Western worldwide, and it must exist even in the Communist bloc in altered form. But in few places does the problem present itself as acutely as in Ontario, for in few places has anyone had the will and the resources to expand universities so rapidly and on so large a scale. Mr Davis stressed this point in presenting the 1966–67 estimates of his University Affairs Department to the Ontario legislature.[10] He compared the province's record in capital projects with the much smaller current capital efforts in Michigan and Ohio. He might well have included the United Kingdom, no laggard when it comes to university affairs. He added that the contribution to total operating revenues coming from Queens Park has risen from $23.3 million in 1961–62 to $31.2 million in 1966–67 – corresponding to 35 per cent and 54 per cent of total revenues. Together with federal aid, this raises the total public contribution to the operating revenues of Ontario universities to $121 million, which, however, is no more than Harvard's annual budget!

There is, of course, one very simple and quite wrong solution. Universities can be absorbed by the state and run as part of the national bureaucracy. One can even develop healthy *lehrfreiheit* within such a nonautonomous or servile system. This is true of France, where the old independent universities vanished with the *ancien regime*, to be replaced by a Napoleonic structure completely

---

9 Vincent W. Bladen, chairman, *Financing Higher Education in Canada*, report of a commission established by the Association of Universities and Colleges of Canada (Toronto University Press and les Presses de l'Université Laval, Quebec, 1965), Table 11, 36.

10 William G. Davis, Minister of University Affairs, Statement before the Fourth Session of the Twenty-Seventh Ontario Legislature, Toronto, 16 June 1966.

centralized in administrative matters. The Gallic *esprit* refuses to be intimidated, and in few places will one hear more pungent criticism of a centralized system. But the criticism goes unheard, as it washes over the monumentally thick skins of the Parisian bureaucrats. To quote the caustic rector of the University of Dijon, Dr M. Bouchard:

Even if the Director-General [of higher education] is a Rector, a Dean or a University professor, the departmental heads and officials at all levels who prepare decisions and transmit instructions are administrators – each dealing only with those questions for which he is particularly responsible. Between them they play the part of a Providence which examines everything, knows everything, prepares everything, arranges everything, whose intervention is a[s] necessary for fixing a lecture hour or a new discipline as it is for equipping a laboratory, and which[subscript]. decides when the golden rain of subventions shall fall. In the corridors of the Ministry, one can watch the mendicant Rectors, Deans and professors journeying from office to office much as in Rome one sees the pilgrims moving from church to church in search of indulgences.[11]

If, as I hear rumoured, there are Quebec intellectuals who wish to see the Napoleonic writ run in their universities, I hope they will ponder this *cri du cœur*. Nor do the German universities enjoy their similar bondage. Lord Robbins tells the story of the director of education in one of the West German *Länder* who boasted that a rector couldn't switch the tiniest item of expenditure from one budgetary line to another without his office's permission. Robbins asked him if this ever caused resentment, whereupon he replied, "Never!" But Robbins heard a muttered comment from behind the hand of a nearby young academic: "Because we are a set of sheep."[12]

The English-speaking countries have for the most part tried out a quite different device: the buffer committee. This is a respected body of intermediaries trusted (in principle) by both academics and politicians. They have the job of assessing need, persuading the politicians to part with the money, and then distributing that money to the universities. There are two main species of this genus, both long-established. The British favour committees, which they name and discuss in a subfusc sort of way, and characteristically they depend on convention rather than on carefully formulated law. Many Americans prefer the concept of a board of regents, and one hears the trumpets sounding in Valhalla

---

11 M. Bouchard, "France," in *University Autonomy: Its Meaning Today* (Paris: Papers 7, International Association of Universities, 1965), 59–60.
12 Lord Robbins, *Of Academic Freedom* (London: Oxford University Press, for British Academy, 1966), 11.

as their roll is read. But the ideas, though different on the surface, are similar in principle and often in execution. Not all jurisdictions employ the device of the buffer committee, but the idea is spreading as its merits become apparent. Ontario has such a committee, though it lacks a properly defined role. Quebec may soon have one, but I confess I can no longer even guess what the province intends unless it be further delay.

To make the buffer committee system work you have to pick the right committee, and you have to persuade universities and politicians alike to let it do the job. Exactly how you do this will depend on the jurisdiction you are in: There are no eternal verities in this down to earth business. You have to pick a formula that fits the local power-structure. And this varies very surprisingly from country to country. Later in these lectures I shall look at one or two successful patterns. But before I do so, I must look at the consequences to the university community of any system of massive public subsidy. Most of these consequences follow in any type of arrangement short of the fully state-centralized plan of Napoleon. To make the buffer system work, those in the universities have to accept certain restrictions on their freedom – *and to impose these upon themselves*.

The first is that they have got to admit, grudgingly or not, that the universities in a modern country form a system. Universities are not isolated individuals able to go their own way without reference to their neighbours. They together constitute a single system meeting a single public need. In Britain we are very much accustomed to this idea. Our system – the word recurs – of centralized admissions, for example, now universal for full-time undergraduates, enables students to pick their universities anywhere in the country, and their local authority grants do the same. They are under no obligation to go to their local campuses, and in general they try to avoid doing so. Hence all our universities are fully national in constituency. From this decision follows certain consequences. We have to spend much money on providing residences and on organizing lodgings bureaus. The policy raised the proportion of students in university residences from 28 to 32 per cent between 1953–54 and 1964–65, and in lodgings from 41 to 50 per cent. The proportion of students living in their own homes fell from 31 to 18 per cent in the same period.[13] We have thus followed nationally a most expensive policy, based on the assumption that it is better for the students to go away from home than to commute from that home to a local university. It may be that this policy was wrong and that the huge capital and operating sums necessary to

---

13 University Grants Committee, Returns from Universities and University Colleges in Receipt of Exchequer Grant, Academic Year 1964–65, London, HMSO, Cmnd. 3106, 1966, 1.

work it would have been better spent on laboratories, offices, or classrooms. The point is, however, that it is a policy, executed with the aid of the University Grants Committee, bearing on all universities alike and arising from concerted action by those universities acting as a rather reluctant system.

It is well known that the academic tradition is highly individualistic; I recall a picture, I think in the *New Yorker*, of the UN headquarters in New York with all the flags of the nations flying one way, except for one lonely flag pointing the other way. It was the flag of the Soviet Union, but it might well have been that of academe. Academics resist uniformity, change, external control, organization. They are not organization men and women but cave dwellers. And they are by nature competitive as societies, even tribal in characteristics. The mere thought that common action by their tribes in confederacy, like the Iroquois, might strengthen their hand, leaves them disdainful. Many will publicly deny this but mentally admit it. In London as head of one college I keep a friendly but very watchful eye on my colleagues in the other colleges. This is the natural atmosphere of the profession – for student and teacher alike. To remember that they are colleagues in the same system with their competitors is not easy. The threat from within to which my title refers is in fact this individualism, this unwillingness to organize.

But to organize is now necessary, at least under conditions of central financing. If one spends public money, one must spend it responsibly. And that means eliminating wasteful competition or duplication of facilities, judging demand, assessing social needs, and seeing well into the future. All these require system-wide consideration and action. That the bulk of their income is from a single public purse gives academics no choice.

Of course this restriction on liberty of local decision, this need to coordinate, does not arise so forcefully if public money is not involved. Waterloo Lutheran breathes a fresher air than Carleton. The rich private universities can afford to be individualists. Harvard, Yale, and Princeton can do this; so can a few others. Significantly, however, their actions show many signs of wishing to complement, and not to duplicate, the state university programs. This arises partly from distaste for state university methods, but largely from the trustee's convictions, reinforced by the professorate, that wealth does not exempt you from public discipline and responsibility. In Britain, Oxford and Cambridge long ago became part of the national system. They have retained, because others have been willing to concede, much of their uniqueness, and they remain to some extent places apart. But they are national universities, dependent like the rest on public moneys and responding like the rest as best they can to common public purposes.

Here in Canada the universities are only part way toward thinking of themselves as a system, or systems (if someone asserts that the francophone universities are separate). They were, for a long time, members or associates of the National Conference of Canadian Universities and Colleges, and since federal aid became a reality, of its executive arm, the Canadian Universities Foundation – both succeeded since 1 August 1965 by the Association of Universities and Colleges of Canada. Meeting together nationally like the learned societies, the senior members of the Canadian universities have long mastered the art of joint consultation and, let me add, of joint dissipation. Out of this habit has come a well-organized federal lobby – amazingly successful by non-Canadian standards – and a mechanism for distributing federal aid. But these bodies, valuable and praiseworthy though they are, do not and cannot coordinate the Canadian university systems because the universities must constitutionally deal with the provinces in which they find themselves.

Hence, under the pressure of financial need, the eyes of all presidents have had to turn toward their provincial capitals, and a new problem – new for some of the provinces, at any rate – arises: how to cope with the provincial government when the latter begin to dominate sources of academic revenue. For the Prairie provinces this is *vieux jeu* because they have always had provincial systems, and so it was in British Columbia until recently, when the complications of growth set in. In Ontario and Quebec, however, there are many universities, and where the provincial governments are deeply involved with private institutions, the problem is real and urgent. In the Maritimes the story is also complex, though not different in principle. But it is in Ontario, with fourteen or fifteen provincially assisted yet autonomous universities, that the problem is classically posed – and it is here that academic history has got to be written in the next few years.

In talking of systems of universities, then, we inevitably mean provincial systems. The need to coordinate, to complement, to not duplicate, is most effective *within* a province, not across the nation, however regrettable this may be – and I do not regret it. Our buffer committees will thus be provincial, I hope, only in a constitutional sense. Clearly an Ontario system of universities is in being; there is a bureaucracy in University Avenue, a buffer committee, a vigorous minister, and a massive commitment of funds – $803 million for capital alone in the period 1966–71, or an average of about $160 million per annum, three-quarters from the public purse. If you compare this, from a population of about six million, with the corresponding figure for Britain of about $180 million per annum from a population of fifty million, you realize the scale of that commitment.

Now the decision-making process in the world of the Canadian universities is anything but systematic. It is individualistic at all levels. Strong and opinionated presidents, aggressive boards, newly invigorated senates and faculty boards, locals of the CAUT: All are habituated to the idea that initiative is local. In the ideal world of local autonomy the university – shall we say of Plantagenet or Alfred because their names have a nice medieval flavour – decides to start up a program of psephology. It does this either because it has anxious politicians on its board or because some expert professor of psephology convinces the senate that Plantagenet or Alfred is the right place to teach it. The board then raises the capital needed from local industry and funds are committed from general revenues to employ staff and run the building. So Plantagenet-Alfred is launched on a new academic venture. It is quite likely that the senate and board will have asked the questions: Does this meet a clear public demand? And is there a university down the road doing the same thing? If so, are we justified in competing? But I can only say that in my experience such conscience-trawling is not very effective. To quote Robbins again, this time his committee's report: "But it is unlikely that separate consideration by independent institutions of their own affairs in their own circumstances will always result in a pattern that is comprehensive, and appropriate in relation to the needs of society ... There is no guarantee of the emergence of any coherent policy."[14] I agree, though I would have been blunter. Local initiatives will produce a coherent policy only if they are taken in the light of stated social needs. No forum exists in Canada whereby these needs can be formulated and whereby the universities can judge these matters. And certainly there is no provincial forum unless, perish the thought, it is the Legislature.

This has been a real issue in compact and much evolved Britain, and I shall later say how the University Grants Committee tries to solve it. It is a major issue in Quebec. I was a member of the McGill Senate for many years. It is a very good body, and during those years it set up many new programs – like, for example, the Marine Sciences Centre, the Centre for Developing Areas, and the Islamic Institute. In all cases we debated the merits of these proposals in a quite enlightened and public-spirited way because we were fairly sure, and events proved us right, that we could get the money from special, nongovernmental sources. But when it came to deciding admissions policies, and such matters as staff-student ratios, we worked in a vacuum. And I may say with shame that as dean of Arts and Science at McGill I never once had occasion to consult or to coordinate my faculty's work with my opposite numbers at Sir George Williams or the Université de Montreal. In Quebec it took a royal commission – the Parent Commission – to undertake fundamental thinking about educational policy. Such commissions pass into history. What is needed is a continuous forum that never

---

14 Committee on Higher Education, Lord Robbins, chairman, *Higher Education*, report of committee, London, HMSO, Cmnd. 2154, paragraph 719, at 233.

stops debating the public stake in the universities. And in my view that forum should itself be an academic body.

What, in outline, do we need to plan in a university system? Obviously the least number of things possible. But even the least is a lot if public money is involved: overall student numbers, for example, and hence admissions policy; special courses, including the provision of professional training; avoiding duplication of specialized topics; library resources; the provision of adequate scholarships and bursaries; research and its findings. One could multiply this list many times. Many aspects of all these questions are capable of local handling and should so be handled. But all of them are problems on which the public at large is entitled to have an opinion, and it is reasonable to expect the government to develop policy on several of them – that is, to assess the public need and to expect the university system to provide for that need.

Yet in only one of these questions is there any long history of public involvement, and that is in professional education, notably in medicine, law, and teaching. In most others Canada and her provinces have been singularly slow to establish strong requirements. This, of course, reflects a formerly colonial position. Canada has always been able, at pinch, to import skilled manpower, capital, and technologies, primarily from Britain and the United States. She has never been driven for any length of time upon her own resources. The long history of active planning of higher education in Britain and France reflects the opposite assumption: that the system must provide all the skills needed on the domestic market and still have a surplus available for export to the less sophisticated countries, a mark of the imperial conscience, if you will. But Canada is no longer colonial, nor France and Britain imperial. Hence these assumptions are anachronisms. There are still distinguished Canadians who do not recognize colonialism when they see it, nor do they realize that colonialism is nowadays not imposed by others but by oneself. I hesitate to quarrel with Ted Sheffield, who knows much more about Canadian education than I shall ever do, nor would I dream of accusing him of colonialism. But I can't accept his view that Canada ought to go on depending on imported university teachers. He is reported to have said: "We are not depending on the production of our own graduate schools, much less on the production of doctorates in our own graduate schools, to staff the universities – not wholly ... We are depending, have depended, will depend and, I think, can successfully depend, on sources outside the country, not just of immigrants, but of Canadians who go abroad and then come back to serve in their own institutions."[15]

15 E.F. Sheffield, quoted by William G. Davis, Minister of University Affairs, Statement before the Fourth Session of the Twenty-Seventh Ontario Legislature, Toronto, 16 June 1966.

The long neglect of Canada's universities by an indifferent society guarantees that this is a statement of fact. But I also feel that it is intolerable, especially now that society is at last blessing our efforts. We are a rich nation, with a per capita income about three-quarters of that of the United States and much greater than those of Britain and France. It should be our objective to be able to meet all reasonable national requirements internally and to be in a position to export both graduates and technology. We do the latter on a small scale now but fall short of meeting our own requirements. Of course, it is good that we would staff our universities with returning Canadians; of course, it is good that any non-Canadians should come here, too, because the university world ought to be international or even supranational. But this is a defensible policy only if we are ourselves strong and versatile, as are the Americans and the British.

Here, then, is what we need to plan. We have to bring our university systems to the point where they can meet and exceed our national requirements in skilled manpower, in technical skills, in ideas and humane scholarship, and in intellectual advance. This means a host of things. It means, obviously, providing places for all qualified undergraduate applicants, and this the Canadian university systems are tackling with the help of public investment. But it is not enough to think simply in numbers. The next stage in Canada's academic history must be one of sophistication. This implies the enriching of physical resources, above all libraries, and specialized laboratories. It calls for the proliferation of graduate schools, and for a great widening in perspectives in advanced study. It presupposes the creation of facilities for Canada's professional education, a spectrum that will broaden rapidly in all Western countries, but especially in rich Canada. I hope that the universities will accept this latter responsibility because I dislike professional education divorced from universities.

We shall not get what I have just spelled out without a formal organization to plan it. Canada's constitution requires that this planning be provincial. Hence we need in every province, but especially in Quebec and Ontario, a body charged with the overall responsibility of planning university development. And the main force of my remarks is that the body should be itself academic in character, though not exclusively so. It must enjoy the full support of both government and the academic community, and it has to be given the powers and the resources necessary for the job. The questions that remain are these: What sort of body will fill this role? And what will happen to university freedom in such a planned system? No system, other than that of complete centralization, can survive if the state does not want it to. All I can urge at present is that we should combine, federate, put our houses in order – and face the state with a reasonably clear conscience. I incline toward statutory or constitutional arrangements rather than those dependent on convention. If the niceties of polite upbringing are finally failing the British, what hope is there in Canada for such a system?

And what, finally, is to happen to these splendid new campuses in Canada? What will happen to their freedom to arrange their affairs as they think best? My fear is that it will die ingloriously. Our reluctance to plan, to combine, may force the provinces to take over. But it is still not too late in Ontario, though it seems to be too early in Quebec. Those who do not hang together hang separately. And whatever fate the Canadian university community may deserve, it doesn't deserve to be hanged.

PART TWO

Remedies: Threat from Without?

Thus far I have tried to make four points: that most universities now depend overwhelmingly on the state for funds; that this means that the state-supported universities in any one jurisdiction have to be treated as a system; that someone has to run this system; and that the academic community, and not the state, should run it. I have also said that I hope we can find a formula that will allow a measure of real freedom to the individual university. These have been laboured and unoriginal thoughts, and I have not been happy making them. As David Monroe always says, the more important education becomes, the more boring it seems to get.

I would like now to look at possible ways of running a university system. We have many good examples. The universities of Britain are a homogeneous system, and their development and operation are centrally financed and coordinated. Yet they individually possess a measure of real freedom, which they exercise vigorously. The nine large state universities of California form another centralized system. They, too, possess far more local autonomy than is usually believed. And both systems – British and Californian – obviously achieve high standards, meet public demands, and are good places to work and study in. Before we speculate on proper Canadian remedies, then, I propose to look at some contrasted systems in the hope of getting useful ideas. My experience of American systems is much thinner than of the British. This will become obvious as I speak. What I have not said, but which I say now, is that the external threat to university freedom does not come from the state alone, especially in its guise as financier. Society as a whole threatens the university by putting demands on it that it ought not to meet. I propose to dispose of the state first – I wish it were as easy as that! – and keep these others for a depressing end to my depressing assessment.

I have said that the device of the buffer committee – a body between government and university to whom the problem of finance remitted – had two poles:
the British soft-shoe concept of a self-effacing committee and the American
drum-roll concept of a board of regents. I may be wrong in suggesting that these
are really opposite poles of a single planetary device, but at least they lie in the
same domain: the no-man's land between state and university.

The British University Grants Committee (UGC) has achieved real fame and
honour. I work under its wing, but I see it through Canadian eyes since almost
my whole previous career was in Canada. I see much to admire – sophistication,
modesty, common sense – and also some things to criticize, such as a very
elaborate procedure for control of building projects. But most of all I see an idea
characteristically British, attuned to the power structure of British public affairs,
and assuming to the full the unwritten conventions on which British public life
depends. Frankly, I doubt the exportability of this sort of thing – but the
committee has done so well that we must look at it attentively.

In its present form it dates back to 1919. It was the creation of a Canadian,
Mr Bonar Law, then chancellor of the Exchequer, though similar committees had
functioned back to 1889. The actual process involved was the circulation of a
Treasury minute proposing the creation of a standing University Grants Committee "to enquire into the financial needs of university education in the United
Kingdom (now Great Britain) and to advise the Government as to the application
of any grants that may be made by Parliament towards meeting them." The chancellor appointed a committee of nine academics, who reported not to the Board
of Education, but to the Treasury. Thus began a long alliance between committee
and Treasury that lasted until 1964.[16] On April 1 of that year the committee passed
to the Department of Education and Science, whose secretary of state today

---

16 University Grants Committee, *University Development 1957–1962*, London, HMSO,
   Cmnd. 2267, paragraphs 517–628, at 170–99, gives a succinct summary of the committee's history and working methods. For more recent developments see House of
   Commons, *Fifth Report from the Estates Committee, Session 1964–65*, London,
   HMSO, 1965. This rather critical assessment of the committee's work was based on
   prolonged public hearings. Pages v–xli contain the report proper; pages 1–280 contain
   the expert evidence verbatim, including memoranda from the Department of Education and Science and the UGC itself. The Estimates Committee recommendations
   (xliii) were referred to the Department of Education and Science for comments, and
   these comments (providing a useful footnote) are in the *Third Special Report from
   the Estimates Committee, Session 1965–66*, London, HMSO, 1965. The tide flows
   quickly, as one soon learns in reading *Parliament and Control of University Expenditure, Special Report from the Committee of Public Accounts, Session 1966–67*,
   House of Commons, Paper 290, London, HMSO, 1967.

appoints the UGC, receives its reports, and speaks for it in the Commons. The
UGC is thus not statutory, and the minister can vary its membership and terms of
reference. These now have added to them the responsibility "to collect, examine
and make available information relating to university education throughout the
United Kingdom; and to assist, in consultation with the universities and other
bodies concerned, the preparation and execution of such plans for the development of the universities as may from time to time be required in order to ensure
that they are fully adequate to national needs." The chairman and the two deputy
chairman are salaried officials, the former full-time, the two deputies part-time,
and carry an enormous responsibility. Of the remaining eighteen members, eleven
are academics, two are persons connected with other forms of education, four
are from industry, and one is from a research establishment. Each serves for a
five-year term, renewable for a second five years. There are numerous standing
subcommittees and advisory panels, as well as ad hoc independent committees
made up of nonmembers of the UGC. A secretariat (including architects) of over
a hundred civil servants functions in support in Park Crescent (an elegant Regency
terrace) far from the secretary of state's offices in Mayfair.

Upon this deliberately self-effacing group of citizens, the government leans
for advice as to all university requirements, capital and operating (nonrecurrent
and recurrent in UGC language). Having decided on the amount of the grant to
be made, the government thereafter by firm convention allows the UGC to
distribute it in block grant form to the universities on its list. The process is
described by Sir John Wolfenden (personal communication) as a "series of
recommendations [by the UGC] which in relation to recurrent grant are always
accepted, never questioned and recognized ... as wholly within our unquestioned
discretion." The UGC attempts to see that the universities spend the money wisely,
but no further public audit is attempted. Operating grants are made quinquennially, with built-in adjustment factors and with occasional supplementary grants
to cover changes in salary scales, the setting up of new programs, and other
unforeseen changes. Capital grants are dealt with continuously and are made
after scrutiny by the committee's own architects and quantity surveyors. Neither
the comptroller and auditor general nor the Parliamentary Committee of Public
Accounts has had access to the committee's books nor to those of the universities.
The Committee of Public Accounts has repeatedly attempted to set aside this
provision, but the Treasury has supported the right of the universities to keep
their books closed. To realize the force of this, try to visualize Mr Watson Sellars,
at the height of his career, being denied access to the books of one of the largest
items of public expenditure, finding his way barred not only by the spender, but
by the officials of the Treasury Board. It may be that this remarkable privilege

is about to end, as the Public Accounts Committee has so recommended (in a report to the Commons published 24 January 1967).[17]

The system has shown increasing signs of strain as the scale of public expenditure has risen. The process whereby new buildings are designed, authorized, built, and equipped strikes my Canada-conditioned eyes as slow and excessively elaborate. The public purse is protected, but it takes a year or two to complete what in Quebec we should have finished in a few months. In its anxiety to justify the trust put in it, the committee has felt it had no choice, on the capital side, but to put protection of the public purse high on its list of obligations. The London colleges, for example, cannot hope to do what government departments do with impunity as regards site and building acquisition in that most expensive city. It is only fair to say that the delays reside at least as much in the offices of the architects, surveyors, and lawyers employed by the universities and on the building sites themselves as in the overloaded offices of the UGC.

The committee is expected to plan academic development in the national interest. This they have done by methods that again presuppose the British atmosphere in public affairs. They unobtrusively saw to it, for example, that proposals for new universities in postwar Britain were handled with proper regard for site, public needs, finances, and academic structure. The eight new institutions, though most of them were conceived and sponsored locally, all bear the mark of this forethought. Academic Planning Boards were set up in each case to ensure that the new universities were from the outset national institutions comparable with the older universities in standards. These planning boards were made up of a chairman and five or six members, all but one nationally respected academics. They were charged with making sure that the new university would be capable of awarding respectable degrees and with determining the range of subjects that were to be taught at undergraduate level in the early years. They drafted the charters and, in consultation with the local sponsors, selected the first governing bodies. They also helped find the first vice chancellors. Thus the new universities, though refreshingly unlike one another, enjoy the respect of their academic colleagues. The success of places like Sussex speaks well for the effect of the background presence of the UGC.

---

17 For a review of the earlier history of this conflict, see Robert O. Berdahl, *British Universities and the State* (Berkeley and Los Angeles: University of California Press, 1959), 117–34. For the last act, see *Parliament and Control of University Expenditure Special Report from the Committee of Public Accounts, Session 1966–67,* House of Commons Paper 290, London, HMSO, 1967.

I have stressed several times the unobtrusiveness of this background presence. There is much argument about the merits of dirigisme, or as Ashby calls it, "crypto-dirigisme,"[18] by the UGC. In fact, academic evolution in Britain is a most complex process. The UGC, by appointing ad hoc independent committees, can assess the public need, advertise the results, and then (in principle) await proposals from the universities. In practice initiatives may flow from government, from the Committee of Vice Chancellors and Principals, from individual universities, from nonacademic bodies, or from the UGC itself. The point is, however, that with minor exceptions financial provision will depend on UGC approval. Thus academic development stands or falls by their decision, in practice if not in principle. Universities file their development proposals with the UGC quinquennially. If the opinion of the committee is negative, the proposals will probably not go forward because the universities, though protected from budgetary line-item control by the block grant principle, cannot afford to resist UGC opinion and may not even want to. Hence Ashby's term "crypto-dirigisme."

Is this committee the voice of the academic community of Britain? The answer must clearly be "no." It is in the main an agent of the state, fulfilling a public duty. And it is to some extent the agent of the corporate universities in dealing with the state. As Ashby and Anderson put it, "the de facto situation in Britain is that there is, of course, an unwritten concordat between university and state, through the medium of the University Grants Committee: one side acknowledges and accepts some measure of state influence and control; the other side agrees to a rigorous code of non-intervention in the university's academic affairs."[19] Bagehot would have comprehended this arrangement though he would have been surprised that the "medium" should be dominated by academics.

The British universities have long felt the need for some form of mutual consultation. No formal organization has been set up for this purpose, and few have been bold enough to suggest that one with teeth is needed. The Committee of Vice Chancellors and Principals dates from 1913 and is an active if rather mysterious body meeting monthly. It neither claims nor in fact possesses any authority. In practice it is becoming rapidly more influential, and steps are being taken to strengthen its hand. It now possesses a secretariat and puts out occasional publications and sponsors studies of the university scene. Its chairman is in close touch with the chairman of the UGC. Sir John Wolfenden has gone on

18 See Tudor David's account of an informal discussion held at Cambridge, 16–18 July 1965, on "Government and University," *Minerva* 4 (1965–66): 111–21.
19 Eric Ashby and Mary Anderson, "Autonomy and Academic Freedom in Britain and in English-Speaking Countries of Tropical Africa," *Minerva* 4, no. 3 (Spring 1966): 317–64.

record that he dines with the chairman of the Vice Chancellors Committee the night before their monthly meeting so that they may talk about the vice chancellors' agenda items, "and," he adds, "this is understood among the vice chancellors as a sensible way of exchanging views."[20] In a mad world, this seems a refreshingly sane procedure.

There will, I am sure, be a great expansion of this form of coordination in Britain in the coming years of dependence on government. Inevitably the University Grants Committee comes to be seen more and more as the voice of the state; equally inevitably, as their dependence on the state increases, the universities will have to learn to speak with a common voice, and to keep their common house in order. In my view the present Committee of Vice Chancellors and Principals can well be the nucleus of such a coordinating body, though consultation at other levels will be necessary. There is also the point that in some few universities the vice chancellor may not be accepted as a suitable voice for the academic body, and it may be that a more democratically conceived committee will be needed.[21]

I am not competent to speak with equal knowledge of American methods in these questions. Here, in any case, genuinely autonomous private universities persist and are likely to persist for many years. This we all should welcome. But even in the USA many students must seek their education in publicly financed universities. State university systems are as characteristic of US culture as are the Ivy League and the Rice University. Private and public can even coexist, as do Stanford, California Institute of Technology, and the University of California. The British and Ontario pattern of heavily state-subsidized yet private, autonomous universities is not so familiar to Americans, who have tended to keep institutions for the privileged separate in their minds from institutions for the multitude. Yet Cornell began as a land-grant college under the Morrill Act, and there are many cases where the complex reality of US education differs from the stereotypes – not least at the University of Pennsylvania, private and proud of it, yet deriving two-fifths of its annual revenues from the Commonwealth Legislature.

Most public university systems of the sort we have been discussing lack the appearance of autonomy retained by the British universities. A state university sees autonomy – or, in more general terms, freedom – as something to be wrung from a powerful parent, the state; it is not something it is in danger of losing, but something it has to gain. Annual line budgets that have to be accepted by the State

20 Testimony cited in House of Commons, *Fifth Report from the Estimates Committee, Session 1964–65*, London, HMSO, 1965, 261.
21 Committee on Higher Education, Lord Robbins, chairman, *Higher Education*, report of committee, London, HMSO, Cmnd. 2154, paragraphs 695–700.

Legislature are still required in some states. Yet both personal freedom of the teacher and the freedom of action of his or her university have in practice been growing. Chancellor Herman B. Wells of Indiana University, for example, points out that "the late Professor Kinsey served for many years on our faculty vigorously expressing ideas on sexual behavior in conflict with the generally accepted mores of our society." And Chancellor Wells enjoys annual block grants.[22]

In fact, of course, as Wells points out, the current trend of university financing in the United States is in the opposite direction to that in Canada and Britain; dependence on a single public source is lessening in the us. Massive federal subsidies to research have transformed the budgets of many of the state universities, as well as enriched the private. This federal support in the case of Indiana now amounts to a third of the total annual income of the university. Most of this support has been one-sidedly scientific, coming from the National Science Foundation and the military services. Recently, however, the Congress authorized the establishment of a council and endowment for the humanities, to be directed by Barnaby C. Keeney (who chaired the Commission on the Humanities that pulled off this coup). If I know Keeney and his associates, this flow will increase far beyond its present proportions.[23] Thanks partly to these large federal subventions, the state universities have become progressively more sophisticated and more versatile, especially in the past decade. Indeed it has become progressively more difficult to maintain their traditional role as teachers of the undergraduate hordes.[24] Getting money from more than one source of funds is a key to independence, and in the progressive states this diversification has been marked by increasingly wise action by state governments as regards the public universities. The latter have thus extended their freedom to plan without arbitrary interference.

In several of the richest states, real sovereignty rests with the board of regents of the state university system, who have jurisdiction in the name of the people over all the campuses of the system, though these may enjoy in practice a degree of autonomy almost as effective as that of the British universities. Patterns vary greatly. In some states the regents are elected by general suffrage; in others they may be appointed by the governor. Americans put much less faith than do the British in unwritten conventions. The "unwritten concordat between university and state" mentioned above does not appeal to a nation used to legal process

---

22 Herman B. Wells, "United States of America," in *University Autonomy: Its Meaning Today* (Paris: Papers 7, International Association of Universities, 1965), 125–28.

23 Commission on the Humanities, Barnaby C. Keeney, chairman, *Report*, New York, 1964.

24 Martin Trow, "The Undergraduate Dilemma in Large State Universities," *Universities Quarterly* 21, no. 1 (December 1966): 17–43.

and the separation of powers between judiciary, executive, and legislature. The strongest systems are built right into the state constitution. Thus in California, which has a state system with fully evolved campus autonomy, the board of regents own and operate the system under the 1879 constitution of the state and are free of political control.[25] The state university contains nine individual universities and three colleges, as well as research institutions. The regents command great respect; they include ex officio members and sixteen distinguished laymen appointed by the governor for sixteen-year terms. These Western aristocrats present a unified budget to the Legislature, which can reduce the total request (not below the previous year's appropriation) but cannot challenge any line items.[26]

Clearly these regents exercise most of the functions that in Britain fall to the UGC, yet they are laymen, except for the president of the system, who is a voting member. This very general provision reflects the deep-seated differences between US and UK assumptions as to proper government. At times it has led to tension between the academic staff and the regents – which brings to mind their recent difficulties with the Berkeley students. Similarly their constitutional status and guarantees are quite alien to British politics. Functionally similar, the two kinds of body are thus constitutionally very different. State boards of regents exercise, by means of committees, full control of academic policies, but these committees, of which the senior is often called a senate, are academic bodies, and by convention – here the practice is more familiar to British eyes – the academic policy of the system is determined here. The heterogeneity of the American university community, wherein lame ducks waddle alongside racing thoroughbreds, makes academic opinion acutely conscious of varying standards and of the need for accreditation, especially of professional and graduate programs. Hence the regents of a state university system habitually exercise through their academic committees much wider power than the British would stomach. The right of authorization for expensive PhD programs, or for new professional schools, typically lies with the regents themselves, as in California. In Britain this right lies with the individual university, although the functioning of it will involve UGC consent if increased costs are involved.

What, then, should Canadians do? Ought they to borrow ideas from the British or the Americans and try to adapt them? Ought they conceivably to borrow from

---

25 Recent events suggest that they are not free from politics! What is wrong in California is not the structure, but the policies followed.

26 I am quoting here from Appendix H of J.W.Y. Spinks, chairman, Commission to Study the Development of Graduate Programmes in Ontario Universities, *Final Report*, Toronto, Department of University Affairs, 1966. Governor Reagan's recent irruption seems to have ignored this provision.

France? Or should they borrow what is good and then work out their own solutions? Before I give an answer, I shall speculate a bit about Canada's special problems. These are very numerous, and some of them look almost insoluble, such as staffing the country's own universities. All have a bearing on cost – and hence raise the question of state support, be it federal or provincial.

The first is the question of scale and its consequences. The decision has been made in nearly all provinces to provide university places for all who can profit. And the latter has been interpreted generously. The lower third of all students entering the Canadian universities are marginal for such education. I don't wish to be too precise about this, but we all know that a high proportion – in some places a half of those who enter – do not graduate. In Britain, by contrast, all but 10 to 20 per cent, will get a first degree. This reflects the greater ease with which the young Canadian gets to college: He lives in a country with an open-door policy, whereas the British characteristically filter more drastically. They set higher minimum requirements, and then reject half the qualified applicants. In the result, a disturbingly high fraction of Canadian university expenditure – and of the energy and patience of teachers – is partially wasted by being spent on those unable to profit from it. Of course, something rubs off but not, I suspect, much. The British get around this by setting up a second tier of colleges – technical and teacher-training – administered by local authorities. The less well-qualified in general find their way into this lower tier of what is usually called the binary system. The UGC and universities have nothing to do with these colleges. The latter offer some degree courses (the degrees being granted externally by London University or else supervised by the National Council for Academic Awards) but devote themselves primarily to less demanding work. Canadian university systems try to cover both functions, as do the state universities in the US. The two-tier structure of the binary system offends my own prejudices, and I accept that the North American formula is ultimately the sounder. Nevertheless, gathering so wide a spectrum of intelligence inside a single system creates major problems for Canada. It commits the provinces to costly provision for very large numbers in a country that until recently starved its universities, which thus arrived in our own day desperately short of buildings, staff, and facilities. I would not wish to change the national open-door policy, but it does pose problems.

High among these is the obsession with numbers, staff/student ratios, wastage, student aid, and all the paraphernalia of a mass-education approach. Discussions of academic policy are mainly about these things.[27] How, that is, to cope with

27 Advisory Committee on University Affairs of Ontario, *Report*, Toronto, 1 February 1964.

an oncoming mass of school-leavers within a single equalitarial framework. Hence one argues about, for example, junior colleges, or institutes (as the Parent Commission preferred), as a means of taking the pressure off the huge classes of early university years.[28] And one hears, in Quebec and Ontario at least, and in some quarters of British Columbia, of another two-tier idea – that of advanced universities dealing primarily with honours and graduate work and of workaday liberal arts colleges for the run-of-the-mill entrant who only seeks a meek and mild general degree. This idea also offends me, and I think it incapable of being carried out. My own conviction is that all "two-tier" arrangements are unsound. If you set up a university system, it must be made up of self-respecting universities. The liberal arts college was a creation of an earlier phase of American education, and locally (though in view rarely) it achieved distinction (for example, at Dartmouth or at Antioch).[29] But nowadays teaching has to be done alongside research if it is to carry conviction. And this means university status, as that term is now commonly used. It is not enough, in thinking about expansion of universities, simply to calculate in terms of numerical formulae, of bodies, and of floorspace: You have to think about how to keep your standards abreast of the next fellow – who in Canada's case is painfully close!

And hence I would put second among the special problems that of sophistication. The Canadian universities exist side by side on this continent with the US universities. It has been possible in the past for Canadians to feel smug about their academic standards. Honours graduates have found ready welcome across the border in the US graduate schools and have been able to compete on equal or even advantageous terms. Even the general graduate has often found his or her feet. It has therefore been easy for Canadians to ignore the great changes that are being carried through on the American campus and to assume that they have some innate quality that keeps them ahead of their neighbours in the undergraduate school.

This comfortable feeling has nothing to justify it. The American willingness to condemn American institutions – loud self-denunciation is part of their way of life – obscures the facts. I have no objective way of proving my conviction, held against highly vocal US opinion to the contrary, that the US high school leaver is far better equipped for university life than he or she was ten years ago and that the undergraduate schools now reflect this fact. But I am sure of this. Add the great capital investment that has been going on everywhere, and the US university now seems to me in my frequent visits an altogether more exciting place than it

---

28 *Report of the Royal Commission of Inquiry on Education in the Province of Quebec,*
    vol. 2, Quebec, 1964.
29 I should record the strong dissent of the Hon. G.O. Arlt on this opinion!

used to be. I am not talking just about Harvard, MIT, Chicago, and Stanford, but about the state university systems. Where in Canada is there a phenomenon like Michigan State at East Lansing? Or like much maligned Berkeley? The fact is that Canadian universities are competing against the most vigorous and exciting universities in existence, and we *must* compete on adequate terms.

By sophistication I mean simply creating the graduate schools, the libraries, the research laboratories, the specialized institutes that are now standard parts of the great university – and increasingly even of the hitherto humdrum US state university. In Canada we have Toronto, we have McGill, we have exciting beginnings elsewhere: We have small pools of real excellence. But only Toronto is yet within striking distance of world stature – because of imaginative leadership, large public financial support, and a very early start (by Canadian standards). McGill has great potential but is hamstrung by the short-sightedness of the provincial government. I mean no idle courtesy when I say that Carleton's beginnings are impressive and exciting. But vastly more resources and time are needed.

As I cannot be expected to repeat the findings of the Spinks Commission, I will say only that we believed that every university in this province must move rapidly toward advanced work – on the master's degree everywhere and on the doctorate where resources justify it. We rejected the view that some of these universities could be kept out of the advanced field; we believed that there is no way of putting a lid on scholarship and that either a university is free to go as far as the intellect can or it is not a university at all. And I believe this to be true also of the rest of Canada's universities. Quebec and the Parent Commission's view that only the big three – McGill, Laval, Montreal – should do graduate work is quite untenable.[30] But, having said this, let me reemphasize the grimness of the job of getting the Canadian universities into better shape for advanced work. I will isolate one problem from among the crowd: library resources. The Spinks Commission estimated (on the basis of recognized standards) that the libraries of the Ontario universities were about nearly 5,000,000 volumes below the standard required for graduate work in those universities *that have already begun such work*. Turned crudely into dollars, these figures imply a capital grant requirement of about $85,000,000 to bring the libraries up to standards similar to those already aimed at in the better university systems. Such calculations should not be taken too seriously. The real cost might be half, or it might be double. But, half or double, it remains a shocking figure.

---

30 *Report of the Royal Commission of Inquiry on Education in the Province of Quebec*, vol. 2, Quebec, 1964, paragraph 349, at 232. What the commissioners recommended was that the other universities should refrain from exercising their charter powers to do graduate work for a few years.

Here, to me, is the real rub. We have not only to meet social demand for university places; we have to diversify, enrich, and ennoble the universities so that they are not inferior to their neighbours. This is another reason why it is crucially necessary for the government of every province to take good advice about its university system – and to find resources to accept it. This advice must come from the academic community itself – not exclusively but in the main – which brings us back again to the theme of university and government in Canada.

First of all we might agree that solutions have got to be found quickly. Fully satisfactory arrangements do not yet seem to exist anywhere. I make these remarks tentatively because I have not followed Duff and Berdahl across the country and must rely on more casual contacts. In Quebec the situation is, and has been, disquieting: Prolonged indecision as to mechanics and, one fears, indifference to the universities needs have led to deep frustration and unease throughout the university community in both cultural groups. Here in Ontario respectable and obviously well-intentioned initiatives by the provincial government have still not created a fully satisfactory scheme. Nowhere in Canada, least of all in Quebec and Ontario, should this situation be tolerated much longer. Since I am partially an outsider I apologize for thus seeming to poke my nose in. But the whole academic world, inside and outside Canada, has a stake in Canada's success. So I hope I will be forgiven for beating the drum.

The answer preferred by most Canadian academics, and seemingly acceptable to most politicians, is the provincial advisory committee, often modelled to a great extent on what is thought to be British practice. Such committees already exist in most provinces. But the British UGC, as we have seen, is nonstatutory and depends for its success on the conventions of British public life. These have no force in Canada; her own ideas on proper government are very different. The common convention of Canadian provincial politics is that office means power, subject only to the constraints of the law and to the vote of the Legislature. It is asking a lot to have politicians delegate this huge and vital job to others and then refrain, in the fate of ever-increasing cost, from using that power to interfere. Frankly I don't think it will happen without guarantees. But since these committees already exist in many provinces, I will suggest a few things about their functioning.

First, the committees must be respected by both the Legislature and the academic community. This means careful thought as to membership. I don't believe that high permanent officials should serve, nor should active politicians. Ideally, I would put my faith in a combination of three elements: lay members, with sympathy for university objectives; heads of universities (presidents make more trouble off than on such committees); and senior professors, with provision for rotation in all cases. I prefer an academic majority but do not feel that this matters if you pick a good team. There should certainly be, among the layman, representatives of the school system. In all this I find I agree with Duff and Berdahl.[31]

Second, in the absence of comfortable conventions, I advocate a statutory role for such committees, with well articulated terms of reference built into the legislation. Those should include the right, *the exclusive right*, to present annual operating budgets for the system to the appropriate ministers; the right, again exclusive, to plan for new developments (including new professional schools) and hence to present annual capital budgets to the ministers; and the right to distribute these moneys to the universities as they think just and to arrange suitable systems of audit.

Third, the committees must have a secretariat, a complete technical staff sufficient to do the job of assessment, scrutiny, control, and audit required by the job. The substantial bureaucracies now existing in departments of higher education should more properly work for the committee than for the minister. One bureaucracy or two is a question that still divides Britain. Since major commitments of capital are always fought out at the ministerial level, it is natural that the minister responsible for university finance should want his team of advisers. But if the committee is to do its job and preserve the freedom of the universities, much of the work now done in Canada by departmental bureaucracies will have to be done by the staffs of the committees. Whether one bureaucracy or two, however, I would plead for the minimum of niggling control. Universities are highly responsible bodies governed by people with strong social consciences and staffed by the intelligent and the dedicated. It is patent nonsense to insist on pettifogging detail of financial control over such bodies. My experience is that such control is more likely to strangle academics than any conscious attack on their freedom. So, in heaven's name, let us keep one publicly financed domain out of the reach of red tape.[32]

Fourth, the operating budgets of the universities simply must be guaranteed several years ahead. The present process of annual budgeting is inefficient, frustrating, and costly. It commits the senior staff of all universities – and of the committees – to a futile, annual rat race. As dean of a faculty of thirty-odd departments, I spent much of the year telling my senior colleagues that I could give them no commitments on anything – until, in fact, it was too late. The

---

31 Sir James Duff and R.O. Berdahl, *University Government in Canada*, report of a commission sponsored by the Canadian Association of University Teachers and the Association of the Universities and Colleges of Canada (Toronto: University of Toronto Press, 1966), 76–82.
32 See Tudor David, "Government and University," *Minerva* 4 (1965–66): 111–21.

British use a quinquennial system, which I think too long. Personally I favour a revisable three-year system, for Canadian jurisdictions, and am not impressed by arguments that this is politically unfeasible. Since it is a necessity for good university governance, it has got to be made feasible.[33]

Now – if this is what is wanted and these conditions can be met – there is an *important* corollary: Such committees must function as agents of the provinces. However academic they may be in composition, they represent the public interest, not the special interest of the university community. The latter also needs a voice. Hence I repeat what I have said twice before: The universities must learn to speak with a common voice and must keep their own houses in order. This needs an interuniversity organization with teeth. Committees of presidents are not nearly enough. I have already noted how angular individualism, our intense local academic nationalisms, make us fight shy of combination. But British experience shows that such combination is inevitable when one is faced with the state. Personally I am an out-and-out federalist. My own college is a member of a federal university and gains immensely from this sharing of interest with others. Of course, we have lost some of our autonomy: We no longer have exclusive control over curricula, and if we want to start something expensive, we have to convince the other members of the university, and that university's governing body, before our bill is sent to the UGC. But, in fact, we are very fairly treated, and the college's Board of Governors and academic board would certainly resist any attempt to dismember the federal structure. What is the use of autonomy if one is starved of money and of students?

It is well known that the Spinks Commission advocated a stronger, more formal American pattern: a federal state university with an academic senate and a board of regents, the first dealing with academic coordination and planning, the latter with finance.[34] Armed with strong enabling legislature, we thought that such a body could reserve for the community the primary role in planning for the future. We did not advocate any amalgamation or dismantling of the existing universities, nor did we envisage any more loss of sovereignty than is, in fact, already lost. Imperial College, University College, the London School of Economics, and Kings College have not suffered from membership in a federal university – in fact, the reverse. I am sure that the London colleges would be in a very much weaker position if they had individually, as fully autonomous institutions, to face the state through the University Grants Committee – though

---

33 I part company with the Duff-Berdahl report at this point (page 81).
34 J.W.Y. Spinks, chairman, Commission to Study the Development of Graduate Programmes in Ontario Universities, *Final Report,* Toronto, Department of University Affairs, 1966, 62–77.

it is fair to add that some of our members, chiefly the large colleges, would like to have a go; there are rogue elephants in all herds. We knew, of course, that we should tread on corns in recommending as we did – and, frankly, we were more concerned that *something* should be done by our brother academics than that they should pick the solution we chose. There are other possible ways, as I have tried to suggest. But whichever pattern is adopted, my strictures about the necessary powers of the chosen instrument will stand.

I come now to another aspect of freedom, as I see yet another threat in the financing of research. Research is not a pleasant frill to be added to the real business of a university, nor is it just an adjunct to undergraduate teaching. It is in fact the core of the university's work, and university financing that does not recognize this falsifies the facts. About half the operating costs of the British universities arise from the advancement of knowledge (research) and half from the dissemination of that knowledge (teaching). These two functions are thus equally supported by Exchequer grants handled by the UGC, and they have never been separated, though costing exercises now in progress by the UGC and the Committee of Vice Chancellors and Principals involve such analysis.[35] Few Canadian jurisdictions yet admit this principle, which is fundamental to the freedom of the scholar and to communities of scholars. Most Canadian justifications of budgets are in terms of the undergraduate teaching "load," and universities are forced to lean on the National Research Council, the Canada Council, or other external bodies for the overt financing of research.

This is quite wrong. The general operating budget of all universities must allow for research costs, and general provincial support for academic research at the universities is therefore extended to the institution, not the individual. The crucial role of the research councils – federal and provincial – should be to support the work of *individual* scholars or teams of scholars who wish to conduct research and to support students who wish to work for higher degrees. This duality contains a most important principle: that the individual member of the university needs to be able to finance his creative ideas independently of his institutions existing programs. This essential freedom is the key to initiative and intellectual innovation. In my opinion all provinces, as well as the federal government, should have such research councils, with terms of reference covering all aspects of research. Without such separate right of access to sources of funds, the creative scholar may fall victim to the natural inertia of big organizations – and universities these days are very big indeed.

35 University Grants Committee, *University Development 1957–1962*, London, HMSO, Omnd. 2267, 1964, paragraphs 159–63, at 55–7.

Conclusion

I wish I felt that I had by now spelled out the full list of threats to university freedom and that I had been able to offer safe remedies. But I see still other hazards. Universities belong in the wide-open world at large; they have to trade in ideas that possess no nationality, and they must hope to get their members, professor and student alike, from a worldwide constituency. Yet they must also serve their parent societies on several scales. Carleton belongs to Ottawa, to Ontario, to Canada – but also (I'm embarrassed to say) to Western civilization. Carleton must often feel the conflict, and universities everywhere feel it. In the final analysis, academics' real loyalties are supranational, yet they have to get their support from the individual state – and in Canada that mostly means, in this context, the provinces. Fortunately, there are many signs that our legislators are coming to feel pride in the international role of Canada's universities: in the flood of students that come here from overseas, in the growing reputation of our scientists, in the cosmopolitan atmosphere of our faculty clubs. Let's hope that this pride grows and that no parochialism emerges.

And I mean, of course, inside as well as outside the university. There is no room for nationalism on the campus. It is right that a country should expect its universities to enrich the national store of knowledge and to cultivate the things the nation does best. It is wrong to expect a university to take a paltry nationalistic view of the world. This has happened all too often in Europe, in Africa, in South America. It is right for a university to have its doors open to every shade of political, religious, intellectual, and artistic opinion, regardless of origin; wrong to espouse one view *institutionally;* right in this country to lay emphasis on the two nearly identical cultures of the Western world, French and English, and to keep both doors open on every campus; wrong to voice vindictive criticism of one or the other on nationalist grounds. It is right to judge American culture on its merits and to absorb those parts of it that we admire; wrong to talk about "Americanization" as if this term had any consistent and prejudicial meaning. In other words, we must be urbane men and women of the world.

And I think we must ask: Whose freedom? I'm afraid we mean freedom for the professors. On the continent of Europe students as well as professors demand this freedom. Here, the professors insist on being paternal. They protect the interests of the young *in statu pugillarit.* There are many signs that the students have woken up to this difference, and they now insistently demand a greater say in university government. I have been depressed by the sourness of much student comment on this problem. Nor is the sourness just Canadian; at Berkeley and at the London School of Economics, much of the tension is said to have arisen from the presence of nonstudents, or nondegree students, in the community. Perhaps they are tired of the middle-aged.

But I confess myself a renegade. The students in the modern university are rather put upon and can with justice claim that their opinions count for little. I sympathize when they call for reform, though not when agitators among them seek to use the campus as a vehicle for partisan politics. How can we carry these reforms through? I have no easy remedy and cannot even define the need precisely, but I feel that we have got to give the student body a larger share in the freedom we prize than is often the case today. At Birkbeck I have two students on the Board of Governors, and fine fellows they are. But I don't believe the problem is best solved in this way in colleges full of school leavers. To ask students to involve themselves in the running of a university is to involve them in what most academics try to escape from: time-wasting committees that come between them and their real work. What students are entitled to is an audible voice in their academic programs – and notice that I say "voice," not "vote." If they believe their programs to be defective in some way they should always be able to express that belief. My own view is that a university where responsible student opinion cannot, as of right, reach its Senate and governors is unfree in the sense I have been using the term. Let me conclude more optimistically by quoting from Monsignor Lussier, former *recteur* of the Université de Montreal and one of Canada's most eloquent defenders of university freedom. He spoke at a McGill convocation back in the 1950s. Then, the problem of universities was to persuade government to finance them. Ottawa had taken the plunge, but we in Quebec were not permitted to accept the grants, and provincial aid in the dark ages of Duplessis was, to put it mildly, exiguous and erratic. Then, the threat we had to fear was starvation. Public indifference was the problem. Our freedom was not in danger, merely our survival. Now, the threat springs from the scale of government support. Can we hope to retain our freedom when we receive such vast sums of public money? It seems perhaps unlikely. But so did the end of the Duplessis era to those at McGill that day Lussier spoke. So it is fitting that I should close with Lussier's memorable words, which he says he drew from William of Orange: "In the absence of hope it is still necessary to strive." And I do not think that hope is really absent.

KENNETH HARE was a professor and dean of Arts and Science at McGill University in Montreal, master of Birbeck College at the University of London, England, president of the University of British Columbia, chancellor of Trent University, professor emeritus at the University of Toronto, and a member of the Research and Development Advisory Panel of Atomic Energy Canada. A meteorologist with the British air ministry during World War Two who emigrated to Canada in 1945, Dr Hare went on to help found McGill's highly successful Department of Meteorology (now the Department of Atmospheric and Oceanic Studies). For the ten years prior to his death in 2002, he chaired the national Climate Program Planning Board.

Dr Hare wrote nearly two hundred books, reports, articles, and commentaries. He is a Companion of the Order of Canada. Among his many other awards are eleven honorary doctorates; the 1973 Patterson Medal from the Canadian Meteorological Service; the 1974 Massey Medal from the Royal Canadian Geographical Society; and the 1988 International Meteorological Organization (IMO) Prize from the United Nations' World Meteorological Organization.

8

Social Science and Modern Man

SCOTT GORDON, 1969

PREFACE

In general, what I want to discuss is one of the most important aspects of humankind's fairly recent intellectual history: the rise of social science. Alexander Pope, in the eighteenth century, announced that "the proper study of mankind is man." Well, proper or not, economists and sociologists have been very busy at it during the past two centuries, and social science is, today, one of the great facts of modern civilization. Needless to say, a lot of other areas of study have also undergone a great development as well, but it is social science I want to focus on as a historical phenomenon, particularly its relation to the rather special problems that emerge in societies like Canada, which are economically and technically highly advanced and which have achieved a high degree of individual freedom and political democracy.

I want first to deal with these things in a very general way, and to discuss the broad problems that humankind seems to encounter in a highly developed society. In the second part I want to focus more concretely on social policy – that is, our efforts to act as collective beings – and to consider how we may develop a philosophy of social policy that is adequate to the modern world.

CHILDREN OF THE AGE OF REASON

I would like to begin by trying to make clear what I have in mind when I speak of "social science," and in order to do so I will have to recall some of the general intellectual history of Western society.

In one way of looking at it, the study of social phenomena is the oldest and most continuous of humankind's intellectual pursuits. The ancient books of religion, like the Old Testament, may be regarded as dealing with the individual's relation to God, but much more acutely they deal with the individual's relation to his or her fellows – that is, with social relations. A large part of the classical writings of the Golden Age of Greek civilization deals with social and political questions. Much of the immense theological literature of medieval Europe is focused on the problems raised by the individual's social relations rather than the problems of his or her soul.

If we were to regard all of this literature as early social science, as some historians do, we would not be able to distinguish between the study of humankind as undertaken by the poet or the novelist, or by the theologian and philosopher, and the study undertaken by the economist, the sociologist, and the statistician. It is true that we all labour in the same vineyard in the sense that we all endeavour to understand the human condition and that we all hope to assist individuals in becoming more civilized beings. So much can be granted. But the nature of modern social science, and the significance of its development, cannot be appreciated if we view it simply as an extension of the ancient study of humankind that has merely given itself some pretentious new names and titles.

My first point, therefore, is that what we today call "social science" is a new intellectual phenomenon in the history of humankind, not much more than two centuries old. A great deal of social science, when it was in its infancy in the eighteenth century, was classified under the headings of "moral philosophy" and "theology," but its true intellectual lineage goes back not to these subjects, but to the physical sciences. When Kepler and Newton and Descartes laid the foundations for modern physical science, they unwittingly laid the foundations for social science as well. When they detached the study of physical phenomena from theology, and made physics and chemistry possible, they also enabled us to detach the study of social phenomena from theology, making economics and sociology possible as well.

This separation of science from theology was a long time coming about, and it was not *recognized* to be an accomplished fact until late in the nineteenth century. One of the striking things that occurs to a reader of the older literature is the strong and almost universal view one finds there that God was regarded as an *immediate presence* in the world. Logically, this should have led people to practise continuous worship and to devote their lives to supplication in fear of divine power. But in Western Europe the view took hold, in some corners, that the Christian God was disciplined and orderly – not the capricious or moody or peevish divinity of the Greek Pantheon or of Israel's Jehovah – and this led to the study of nature as a manifestation of His divine discipline. For a time, the theistic and scientific attitudes were fused. To put questions to nature by means of careful observation and experiment was regarded as equivalent to conversing with God. On this basis, scientific knowledge grew and grew, rapidly and deeply. By the time it was realized that it was not God who was answering the questions of these investigators, it was too late to go back. Science existed, and it had its own credentials of legitimacy, independent of theology. Rationalism and empiricism were firmly established as the basic modes of knowledge. In the eighteenth century, the study of social phenomena began to place itself upon the same foundations.

The scientific approach is such a large part of modern life that it is difficult to believe that man's intellectual attitude was ever different. I want to take a moment to emphasize this point. To give some idea of how the educated mind worked even as recently as the end of the seventeenth century, I include an account of the medical treatment of King Charles II upon his final illness in 1685. The account is based on the records of a Dr Scarburgh, one of the king's physicians, and is contained in H.W. Haggard's *Devils, Drugs and Doctors*:

At eight o'clock on Monday morning of February 2, 1685, King Charles was being shaved in his bedroom. With a sudden cry he fell backward and had a violent convulsion. He became unconscious, rallied once or twice, and after a few days died. Seventeenth-century autopsy records are far from complete, but one could hazard a guess that the king suffered from an embolism – that is, a floating blood clot which had plugged up an artery and deprived some portion of his brain of blood – or else his kidneys were diseased. As the first step in treatment the king was bled to the extent of a pint from a vein in his right arm. Next his shoulder was cut into and the incised area "cupped" to suck out an additional eight ounces of blood. After this homicidal onslaught, the drugging began. An emetic and purgative were administered, and soon after a second purgative. This was followed by an enema containing antimony, sacred bitters, rock salt, mallow leaves, violets, beetroots, camomile flowers, fennel seed, linseed, cinnamon, cardamom seed, saphron, cochineal, and aloes. The enema was repeated in two hours and a purgative given. The king's head was shaved and blister raised in his scalp. A sneezing powder of hellebore root was administered, and also a powder of cowslip flowers "to strengthen his brain." The cathartics were repeated at frequent intervals and interspersed with a soothing drink composed of barley water, liquorice and sweet almond. Likewise white wine, absinthe and anise were given, as also were extracts of thistle leaves, mint, rue, and angelica. For external treatment a plaster of Burgundy pitch and pigeon dung were applied to the king's feet. The bleeding and purging continued, and to the medicaments were added melon seeds, manna, slippery elm, black cherry water, an extract of flowers of lime, lily-of-the-valley peony, lavender, and dissolved pearls. Later came gentian root, nutmeg, quinine and cloves. The king's condition did not improve, indeed it grew worse, and in the emergency forty drops of extract of human skull were administered to allay convulsions. A rallying dose of Raleigh's antidote was forced down the king's throat; this antidote contained an enormous number of herbs and animal extracts. Finally bezoar stone was given. Then, says Scarburgh: "Alas! After an ill-fated night his serene majesty's strength seemed exhausted to such a degree that the whole assembly of physicians lost all hope and became despondent: still so as not to appear to fail in doing their duty in any detail, they brought into play the most active cordial." As a sort of grand summary to this pharmaceutical debauch, a mixture of Raleigh's antidote, pearl julep, and ammonia was forced down the throat of the dying king.

Now what are we to make of this? We cannot dismiss the physicians of Charles II as fools. On the contrary, they represented the best medical knowledge of the time, and they were not dealing with abstract metaphysics but with very practical matters. Their "knowledge," however, if we can give it that name, seems to have been nothing more than a collection of ancient nostrums. These physicians lacked a sound foundation for their practice because the spirit of scientific study of the human body had not yet been established. If one considers how far removed modern medicine is from the account I have just read, one can get at least a slight idea of the intellectual change that has taken place in the last three centuries.

There is another aspect of this intellectual change that I want to bring to attention, one that is more difficult to explain briefly but is very important for what I am trying to get at. In order to understand the mind of the pre-scientific era, one must understand the general belief in the existence of occult powers in the world. A book that is especially revealing for this purpose is Aldous Huxley's *The Devils of Loudun*. It is an account of a celebrated case of "demonic possession" that took place in the French town of Loudun, near Tours, in the early seventeenth century. The nuns of the town's Carmelite convent suddenly began to act rather strangely, and the local priest, one Urbain Grandier, was accused of having entered into a pact with the devil in order to torment them. After interrogation and torture, the unfortunate Grandier was eventually burnt alive for witchcraft.

The important part of this dark story is the care with which the charge was investigated by the ecclesiastical authorities. The church demanded hard evidence, and it got it: The nuns "spoke in tongues"; "stigmata" appeared on their bodies; they performed feats of incredible strength and endurance while "possessed." In fact, we don't require as much proof today in modern courts of law; we hang people on less evidence than that on which Grandier was burnt. The difference between our century and the seventeenth is not a matter of evidence and proof but the simple fact that there is no place for occult powers in our mental image of the world. Science has exercised the devil by leaving no room for him in its model of reality. It is not a matter of one age being illogical and another logical. It is a matter of fundamental belief – one's basic image of the constitution of nature.

How difficult it is for us to grasp the mind of an age that believed in occult powers is indicated by the effort, a few years ago, to turn Huxley's book into a stage play in New York. It was a failure as a play despite the acting talents of Jason Robards and Anne Bancroft because the playwright and director simply could not bring themselves to believe that anybody had ever believed in witch-craft. In an effort to make the events at Loudun three hundred years ago intelligible to a twentieth-century mind, they interpreted Huxley's book in modern terms. The demonic frenzies of the Carmelite nuns became a simple case of sexual repression among ladies of enforced celibacy. The investigative tenacity of the church inquisitor became a simple matter of ambition to get on in the world and be promoted in the hierarchy by doing a thorough job of his assignment. As a result, the play conveyed no understanding of the seventeenth-century mind at all.

The theme of the conflict between medieval theology and the rational empir-icism of science was also explored in *Lamp at Midnight*, a Broadway play on Galileo's celebrated struggle with the church. It had the great advantage of Tyrone Guthrie as director, but it too only succeeded in proving how hard it is for the modern mind to grasp the system of thought that was held almost universally by intelligent and educated men in the pre-scientific age.

Why am I wandering around in the dark mental processes of the seventeenth century like this? Because I want to emphasize that the intellectual attitudes we take for granted in modern civilized societies are recent in the history of human-kind. A momentous change has taken place in our mental life in the past few centuries. Intellectually, we are not the descendants of the Golden Age of Athens or of the Judaeo-Christian tradition in theology. We are the children of the Age of Science and the Age of Reason.

But we are not quite sure what that means. The great historian W.E.H. Lecky wrote a large book, *The Rise and Influence of Rationalism in Europe*. When we come to the end of its eight hundred pages, we are sure that something tremen-dous happened, but what it is and how it occurred remains a mystery. All that Lecky can say, when we come down to it, is that there was a change in our "predisposition to believe." That is to say, we do not believe in occult powers today because we are not predisposed to accept such arguments even if they are supported by evidence. The great eighteenth-century philosopher David Hume expressed the modern temper exactly in his famous essay on miracles. Should we believe in miracles, he asked, even when presented with evidence? Suppose that all the historians and chroniclers agreed that Queen Elizabeth had returned from the dead. What should we believe? This was Hume's advice: "I should not doubt her pretended death, and of those other public circumstances that followed it: I should simply assert it to have been pretended, and that it neither was nor possibly, could be real ... I would ... reply, that the knavery and folly of men are such common phenomena, that I should rather believe the most extraordinary events to arise from their concurrence, than admit of so signal a violation of the laws of nature." Here is the heart of the matter: There are *laws of nature* that cannot be violated by human or devil or God.

Once the physical sciences had succeeded in establishing this conception of the physical world, it was possible to extend it to the world of human behaviour and social phenomena. There are laws of human nature and social nature, too, and so there can be social science, just as there is physical science.

The victory of the scientific attitude has not, of course, been complete. There still exist mystery sects like the Rosicrucians, and astrology still enjoys a considerable body of devotees. Even in practical matters like medicine, we have Christian scientists, and Queen Elizabeth II has recently appointed a homeopath to the staff of physicians to the royal household. Even among the intelligent and the sophisticated, there are those who believe they can attain direct cosmic revelation via Zen Buddhism, or hallucinogenic drugs, or other "mind-expanding" experiences. There are still people who believe literally in the existence of occult powers. I read in the Toronto *Globe and Mail* of 25 January 1969 (not 1669) that three Roman Catholic priests were called to investigate certain strange happenings in a house in Acton Vale, Quebec. They reported, it is quoted: "In our view, it is the case of a diabolical phenomenon, a rare phenomenon, but possible with divine permission ... The Devil, if God allows it, can manifest himself tangibly ... [and] the gravity of a diabolical infestation depends on the latitude God has given the Spirit of Evil to try His servants." In Switzerland, a man and woman belonging to a sect described as the International Community for the Furtherance of Peace were jailed recently for beating a young girl to death in an effort to drive the devil out of her body.

I think it is fair to say though that, so far as physical phenomena are concerned, the modes of thought of rationalist science are now deeply established. Even the members of the Flat Earth Society consider it necessary to offer alternative mechanical models of the universe to explain their belief that Apollo VIII did not go round the moon and back. But by comparison with physical science, the rationalist roots of social science are still shallow. Large numbers of people view social phenomena as manifestations of forces that are really the political equivalent of demonic powers. The conspiratorial theory of politics enjoys a certain substantial vogue. A few years ago, Arthur Miller wrote a play, *The Crucible*, about the New England witchcraft craze of the seventeenth century; it was a much more successful work of art than the effort to dramatize Huxley's *Devils of Loudon* or Galileo's struggles with the church in *Lamp at Midnight* because it had an authentic modern referent: the revival of medievalism that was inherent in the political hysteria of McCarthyism in the United States in the 1950s. One would like to think that this is a cast of mind confined to the ignorant and the gullible, but alas, one finds otherwise intelligent and skeptical people embracing political philosophies that they regard as disclosing in one flash of light the whole demonology of the social and economic world in terms of categories such as the "establishment" or "imperialism," the "military industrial complex," or sometimes, with grand comprehensiveness, the "system." Not without evidence, of course – evidence almost as good as that which the priests of Acton Vale saw with their very eyes. Nor can we assume with assurance that pre-rationalist or anti-rationalist modes of social thought will always remain a minority comprehension in a modern nation. There is, after all, the experience of Nazism to give one pause.

Social phenomena are complex and no more self-evident than physical phenomena. To the naive observer the flies that gather on the windowpane are obviously trying to get *out*, and the moon is more valuable to humankind than the sun because it shines at night when the light is really needed. The social scientist tries to pierce the obvious, to discover the laws of social phenomena, but there are many who hold the view that to "unmask" the conspirators and the manipulators of the world is all that needs be done.

I shall not go much further with this, but perhaps I have succeeded in indicating the drift of my argument. Social science, to my mind, is an outgrowth of the rationalistic age, which was initiated and established by physical science. The rationalistic study of humankind has, however, not driven its roots as deep into the civilized intellect as has the scientific study of physical phenomena. It could easily be uprooted in a prolonged political hurricane.

I have been describing social science so far in the singular, but it is, of course, a plural subject with a number of branches represented by different departments in a typical modern university. One will perhaps not be surprised if I claim that the virtues and merits I see in social science generally are particularly notable in my own field of economics. Economics is not only a rationalistic study of man, but it is the study of man as a rational being. To the economist, the buying and selling that goes on in markets, and the producing and consuming that goes on behind and before them, are conceived of as manifestations of humankind's capacity for the rational organization of daily life. What makes sense to an economist is the view that humans are maximizing creatures trying to achieve some definite objective as fully as they can in a world that presents them with various constraints and limitations. Some important consequences flow from this, and these I would like to discuss briefly.

First, since we cannot have everything we want, we must make choices. The constraints and limitations imposed by the external world force individuals to be rational – that is to say, to make logically effective choices. Some economists today even define the content of economic theory as "the logic of rational choice." It isn't a bad definition; it catches the spirit of a lot of the work that economists do. It is deeply embedded into the structure of economic theory that this process of rational choice will produce variety. We will not find a rational person or a rational society devoted exclusively to one thing. The society that dedicates itself without reserve to power, or prestige, or glory is as irrational is the individual who is dedicated to whisky. Whenever someone says that something is immeasurably important, or infinitely valuable, one can see an economist's hackles rise. Economics is the enemy of absolutes, and this applies to political and social aims as well as to material ones.

Second, it is inherent in the structure of economic theory that only individuals can make value judgments. A society or a nation is not a sentient organism able to enjoy and appreciate or make aesthetic and moral determinations; only men and women can do that. The significance of this individualistic postulate is that it quickly leads one to the corollary that all individuals should be treated equally as valuing beings. Consequently, there are strong democratic and egalitarian elements inherent in the basic logic of economics. With very few exceptions, economists have been committed democrats since Adam Smith's time.

Finally, I wish to point out that economics contains a strong cosmopolitan element. We talk about the national income and the national welfare, and we advise on policies that are in the best interests of our own nation state. But the nation is really a pragmatic rather than a fundamental unit in economic theory. From its earliest days in the late eighteenth century, scientific economics has had an international orientation, and one of its most notable achievements is the demonstration of the mutuality of the economic interests of individual nations.

In sum then, I see economics (and I think I might be able to say the same for sociology as well) as a study of humankind that is committed to liberalism, democracy, and cosmopolitanism. At the end of the eighteenth century, the English political philosopher Edmund Burke moaned that "the age of chivalry is gone. That of sophisters, economists and calculators has succeeded, and the glory of Europe is extinguished forever." How wrong he was! The age of chivalry was just beginning, and "economists and calculators" were destined to play a large role in it. That role is not yet ended.

MODERN PROBLEMS

I have been dealing, in general terms, with social science and intellectual history. I would now like to turn to the specific and focus attention on more concrete issues of contemporary concern. There are, it seems to me, a number of developments that have emerged as problems in economically advanced and politically demo-cratic societies. For my present purpose, I have attempted to package them under the following labels: (1) the Brave New World Problem; (2) the Affluent Society Problem; (3) the Entrenched Oligarchy Problem; and (4) the Problem of Profes-sionalism. Each of these will be discussed in turn.

The Brave New World Problem

A one-armed social scientist would be a terribly maimed creature, for there are hardly any of us who can get very far without saying, "on the other hand." Having just sung the praises of social science and covered myself and my colleagues with honour as the most rational and humane spirits of the modern age, it is only to be expected that I will now go on to say, "however, on the other hand ..." There is an obverse to the face of our intellectual heritage that I have been portraying, and it seems to become more important every day that we take note of it.

I have called this "the brave new world problem" because the best presentation of it that I know is in Aldous Huxley's novel of that name written in the early 1930s. Most people seem to remember this novel as a picture of society that is horrifying because motherhood has been made obsolete by science. The inhab-itants of Huxley's world (it is not certain that we should call them "people") are of two sexes and possess the requisite equipment and capacity for sexual enjoy-ment, but they do not do so for the purpose of human reproduction at all, not even incidentally, or, indeed, even accidentally. The production of life in this way is regarded as obscene and has been outlawed. Science has developed much neater, and more efficient, methods of providing the labour and specialized skills required by an industrial society. The required humanoid organisms are produced in test tubes under controlled laboratory conditions where nothing is left to chance. It is a eugenist's dream – and a humanist's nightmare.

If we look a bit closer at Huxley's "brave new world," however, we find that what makes it repulsive is not the success of the biochemist in synthesizing the human reproductive process. This aspect is not really even very shocking when we come down to it. After all, the modern educational system is not essentially different from Huxley's test tubes. We get the raw material out of a womb, but we then convert it into "human capital" by running it through a mill that grinds, and shapes, and stamps it out into a well-trained engineer, or a computer programmer, or a literary critic, or an economist. We don't even have to contend against parental love in carrying out this process; the modern parent is anxious to shove the little ingot of his adoration into the maw of this machine.

No, what is unsatisfactory in the "brave new world," when one comes down to it, is that the dream of social science has come true. Everyone is well fed, well clothed, well housed. There is a great deal of leisure, and there are many opportunities for enjoyment. There is even provision for variety in tastes; some girls are more "pneumatic" than others. Everybody is satisfied and happy. Now what can be wrong with that? It is a utilitarian heaven; isn't that what we have been striving for all along?

Nevertheless, this "brave new world" is horrible, as Huxley meant it to be. What is essentially repellent about it is its *flatness*. There is no striving, no yearning, no dreaming or creating. All the tally-ho is organized so that there should be no disappointment, no misadventure, and no pain. Tennyson had his hero Ulysses sigh, "Must we forever climb the climbing wave?" as if he found it a burden, but the plain fact is he wanted to climb; indeed, he was compelled to by his human nature. Humans are romantic beings. They seek adventure and danger, fame and glory. They are like Don Quixote de la Mancha, and if there were no giants or dragons in the world, they would create some so that they might fight them.

This is one of the oldest and most persistent themes in our literature. If you read the English poets and novelists of the early nineteenth century, you will find that they loathed the world of industrial capitalism and material progress that was coming into being and that they were contemptuous of the philosophy of utilitarianism on which the new social science was founded. Carlyle called it the "pig philosophy," but he was only a little more violent in expressing views that were shared by Coleridge, Wordsworth, Tennyson, Dickens, Ruskin, and the rest of the English Romantics.

In essentials, the Romantics were wrong. Economic and material progress is not the enemy of civilization and higher humanism. It would be truer to regard it as a precondition. Poverty is not an aesthetic or a moral virtue. Suffering and starvation do not make individuals wiser and more humane. Fortunately for us today, the great nineteenth-century contention between the utilitarians and the Romantics was won by the utilitarians. The Romantics may have dominated the world of literature and music and philosophy, but the utilitarians dominated the economy, including, to a somewhat lesser extent, the state.

Nevertheless, the nineteenth-century Romantics had a finger on something of importance, and we are now being forced to recognize their insight into the human condition. The "brave new world problem," as I have called it, is that we have no reason to believe that humankind will be satisfied with a state of economic plenty and security. To the adventurous spirit, these are merely bourgeois virtues. Humans need challenges – and enemies.

I sometimes think how simple was the world of my youth compared to that of today. We had two great enemies – the Depression and the Germans – big enough, and evil enough, and dangerous enough for anybody's taste. There is no equivalent for them in today's world. Most of our sons and daughters have been brought up in a world of plenty – unlimited food, good clothing and shelter, personal security, education of high quality – and, as a consequence, they feel deprived. The Dutch philosopher Johan Huizinga wrote a book some twenty-five years ago called *Homo Ludens* (man, a game-playing animal) in which he pointed out the significance of play in human culture. Today we are very much in need of some good games that would provide the excitement and the thrill of contest but not undermine economic progress, political democracy, or the development of humans into more sensitive and civilized creatures. The physicists have made it pretty dangerous for us to play war anymore, and besides that, a lot of us are getting too civilized to enjoy it.

The Affluent Society Problem

Under this heading I want to consider a social problem to which John K. Galbraith's book *The Affluent Society* brought widespread public attention some ten years ago. It is a very peculiar problem because it almost seems to reverse the general and obvious rule that a wealthy society can provide more material benefits for its citizens than a poor one can. A society that is progressing economically and steadily increasing its general command of economic resources may in fact become less capable of serving a certain range of human needs even though, in principle, it is necessary only that the requisite amount of economic resources be devoted to them.

As a society develops economically, and especially as it becomes more urbanized, its need for what economists call "collective goods" rises. By "collective goods" we mean goods and services that cannot be provided individually to consumers in response to their individual preferences and needs. A standardized good has to be provided generally for all members of a given community. It is possible for me to exercise my individual taste for food or clothing – I simply go to the shops and buy what suits my own peculiar wants, and every other member of the community can do the same. It is easy for an economy (of any type) to meet the diversity of such needs. But I cannot exercise, in the same way, my preference for something like street cleanliness. I could sweep the street outside my own home, but that is not really what I want; I want the streets of my community *generally* to be clean. In brief, there is no private property in street cleanliness; all members of the community enjoy its benefits collectively.

There are, of course, many goods that are individually consumed, like shirts and socks and steak, but there are also many that are inherently collective, including a large proportion of civic and other governmental services and some publicly supported goods and services, such as the educational system and various cultural and recreational facilities.

The main problem with such collective goods is that it is difficult to manage them and to finance them. The same person who would not drop a cigarette butt in his own driveway will cheerfully empty the ashtray of his car in the public roadway. The same person who would regard it as barbarous not to send his children to school will wiggle like an eel to avoid the taxes that must be levied to pay for such collective goods as schools. (The city of Youngstown, Ohio, had to close its public school system for the last month of 1968 because it did not have the money to pay its expenses. This occurred not in Appalachia or in Mississippi, but in a modern and prosperous industrial city that enjoys the full fruits of the past decade of rapid economic growth. The people of Youngstown simply refused to vote the taxes necessary to pay for their schools!)

There is another aspect of this problem that will, I think, greatly exacerbate the difficulty of providing an adequate level of public services and other collective goods. It arises from the fact that a large proportion of these goods and services are "labour intensive," as economists say, and it is not possible to increase by much the productivity of labour in such lines of activity. This gives rise to what has been called "Baumol's disease," after William J. Baumol of Princeton, who used the idea a few years ago to explain why the performing arts are experiencing greater and greater financial difficulty as the society they serve becomes wealthier and wealthier.

Let me try to explain this phenomenon by reference to the problem of education – where, I believe, it will have some of its most acute impact in the next few years.

As a society progresses economically, its output per person rises. So the wages of automobile workers, and steelworkers, and textile workers, and others go up. But this means that the salaries of teachers and professors must go up, too, if for no other reason than to draw the requisite workforce into the education industry. But if we maintain the same ratio of teachers to students as before, the cost of providing the education per student will rise, and it will keep on rising as long as economic progress continues, even without any improvement in the quality of the educational services provided. Automobiles and shirts may not rise in price because technical improvements mean an increase of car and shirt output per person, but if we do not increase the number of students "processed" per teacher – and, in my opinion, we cannot do so without reducing the quality of education, particularly at elementary school levels – then we have to be prepared to face the necessity of providing *more money per student every year* just to maintain the existing quality of education.

This problem is not peculiar to education. It will be faced by all parts of the economy that are labour-intensive, from barbershops to ballet companies. Unfortunately, since a large part of the public services financed by taxation are labour-intensive, we may well discover that they are squeezed between the increasing costs due to "Baumol's disease," on the one hand, and the reluctance of people to tax themselves for the provision of collective goods and services, on the other.

This problem is already with us: "Private affluence and public squalor" it has been called. The public sector of our society becomes more and more squalid as the private sector becomes more and more affluent. The picture of community life, and particularly urban life, that this trend generates is not attractive. I have the impression that this problem is, so far, more acute in the United States than in Canada, but it is a general problem inherent in the characteristics of economic progress itself. This problem of public finance is not so serious for those levels of government that receive a large proportion of their revenues from progressively scheduled income taxes, for these will automatically yield more revenues as economic growth takes place. It will be the junior governments, and especially the cities, that will really feel the pinch, but even at the federal level, the willingness of the public to levy increased taxes upon themselves is a precondition of social progress in a modern world. Any economically advanced society that fails to develop the higher level of community consciousness necessary to support a marked improvement in the finance and administration of public services and other collective goods will be an uncivilized place – dirty, ugly, ignorant, and unsafe – despite, indeed partly because of, its technical and economic progress. Perhaps I should have called this "the King Midas problem."

The Enriched Oligarchy Problem

I would now like to go on to discuss the problem of maintaining and promoting a high degree of social mobility in our society. For the past two centuries or so, humankind has been living in exceedingly fluid societies. Revolutions have taken place all over the world – economic revolutions and political revolutions – and today there is hardly a corner that has not experienced the displacement of old, hardened institutions and the establishment of new economic systems, new social practices, and new political authorities.

In Canada, and in the countries that have been of principal importance in Canadian social and economic development – that is, Great Britain and the United States – the revolutionary developments that created the mobility and fluidity I am talking about were almost exclusively economic in origin. It is true that the British went so far as to cut off a foolish monarch's head in the seventeenth century, but nothing really changed very much so far as the mass of the people were concerned. The United States was born in a revolution that had immense political and international consequences, but, again, I don't think it can be said that the structure and dynamics of American society were much affected by it. The Daughters of the American Revolution were not so silly as they seemed a few years ago when, despite their name, they passed a declaration condemning all revolutions. As far as Canada's only effort in that direction was concerned, we didn't even get as far as to knock off a bishop's mitre.

The extraordinary social fluidity of these countries has been due to their industrial revolutions, not their political ones. In England, before the late eighteenth century, there existed a fusion of economic and political power that was almost complete. Its basis was *land*. Ownership of land conferred wealth and economic power, and it determined social status and political authority as well. What the industrial revolution did was to permit the growth of economic wealth on a large scale outside the orbit of landed power, and this produced in the society a degree of mobility hitherto unknown or even dreamed of. North America was an even more fluid society than Britain. Except in the American South and possibly in French Canada, social and economic power never did become firmly connected with land, and, anyway, since land was not limited in supply, there could be no monopoly of it of the sort necessary to social exclusiveness.

As a result of the economic growth that has characterized the past century, our societies have continued to be quite fluid. Not perfectly so, of course. Indeed, far from it. We have never been even within telescopic distance of a society of complete equality of opportunity, but we are now a lot closer to it than at any previous time in human history.

In the late nineteenth century, many Americans became exceedingly worried that their society might be closing and hardening. They saw the development of an entrenched oligarchy of plutocratic businessmen using the newly developed laws of corporate organization to establish "trusts," as they were then called, and to fix themselves forever into economic and political power. Mark Twain, the great iconoclast, wrote about it in his first novel, *The Gilded Age*, in which he not only flayed the shallow mammonism of his society, but also sounded the alarm that the men of business had corrupted politics and were seizing political power for themselves. He didn't think much of the intelligence of congressmen and senators and even less of their morals. He wasn't alone in this; the literature and journalism on this theme was a flourishing industry at the time.

The rule of the trusts didn't take place in the United States partly because they were attacked by law, partly because of the growth of trade unions as independent centres of power, but mainly because the economy continued to expand and to generate innovations in products and in methods of production that kept the established business enterprises off balance and prevented them from consolidating their power. It may be that we can depend on continued economic chance to keep advanced industrial societies from developing into hardened oligarchies, but there are times when I am not optimistic about this. It seems to me that certain developments have taken place already, and are continuing, that will have a strong tendency to reduce social mobility in countries such as Canada and the United States. I can't talk about this extensively here, but I would like to sketch the outlines of what I have in mind.

The most important development in social organization during the past half-century or so has been the growth of bureaucracy. I am not referring only to government when I use this term. The bureaucratic form of organization has become solidly established in modern business and industry, in trade unions, in the professions, in education, and in almost everything else. It is in these bureaucracies that power resides. The political, economic, and social functions of our society are becoming increasingly concentrated within a limited number of these bureaucracies, which tend to become, as a result, the dominant established institutions of society, just as the church and the aristocracy were in earlier times.

Modern bureaucracies may appear to be very different from the medieval church and aristocracy but they share certain common characteristics in respect of the crucial question of the recruitment of new members to occupy senior positions of authority within their structures. Like the church, modern bureaucracies recruit into themselves people who appear to be reliable perpetuators of their established practices. Senior bureaucrats invite people who are like themselves to share and to inherit power. Like the ancient aristocrat, the modern bureaucrat is particularly anxious to see to it that his own children are well placed. I am not saying that deputy ministers and general managers hand over their jobs directly to their sons or that union presidents bequeath the union to theirs. That is not necessary. The same general result is produced if the bureaucrat in one establishment enables his son to get a good start on the hierarchical ladder in another. In our society, it is virtually impossible for the children of a successful person to fall down into the pool of common labour, unless they are determined to do so. The children of the lower classes have to work hard to be successes. The children of the middle and upper classes have to make great efforts to be failures.

The result of this is that the bureaucracies that make up the established institutions of modern society tend to become dominated by entrenched oligarchies. The children of the poor and the rejected have never had a fair shake in the social crap game; they are going to get an even worse one if we do not make strong efforts to increase the fluidity of society. There is one feature of modern social organization that could be used to exert a great deal of leverage in this direction. All the bureaucracies depend upon the educational system for the training and certification of its recruits. If the educational system were to increase its own fluidity, it could have a multiplied effect upon the social mobility of the whole society.

The Problem of Professionalism

Another development in modern society that I would like to comment on briefly is the trend to organize everyone into professional categories. This is not confined to the formally licensed professions, such as medicine or law, but is much more general. The modern craft union goes back historically to the old medieval guilds. Today we have organizations not only of plasterers, electricians, and doctors, but of morticians, real estate salesmen, air traffic controllers, university registrars, and so on. Everyone belongs to a guild or syndicate of one kind or another.

Some of these associations are very loose affairs whose programs are primarily social or educational, but many of them possess some form of regulatory power over the practice of the profession, and many more aim at achieving such power. Sometimes this power is exercised in order to protect the general public from quackery or fraud, but more often than not its object is to protect the practitioners of the profession from competition. When an association announces that it is adopting a "code of ethical practices" in order to "raise professional standards," you can usually be pretty sure that a drive is afoot to create a cozy little monopoly and to limit entry into the profession.

Many of these organizations have even achieved legal status for their regulatory powers – they act as arms of the state in policing the profession. And often we grant this power without even making sure that the regulatory activity will be carried out in a fair and nondiscriminatory manner. The result is a weird tissue of ambiguities. We attack some restrictive and discriminatory practices with the law while at the same time we give to others its support and sanction. Professional and trade syndicates have been a potent force working against the social mobility of disadvantaged groups in our society, and I see no reason to believe that they will not continue to be so. This has been more of a problem in the United States because of the widespread discrimination against blacks, but it has not been without significance in Canada, and it may continue to grow as such associations proliferate and acquire status and power.

I have singled out this problem for some special comment instead of treating it as an aspect of the social mobility question because of the special significance of the development of professional specialization in the field of knowledge. This is a fairly recent development – only about a hundred years old, I think. Before that time there were people who were biologists or chemists or physicians or economists, and they labelled themselves as such but not with the degree of exclusiveness in use today. If Joseph Priestley had called himself a chemist or John Stuart Mill had called himself a political economist, this would have been more a prideful claim to the possession of a body of knowledge or a skill rather than an exclusive designation. Up to about the 1870s, most educated people were well read in all the various areas of human knowledge; to be a biologist, say, or a chemist, was merely to be especially well read in that field.

Today, by contrast, a professional designation in a particular field of scholarship or science is virtually a certificate of ignorance in all other fields. The academic scholar nowadays is the kind of person who can see a fly on a barn door at fifty feet but can't see the door or even the barn. Most research work is carried out by ignoramuses of genius, who root out little truffles of empirical fact from the body of mother earth like a perigord pig on a leash and who are about as equally concerned with the human significance of their work. There is the story (it may be apocryphal, but it could easily be true) of the scientist who was invited to attend a conference on "the future of man" and declined the invitation on the ground that this was not his field!

I hate to give up any area of knowledge to the "authorities" in the subject. It seems to me that there is an inherent medievalism in doing so, a danger of turning science into a kind of religion. It is especially dangerous to leave social science to the social scientists. There is very little in the social sciences that can be left exclusively to the economists and sociologists on the ground that it is purely technical. The welfare and the future of humankind are always involved, even in the most arid of our researches.

What disturbs me most, however, is not that professional men in other fields do not discuss social questions, but that they so often do so with ignorance and prejudice, and the with sublime assurance that usually accompanies these. Medical doctors will discourse on the economics of health services with less detachment than a drug dealer can muster. Professors of English literature will talk about the economy as if they could simply imagine it, like the plot of a play. Philosophers skilled in logical analysis will abandon everything they have been taught, and have been teaching to others, in favour of assertions about society beginning with "It is obvious that ..." and followed by some private piece of unsubstantiated, and often unsubstantiable, intuition. Some intellectuals have even rejected the principle of scientific objectivity generally and totally not only in social questions, but for all fields of knowledge. Three admiring students of Herbert Marcuse, for example, write that "the essential element in Marcuse's teaching is that knowledge is partisan" and that "scientific objectivity, intellectual neutrality, and value-free thinking" are "mere pretensions" that "betray the goals of knowledge." I tremble when I think of the other gods we are expected to worship instead. According to this view, Lysenko's practice of faking his genetics experiments in order that the results should agree with Stalin's political ideology would be the new wave of intellectual development.

I have probably gone far enough in this vein – one can plainly see that I am vexed, and I have probably bruised enough sensibilities already. I began by discussing the development of social science as a bright chapter in humankind's efforts to free itself from myth and tyranny, and I have now come around to saying that this great light has been dimmed by the development of intellectual professionalism, which has led some of our best intellects to resign altogether from the discussion of social questions and others to discuss them as simpletons and arrant drivellers.

I will turn now to the problem of developing rational policy in a modern society.

BLUEPRINTS VS. LITTLE STEPS

Someone once defined an economist as a man who is frequently in error but never in doubt. There is enough truth in that to sting. A few years ago we used to play a little game of suggesting appropriate collective nouns for the various academic disciplines. We refer to a "herd" of horses, a "pride" of lions, and a "flock" of geese; what should we call a group of chemists or historians or social scientists? The best of these terms that I can now recall was a "fall-out" of physicists and a "pretension" of economists. When one thinks of it, it really is pretentious to be a social scientist at all, to believe that one can make some sense out of the behaviour of that perverse, stubborn, opinionated, bigoted, and willful creature *Homo sapiens,* and even more pretentious to believe that some members of that species may find, and persuade others to be guided into, the paths of righteousness. In the course of the past century and a half, social scientists have suffered some heavy disappointments, but we are still plugging away and still believe that the world may be constructively changed by what we do. We are optimists, and that is perhaps the greatest pretension of all.

I noted earlier that the rise of social science in the nineteenth century was not viewed with enthusiasm by the established humane disciplines: literature and theology. The past hundred years or so has not stilled their criticism of our approach to the phenomenon of man, and we still find it expressed, sometimes sharply, today.

Some of these criticisms are merely puerile – like the recurrent theme of some humanists that social scientists talk nonsense because they often employ repellent technical language or jargon. During the past three years I have been on the

Board of Editors of an academic journal whose interests lie primarily in literary interpretation, and I have had to read many manuscripts coming from the pens of literary scholars. I can offer the assurance that economists and sociologists have no monopoly on obscurantism or on professional jargon. The examination of the condition of humankind by means of the literary imagination is frequently opaque and badly written. Some other criticisms that I have seen of social science seem to be more profound than this, but they often call for one to try to understand humankind and to meet its problems on the basis of pure intuition, rather than scientific knowledge, as a methodological principle. Even worse, they sometimes tend to enthrone ideology and doctrinal authoritarianism as the guides, or perhaps I should say the goads, of human action.

Nevertheless, as I have tried to point out, there are some insights of great value to be found in the humanist perception of humankind's nature, which social science has neglected. It may well be that the more we grow in economic wealth and the more we develop our society into one of industrialization, high technology, and urbanism, the more we should tune our ears to what the humanists say about the state of our civilization.

I am returning to this now because I am going to discuss social policy – that is, collective action to come to grips with our collective problems – and I want to emphasize the necessity of taking a large and comprehensive view of the objectives and effects of social policies. To say this, in such a general way, would seem to be merely to utter a platitude. But I think that there is little doubt that one of our major difficulties in doing what should be done in society is due to the fact that almost all of the policies initiated by governments are specific and ad hoc. They are directed at immediate and concrete economic or social or political problems, and little or no attention is paid to their larger and cumulative consequences. Politicians and civil servants pride themselves on being "practical men" and are impatient with people who raise issues that they regard as being "philosophical" or "academic." My point is that, in the long, run, it may prove to be very impractical not to be philosophical. The theme that will be the basis of what I have to say is that those who advise on, determine, and administer the policies of governments must be urged to adopt a much wider angle and a much longer focus of vision than they have customarily taken if we are to deal adequately with the human problems of living in a modern society.

One of the things that I would like to do here is to try to make this view of the requirements of modern social policy concrete enough for use as a practical guidance principle. In order to do so, however, I will have to begin by discussing more generally the philosophy of social policy implied in this view. The first point that I must make is a disclaimer. When I say that our social policies must be guided by more comprehensive and longer-range goals, I do not mean that they must embrace the totality of life or that they must be cast into the framework of the grand sweep of history. At first sight, it may seem as if such a disclaimer is unnecessary. Who is audacious enough to believe that he or she could prescribe, once and for all, the blueprint of the ideal society? But whether it is audacious or not, it has been one of the most common themes of social philosophy since Plato. You could fill a sizable bookcase with the writings of men and women who, over the course of Western history, have dreamed of the perfect state and have committed their visions to paper. You could fill a whole library with the books that have been written as commentaries on these visions.

This is not a matter of interest only to people who dig around in libraries. During the nineteenth century dozens of communities were founded, most of them in the United States, by people who wished to turn their dream of social perfection into reality. Other dreamers, instead of going off into the American wilderness, set about to revolutionize their own societies and turn them into ideal states, and some of these dreamers succeeded, at least to the extent of creating the revolutions.

Moreover, this is clearly not a matter of only historical interest. The utopian cast of mind, if I may call it that, is an important feature of contemporary controversy in Western social philosophy. The view that the particular evils of our society reflect a rottenness that is total; that reform of existing society and gradual progress are not possible; that one must start with a clean slate and build the new society without being constrained by existing institutions; that revolution is justified in itself because it "cleans the slate"; that in order to build a just society one must create a "totally new individual": These are ideas that one will find expressed today on almost every college campus in the Western world. Some people who hear them identify them as Marxist doctrine and regard their exponents as simply a new wave of the "Communist conspiracy," but, in fact, many of them are anti-Marxist and anti-Communist. Marxism, after all, is not the only version of utopian romanticism in the history of political philosophy. When people start talking about how terrible contemporary society is and advocating its wholesale reconstruction, they may not be Marxists or Communists; they may not even be Christians!

They may not be fools either, but the chances are that their prescription for social policy is very wrong and may be productive of much suffering and evil. During World War Two, the philosopher Karl Popper wrote an important book called *The Open Society and Its Enemies*. The theme of the book is that the enemies of political freedom and social progress are those who have fallen under the "Spell of Plato" and dream of creating a new society according to a specific blueprint. In their effort to wipe the slate clean of encumbering institutions, such people would cheerfully create misery and death on a wholesale scale. In their effort to create the new individual, they would turn education into indoctrination. In their desire to carry the blueprint into realization, they would clamp an iron tyranny upon all people, and anyone who demurred would be shot as a "counter-revolutionary." When I first read Popper's book some fifteen years ago, it seemed to me that he had presented an exaggerated picture. I no longer think so. I am reminded again of poor Urbain Grandier, who was fearfully tortured and burnt at the stake for the good of his soul by men who had the best interests of society at heart. We have to recognize that great evil can be done in the name of righteousness, that visionaries can be vicious, that a person who yearns for the millennium will welcome a cataclysm and may not shrink from offering up human sacrifices.

Karl Popper's recommendation was that we avoid the evils of utopianism by adopting as our philosophy of social policy what he called "piecemeal experimentation." This view has been given further expression and development in recent years by the American political scientist Charles E. Lindblom, who uses the term "discrete incrementalism" to express the policy approach he advocates. The basic idea is that a society will best combine progress and freedom if its social policy consists of limited specific programs devoted to limited specific problems and undertaken by specific governmental agencies, without any effort to knit it all together in any comprehensive way. By this means, it is argued, we may experiment over a broad front affecting a great variety of policy efforts, and we can then follow through on those that are successful and abandon, without loss, those that are not.

I have great difficulty in accepting either of these two polar positions on the philosophy of social policy. I am willing to accept the view that the utopianism of comprehensive social planning would be a retrograde and possibly very dangerous philosophy, at least for a society such as ours that is already economically advanced, democratic, and socially progressive, and therefore has much to lose of great human value. It does not follow however that the only way in which we can preserve our achievements and make further advances is by confining social policies to narrow limits and short-range objectives. It seems to me that we can do better than this and that we can do it safely. A social scientist, if he or she is realistic, will realize that to sit down to write the constitution of utopia is equivalent to nominating oneself for dictator, or, if you like, "philosopher king." But I don't think it is unrealistic for us to take the view that we can develop our specific social policies within an integrated framework of goals. The weakness of our economic and social policies at the present time is that they are in fact *too much* what Popper and Lindblom prescribe. They are too "piecemeal" and "disjointed," and we could do better if we were prepared to be somewhat more comprehensive.

I would now like to give some brief illustrations that may help to make my argument here more tangible. My illustrations will be two areas of policy that have been of exceptional importance since World War Two: housing policy and taxation policy.

Like most other countries, Canada has been engaged, over the past twenty years or so, in encouraging the construction of housing units by a variety of public policies. Housing policy has been, in the United States as well as in Canada, a clear case of the sort of thing that Popper and Lindblom have advocated: specific policies strongly focused on specific problems and restricted to that focus. The problem of housing policy has been construed as the problem of building houses; it's as simple as that. Accordingly, policy in this area is merely a matter of making financial and other effective arrangements to draw the appropriate volume of the nation's productive resources into housing: The policy is measured and evaluated in terms of the number of units constructed.

The difficulty with such a policy approach is that when one builds houses, one is also engaged in the process of building a city. If we have a housing policy only and do not have a more comprehensive urban development policy into which housing fits, then it is unlikely that the city that will emerge will be the best possible city that civilized humans can conceive and create. It may in fact turn out to be a very bad city indeed. Much of what has been written about the tawdriness of suburban living in North America is true, and much of the agonizing that has been going on over the decay of the central city is well founded.

A great many of our problems with respect to this aspect of modern life stem from a quite extraordinary gap between our image of humankind and the contemporary economic reality. We still think of humankind as labouring under the curse of Adam and Eve – expelled from the Garden of Eden and condemned to produce their bread by the sweat of their brows – and for most people that means being a farmer. Our literature and our philosophy alike have glorified the agriculturalist. Being "close to the soil" and "in communion with mother nature" are viewed as superior ways of life that carry with them virtue, goodness, and wisdom as necessary adjuncts. Some, at least, will remember the schoolroom in which you read Oliver Goldsmith's *Deserted Village* as an elegy for a bygone golden age of rurality and the novels of Charles Dickens as warnings of ineffable evil and misery inherent in city life. What is the widespread desire to own a suburban house on its own lot, with its own trees and garden, but a modern version of the family farm of earlier times? The ranch-style bungalow is a surrogate for a ranch.

One of the major problems of modern times is our inability to shake ourselves free of powerful rural images despite the fact that we are an urban and industrial people. Professors Harvey Lithwick and Gilles Paquet, writing recently in their collection, *Urban Studies*, arrive at the conclusion that: "many of our present problems in both the urban and the regional environment stem from what may be called an agrarian or peasant view of economic reality. The changes brought about on the spatial organization of society as a result of economic development make this view archaic and irrelevant. Since it prevails in the hearts and minds of our policy-makers, it is little wonder that we have been notoriously unsuccessful in coping with both our urban and our regional problems." This is, I think, a trenchant evaluation of the case. A colleague of mine at Indiana University, Professor Jerome Milliman, has pointed out that of the large expenditures made from the federal treasury in the United States for the purpose of social and scientific research, the US Department of Agriculture had $262 million to spend in 1968, while the Department of Housing and Urban Development had less than $1 million – this in a country in which less than 7 per cent of the population live on farms and which produces agricultural "surpluses" that it finds difficult to get rid of. The situation in Canada is not appreciably different: The Department of Agriculture of the federal government is one of the largest anachronisms to be found in any modern state.

We have to come to grips with the modern human as a city dweller in our social policies. The problem will be a real test of our ability to engage in comprehensive social planning and direction without falling into the error of constructing hard utopian blueprints. It is of more than passing interest that utopian philosophers have usually cast their visions of perfection in the form of ideal cities – from Plato's *Republic* to Ebenezer Howard's *Garden Cities of Tomorrow*. There is a danger of totalitarianism in the idea of city planning that it would be foolish for us to neglect, but we have to risk it. Great cities will not automatically come into being as a result of housing policy and urban-transport policy and city-services policy and so on, all pursued in a piecemeal and disjointed way. We have to have urban policy. Modern humans do not merely need housing and buses and sewers. They need a CITY in which to live.

I might add, before leaving this topic, that Canada is, at the present time, in a much more fortunate position than the United States. Canadian cities, it seems to me, are by and large promising: They have not yet met the needs of modern humans, but they have not yet been ruined. Many American cities have become degenerate – so much so that some American social scientists have recommended that their centre be turned into parkland with the focus of urban development shifted to the suburbs altogether. This, to my mind, is a council of despair and would amount to abandoning the opportunities of city life in the effort to solve some of its problems. The seriousness of the situation in the United States is indicated by the decision of the Nixon administration to create a Cabinet-level Urban Affairs Council under the direct chairmanship of the president. It represents a major effort on the part of the national government to cope with the problems of city life. We will have to come to that in Canada, too. I must add here that the urban problem in the United States intersects on so many planes with the racial issue that it is impossible to discuss the one without the other. Canadian cities have problems, but American cities are in a continuous state of explosiveness that reflects the racial crisis now dominating American domestic life and thought. The new focus on urbanism that is emerging in American social policy is in large part a result of this intersection.

I now want to go on to discuss the other case that I have chosen to illustrate the argument put forward earlier: taxation. I have chosen this topic partly because of its importance as an instrument of public policy but also because it was the object of a royal commission investigation a few years ago that is of exceptional interest. The report of the Carter Commission is a remarkable document in the history of public finance. But it is more than that; it is a landmark in the history of social policy.

What makes the Carter report outstanding is its attempt to bring order into our system of taxation by providing the guidance of a set of general principles and general social goals. Traditionally, taxation has been used in the past as the string-pull for ad hoc economic and social policies of all kinds and descriptions. Whenever it has been decided to encourage one line of activity (like prospecting for uranium) or to discourage another (like the consumption of alcohol), it is the power of the Royal Fisc that has been most often brought in to do the job. In this area we have been practising for many years the principles of social policy that Popper and Lindblom preach, and the result is absolute chaos. We now devote more highly trained talent to attempting to understand the tax laws, and to loophole them, than we do to administering them. Economists themselves have been an important factor in this accumulation of the ad hoc. One of the things that economists feel fairly confident about is the economic analysis of the probable effects of taxes and subsidies, and since hardly anybody else seems to be able to talk sensibly about such matters at all, there has been a fairly clear field. But, typically, economic advice on tax policy has been confined strictly to narrow specifics. I am quite sure that if, a few years ago, an economist in the Department of Finance or of Revenue had raised the issue of the general principles of taxation in relation to general social goals, the message would have come through to him loud and clear from on high: "There is no future for you here; get thee to a university."

But royal commissions are allowed to be philosophical about public affairs, if they choose to be, and the Carter Commission chose to be. I cannot here enter into a discussion of the commission's proposals. It is sufficient to say that by adopting the view that equity in taxation demands that people should be taxed according to their incomes and that a person's income is measured by his or her acquisition of power to command the resources of the economy, the commission laid the foundation for a coherent system of taxation. It could, in my opinion, have gone further than it did in elucidating the basic principles of social policy that taxation should serve: The commissioners could have been even more "philosophical," especially in defining the economic and social role of the modern business corporation and providing thereby better principles of corporate taxation, but this is a minor defect compared with the achievements.

I hardly need to mention that the public reception of the Carter report has not been in accord with this interpretation of its merits. Most of the academic economists leapt to their feet and shouted "Bravo!" but almost everyone else hissed. Some of the latter reaction is a bit hard to understand. It may have been nothing more than the simple ignorance of conservatism. (A French commentator on early-nineteenth-century English politics once observed of Lord Liverpool, who was first lord of the Treasury, that had he been present in heaven on the first day of creation he would have exclaimed, "Mon Dieu! Conservons le chaos!") I suspect, in addition, that peculiar vested interests accumulate around any complex and disjointed taxation system. After working the loopholes for many years, people become convinced that they are pretty good at it and that they pick pockets more deeply than they are picked from. The academic social scientist may believe that it is desirable to have a fiscal system that anyone can understand, but there are many taxpayers who think that it is in their interest to have one that no one can understand.

It seems very unlikely that the proposals of the Carter Commission will be directly implemented in Canada. Some academicians would count it a failure if we did not set about the wholesale reconstruction of the system according to the Carter plan. If I have made my argument clear earlier, one will understand that I do not share this view. The role of general principles in social policy is not to present a blueprint for the construction of a wholly new structure. They are much more effective as guides for the gradual reconstruction of the old. We are not likely to tear down the old taxation system and erect a new one in its place and, if we did, we'd immediately set to work to make alterations in the new one.

We will always be making changes in our social policies, in taxation, and in other areas. We need an architecture of social policy to guide not a master builder but the more pedestrian alterations carpenters, who are constantly at work in a progressive society. The Carter report will do its work if it acts as a general guide for the changes in taxation policy that will be made year by year in the future. Observers of tax policy and of public policy in general will observe Canada with great interest.

One of the reasons why the taxation system tends to become encumbered with all sorts of diverse (and sometimes incompatible) objectives, instead of being used as a straightforward instrument by which to raise public revenues in a clear and equitable way, is because social policies in Canada have to be carried out within a political system of divided jurisdiction. The federal government can attempt to accomplish many things by fiscal policy that the Constitution would constrain it from doing by other means. Federal states whose constitutions are old have had to be innovative in coping with the problems of the modern world, and most of the room available for exercising ingenuity in bypassing the restrictions of old constitutions has existed in the fiscal area of governmental power. I think that it is fair to say that Canada has been as ingenious as most federal states in coping with the problem. Yet one cannot avoid the conclusion that one of the major barriers against the development of social policies appropriate to the modern world is the archaic form of the federal system. The federal system in Canada was enacted at a time when the nature of Canadian society was very different from what it is today. It may have been suitable when Canada was a nation of farmers, but it is not suitable for an urbanized industrial society.

In modern society, it seems to me that there are two levels of government that are meaningful: the nation and the city. The nation corresponds, in a broad way, to the political self-consciousness of a people; it is an area within which there is a free flow of goods and services and of their factors of production; it represents, in most cases, a satisfactory scope for the development of economic and social policies; and, in a world composed of nation-states, a national government has an important role to play in controlling the country's relations (both friendly and hostile) with other sovereign powers. The city is important because it is the actual environmental entity in which most people live and work. By contrast, the province (and the individual state in the United States) is, in the modern world, an anachronism. It does not correspond to anything that can provide an effective scope for social and economic policy. I am all in favour of a high degree of governmental pluralism, but I cannot see what merit there is in carving up the country almost arbitrarily into large geographical segments and giving those segments quasi-sovereign political powers. Political divisions of this sort can be only troublesome for a nation that ought to develop coherent social policies, and they may even actively frustrate the functioning of some policies of great importance. (If a province, for example, in an effort to attract persons of wealth and influence, offers them the incentive of low or zero inheritance taxation, it will work powerfully against the achievement of greater economic equality and social mobility that should be one of the modern state's primary aims.)

It is for this reason that I do not think that one should dismiss out of hand the suggestion of some of the French Canadian separatists that Canada should be reconfederated into two almost sovereign nation-states. Some of the suggestions that have been made are clearly retrograde and would be a threat to economic development and social progress, but the idea of separatism is not inherently bad. When the British North American provinces united into a confederation in 1867, those who conceived the constitution had in mind the need to avoid the chief weakness that had manifested itself in the American federation: the excessive power of the individual states. But the events did not unfold according to this scenario. For a variety of reasons, many of which could not have been foreseen, governmental power became decentralized in Canada while the opposite trend was taking place in the United States. Today, Canada is a weak federation and the United States a strong one.

Now I do not want to be misunderstood on this point. I am not saying that French-English separation is the *only* way of achieving a framework of governmental organization that can be adequate to the demands of modern social and economic policy. It is possible that within the framework of the existing constitution, Canada as a single nation could regroup its governmental powers in a satisfactory way. What I *am* suggesting is that separatism might be another way of doing this – more radical, perhaps more dangerous, but not by any means impossible or entirely undesirable. In any case, if a modern industrial society is to meet the social challenges that such a society generates, it must accomplish somehow a form of governmental organization that permits the formulation and effective implementation of social policies at two fundamental levels: that of the nation and that of the city or metropolis. Power, finance, and political and bureaucratic talent must flow toward these two poles of social development, and the political entities that are, socially and economically speaking, nonentities – that is, the provinces – must correspondingly be reduced in importance.

I have become increasingly more specific, but I have, I think, come to the end of what I can fruitfully do here in that direction, and I want to return now to more general topics.

THE ESSENCE OF LIBERALISM

A large part of my time as an academician during the past twenty years has been spent in the study of the history of economic and social thought. One of the viewpoints that people who work in this field are likely, after a little while, to adopt is that there is nothing new beneath the sun. We have neat labels for particular viewpoints or sets of ideas, and it is fairly easy for us to stick one or more of them onto any contemporary argument and thereby identify it, just as a biologist would identify an insect. We have a fairly large selection of labels to choose from, such as liberalism, capitalism, socialism, communism, conservatism, individualism, pluralism, anarchism, utilitarianism, romanticism, fascism, and so on.

The trouble, however, is that the common, and even the academic, meanings of these labels do not stay constant. Anyone who has studied the political and economic thought of the past two centuries must be aware of the great changes that have taken place in political terminology. Many important words have acquired new connotations and some have changed their meanings almost completely. George Orwell wrote about this in his novel *Animal Farm*, suggesting that perversion of language may be employed as an instrument of political tyranny, and there is no doubt that he was on to something. But the terms we use in political discourse can also go through great shifts of meaning, even the 180° ones that Orwell satirized, as a result of an evolutionary process. The deliberate perversion of political language for nefarious purposes is undoubtedly an important feature of the Age of Propaganda in which we live, and it has made rational and informed discussion of social questions more difficult. In contemporary political discussion words are regarded as invested with ideological content, and many of them are viewed by some as "codes" for disguised or unconscious political ideas. In some circles, for example, "order" is a bad word and "protest" is a good one, while in others it is the other way round. Some people seem to believe that one makes a coherent political argument by shouting or displaying in print a single word like "fuck" or "shit," and perhaps they are right if they get an emotional and irrational reaction from others by doing so. Personally, I feel rather deprived by this development; it means that one cannot employ profanity for art or emphasis without risking a political identification. For a Nova Scotian like me that represents a definite decline in the standard of living. It may be that, in time, these extremities of speech will enlarge and enrich the language, but in the meantime we find ourselves almost incapable of rational political discourse because of the wholesale destruction of objective terminology.

Nevertheless, we must keep on talking about political and social problems. To fall silent in the face of intellectual bullying is no different from being silenced by the censor or the political police.

This is by way of edging around to the terminology that I find it necessary to employ in order to indicate what is, in my view, an appropriate philosophy of social policy for the modern world. I have struggled with the problem during the past few years and have had to discard some old and favourite pieces of intellectual lumber. The central pillars remaining are "rationalism" and "liberalism."

I am aware, of course, that there are some quarters where these terms, especially "liberalism," is a stench in the nostrils. In some contemporary discussion in the United States, "liberalism" denotes only the vileness and hypocrisy of those in established positions in the society: Some people use it as if it were a strong, rich, four-letter word. And this is not confined to the practitioners of "guerrilla theatre" in the streets but has extended itself into intellectual discussion.

A short while ago I wrote an article on John Kenneth Galbraith in an academic journal that circulates almost exclusively to economists. Among my "fan mail" arrived a postcard from New York saying, "Good for you – that article on Galbraith. He has been the *Lolly Pop* for all Lazy Parasitical Middle Class Sweet Liberals. He is the Rasputin of the Liberal Escapists." I reread my article quickly to see what could have caused such a remarkable outburst. I can conclude only that my correspondent was already loaded and that I had simply touched his hair trigger somehow. There seems to be quite a bit of political emotion primed and ready in our society at the present time, and if I had Jeremy Bentham's ability to invent new words altogether, or Marshall McLuhan's talent for obscurity, I would be tempted to talk about modern social problems in one, or both, of these styles. But that wouldn't really help.

"Liberalism" is a difficult term to use in expressing a modern social philosophy, not only because it makes some people see red (in two different senses for two very different opponents of it) but because it is one of those terms that have gone through the evolutionary process of alteration in meaning that I mentioned earlier.

The early-nineteenth-century philosophy of liberalism was highly individualistic. Society was conceived of as fundamentally a collection of individual persons, and individual freedom to pursue one's own interests was regarded as a principle that not only had a sound philosophical foundation, but would work more effectively than any other to promote the practical objectives of economic progress. The early-nineteenth-century liberals were not doctrinaire laissez-fairists – they did not advocate that there should be no state interference in the economy – but they did view the role of the state as small, and, generally, they were skeptical of the idea that the state as an institution could be an instrument for the effective promotion of human and social objectives.

It was the liberals themselves who undermined this position by working so effectively to increase the democratic representativeness of the state and to improve its administrative capacity. By the latter part of the nineteenth century, the term "liberalism" was adopting other connotations and resonances – it was being invested with the ideas of equality of opportunity, economic security, humaneness, amelioration, generosity – and the state was being invoked as an institution that should take upon itself the duty of promoting these social objectives. From being a philosophy that looked upon the coercive power of the state as an evil always to be deplored though sometimes necessary, liberalism became, in the English-speaking world at least, the leading philosophy of the positive, active, interventionist state that uses its power for the purpose of promoting a wide range of desirable social ends. This shift has been so complete that, today, the set of political ideas that used to be called "liberalism" is now most commonly called "conservatism." (In the game of political philosophy it is hard to identify the players without a historical scorecard.) Some modern writers on political philosophy reject this political infidelity of our language and wish to restore the older meaning of the term "liberalism" as a conveyance for the idea of strict individual freedom and responsibility, but they succeed only in confusing the discussion of important matters by attempting to exercise a proprietary interest in words.

The essential theme of liberalism, both old and new, it seems to me, is that the only valid purpose of society is to serve the welfare of the individuals of which it is composed. Only individuals are valuing entities. Societies, races, nations, and so on, even families, are collectivities; they are not sentient organisms, and it is invalid to ascribe to them qualities of sense and sensibility that apply only to individual beings.

Considered in these terms, it is plain that nothing fundamental hinges upon any abstract conception of the proper role of the state in modern life. The state is merely instrumental. It is not the embodiment of the "national soul"; it does not represent the "genius of the race." Phrases such as these (and there are lots of them) are meaningless. There is, as a consequence of this view, no merit as such in having a large or small scope for state action; it all depends on what will best serve the welfare of the nation's citizens considered as individuals. At the present stage in modern society, we need the services of a large and active state because there is much that we wish to accomplish that cannot be done otherwise. The liberal philosophy is essentially one of grappling with the affairs of the world in a rational and pragmatic way, without the constraints of dogma. But even more so it is the realization that the political work of humankind will never be finished. We must go on and on. The road may be marked as leading to utopia, but one of its essential features is that it never gets there. A great deal of what is fundamental in the political philosophy of liberalism was well expressed by Sir Wilfrid Laurier many years ago. Of all the writers on this subject, I find that he remains fresh and relevant, and I want to quote him here:

The principle of Liberalism is inherent in the very essence of our nature, to that desire for happiness with which we are all born into the world, which pursues us throughout life and which is never completely satisfied ... We constantly gravitate towards an ideal which we never attain. We only reach the goal we have proposed ourselves, to discover new horizons opening up, which we had not before even suspected. We rush on towards them and those horizons, explored in turn, reveal to us others which lead us even further and further ...

This condition of our nature is precisely what makes the greatness of man, for it condemns him irrevocably to movement, to progress ... There is always room for improvement of our condition, for the perfecting of our nature, and for the attainment by a larger number of an easier life.

Then he goes on to sound a warning:

Experience has established that invariably, imperceptibly, abuses will creep into the body social and end by seriously obstructing its upward march, if not endangering its existence ... There will always be men found, who will attach themselves with love to these abuses, defend them to the bitter end and view with dismay any attempt to suppress them. Woe to such men if they do not know how to yield and adopt proposed reforms! They will draw upon their country disturbances all the more terrible that justice shall have been long refused ... Wherever there is repression, there will be explosion, violence and ruin. I do not say this to excuse revolutions, as I hate revolutions and detest all attempts to win the triumph of opinions by violence. But I am less inclined to cast the responsibility on those who make them than on those who provoke them by their blind obstinacy.

This passage is from a speech of Laurier's to the Canadian Club of Quebec in 1877. He had just become leader of the Liberal Party, and he felt it necessary to say to his French Canadian compatriots that liberalism was not a religious heresy, that Catholics are more likely to suffer damnation on earth if they oppose social change than they are to do so in the afterlife by embracing it. It was a frankly partisan speech, and Laurier did not distinguish between the Liberal Party and liberalism as a political philosophy, but this does not diminish the wisdom or the modern relevance of his reasoning.

It is clear from what I have been saying on my own account, and from the passage I have quoted from Wilfrid Laurier, that reform and change are essential to the liberal philosophy. But make no mistake about it. This is no effort to preserve the status quo by giving small concessions that will hush the demand for far-reaching and fundamental social change. The history of the past two centuries gives eloquent testimony to the fact that it is the liberal rationalists, not the revolutionary romantics, who have been the true radicals. While most of the rest of the world has been engaged in the fruitless process of exchanging one tyranny for another, the countries that have adopted a liberal political philosophy have moved long distances along the road to a civilized and humane society, and they have also kept open the opportunity for continued progress in this direction. This is no cause for complacency. We are not civilized enough by any means. Our society is still very far from being generous and just. Liberalism still has a great deal of work to do.

I cannot, at this point, embark upon the description of a detailed agenda for liberal action in the modern world. If I were to do so, I would take up again the four large "problems" outlined above, and I would lay the greatest emphasis upon the need to prevent our society from hardening into entrenched oligarchies of wealth and power. Especially, I would talk long and loud and strongly about the obligation that falls upon the educational system to widen the opportunities for advancement and to increase the fluidity of our society.

I am not unaware of the difficulties, both philosophical and practical, that one encounters in translating the philosophy of liberal rationalism into social policy, and, indeed, I have scattered a few of the larger ones here and there in this paper. I return to the theme with which I began: The social sciences have a special role to play in making a political philosophy of this sort coherent and practical. They are committed, it seems to me, to a liberal point of view, and they are an essential part of our long struggle to bring reason and truth to the study and discussion of social questions.

Humans are perverse beings – full of superstitions, and grand and petty passions, and assorted bigotries – but they are also endowed with the capacity to reason, and they can be gentle and generous upon occasion. We have had some very dark periods during the past two centuries, since the modern economic and social world began to come into being, but liberality and rationality have survived and, on the whole I think, have expanded and deepened their capacity. It is the special task of the social scientist to carry them further, but it is an obligation that does not belong to him or her alone. To bring the spirit of science to the discussion of human affairs, to dispel the mists of dogma and mysticism in the study of social questions, is a prime responsibility of all individuals of learning.

I cannot honestly say that we can be proud of the way in which intellectuals, especially those of academia, have been meeting these responsibilities in recent years. I do not wish now to enter into a recital of their failings, but there are times when I think that their entire commitment to the search for truth is in grave danger. Some large part of that danger, it seems to me, is due to their pursuit of narrow professionalisms, their implicit rejection of the wider responsibilities of scholarship. I have been thinking lately of the legend of Dr Faustus and reflecting upon the fact that Faustus was a professor – a man of learning, a scientist, a good research man. As one will recall, he sold his soul to the devil. But none of the artists who have written the great statements of the legend tell us plainly what it is that Faustus got in exchange. This may be the reason why the story continues to have such great evocative power: The soul of an intellectual can be sold and paid for in many currencies – wealth, power, fame, popularity, fashion, youth, certainty – all of which will serve. In most versions of the story, Dr Faustus is saved from hell at the eleventh hour by the love of a pure maiden. Well, salvation is not quite as easy as that, and even if it were, there probably aren't enough pure maidens to go round. Altogether it is an implausible ending to a great dramatic statement. But this is not what seems to me to be the legend's greatest weakness. As I read it, the story implies that if the intellectual goes to hell, he goes alone, and the other good people remain behind to mourn his personal folly. This is a profound error. If the intellectual goes to hell, he carries civilization down with him.

Now this may be a good place for me to end – because I have come back to my beginning. When I started this paper, the gates of hell were opened wide, and I discussed the demonic possession of the nuns of the Carmelite Convent at Loudun and the great witchcraft scare and other assorted intellectual frenzies of the sixteenth and seventeenth centuries. And then those gates closed with the arrival of the eighteenth-century enlightenment and the dawn of the Age of Reason. Now it seems as if I see them opening again, and one will wonder whether I am obsessed with thoughts of the devil and likely to undergo an imminent religious conversion. Have no fear. I do indeed hear the hinges creaking sometimes, and it seems to get pretty hot in academia upon occasion. But the only bolts and bars that can suppress humankind's barbarity are reason of mind and liberality of spirit. Whatever the attacks made upon academics, and from whatever quarter, these are their proper weapons, and, with them, we shall overcome.

SCOTT GORDON is Distinguished Professor Emeritus (Economics) at Indiana University and Professor Emeritus (Economics) at Queen's University. He organized the first economics department of Carleton College (now Carleton University) and served as department chairman for six years. He then joined the Department of Economics of Indiana University and, from 1970 to 1973, served as chair. He was later cross-appointed to the Department of Economics and the Department of the History and Philosophy of Science. Dr Gordon remained on the graduate faculty of Queen's University for twenty-six years.

In 1988 Carleton University held a symposium in Dr Gordon's honour, which was published as a festschrift. At its convocation, he was awarded the honorary degree of LL.D. His other honours include receipt of a 1965 Guggenheim Fellowship and the presidencies of the Canadian Economics Association and the Western (US) Economics Association. In 1990 Dr Gordon was invited to give Indiana University's Distinguished Faculty Research Lecture.

9

The Changing Economy of Canada

JANE JACOBS, 1970

PART ONE

The problems of Canadian cities are not as severe as those of cities in many other countries. But to this can be added the ominous word "yet." Canadian city problems are not that different in kind from those of other places, and solutions being attempted here are not yet that different from many attempts that have failed elsewhere, including the United States and the United Kingdom, two nations closest to Canada in their history and institutions. Marshall McLuhan says Canadians have a built-in early-warning system; they need only look south of the border. When he said this, he was referring specifically to the calamitous effects of expressways on American cities, but his comment can also be taken more generally.

Canada's economy and therefore its society is urbanizing; a larger proportion – as well as a much larger number – of its people live and work in cities than formerly. This trend is expected to continue, not halt or reverse. Indeed, if Canada were not urbanizing, the country would be in dire economic trouble, with worse to come. No country develops its economy much, or combats poverty with even tolerable success, or improves its standards of living, opportunity, and choice greatly by concentrating on agricultural and raw materials and depending on others to supply goods and services that draw more heavily on human resources. An economy that puts to use the main resource nature has given us – human ingenuity – must have cities where new kinds of goods and services are added to old and where, to a great extent, these goods and services are produced, too, after being incubated.

A successfully urbanizing economy has far-reaching effects, of course. It provides work and the fruits of work for people who would otherwise be increasingly underemployed and poor in the rural world, people who cannot be supported by the unchanged work of the countryside and seaside or in mining and rural market towns. Cities stimulate rural work itself by two means. Some of the work originated in cities is spun off into towns, which are then said to have attracted industry. At the same time, an urbanizing economy provides prospering and expanding markets in its cities not only for the work spun off to the country, but also for other rural products. And, of course, vigorous cities themselves take in streams of people from the rural world who would otherwise be idle; their brains and hands are needed.

In Canada, as anywhere else, the most depressed regions, with the largest numbers of underemployed and poverty-stricken people, the fewest opportunities for the young, and of course the greatest needs for equalizing funds from the federal (and provincial) governments, are those regions in which the proportions of city workers are comparatively low.

Conversely, those equalizing funds, without which many Canadians would have intolerably low living standards and closed-off opportunities, are derived most heavily from the most urbanized places. It is in the most vigorously urbanizing region, too, that by far the greatest numbers of Canada's new immigrants find economic opportunity and the social and political opportunity to share in this country's sanity and freedom.

Successfully urbanizing economies produce substitutes for many specific natural resources over the course of time; unlike stagnant economies, they are capable of shifting forms of natural exploitation before disastrous or irreversible depletion sets in and have often done so. Even as cities are accused of being irredeemable enemies of nature, the very impetus to conservation wells out from cities.

We should not, it seems, regard urbanization with foreboding, yet when we see the pass to which the air, the water, the land, and the people, too, have come in many highly urbanized economies, we have good reason for fears and forebodings. I am not going to try to chill anyone with an account of how massive and intricate – in some instances how apparently hopeless and out of control – the problems of late-twentieth-century cities have become and the further perils they pose. We all know about these things – if not by first-hand experience, then by reading the papers and watching television.

To me, the truly alarming fact is not that these problems are numerous, massive, intricate, and dangerous. We know that people – certainly intelligent, capable, free people – are quite able to deal constructively with massive, intricate, and dangerous city problems and that they have often done so. Were this not true, our cities would still be swept with horrible and uncontrollable epidemics at frequent intervals, our food supplies would be desperately unreliable, and every fire would hold the threat of the Great Fire of London.

What does alarm me is that the problems are not being solved. We must not fool ourselves about this. Studies of problems, no matter how impressive, widespread public awareness of problems, and legislation banning problems are not at all the same things as creating relevant solutions to problems and putting them to use.

In the United States we used to laugh at the Soviet encyclopedia, which claimed that virtually every useful invention from the sewing machine to the telephone had been thought up by this or that obscure nineteenth-century Russian gentleman. Perhaps it was so, but the ideas were not put to use.

In North America the material for a similar encyclopedia is rapidly accumulating, much of it having to do with city problems. While old mistakes are repeated and hopeless doctrines clung to, great numbers of new ideas go unused, or are neglected, or, in some cases, are co-opted, as we say, and then warped out of all relevance. The bitter accusation by young people in the United States – and its echoes here – that society lacks meaningful work for them to do is sometimes dismissed as a frivolous symptom of affluence. It is not frivolous, and it is a symptom of the stagnation of establishment approaches toward unsolved city problems and undone work.

Great apparatuses exist for controlling cities and presumably for solving or ameliorating their problems, too. Beginning with the ascendancy of city zoning law somewhat more than half a century ago, accompanied later by the great ascendancy of formal city planning bodies, and still later by the immense proliferation of experts and agencies, enormous efforts have been directed to shaping cities and determining their quality of life. Seldom, if ever, have human beings enacted so much law, called into being so many agencies, and allocated so much public money to reap results so unsatisfying or ineffectual. It is hardly a reassuring fact that so much effort has been made. It tells us that we have something a good deal more baffling and serious to face up to than we would if our only trouble had been that we hadn't tried.

In a recent speech, the prime minister did me the honour of quoting something I had written about Toronto, which is my home. I had called it "the most hopeful and healthy city in North America, still unmangled, still with options." Like McLuhan, I had been warning of the havoc an expressway would wreak upon that splendid city. The prime minister, however, attached a different moral to the description; it applied, he remarked, equally to Canada as a whole. "We are a healthy and hopeful country," he said, "still unmangled, still with options."

It pleased me that he chose to extend my words to that meaning, too. It is true not only that Canada is still a healthy and hopeful country, but that it still has options. When a "yet" is added to the statement that the problems of Canadian cities are not nearly so severe as those of many other countries, the "yet" can be ominous as I have suggested, or it can be wonderfully hopeful.

I choose to hope, and this not merely because I happen to be optimistic by temperament nor merely, either, because this is a country where time has not yet run out in failures, but mainly because of a certain strong quality I keep seeing in everyday Canadian life: so many taken-for-granted attitudes, so many civilized and sensible actions that have gradually summed themselves up in my mind as evidence of a sane society. There is so much plain, good sanity here, so much reasonable caution as opposed to haring after this panacea and that, so much willingness to stop and look at the reality before mindlessly repeating mistake upon mistake upon mistake.

If this quality strikes some as a dull or boring attribute to single out, I would roundly disagree. After all, sanity means being in close touch with reality, not governed by delusions; delusions, for all the surface excitement and sound and fury they can cause, are not very durably interesting, while reality, as it unfolds, is inexhaustibly so. In an unsane society, one must forever batter away absurdly at delusions and futilities or else adopt the other classical response: the unutterably boring surrender to pointlessness known as apathy. There is nothing more frustrating than to be continually hurt in the concrete while you are continually assured, by persons out of touch with those realities, that you are being helped in the abstract.

The people who best understand the realities of city problems, who first watch them unfolding, and who know most realistically whether efforts supposedly being made on their and the city's behalf are actually to the point, are ordinary people in closest touch with the realities. If anyone has a chance at the sane view, it is they. To suppose bureaucracies and their officials, no matter how trained or learned, have a more valid vision is itself a delusion, perhaps a fatal one.

A little community within London, the Isle of Dogs, recently gained fame far and wide by acting out the frustrations felt perhaps universally in communities within cities, where it is bad enough to enjoy almost no self-government in practical terms and so much the worse to see the botch made by those who do have the power. The local tenants' councils defiantly declared the Isle of Dogs' independence to run its own local affairs. "We are grappling with a really vast problem," one of the community's leaders, a longshoreman, told a reporter, "that of ordinary people trying to overcome bureaucracy."

Just so: ordinary people trying to apply sanity in their daily affairs. In a listing of city problems, I myself would give highest priority to the problem of bureaucracies. Far from being the doctors, they are a large part of the disease. Or to put it another way, the extreme lack of local self-government within city neigh-bourhoods and communities is an immense city problem.

The power to make decisions has gotten too far away from the realities. Simply because modern cities are so complex and large, centralized city government becomes increasingly unworkable. I think it has been no coincidence that city problems have increasingly mounted unsolved as attempts to solve them have become increasingly handed down from above.

Intelligence has been defined biologically as "the breakdown of the instinctive fixity, increasing the potential for recombination, both within the organism and the environment." When we fail to solve problems, intelligence is not breaking through. To be sure, we are not clinging to an "instinctive fixity" instead because we human beings cannot return, even if we would, to the fixed instinctual behaviour of animals. Rather, we are victimizing ourselves and our cities with something that does not serve as well as either intelligence or instinct: the phenomenon of bureaucratic fixity. We have got to achieve, somehow, a break-down of the bureaucratic fixity, increasing the potential for recombination, both within the enterprises and institutions of the city and within the community environments – which is a fancy way of saying we need to use some new approaches emerging from below.

I am going to mention some approaches of this sort. In a way, I am hesitant to do so. Either they will be ignored or dismissed, which has been pretty much their fate thus far, or else they will be discussed (by people in bureaucracies) in terms of applying them from the top, wholesale, whether they fit with the given realities and self-expressed wishes of a community or not.

My purpose, of course, is quite different. It is to indicate, first, not only that home remedies differ from prescriptions being handed down from aloft, but that they are superior. This superiority is not owing to the fact that people at the bottom are smarter – although sometimes they are – but rather to the fact that they have the advantage of the worm's eye view. Since people in city neighbour-hoods do not need to be told any of this – they know it already – why bring it up? Perhaps I am foolish enough to hope that people at the top will see it is their proper function to let new approaches arise and be tried, where and by whom they are wanted, and even to help and encourage these experiments if they are asked to do so. Perhaps I am foolish enough to wish that city bureau-cracies could be the servants rather than rulers of the people.

One thing I am decidedly not doing is attempting to make a catalogue, under any pretext, of prescriptive answers to city ills. My whole point is that specific answers are infinitely various; the very intricacy of the problems arising should tell us that. I am hauling out only a few samples of new approaches to only a few problems. These are just samples of the intelligence available if bureaucratic fixity could be broken through.

Let me begin with one variety of housing problem – how to add new housing into already built-up parts of cities – and with one new approach to this that a good many city communities have attempted to invoke, almost wholly without success.

The current methods, unfortunately, sacrifice much good and reclaimable housing along with bad housing. This is true whether the new construction is carried out by private developers, who require nothing from government but permission, or whether it is carried out under public programs of slum clearance, public housing, or urban renewal. The old rationale for the gratuitous destruction was that large-scale project building was desirable in itself as a method of creating better, planned neighbourhoods. "You can't make an omelet without breaking eggs." Experience has taught almost everyone, except a very few rather old-fashioned planners, that the omelets aren't all that good.

But the gratuitous destruction of good buildings continues nonetheless, and if the scale of destruction by public programs has diminished, this is owing less to the significant use of new or different ideas than it is to diminished programs for construction itself. The rationale that now justifies destruction of good buildings to construct new housing in built-up city areas is economic. The sizes and shapes of sites required for economic new construction, it is said, justify destroying buildings that interfere with this need. You can't make an omelet without breaking eggs.

Ironically, the economic consequences of breaking all these eggs have been pretty bad. Recently the minister of housing, Robert Andras, pointed out that Canadian urban renewal programs have resulted in a net loss of housing – especially of the kind already in shortest supply: low-cost housing. In the United States the results have been the same although on a much larger and more disastrous scale. The sanity of Canada made itself felt at an earlier stage in the proceedings, or perhaps the built-in early-warning system has been working.

At any rate, the result of gratuitous destruction, on whatever scale, has been a net loss in moderate and low-cost housing. The method, in short, simply inflates the cost of city housing. And of course one side effect is that displaced people, if they are poor, have been overcrowded into other neighbourhoods that have then deteriorated from the overcrowding and from the absence of any means of injecting new construction there, except by repeating the same process over again.

It is no real answer to neglect new construction of housing in the built-up parts of cities and to concentrate instead – not just also but instead – on large vacant sites on city outskirts. The fact is that built-up parts of cities do need new housing. Old buildings wear out. Fires happen. Vacant lots better not left vacant do exist. An industrial building here or a commercial building there is vacated;

housing may be the logical substitute in many cases, yet the older buildings may not be convertible to housing. In short, normal attrition requires construction. Furthermore, out there on the outskirts, the same dilemmas are only being postponed. The new developments and suburbs will not stay new forever. Their turn for attrition will gradually but inevitably come.

Down on the streets, those gaps where housing might be inserted without destroying anything useful are very real. They are so real that naturally the thought occurs: "Fill the gaps and don't destroy anything good or reclaimable." People in a neighbourhood know exactly where the gaps are. And it seems sane, to anyone taking this worm's-eye view, to stretch the construction money as far as possible by making all the new construction a net increase in the supply of habitable housing. I dare say this even looks sane from the bird's-eye view.

Another reason those wonderfully real gaps loom so importantly is that people detest seeing their communities destroyed or ruthlessly shaken up. There may be some communities that feel differently, but if so they must be few. It is almost a foregone conclusion that, whenever people are invited to engage in what is called participatory planning for their local area, or whenever they impose themselves uninvited into the decision making, they will concentrate upon improving the neighbourhood. Destroying good and useful things in it, as well as tossing people around for that dubious purpose, does not strike ordinary people as representing improvement. I make these rather categorical statements because I have heard just these reasoning processes and just these aims in so many American city neighbourhoods since the time I first heard them voiced, fourteen years ago, in a poor neighbourhood in Philadelphia. A few years ago I heard much the same thing in London and in Glasgow, and now I have heard it in Toronto and Montreal, and people tell me they hear this talk in Halifax. No longer do only poor neighbourhoods look at gaps and propose that they be filled, although that is where the idea seems to have started perhaps because the poor are always most threatened and first threatened by doctrines devised on high.

But standing in the way is the rationale against it. I know of only one community – I shall come to it in a moment – that seems to have prevailed. Gap-filling is always brushed off, participatory planning or no. Naturally this makes people who have experienced participatory planning quite cynical about that, too. I know architectural students and young architects in the United States who enlisted with high idealism to help neighbourhoods engaged in participatory planning and now will have none of it. They are as bitter as their clients. As one of them put it to me in Pittsburgh, "I know by now what they are going to say they want, and I know by now the city will tell them they can't have it. It's immoral to kid people along with the idea that if they participate the system can work for them when it can't or anyway doesn't." Here is a little clang from the

early-warning system: Participatory planning requires revision of much besides
the process of making plans.

The one community that, so far as I know, is getting a gap-filling scheme is
in New York. Far from being economically unfeasible, the scheme costs less than
a third as much as a plan originally proposed by the bureaucracy yet adds almost
twice as much net housing because none is subtracted. That particular bureaucratic scheme called for large-scale clearance under the rationale that a new,
instant community would be better than the one that had grown organically, so
it is not surprising that the differences in cost proved so great. However, and this
is more significant, the gap-filling scheme proved to be more economical than
the theoretically more feasible schemes: the so-called vest-pocket constructions
proposed by the bureaucracy as alternatives. These destroyed only such housing
as was deemed necessary to fill out sites for economical building, which turned
out to be quite a bit one way and another.

So far as what that gap-filling scheme demonstrates about costs, it is hopeful
but otherwise not. The city served notice that the approach would be allowed
only in that one place by adding a new provision to the building code making
its repetition or adaptation elsewhere in the city impossible. Don't ask me why;
it really passes my understanding.

But the presumed economic unfeasibility of gap-filling, the rationale that
usually prevents it – how was that overcome? The architects employed by the
community designed a rather small building, standardized in its construction
system, stairs, and utilities, but otherwise capable of very flexible interior planning so that the one type can serve many different requirements and purposes.
These include duplexes and studios, as well as flats for large families or small,
and convertibility to retail shops or workshops, for this neighbourhood was
looking ahead to kinds of changes that might be wanted in the next generation.
To the basic forty-foot-wide building were added buildings of two somewhat
different proportions in depth and width but that were otherwise the same. Singly,
or in combination, these three building units could make use of every available
site on the site's own given terms.

In short, the solution was to design a flexibly usable, relatively small building
that could be reproduced – in this case, about fifty are being constructed – so
that the high costs of custom building could be avoided but so could the need
for synthetically contrived sites.

The neighbourhood had no problem in getting the architects to understand
what it wanted and to respond relevantly and ingeniously to the need and had
no trouble finding a builder willing to undertake the work.

Since coming to live in Toronto, I have learned that gap-filling may have more
possibilities than I had every imagined. The New York scheme is rather primitive

compared with what it seems can be done. In Toronto are architects capable of designing handsome, pre-engineered structural and mechanical modules, even more flexible in their interior planning – for instance, stairs and utilities can go anywhere – and in their adaptability to fortuitous sites. The basic unit could be as small as twenty-two square feet and could be used in multiples horizontally and vertically. It would appear, also, to be potentially even more economical than buildings going into the New York scheme. I don't want to convey the impression that there is any plan afoot to do gap-filling this way – but why not?

Historically, new approaches undertaken for one reason have often solved other problems as well or cast a new light upon potential means of solving them. Gap-filling might well lead to construction improvements and savings generally.

When zoning first began, the codes were concerned with a kind of performance: with prescribing setbacks to preserve light down in the street and hence also to limit bulk. Then the notion came along of using zoning to control the uses of buildings or other facilities allowed on the land. Zoning and land planning became indissoluble partners. Indeed, zoning is the major tool for enforcing planning – and planning means mostly land planning. Thus land-use zoning is supposed to protect given uses against harmful neighbours, to keep incompatible uses separated, and to imbue cities with a functionally and esthetically pleasing order. In my neighbourhood in Toronto a women's club wishes to buy a fine old house for its quarters. Far from being objectionable to the ratepayers' association or other persons in the community, this proposal was welcomed because it assured that the house, widely appreciated for its attractiveness and idiosyncrasy, would be preserved instead of falling to supply a parking lot or a fragment of a high-rise site.

But a club is a land use, and it is a member of a category of land uses – in this case, clubs. A zoning variance granted for the women's club would automatically make the area vulnerable to requests for variances for other clubs, some of which could be noisy and garish. Spot zoning, making an exception for one thing, is of course frowned upon. It has a bad name. If it were widely indulged, the whole system of zoning would break down. Hence the vulnerability of a street when one exception is made; the exception is a powerful argument for the land-use category as a whole.

But the trouble, really, is not with the problem of exceptions. The trouble is that land use, per se, is a quite irrelevant criterion in this case, and so is it in many another.

The relevant criterion, rather, is performance. Moreover, it usually is. Land use is a shield through which many an assault in the form of bad performance easily penetrates, while many a harmless neighbour is gratuitously forbidden.

Ordinary people, as in this illustrative case, often couldn't care less about land use and its classifications. What they want is protection against bad performance: against pollution, noise, excessive traffic, shattering of neighbourhood scale, destruction of landmarks, and so on.

Land use is a sensible fact with which to begin if an agrarian economy is concerned. But it poses one insane little dilemma after another in cities. Where it actually does provide protection, it does so only by rigidly segregating various things from one another in a manner much more suitable to a farm than to a city: Here will be the orchard, over there the barnyard and feed lots, beyond that the bean fields, then the pastures, and so on.

If a neighbourhood is interested in performance, instead of categories of land use, why should it not be allowed to hammer out performance standards, commission an intelligent lawyer to write a performance zoning code, and then be allowed to apply it? No doubt the first homemade codes would have bugs in them, but the present system is almost all bugs.

Based upon what I have picked up listening to and about zoning disputes, people seem to be interested in one or more of six different kinds of performance:

1 Noise. Standards could be set according to the number of decibels allowable outside the building. That, of course, includes what penetrates from inside the building.
2 Pollution. In the present stage of the technology, standards could govern the solid particulate matter and sulphur dioxide emitted.
3 Scale. Many streets, especially those intimately scaled, are disintegrated visually by an out-of-scale building. In practice, it always seems to mean one too large. Usually the relevant standard would be the length of street frontage allowed a building. A small scale frontage automatically takes care of height in most cases; differences of a few storeys in height are not what disintegrate street scale, as one can see by looking at intimately scaled streets. A street with identical or very similar uses can be rendered chaotic by incongruities of size; conversely, a street can assimilate an astonishing diversity of building designs and of uses and yet be attractive and harmonious because of the harmonious scale.
4 Signs. Standards could apply to sizes, beginning with discreet plaques, and to illumination.
5 Traffic generation. Standards could designate the number of parking places permitted. When people seek protection against traffic generators, they seek protection against automobile and truck traffic, not against pedestrians. Retail uses that go into the same land-planning categories can differ enormously, for instance, in the kind of traffic they draw: automotive or foot.
6 Destruction. As everybody down there on the street knows, what is removed to make way for something is a vital aspect of performance. Standards could designate what

is to be protected, such as local landmarks, buildings of particular esthetic value, trees over a certain girth. In times and places of severe housing shortage, protection could cover habitable housing.

Standards could vary as the neighbourhood or community thought appropriate, and the various kinds of protection would be combined as considered appropriate.

Now if this approach were used by local communities that wanted it, we might expect that the effects would, in time, be felt upon new development, too.

Today, land-use planning and zoning are permitting look-alike sprawls around almost every city in North America, no different around Toronto than around Dallas or Richmond. As Peter Swann, director of the Royal Ontario Museum, has remarked of the United States, things are "petrified by the accountants who have seized high position." The developers blame the public officials: "They made us do it like this." The public officials blame the developers: "They did it." Wherever the blame belongs, the situation says as clearly as possible that the right to create the environment is being monopolized by a very few people or else by people who are really interchangeable cogs.

An alternative to this authoritarianism is not laissez faire. A municipality opening and servicing a new area could, if it chose, lay out the street patterns, allocate spaces for parks and other public facilities certain to be needed, and – presuming it already had the advantage of experience with performance codes worked out by city neighbourhoods – set performance standards for the various streets. Anything not performing harmfully that happened already to be on the land could be left there. The remaining land could be sold by the municipality to large purchasers and small, and within the protective performance codes, enterprises and people could be as diverse and as ingenious as they liked in how they used the land and what for.

Under such an arrangement, uses would not be frozen in new developments for two generations or more, as they typically are today. Possibly humankind would have learned again how to build and manage organically growing city areas.

Legislative bans against pollution mean little, as New York found out when it tried to ban apartment house incinerators – unless alternative ways of handling wastes are available. To combat pollution of almost any kind requires new goods and services, new organizations for waste handling, new methods.

The key to combatting many kinds of pollution is waste recycling. According to the summary of a report from China published earlier this year in the *New York Times*, people in Shanghai have the right idea. Some enterprises are making building materials from slag, others are turning out more than fifty different chemicals from former wastes, textile companies have found a way to use dye water a second time, and so on. The policy, taken as a whole, is described as reusing wastes, "instead of allowing them to pile up as garbage or to foul the city's air and water."

The report goes on to say that these developments were not handed down from above by "experts behind closed doors" and, indeed, makes a great point that higher-level obstructionism or ignorance had to be overcome by workers who were in direct touch with the wastes. Perhaps this can be dismissed as a flourish of ideology, but the point about the importance of the workers in direct touch with the wastes checks with much experience on our own continent.

The pitifully few advances in waste-recycling made in North America – for example, conversion of fly ash to cinderblock, return of waste paper to mills for reprocessing, conversion of garbage into lightweight dehydrated compost, the now large and prosperous industries that reclaim and sell automobile engine parts or second-hand production machinery – all these were contrived and carried out by people in lowly positions, in direct touch with wastes.

Back in the early 1960s, a coal-burning electric power plant, in cooperation with a large American chemical corporation, developed and successfully tested equipment for capturing sulphur dioxide in fuel-burning stacks and converting it to sulphuric acid. Left at that stage, which is about where it is still, it is rather like those sewing machines and telephones invented by the nineteenth-century Russians. To get it into use, somebody in this large city and that – probably a good many somebodies – has to risk successfully finding customers for sulphur dioxide-capturing equipment, has to install the equipment, service it, pick up the sulphuric acid, and channel it back to wholesalers or re-users. Someplace, those somebodies have to find capital to start their organizations or to add this new work appropriately to something else they are already doing.

It seems very few understood how helpless large and seemingly all-powerful corporations often are in the absence of small and humble organizations. Some years ago the president of DuPont, reminiscing to a *Fortune* magazine editor about the marketing of moisture-proof Cellophane, recalled how the company had depended upon very small customers, and a lot of them, to put it to use, find out its applications, get it to market. The product would have failed, he said, had the company had to rely upon large users. Later, large customers followed. I was reminded of this by a *Scientific American* article in December 1969, written by two DuPont researchers, describing materials for overcoming various types of mechanical noise. DuPont makes the materials. As a practical matter, they commented, widespread application depends upon the growth of many servicing organizations to prescribe, design, and install the materials.

So much ingenuity is needed to solve city problems, so much undone work must be undertaken, so many new approaches must be tried that, to me, progress seems inconceivable unless there is a great liberation and application of ideas from below. The best place to begin, perhaps, would be with the people who are clamouring to try things their way. The old approaches certainly are not working.

Apart from trying to show that new approaches are possible, arising from close contact with the realities, I have had another reason for trotting out some. illustrative samples. This other reason has to do with Canadian economic development; I will touch on the connection, along with some other things, in the next section.

PART TWO

Thus far, I have expressed the opinion that the mounting problems of contemporary cities, although intricate, massive, and numerous, are soluble; if this hope at present seems forlorn in some places, it is nevertheless realistic here. The problems of Canadian cities, though similar in kind to those of other countries, are not yet at a disaster stage, and, more important, Canadian society is not a mere duplicate of any other, certainly not of America's. It has strong and distinct qualities of its own. It has a refreshing sanity; it is not demoralized.

But as I have also pointed out, we may well be alarmed that so many city problems – here as elsewhere – are not actually being solved. I have ventured that I cannot see where solutions are going to come from unless they arise from people in close, normal touch with the realities down on the city streets. As a practical matter this means, among other things, less analysis and fewer prescriptions from above, less control of neighbourhoods and communities within cities from centralized governments, and much more reliance on local understanding of problems and on local prescriptions and experiments, which means more local autonomy.

The usual objection is that city localities – neighbourhoods, wards, districts – are shortsighted, selfish, and either oblivious to the good of the whole or opposed to it. In some cases this may be true. But one of the compensations of growing older is that you get to see how so many things turn out, and from what I have watched happen during the past several decades, I have quite an opposite impression. In cases of conflicts between central authorities and neighbourhoods about all kinds of matters, from school locations and park facilities to urban renewal schemes, the warnings and predictions of protesting neighbourhoods are astoundingly often confirmed by events and time, while it is the analyses of the bureaucracies that, astoundingly often, have gone wildly agley. It seems a strange use of the language, too, to describe people battling for their neighbourhoods as selfish, particularly when the term is applied to them by people who are, quite by the way no doubt, advancing their careers and power by overriding the objections of their victims. I am also impressed by how often the good of the neighbourhood corresponds with the good of the whole. The whole city, as time inexorably demonstrates, is not an abstraction unaffected by the fates of its parts.

The stock argument–the clincher–of those who think neighbourhood power would be impractical or ruinous is to bring up the question of highways, pointing out that no community within a city would allow a highway to be cut through it, if it had the power to say no.

But time has been dramatically vindicating the city communities that have tried, almost always unsuccessfully in the past, to stop expressways. As the pollution has mounted, the traffic problems have been compounded, as public transportation has decayed. And, as the direct and indirect costs of expressways in cities have soared, the protests have come to look, in retrospect, more and more sensible. Recently, communities protesting expressways in American cities have been winning. At last count, seventeen cities were halting partly completed expressway plans. But the change, which in many instances is too late, has come about only because such appalling harm has already been done by the programs, at such fantastic social and financial costs, while the practical problems of city traffic are still not solved.

And what was the good of the whole, for which all the sacrifice was made by the communities ripped asunder? Certainly it was not the good of whole cities, for it is precisely the demonstrated harm to them that has become so evident. It seems to me that only very special interests indeed have been benefitted, interests such as those touched upon by a chairman of the American Petroleum Institute, M.J. Rathbone, who was quoted in 1961 in the magazine of Standard Oil of New Jersey as follows: "If every car travelled just another hundred miles, the consumption of gasoline would rise almost one per cent. This would mean only three or four more minutes behind the steering wheel each week for each driver, but it would add up to 10 million more barrels of gasoline consumed in a year. As chairman of the American Petroleum Institute, I most heartily endorse the Institute's new travel program as a stimulant to the greater consumption of gasoline and motor oil."

There is more than a symbolic relationship between the destruction of city neighbourhoods and the threatened ecology of the Arctic. There is a direct cause-and-effect connection. No doubt it can be said the caribou are selfish, short-sighted, and lack appreciation for the good of the whole.

Suppose it had been truly necessary for officials in the United States and elsewhere to heed city localities when their people objected to plans that hurtled expressways through, cannibalized parks with parkways, narrowed sidewalks, cut street trees, widened roads, destroyed houses for parking lots and rezoned streets for gas stations. Then it would also have been necessary to turn to other means for solving city traffic problems.

Other means have been available, not only those, like subways, that were already well developed before everything had been sacrificed to the automobile, but many others that have not been used: Carveyors, automated StarRcars, dial-a-buses, minibuses, trailer buses, cableways, Rotobugs, geotubes, hovercraft. In 1969, when the Metropolitan Transportation Authority of New York began pondering a "people mover" for a crosstown subway link, it was reported by the *New York Times* to be studying 115 different possible methods and devices. Most of these schemes are already ten, twenty, or even thirty years old. Presumably one of them is a system, a Carveyor, that was fully developed and successfully tested for a subway link seventeen years ago, but was so economical and required so little labour that it was dropped as being too upsetting to the status quo. That authority takes about two years of thinking and a study grant from the federal government to decide whether to ask for another grant to redecorate two subway stations, so none of us should hold our breath while it decides how to pick and choose among the 115 schemes before it.

I do not think necessity is the mother of invention. Creation is not quite that pat. Rather, necessity often compels people actually to accept inventions, put them to use – an important difference. If a city today wanted to change its approach, a modern complex of services, vehicles, and methods could be developed rather quickly, both to get swiftly from place to place and to use rapidly and flexibly when one gets there. A systems analysis undertaken at the behest of the us Department of Housing and Urban Development, described in *Scientific American* of July 1969, concluded that an entirely new system of transportation – the one the analysts chose was the StarRcar system of small, automated capsules – would be cheaper than adding to either an expressway or subway system; could be developed in no more than the time it takes to build expressways or subways; would move people more swiftly than any of the present methods; and would overcome a great many problems that expressways and heavy dependence upon automobiles compound. Possibilities like this should, of course, surprise no one who believes progress is possible. Nevertheless, no matter what the possibilities, it seems that current bureaucracies, in Canada as elsewhere, are not going to permit progress in city transportation unless and until they are forced to by effective community opposition to expressways.

Increasingly angry talk about banning automobiles in downtowns entirely is understandable in view of growing desperation, but here again, as in the case of pollution, a constructive and practical solution requires new goods and services. Then, the automobile could be used, too, although it would not be as convenient for most purposes in a city as other methods of movement since all other community values, city amenities, and functions, including really good transportation, would not be sacrificed to the automobile.

Ironically, there is no more dramatic illustration of the need for more local autonomy within cities than the stock objection, "they won't allow new highways."

Cities of our time that actually do begin to take the lead in solving their problems will almost surely have new growth industries. The very kinds of goods and services I have been touching on here – innovative transportation vehicles and services, gap-filling construction schemes and products, waste-recycling equipment and services – are growth industries of the future.

For this reason, Canada ought to be especially interested in pursuing new approaches of this sort. Virtually every analysis of the Canadian economy nowadays emphasizes the need for less reliance on natural resources and more reliance on production that makes use of human resources. As Dr L.G. Cook of the National Research Council of Canada has put it, the future demands "businesses in which one is not selling pounds of anything but rather a capability to *do* something."

Canada's historically heavy dependence upon natural resources – an unusually heavy dependence for an advanced economy – can hardly continue indefinitely. Consider, for instance, what is happening in the case of wheat. Some of Canada's former customer nations are now growing their own wheat, and in future some customers will probably even become wheat exporters themselves – much as Japan, once a rice importer, now supplies its own needs for rice and exports it, too. No one can deplore the Green Revolution in developing countries, but this means change in Canada.

Dr Cook points out, in a recent issue of *Science Forum*, some of the other difficulties that may lie ahead. "The whole raison d'être for the aluminum industry in Canada," he writes, "was the existence of cheap electric power on a large scale. The discovery of uranium fission has now removed that economic justification. Cheap electric power on a large scale will, in the next decade, be available anywhere. Over the next two decades, Canada's large aluminum industry may not only cease to grow; it may well decline as importing and bauxite-owning nations insist that the reduction stage be carried out in their own country.

"It may seem incredible," he goes on, "that the pulp and paper business should stop growing, or even be reduced to buggy-whip status, but the march of synthetic polymer technology and alternative communication technologies makes this possibility more real over a 10-to-20 year span than one would like to think. The wool, cotton and silk industries probably never thought it could happen to them – but it *is* happening to them."

To these possibilities we may add another: The most rapidly growing market for mineral products, and probably the most reliable one, too, in the foreseeable future, is Japan's. Australia, where immense mineral discoveries have recently been made and are being developed, is inevitably going to be a heavier supplier of the great Japanese market than Canada. The Australian finds include, among others, what seem to be the largest and richest nickel deposits yet discovered.

Now let me consider quite another kind of change outside of Canada. Historically, Canada has depended rather heavily for innovations on cities outside, first those of Britain and then those of the United States. Of course, Canada's own contribution to development of the pool of new goods and services and methods has been large, but it has been contributed, to a great extent, by exporting Canadian talent to the United States.

The United States has thus been both a reservoir of opportunities and a reservoir of innovations. But the reservoir is drying up. Extremely troubling things are happening to the US economy. It is stagnating. I am not talking about a recession or a depression or even about the effects of the Vietnamese war, but about a condition that has been in the making these past fifteen years or so at least and that is surely not going to be easily or rapidly reversed.

A stagnating economy concentrates too long and too heavily on production of already established goods and services, and depends too long on its already established and successful organizations, at the expense of opportunities for new ones. The old services of all kinds work increasingly badly, as they fail to keep up with needed changes. Mistakes are repeated because there seem to be no available alternatives. Idleness grows, along with the undone work. So does unproductive make-work. Costs of the associated social problems begin to affect everything until every pursuit seems caught in a vicious circle. All these symptoms of stagnation are now deeply entrenched in the US economy.

In the two world wars, American industries were rather briefly and temporarily diverted to war production. They swiftly and knowledgeably reconverted to civilian work. But that cannot be repeated now. It is too late. America's war production has been growing unremittingly for twenty years. Many of the enterprises have never done any other work; others have long since come to depend primarily on war contracts. If the executives of these enterprises thought they could successfully turn out civilian products, they would hardly lobby so desperately as they do to keep the war orders coming. Whole towns now live on war production as their normal way of economic life. In some cases, whole cities now do. In a sense, American military expenditures are now a "welfare system" for war workers, war industries, and war-supported communities. The alternative work they might be doing, or might do in future, has not been developed, is not waiting in the wings ready to take over.

This, of course, has not been for lack of capital to develop new and needed goods and services and to overcome practical city problems. American capital is not going into new American economic development, apart from some exceptions. One reason there is such an abundance of American capital for buying up

Canadian resources and enterprises is that development work needed in America is being neglected by American capital. To me, the trip to the moon looks rather like the magnificent feats of fifteenth- and sixteenth-century Portuguese navigation, carried out while the great body of the Portuguese economy failed to develop.

The stagnation is good for no one, including Canada. The stable, prosperous, creative neighbour to the south has changed, and among other things, it cannot be depended on now to cast up streams of innovations that Canada can then adopt, too.

All of this, along with Canadian desires to retain the country's independence, only reinforce Canada's needs for indigenous development, needs that would exist in any case. All analyses of the economy seem to agree on this. As Dr Cook puts it, certain existing primary industries on which Canada has long depended must be kept in the next ten to twenty years from sliding downhill or even disappearing, specifically so that Canada can win that much time in which to build up a new industrial base. Composed of what? All the prescriptions advise that the changing economy must include modern, high-growth-rate industries.

The trouble is that all the prescriptions I have seen then proceed to discuss only industries that already have established high growth rates. For instance, Dr Cook mentions computers, Xerox machines, television, drugs, and Technician blood analyzers as the kind of things he means. Similarly, an economist who recently advised a committee of Parliament concerning the need for new Canadian industries went on to say, according to the Toronto *Globe and Mail*, that Canada must get in on the ground floor of some growth industries, and he advised getting into computers.

But one can't get in on the ground floor of the computer industry now. It is too late. By the time a growth industry is already established as a growth industry, it has already passed through major stages of experimentation, development, and very rapid growth. Growth industries usually require relatively small amounts of capital in their initial stages, which is one reason their founders can establish them at all. Very few people believe in a thing until they have seen that it is a success. And for every successful growth industry, there are many failures.

After a growth industry has already made a success, it will take very large amounts of capital, indeed, to catch up with it, let alone compete. It also may require severe protectionist policies to buffer the domestic market from the already well-established foreign competition. And what does a nation imitating an established growth industry have, in the end? The chances are it does not have much of an export industry because there are already the longer-established foreign enterprises with which it must compete.

To be sure, imitative industries do become exports from the imitating nation but usually for one or both of the following reasons: (a) labour costs in the imitating nation are much lower than those in the country or countries it is imitating; or (b) the imitating nation has employed significantly different methods of production or significantly different materials, or has made dramatic improvements in the product itself, any or all of which mean that it has cast up innovations of some sort; it is not simply imitating an established good thing.

There is no way around it: To get in on the ground floor of a growth industry means undertaking things that have not yet been proved successful. It means sinking capital into originality, not imitation, but this is advice that Canadian advisors seem to neglect.

Another feature of many prescriptions for new Canadian industry disturbs me. They dwell too exclusively upon technological work. To be sure, urbanizing economies make many technological advances, but it is not a mark of a highly advanced economy that it specializes upon technology. Rather, it includes technology. The really great difference between an advanced economy and a less advanced economy is the far greater comprehensiveness of all kinds of work in nontechnological as well as technological areas. This is not simply a matter of size. Denmark, with a population of only some five million has an extremely comprehensive economy and an extraordinarily varied range of exports, too.

Furthermore, as I pointed out when discussing antipollution or waste-recycling work, while waste-recycling requires much technology, it also requires much new work that can hardly be called technological at all. One is as necessary as the other. I should say that almost any kind of work that can make a go of it is apt to prove useful, particularly if it serves other work, no matter how humbly. Work in which Canada is doing its own new thing, not copying, should be most valuable of all.

Still another element that disturbs me in the prescriptions for Canadian industry is what seems to me a lack of attention to the need for greater economic interaction among Canadian cities themselves and to the opportunity for this that originality and innovations affords. North-south trade is not, it seems to me, merely a matter of geography. When Canadian cities are producing more innovations, they will sell more to each other. Another mark of an advanced, urbanizing economy is that an increasingly large proportion of its production is done for domestic markets, and the heightened intercity trade within an innovating, advanced economy is one of several reasons for this. Another, of course, is that as domestic markets grow, it becomes worth while to manufacture many former imports domestically.

Still another thing that disturbs me is the great emphasis here upon attracting industry as a form of development. So much capital and effort seem to go into luring established industries into depressed rural localities, while so little, relatively speaking, seems to go into indigenous city enterprises – yet the cities are the reservoirs from which plans for Canadian towns and rural areas in the future will have to come unless, of course, companies incubated in foreign cities are going to be depended upon to rescue rural Canada.

The goods and services created in a city, and exported from it or transplanted from it, do not come out of thin air; they arise in quite systematic ways within the local economy of the city. Often an exported product or service is first produced for people or enterprises within that city itself and then subsequently is exported to cities within the same country and sometimes to cities abroad.

This pattern is what I have in mind when I suggest that unsolved city problems are potential economic opportunities for cities that use some originality. Cities copy each others' solutions to problems, but they also import the new goods and services that helped solve them. I am not suggesting that the whole of an urbanizing economy can by any means be built upon finding new approaches and effective solutions to persistently unsolved city problems. There is more to life than that, including economic life. But it is part of the need and part of the opportunity. How important a part we can see if we put the matter negatively. If cities here were to sink under expensive, and otherwise wretched, problems of mounting pollution, insufficient housing, elephantine transportation difficulties, unrest, anger, and poverty, not much else in the economy would enjoy very promising prospects either.

A city employs two major growth and development mechanisms, each of which builds upon the other. The city generates new exports, as just mentioned, and it also replaces former imports. Then it generates more new exports and replaces still more imports, and so on. Cities are unique, among all kinds of settlements, in growing in this fashion. Indeed, any settlement that grows this way becomes a city.

We think of cities as commonplace, yet among all the millions of settlements the earth has seen, relatively few have grown as cities. This is as true in Canada as in other countries. Among settlements that do grow as cities, many do so only for a brief while, then stagnate.

It is quite easy to create a company town that dies when the factories close or the mines shut down. It is not hard to create a market town that dwindles when the surrounding hinterland loses population. It is easy to create a suburb that depends on the already existing fact of a city.

But to create a city, an economically self-generating settlement, is an entirely different matter. It is incredibly difficult to do deliberately; it almost never happens successfully by plan. Indeed, it is immensely difficult to revitalize a stagnated city, as Britain has learned from its attempts to revitalize cities in its north.

Cities are amazingly tough in some ways: capable of surviving disorders, pestilence, and the destruction of war. They have often survived longer than the nations of which they were originally a part. But they are also, obviously, very delicate in some ways, or else they would not stagnate, lose their capacities for self-generating growth. If their capacities to keep generating exports and to replace imports are destroyed, or seriously obstructed, then jobs decline, poverty increases, and, of course, the very resources for developing new work wither, too.

Simply to maintain its export base – the goods and services the city sells to other places in its own country or abroad or both – let alone grow, a city must continually generate new exports and new exporting organizations. Merely expanding the old ones does not suffice indefinitely although it may for a while. Inevitably, some of a city's former exports become obsolete over the course of time. Some are eventually produced in former customer cities. Still others become transplanted from a city out to a town or the countryside.

The way a city's new exporting organizations typically begin is by producing something first for the local market, as has already been mentioned, then supplying the same thing more widely; or by adding some new product or service for export to something different first produced for the local market; or, finally, by drawing heavily upon other local producers and suppliers to produce something that can be exported. The city's own local economy is its greatest economic resource.

The other growth mechanism, import replacing, helps in time to provide new foundations for export work, too. As a city's exports grow, so do its imports increase. When the local market for some imports grows large enough, the imports can be produced right there instead. Then, in place of those former imports, the city can import still other things.

Among the "other things" it can now import are apt to be innovative goods and services from other cities. The more vigorously the various cities in a nation can maintain these processes, the better it is for each of them – and the more encouraging to new types of goods and services. Vigorous cities need vigorous customer cities and vigorous intercity trade.

Quite apart from the many new goods and services that arise in cities in the course of generating exports and replacing imports, the processes themselves are vital, considered as sheer mechanisms.

Now, in the light of these mechanisms, let me consider the question of national grants made to cities in order to help them with their problems.

National governments have massive amounts of public money to deploy, compared with provinces or cities. Cities have massive needs for public money. It has seemed plausible, in many countries including Canada, to make national grants to cities and towns for specific kinds of city problems. Thus we have national urban renewal programs, national housing programs; in the United

States, national highway programs affecting cities; no doubt national grants to cities for air and water pollution will come; and so on. Quite apart from the question of the usual quality of the programs themselves, I think there is a defect in the very strategy. It seems to me to work against the vital city economic mechanisms, rather than with them.

The trouble is precisely that the strategy is national. This means the programs ensure that various cities will be concentrating on the same collections of problems in much the same ways.

Some of this standardization is built into the prescriptions themselves. That is, it is built into the choice of problems and the way they are defined. If grants are given for urban renewal, and urban renewal is defined as dealing with objects and facilities in certain ways, then that is how cities will necessarily spend the grants, and some of their own money, too. If grants are given to combat water pollution from sewage, and the problem is defined as need for sewage plants, then that is what will be done. There might be other, better ways to combat the sewage problem; but if so, that will be academic.

Still more standardization is necessarily built in. Whenever money is allocated for specific purposes, the grants must be policed against being used in ways the law does not allow, against gratuitous waste, against egregious mistakes. If they are not policed, the granting agency is soon going to be in trouble. A good many "correct" answers must therefore be routinized.

What all this means, in sum, is that each city participating in a given grant program must respond with methods, goods, and services, whether imported or locally produced, very similar to those of all other cities participating. And what this means, in turn, is that the very stuff of differential export generating and import replacing is being discouraged in a country's cities.

The defect is much more serious than the size of the grants alone would suggest. Since such grants are always directed to glaring practical problems, they are automatically directed to activities that have already become backward or stultified. But these are precisely the problems, along with their associated economic activities, that most require development work, not premature prescriptions with their accompanying standardizations.

To be sure, additional theoretical reasons are sometimes given for such grants, apart from the fact that a bad problem exists. Thus it is often urged that housing grants of one kind or another are justified because "shelter is a necessity." So is clothing, but nobody urges that national grants be made for clothing programs on that account. If the clothing industries were performing as poorly as the building industries, we might have such programs. I think there is no getting around the fact that the grants are associated with problem activities, hence backward activities.

The grants do not work well empirically. The larger and the more prescriptive they are, the more do solutions seem to retreat. Canada is fortunate not to have become as deeply enmeshed in this strategy as either the United States or Britain. Provincial grants to cities, tied prescriptively to specific problems, are probably not as bad – if they genuinely vary from province to province – simply because the writ of a province does not run to as many cities. Otherwise, they share the same defects as federal grants tied to specific city problems.

I am not suggesting that there is no place for federal or provincial programs or that these should be kept out of cities. There is much scope for outright programs, of course: for example, the federal government's Canadian Broadcasting Company, Canada Council grants, the Ontario GO trains, and many others that will likely increase further in number and in kind as years go by. But outright federal and provincial programs are a very different matter, in their operation and in their effects, from supposedly city-administered grants with directions attached to them. It is these that work so badly.

It still remains that there is money to deploy for city problems, and cities need it. If my reasoning is correct, it would be far better to return such money to city governments with no strings attached, to use as they see fit, for problems as they define them. The cities that pay most heed to new ideas coming out of their own local communities and economies would probably be the cities using the money most wisely and with greatest originality.

I understand that fifteen years ago or so, at a time when Calgary was growing at an extraordinarily rapid rate, somebody projected that Calgary was destined to reach a population of twenty million in another generation. No city grows at a constant rate. Thus to try to predict future size based upon the current rate at any given time cannot help but give a false projection. For one thing, the process of replacing imports is inherently episodic; it happens in bursts, creating episodes, but episodes only of unusually rapid growth. For another, the vigour with which the city is going to generate exports, the rate of expansion of given export work after it has been established, and the rates of loss of older export work are all inherently problematical until they are happening.

When one city in a nation grows absolutely gigantic, as often happens, while at the same time many others are growing very slowly or even declining, the situation may be considered just fine by enthusiastic boosters in the gigantic city. It is not just fine; something is seriously wrong, but it is useless to search for the trouble in the gigantic city or to try to right the imbalance by halting its growth. Supposing the effort succeeded, the whole country would then probably be stagnant. The difficulty lies in the cities that are growing so slowly or stagnating. They are the ones that require understanding; theirs are the deficiencies that need remedy. Why have they lost their capacity to generate new exports?

The fates of other kinds of settlements can be easily seen and explained in terms of natural resources, or specific factories, or a particular form of trade that rose and fell. But with cities, one must return always to that problem of continuing creativity, based in the city's own local economy. A city with mounting problems that do not get solved is surely repressing or starving the ingenuity of its own potentially creative people. A stagnating city has done the same. Ingenuity, cropping up from the city population itself, is the great natural resource of a city. It is the only effectively renewable resource, too. A true urban renewal is one that liberates a people's ingenuity, lets them try new things for solving their own problems.

JANE JACOBS is an author, urban advocate, economist, ecologist, and philosopher whose most influential work, *The Death and Life of Great American Cities* (1961), transformed city planning in North America. Ms Jacobs began working as a writer and editor for the trade magazine *Iron Age* (now *New Steel*) and as a pamphlet writer for the US wartime administration before becoming associate editor for *Architectural Forum* magazine. Through the 1960s, she established her lifelong commitment to citizen activism and was instrumental in saving two New York neighbourhoods from demolition. She moved to Toronto with her husband and children in 1968, where she continues her activism on behalf of healthy neighbourhoods as well as her influential writing.

Jane Jacobs has turned down numerous honorary degrees, but in June 1998 she became an Officer of the Order of Canada and, in 2000, was awarded the Order of Ontario as well as the Vincent Scully Prize in Architecture from the National Building Museum in Washington, DC.

10

Development, Environment, and the New Global Imperative

MAURICE F. STRONG, 1971

THE NEW TECHNOLOGICAL ORDER

The basic premise I would like to elaborate here is that "development" and "environment" are not separate and distinct fields but are manifestations of the same basic phenomena, the consequences of humankind's mastery and use of science and technology. They derive from the basic fact that humankind's accelerated development and use of science and technology since the industrial revolution have produced the world's first technological civilization. In these remarks I will attempt to outline my thinking about this technological civilization as inherently a global civilization, the contradictions and imbalances it has produced, and the historical processes by which these have come about. I will also explain why I think that the conditions under which we must seek to deal with these problems are entirely new, that the multiplicity of interacting relationships on which our technological civilization depends for its essential equilibrium cannot be dealt with adequately by traditional means. Finally, I will examine the implications of this for the structure and operation of the institutions through which we conduct our international relationships, with particular reference to the United Nations.

There is no universally agreed upon definition of either development or environment. Both the "development" and "environment" fields originated with a narrower and simpler range of concerns than they are now generally acknowledged to encompass. Originally, development was concerned principally with providing external capital and technical assistance to foster and support economic growth in the recipient country. Later, attention began to be directed to the need to effect basic changes in the trading relationships between less developed nations and the more industrialized countries. More recently, attention has been focused on the important implications of population growth, the problem of development management, the significance of the science and technology gap between rich and poor nations, and a series of other issues ranging from the problems of the brain-drain to the role of foreign investment. As we begin the second development decade, we now appreciate that our concern for development must embrace the whole complex of relationships between the less developed and the more industrialized regions of the world.

Similarly, environmental issues arose originally out of the concern of small groups of conservationists for the protection of species of wildlife and the natural landscape and later out of the concern of many individual communities with the local and visible problems of air and water pollution. It is only recently that people in the industrialized world have begun to become aware of the complexity of the ecological relationships through which human beings interact with their natural environment and the magnitude of the problems they are creating by their interventions in the ecosystems that are vital to their own wellbeing – indeed, their very survival. The most powerful image of our age is the vision of Earth from outer space – an incredibly beautiful, finite, vulnerable sphere that provides the home and enshrines the hopes of all humankind.

It must now be clear that despite the differences in the origin of our respective concerns for development and environment and in the perspectives that they provide of our problems, the fundamental object of these concerns is the welfare of humankind itself. Whether we are pursuing this object under the banner of development or under the banner of environment, the common essence of our task is to manage the power that science and technology give us for the maximum benefit of all humanity.

But it is much easier to agree on this broad objective than it is to understand the kind of actions required to bring it about and even more difficult for us to organize ourselves in such a way as to take those actions.

From the time primitive humans discovered how to use fire and fashioned their first crude weapons and tools, their technologies have been affecting the natural environment significantly. But the scale of humankind's interventions has now grown to the point where they have already produced vast and disruptive changes in the original natural ecosystems of the planet we inhabit and will be decisive in determining its future. The essence of this new technological order is barely two hundred years old, but it has already modified our global existence more profoundly than any earlier human activity in the history of human existence. At the core of this new order is knowledge as Sir Francis Bacon saw it – knowledge as power.

By discovering the mathematical laws of energy and development and techniques of controlled experiment, humans have little by little substituted infinitely more powerful and exact means of production for the old interaction between materials, natural energy, and human labour. Set to work as an instrument of the nation-state, this new system of power and production has been pressed forward by the arts of war until, in its latest incarnation of nuclear energy, it has put into human hands the instruments of total destruction. Set to work in the service of the commercial drives of the market economy, it has elaborated the fantastic array of both essentials and luxuries, whose sale at a profit permits further investment and sets the scene for higher material standards and rising expectations.

One of the products of the advances of technology has been the dramatic improvement in human health and life expectancy. Here, too, the present gap between the epoch of falling death rates and the later fall in birth rates – a fifty-year gap in Europe, North America, and Japan – is creating yet another unprecedented human event: a surge in population expansion that could carry the world to ten billion by 2015, to fifty billion by 2100. After taking perhaps forty millennia to reach the first billion human beings, we are now adding a billion every twenty years. By the year 2000 this could take only seven years and by 2010 only five. Demographers tend to believe that ten billion "earthlings" are about the physical limit for modest but reasonable living standards. Some say we are already approaching the limit of a level of world population at which humankind can expect to sustain a decent standard for all. Certainly at a level of fifty billion we shall be back at the animal limit of a primordial and bloody fight for survival.

What are then the consequences for humanity of this incredible thrust of power, production, and population? First of all we have to see that our unrestrained service to the "idols of the market and the idols of the tribe," to quote Francis Bacon again, does not necessarily produce either a humane or a rational society. The nation as a society of loyalties and common traditions has provided a unifying and enriching element in humankind's progressive revolution to its present state. But narrow and single-minded pursuit of national sovereignty for its own sake can be a dangerously destructive and divisive force.

From the time of our tribal origins, the protection and extension of sovereignty has provided the impetus and rationale for a series of vicious struggles in which the more powerful have exploited their might to eliminate or subordinate the rights and sovereignty of the weak. The "idols of the tribe" continue to be a powerful and divisive force in the relationship within nations as well as amongst nations, and it may seem paradoxical that while the inheritors of the technological civilization are universalizing our culture and widening the area of our interdependence, there has been a resurgence of what might be called "cultural nationalism." Vigorous attempts of such groups as the Basques in Spain, the

Welsh and Scots in Great Britain, and, of course, the French in Canada not only to preserve but to assert their own distinctive cultural values and language are at least in part a reaction against these universalizing forces that would rob them of their sense of uniqueness and identity. This has set up tensions within many societies, in some instances threatening the very existence of states. Nationalism has also generated powerful resistance within a number of countries to the extension of supranational economic units like the common markets in Europe and in Latin America and to the full economic integration of Eastern Europe.

The "idols of the market" have been a powerful and positive force in meeting human needs throughout most of our history. But we are now seeing that the unrestrained pursuit of wealth and market power cannot of itself produce the good society. To say this is not to denounce the uses of enterprise or to deny the value of the market. It is simply to say that it is no longer possible to reconcile a just and equitable economy with the practice of the degree of laissez faire on which the economies of most of the highly industrialized nations has been based thus far. The whole incentive system on which the market economy is based attracts resources into the areas that have the most immediate prospects for profit. The relentless application of cost-benefit analysis determines the patterns of investment and economic developments. This gives priority to the establishment of service stations and breweries and cigarette factories in the newly developing nations over schools and health services.

While I have a great respect for the dynamism and creative power of our market economy and for the good things that it has made possible for us, it has also severely distorted our system of values and created many of the imbalances that now threaten us. If we are to remove some of these imbalances, we must challenge and, if necessary, change some of the attitudes and concepts on which the power and structure of our society is now based. These include the right of one person or one group to initiate an economic action without taking into full account the social costs to the remainder of society. This in turn will necessitate a much better and more integrated system of calculating and allocating the overall costs and benefits to society as a whole of actions that have previously been dealt with purely in a strictly economic context by the parties directly involved. To do this we will require a much greater degree of social and political intervention in the market economy than most Western nations have yet been prepared to accept. But perhaps even more important is the need to devise a much more effective mechanism for the interaction between social and economic decision making in our societies. The expansion of the traditional bureaucratic systems of government represents neither a desirable nor a feasible alternative, as they are simply not geared to deal with the kind and complexity of relationships we must now evolve.

The environmental crisis is requiring us to realize that any uncontrolled industrial system, national or global, can so ruthlessly exploit humankind's physical environment that the manufactured goods offered as proof of rising living standards are produced at a cost of ever-declining standards of clean water, pure air, natural beauty, and the plant and animal life on which humans depend for their own survival and wellbeing. In short, the drive to produce, like the drive to national defense, yields irrational and destructive results unless it is placed under proper human and social direction.

I would like now to examine the degree to which technology at the service of nationalism and commerce has given us today's imbalanced world society. I want to look particularly at what I regard as the most important imbalance of all: the "gap" between the more industrialized nations of the world and the two-thirds of the earth's people who live in the developing nations of Africa, Asia, and Latin America. Let me suggest now how it came about.

The first states to make the transition to the modern technological order were of course the states of Western Europe and North America. The Atlantic powers began to industrialize and urbanize their societies in the first half of the nineteenth century. It was, as anyone with a sense of history or taste for the novels of Dickens and Balzac will recall, a time of agonizing upheaval and exploitation as well as of growing wealth and national self-confidence. The 1840s were the "Hungry 40s," a period of great pressure and hunger and unemployment. They culminated in 1848, the year of revolutions, and many who surveyed the emerging social order at that time – among them, preeminently, Marx and Engels – doubted whether a system so violently at odds with itself could possibly endure.

The chief reason for its endurance after the 1840s was the vast new input of wealth and resources that the Atlantic world enjoyed during the rest of the nineteenth century. All the world's temperate farming land was open for Western settlement. Forty million migrants left Europe's uncertainties for a new land and new lives. The whole world, most of it under European colonial control, was open virgin territory for Western trade and Western investment in mines and plantations. The world market circuit came into being with raw materials flowing to the Atlantic states, Latin America, Africa, and Asia – paid for by Western manufactures and Western capital.

This great expansion created for the first time a single global economy based upon advancing technology. But it also ensured that the 20 per cent of the world's people who were white and Atlantic-based would control – as they still do – some 80 per cent of the world's resources. The technological drive, based an power and capital and directed principally by profit and national interest, gave us the world economy we have today – a single system, yes, but one shaken from end to end by the imbalances and injustices with which our planet's rewards and advantages are distributed. The continued evolution of our economic life under the impetus of universalized technologies is leading inevitably toward even greater specialization and interdependence and consequently greater internationalization.

Nor can we expect a continued dominance of unmodified national interest and profit to set right the manifest imbalances. An uncorrected market system that has managed without social imperatives or moral control cannot but leave the balance of advantage with the already richer powers – in other words, with the ex-colonial Atlantic powers, to which we must now add Japan. Moreover, the developing nations of today, when they seek to enter the technological order, are seriously disadvantaged by the fact that they come late to the modernizing race and that they must cross the threshold of modern technological order in the wake of other more powerful nations. For those nations that made the transition first have built a whole world economy on the basis of their own needs, drives, and achievements. It accommodates only very inadequately the needs and aspirations of the majority, who are latecomers to the modernization process.

When developing governments cast around for alternatives, they find themselves blocked by the entrenched positions of the already modernized nations. In a sense, one can say that they have already arrived at the stage reached in the 1840s by the now-industrialized states, but no vast input of free land and open trade awaits them today. There can be no massive migrations to new settlements. The earth's surface is allotted, all of it under some other nation's control, and one by one the borders of the more privileged nations are closing to all but a selective few of the most highly skilled and trained immigrants. Everywhere there are artificial restraints on the opening up of markets to newcomers. The more industrialized world already controls some 80 per cent of world trade and 90 per cent of the trade in manufactures. And it continues to maintain tariffs and quotas against the exported textiles, clothing, and simple machines that the infant industries of the less developed countries are able to produce competitively.

Even down to such elements as commercial services – banking, marketing, insurance, shipping – the whole system is largely under the control of the industrialized countries of the West and Japan. It is not easy for a poor land to break in, coming late, technologically backward, short of capital, swarming with people, operating perpetually under norms and standards devised and imposed by others.

But the most ominous disparity of all is in the field of research and development. For it is today's research and development that produces tomorrow's technology, which in turn is the source of tomorrow's wealth and power. Yet some 98 per cent of the world's expenditures (excluding the Communist countries) on research and development continue to be made in the more industrialized countries and only 2 per cent in the developing nations. More money is in fact being spent on research and development of synthetic products that compete directly with some of the principal commodity exports of the developing world than is allotted for the entire research and development expenditures of all developing countries combined. Some individual multinational corporations have research and development budgets that exceed those of all developing countries combined. And only a very small amount – less than 1 per cent – of the research and development expenditures of the industrialized countries is specifically directed to the solution of problems of importance to the developing countries.

The report of the Commission on International Development, headed by Canada's own Lester B. Pearson, identified this as one of the most important elements in the development gap and urged industrialized countries to devote a significant share of their research and development resources and facilities to projects specifically relating to problems of developing countries. The creation by the Canadian government of the International Development Research Centre, with Mr Pearson as its chairman, represents in my view one of the most promising initiatives Canada has taken in the field of international development. It is directed squarely at what I believe is the central problem of the developing nations, that of increasing their own scientific and technological capability.

It is encouraging to note that other governments are beginning to follow Canada's lead in this field. But it will require a massive reordering of the research and development priorities of the industrialized countries if the present techno-logical bias against the interests of the developing countries is to be removed. Indeed, all the efforts under conventional aid programs to help increase agricul-tural and industrial production through massive infusions of capital and technical assistance will prove to be but temporary palliatives if we do not tackle the problem here at its roots.

In fact, we are only now, I believe, beginning to see that the real problems of underdevelopment are deeply rooted in the pattern of our lopsided technological advances over the last two centuries.

To go back to the two earlier points: the unparalleled wealth that was opened up to Atlantic developers in the nineteenth century; and the powerful, uncon-trolled drive for wealth in markets that gave rise to today's modern industrial system. The sense that resources and land were all but unlimited, together with the driving ambitions of the industrial pioneers, combined to bring into being an inconceivably wasteful and perilous economic and technological system. For the old concepts of thrift and care, we substituted waste and planned obsoles-cence. Millions of acres were eroded by careless, mechanized farming. Poisons were released from factories into air and water. Blankets of unwholesome smog enveloped some of our largest cities. Lakes died. Rivers and oceans were awash with the mounting residues of a gluttonous society. Above all, that tyrant the automobile filled the air with fumes, covered the soil with concrete, and helped to bring into being that painful phenomenon, neither city nor countryside, of the sprawling, faceless, graceless "conurbation."

This high-consumption, high-pollution society has come into its own only in the past twenty years. Before that, the majority's claim on national wealth was still modest, and periodic recessions retarded the growth in the use of resources. But now, after a twenty-year boom, average income per capita in the Atlantic area is between $1,200 and $2,000 – in North America, some $3,500. There is a car for every two persons in the United States, and cars are increasing more rapidly than people. Whatever the damage to the environment – and it is great and growing – it can be argued that living standards have never been so high. At least, the ideal taken round the world by every means of advertising and the mass media is the high-consumption society in its Atlantic incarnation. Now the concern for environment is leading even those who have been extolling the advantages of this society, and encouraging and assisting others to acquire them, to have their doubts.

Although environment has rapidly become a major preoccupation of both publics and governments in the industrialized countries, it is still endowed with no such magic in much of the developing world. Environment is still seen by many as a rich man's problem, a disease they would be prepared to risk if it is a necessary accompaniment to the economic growth that they want and urgently need. They are understandably concerned about how the preoccupation of the industrialized countries with environment will affect their priority task of meeting the basic and immediate needs of their peoples for food, shelter, jobs, education, and health care. They have also been concerned that those whose industrial technology has produced the major part of today's pollution should assume the major cost of dealing with the environmental consequences. They want to be surer, before jumping enthusiastically on the environmental bandwagon, of just how it is likely to affect their own interests and their own priorities.

But there is a growing recognition, in both the developed and developing countries, that there is much more to the environmental crisis than industrial pollution and that the environmental problems of poverty are even more acute and more widespread than the environmental problems of affluence. In developing countries environmental problems are seen as integral aspects of their fundamental problem of development, and we must be prepared to understand them in this context. But in all societies it is the poor who stand to gain most from enhancement of their environment; they have fewer resources to waste on costly mistakes or remedial action and fewer alternatives to escape the consequences of environmental neglect.

There is growing evidence, too, in the experience of the developing countries that economic development that ignores environmental and ecological considerations can give rise to economic and social costs that negate or seriously impair the purposes they were intended to serve, and equally that effective environmental planning and action can make a positive contribution to development.

Vast tracks of formerly productive land have been desecrated by water-logging and desalination in countries like Algeria and Pakistan as a result of large-scale irrigation programs that were designed to increase their productivity. The benefits of the Kariba Dam in Zambia were accompanied by unexpected costs in the loss of the livelihood of farmers and fisherman. The Peruvian anchovy fisheries have suffered drastic depletion because of exploitation practices that ignored ecological factors. An insecticide program in Peru resulted in virtual destruction of the crop it was designed to improve. Indeed, the environmental resources of a country represent its irreplaceable base of natural capital and are the very foundation of its development. The developing countries least of all can afford to misuse their environmental capital.

It must be equally apparent to those in the industrialized world who are concerned with the threat to our common environment from pollutants that disperse widely through the oceans and atmosphere that effective control of these substances requires the cooperation of all countries. The banning of DDT in Canada, for example, will not in itself protect Canadians from the ultimate consequences of DDT contamination so long as it continues to be used in large quantities in the countries of the developing world. But in these countries it is a vital ingredient in the "green" revolution, on which they depend for so much of their vital food supply, and there is as yet no available substitute for it. How can we expect these people to accept costs and constraints that affect their vital and immediate welfare simply to reduce the risks of an already uncertain and unpromising future? We can only expect from them the cooperation on which international collective action must depend if we can work out arrangements that clearly take account of their own needs and priorities.

We have rather vaguely and naively been assuming that it is possible to extend the high-consumption society to everyone. There are now real doubts as to whether this is feasible, and it certainly is not a likelihood in the foreseeable future. The planet's finite supply of a number of critical resources is bound to impose limitations on the extent of our quantitative growth. This poses the problem of equitable use of the earth's resources. We are already altering significantly various critical chemical balances in the atmosphere and possibly the oceans. We are faced with sudden catastrophic and often unexplained mega-deaths of fish, birds, and wildlife, which play a vital part in the natural ecosystems on which human beings themselves are highly dependent. We are finding that such substances as DDT and mercury accumulate in quantities that are dangerous to both human and animal life in places that are remote from the sources of their emission.

These are risks that are now being perceived by people of the industrialized world. But what if we were to extend the system that produced them to the whole of the rest of humanity? Is this really a viable proposition? It has been estimated that one American uses more electric power than fifty-five Africans and puts more toxic waste in the rivers and oceans than 1,000 Asians. There are some who doubt whether it is sensible at all to extend to the rest of the world the material standards that would even approach the present standards of North America and Western Europe. But it is not necessary to be that pessimistic to appreciate that this could not be done without vast changes in the organization and structures through which human beings carry out their economic and social relationships, and this in turn can only come about through a major reorientation of attitudes and values.

Indeed, we have reached a watershed in the history of humankind. We now have in our hands the ultimate power to destroy ourselves or to achieve a decent standard of life for all. Having opened up Pandora's box, we have no alternative but to control the power that is now in our hands. For it is quite clear that its uncontrolled, uncoordinated use will make human life intolerable, if not impossible.

The attitudes and practices that we have followed throughout the period of our history in which the main threats to human beings have come from nature are no longer adequate for a period in which the main threats to both humankind and nature come from humans themselves.

Let us then examine our ability to manage this power and what it requires of us in terms of attitudes, values, and structures if we are to use it wisely and beneficially. What are the real chances of our being able to respond to these requirements in time for us to be able to take the high road to a peaceful and prosperous life for the whole human family rather than the low road to anarchy, disintegration, or total destruction?

Let us look more closely at some of the important areas in which international action will have to be taken to deal with environmental problems. It is useful to recall that most of the earth as life-sustaining biosphere is beyond the control of any nation. Some 70 per cent of the world's surface is covered by ocean. The oceans, in which life first began, continue to be a critical element in the maintenance of the natural cycles on which human life on this planet depends. They are a vital factor in determining the delicate heat balances, chemical balances, and moisture balances that are critical to the capacity of the biosphere to sustain human life. The ocean fisheries are the main source of much of the protein on which the world's growing population must rely to a greater and greater extent in the future. Yet the oceans are still largely a no-man's land that – except for agreements covering their use for surface transportation, the recent treaty banning the use of the sea floors for nuclear weapons, and some conventions concerning ocean fisheries – are largely bereft of the rule of law and the kind of control that nations exercise over their national territories.

The pollution of some of the more enclosed seas, such as the Baltic, the Mediterranean, and the North Sea, is reaching the point where it is posing a serious threat to the ecology and economies of the countries that border them. There is mounting evidence that even the great vastness of the open sea is showing the unmistakable marks of our use of them as a depositary for the growing tides of refuse human civilization is producing. Some of this results from spillage of oil from tankers, some from offshore oil drilling operations, but most of it flows quietly and undramatically from the sewers of the great cities: the effluents from industrial plants and the run-offs from chemically treated lands and forests. No one knows just how much waste is being poured into the oceans. What we do know is that it is beginning to affect significantly many of the critical ecological relationships and to impair the beauty and utility of the ocean beaches. We also know that the amount of waste being dumped into the oceans is growing at exponential rates.

In a special category are those toxic substances that are being disposed of in increasing quantities by deliberate dumping into the ocean. Again no one knows just what substances or how much of them are being dumped or where they are being dumped or how long their containers will keep them from being released into the oceans.

What is clear is that all of these activities represent a threat to human life and wellbeing that we can no longer ignore and that can only be dealt with by collective international action.

Even some of the most elementary steps have not yet been taken. For example, there is as yet no international agreement providing even for the registration of those poisonous substances that are dumped deliberately into the ocean so that their nature, quantities, and location will be known, quite apart from agreement to refrain from such dumpings. We have not even begun to reach agreement on the collection of data on the kinds and quantities and sources of waste materials that drain into the oceans from the world's land masses, nor do we yet have the means of monitoring, on a regular, systematic basis, changes that may take place in the composition of the ocean waters and changes that occur in plant and animal life of the oceans that signal important consequences for humans themselves. Although some work has been done in all of these areas, it is still at a very preliminary stage, largely uncoordinated, and inadequately financed. Much of the work that needs to be done can and must of course be done by national governments. But there must be international agreements on common guidelines and criteria for carrying out the required tests and measurements, and on mechanisms for collecting the data from a variety of sources as part of a network that will assure adequate global coverage and for the evaluation of the data and dissemination of its results to all who require them.

But even existing knowledge, with all its deficiencies, is sufficient to enable us to make a start toward obtaining international agreement on such urgent matters as deliberate dumping of poisonous substances into the ocean. The meeting of the twenty-seven-nation preparatory committee for the Conference on the Human Environment in February 1971 in Geneva agreed that an intergovernmental working group would be established to facilitate international action in dealing with the whole range of problems in the field of marine pollution and, in particular, to agree on a master plan within which priorities for action could be established and responsibility for carrying out such actions clearly assigned. In this way the Stockholm Conference has already served to accelerate and facilitate action.

At the last session of the General Assembly a resolution was passed calling for the holding of a conference on the law of the sea in 1973. This conference would be called upon to deal with the whole complex of legal questions concerning control of the seas from the point of view of exploitation of its resources as well as marine pollution. It will consider a revolutionary proposal for the establishment of a sea-beds regime that would, in effect, subject the ocean to direct international control. The scheme as now envisaged provides for revenues from the exploitation of the mineral resources of the sea to go to the United Nations, with a major portion of them to be directed to assisting the developing countries. It is apparent that the implementation of this scheme would bring a completely new dimension to the structure of the international system of organizations. If it were endowed with the powers envisaged by its sponsors, the sea-beds regime would indeed become potentially one of the most powerful organizations on earth. It is precisely for this reason that agreement on it will take a long time.

In the meantime the world cannot and need not wait for agreement on the creation of such a regime in order to begin to deal with the urgent problems of marine pollution. Any actions taken in this area can be conceived of as steps toward realization of the larger goals envisaged for the creation of the sea-beds regime. Indeed, I am convinced that the creation of such a regime will be much more likely to command the kind of support it will require if it is approached on as step-by-step basis and if agreement on marine pollution is seen as the most logical first step along this path.

The atmosphere – its contamination, its composition, and its temperature – is another intrinsically international concern. Emission of toxic substances into the air from the industrial heartland of Western Europe is resulting in accumulations of polluted air that threaten the forests of Scandinavia. We are only beginning to perceive the effects on the atmosphere in different parts of the world of the emission of millions of tons of toxic substances, carbon dioxide, carbon monoxide, and particular matter from the exhausts of automobiles, the jet streams of aircraft, and the chimneys of factories and homes throughout the world. We now know that air pollution causes damage amounting to hundreds of millions of dollars annually to buildings, forests, other forms of plant life, and to human health. We also know that our interventions are materially changing the composition of the thin band of the earth's atmosphere that acts as a filter for the energy we receive from the sun, reflecting much of it back into space and thus determining the delicate heat balance on which our planet's ability to sustain life is based. Scientists are not yet agreed on the net effects of these changes in the atmosphere – whether they will result in reducing the earth's temperature enough to produce a new ice age or in increasing its temperature enough to melt the polar ice caps and inundate much of the present land surface of the globe. We do know that it only takes a few degrees of change in average temperature to produce such changes, which would be catastrophic for human life. We know, too, that our activities are now affecting the atmosphere on a scale that could possibly bring about changes of this magnitude.

It is clear that we are now taking great, perhaps decisive, risks with our future, risks of consequences that will be too late to reverse if and when they do occur. Accordingly it is imperative that we have more knowledge of the extent and nature of these risks. This in turn requires vastly expanded networks for the gathering, evaluation, and dissemination of data and facilities for carrying out research based on this data, all on a global basis. The program and facilities already in place in many countries and within such United Nations agencies as the World Meteorological Organization (WMO), the World Health Organization (WHO), the Food and Agriculture Organization (FAO), and the United Nations Educational, Scientific, and Cultural Organization (UNESCO) provide many of the ingredients on which such global knowledge systems can be based. But international agreement is needed on how those elements can best be utilized to provide the kind of information and evaluation that will be needed by the world's decision makers.

And the gathering and evaluation of data is only the first step. The task of achieving international agreement on limiting emissions of the substances that produce the dangers to both atmosphere and oceans to which I have referred will be an even more difficult one. But it is an obligation from which there can be no escape and no alternative to international action.

Even in fields in which both the sources of pollution and its principal or immediate consequences are national, there is a need for international cooperation. No nation can afford to impose controls and standards on its industry that burden it with costs that impede its ability to compete in international markets. But if all countries agree on the adoption of common guidelines, each country will be able to implement the necessary measures in its own country without impairing the competitive position of its industry. Even such local problems as soil erosion and noise pollution can benefit from the international exchange of experience and the application of technology that can be made available from international cooperation.

Machinery must also be developed for the arbitration and settlement of international disputes involving the actions of one country that impair the environment of others. Pollution of water and air from industries in one country that derives the benefits produced by the industry impose massive economic and social costs in other countries. The number of such issues is bound to mount rapidly and will require new mechanisms – environmental courts, if you will – to reconcile the interests of all parties affected.

I have talked about the substantial growth that I foresee as necessary in the nature and the scale of the functions that must be performed in relation to environment by the international system of organizations in the period ahead. I am convinced that a similar review of such fields as telecommunications, the increasing complexity of common problems of the development and use of the world's food resources, mineral resources, and energy resources, and the vastly expanded requirements of traffic in the air and on the oceans would reveal corresponding increases in the range and complexity of requirements for international collective actions.

Thus the growth of the new technological order is creating a complex network of relationships that are essentially global in character and subject to a degree of interdependence that is totally without precedence in human experience.

In the second part of this paper I will discuss the ability of the existing international structure, particularly the United Nations, to respond to the need for the new dimensions of international cooperation that this demands of us.

THE FUTURE OF INTERNATIONAL COOPERATION

Thus far I have put forth my views that the problems of underdevelopment in Africa, Asia, and Latin America and the newly perceived problems of humankind's relationship with its natural environment both derive from imbalances created by our use of the power that science and technology has placed in our hands, that these problems are essentially global in nature, and that they require us to deal with a complex system of interactions across traditional, political, sectoral, and disciplinary boundaries. I would like now to examine how well we are now organized in our international relationships to deal with these problems, particularly within the United Nations system, what new measures may be required in the future, and the changes that will be needed in our own attitudes and values to make this possible.

The quarter of a century since the end of World War Two has seen vast changes in the political structure of the world. The colonial empires of the European powers have been almost completely dismantled, and most of the world's people live in independent nations. The number of nations has doubled from 65 to 130, so that almost the entire world is now organized on the basis of independent nation-states. Nationalism has shown itself to be a powerful continuing force in world affairs.

Yet despite the persistence of vigorous and sensitive nationalism during the past twenty-five years, the world has seen an unprecedented increase in the number and the role of international organizations. The number of intergovernmental organizations has more than doubled to 229, and there has been an even greater growth in the number of nongovernmental organizations, which, at the end of 1969, had reached 2,188.

The United Nations and its family of agencies has clearly established itself as the principal focal point in this network of international organizations. The total of the regular budget and voluntary contributions of the United Nations system rose from $27 million in 1946 to $695 million in 1970, and the total number of full-time employees increased to some 19,600. Anyone who has visited the headquarters of these agencies in recent years cannot fail to have seen the visible evidences of their growth in the continued expansion of their buildings and staffs. Much of the impetus for the growth in international organizations since the end of World War Two, and particularly the growth of the United Nations system, has come from the commitment to international development. Almost all of the newcomers to full membership in the community of nations were from the developing regions of the world. A total of over 100 of the 127 member nations of the United Nations today are accounted for by countries with average per capita incomes of less than $500 per year. It is natural then that in all those world organizations that reflect this new alignment of political forces, there has been a heavy emphasis on those programs and activities that are designed to meet the development needs and aspirations of the low-income countries.

Indeed, one of the principal products of the post-World War Two experience in international development has been the creation of a system of organizations and relationships within the international community for the international transfer and utilization of financial and human resources. Some two-thirds of the total budget of the United Nations and its specialized agencies, even those with relatively narrow functional responsibilities, have become increasingly involved in providing technical assistance to the less developed countries.

But the very growth in the extent and the complexity of these activities has created very great difficulties within the system itself. These difficulties have nowhere been better elaborated than in the report of Sir Robert Jackson on the development capacity of the United Nations system. The basic question proposed by the Jackson study is the ability of the United Nations to make the changes necessary to enable it to carry out effectively the much larger role in international development that it can and should play in the future. The United Nations is now deeply involved in the attempt to deal with the issues that Jackson identified. Its ability to do so will obviously have an important bearing on the extent to which governments will be prepared to entrust it with the new and enlarged tasks that must be performed within the international system in the years ahead.

Two of the most powerful and effective international institutions that have been created are the International Monetary Fund and the International Bank for Reconstruction and Development, commonly called the World Bank, which arose out of a meeting at Bretton-Woods, New Hampshire, in July 1944. Both these organizations are technically part of the United Nations system, but they operate for all practical purposes independently. The important distinction between them and most other United Nations agencies is that their membership is based on a formula that attaches such weight to economic and financial factors as to assure the wealthy industrialized nations majority membership of their governing bodies. They are also not so universal in their membership, as the USSR and other Communist countries, except for Yugoslavia, have thus far not sought membership.

In the monetary field, the International Monetary Fund (IMF) has gradually acquired some of the attributes of an international central bank. Its members have come to accept a degree of intervention in their own economic and monetary policies that would have been regarded as an unthinkable affront to national sovereignty only a few years ago. It has played a major part in maintaining a relatively stable international economic and financial environment, which has contributed immensely to the economic growth of both industrialized and less developed countries. It has also interested itself especially in the affairs of the less developed countries. Its compensatory financing scheme has provided short-term assistance for those less developed nations that were experiencing short-falls in foreign-exchange earnings due to unexpected drops from their principal commodity exports. The agreement to permit it to create what is in effect a new form of money, special drawing rights (SDRs), is one of the great milestones in the evolution of the international system. One of the important potentialities of this new means of creating international credit is that it could be used to provide an indirect means of transferring resources to the less developed countries. Although the principal members of the IMF have not yet shown a disposition to permit SDRs to be used for this purpose, there is growing evidence of support for it. In my view it offers one of the most promising methods of increasing the transfer of resources to the less developed countries under conditions that are devoid of the normal political and psychological connotations of "aid."

The World Bank has become by far the dominant institution in the field of international development and one of the principal sources of direct capital assistance. From its early role as a banking and financial institution involved in development leading it has evolved into a more comprehensive development institution that has assumed, particularly under the leadership of Mr Robert McNamara, the role of a leader in the international development field. This has been facilitated by the substantial increases in the amount of soft loan funds made available directly to it by governments that now account for a larger portion of its lending activities than the funds derived from its borrowings in the financial markets.

The bank's assessment of the development plans of the less developed countries is accepted as a leading criteria by most bilateral donors in determining the extent and nature of their own support of these countries. It has established a reputation for objectivity, integrity, and devotion to the economic rather than the political aspects of development. Accordingly it has succeeded where individual countries could not in having its borrowers adopt policies and accept constraints designed to improve their economic performance as a condition of the World Bank's financing. It has organized consultative and consortia groups for the principal countries receiving aid to permit better coordination of the development plans of the recipients with the resources available from donors. The bank has succeeded in retaining the confidence of investors in its securities and of donor countries as an effective means of dispensing their aid funds through the International Development Association. This has enabled the bank to expand its resources, to double its lending activities during the past four years, and to extend its influence in the international system substantially. Partly because of this and partly out of disagreement with its policies, it has been subjected to criticism and resentment in some developing countries, but it nevertheless continues to command a high degree of respect and support throughout the developing world.

The willingness of the donor countries to support the World Bank illustrates another important reality: the fact that donors are much more prepared to support those international institutions in which they are able to play a dominant role than those in which they are a minority. This is further evidenced by the unwillingness of the industrialized countries to support the United Nations Capital Development Fund and by their clear lack of enthusiasm for the United Nations Industrial Development Organization and the United Nations Conference on Trade and Development, in all of which the developing countries are in a majority position.

Another illustration of this donor bias in favour of the institutions they can dominate is the regional development banks, which are becoming a more important factor in the international development system. The Asian Development Bank was able to attract initial capital of almost one billion dollars by permitting the full membership of nonregional donor countries, whereas the African Development Bank, which began some several years earlier in 1963, has had to accept severe limitations on its resources and scale of its activities because of its inability to attract resources from countries outside the region without providing for their participation in decisions concerning the use of the funds.

The United Nations Development Program (UNDP) occupies a special place within the United Nations system. Unlike the World Bank and the IMF, it operates clearly as part of the UN system. The socialist countries participate actively in it, and while the more industrialized countries have a majority of one on its Governing Council, it is seen by virtually the entire membership of the UN as "their" organization. This in itself gives it an extremely important role, but it is important also for the fact that it is the principal instrumentality through which funds are channelled to the support of the development activities of the specialized agencies. The specialized agencies are the executing agencies for almost all projects carried out using UNDP funds, and UNDP-financed activities now account for a large share of the programs of such important specialized agencies as the FAO, the WHO, UNESCO, and the International Labour Organization (ILO). Thus the UNDP's control of such a large portion of the funds that go to the specialized agencies gives it a substantial potential for influencing and coordinating the development activities of the entire United Nations system. It is the degree to which the UNDP seeks to use this power to influence and coordinate the development activities of the specialized agencies that has provided the principal source of tension and controversy with the United Nations in its attempt to reconcile the issues pointed out by the Jackson capacity study.

This poses a real dilemma. Under the stimulus of budget stringency in most of the donor countries and a general disenchantment with the United Nations, governments are showing themselves unwilling to support continued expansion of the development activities of the UN without evidence that the UN can subject these activities to a greater degree of coordination and rationalization. The UNDP is the principal instrument available to perform this role. If it can demonstrate that it can do so effectively, there is no doubt that it can command increasing financial support in the future, and this in turn will provide support for the further expansion of the development activities of the agencies. Some major donor governments, particularly the US, are now showing a disposition to increase the portion of their foreign aid allocations that are devoted to multilateral aid, and the UNDP clearly has an opportunity to lay claim to a significant share of these increases. Indeed, this is the reason why UNDP administrator Paul Hoffman, the grand old man of development assistance, with his characteristic foresight commissioned the capacity study.

Coincident with the changes being made as a result of the Jackson study in the mechanisms for dispensing development aid with the United Nations system, agreement was reached at the last General Assembly on a development strategy for the second development decade and on a number of targets for the realization of this strategy. A committee on development planning was set up to supervise its implementation. Many countries now feel the need for a greater degree of coordination and cooperation in the harmonization of policies amongst both more industrialized and developing nations if the objectives of the second development decade are to be achieved. Some have expressed doubt that this can be done within the United Nations system. Proposals are being made in some quarters for the establishment of new coordinating mechanisms outside the United Nations.

Both in its response to the challenge of the Jackson capacity study to improve its effectiveness in dispensing development aid and in its response to the pressures for greater coordination of aid, the United Nations faces a formidable challenge. Its ability to respond successfully to this challenge is directly related to the role governments will permit it to play in meeting the vastly increased needs for international action in many other spheres of activity.

It should not be taken for granted that all of the new activities required to deal with international environmental concerns will take place within the United Nations system. Indeed, there are some who believe that the United Nations is not capable of responding effectively to the new responsibilities that this would require it to assume. This view has powerful advocates: some of the leading industrialized countries, including US diplomat George Kennan. In fact, the industrialized countries of the Western world have already assigned substantial responsibilities in the environmental field to NATO and the Organization for Economic Cooperation and Development (OECD). It would be easy for them to succumb to the temptation of letting such organizations in, which would make it so much easier for them to establish the political and economic common denominators required for action because of the principal instrumentalities of these organizations' approach to the solution of international environmental problems. The negative attitude of some developing countries toward United Nations activities in the environmental field and the apathy of others could encourage this. In my view this would be a mistake both for developing countries, who would then be deprived of a voice in decisions that will vitally affect their interests, and for the industrialized countries, which have the most to lose by the deepening and destabilizing division between rich and poor nations that would inevitably follow. And for the United Nations it would represent the loss of a unique and probably irretrievable opportunity to achieve the new dimension of relevance and usefulness it so badly needs at this critical juncture in its history.

I am convinced that much of the action required to deal with environmental problems must be taken on a regional level. Many of the conditions affecting the environment have a distinctive regional character. The specific problems of each of the regions of the world will often respond best to a regional approach. But environmental problems embrace all of the countries within each region and can be dealt with most effectively by those regional organizations in which the maximum number of countries in the region participate. Thus while the OECD and NATO in Europe both have a high degree of competence in carrying out research and analysis in environmental matters and can help provide an impetus to political action, they do not include the more universal political constituency within the European region that the United Nations Economic Commission for Europe possesses and that is an essential precondition to any effective collective action within the region. The unique character of the United Nations, with its regional organs embracing the largest political constituency in each region while being part of the global United Nations system, gives it special opportunities to serve the interests of each region. And it is my hope that any international action in the environmental field will serve to reinforce and strengthen the role and capacity of the regional system of organizations. The situation in Latin America is a special case in that the United Nations presence is complemented by a powerful and long-established inter-American system of organizations that, while it does not include all of the countries of the region, provides nevertheless the most comprehensive regional machinery that exists anywhere. It could be readily adapted to the requirements for large-scale cooperative environmental action within the region.

Both development and environment deal with a whole complex of sectors and functions that in turn involve a large number of specialized policy and operational organizations. Both fields involve the application of multiple disciplines in the identification both of problems and of their solutions. They involve the interaction of economic and social factors and large-scale utilization of technology. In the international development field we have twenty-five years of experience to call upon; we also have some deeply entrenched institutional interests and attitudes that are not easy to change. Within the environmental field our problems are more recently perceived, and we are only at the initial stages in our attempts to deal with them within the international systems of organizations. That is not to say that the existing international organizations are not now involved in dealing with these problems. Indeed, much of the work of such specialized agencies as UNESCO, the FAO, the WHO, and the WMO is in programs and activities that relate directly to important environmental concerns. Accordingly, in determining how the international activities in the environmental field will be organized and coordinated, we are not devoid of some of the same problems of jurisdictional conflict, overlap, and duplication of activities that affect relations in the development field. The United Nations Conference on the Human Environment, which will be held in Stockholm in 1972, does provide us, however, with a basis for taking a fresh new look at all of these activities and for considering ways of dealing with these issues in the future that will take full account of the lessons of the past.

It is clear that to deal with the problems of the human environment will require a vast increase in the scale and scope of international cooperation. The first and most important task we face is the political task of agreeing on what the principal problems are, then what action we must begin to take to deal with them, and how and by whom these actions will be taken. This is the essential task of the Stockholm Conference. It will draw upon the world's scientific-intellectual community to identify the major issues requiring the priority attention of governments and produce a comprehensive plan of action to provide governments and international organizations with an internationally agreed upon basis for establishment of action priorities and the allocation of responsibilities and resources to meet these priorities. These actions will not in most cases represent final solutions to environmental problems, but first steps in what will be a long-term and continuing process, not just of identifying and resolving problems but of planning to foresee and avoid them. But while each particular action or component of an action program can be taken within a separate organization – and indeed I believe firmly that new organizations should not be created to carry out functions that can be performed effectively by existing organizations – all components must be related to each other within a network or "system." Each such system would be based on particular policy or functional objectives and would contain within it all the variable elements that can affect significantly the objectives of the system. The systems in turn would have to be related to each other as part of larger systems again designed around particular objectives. These systems must be designed to facilitate the communication of essential information, the evaluation of critical overall trends and results by decision makers, and the response of all the elements in the system to the decisions made.

This suggests that what is needed to deal with the task of improving humankind's global environment is not a new specialized agency or operating body but a policy evaluation and review mechanism that can become the institutional "centre" or "brain" of the environmental network. It might be charged with responsibility for maintaining a global review of environmental trends, policies, and actions, determining important issues that should be brought to the attention of governments, identifying gaps in knowledge and in the performance of organizations carrying out agreed upon international measures for environmental control. It would have to be sufficiently competent, both politically and technically, to give it a high degree of credibility and influence with both the governments and other organizations in the international system. It would have to have access to the world's best scientific and professional resources in evaluating the information that would be available to it through the world-monitoring networks operated by other agencies, both national and international.

If it were to be an effective instrument for coordinating and rationalizing environmental activities throughout the international system, it would not, in my view, undertake operating functions in which it could compete with the organizations it must influence. It should, however, exercise a sufficient influence on the funding of international environmental activities by national governments that it will be able to exercise a coordinating influence on the environmental activities of the agencies. This function would be further strengthened if it were to be allied to a world environmental fund, which would permit central funding of at least some aspects of international environmental activities, such as research and technical assistance.

In my view the most important first step that must be taken at this stage is to agree on an effective means of performing this policy review and coordination function. Our experiences in international development have taught us that it is virtually impossible to superimpose such a policy review and coordination function on a system of organizations in which deep and extensive vested interests have already been established in separate and competing organizations. It also takes account of the reality that effective coordination within the United Nations system, as now constituted, must involve coordination within national governments. The Secretary General of the United Nations has none of the normal powers at his disposal with which heads of national governments can exercise central control over their component ministries. He has the power neither to appoint their principal officers nor to control their budgets. The heads of specialized agencies are appointed by their own governing councils, which are in turn the direct representatives of member governments, and their regular budgets are funded by direct contributions from member governments.

As I indicated before, the UNDP has a significant potential influence over the specialized agencies in virtue of the substantial portions of their activities that are financed by the UNDP, but in practice this is not used to any considerable extent to influence the policies or programs of the agencies.

It must be said that governments themselves often suffer from the very lack of coordination that they frequently attribute to the United Nations system, despite the fact that, unlike the United Nations, they do possess the inherent means of coordination. There is a deeply entrenched relationship between each of the specialized agencies and the corresponding department of national governments – for example, the FAO with departments of agriculture, the WHO with departments of health, the ILO with departments of labour, and so on. Only a few governments seem to have succeeded in maintaining, in the governing bodies of the agencies, a consistent set of policies and objectives. The record is replete with conflict between the positions taken by the representative of a government in one specialized agency and representatives of the same government in other agencies.

Budget stringencies and proliferation of demands for the financing of international activities are now causing most governments to look hard at the financing of international organizations and the coordination of their policies in respect of them. Governments need a basis for effecting such coordination. An internationally agreed upon plan of action, such as that which we are hoping to produce at the Stockholm Conference in the environmental field, would provide governments with a rational basis for the coordination of their own positions in each of the individual organizations involved to prevent the overlap and duplication that too often characterize their activities. Given the realities of the present international system, the only way in which a central policy unit within the United Nations Secretariat can exercise a coordinating influence over specialized agencies is by influencing the member governments. It is only through this interaction between its influence on governments and its influence on other components of the UN system that any policy coordination and review organ can expect to operate effectively. If through the Stockholm Conference the United Nations can demonstrate its ability to deal usefully and effectively with the important environment issues requiring international action, it could have an exemplary and revitalizing effect on the whole United Nations.

The attempt to foresee the future is no longer a matter for casual speculation but an imperative for those who are responsible for leading and directing the nations and the powerful institutions of our society. As a result, there has been a proliferation of forecasts and of forecasters. One does not need to choose between them to see that one common denominator in all their predictions is a vast expansion in the kinds of activities that are inherently international.

The big question, then, is where will this lead us. Will the dreams of those who have long seen world government as the ideal finally come to pass? And will the United Nations become the nucleus for such a world government?

Let me look at the realities. In my view world government is neither feasible nor desirable if by it we mean a central world authority to which all other levels of government would be subservient. The world today is a system of nations. Nation-states are the repositories of most of the world's political power. All nation-states have an institutional commitment to maintaining their sovereignty and integrity, even in cases where an objective analysis of the interests of the people might dictate otherwise. There is nothing in the existing situation or in our understanding of the behaviour of institutions toward the power they possess that would encourage us to think that nations will easily or lightly surrender sovereignty over any of the important areas and jurisdiction that they now possess.

One of the deficiencies inherent in the nation-state system is that nations are organized around control of territory. They are therefore necessarily confined in the jurisdiction they exercise to the territory that they control. Many of the issues with which we must cope in the future are ones in which exercise of power and jurisdiction is essentially of a nonterritorial or extraterritorial character. This is of course demonstrably true of outer space and the use of satellites. But it is also true of the control of broadcasting frequencies, the control of the oceans, and of the atmosphere.

The fact that the large private business corporations are organized around performance of functions and the control of financial and technological resources rather than territory has enabled them to take full advantage of the new technological order in extending their activities and their power throughout the world. They are able to move money, skilled manpower, and technology across national boundaries to their own advantage and to avoid or offset effective jurisdiction over their affairs by any of the individual nations in which they operate. The large "multinational" corporations have indeed become the repositories and the practitioners of much of the world's technology and therefore the possessors of much of its power. Some of these corporations have financial resources and staffs that are larger than the majority of the member states of the United Nations and greater than that of any international intergovernmental organization. A few of them have research and development budgets greater than the entire research and development expenditures of all developing countries combined. International action will undoubtedly be necessary to assure that the vast and growing power of these multinational corporations will be used to serve the needs and aspirations of the larger human community.

The evolution of new international machinery to deal with the complex problems of an increasingly interdependent technological civilization will not come about through the surrender of sovereignty by national governments but only by the wilful exercise of that sovereignty. And it will be only to the extent to which nations find themselves incapable of exercising their sovereignty effectively or advantageously on a unilateral basis that they will agree to exercise it collectively by agreement with other nations. As such agreements invariably impose constraints on the individual exercise of sovereignty, all nations enter into such agreements only reluctantly. It is seldom that nations enter into arrangements that restrict their ability to exercise their sovereignty until circumstances compel them to do so.

Two of the principal manifestations of the technological order in our social and political relationships are greater complexity and more universalization. This is already forcing substantial modification of traditional jurisdictional patterns within the nation-state system, exerting pressures for delegation of responsibilities downstream to political units closer to those most directly affected by decisions in matters of local concern – that is, local governments – at the same time as pressures are being generated for delegation of other responsibilities upstream to international organs. A good example is Great Britain, where the government is actively seeking membership in the European Common Market to which it will have to delegate important responsibilities, while at the same time it has set up a special commission to consider giving more autonomy to Scotland and Wales.

This does not necessarily mean that the role of national governments will be diminished, only that the total activities of governments are growing in magnitude and complexity to the point where they can no longer be carried out effectively by highly centralized mechanisms that concentrate all power at the national level. There will have to be a greater sharing of the burdens of governments by allowing responsibility to flow to the level on which it can be exercised most effectively.

But it seems clear that the nation-state will remain the principal source and dispenser of power within this system, and on the international level, if not internally, the organization charged with carrying out particular responsibilities will continue to be the servants and not the masters of nation-states. There would be such a degree of interdependence and interaction between international organizations and their counterparts within nations in this kind of world system that the incentives to resort to war as a means of settling disputes could be greatly diminished. In time this might bring a diminution of the sense of mutual threat and in turn provide a basis for real progress toward disarmament and a diversion of military expenditures to peaceful purposes.

This is one of the basic dangers in the present situation. The threats to humankind's existence from nuclear warfare can be avoided right up until the moment someone pushes the button. But the threats to humankind's survival that derive from our intervention in our natural environment are of a different nature. They require us to begin to act now to avoid dangers that will not materialize until the next generation or even beyond – but still within the lifetimes of our own children or grandchildren. Such dangers as contamination of the world's air and water supply to the point of affecting our genetic development and impairing the very qualities that make us human, changes in the world's climate that could destroy the heat balance on which human life depends, the large-scale destruction of plant and animal species: All of these will be beyond remedy by the time they are perceived as imminent threats. To deal with issues that involve cause-and-effect relationships so far removed from more immediate and pressing priorities will require a degree of enlightened political will on the part of the peoples and nations of the world.

Our recent experience in dealing with some specific issues also provides some hopeful examples of what can be done. The treaties that provided for cooperative scientific exploration of the Antarctic continent and its insulation from military activities and the treaty banning nuclear weapons from the sea beds and from outer space demonstrate that important international agreements can be reached both for collective positive measures and for the avoidance of mutual hazards. The interesting common denominator in all of these agreements is that they dealt with areas of concern in which the individual interests of nations had not yet developed to the point of significant conflict. I believe there is an important lesson for us in this that should encourage us to proceed as quickly as possible to seek agreements for further such protections.

The only practical hope is that humankind will respond to a common concern for its own survival, an acknowledgement of the essential interdependence of all peoples, and an awareness that cooperative action can enlarge the horizons and enrich the lives of all peoples. This is a tall order, indeed, but our history should not lead us to be overly pessimistic. After all, humans have shown their ability to transfer their loyalties and allegiances to ever larger units as they have ascended the hierarchy of collectivities from family to tribe to town to city to city-state and then to nation-state. We have not had to shed our allegiances to the other collectivities but simply to modify them and enlarge them, such that our system of allegiances and values can now be based on neither ideological conformity nor central world government. Rather it must involve a series of multidimensional relationships between a large number of organizational units – some of which will continue to be organized on the basis of territory and some of which will be organized on the basis of particular objectives, functions, and sectors – operating both within nations and internationally in fields of activity that cannot be carried out effectively within the confines of individual territories.

There are only two ways of creating the kind of network of organizational relationships that would enable an interdependent technological society to function effectively. One is the imposition of such a system by the force of the two superpowers acting in consort. This is scarcely possible and certainly not likely and in any event would not provide a durable basis for the maintenance of such a system. The only real and permanent alternative is the voluntary consent of the majority of nations supported by the collective will of their constituents.

This would not be possible in a world that continued to preserve the vast disparities between the wealthy minority, who live in the more industrialized nations, and the majority of the world's people, who live on the margins of poverty and despair in the developing countries. We must be prepared to accept a system of power and responsibility on a global scale that represents a more equitable balance than now exists between the distribution of people and their needs, on the one hand, and economic and military power, on the other. A better system of sharing the world's resources and opportunities is an indispensable prerequisite for workable world community.

This can only be brought about by those nations of the industrialized world that are the most wealthy, the most privileged, the most educated, and the most able to see the consequences of continuing on such a course. No group that has such a monopoly on wealth and power and privilege will relinquish it easily. But we are not talking about relinquishing it altogether, only sharing it more widely and using it more wisely. Surely if our sense of moral and ethical values does not lead us to this conclusion, an objective analysis of our own long-range self-interest should compel it.

Programs of international development in their present state represent but the first primitive steps toward the extension into an international relation of the principles of equity, justice, and mutual responsibility, which we have come to accept as a basis for our relationships within national societies. We must devise more sophisticated and objective methods for the transfer of resources to developing countries and for improving their ability to deal with the industrialized world on a more equal basis. The charity syndrome engendered by the donor-recipient relationship inherent in conventional aid programs is no more satisfactory or durable a basis for the relations between rich and poor nations than it was between rich and poor people within our national societies. Our experience in building our national societies shows clearly that the wealthy do not have to become poor in order for the poor to improve their lives. It is not a question of whether the rich can afford to share their wealth but whether they will be wise enough to appreciate in time how very much it is in their interest to do so.

The accelerated impact of the technological order has made it imperative that this generation make some choices that will probably determine the course of humankind's future on this planet. This requires that we give our urgent attention to the task of devising better methods of applying both knowledge and values to our processes of political and social decision making on a global basis. I am convinced that the United Nations Conference on the Human Environment must move us decisively toward this objective. For our hopes for the future of humankind must rest on our confidence that a greater understanding of the consequences of our actions will be accompanied by the will and the wisdom to make the right choices.

MAURICE STRONG is a senior advisor to the secretary general of the United Nations and a former senior advisor to the president of the World Bank. His numerous public and private sector positions have included chairman and CEO of Ontario Hydro; secretary general of the UN Conference on Environment and Development (the Earth Summit); under-secretary general of the United Nations; executive coordinator of the United Nations Office for Emergency Operations in Africa; and membership on the World Commission on Environment and Development. His volunteer activities have included positions with the International Union for the Conservation of Nature and Natural Resources; the World Council of Churches; and the Vatican Society for Development, Justice, and Peace.

Mr Strong is a Companion of the Order of Canada and a fellow of the Royal Society (UK), the Royal Society of Canada, and the Royal Architectural Society of Canada. He has received numerous awards and honours, including the Swedish Royal Order of the Polar Star, the Freedom Festival Award, and the first Pahlavi Environment Prize. He has been awarded honorary doctorates from over forty universities around the world.

II

Untitled

MORDECAI RICHLER, 1973

PART ONE

Recently I spoke at the University of Toronto. At the dinner preceding my talk, I sat next to a dean's wife, a most solicitous lady, who enquired whether I had a degree from the University of Toronto myself.

"Madam," I was obliged to reply, "I have no university degree whatsoever."

Affronted, she then demanded, "Then how on earth did you learn how to write? Did you attend night school?"

No, not quite.

In 1949 I was really determined to get into McGill, but my marks were so bad I didn't even bother to apply. The truth is, I just managed to scrape through Baron Byng High School, having put in too much time at the Mount Royal Billiards Academy and the System Theatre and not enough in the classroom.

After my high school examination results arrived in the mail, a bitter blow, my older brother sent me along to a psychologist friend of his to write a battery of aptitude tests. The psychologist's lab was on the McGill campus, and when I arrived he was putting rats, some of them methodically starved, others methodically blinded, through a maze. The overheated room was charged with squeaking and smelled of dung. Glad of company, the psychologist put on a little show for me. Two rats, one blind and starving, the other with a bleeding paw, were set down on the overturned lid of a garbage pail. We waited until the blind starved rat had sniffed out the wounded one, and then I sat down to write my tests. I was summoned to the psychologist's home the following evening.

"Have you ever thought of doing something else?" he asked.

"Like what?" I wanted to know.

"A job," he said.

No, I hadn't actually, and I did manage to get into Sir George Williams College as it then was. I survived for two years, experiencing, among other illuminations, a class on the modern novel. Come examination time, we were asked if *Sons and Lovers* (by H.G. Wells, D.H. Lawrence, or Ellery Queen) was a (thriller, psychological, or comic novel).

I should point out — hastily – that standards at Sir George Williams, now a recognized university, have improved immensely since 1949, but at the time it was a pathetic place. We were taught grammar (English 101) by superannuated high school teachers and poetry by good-natured but inadequate ladies who flushed at the mention of Keats. The university was, and still is, run by the YMCA, and in those days taking time out to pee in any toilet higher than the second floor was to risk your heterosexual integrity.

However, it was at Sir George Williams that I discovered that my intelligence tests were no fluke. They couldn't, as I had hoped, be laid down to unfavourable conditions. For once established at the college, I was sufficiently intrepid to submit to another battery of tests, these designed to determine what, if any, natural aptitudes I possessed.

The one question I still remember, because it was so cunningly composed, asked, if given a choice, would I rather have dinner with:

- a four-star general
- a Hollywood starlet, or
- a Nobel prize-winning writer.

No fool, I could see what they were getting at, but I had to be honest; appetite always before ambition.

Bent glumly over the results of my test, the guidance counsellor asked me, "What exactly do you want to do?"

"I want to be a writer," I said, and in order to fill that office with integrity, it seemed to me I had to put picayune Canada, the stifling Montreal ghetto, and all these things stood for behind me. Ironically, I suppose, I was to carry picayune Canada, and the stifling Montreal ghetto, with me everywhere: through the consuming years in France, Spain, Italy, Germany, and, finally, England. But that's another story and one that I've already written.

My good friend Robert Fulford, the editor of *Saturday Night*, once said that the trouble with our generation of Canadians, a cultural-internationalist of the fifties, was our conviction that the only thing for the talented to do was to "graduate from Canada." I don't agree. I'm not denying the charge, far from it, but I don't think we were wrong.

Let me put the case for my generation this way:

Elsewhere – that was the operative word, the built-in insult. Canadians of my generation, sprung to adolescence during World War Two, were conditioned to believe the world happened elsewhere. You apprenticed for it in Canada on the farm with a view, then you packed your bags and lit out for the golden cities: New York, London, Paris. Home was a good neighbourhood, but suburban, even bush, unless you happen to be a hockey player. Of all our boyhood heroes, from Joe DiMaggio to Humphrey Bogart, only hockey players were Canadian and undoubtedly the best. While we did have other indigenous heroes, they were badly flawed by being pint-sized versions of an altogether larger British or American presence. They were world-famous – in Canada. Put plainly, any candidate for excellence was bound to be suspect unless he proved himself under alien skies. The Canadian kid who wanted to be prime minister wasn't thinking big, he was setting a limit to his ambitions rather early.

In the late forties, I need hardly point out we were embarrassed to be Canadians, and charged with it we always had a self-deprecating joke ready.

At Sir George Williams, when we began to read the *New Republic* and the *New Statesman*, and one or perhaps two of us dared to venture out loud in a tavern, "I'm going to be a writer," the immediate and crushing rejoinder was, "What? You're going to be a *Canadian* writer?"

Sir George, in a sense ahead of its day, actually had a course on Canadian writing. Yes, when today's young militants were still in their swaddling clothes, devouring American-made baby foods (colonized in the crib, as it were), I was already collecting evidence, a student of Canadian Lit in the forties. We did not, I must admit, have a text. In fact, it was our pioneering venture to develop a Canadiana bibliography. We were supposed to scan the libraries for Canadiana, any Canadiana, listing the books' dimensions, number of pages, and whether or not there were illustrations. I *do* hope this bibliography is not still in use anywhere. For, at the time, we found it easier and much more fun to invent titles and authors rather than hunt them down.

At the time, I first became aware of the conflict between my Jewish heritage and Canadian upbringing, the tensions out of which I was to forge my novels.

I was to be reminded of this on my first trip out West, many years later, when I came across Murray Donnelly's biography, *Dafoe of the Free Press*.

When Dafoe was only a child, in 1865, Donnelly writes, his parents, beguiled by colonization literature, went to settle on an Ontario farm:

The pamphlets they carried with them were full of enthusiasm and glowing descriptions of the new land between the Ottawa River and Georgian Bay, and predicted that the area would eventually have a population of eight million. Canada, Canada, forever tomorrow country ... They knew little of the true nature of the land their Protestant god had created in the highlands of Ontario. They did not know, although the evidence mounted as they travelled, that the seemingly fertile soil was strewn with stones and was actually little more than a shallow sprinkling of earth on the solid rock of the pre-Cambrian shield. They did note, as they struggled up the Hastings Road, that one in three homesteads had already been abandoned, but concluded that this was due to a lack of stamina on the part of the owner or to a false desire for the ease and sensual delight of the city.

Now, endure, endure, says the Canadian experience, but what I learned on my grandmother's knee was "enjoy, enjoy: life is short, the grave without light."

But to return to the forties.

After classes, we used to divert ourselves playing the Canadian Identity Game, trying to trap the elusive nuance that made us different from the Americans. A friend came closest. If, he ventured, it had been a Canadian marine who had broadcast the last ringingly defiant message from Wake Island in the darkest days of World War Two, he would not have dared, "Send us more Japs," but instead, "No offence intended to any ethnic group, but could you allow us more Japanese, please?"

In those days there were several Canadian "little magazines," but we would have considered it a stigma to have our stories published in any one of them. We also, on scrutinizing the fiction published in *Canadian Forum*, took it for granted that it had already been turned down by *Harpers* and the *Atlantic Monthly*. And the most shattering criticism you could make of another man's poetry was to say, "Ryerson is publishing it in Toronto."

London and New York were the places we looked to for all our excitement. We had never had, in the literary history of our own country, a magazine that young intellectuals might have responded to, like *Partisan Review, Horizon, Story,* or *Penguin New Writing*. Perhaps what really bound us together in those days was a shared sense of how comic our country was. We appeared to be surrounded by the ridiculous: a political party called Progressive Conservative, the cult of Barbara Ann Scott, hunt balls in Montreal, Beverley Baxter's schmaltzy "London Letters" in *Maclean's*, the Native Sons of Canada, the Imperial Order of the Daughters of the British Empire, and so forth. Though, to be fair, we had yet to be saddled with the Canadian-born governor general: in the absence of real linen, our own drip-dry monarchy symbol.

Now no country is without its buffoons, inanities, and outlandish conventions, but what seemed to make ours different was that only the most private and isolated voices were raised in protest. Here a professor, there a poet, and, between, thousands of miles of wheat and indifference. So when we discovered, in the early forties, the CBC *Stage* series, those plays of Lister Sinclair and Len Peterson that were produced by Andrew Allen, with John Drainie usually playing the lead, we used to gather gratefully round the radio on Sunday nights. Andrew Allen was a name we respected. His writers shared our hopes; their concept of humbug was mine. We would have been honoured to work for Allen, and many, scattered long since, got their start doing precisely that.

The CBC *Stage* series was the one part of our formative intellectual experience that was distinctly Canadian, not shared with the other Americans, and for that I shall always be grateful. But, on reflection, if the adaptations from, say, Kafka, Chekhov, and Ibsen were a pleasure to listen to, the standard of production high, it must be said that original plays were not as good as we thought they were. The playwrights of that golden age of Canadian radio were liberal intellectuals, sociologists who wrote, rather than the makers of flesh-and-blood art. All the same, in a land where there were no more than thirty bookshops from coast to coast, these productions were significant.

Significant but hardly sufficient to detain us.

So, putting Canada behind me in 1951, I sailed for Europe without regrets. If I were to be published at all, it was not going to be by Ryerson or anybody else in Toronto. Like many of my intellectual contemporaries, I was mistakenly filled with scorn for *all* things Canadian. If we were indeed hemmed in by the boring, the inane, and the absurd, we foolishly blamed it all on Canada, failing to grasp that we would suffer from a surfeit of the boring, the inane, and the absurd wherever we wandered.

This is one of the themes I tried to cope with in *St. Urbain's Horseman,* and, if you'll pardon me because it's not something I like to do, I'll lean briefly on the novel here:

Jake, Luke, and others of their generation were reared to believe in the cultural thinness of their own blood. Anemia was their heritage. As certain homosexuals pandered to others by telling the most vicious anti-queer jokes, so Jake, so Luke, shielded themselves from ridicule by anticipating with derisive tales of their own. Their own certitude was that all indigenous cultural standards they'd been raised on were a shared joke. No national reputation could be bandied abroad without apology.

Adrift in a cosmopolitan sea of conflicting mythologies, only they had none. Moving among discontented Commonwealth types in London, they were inclined to envy them their real grievances. South Africans and Rhodesians, bona fide refugees from tyranny, would come to raise a humanitarian banner in exile; Australians, who can allude to forbears transported in convict ships; and West Indians, armed with the most obscene outrage of all, the memory of their grandfathers sold in marketplaces. What they failed to grasp was the ironic truth in Sir Wilfrid Laurier's boast that the twentieth century would belong to Canada. For amid so many exiles from nineteenth-century tyranny, heirs to injustices that could actually be set right politically, thereby lending themselves to constructive angers, only the Canadians, surprisingly, were true children of their times. Only they had packed their bags and left home to escape the hell of boredom. And find it everywhere.

Nevertheless, what many expatriates felt on return visits to Canada was that those in the arts who had stayed behind were faint-hearted, and middle-aged before their time, settling for being big fish in a small pond.

Well, yes, possibly, but not quite.

Naturally, there are many who still appear to be whales because they discreetly limited their splashing for the shallow standards of the Canadian pond, but as a Canadian who lived in London for almost two decades, I must admit that while many expatriates are well known, nobody has made themselves artistically indispensable there. We have not surfaced with a Conrad or a Joyce. And, meanwhile, at home, we always had Northrop Frye, Morley Callaghan, and Robertson Davies, among writers, and such dedicated advocates as Jack McClelland, John Grey of Macmillans, and Robert Weaver of the CBC.

But I must insist that others in the arts who stayed at home did so out of necessity, not without self-apology, promising themselves that next year, or the year after, they would try London or New York, testing their talents against the larger world. Alas, next year, or the year after never came, and a decade later many felt themselves compromised, self-condemned, a big bat in the minors forevermore, until, with hindsight, they redeemed themselves in their own eyes by becoming the most impassioned of nationalists, declaring that for all seasons there is nothing like home, which, I fear, was no more than self-justification.

And there were others, luxuriating in provincial celebrity, who were, I think, irresponsible. Take, for instance, that engaging poet, famous in Canada, and largely unknown abroad, who has been playing the campus circuit for years telling the students that the best damn poetry in the world is being written here.

Nonsense.

The rest of the world does not suffer from a tin ear, and if the best damn poetry was indeed being written here, they would have heard, and, furthermore, they would have clapped hands.

Something else.

If, in Paris, I wished to discover many neophyte writers with all the faults of genius – that is to say, they screwed and drank prodigiously, never paid the rent, and happily belted their wives about the room, but, when you came down to it, still couldn't write worth a damn. So, on many a return trip home, I found artists who were long, marvellously long on integrity, but conspicuously short of talent. Say, the ebullient National Film Board or CBC drama director who assured me he would never, no matter what, sell out, as it were, to Hollywood, New York, or London. Or the journalist, equally charged with patriotic fervour, who would not, come hell or high water, write for *Life*, *Playboy*, or *Esquire*.

It was rather as if the late Sam Bronfman said he would not be canonized no matter how much the Pope pleaded. Or if Judy LaMarsh declared, whatever her financial difficulties, she would never become a courtesan. Some sacrifices, however ardently proffered, are simply not called for.

For many nationalism was self-interest, not so much a badge of honour as a shield for mediocrity.

This was, and still is, a small pond – it's yours, it's mine; it's home – but it's certainly not the world.

Or is it?

Since the fifties, as we all know, there have been changes in the Canadian cultural climate, enormous changes, some of them hopeful, others mind-boggling. Which is to say, we now boast, among other things, a Committee for an Independent Canada.

Toronto, September 1970. Only three hours after I landed in the city, still woozy from a transatlantic flight, I found myself in the thin frontline of the newly joined battle for Canada's soul, at a press conference, in the Royal York Hotel, knocking back drinks with other reporters. One of them, long on appetite, short on a sense of occasion, whispered to me, "After this, the Niagara Society is having a wine-tasting upstairs."

I had come to hear the spiritual great-grandsons of the Fathers of Confederation; a witness to the formation of the Committee for an Independent Canada. "We believe," they declared, "that Canadians today share a surging mood of self-awareness ... A society has evolved, unique in its quality of life – a kind of civilized resistance to the similarly blessed but much more violent land to the south of us."

Immediately this statement was made, a sagacious reporter bobbed out of his chair. "What," he asked, "does Washington think of your plans?"

Under the klieg lights, TV cameras whirring, sat co-chairman Jack McClelland, the country's leading publisher, and Claude Ryan, the editor of *Le Devoir*. After more than a hundred years, Canada's two founding races, the English and the French, had got off the fence and finally decided they liked the country well enough to stay, and now, understandably enough, they wanted the freehold back. A second chance for indigenous, rather than foreign, capitalists to exploit the rest of us.

I fail to see how the populace can be roused to do anything about it. In my demonstrating days, revolutionaries argued for a fairer distribution of the wealth, not the joys of being exploited by homebred capitalists over one who was a foreigner. An issue that I, being old-fashioned, still consider a matter of indifference to the working person. After all, if I were repairing telephone lines for the telephone company, it would not exercise me whether the bell tolled for Canadian or American shareholders but, rather, which group of coupon-clippers was willing to offer a better deal to the workers.

Even so, I do agree that, in 1970, there was a new sense of self-awareness in Canada and that the spirit of nationalism was rampaging over the land. Its murky underside, anti-Americanism, was sometimes justified but more often embarrassingly coarse, as when an incensed professor protested against Pierre Elliott Trudeau's right to escort Barbra Streisand to the Manitoba Centennial party at the National Arts Centre. "Since it is a Canadian birthday," he wrote to the *Citizen*, "one might have at least expected him to appear with a Canadian. But Pierre-baby is a realist. He knows where it's at ... when you're prime minister of a colony, you appear with one of the princesses of the empire. It's called pragmatism, baby."

Which philosophy, admittedly yet another dirty foreign influence, possibly explained why Trudeau, venturing north later in the year in the hope of establishing our jurisdiction over the Arctic, schlepped Elizabeth II with him, not Barbra. Looked at another way, you can sweet-talk a nice Jewish princess into a weekend in Ottawa, but you can't lead her into the black-fly country. With the Queen, however, it's duty above all.

The new nationalism, to its credit, ensured a welcome for thousands of American draft dodgers, but other American émigrés were beginning to feel the heat, as witness the case of Warren Tallman. In 1970 our militant academics came up with a round-robin letter objecting to Tallman's appointment to the governor general's literary awards committee. It was the crime of the affable professor, an astute critic of Canadian literature, that in spite of ten years' residence in British Columbia, he had retained his American citizenship, just as I held onto my Canadian passport for twenty years in England. Without incident, mind you. Tallman was also vulnerable to the dastardly charge of "cultural imperialism," the evidence offered being that he wrote of Canadian fiction, *our thing*, as it were, as if it were part of "the true North American tone," which I should have thought self-evident.

But to return to the Committee for an Independent Canada.

It was my good fortune to hear from them directly shortly after my return to Montreal with my family in July 1972. Their letter, which actually originated with the committee's cultural think tank, began, "Dear Author, You have been chosen, along with seventy-nine other major contemporary Canadian authors, to present your views ..."

Seemingly, if twenty years ago the flower of Canadian letters, like the British Liberal Party, could fit snugly into a taxi, now, on my return to Canada, a veritable charabanc was called for.

This is not to say that nationalist hyperbole has caught me by surprise. In my long absence abroad, I was often pulled home, back to Canada, twice for a year's duration and, more often than I can count, for stays of three weeks or more.

In 1960, home for a year, I accompanied my pregnant wife to the doctor's office.

"What do you do?" the nurse asked me, her expression severe.

"I'm a novelist."

"With what firm?" she asked. There was, at the time, a touching confusion about novel writing amongst some Canadian publishers as well. When I met Marsh Jeanneret, director of the University of Toronto Press, he told me with a certain *hauteur* that his was a cultural press.

"What exactly do you mean by that?" I asked.

"We don't publish cookbooks or novels," he replied.

I laughed, mistakenly, alas, for Jeanneret, who was about to publish the *pensées* of Yousuf Karsh, was not putting me down. The director of the University of Toronto Press was in earnest.

Toronto, Toronto.

In 1963 it seemed all but impossible to get an honest drink served in a well-lit place. Coming in out of the afternoon sun, you stumbled through bars that were in almost total darkness to be served by girls in long black net stockings. In something called the Bombay Bicycle Room, for example, the waitresses wore saris and offered young men in horn-rimmed glasses, their breast pockets brimming with ballpoint pens, the loan of a pith helmet to go with their gin. Then there was the Ports of Call. Once a sleazy hotel where sour men met for a beer, this place had been rebuilt as a sexy but safe fantasyland, Genet made palatable for Orangemen. Outside the Ports of Call there squatted a wooden South Seas idol, whose stomach flap lifted to reveal a telephone. Inside, among other wonders, there was the Bali Hai, complete with a ship's bridge, waterfall, and Rotarians; a Gay Nineties room; and a Last Chance Saloon, where the sheriff showed the B'nai Brith bad men to their tables, and the inevitable girl in tights served the drinks. But just to show you that British cultural influence was still a living force, there *was* a pub, the Dickens Room. According to the original Ports of Call publicity release, the Dickens Room "was furnished in the style of his period – Tudor." And, damn it, so it was.

But, much more significant, intellectuals in Toronto seemed, at the time, marvellously well read and outgoing, not yet defensive or confined by nationalist blinkers. While in New York there was an arrogant and parochial tendency to put down anything beyond its environs as "off-Broadway" and in England it was modish in some circles in those years to dismiss all things American as characterized by more energy than art, I found Torontonians charged with a bracing curiosity about the new French novel and English, American, and Italian letters.

On yet another trip to Toronto, I tangled with one of the new nationalist zealots, a novelist-cum-publisher. He would not, he told me heatedly, read any American novels because they were all contaminating.

"Not even Saul Bellow?" I asked.

Not even Bellow.

Bellow, he argued, had a publisher that was owned by a multinational corporation – RCA, I think it was – and this corporation also manufactured electronic equipment that was being used in Vietnam; ergo, old Saul was no better than any other imperialist fascist dog.

But I could have replied, equally perversely, that his publishing firm, albeit radical, was financed by Maclean-Hunter. *Maclean's* welcomed advertisements from Kotex; ergo, he was riding to revolution on a menstrual floodtide of exploited Canadian women and, therefore, was just another male chauvinist pig.

Even in my absence, I subscribed to any number of Canadian newspapers and magazines and was dismayed, if not exactly astonished, to discover that in the pages of *Canadian Forum*, nationalism was also running riot. In a review of Robertson Davies' *Fifth Business*, the author is adjudged a rotter because, in his novel, he is nasty to Canadian ladies.

More recently, since my return to Montreal in July 1972, in fact, a new literary periodical, *Northern Journey*, has come my way, and in a fighting editorial, Fraser Sutherland writes:

We're no longer a colony, Great Britain's outer reef. No one writes rhyming couplets about bull moose anymore. We have built a small, rather fragile island that needs the constant tide of foreign influence to wash away the refuse. Yet the local element, our most vulnerable resource, must be preserved. If we don't build dykes to ward off the tidal wave of second-rate American influence, we will be swamped. We'll lose our culture and in doing so, ourselves. We've come too far and, by God, it's not going to happen. If that's insularism, then here's to Prince Edward Island; if that's parochialism, then here's to Grey Nuns.

Now that's fine rousing stuff until you turn to the first selection in *Northern Journey,* our dyke to ward off the tidal wave of second-rate American influence. It's the opening chapter from a new novel, *Fetish Girl,* by Sylvia Bayer.

Ursula, seated by the poolside of an out-of-the-way motel, spies a marvellous man: "Gazing, Ursula felt the animal moisture already gathering in her mouth before her eyes dropped to his bathing trunks. Zowie! Her heart seemed to turn over as she saw they were of gleaming black latex. God, perhaps he was a rubber fan too!"

Ursula, after recalling her last affair with "the handsome lout for whom she had fallen at first sight ... simply because he was wearing a calf-length belted trench coat of heavy lustrous black latex, with narrow riding boots to match," decides she must have the stranger by the poolside.

But, alas for Ursula, there's a surprise in store, a newcomer:

The newcomer was kneeling before the man, fondling his hand ... A fetish pair! No doubt of it now. Oh, woe is me.

She looked again at the newcomer's contours beneath the tight rubber leotard, suddenly seeing their male conformation – the narrow hips, the swelling torso.

Oh my God! she thought, it's a boy! He's gay! Dammit to hell, my lovely fetish man is gay!

In the short note preceding the excerpt from *Fetish Girl*, Miss Bayer writes: "I am delighted to see this opening chapter of my eighth published novel appear in a serious literary magazine in my native land, and only hope that this example of frankly commercial genre won't be too out of place here. After all, aphrodisiac writing is genuine 'pop' art, isn't it? And this has the distinction of being the first book ever written for rubber fetishists."

Possibly, just possibly, another *Canadian* first, and in his long polemical editorial, Fraser Sutherland quotes, with disapproval, a remark of Morley Callaghan's, a remark I, on the other hand, commend to all of you. "Forget all about the words 'identity' and 'culture,'" Callaghan said, "just never mention them. Seek only excellence and in good time people all over the world will ask about Canadians."

Alas, Canadian writers are no longer so engagingly sane. This is clearly maple-leaf power time. Today's embittered young intellectuals, especially the nationalist hardhats of English-speaking Canada, are seething with *machismo*; and yet there is hardly a new writer in Quebec who is not an impassioned separatist. And yet – ours was to be a tranquil land, serene beyond compare. Not so much a melting pot on the boil as a vertical mosaic, the WASPs of the pinnacle, the adorable, saucy French Canadians, toting the bales.

Canada's most distinguished literary critic, Northrop Frye, attempting to pin-point what is peculiar to the Canadian psyche, has alluded to a painting inspired by the prophesy of Isaiah, "The Peaceable Kingdom," which illustrates the treaty between Indians and Quakers and a group of lions, bears, oxen, and other animals. Frye writes that the Canadian tradition as revealed in literature might well be called a quest for the peaceable kingdom.

Yes, possibly, but following the yellow brick road, we have recently run afoul of a threatening landslide and dangerous overhanging rocks: Quebec separatism and, in English-speaking Canada, militant nationalism. There is much in the new mood that is encouraging, but it is, I think, badly tainted by bravado and an embarrassing penchant for overselling cultural geese, proffering them as swans. If, in my day, respectability for a Canadian writer could only be gained by publication abroad, today, on the new scale, to be published *only* in Canada is no longer a stigma, a measure of parochial content, but instead a badge of patriotic purity.

When I started out, Morley Callaghan meant more to us than any other Canadian writer; he had been to Paris with Hemingway and Fitzgerald and published as an equal. To us, merely apprenticing at the time, it meant that it was possible to be Canadian *and* first-rate. It settled, in our minds, that if you wrote well enough about Toronto or Montreal, the larger world outside *would* pay attention. Today, I fear, if a younger Callaghan were to emerge, say, out of Regina or Halifax, and accomplish as much, he would be denounced as a turncoat, fraternizing with American imperialist dogs. There is less modesty in today's literary community, more truculence. Out of rejection, there has sprung self-pity and a certain shallow defiance. The present mood, I think, can best be illustrated by a little classic of a Jewish story, and forgive me if it is familiar to you.

It is the story of a determined Jewish boy who was set on becoming a radio announcer. To this end, he enrolled in the best schools, studying day and night for years. On graduation, however, he was turned down by CBS, NBC, and all the other American networks. He returned home, totally crushed.

"Why wouldn't any of them hire you?" his mother asked.

"B-b-b-because," he said, "th-th-they're all anti-Semites."

Similarly, too many Canadian novelists, turned down abroad, do not question their own talent. Instead, they take this as proof of the prejudice against all things Canadian.

Nonsense.

The trouble is not with the world outside, the problem is that there are far too many novels and collections of poetry being published here that can be of interest only to the writer, his family, and friends. Their outstanding merit is that they are homemade. Or, put another way, if Morley Callaghan, *pace* Edmund Wilson, was, for a period, unfairly neglected – or forgotten – abroad, other indigenous writers have been very, very fairly neglected indeed. Barely good enough for domestic use, they are frankly not for export. The sour, and to some Canadians unacceptable, truth is that while there is arguably a measure of indifference, there is certainly no international cabal against our novels and poetry, as witness the general response to Robertson Davies, Richard Wright, Leonard Cohen, Margaret Atwood, and, most recently, Alice Munro.

I am, for present purposes, mainly concerned with cultural nationalism and its coarsening, self-inflating effect on writers, filmmakers, publishers, and the academy. But, to begin with, it is necessary to take a brief look at primary sources.

Obviously, one form of parochialism has spawned another. Undoubtedly, the present bellicose mood in English-speaking Canada was prompted by the turbulence in Quebec. For years, smugness was all. The short, uninspired Scots Presbyterian answer to the French Canadian case, a reply no friendly suburban bank manager could improve on, was that should the provinces secede, Quebec's standard of living would tumble and, oh, yes, oh dear, the St Lawrence Seaway would be difficult to run. It was rather as if an impotent husband, being shown the bedroom door by his wife, a woman of tiresome appetite, were to remind her of the equities they hold in common and plead they remain together for the children's sake.

It wouldn't wash.

The separatists, and many French Canadians who weren't, insisted that they were a true nation, and the rest of us – quasi-Americans. And so, belatedly, English-speaking Canada was driven to scrutinize its own soul, the upshot being self-discovery, sometimes rancid self-discovery, and a sharp turning against the other America.

Suddenly, there was a sea change. If, as French Canada scornfully charged, we were in fact spiritually puny, the fault then was most happily not in ourselves but in the stars and stripes. America, America. Washington, ever our rapacious landlord; Wall Street, the usurious shop where we pawned our ore and our oil. For years and years, of all the client states in the school of American economic dominance, we were not so much the rank-one boy as teacher's pet; no nose picker or truant, like Fidel, or irretrievable delinquent, like Ché, but the freckled fink who volunteers to wipe the blackboards clean and never omits to practise the Ten Rules of Hygiene as set down by the junior Red Cross. So we never had to stay in after school to endure a Santo Domingo. Or be punished with a Bay of Pigs. Instead, we were blessed with branch plants by General Motors, Ford, and the rest. Flattered, we did not come to school merely with apples. Instead, we laid everything on the table: if you need oil, come and get it; iron ore you want? Take. Pulp and paper? Enjoy. Natural gas? Uranium? Nickel? Help yourself.

Our problem, unique in the Western world, perhaps, was not an indigenous buccaneering capitalist class, indifferent to those whom they exploited, yet bold and imaginative. Nation builders. Our problem was the Scots, the most inept and cautious capitalists in the West. Not builders, but sellers.

If the pre-World War One American boy, at the age of sixteen, was dreaming of how to conquer and market the rest of the world, his Canadian equivalent, at the same tender age, was already looking for a position with an unrivalled pension scheme. As a result, the United States now owns much more than 50 per cent of our basic industries.

If we are, with a tip of a hat to Walter Gordon, more acutely aware of our national dilemma now than we were ten years ago, it is also true that the problem is fundamentally unchanged. Namely, is it possible to operate a cautious, small, corner grocery of a country on the same continent as one of the most voracious supermarket nations? Is the corner grocery worth defending? Is there anything on the shelves but wheat, copper, ore, and yearning? Is there a tradition to cherish and pass on, something more than a reputation for honest trading?

I believe there is a tradition evolving at last and that it is worth defending. But hysteria is no shield, chauvinism an unacceptable armour. Canada, Canada, count your blessings.

Because we are Canadian citizens, we have never had to acquiesce to a Suez conspiracy, on the one hand, or to the obscene war in Vietnam, on the other. Somebody else's government bears the guilt-load for the suppression of freedom in Czechoslovakia. Rhodesia's not our shame. We are the progeny of a thinly populated country, basically decent, with no compromising say in the world's calumnies. This I should think is a moral pleasure that far outweighs our artistic shortcomings. And the same, if you like, could also be said of Sweden, Norway, and Denmark, with one crucial difference. They are culturally sheltered by language; we, English-speaking Canadians, are not. Neither are we quite so independent.

We are, in fact, in a humiliating position of having shaken our British swaddling clothes in the thirties not to risk the rocky road to true independence, but only to end up sucking our thumb in Uncle Sam's comfy lap, now to complain that the goodies bestowed (and eagerly consumed) have given us a stomach ache, and we are willing to regurgitate if only we can have some of Canada back. Say, half.

We have given the US not only our iron and oil, whiskey during Prohibition, eight-year-old Saul Bellow from Lachine, Quebec, Deanna Durbin, Bobby Orr, pitcher Ferguson Jenkins, Walter Pidgeon, Kenneth Galbraith, the Royal Canadian Air Force exercise book, Jack Kent Cooke, and the musical score for *Hair*, but, above all, *Superman*. He was drawn by Toronto-born cartoonist Joe Schuster, which makes Superman's assumed identity, a bland Clark Kent, not merely understandable but artistically inevitable. Today, however, Canada, traditionally seen as mild Clark Kent, has done a quick change in the political telephone booth. We emerged from World War Two into a fleshpot of prosperity, but the big payday was bought by mortgaging the land to America, and today's politically conscious young Canadians are indignant to be left with a debt. Indignant and unforgiving.

And so, to mollify French Canada, appease the young, *and* pardon ourselves – in the exigent and, I believe, admirable hope of keeping Canada one – new answers, some grandiose, other truculent, have been offered. "I hold that Canada," Bruce Hutchinson wrote in *Maclean's*, "admitting all its troubles and blunders, is the luckiest nation on earth, with the richest estate and the fairest prospects."

Richest estate. Now look here, this is home, but it is still a cold country. The winters are endless. Hugh MacLennan, who yields to nobody in concern for the country, has already put the icier reality to us. "Canada's geographical vastness is deceptive," he wrote. "At the moment little more than 4 per cent of the whole country is under cultivation, and it has been estimated that only 7 per cent ever will be."

Even so, we now boast a fistful of militant new publishing houses and magazines. A Canadian Film Development Corporation. A National Arts Centre. And, in the universities, the proliferation of Canadian literature courses and a burgeoning rebellion against the hiring of American professors.

I will confine my observations here to the Film Development Corporation. Like the admirable Canada Council, it is there to create favourable conditions and to provide financing, no more. It can be only as good, or as bad, as the talent to hand, and so if it has not exactly distinguished itself so far, it must be allowed that these are still early, formative days. The best, hopefully, is yet to come – and, in any event, anything would be an improvement on the project's launching statement by former state secretary Maurice Lamontaigne. "The feature films that Canadians see," the minister said, "come almost exclusively from abroad. This," he added, "is not good for the Canadian identity or our cultural life."

Well, no. It *is* good for our cultural life to see the best films wherever they come from, and whether or not we succeed – as I hope – in establishing an industry of our own, most of the best films, like most of the best books, will continue to come almost exclusively from abroad.

This is not a pejorative statement but a recognition of facts. Canada is small, the world is big, and no nationalist can alter that. *And* what did the baffling Mr Lamontaigne mean by "not good for the Canadian identity"? In my time, I've gone to the movies to neck or avoid work or to be entertained or moved, but I've never gone to look for my Canadian identity. Come to think of it, where *do* you look for it? Under the seat? On the screen? In the gents? These days if you start flitting from seat to seat, there's bound to be trouble. Some nervy lady is sure to send for the usher.

Which is not to say I'm against the Canadian film industry or, for that matter, a Canadian identity, but rather that I'm for more realism, less hyperbole.

Digging into my own past experience, I would divide Canadian filmmakers into two rough groups: Mr Clean (the National Film Board, CBC-TV) and the Little Greasers or independent producers. The indies, as *Variety* calls them, largely subdivide into three classes:

1   There is the Toronto-based production company that has made indecently large profits out of TV commercials or has perhaps produced a puerile but money-spinning series about Indians or Mounties and has now set its sights higher, so to speak. They want to make skin flicks, but with Canadian content – that is to say, featuring our very own pubic hairs.

2   Then there is the indie who has made a clean break with his past in a soul-destroying advertising agency, rented an office, and registered a company: Award Films or Now People Productions. He has let his hair grow some, taken an option on a paperback or two, or, still better, he has ventured into a public library and discovered a classic (a book in the public domain) that can be updated and reset in Montreal or on the Prairies. Say, *Crime and Punishment*, the student now a separatist militant, the inspector a Westmount WASP.

3   The third and most pernicious type of indie, comprised of a partnership of Hollywood and British film hangers-on, losers, has discovered that there is nothing but TV hackwork available in Hollywood or London but that innocent Canada might just possibly be dazzled by a bunch with film experience – any film experience. Michael Spencer and Gratien Gelinas, who head the corporation, both honest men, charged with goodwill, are to be pitied: They tread among thieves in the jungle.

And so far, *Goin' Down the Road* aside, it must be said that our English-language productions have lacked not only distinction, but usually distribution as well. And the French ventures, sometimes highly profitable, have largely been skin flicks. I've only managed to catch one of them, *Love is a Four-Letter Word*, and there are two ways of looking at it. The film is odious. Everybody connected with it should hang his head in shame. Or, on the other hand, it is offered as proof, as if it were needed, that our indigenous tits, nicely bilingual, are as lovely as any made in Denmark. Furthermore, if *Love* and other salacious films were shown to prospective immigrants at Canada House in London, instead of the usual worthy Film Board documentary, we would undoubtedly recruit more settlers to this country.

All the same, the Film Development Corporation is not only a highly promising venture, but one long overdue.

For the rest, however, I still think there is a tendency for the nationalists in this country to evade the real issues and to protest too much, even as Quebec has overstated its own good case. Which is to say the Québecois is no more a "white nigger" than all our cultural inadequacies can be blamed on Americans, most of whom are blithely unaware of Canada's existence, let alone that it is presently ridden with problems other than the rising costs of waterfront land in the Maritimes.

The self-regarding theory of the Québecois as the "white nigger," most recently expounded by Pierre Vallières in his *Nègres Blancs d'Amérique,* originated, as you probably know, some years back with Andre Laurandeau when he was editor of *Le Devoir.* M. Laurandeau advanced the idea of the *"Roi Negre"* – that is to say, that the real rulers of Quebec (the English) used the French Canadian chieftain (Maurice Duplessis) to govern the province, just as colonial powers used African puppets to keep their tribes quiescent.

The analogy, albeit a clever one, strikes me as shaky on several counts. While I agree that the role of the WASPs in Montreal during the Duplessis era was, to say the least, disgraceful, the French Canadians, unlike the southern black, had the vote. They were not held back from the polls. So if I was raised in a notoriously backward and corrupt province, it was, however artfully you sliced it, an overwhelmingly French Canadian electoral majority that boosted the government into office and kept it there and kept it there. The affluent English-speaking community may have been more than pleased about it – there's no doubt they behaved arrogantly, even dishonestly – but the shame, such as it is, is largely French Canadian, and raising the injustice-collecting ante, blaming English-speaking Canada every time it rains on Sunday, does not enhance Quebec's case.

Neither does it behoove English-speaking Canadians, who wantonly shed most of our natural resources years ago, tripping over themselves to strip down for American investors, to sob, long after the affair is over, that they were in fact raped. Which is not to say that our branch-plant economy is not in need of adjustment. "This state of affairs," Walter Gordon has said, "threatens our existence as a nation."

I happen to agree, but economic sense, in this case, makes cultural nonsense. I'm all for buying back some of Canada, as Mr Gordon proposes, so long as he, and the committee, out seeking the wherewithal, do not oversell the intellectual portfolio to us in the process, writing letters to me and seventy-nine other major Canadian writers.

Providing we are willing to pay the price, which I strongly doubt, we can legislate against foreign ownership, nationalizing wherever necessary, but

Canada cannot quite so easily pass a bill declaring indigenous pap to be soul food, pronouncing second-rate novelists (a poor thing, but our own) to be as necessary as Melville, Faulkner, or Fitzgerald. "There is no Canadian writer," Northrop Frye reminds us in *The Literary History of Canada*, "of whom we can say as we can say of the world's major writers, that their readers grew up inside their work without ever being aware of a circumference."

Classics aren't made by decree. Or by ruling the available set books and feeding them to students from coast to coast. Proliferating Canadian literature courses notwithstanding, the sad truth is that we have still produced almost no art of any but domestic significance.

But I would like to add – no, emphasize – that there is more good and honest writing being done in Canada today than there was twenty years ago. Or, put another way, there is certainly no need to be ashamed for the neighbours. If twenty years ago, Canadian writers suffered from neglect, what we must now guard against is overpraise, the largest insult. The dirty double standard. One test for Canadian writers, another, more exacting litmus applied to foreigners. I don't know, I can't be sure, but I hope I speak for everybody else in the small Canadian literary house when I say either we are talented enough to pass muster or we are not. We do not stand in need of a nationalist's dog licence. We don't want to be read as village gossip because you recognize the street names in our novels or can nod over the weather conditions. We wish to be read because we have something fresh to say about the human condition – or not read at all.

PART TWO

In a more decent age, long past, if Canadian writers ran into each other at all it was in bars, the CBC canteen in Toronto, or at the rare publishers' cocktail party. Nowadays, we literally collide at Prairie airports and in hotel elevators in the Maritimes. This one returning from a boffo night in Fredericton, where he has pronounced on the Canadian arts, claiming it's charged with vitality, his own hairy chest being a case in point; and that one bound for a gig in Vancouver to demand the students read more indigenous poetry, beginning with his own, preferably. The truth is that each one of us has become an act, another performer on the touring CanLit writer's circuit. Playing the campuses. A sort of higher vaudeville belt with its own headliners and audience warmer-uppers. Every writer shamelessly armed with a rate card, seemingly indifferent to the danger that one day he may be better known for his one-liners than his more serious literarily output.

Now I do not altogether approve. Writers, I strongly believe, should be read but not necessarily seen. They are, in my long experience, largely tiresome company, the most boring fellows, hoarding the best of themselves for their work, and quite properly so. The present danger, a distinctly American one, is that they may settle for becoming personalities, better known for doing their thing, as they say, than for their own things. Norman Mailer, a large but reckless talent, is a case in point, arguably not so much a novelist any more as a man of outsize appetite living through his own novel. A lesser but still engaging case is George Plimpton, acting out and transcribing his own fantasies, serving as his own fictional hero. I have more regard, I must say, for those novelists who send their books out to market and severely limit their own public appearances. I think that writers should be wary, necessarily wary, of talking too easily about writing, lest they lose it. Put plainly, I take my stand with A.J. Leibling, a superb stylist, who, when he was once sent a batch of how-to-write books for review, returned them to the editor with a note that said, "The only way to write is well and how you do it is your own damn business."

My stand-up act has now carried me as far as Edinburgh, to Toronto more than once, as well as to most of the university towns adrift on the Prairies. As a result, I may have written less, but I have learned which English faculty has the most superlative wine cellar and where the most compulsive bores lurk. I now know enough to bless those campuses where they offer you a double Scotch before thrusting you on stage and to come forearmed against those that don't. I have also discovered that if a handful of Canadiana scholars are men of singular dedication, and acumen, still more, farming your novels for sometimes self-serving critical dissertations, always definitive, tend to look on you as a tenant farmer, even a poacher, on the land you cleared in the first place. I have been congratulated for writing *The Sacrifice*, otherwise by Adele Wiseman, and rebuked by more than one matron for having committed *Beautiful Losers*, by Leonard Cohen, but then out in British Columbia, especially, they tend to get their literary Jews mixed up.

In Winnipeg, incidentally, I was once charged with the question "Why do Jews and homosexuals write so much?" to which I could only reply, "Was I expected to answer that in my office as Jew or homosexual?" And for years, on one Canadian campus after another, I have been treated as a turncoat, criticized for being an expatriate luxuriating in England for almost two decades. "This country," I've been told more times than I care to remember, "has always been big enough for me, but not for the likes of you, what?"

Then, finally flattered into a decision, I came home in July 1972 (me, my wife, and my five children), only to be confronted by a fresh accusation.

"Why did you come back, Richler? Things not working out for you in London anymore?"

I'm back because I am a provincial, and this is my province. Or, put more crudely, the pithead, the place where I mine not all, but most, of the ore.

When I was in Montreal for a year in 1960, I spoke at two or three synagogues, and it was the question period, as one might have expected, that made for most of the action. One evening, an indignant man leaped out of his seat to say, "I'm a dentist."

"That's very nice," I replied.

He said, "One of your cousins comes to me."

May his cheques bounce, I thought.

"You probably don't remember me," he said, "You think you're such a big shot now, but I'm from St Urbain Street too."

"What's your question, please?" I asked.

And he said, "Now why in *The Apprenticeship of Duddy Kravitz* did you write that we call the French Canadian kids 'frogs'?"

"Didn't we?" I asked.

"That's not the point," he said. "It isn't very nice. In fact, it's very bad publicity for us with the frogs."

Visiting campuses, I find one question, absolutely unanswerable, surfacing again and again.

"Sir, is there such a thing as a Canadian identity? If so, define it. If not, why not?"

I am not, I think, self-pitying, but I do feel, over the years, I have carried more than my deserved share of labelers. And what I now take to be the present word, that I'm a professional Canada-knocker, I object to strongly. Mind you, I realize I'm fair game. Even in season. And I'm not without humour on the subject. After all, before it was ordained, in some circles, that I supported my family by carving up Canada for the delight of foreigners, I was taken to be this country's leading literary anti-Semite.

After *Son of a Smaller Hero*, following *The Apprenticeship of Duddy Kravitz*, I was asked again and again how could I write such awful things about my people. I did not then, nor do I now, think the things I wrote about my people were awful, but when I was younger, and more easily aroused, I used to answer these charges in detail, explaining time and again why I was not an anti-Semite.

I wish I had known then, as I do now, William Faulkner's answer to a similar charge. And, if you'll pardon the brief digression, let me tell you that story now.

I can't be sure, but I do hope you have heard of, maybe even read, Daniel Fuchs, a very talented American novelist of Jewish origin who wrote a trilogy about Williamsburg, in Brooklyn, before disappearing into Hollywood as a young man. Fuchs had been in Hollywood only for a few weeks, an apprentice screenwriter, when the producer, Jerry Wald, told him he would be collaborating on a script with William Faulkner. Faulkner was one of Fuchs's literary idols, and so he was, quite properly, terrified. Then, as things turned out, Faulkner did no work for the first two weeks; in fact, he was drunk most of the time. Finally, Fuchs confronted him.

"Mr Faulkner," he said, "I don't think this collaboration is working."

"Quite right," Faulkner said.

"Furthermore," Fuchs said, "I don't think it's working because you don't like Jews. You're an anti-Semite."

"That's true," Faulkner said. "But, you see, Mr Fuchs, I don't like gentiles either."

Playing the Canadian campus circuit, mindful of nationalist zealotry, I have warned students again and again that if twenty years ago Canadian writers suffered from neglect, what we must now guard against is overpraise. The dirty double standard. One test for Canadian writers, another, more exacting litmus applied to foreigners. Good Canadian writers, I told them, stand in no need of a nationalist's dog licence, and the rest are simply not worth sheltering.

But, more recently, venturing into balmy, sun-drenched California, deep in the Berkeley hills, I discovered, to my dismay, that I could speak in two voices. I found that, once having explained our nationalist conundrums to American students, some of them baffled, others bored, I was making a plea for our writers, asking that Americans, subject to their own brand of parochialism, no longer dismiss anything written north of the border out of hand.

And so, I found myself insisting that there was now a sufficient number of Canadian writers who needn't be read as a task, but could be looked to for literary pleasure.

Problems.

An American or British writer can lecture abroad and take it for granted that any literate audience will readily grasp what he is about if he mentions Wall Street or the City, Broadway or the West End, Harvard, Oxford, a home run, a sticky wicket, Babe Ruth, Queen Elizabeth, and much more. But I had to assume that I'd lose most of my audience if I mentioned St James Street, Westmount, Carleton University, Howie Morens, or John A. MacDonald, without explaining my references at tedious length.

Look at it this way. If, instead of F. Scott Fitzgerald, a writer out of Ottawa had written a story called "A Diamond as Big as the Ritz," he would have had to title it, "A Diamond as Big as the Chateau Laurier, the Most Exclusive Hotel in Ottawa, the Capital of Canada." But within this frustration lies, I think, our greatest strength. Our largest advantage. Canadian symbols are not yet hackneyed. The mythology is still to be fabricated.

Unfortunately, instead of exalting in this rare situation, the inherent freshness of our native material, too many Canadian writers have taken it as a cause for petulance, self-pity, and even meanness of spirit. They are, they feel, not accorded instant recognition abroad merely because they are Canadian. It is, if I understand one nationalist argument correctly, because we are colonials, far removed from the centre of imperial power and taste-making, that is to say New York, that our work is largely ignored. But Doris Lessing is also a colonial, and so is V.S. Naipaul. Camus emerged out of Algeria, Borges from Argentina, and even James Joyce came out of a colony, if you like.

Years ago, I once wrote that to be a Jew and a Canadian was to emerge from the ghetto twice, for self-conscious Canadians, like some touchy Jews, tended to contemplate the world through a wrong-ended telescope; and that observation, unlike some others I would prefer not to recall, seems to me even more valid now. So, as Jewish audiences tend to chide me for having written *The Apprenticeship of Duddy Kravitz* – "Why did you have to call him Kravitz? Couldn't you have given him an Italian name?" – so Robertson Davies has been reproached by at least one reviewer of *Fifth Business* for maligning Canadian womanhood *for them*, for the foreigners.

Many nationalist Canadians, I feel, also share with certain Jews a subscription to plot theories, the former espying the CIA under every bed, the latter, anti-Semites; and both groups enjoy a neurotic, a conveniently neurotic, misconception of the larger world outside. A penchant for special pleading.

In Toronto, three years ago, a militant young nationalist said to me, his manner outraged, "Do you realize that of all the books on sale in Canada, only 20 per cent are in fact written or printed here?"

Considering the quality of much Canadian writing, it was, I suggested, a lot.

As it happened, the man was also a dedicated partner in a new publishing firm. The books they brought out, uncompromising stuff, were largely political, stoking the nationalist fires. "We can't get booksellers in Chicago or Pittsburgh to take them," he said. "The *Saturday Review* won't review them, either."

"But," I protested, "outside of Canada, surely most books on our domestic affairs would only interest the specialist."

"Didn't we," he countered, "consume masses of books about American politics?"

"Yes, but this is, after all, an American age. Like it or not, whatever the nefarious Nixon ordained on the South China Sea, in Berlin, or even on the matter of the domestic bank rate impinged on all our lives. Ottawa's obloquy touched only the Canadian cognition."

Unsatisfied, he carried on to excoriate all things American, making it clear what he felt about people like me. Cultural cop-outs.

In these overheated days, intellectuals in their late thirties, or, like me in their forties, are commonly cast by the young nationalists as cultural colonials, lackeys of the US cultural establishment. The truth is, we belong to a generation that cannot honestly rise to all-bracing anti-Americanism, abominating everything from the war in Vietnam to *Peanuts*, for we must recognize that the very best, as well as the worst, influences that shaped us were inevitably American.

Morley Callaghan has said, "Canada is a part of the North American cultural pattern. We in the North should have a different literature than, say, Southern writers ... We have our own idiosyncrasies here, you know, our own peculiar variation of the cultural pattern ... But it is still definitely American."

Now, I emphatically agree, which is not to say Callaghan, and me too, for that matter, have ever been anything but Canadian writers. What it is to say is that, looked at objectively, or from the distance of Europe, the difference between a Canadian or United States writer amounts to no more than a nuance. We are, after all, all of us North Americans.

It is also to say that it is possible to be a Canadian writer and not accept that Leacock, albeit a funny fellow, is the rock on which any literary church can be founded, or that Frederick Philip Grove, our great Canadian unreadable, is a classic by anything less than the most picayune standards.

Grove's problem, bluntly stated, is that he couldn't write very well. Even his advocates allow that his dialogue was wooden, his characterization thin, and his prose no more than passable. The only mystery he left us, sufficient for some scholars, was the place of his birth. But there are Canadian critics who will continue to praise him for nothing more than his accurate accounts of Prairie blizzards and summer storms, making a case for him not as a literary figure but as the Percy Saltzman of his time.

I, on the other hand, would recommend Grove to you as the quintessential Canadian neurotic. Grove, we are told, wrote his novels in exercise books, writing on both sides of the page. When they were turned down in New York again and again, he concluded it was not because he was inadequate, but rather because New York editors, being dense, only read one side of the page.

Similarly, young novelists today who have their manuscripts turned down in London or New York, tend not to question their own talent but to lament that it is only because they are Canadians.

When, as is often the case, a Canadian novel is not published outside of Toronto, then the trouble is not the literary, homosexual conspiracy in London, or the Jewish den of thieves in New York; it is, put plainly, that the novel is not good enough. There are far too many novels, and collections of poetry, published in this country whose only virtue is that, like Bright's wine, they are conceived in Canada, but they don't travel well. And when their publishers, largely the new young presses, discover that they can't unload them in London or New York, they are prone to cry unfair. Nobody wants to know about Canada. But the truth is, most British novels are not published in the United States as well, and very few American novels, fewer than ever in fact, are also brought out in England. Most are judged too parochial to make the transatlantic trip.

In this sense then, Canada is not a special case. With some exceptions. For what I have said of Canadian novelists and poets cannot, to be fair, be applied to the indigenous nonfiction writer who tackles a specifically Canadian subject with gusto. Say, Peter Newman on Diefenbaker or Pierre Berton on the CPR. These are obviously limited subjects and cannot hope for a large audience beyond our frontiers. But even this does not suggest a cabal against Canada. After all, when did you or I last read a portrait, however entertaining, of an Australian prime minister or the story of the construction of a Swedish railway?

Mind you, there are specifically Canadian problems. Economic problems. But they largely apply to English-language publishers here, not the writers. Canadian publishers, good and bad, suffer from an impossibly small market base, so that a singularly well-reviewed literary novel that sells anything over 2,000 copies here is doing very well indeed. As well, I'd say, as a novel that sells 20,000 copies in the United States. Then, to add intellectual insult to economic injury, the going largely depends not on the blessings of Toronto or Montreal newspapers, but, as any bookseller will tell you, on the verdict of the *New York Times Book Review, Time,* and *Newsweek,* should they deign to notice. A case in point is Richard Wright. When first published here, Wright's *The Weekend Man* was largely overlooked and sold less than a thousand copies. Only after the novel had been deservedly praised by American reviewers did it enjoy a second coming in Canada. The case of one of the most engaging Canadian films I've seen, *Goin' Down the Road*, is something else again. Don Shebib's film was lavishly praised in Canada but did not win adequate distribution here until New York reviewers stood up to clap hands. Making it real.

The continuing need for New York to make it real has caused many resentments. It is, of course, humiliating and ultimately unacceptable that foreign critics should ordain what's saleable and what isn't in the Canadian arts, but in this imperfect world it's only fair to say that, at the moment, New York reviewers are generally more perceptive than all but a very few people who write about the arts in our own newspapers. It should surprise nobody that the average Canadian reviewer is no more prescient than his equivalent in, say, Cleveland or Denver or, come to think of it, Leeds or Newcastle.

Ironically, though Canadians are now buying more books than hitherto, even more Canadian books – and recently the literary scene was much enlivened by the appearance of a handful of enthusiastic new publishers, among them Anansi, New Press, and Mel Hurtig – there is a continuing crisis in Canadian publishing. Our oldest house, Ryerson, has been swallowed by McGraw Hill, and easily our most important publisher, McClelland and Stewart, all but didn't survive its last financial crisis.

Over 80 per cent of the books Canadians buy are written and published outside the country. In 1969, according to one of the most admirable of nationalists, poet and publisher Dennis Lee, US subsidiaries did 59 per cent of the dollar-volume of book sales in Canada. Canadian firms enjoyed less than 20 per cent of the sales, but they published almost 90 per cent of Canadian fiction and poetry.

Both the takeover of Ryerson and the figures quoted above enraged the young nationalists but fail utterly to rouse me. In my view, it has always been a stigma to be published by Ryerson, ineffectual purveyors of fifth-rate Canadiana for years, and the company's demise, long overdue, can only contribute to the nation's cultural health. I cannot accept the nationalists' cry that Ryerson, hitherto the inviolate old maid of Toronto culture, was raped by agents of the imperialist monster to the south of us. For, to my mind, the wonder of it is not in the infamous act itself but that anybody can be so debauched as to find Ryerson sufficiently tempting to ravish.

O Canada, there is hope. If we are indeed being plundered by a satyr of such omnivorous appetite, we may yet sell them Spring Thaw, *Front Page Challenge*, the Mounties' Musical Ride, and other cultural treasures most of us could do without. Even as things stand, we are not doing too badly. We have already dumped Guy Lombardo on them, as well as Robert Goulet and, God forgive us, the California Golden Seals. In fact, even as we complain about American domination, we are quietly intervening in American mythology and pop culture. Were I a devil's advocate, I could even make out a case for unseemly Canadian manipulation of that very scene we claim is smothering us. Louis B. Meyer and Jack Warner, makers of the Hollywood dream, both emerged out of Canada. The popular myth of a couple of years ago, *Love Story*, was perpetuated onscreen by a CBC-trained director, Arthur Hiller. And the most successful and well-loved Western series ever, *Bonanza*, relied for its father figure on Canada's very own Lorne Greene. Or should I say Dr Greene, now that the sapience of one of our oldest universities, Queen's, has seen fit to honour that Forest Hill sodbuster for this and his other artistic endeavours?

Worse news.

Amidst a plethora of obscene, drug-addicted rock'n'rollers, the last shining morning face in American entertainment is Ottawa's own Paul Anka. The *Police Gazette*, a time-honoured American institution, is actually edited in Montreal. Harlequin doctor-and-nurse novels, written and published here, are devoured in small-town America. Until *Screw, Swinger, Suck*, and other salacious tabloids came along, our own *Justice Weekly* was in the vanguard. *Justice Weekly*, for many years the only journal to publish endlessly saucy spanking letters, came out of Toronto, from Hogtown with love, the pervert's *New Statesman*.

Now, that's quite enough.

But what, I wonder, would Robin Matthews, were he an American nationalist, make of such blatant cultural tampering from without?

To return to more serious matters: our own English-language publishing scene.

If, as Dennis Lee maintains, Canadian-written books account for almost 20 per cent of our total sales, then I, for one, am gratified, not inflamed. Our country may be unequalled as a producer of pulp and paper, but so far the finished product has been put to its most original uses elsewhere.

Meanwhile, it's worth noting that the writers themselves have never had it so good.

I am very weary, indeed, of reading tracts, larded with self-pity, about the poor novelist's plight. After all, novelists are not drafted for duty; they volunteer. Too many volunteer, which is largely the trouble. For as surely as this is expansion time in hockey, allowing many a mediocrity his season on ice, so it is the retrenchment hour in fiction, hardback editions of novels selling on nothing like the scale of twenty years ago.

But if novelists, new and established, are generally an indigent lot, given to moonlighting as teachers or journalists, then it must be allowed, contrary to popular belief, that the small Canadian club is more fortunate, and sought-after, than most. Indeed, it's safe to say that never have so many CanLit bounty-hunters been out combing the woods for so few fawns, ensnaring novelists only to pelt them with cash awards and essays, even books, in praise of.

The latter, it's true, are sometimes embarrassing. There has been a book published about me here that amounts to no more than a selection of newspaper reviews of my work. My mother was touched, it will be a souvenir for my kids, but, as for the rest of you, I'd rather you read *my* books, not their reviews. And in George Woodcock's little book about me, he has it that I was born in 1921, ten years early, and didn't drop out of Sir George Williams without a degree until thirty years later, as if my academic record weren't bad enough. He also ventures that I didn't leave Canada until after the publication of my first novel, *The Acrobats*, noting that the novel's publication aroused very little attention here. "It may have been this cool reception in his own country," he writes, "except on the part of those who conducted literary programs for the CBC, that led Richler to return shortly afterwards to Europe." Actually, a shrewd young man with reliable antenna, I left Canada before the book's publication, and if I'd eschewed all those countries where *The Acrobats* had a cool reception, I'd still be a travelling man.

Neither am I impressed with the indigenous trade journal *Canadian Literature*, which I count little more than an academic make-work program for those who have bet their tenure on Canadiana, and the more recent *Books in Canada* seems to me a nonstarter, even as fan mags go. Alas, these publications do not make literary reputations, but inter them. Looked at another way, not every goose forcibly overstuffed will yield succulent pâté. Many merely burst.

The Canadian novelist, to be fair, is far from totally blessed. We suffer, as I have already pointed out, from a domestic market smaller than the American one, considerably less literate than the British. But taking, as we should, the entire English-speaking world to be our potential oyster, we are, on balance, a very lucky bunch.

So in these far from burgeoning days for serious fiction, my heart does not go out to my Canadian colleagues, but to the Finnish, Czech, or Turk practitioner, limited by languages not widely shared. His or her troubles are further compounded because these days even the best publishers are generally loathe to commit themselves to translations of literary novels, the costs being all but prohibitive, the market small. Neither, so far as I know, are naysaying Finnish, Czech, or Turk novelists rewarded by a proliferating prize system, the manner of cornucopia we now take for granted here.

For novelists, Canada is a gravy train. There are more than a sufficient number of Canada Council awards available: junior and, for toilet-trained writers, senior. In 1968 I served on the arts panel myself, along with Eli Mandel and Ralph Gustafson, and I can assure everybody that this delicate chore is handled with tact and uncommon generosity. In our term, typically, there was a larger pot than players deserving. We finally came down to gambling on good spellers and those who showed a whisper of promise. There are other awards, too. The Montreal prize and eight annual awards, worth $2,500 each, from the Quebec Department of Cultural Affairs. Quebec also offers the Prix David for writers, English- or French-speaking, over forty, and Ontario is also willing to shake the tree for its own.

There is also the Governor General's Awards and another bauble, one that still stubbornly eludes my grasp, the $1,000 Vicki Metcalf Award "for writing inspirational to youth."

And, in 1972, the Canada Council rode to the rescue of our beleaguered publishers, English- and French-speaking, with a new million-dollar program for Canadian book publication, translation, and purchase. Block grants of almost $400,000 were offered to forty-nine Canadian publishers to support their programs and, under a new book-purchase scheme, $500,000 was made available to buy Canadian works for free distribution in Canada and abroad. About two-thirds of the books bought will be distributed to embassies, foreign universities, and cultural centres in kits of two to three hundred titles. But even this was not without its amusing nationalist delight.

The books, you see, were only to be bought from bona fide Canadian publishers and, until recently, that did not apply to one of our most important houses, Macmillan of Canada. It made for an outlandish situation. It would have meant that those packages of two to three hundred Canadian titles could not have included anything by Morley Callaghan, Robertson Davies, Hugh MacLennan, or Ethel Wilson. For, over the years, they were all published by John Grey of Macmillan. John Grey not, as one would have thought, one of the most prescient and conscientious of publishers, an acknowledged gentleman in the trade, but, on the new standard, an imperialist lackey. Fortunately, Maclean-Hunter has since bought Macmillans, belatedly stamping Callaghan, Davies, MacLennan, and Wilson with the nationalist's good-housekeeping seal of Canadian approval.

Even so, our hungering nationalists are still far from satisfied. In a policy paper on book publishing in Canada, issued by the Committee for an Independent Canada, they make the following demands:

That within ten years any publishing or distribution company operating in Canada be required to increase Canadian ownership and control to the standard presently set for the broadcast industry, which is 80 per cent, or cease to operate in Canada.

That all mass paperback distributors in Canada be required within one year to increase to 10 per cent the percentage of Canadian-written and manufactured books displayed in every outlet, and that this percentage rise to 25 per cent in three years and be subject to regular review.

Others, more militant, would even seek to impose a Canadian-content and display quota in our hardback bookshops.

Now, look here, this would be cultural dictatorship at its worst. It's not merely impractical; it's absurd. Do you believe that your cultural needs, or mine, can be satisfied, *25 per cent satisfied*, by Canadian content? Have we, honestly, such a pool of talent available yet?

The Canadian publisher's economic problem springs from our thin population. When Canada can provide an English-speaking audience of thirty, rather than fifteen, million potential book-buyers, then foreign authors will sign separate publishing contracts for Canadian rights as they do now for British and American, and our publishers will be home free. It's population, not indignation, that will eventually bring an end to subsidiaries. Subsidiaries, I should add, that are hardly sinister agents of American imperialism but honest merchants filling a real need.

Content or display book quotas will not invigorate the country's cultural health but, instead, compromise it. It amounts to nothing more than a licence for the second-rate and might drive whatever readers we have left out of the bookshops.

After all, it is not as if hugely talented Canadian manuscripts are going begging. On the contrary. Such is the yearning for Canadiana, and the dilettante attracted to art publishing by the number and generosity of Canada Council grants, that the market is being inundated with books whose jackets are a joy to behold, end papers elegant beyond compare, but actual content, deplorable. And not a year goes by without three new anthologies of Canadian short stories appearing: the same stories, the same authors, but placed in a different order, collected by yet another editor, and issued under a new imprint.

Neither will Canadian content quota help our newly aroused playwrights, now shamelessly set on gaining by stealth – or legislation, if you like – what talent alone has denied them.

The Canadian playwright's mood, wrote Tom Hendry in the January 1972 issue of *Saturday Night*, has "changed with a vengeance. At two conferences last summer ... the playwrights drew up manifestos. They demanded that theatres receiving subsidies be required to produce 50 per cent Canadian material by the end of 1973."

Well, God help us, is all I can say. As things stand, Canadian theatres, from the National Arts Centre, through Stratford, the Manitoba Theatre Centre, and the rest, are pleading, scratching, digging, and weeping for acceptable, even actable, Canadian material. Hardly a month goes by when I don't hear from one or another of them asking for a play, and I daresay it's the same for every other Canadian writer. The truth is, armed with a not inconsiderable bankroll and the best will in the world, they still cannot find sufficient Canadian material of quality, and I defy any nationalist to show me an indigenous play of talent – even of promise – that lacks for production.

I have not yet been to see *Creeps* but have seen this season's other success, *Leaving Home,* by David French. It is a young man's promising first effort and deserved a production. I have not come here to knock it but must say that we still have a long way to go because I can see as good a play any week of the year on British television.

So I am appalled at the thought of a theatre on which a 50 or even 25 per cent Canadian-content quota is imposed – we haven't got the horses yet – and, in the final analysis, I must insist that Chekhov, however questionable his Canadian credentials, still has more to tell us about the way we live now than any Canadian playwright I can think of.

If there's a crisis in publishing and our playwrights' grasp now easily exceeds their reach, then, in the larger world of magazines, it's still doom-watch time.

Maclean's, our national magazine, has recently acquired its fourth saviour in as many years, the astute Peter Newman, who in his office as editor, has swiftly transformed it into the sort of inspirational journal that might honourably be issued by a national Chamber of Commerce. After Information Canada, Canada Hurrah. Each issue opens with a hymn of praise to our land by a writer of repute. In one issue, Al Purdy wrote, "Far beneath the noisy DC-8, ice floes reeled away south. Black and white Arctic hills surrounded us on both sides. This was the first time I'd been to the Arctic, and I was so excited I could hardly sit still ... In Cuba, England, France, and other countries, I'd felt like a stranger; but here I'd never left home. And I thought, what an odd feeling this is to have in a region most people think is desolate and alien. But I felt as if the Arctic was just a northern extension of Canada."

Can Purdy, his poet's third eye undoubted, can Purdy, I wondered, really distinguish at, say, 30,000 feet, our heart-warming bilingual ice from the pernicious imperialist ice of Alaska or the repressive Communist ice of Siberia?

Love, love, love. "Why I believe in *Maclean's*," Newman sang of his employer in his first editorial, "and why *Maclean's* believes in Canada."

Yes, *Maclean's* believes in Canada. In you and me, baby.

My God, what is it about the rich that they adore us so much? What have we done to deserve it? In Montreal the Bronfmans have brought us the Expos, a major league baseball team, and every day in summer the *Gazette* publishes a table of this year's attendance as compared to last. Last season, God forgive us, we ran some 35,000 paid attendance behind 1971, and I feel awful. A bum Canadian. And though the season has not yet begun, I've already resolved to attend more ball games lest the Bronfmans feel their love is unrequited.

Similarly, I feel dreadful because Newman loves *Maclean's* and *Maclean's* has the hots for the rest of us, but I still find the magazine something of a post-Rotarian bore.

Maclean's believes in Canada.

Now let's cut the crap. Maclean-Hunter believes in Canada because over the years, through its innumerable business publications and other interests, it has managed to extract a fortune from it. I take it that the Molson family, E.P. Taylor, the Southams, the Bronfmans, the Eatons, and all those that rode the uranium and oil booms, also believe in Canada, and for the same bloody good reason.

I am not touched.

Neither am I impressed by *Maclean's* electing itself our national conscience, the ultimate authority on what's truly Canadian, if only because I find its taste, intelligence, and moral credentials wanting.

Look at it this way. In Jerusalem there's a group of ultra-Orthodox Jews, the Guardians of the Gate, who arrogantly take themselves to be the conscience of all Jewry. On Saturdays they move out into the city slashing the tires of those who drive on the Sabbath. They are obdurate, fanatical, and an embarrassment, but their integrity is unquestioned. If they are impatient, even violent, with those who don't observe the Sabbath, they do not themselves prosper the rest of the week by dealing in salt pork. But *Maclean's*, our self-elected conscience, is in fact dependent for its continued survival on the full-page advertisements of the multinational, American-based corporations. In a word, it's the bogeyman himself that pays the piper.

There's also been an occasional lapse of journalistic responsibility. In a recent issue, "The Great God Bless America Issue," the front cover proclaimed a story, "The CIA at Home in Quebec?" And on page 22, there was indeed an article titled, "An Analysis of American Intervention in the Matter of Quebec," with the subtitle, "In the Beginning There Was the CIA," and, underneath, a large photograph of a CIA crest, which was pretty sinister stuff.

But if you actually persevered through the text itself, panting breathless, after red herrings, you found the author ruefully concluding that few observers persist in the belief that there *was* an operational contact between the CIA and the FLQ. Unembarrassed, he goes on to venture in true publish-and-be-damned spirit, "that it is highly unlikely that the United States, whatever its good intentions now, would remain indifferent if there were established in Quebec, constitutionally or by force, an independent state that showed itself in any way hostile."

Well, to each his own insights.

The traditional, not unjustified complaint of *Maclean's*, like the more intellectual *Saturday Night*, and indeed all Canadian magazines, is that they must endure the unfair competition of the so-called Canadian editions of the *Reader's Digest* and *Time*, which, between them, accounted for more than 51 per cent of all Canadian advertising in 1971.

If, as recommended by the Special Senate Committee on the Mass Media, the special tax privileges of *Time* and the *Digest* are withdrawn, then undoubtedly more advertising would accrue to *Maclean's* and other Canadian magazines. The financial position would brighten, but not necessarily the editorial content, and that's the real problem.

Maclean's is an anomaly. The American magazines it was modelled on (the *Saturday Evening Post* and *Colliers*) succumbed long ago. Even its French edition, *le Maclean,* seems to me, under present conditions, as ill-advised and subtle a gesture as it would be for the Israelis to attempt to mollify the Left Bank Arabs with a journal called *Shapiro's*. Peter Newman, still one of our most readable political commentators, is lumbered, as were previous *Maclean's* editors, with too large a circulation, obliging him to bring out a magazine that satisfies nobody. Alongside the one, or possibly two, interesting articles per issue, he must run old-fashioned pap about "Spring!" "The Gorgeous Sexy Life After Thirty," and so forth, all aimed to satisfy what Terry Southern once called Mr and Mrs Front Porch. So, not surprisingly, sophisticated Canadians could dispense with *Maclean's* more readily than they could do without better written, more informative American or British magazines.

The pity is Canada does desperately need an intelligent magazine to help bind it together, but what's called for, in the absence of a national newspaper, is a weekly, a newsweekly all our own, not a monthly booster's bulletin, larded with sentimental colour photographs of rocks, trees, and lakes. *Our* rocks, *our* trees, *our* lakes, before they run into infamous Michigan, perfidious Vermont.

There is more hope, I think, in the batch of new magazines that have emerged in the last five years, many of them regional. Easily the best, the radical *Last Post*, surfaces again and again with lively and even necessary pieces about the role of the "*Time* lobby" in Canada or hockey as big business. Other new, freshly written magazines are more specialized. *Take One*, a film journal, *Content*, a monthly for journalists, and *This Magazine Is About Schools*.

Which brings me to the problem of our universities, where Canadiana courses are proliferating and there's a burgeoning rebellion against the hiring of American professors.

What troubles me about Canadian literature courses is not that they are now part of the curriculum, for they very well should be, but that in order to fill them out there is, I fear, more sawdust than wheat going into the literary loaf. From what I've seen of CanLit courses at various universities, there are too many novels actually being studied that are, as *Time* once remarked in a different context, more to be remaindered than remembered. Some of our writers, say, Grove, have some sociological, but no literary, importance. Possibly, the solution is a two-tier system, much of our literary past being studied as social history, with no pretence that it has aesthetic value. I would also think it is a good thing to stir some of our better Canadian novels into a course on the modern North American novel in general, which is, I think, already being done at Carleton.

Canadian literature, as I see it, is a still tender if promising flower, and I'd hate for the academy, like the proverbial Jewish mother, to smother it with too much affection, making claims that are overlarge for the material to hand. If contemporary literature, anything written in the last fifty years, can be called a living museum, then I look to the academy as the museum guards. All I ask, then, is less nationalist hyperbole, a more honest count. Rather ignore us again than claim too much, for, in my experience, a writer can better endure, even luxuriate in, lack of appreciation than survive overheated praise.

I'm even more distressed by the quality of much of the campaign against American domination of our universities. For there is a case to be made against American domination. Certainly, against the spread of American textbooks, with American examples, in our high schools and universities, but it renders itself ridiculous – incidentally, making satire redundant – when somebody, in this case, Robin Matthews again, argues against the presence of texts in Ottawa schools that use illustrations of dinosaurs from American rather than Canadian museums.

The problem of the presence and number of American professors actually teaching in our universities is something else again. The American professors, we are told, have funny accents, are too clever by half, and are fiddling the income tax. Let one in, and they all swarm over you. What's needed is a quota system. The argument is not only familiar to me, but it is also repugnant. The same used to be said of the German Jews.

Now this Canada of ours is a country of immigrants: We are all, save the Aboriginals and Inuit, newcomers here, so why make the Americans a special case? Is it because many of them, after some years here, have still to surrender their US citizenship? Well, then, let me counter that in my many years in London, nobody at the *Observer*, *New Statesman*, or *Encounter* ever suggested to me that I'd best apply for British papers if I wanted to write for them again; and on any British or American campus I have ever visited, I met Canadians, still citizens of this country, who had been teaching for years there without incident.

It might serve us well to remember that only ten years ago, in 1963, nearly 50,000 Canadians emigrated to the United States, swelling the number of Americans of Canadian origin to some three-and-a-half million, an unnervingly high proportion of whom are doctors, scientists, engineers, professors, and businessman – doubly precious, I should think, to our country's development. A.M. Lower wrote, "It has tended to be the more able and especially the spontaneous ... who have gone ... Canada has retained the withdrawn, the sedate, and those with the least energy and ability."

Now that's a very harsh judgment and one I cannot endorse myself. Nevertheless, shouldn't we be grateful, rather than churlish, because so much of the traffic is now moving the other way?

This is not to say, mark you, that universities out to hire professors should at any time favour an American over a Canadian candidate. All things being equal, they should certainly opt for the Canadian. But, as a general rule, surely it is the moral responsibility of each university to seek out the best person for the job, always putting excellence before country of origin.

Finally, such is the heat of our present nationalist fires that they have now even seared Parliament Hill.

In a report published in the *Montreal Gazette*, on Monday, 19 March, it was revealed that the government plans this spring and summer to make a general reassessment of its multimillion-dollar aid to Canadian cultural affairs, probably leading to more money for rising, innovative young artists and artisans of all kinds.

Hugh Faulkner, federal minister for cultural affairs, declared that it won't matter much how resources are protected from American takeovers if cultural affairs succumb to New York and Hollywood influence. Helping the arts, he said, was the key to building a distinctive Canadian cultural identity. It was his immediate goal to ensure wider distribution of Canadian films and books. They are not, he said, getting into the theatres and bookstores of most communities outside the big metropolitan areas. This was, in his opinion, because of the heavy US control of newsstand and bookstore distribution and American or other foreign dominance in chain movie-house bookings.

Some newer Canadian publishing houses, he said, are doing good work in getting Canadian writers and Canadian material between book covers. But again the finished product isn't getting onto the pocketbook racks of neighbourhood drugstores and newsstands.

Mr Faulkner, I'm afraid, has been sold a nationalist bill of tainted goods. Special pleading yet again. For, since when have serious political books, or literary novels, been displayed in neighbourhood drugstores or newsstands anywhere? In England or the United States? In my experience, they have always been confined to good bookshops, which are, for the most part, limited to big cities.

And since when, I must also ask, have art films, anybody's art films, played in the boondocks? Again, seldom in my experience. Film producers, distributors, and exhibitors, Canadian and foreign, are largely cut from the same grubby cloth. Propelled by greed, their demands on life are touchingly simple. All they ask is a profit. When sodomy is saleable, that's what they'll make; when mindless violence brings in the crowds, that's what they'll exhibit. And as soon as Canadian films are boffo, they will run them with pleasure. Meanwhile, the situation isn't helped any by still more hyperbole, say the *Maclean's* reviewer hailing Paul Almond as no less than Canada's answer to Fellini, Bergman, and Antonioni. If that's our best reply, I think, better no comment.

Mr Faulkner, who holds art and artists in refreshingly high regard, concludes, "It's really up to us. We can go on for the next twenty-five years or more borrowing our thoughts and styles – our clothes, ideas, books, and plays – from the United States. But if we do that we will just be a pale reflection of that society. That's not what I want."

Now that's not what I want either, but I'm afraid we emphatically disagree on how best to avoid it.

My quarrel with the nationalists is that they – obviously thinking very little of us – would put barriers above all, erecting a great cultural wall of Canada, jamming the airwaves, sealing off the frontier, sheltering us from all things American, in the slender hope that something better, something distinctly our own, would emerge from the airless land we'd be left to linger in. On the other hand, it is my case, that this is to license mediocrity and twice bless the second-rate, endorsing just about anything that is our very own.

We are not, as I have remarked, lucky enough to be Sweden, Norway, or Denmark, sheltered by language, but a small honest grocery of a country living next to a supermarket of voracious appetite and precious little concern for its neighbour's problems. Self-indulgent cultural nationalism, lashing out at all things American, is ultimately a futile exercise. Short of scissoring the continent apart at the forty-ninth parallel, setting Canada adrift in the Atlantic, we will continue to share it with the other Americans, and must learn to live with that. For, even if we gain, as I hope, a larger measure of economic independence, redeeming our political self-respect, we will go on being culturally entwined with the United States for years to come. After all, we are 20 million; they are more than 200. And most of us do share an English-speaking culture, the larger tradition. If only we could graciously come to terms with this – rejecting the shoddy, be it American or Canadian, absorbing and learning to transmogrify excellence wherever it springs from – then it is fair to say Canadian writers, filmmakers, and other artists are in a most enviable position.

Such is the cultural yearning that the advantages and the money are out scouring the woods for us. Myth makers are urgently needed; and, furthermore, applicants needn't be unduly inhibited. The young writer, for instance, who is settling down to a novel in the Maritimes, hasn't the ghost of Faulkner peering over his or her shoulder. Henry James didn't come before. Or Twain. Or Fitzgerald. If the literary house is haunted, it's only by the amiable Leacock, the dispensable de la Roche. For the rest, the tradition is yet to be made. It's virgin land. Up for grabs.

So let's not be diverted into chauvinism, a stagnant stream, and accept or burnish cultural wooden nickels, even if they are stamped with the maple leaf. Literature is more than a local address, or familiar street names, or good intentions. It's what, hopefully, makes our short passage here more endurable. And, finally, to my fellow artists I say eschew the cultural policy of the closed door, reject the proffered nationalist crutch: Instead, seize the day.

MORDECAI RICHLER is the author of ten novels, including *Barney's Version* (1997), *Solomon Gursky Was Here* (1989), *Cocksure* (1968), and *The Apprenticeship of Duddy Kravitz* (1959), as well as numerous screenplays, essays, children's books, and over three hundred journalistic pieces in a wide range of publications in Canada, the US, and Britain. His most recent book, *On Snooker,* was published in 2001.

Mordechai Richler received countless literary awards, including two Governor General's Awards, the Giller Prize, the Commonwealth Writers Prize, the Stephen Leacock Memorial Medal for Humour, the QSPELL Award, the Screenwriter's Guild of America Award, and the Ruth Schwartz Children's Book Award. He was made a Companion of the Order of Canada just months before his death in 2001.

12

Life as an Artist in Canada

JOHN HIRSCH, 1975

PART ONE

There have been innumerous growing-up books lately full of nostalgia: growing up black, growing up Hungarian, growing up Jewish, growing up Canadian, and so on. I'd like to share my experiences growing up in theatre in Canada. Somewhat nostalgically, with a curiously Canadian mixture of disillusionment and continuing, persistent, idealistic illusion. Everything I can remember about my early childhood and my experiences through school while still in Hungary pointed to what I am now doing. I always wanted to work in the arts. I painted, I wrote, I directed plays.

There was a strong theatrical atmosphere in my family. My great-uncle was a well-known operetta composer. As a child I always went to the movies a great deal and to the theatre. I was always interested in music. I wrote stories – right from the beginning of my life. I can remember very sharply that I wanted to be a director. At the age of three I danced for Nijinsky at the time when he was completely crazy, and I still remember this great, fat, immobile, bald man sitting in the corner of the room at the piano. My mother's friend, who was called Mrs Mozart, and I were dancing to the tune of "Who's afraid of the big bad wolf?" in 1933. And from then on, not a summer passed, not a moment passed of my life, when I was not doing something that was connected with theatre.

A very important determining factor in my life was, I think, my choice of country. Immigrants are rather in the same position toward their adopted country as adoptive parents toward their chosen children. They can say, in the same way, others are stuck with their relationship, but I chose you. This makes for an element of passion and determination in the relationship that the native-born do not always have. After a postwar stay in a camp for refugee orphans in Bavaria, I was headed for an Israeli-bound ship in Marseilles, the wandering ship that became the *Exodus*, when I suddenly decided to visit Paris before going east, so I took off alone on the train. I had just turned sixteen. The stay in Paris turned my thoughts determinedly westward: toward the West in general and Canada specifically.

In those days, when I was sixteen and living in Paris just after the war, it was a tremendously difficult time. One was a displaced person; the police hunted you everyday, so you had to move from hotel to hotel, staying with various friends, always getting up at five o'clock in the morning before the police came, knocked on the door, and asked for papers. Finally, I found refuge in an orphanage just outside of Paris, and from there I made excursions into various embassies in Paris to put down my name for immigration. Immigration to Brazil, Argentina, United States, Canada, and what-have-you. Every time you went you had to fill out a form, and the next time you went, you had to have a medical examination, and they took blood, and after you had gone to fifteen embassies, you had to lay off for a couple of months because you couldn't walk, you had to recuperate! However, the Canadians came through first. They took my blood three times and decided it was good. So I finally came to Canada.

Now there are immigrants who never identify with the new country, and there are immigrants who overidentify with the country. Some immigrants live forever in exile. They always think of the days when they're going to go back, when they'll drive their huge Cadillacs through the small town where they came from and there'll be virgins and old men and everybody waving to them and saying, "Look how well he has done. Isn't that marvellous?" There are other immigrants who are only here for a time, just for a short time, and then they can go back, and indeed they can go back. I was an immigrant who could not go back. There was no possibility for me to go back. Therefore, I had to become, almost by necessity, a passionate patriot. And I became a passionate patriot before I could speak the language, before I knew the country, before I knew where I was. But I just had to belong. And it was very difficult to belong in Winnipeg. Because I arrived in the fall, the weather turned to forty degrees below zero in almost no time at all. The Canadian Jewish Congress outfitted me with clothes that came from some wholesaler on McDermott Avenue, who was tremendously altruistic, but who made sure that the coats were approximately the thickness of potato bags – and if you've ever been to Winnipeg you know what that means when you walk around in the streets.

It was a very difficult place to love, but I was determined to love it. I really felt like a plant that had been plucked out from its earth, and I was carried aloft, the roots screaming, really, for some place to settle in, for some place to call home. And the home turned out to be Winnipeg. Some people at that time said it was the middle of nowhere. The weather man in Winnipeg used to call it the heart of the continent. Some people, I'm afraid, called it the asshole of the continent, and most young people who were sitting around in Childs restaurant, which was the gathering place of the local intelligentsia, called it just that. But more about Childs shortly.

I found a marvellous family, the Shacks. Mr Shack was a supervisor of the hydro steam-heating system and spent most of his days underground, which was a good job in Winnipeg. My sister was Sybil Shack, a passionate patriot, a Prairie lady, and my mother was really a Tolstoy without a beard. She is eighty-four now. She is one of the most remarkable creatures that I have ever encountered. The house is full of birds, plants, dogs, cats. She feeds people all the time, and she loves the gory murder stories and wrestling on television, the ideal kind of contradiction, the ideal way to live, I think. She, at an early age, stood in front of the Winnipeg City Hall, in the 1919 strike, and spoke from a soap box. She's always against the government. She will now be against Mr Trudeau, and, I'm sure, at the back of her mind there is someone whom she's pushing. She doesn't know who, but she knows that the government is wrong, and this is the feeling that I was brought up with in that house. They're patriots, they're marvellous Canadians. Every time I talk about being Canadian, I have a slight difficulty because I am really a Manitoban; I am really a Winnipegger. And as I am growing older and farther away from Winnipeg, I really feel like Kennedy, when he went to Berlin and said, "Ich bin ein Berliner," and I'm becoming quite as passionate about being a Winnipegger. Winnipeg is a remarkable place. It is the Baghdad of the Prairies, and I don't know if anyone has ever called it that, but I do so.

And it was especially so in those days in 1947, when the place, the university, was still full of those people who came back from the war. The famous Childs restaurant was at the corner of Portage and Main, with a space that still looks, but then even more looked, like a huge railroad station. The tiled floors, pillars that were covered with mirrors, the two huge plate-glass windows in the front, always frosted in the wintertime, the long counter with the marble top, the waitresses in black uniforms – little white aprons and little white sort of things on their heads – ran up and down and served innumerable cups of coffee and pancakes. It was the place where people went early in the morning, sometimes two, three o'clock. It was the only place that was open.

My problem was, when I arrived, that I didn't speak English, and it was difficult for me to communicate with people. However, I gravitated to Childs restaurant almost immediately because that was the place where the "intelligentsia" met, and I use the word with a purpose because it was very much like that, in the spirit of nineteenth-century Russia. Around the tables you could find people like Adele Wiseman, who at the time was somewhat becoming a joke because she had been working on this huge novel that no one had ever seen but everybody talked about, the novel that later became *The Sacrifice*, which won the Governor General's Award. At the same table sat Boris Margolis, who was working on a thesis in history that also had been going on for decades, so it seemed. And then there was James Rainey, who came from the East to become an assistant lecturer at the university. James Rainey was a very young man at that time, from Stratford, Ontario, whose mother took him to a blind tailor before he was sent out to the West and ordered him a blue serge suit, and in that blue serge suit and a raincoat, with an alarm clock under his arm, Jamie arrived in Winnipeg. The alarm clock was brought because he hated teaching so much that he couldn't trust the alarm system in the university, and every time he walked into a lecture, he set his clock exactly to forty-five minutes, and when the bell rang, he walked out.

It was in Winnipeg, at Childs restaurant, that you could see Jamie writing his poems in the middle of the night. There were also people like Jack Woodbury, Jack Ludwig, Margaret Lawrence, Roman Kroitor, a lot of very exciting and interesting people. Just the other night I was talking to a friend of mine, and I said, "Isn't it strange that the people who belong to the Bloomsbury group were constantly scribbling about what they were doing, how they were doing it, for posterity." And, indeed, all these marvellous biographies and autobiographies are coming out just now. People who were in Paris and sat around Gertrude Stein and Janet Flanner and all those people constantly were aware at the time when they were living that they were important, that they were history. But to no one did it occur in Winnipeg in 1947 at Childs restaurant that they were history. Now it is funny, but then it was not. I think that this kind of lack of arrogance, this lack of self-awareness, was totally deficient. I ran into it headlong.

I had just arrived, and I got into Childs restaurant, where people were sitting around planning to go to London, and I couldn't. This was just too much. I had been wandering around long enough. I could not understand why all these people wanted to go away. No one wanted to stay. They kept running down the place, they kept saying how terrible it was and how everything that was worthwhile, everything that was to be emulated, was in London. And so people were planning, saving their pennies to go to London. Nobody wanted to stay in Winnipeg ever. And that was terrible because I had just got there. And I also knew that I had to stay there. I was determined to stay there, and I began to love the place. I began to love the place when I realized that here there was space. Here there was room. Here there was a mixture of people who lived reasonably peacefully together, and nobody was killing one another, and I was not used to that kind of an atmosphere. But here there was peace.

It is true that a friend of mine, John Adamson, who was born and brought up in the South End had never in his life crossed over to the North End, and he did so only because I lived there. To him it was a tremendous kind of adventure. But you see, again, I did not quite understand that because I was not aware of the historical schism that caused that kind of separation, which was the 1919 Winnipeg Strike. The South End and the North End were battling, and it's only now, fifteen or twenty years later, that I understand why John never, ever went to the North End.

In time I became a real lover of the place. Landscape shapes us as much as anything else, and the second-strongest shaping factor in my life, I think, has been the encounter with the Prairie. To me, it was an incredible kind of encounter. The rocks, the lakes, the Aboriginals paddling along in the morning, harvesting the wild rice, the sound of the loon, the scent of mushrooms, the fish just out of the lake. Looking at the pine trees, looking at the sky, made me realize where I was. Those trips from Winnipeg to Brandon in the middle of the winter when, suddenly, I felt as if I was riding across the concrete sea, the snow-covered sea without any kind of signpost. This incredible infinite kind of landscape that still, when I think of it, gives me goose pimples because of the hugeness of it is something I will never forget. And it formed me and shaped me. And my love for the place grew a great deal.

The only thing I've wanted to do all my life, ever since I can remember, is to be in the theatre. That's all I really wanted to do. I wanted to direct plays, put things together, tell stories, communicate colour, movement, to people. And I arrived in a community where there was no theatre, and every time I spoke to people and said I wanted to become a director, they laughed at me because that wasn't a kind of available category. There was no theatre except the little theatre. Four times a year, for two nights each, a play was put on in the Playhouse Theatre, and six or seven hundred people attended. Most of the plays that were put on were by either Shaw, J.P. Priestley, Noel Coward, or sometimes, but very, very seldom, Gilbert and Sullivan. And this was again very strange to me because I wanted to be a Canadian.

I used to be a Hungarian. I couldn't be nothing. And I was young and had to fit into something, something that I could hold on to. Again, this tremendous desire to belong. But, culturally, it was really an impossibility to do that. The only time there was anything resembling an original Canadian thing that I can remember was done by George Broderson, who was a marvellous man. In my eyes, his claim to fame was that he actually shook Bernard Shaw's hand. Then, he was in an amateur production in Oxford. But it was George Broderson who took Gwen Pharis Ringwood's play, *Dark Harvest*, and put it on, and that was the first time I had seen anything that was Canadian. The rest of it was a rather terrible imitation, and now I could understand why people wanted to go to London. What was the point of living in the middle of an imitation. You might as well go where the real thing is. That's where it was all happening, not in the little theatre. There were also poetry readings in the Business and Professional Women's Club in the evenings, where some university professors and ladies with feathers on their hats and little pieces of fur and gloves sat and listened to *Murder in the Cathedral* as it was read by graduate students, and that was also very interesting.

Then the climax of the year, theatrically speaking, came when the Dominion Drama Festival had a contest, and from Brandon and from Flin Flon and from Dauphin and from Winnipeg, we put on plays. So you had Shaw and Coward and J.B. Priestley, and for this there were people who came from England to adjudicate us. This was always a very marvellous kind of an occasion because everybody could put on evening gowns and white gloves and tuxedos, and there was a kind of an imitation garden-party/Buckingham Palace atmosphere. As long as the adjudicator had a reasonably good English accent and a tuxedo, everybody listened very carefully. I felt myself in a very strange atmosphere because I thought that this was a country, and on the streets in the North End I knew where I was. In the Nordic pool hall shooting pool, I knew who I was and where I was. There were also a lot of people around who belonged to the place and who had a sense of belonging. But there was this feeling among the elite: They were always talking about some other place and wanting to be somewhere else. And this business of adjudicators bothered me even then because I lost once, I must admit.

It is true that Pierre Lefebvre and others came out, but also along with those people, sometimes people came who were from music halls. Very good artists, but I'm sure they were out of a job, and somebody asked them to come and travel across Canada and tell all these natives what to do and how to do it. I was offended by that, at times. I realized at that time that if I am going to be working in the theatre and make a living working in the theatre, I have to start one. It was an arduous kind of a process because I was living in a society where the artist was not really accepted. The artist was not accepted because he did what he wanted to do and because he enjoyed it, and for that you must not get paid. Work had to do with punishment. Work was something that people did because they had sinned, probably, and this was the way to get rid of all of that. They had to work, and I was looked upon as a frivolous creature because all I wanted to get paid for is fun. I just wanted to have fun. I wanted to do what I wanted to do, and I wanted to get paid for it, and that was sinful. And there it was.

Music was alright because music had to do with church and education, and "Hear, Hear" or "Hark, Hark, the Lark" went on for three weeks every spring at the Winnipeg Auditorium. Thousands of children, one after another, coming "Hark, Hark, Lark, Hark, Hark," and again somebody from the Royal Academy of Music was sitting out there, I think three people, giving marks and then coming on that Joanie was the best "Hark, Hark," and so on – and that was alright. Money was given for it, and people thought that was fine. But to put on plays – that was a different matter altogether. To get paid for acting or for directing was really just beyond the pale.

Well, I decided, what the hell. I'll have a try at it because that was the only thing I wanted to do, and that was the only thing I knew how to do. And then one had to go and begin a political kind of a campaign. You had to figure out who were the people who were interested in charity and education and good works. Therefore, one went to those people and, bless their hearts, the Junior League of Winnipeg helped me out. I went to the Junior League, and I said, you are interested in education, you are interested in children, you are interested in culture, what about giving me $300, and I'll start a puppet theatre. Kathleen Richardson, Bev Gurley, and a lot of marvellous girls from the Junior League, bless their cashmere sweaters and one-string pearl things, they helped, and they took a chance. And it was a momentous and revolutionary step in my career and, as it turns out, in the life of the city because we did start a puppet theatre, and we got paid. All three of us who put those puppets together, who made the theatre, all of us got paid ten dollars a month, and for that – that was big money in those days – we toured community halls, schools. And, lo and behold, the children loved it.

It was the first time that I realized that in this particular country – and I'm talking about Winnipeg – you got to prove somehow what you were about. You have to show what you are going to do, and support will come forth, and it did. Because next year, the same Junior League allowed us to start a children's theatre, and we went on and did the same thing as we had done with the puppet theatre. But now actors got paid, and there was a possibility for actors who worked at Arthur Murray's Dance Studio, Chan's Chinese restaurant – they all had a chance now – to spend at least a couple of hours every night doing what they really wanted to do, so the Winnipeg Children's Theatre was started.

It was an interesting and extremely exciting time for me because I realized that the period of pioneering that went on there in terms of the land, that incredible effort that it must have taken for people to settle there, to make a home, that period of pioneering was still possible and was still available for me, a nobody from nowhere, a Jewish orphan from Hungary to come here and actually have the opportunity to start all these things, to tell people that there are things that they have not heard of, but they will love it when they see it. It was monumental arrogance. Nevertheless, I was sure that children do love puppets and children do love theatre, and only if you can show it to them once, they'll get hooked. And they did. And the city slowly began to be proud of what we were doing, and these two organizations started, and they're still there.

Then came the battle of the Rainbow Stage, the musical-comedy theatre. The city built a musical-comedy bandshell in Assiniboine Park, and they were going to have Ukrainian dancing, Hungarian pancakes, baking, and all this ethnic BS going on all summer long. But after a week, they ran out. They had nothing to do. They built this tremendous thing, and there was nothing to do. They tried everything, but people wouldn't come. I went to the City Hall, and I said, "What we need is an open-air, musical-comedy theatre, and I need $2,000 to start it." Jimmy Duncan, may he rest in peace, who was a great exponent of Gilbert and Sullivan, and Barry England, and all the rest of it, every year they did one of those things, you see. Kelvin High School did one. Suddenly they said, "Yes, this is a good idea, let's put on musical comedies out there." But we needed money, and we needed something that was never heard of: It was called "subsidy." The city was asked to put money toward the employment of actors, my God, and to hire an orchestra, my God, to buy costumes, scenery, all that! Well, I went and I asked them for this $2,000, and Douglas Chisholm was one of the aldermen and the head of the Treasury Board of Winnipeg. He said to me, "When you can prove it to me that you can get as many people to a musical comedy in Assiniboine Park as I can to a yo-yo contest, I will give you $2,000" – which is, by the way, not too far from what one of my superiors said to me the other day at the CBC!

Well, at the end of that summer, we had proven to Mr Chisholm that we could get more people out to Assiniboine Park than the baseball club got out to the baseball games, and that was a fantastic victory for us. We also made sure that he didn't get re-elected, and we did it through all kinds of ways and means. The battle to get acceptance as an artist, the battle to get acceptance for cultural institutions that serve people, that benefit people, very much the same way as libraries, sewers, whatever, in this country has been an infinitely long battle. And the battle goes on, and it is a marvellously worthwhile battle. But it's very fatiguing, and it doesn't much change. But we won and Chisholm didn't get re-elected, and he still remembers that.

The theatre is still there, and it was marvellous on a Sunday, on a summer night, to be in Assiniboine Park while we were doing *Chu Chin Chow* or the *Wizard of Oz*, or whatever, or one of our own new musicals, such as *Do You Remember?*, which was about the city. To seat three thousand people, with babies going to the washroom every five minutes, running to get popcorn, sitting there on their own pillows, putting newspapers over their heads when the rain started – to see this was marvellous, and it was a reward beyond any monetary reward that anybody could get. Because there had been nothing there before, and now there was something there. And people came from all over the city, and it was not just the six hundred people who turned out four times a year to the little theatre to applaud. But they were people. The cleaning ladies were there, and the garage mechanics were there. It was for the people – and it was great.

Now for me that was not quite enough because I had to stay in Winnipeg. As I said before, I really love the city. We then started a kind of guerilla action within the little theatre. One had to infiltrate it because it was an existing organization and through patient work one had to convert it into something that one wanted, which was a professional theatre. This happened over the dead bodies of all the housewives that used to act once a year and who thought of themselves as Sarah Bernhardts. It had to happen over the dead bodies of all those, bless their hearts, professors of English at universities who were really Peter Brooks underneath it all, but they had never had a proper chance. Now there was no work for them because this upstart comes along and says that we have to do professional theatre, and you have to work at it all day and full time, and we did. We got ourselves a burned-out golf school and started rehearsals and started to work for the little theatre, and that happened – by us, Tom Hendry and myself and a couple of brave souls. Simply using the people who were in Winnipeg, young people and old people who wanted to become professionals, and we gathered people, and some of them you know. Gordon Pinsent came from an Arthur Murray dancing school; that's what he did. He only just wanted to act and be a writer, and he came and worked. James Blandit, marvellous actor now, at the age of fifteen, Saturday night, he used to sing in Chan's Moon Room on Main Street for $10. He came in and became an actor. Then we used a lot of older people who worked for CBC Radio, and out of that nucleus we began to do plays.

Within a year, the little theatre turned into Theatre 77, and the work of convincing the city that this was a good thing, that we were trying to create something indigenous, that we were trying to create something that was their own, went on. In rain, in snow, on icy roads, through mud and snow storms, we went with a small Morris Minor delivering posters, selling tickets, and creating this crazy theatre, which became the Manitoba Theatre Centre, first of the regional theatres in Canada, the first on the continent, and in a few years' time, lo and behold, we really got the signs of approval, the kind of a stamp, because from New York people came up and took a look at it, and from then on it was easy sailing.

The Ford Foundation came and looked at this thing and said that this was a model, this was something that ought to be emulated. We had a theatre that put on plays six times a year, running two weeks each. We had a studio theatre, where we were doing difficult plays, and we were doing original Canadian works. We had a children's theatre that performed four times a year. We had a touring company that went into high schools and elementary schools to do programs that had something to do with the curriculum that was taught at that time. We had a bus that went twice a year around the province and did one-act plays. It was an incredibly ambitious program, the result of an incredible amount of work.

During all that time Tom Hendry and I spent a hell of a lot of time talking to any group that wanted us to talk to them, from United Church basements where we talked to ten ladies, to Hadassah Bazaars where we talked to four hundred. From Rotary clubs to Kiwanis clubs, we were everywhere. We talked and we talked and we talked, and we told people that what we were going to do, what we were going to give them, would be to their liking, that they'd acquire a taste for it, that it was homegrown, that it was ours, that one of these days they'd be as proud of this theatre as they were of the Blue Bombers. We told them that what we were trying to create was a husbanding of our human resources. We told them that we were interested in showing their past, our present, and, possibly, our future through this. We told them that it was educational. We told them that it was good for their children. And slowly, it was accepted.

The Canada Council came along, and along with it Peter Dwyer, a man who was a remarkable person, an extremely cultivated, educated human being, who put his faith in people, not in institutions. Wherever there was anyone with any promise, any imagination and ambition, Peter could grasp it and would see that person was supported. Through that support, through that very personal individual nurturing of people, institutions were created, and to a great extent it is due to Peter and to the Canada Council, through Peter, that the Manitoba Theatre Centre was born. It was a remarkable achievement helped by this remarkable man and by a community. In my wildest dreams I couldn't have imagined, in 1947, that barely ten, fifteen years later that city of Philistines, a city nowhere, a city in the middle of nowhere, would come forth and build a theatre for their own company. And, up to that time, it was the only company, really, in this country, and the only company until that time, on this continent, that had a theatre built for it before the Centennial madness came around building buildings, and hoping that there were people to fill them. It was the first time that it happened the other way around.

Now I stayed in Winnipeg after having built that theatre and the musical-comedy theatre and the children's theatre, and I realized that I had to leave, I had to grow. One of the great dangers an artist suffers in Canada is that it is too easy. Now it is very strange, after what I've said, that suddenly I say it is too easy, but it is. You can become a very big boy in a very short time, if you have a lot of energy, because there are marvellous things to be done. But it's a very damaging situation for a young man. I got the Order of Canada at the age of thirty-five, and I thought it was slightly ridiculous because I was not ready for the pigeons yet. It's too early to become a monument. I had to go away, and I also had to go away because the kind of acceptance, the kind of challenge that one is looking for as an artist, is not available. So I left the country … no, I didn't leave the country; I went to Stratford, and I became an associate artistic director. I have done interesting things there, some new things. I tried to Canadianize the place, but I was premature in my effort. It was not possible at the time.

I tried to get young actors from the National Theatre School to come and work there, and they did come, but they really weren't received too well. I tried to do Shakespeare in a Canadian kind of way. I don't mean in a self-conscious and embarrassing kind of way. I just mean that I wanted to have these plays done with a Canadian sensibility, or a Winnipeg sensibility, or a Winnipeg/Central European sensibility. Obviously I did not succeed very well. I also did one of the first successful – I suppose *the* first successful – Canadian productions of James Reaney's *Colours in the Dark*. And again, it took a tremendous amount of battle to get that play done there. Nobody wanted to do it. They said it was parochial, local, provincial; nobody was interested. To me it was a beautiful, marvellous work because it was local. Provincial. That's why it was beautiful because it was written by a man who was writing about what he knew. He was writing about his own mythology. Through it, he was working out his own mythology, and that was an exciting, absolutely incredible experience.

Curiously enough, the theatre for the first previews was filled up by people from Stratford and the little hamlets and villages. They were roaring and laughing and having a marvellous time. But then, as somebody told me afterward, who was a stalwart, Stratfordian designer, these were not the kind of people we wanted in the theatre, which just about put the cherry on the top of that particular sundae. They were not the kind of people? I never felt at home in Stratford because it was not Winnipeg, it was not Canada for me. I felt very strange there. It was very difficult to be yourself. I think Guthrie, Tony Guthrie, did a marvellous thing, and his genius consisted of having started something and leaving it. He wanted that theatre to become a Canadian theatre. This is what he wanted. He started a magnificent thing, and he left. It's too bad that it took years and years to become – or perhaps it's still not – really a Canadian theatre.

When I talk about Canadianism I'm not talking about chauvinism, I'm not talking about nationalism. I'm talking about self-actualization, I'm talking about self-awareness. I think that, all my life in this country, I was forever overcome – and that's the word, really – by the beauty of it, by the size of it, by the fantastic opportunities that we have here. I spent a year travelling in Asia and, after a year away, and in the early morning at four o'clock, I got off the plane straight from Japan, and I was really in tears because, suddenly, I saw all this space, and, after Tokyo, this was incredible. This was miraculous, that any group of people could be as fortunate as we are to have this space, to have this air, and from the airport I went to English Bay, and I left my bags at the Sylvia Hotel, and I walked around Stanley Park, six miles, seven o'clock in the morning, and I met one person. One person. And after Bombay and Calcutta and Tokyo, to meet one person in the heart of the city walking along the periphery of this magnificent park was a mystical experience for me that I will never forget, which is at the base of my whole appreciation of this country.

To this day I do not understand why we cannot say more openly, and repeat it more often, how much we love this place, how marvellous it is for us to live here, how worthwhile it is to be in a place where there are still opportunities, where there are still possibilities, where you can still have some kind of an effect, where you still have a voice, and the voice is heard, and you can still make things. To be in a place where institutions still can be changed. It is not nationalism that the artists today want in this country, just self-awareness, just a constant emphasis on who we are. Health consists for an individual in self-knowledge. It consists of a constant reexamination of the process of growth, it's relationship to others. It is essential that we should, as a nation, as a group of people living here, pay a hell of a lot of attention to ourselves, healthy intro-spection, and pride. Seems to me that today I have a terrible sense that we don't have much time. I have a sense that we're living in crucial times in this country. Something in the next decade might happen, and if it doesn't happen, I think we are just going to become part of a huge mess, huge other thing, and this is why, perhaps, we have to accelerate the definition of ourselves. This is why we have to go as artists to create those myths that are there to be created, to give sound to those ideas and voices that, so far, have not been heard.

I am haunted, absolutely haunted, by all our past going down the drain unrecorded, unmarked, torn down, and it is only through the imaginative han-dling of our past that we can gain the kind of strength that we need for our future. The stories that people are telling, history, old buildings, all the rest of it, which gives us the ground to stand on, I think, is disappearing. There are thousands of subjects in my head that I would like to put forth because I know that they would be illuminating, would give strength, enabling us to define ourselves as human beings, living in a group here in this kind of a place, but there's so few of us used to doing that. We don't think it is somehow our right.

We were brought up, most of us, I think, on other people's histories, on other people's memories, told that those experiences elsewhere were more valuable, more valuable than our own. Theatre, I think, is necessary. It's not peripheral, it is essential, it is a constant ritualistic recreation of the past presentation of what is happening now, and perhaps it can give some kind of indication of what is to come. We need a group of people who think that the activity is important. We have to convince governments that art and the artist are important, that the artist is not a special person, not a unique kind of a creature, not an aristocrat, but a necessary member of a society. Artists are needed because they present the dreams, they present the visions. And it is in those dreams and in those visions that a nation, a group of people, living at a particular time, can find itself.

PART TWO

In 1954 I went to work for the Canadian Broadcasting Corporation in Sable, Winnipeg, as a television producer, the youngest in the country. There couldn't have been more than a dozen of us in all, and I am sure that most of us were under thirty. In the next two years, I learned to produce television shows, everything from *Pets Corner* to *Hubby Highlights*, with panel shows, ice reviews, folk dances, dramas, Santa Claus parades, baseball games, and Auden's "New Year's Letter." I left the CBC two years later when one of my bosses called me into his office and told me that I must stop producing programs for "eggheads," which was a 1950s phrase. He told me that if a program wasn't understood by his fourteen-year-old daughter, he didn't want it on the screen. As it happened, the girl was a student in my sister's school, and I quickly found out that the child, to be charitable, was slow.

That was in 1956, and now almost twenty years later I am with the CBC once again. I'm back in Canada, aware of the tremendous growth of this country over the years and aware, with a bit of a shock, how in some respects we have changed so little. The mandate of the Canadian Broadcasting Corporation dedicates the corporation to "public service." These two vital words must be redefined from time to time, especially in such a rapidly growing country. What is the public, with a capital P? Is it my friend, Ramona McBean, who at seventy retired to live in Victoria; hundreds of young Greeks who hang out at the pool halls on Pape Street in Toronto; the couples in Don Mills, who settle down on Friday nights in front of their television sets to watch the *Baby Blue* soft-porno film; the people of Red Deer, Alberta; my friend, the PhD, who watches only wrestling on the tube; or the twenty-three-year-old Lawrence Welk addict?

In trying to provide programs for a potential audience of seven to ten million people who happen to be spread across three thousand miles and who behave more and more like citizens of the proud Italian city-states of the Renaissance, you're really up against it. And having accepted the role of the Pope of Drama for four years, let me tell you, spreading Catholicism is pretty tough. By tradition, the most troublesome area in broadcasting is drama. You can't complain about the weather report. The people who used to ask for more uplifting news are by now thoroughly conditioned to the fact that wars, floods, fires, plagues of all sorts are here to stay, and only when corruption in Canada, not in the States, is reported by Lloyd Robertson do people complain about the CBC bias.

But drama, by definition, implies a presentation of conflict, a juxtaposition of opposite views in a highly personal way. They're confronted with the total subjectivity on the part of the creator, where the strength of a unique vision, coupled with skill to communicate that vision through intellectual and, above all, emotional means will affect the viewer. Drama must involve; therefore, it will disturb, one way or another. It will push the viewer into activity, and that is why it is pornographic in a Platonic sense. It has to move if it is any good. The audience will have to think; the audience will feel joy, sorrow, pity, anger, and, a lot of times, outrage because, perhaps, at times, they will recognize themselves on the screen. In Canada, for years now, we have been used to a contemplation of other people's realities, the imaginative interpretation of other people's realities. *Kojak* is an American Slav; the problems of Archie Bunker are super funny in a comfortable way because he is an American bigot facing American racial problems. *Upstairs, Downstairs* deals with the nineteenth-century marzipan relationships between servants and masters in London and not in twentieth-century Toronto, where the dealings are with West Indian maids and nannies out of Scotland. Those American doctor shows are full of Puerto Rican and black nurses and patients who are not Canadian ethnics but Americans. Everything is once removed from us in those shows. They're not quite us. Their violence is not our violence. Their sexuality not our sexuality.

The truth is that we haven't yet seen ourselves reflected on the tube in our living rooms. We used to be more or less noninvolved spectators of other people's problems. And this is, I believe, what caused this flood of mail, these voices of outrage against programs such as *Baptizing,* by Alice Monroe, *Ten Lost Years*, Barry Broadfoot's piece, and the *Farm Show*. People are outraged because for the first time, very directly, there was something up there that was talking about them. *Jamie Boy* I don't think disturbed people because one of the characters said, "Fuck the apple crisp." I don't think that; that's not what did it. What happened was that here was the Canadian working-class on the tube talking the language that I think they talk, dealing with problems that they deal with, and that was something new and very disturbing. And, consequently, all the squawking and outrage.

It is assumed by most people, I think, even within the Canadian Broadcasting Corporation, that our Canadian public, whatever that public is, would like to see programs like the American programs, but done in Canada, and some Canadian films have already achieved this marvellous made-in-Japan souvenir quality. In one of these films, shot entirely in Canada with subsidies provided by the Canadian government, there's a scene in a police station, and, lo and behold, on the desk there is the tiniest American flag, to give the Canadian audience the feel that they are really watching an American film. And to reassure the American audience, with a market of two hundred million, that despite the strange, never-identified look of Toronto, they are watching an American product. And we subsidize films like that, which I think is immoral.

All of this leads me to the hard realization that if we, in the corporation, are honest, we must stop imitating American products. It is a disastrous road, even if we contemplate it, and here are the reasons. First of all, we are a public network. A public service network, and not a commercial network. Our function is not to program for profit – that is, the essential aim is not to sell soap, sanitary napkins, laxatives, and dog food to a conditioned and therefore pretty defenseless public – but to create television drama that entertains without being inane and soporific, intelligent without being dull and didactic, reflective of this country as a matter of fact, without the terrible self-conscious, artificial way that in my mind evokes informational films of beavers and of Ukrainian ladies in full national costumes painting Easter eggs in weather forty degrees below zero on the corner of Portage and Main, accompanied by those great three-piece orchestras playing pseudo-Aaron Copeland on the soundtrack, which is the kind of thing that we have been used to in the past. A public service that recognizes the fact that there is no capital-P public. They're individuals, a hell of a lot of individuals. And a public service that is not afraid of creative artists. A public service that realizes that it's function is to encourage a group of creative artists to express themselves and to enable them to communicate these expressions to the largest number of Canadians.

In short, you have to put your faith in the creative artist, the people with individual vision, with voices, with commitment. And only they are going to provide you with programs. A creative community of people made up of the people of this country with different backgrounds, tastes, minds, visions, and interests who are obsessed with expressing themselves and communicating it to you. And the best you can hope for is that all these different people – who are united by some common aim, by some crazy idea that this country, this impossible country, somehow can be united in a mystical way, perhaps in some kind of religious way, some way – that the common aim of these creative people can place mirrors on the walls of this house, where, up to now, we could see ourselves only through other people's images. This common aim would include the unearthing of a strong but buried and seldom-expressed love of this place. Only through the work of individual creators will the public, made up of ten million individuals, be properly served, only when programs are offered to this infinite mix of people making up the Canadian nation, programs that begin to open up new horizons into our own self-knowledge.

The public is there to watch. Even on the basis of the marketers, over 50 per cent more of the public watched CBC television drama this past season when it attempted some small steps forward than had watched it last season. *Baptizing* and *Ten Lost Years* drew bigger audiences, more letters pro and con, and more enthusiastic response from very intelligent and bright people than the usual home-made or imported fair. Those who objected to the programs and stirred up their parliamentary representatives to object to them have made most of the newspaper headlines. But their opposite numbers are no less vigorous, if somewhat less well known. We have received avalanches of letters from Winnipeg, Moncton, Rapid City, Manitoba, Calgary, Saskatoon, Toronto, North Bay, Vancouver, Cornerbrook – you name it – all congratulating us on what we have done. And it is not the ultimate thing. It is not the greatest thing, but it is a step in the right direction.

You see, when I went to the CBC, I was told once again that Canadians are really not interested in Canadian drama, that we should really be doing the police series and all that kind of stuff that we buy from the States. And it came as a tremendous surprise to me that on Sunday nights people watched, in huge numbers: *Baptizing* was seen by two and a half million people. That's a fantastic number in this country. To give you some kind of an idea, some kind of comparison, when Katherine Hepburn's *Glass Menagerie* was last shown with all the hoo-ha and all the publicity, 2,200,000 people watched. *Ten Lost Years* was watched by 2,200,000 people, and the reaction was really phenomenal, for and against.

The problem is that most people at the CBC are conditioned to react to negative things. They get scared. They really don't see that the mere fact that two and a half million sat from 9:00 to 10:00 P.M. watching *Baptizing* is an incredible experience for the CBC and a very positive kind of thing. Fifty-five per cent loved it, 20 per cent hated it, and 25 per cent, well, they didn't mind. But the uproar and the panic and the terror that ran through the place because there were letters and phone calls just blew my mind because I'd been brought up in show business, and as long as they mention you, that's all you care about. You know, who cares? As long as people are paying attention; that's what you're after. This doesn't mean that you have a licence to go out and grab, through sort of titillating the public and being sensational, I don't mean that, but if you believe in the stuff that you're doing, if you feel that it's important, that the people who do it are committed artists, and when all those people actually watch it, and some of them hate it, well, you have succeeded! You have really done something.

After all, we are talking about Alice Munro, we are talking about Alan King, and the girl who appeared naked on the goddamn show was Alice Munro's daughter. If she didn't care, why should somebody in Red Deer care? And, after all, if you have seen a naked girl who is fourteen years old, what's the big deal?

But we got, from Red Deer, a letter signed by 250 people, and they were objecting to representation of normal sexual relationships because it was not normal. Something to that effect. This was the really damned of it. Now, what I am puzzled by is not the reaction of the public and not the reaction by people in parliamentary committees and all the rest of it, but by some of the people within the CBC. Because, after all, if you're in show business, once again, you want attention. Not by dropping your pants or making rude noises, but by doing works that will arouse in the right kind of way, will disturb, perhaps, in the right kind of way. Anyhow, the phones were ringing like crazy for days. I couldn't do anything else but listen to these panicky people saying, "Well, two hundred more phone calls from Couchiching" or anywhere. Nobody ever congratulated me on the fact that two and a half million people watched. It's another Canadian thing, isn't it? I thought there would have been a delegation with little flags coming to say, "Gee! You did it! Oh ho! Look at all these people watching!" Nobody. No, sir. Phone calls, phone calls.

Anyhow, it seems to me that we are a bit behind the times in English Canada in this respect. In French Canada they have a good five or ten year start. For whatever reasons, having much to do with early definition of identity, it was among the French Canadians and, first of all, in Quebec that Canada began to define itself articulately in the arts. "The playwright is the spokesman for the nation," said Gratien Gelinas in an interview nearly ten years ago. "It is through the process of viewing ourselves as we really are, or synthesizing and crystallizing who we really are, that we in the end become ourselves." In that same interview, Gelinas compared English and French Canada's attitudes toward art in general – but particularly toward theatrical creativity – to the attitudes of a young man and his kid brother toward romance. The young man is enthralled by the passionate scenes in a movie, for instance, Gelinas explained, while the kid brother turns his nose up at all that silly stuff. And the older brother says, "But just give him a few more years."

Well, these few years have now passed, and in English Canada we are engaged in a passionate affair, or English Canada is engaged in a passionate affair with its theatrical creators. This creativity as yet only amounts to the topsoil of talent and expertise, a top soil that is every moment in danger of being washed away by this golden stream that continuously flows from the south. But while this topsoil was developing, we neglected to cultivate it. Right now we cannot supply enough new and good material, even for the live theatre companies that have multiplied throughout the century, throughout the country. Sorry. Here we come to the crux of the whole problem with television drama in this country. Neglected cultivation. Television drama is normally intrinsically connected with theatre and draws its forces from the theatre and the film industry. But in Canada, dramaturgy is still in its infancy, and the film industry, in spite of some valiant efforts, again firstly in Quebec, is almost nonexistent. So television's usual sources of material are not here. A truly national television drama program of broad and popular scope needs a minimum of 100 to 130 hours of material annually. Of this, not more than 15 to 20 per cent can be taken from already existing play and short story adaptations.

Now, may I point out to you that in Yugoslavia the television network produces 300 hours of original drama a year. In Hungary they put out ten feature films every year and twenty films for television. They're very poor countries. In Canada, we do barely seventy hours a year. Seventy hours. That's an incredibly low amount. There's a general misunderstanding that the CBC could go right out there and get all the stuff because it's out on the street. And it's true that there is tremendous talent in the country, and there is a tremendous interest on the part of young writers to create for television, but there are no channels. There are no means by which this talent and this desire to create, to produce something totally and specifically and deliberately Canadian, can be developed and trained. We have not been in the habit of thinking in terms of training. We have been importing people forever and a day. Do you realize that the CBC does not train directors, television directors or film directors. It's a corporation with a budget of $300 million a year, and not for the last ten years did they pay any attention to training directors, tape directors, film directors, writers, anyone like that. How on earth they thought they'd be able to produce programs without some kind of continuous and consistent training program, I really don't know. But we are suffering grievously from this neglect right now.

There was a golden age of Canadian television. It's not a myth. Indeed, there was a time when Canadian television did produce a considerable body of very good dramas. These included both adaptations of classical dramas and also original material. But most of the people – involved in the starring – left the country, little by little. And the corporation neither took steps to retain them here nor cared that there be some kind of an aftergrowth. So the flowering just stopped. Most people went with Sydney Newman to the BBC, and the renaissance of important television drama began in England. Today, we have in Canada very few experienced writers for television. Practically no tape directors – because they were not trained over the last ten years – who have sufficient maturity, experience, and skill, and taste, and judgment to produce really good tape dramas. Those who were capable have mostly gone elsewhere; very few have returned.

Now, should we get into the field of training these people? If we do, what are we training for? Unless there is a commitment from our national broadcasting system to enlarge and enrich its programs and unless we can make sure then that there is enough scope and field of endeavour for these people we train, they will once again be forced to leave because they will have acquired skills that they cannot possibly use here. It's a circle that can be either vicious or inspiring. Now, there's a facile solution. If there are no writers, directors, and experienced television actors, then we need only turn abroad for our supplies. And forget about any ambitions of national self-definition through this most powerful of all identity-making media. But if we do decide to train and retain a backlog of creative writers – imagine that – and film and tape drama makers, then a whole new field lies before us, for practically the whole field of our history and self-image lies as yet untouched, undeveloped, waiting to be explored, cultivated, and made fruitful. The work to be done offers a fantastic challenge.

When I came to the CBC, I was told that the corporation was embarking on a new policy involving an enormous growth in drama. A growth whose focus I could see as the development of just such self-awareness. Drama was to be increased over the next five years from 70 to 120 or 130 hours yearly. This policy has now been abandoned. The reason it has been abandoned is that it's cheaper to buy foreign-made products. You can buy an hour and a half show for $12,000 or $15,000. To produce the same show in Canada would cost $140,000, and the reason is simple. The foreign show, which costs an average of $250,000 to produce in Hollywood, has already covered its costs and presumably made a considerable profit in the 250-million-person market in its country of origin. Whatever the Hollywood makers can get for what they sell here is pure gravy. So naturally they will sharply undercut our native market. Similarly, you can buy an American half-hour situation comedy for $5,000 to $7,000. To produce a Canadian half-hour, it costs $60,000.

You see, in the States, there is a fantastic industry. People invest. There is a huge manure pile of programs, and out of it comes the few exceptional pieces that the networks buy there and then we re-buy. Once again, if the CBC means business, if it is really going to develop native drama, then it has to go at it in a big way. The budget of the English drama department in Canada, which is there to produce seventy hours of drama, is less than Universal Studios spent on seven movies-of-the-week. If we want our own stuff, we'll have to pay for it. If we are not paying for it, we should stop titillating our writers, our public, our directors, and forget about it. You can't do it in a half-assed way. Either you do it properly, or you don't do it.

I have a feeling that we must do it. We really have no alternatives, it seems to me, unless we want our airwaves inundated by American and British products. And it's a decision that is not in the hands of the CBC. It is in the hands of Parliament; it's in the hands of the people of this country. If we want to be culturally independent, if we want to express ourselves, then we have to do it by paying for it, and we cannot do it on the cheap.

There is also the problem of what we are going to produce. What are the kind of things that we should be doing on television? Obviously, we have to do situation comedies. We have to do soap operas. We have to do classical plays. We have to do one-shot affairs, one-shot plays. Now, in the past season we have produced a kind of a soap opera. We are trying to produce a soap opera because, apparently, it is a genre that people enjoy, and through it, through the genre, we can say a lot of things about the country. Whether we have been successful or not, I really don't know, but it's an interesting thing to do. We have produced one-hour anthologies, plays, individual pieces, and here we have been extremely successful. We have produced hour-and-a-half plays mainly taken from the theatre because these plays were successful in the theatre. Because they are important. Some of them are good, some of them are not so good, but they should be shown to a lot of Canadians, and we have done that, and the response, again, has been exceptionally encouraging.

Next season we are starting a situation comedy called *King of Kensington*. It tries to reflect the country week by week. It's going to be recorded on a Thursday, and hopefully we can show it the next Monday. We are doing six hour-and-a-half plays, things like, *Of the Fields Lately*, *Lulu Street* by Ann Henry, a new play called *Fellowship* by Michael Tate, *An Enemy of the People*, *Captain of Kopenick*, and a play called *The Marriage of Mississippi*. We are planning hour-long shows. We are doing an hour on the trial of Tim Buck. We are doing an hour on Nelly McClung. We are doing *Six War Years*. We are doing the *Trial of Woodsworth*. We are doing some comedies by young writers. We are planning to do a series about Canadian history called *Strange Empire* based on the book of the same title, which deals with Riel and the West in a new kind of a way, in a very exciting kind of way, and all of this needs support. All of this needs an intelligent and articulate audience.

It seems to me that, in this country, most people will voice their opinion only when there is something to complain about. Nobody really supports, and I think there needs to be constant support, critical, but we need support. When Sydney Newman went to the BBC and started doing plays that involved real situations, real people, reflecting the country, he had great flack from the Midlands and all over England, and he organized a group of people called "Friends of Adult Television," and every time they were going to do something where they expected any kind of a flack from the vicar of Lower Chiswick or whatever, there were two hundred letters coming in and saying that this is the most marvellous thing that these people have seen, and within a couple of years, the public got used to looking at these things and the great BBC armchair-theatre television drama came into being.

We need exactly the same kind of support here. The drama department is very important within the CBC because, in a very simple way, in a very emotional way, it can present the problems of this country, the joys of it, the pleasures of it, to an audience. Drama that is accessible. Drama that would arouse, create interest, at times disturb. But it cannot be done without a group of people who keep saying, "We want this. We want more of it. We'll come along with you on this voyage of discovery." Because that is what we are embarking on. If there is pioneering left in this country – and there is, I believe – it is this tremendous pioneering voyage of discovery into our own psyche led by artists, the wagon train into the interior of the Canadian being. That is what we are talking about, and it cannot be done without support. We must organize. We must try to make the Canadian Broadcasting Corporation a public-service organization. Try to free it from the terrible and obscene – in my mind – commercial kind of a cast that it still has.

I was ill last week. I was in bed for a whole week, and I looked at television all the time – and I was horrified. I was horrified because a documentary on the starving people in Ethiopia was interrupted for an advertisement for dog and cat food. Because the Vietnam terror was bookended by shampoo advertisements that hailed this new shampoo because it had milk in it. And I think that is obscene. That is the ultimate obscenity. The kind of cheap, mindless violence for which we pay and that we put on our networks because it brings profit is immoral, and no public network should get mixed up in that kind of immorality. We can get what we want. But we can get it only through political action. The CBC cannot from one day to another turn into a public-service broadcasting system because the CBC needs the $50 million annually that could make it into that, or maybe even $100 million. But if you think how important this image-making, myth-making machine is, what it could do for this country, surely that is not too great an expenditure.

A fellow Winnipegger, Marshall McLuhan, said, "We shape our tools and then our tools shape us." Here is the most potent, most important tool that we have, and we allow it to shape us in a way that is not to our liking. We allow it to be an instrument of cultural imperialism to which we acquiesce; we allow this to happen. I have talked about the possibility of this country disappearing and becoming part of the United States, but I don't think that there will need to be a forceful takeover. We will just crumple. We will just lean gently and comfortably into the arms of the Americans. Why? Because we are being infiltrated, and we are paying for the infiltration. Because our school children across the country think that Truman and Churchill were Canadian prime ministers. Because they think that *All in the Family* really is a Canadian program. Because they think that Gerald Ford is the head of the Liberal Party or something. This is what is going on. And we have the tools to say what we want to say. We have the tools to communicate what we want to communicate, yet we don't use them, and we will only be able to use them if we, the people, demand that we need this instrument to express ourselves and are willing to pay for it. It's worth paying for. Very little money is required.

I envision three million people across the country sitting down in front of their television sets every Sunday night and then writing to the people in Parliament, to the CBC, that they like what we're doing, or sometimes don't like what we're doing, and asking us for more of this and more of that but, above all, acting as a vital force in returning the CBC to the people, to Canadians, in getting the CBC to create an organization where the best brains and the best hearts of the country are working toward national unity and toward creating an exciting network, a public-service network. Only through support can this happen.

JOHN HIRSCH, theatre director and administrator, made an indelible mark on the development of theatre in Canada. In Winnipeg, he co-founded the country's first regional theatre, the Manitoba Theatre Centre, and became the company's first artistic director. He went on to become co-director, associate director, and finally sole artistic director of the Stratford Festival. Between his two stints in Stratford, John Hirsch became the head of CBC television drama. His projects were by no means limited to these institutions, however. He oversaw productions throughout Canada – at the National Arts Centre, Toronto Arts Productions, Young People's Theatre, and the Shaw Festival – as well as abroad. He taught theatre at Yale University and was a visiting lecturer at other American universities.

John Hirsch became an Officer of the Order of Canada in 1967. His productions won a number of awards in the United States, including the Obie Award, the Outer Circle Critics' Award, and the Drama Critics' Award. John Hirsch died in 1989.

13

History and Social Change:
Some Myths and Realities

GUY ROCHER, 1976

PART ONE

I am a sociologist who has spent a large proportion of his life studying and writing on the evolution of Quebec within the Canadian and North American context. In various ways, Quebec has been my laboratory because I have been sometimes puzzled, at other times optimistic, and at some other times disturbed and concerned by what was going on both within that society and within its relationships with its broader environment. Moreover, it has happened at some points in time that I have been both an actor in the change that was taking place and an observer of that change. For instance, as a member of the Royal Commission of Inquiry on Education, the so-called Parent Commission, I tried to understand the main trends of the evolution of the Quebec educational system in the past, the role it played in the history of French Canada, the factors that both shaped it in the past and impeded its evolution at the beginning of the twentieth century. At the same time, my colleague-commissioners and I were looking into the future in order to propose the outlines of a new educational system that would be more in line with the type of society that we can imagine and hope for in the future. To me, this experience was both applied sociology and policy making, one feeding the other and calling for the other.

Therefore, with this experience as a background, I thought at first that I should take this opportunity to explain once again the recent evolution of Quebec and discuss some of the issues raised by its future. But after working at this task for a while, I developed a strong reaction against what I was doing. Several times in the past, I have complained about the fact that we, Quebec sociologists, were generally bound to speak only about Quebec when we were invited to the other Canadian provinces, to the United States, and to Europe. Never or almost never were we invited to deal with any other, broader topic, and never were we invited as plain sociologists. It seemed that we were labelled forever as Quebec sociologists. I remember, for instance, a couple of years ago, attending a seminar with a dozen Quebec sociologists at one of the Ontario universities, where our colleagues had organized a one-term-long seminar on Quebec society. And we finally reacted very negatively and overtly against the fact that we were always invited to talk only about Quebec, and never as sociologists who were also interested in other topics of a more general nature.

But this time, the choice of the topic was left entirely to me. Yet I was again reacting as a Quebec sociologist. Hence, when for the first time as far as I could remember, I was invited without any specification as to the subject that I was expected to deal with, I found myself falling back on the traditional topic of the Quebec sociologist. This time, I could not blame anybody but myself for not taking this opportunity to feel free to present the subject of my choice. This, by the way, is a good illustration of how sociologists belong to the society that they study, and how they are themselves submitted to the expectations of others or to the expectations that they think others have, expectations that create what we call the social control and the cultural patterns of the society.

Now, instead of coping once again with the evolving situation in Quebec, which, I don't deny, might be interesting, I thought that I should engage in what might be for me a new venture, consisting paradoxically of presenting a topic that is of immediate interest to me.

But, as will be seen, the reflections of a sociologist, even when he wants them to be as general as possible, are never completely disconnected from the actual society he is living in. As a matter of fact, if I have been concerned over the past years with the meaning of history, this interest sprang directly from the experience I had of a society like Quebec's, which was evolving very rapidly. Events like the so-called Quiet Revolution in Quebec, the protest movements of various sorts among the youth in North America and Europe during the 1960s, the growing number of independent nations, the impact of socialism as well as of nationalism in the modern world, the constant threat of the atomic destruction of millions of people, the expanding areas of influence of the socialist ideologies: All of this has served as a background to the questions that have progressively become the main concerns on my mind. The questions all those events, and many others, raise, it seems to me, can be put in the following words: Are we sure that the history of humankind has some meaning? How can we be sure, first, that it has a meaning and, second, that it has the meanings that we say or that we think it has?

These are questions that philosophy more than sociology has dealt with in the past. But the more I come to know sociology, the more I must admit that it has been deeply influenced by the philosophers, particularly the philosophers of history, who have been wrestling with those questions. Names like Auguste Comte, Hegel, Karl Marx, Herbert Spencer, Spengler, and Sorokin are regarded by us as the forefathers of our discipline.

I think it is extremely difficult for a person, both as an individual and as a member of a collectivity, to think of history as being meaningless and without any goal. If I can use here the word "archetype" in the sense that Carl Jung gave to that word, which refers to a representation that goes back to a remote past and is very largely shared among humankind to the point that it now seems to be inherited, I think we can say that this idea of the meaningfulness of human history is one of the great archetypes that is to be found in all societies and at all periods of history. Indeed, the roots of this archetype are not necessarily the same in all societies, probably because we cannot go back far enough in the past to uncover the common roots of this widely spread archetype. Each civilization has a specific history of the meaning of its own history and/or of the history of humankind. Here I will trace what I think to be the main historical roots of that archetype in the Western world. I will more specifically identify three great currents of thought that have fed this archetype: they are the Judeo-Christian religions, scientific positivism, and the socialist ideologies. Let me now expand on each of them.

The Christian religions, whether they are Catholicism or Protestantism or Oriental Christianism, have all inherited from the Jewish religion a profound conviction that the history of humankind has its meaning in its relationship with either the will of God or the kingdom of God, of which it is a part and in which it finds its purpose and its end. Before Christ, the most meaningful events taking place, from that perspective, were the difficult and uneasy relationships between God and his chosen people: the people of Israel. Obviously, at the time they took place, those relationships between God and this not very numerous and hardly known people were kept unknown to the very large majority of the men and women who lived outside of Israel at that time, and they had no historical importance and no historical significance at all in the sense that they had no practical immediate impact on the great historical events of that time. The evolution of great civilizations of that period, in Mesopotamia, Egypt, the Roman Empire, was untouched by the history of the relationships between Israel and God. Yet, in spite of that, the Christian tradition has magnified those relationships to the point of making them the centre of the history of the world at that time and up to now.

On the foundations of this heritage from the religion of Israel, all the Christian religions have evolved their own eschatology and their own teleology – that is,

they all have developed a more or less explicit scheme or explanation or interpretation of past history, ancient and recent, and they all have an explicit or
implicit representation of where the world is going and/or should go and why.
In the Christian tradition, the visible history of humankind is regarded as one
aspect or one dimension of the history of the kingdom of God, the latter being
partly visible and partly invisible, partly historical and partly over and above
history. Through their actions and deeds, consciously or unconsciously, human
beings have engaged in the necessary evolution of the kingdom of God, so that
one's own personal life has a meaning both in itself and through the meaning
that the history of the city of God gives to the history of the city of humankind.

Obviously, within the Christian tradition, the meaning of individual and collective history has given rise to a great variety of interpretations and has been
implemented in a great variety of types of behaviours. More than anyone else
maybe, Max Weber has demonstrated the different economic behaviours that
spring from the different conceptions of "the calling" and of the evolution of the
kingdom of God in its relation with human history to be found among three
branches of the Christian tradition of modern times: the Puritan, the Lutheran,
and the Catholic. Max Weber has especially emphasized how, among the Puritans,
the doctrine of predestination, the notion of a calling in this world, and the link
that was made between success in this world and salvation in the eternal life
contributed to developing an economic behaviour and motivation that served to
pave the way to modern capitalism. The Weberian interpretation of this historical
role of the Puritan ethic, the meaning it gave to the lives of many men and
women, individually and collectively, is far from foreign to North American
history, Canadian as well as American, past and still recent. Although Max
Weber's thesis has been challenged in many ways and has been one of the most
discussed hypotheses in the social sciences, it remains on the whole one of the
most enlightening contributions of the social scientists to the understanding of
our contemporary history.

In Quebec some historians and social scientists have shed some light on one
current of thought within the Roman Catholic Church that has been quite deeply
influential on the image that the French Canadians have developed of themselves,
of their historical calling in North America, and that has served to justify their
status and their peculiar position on the North American continent. This current
of thought was rooted in a relatively long tradition that all the historians and
social scientists who have dealt with it have not totally seen. This tradition can
be called the non-Jansenist, rigoristic branch of the French Roman Catholic
Church, which in the sixteenth and seventeenth centuries developed against
both the Gallican anti-Papist and anti-Roman ideology that was predominant at
the Court of Versailles, especially under Louis XIV and Colbert, and against

Jansenism, which was mostly centralized at Port-Royal and which represented for awhile a kind of official opposition to the court. The non-Jansenist rigorism had much in common with Jansenism, so that it has often been confused with it. But one of the main differences with Jansenism was the strong Papist component that was not to be found in Jansenism. Moreover, the non-Jansenist tradition was somewhat a secret society that was identified under the name of La Societé du Saint-Sacrement de l'Autel.

It is this non-Jansenist rigorism, strongly Papist and much more otherworldly oriented than Puritan Protestantism, that was highly influential in the Roman Catholic Church in the first period of the French colony of New France. Bishop Laval, the first bishop of Quebec, who largely contributed to shaping the Church of New France, was one of the representatives of this current of thought in New France.

In New France the Catholics belonging to that tradition were characterized by very rigoristic morals, including a strong opposition to the use of alcohol in the fur trade with the Aboriginals; they were very strongly in favour of the settlement of both the French and Aboriginals on farms, where they would all lead a good, Christian, regular life, instead of travelling across the continent and living in the woods without enough control and out of sight of the religious authorities.

For several reasons, this religious rigorism came to a clash with the Gallican ideology that was progressively taking root in New France, especially at the end of the seventeenth century. And it was the latter, the Gallican ideology, that finally became the dominant, official position of both the church and the state in New France by the end of the French regime. Yet the non-Jansenist, rigoristic tradition always remained in the background, mostly among some groups of the clergy, and it inspired what might be called the rightist wing of the Roman Catholic Church throughout the eighteenth and the nineteenth centuries. By the second half of the nineteenth century, it was this rightist wing of the Roman Catholic Church that had become dominant in Quebec, although it was still at times strongly opposed by the liberals of that period, who were largely inspired by the anticlerical and more or less openly atheist French intellectuals. But the rightist wing triumphed over its opponents by the middle of the nineteenth century. It was therefore the rigoristic, Catholic tradition that inspired the clerical domination of the Roman Catholic Church in French Canada, starting with the second half of the nineteenth century and lasting about one century – that is, until the second half of the twentieth century. And one aspect of this domination of the Roman Catholic Church was the so-called ruralist image of the calling of French Canada that became predominant by the end of the nineteenth century and at the beginning of the twentieth – that is, during the period of the industrial revolution in Quebec. As we know well, the industrial revolution in Quebec was not initiated by the French Canadians. They were not at all instrumental in that revolution, which was effected largely through British, and later English Canadian, and finally American capital and technicians, while the French Canadians were providing mostly the labour force – and still more a cheap labour force. It was to justify this situation that the idea was developed that urban and industrial life was identified somehow with materialism, which was itself related to Protestantism. The Catholics, for their part, were said to be inspired by a more spiritual view of life and were consequently to stay out of the big cities and the manufactures and to keep on with the traditional way of life that had evolved on the farms and in the rural parish. The latter became the ideal model of French Canadian, Catholic individuals and their collectivity.

Thus some sort of a philosophy or a theology of history applied to the French Canadians was made explicit by some theologians at the beginning of the twentieth century. And this theology of history had a long-standing influence on the economic and political attitudes of the French Canadians up to the 1950s or the 1960s, and it is probably still influential in some quarters of the French Canadian population.

These are just a few illustrations of the impact of the theological representation of history and of the theological interpretation of the evolution of humankind and of specific societies or groups within society. This is history as seen *sub specie aeternitatis* – that is, as it is supposed to be seen from God's viewpoint. Starting with the Jewish tradition, as I noted earlier, there is a long unbroken tradition of such a representation, which goes through the Roman Empire, the Middle Ages, the Reformation, the Counter-Reformation, and up to our times. Bishop Bossuet, the great writer of the French classical period, who was also the prestigious preacher at the French Court in the seventeenth century, has probably made more explicit than anyone else this representation of history as the implementation of God's will.

While the theological interpretation of history has a long tradition that goes back several thousand years, the positivist, or scientific, tradition is much shorter. Or, at least, this is how it appears to us because in the Western world we still believe that the beginning of science goes back only as far as the fifteenth or sixteenth century, or even the seventeenth century, with the end of the Middle Ages and the beginning of the so-called Renaissance. In fact, it is certain that scientific knowledge was already of prime importance among the Greek philosophers some 2,200 years ago and that it might have been quite lively in at least some periods of the Egyptian civilization. But it happens that throughout history the scientific tradition has been more broken, less continuous, and less ubiquitous than the theological and religious one. There have been periods in the history of the Western world – for instance, part of the Middle Ages, especially the low

364 Guy Rocher

Middle Ages, from about the sixth or seventh century to the eleventh century – when scientific knowledge almost disappeared or at least was kept in the background and could not be practiced in the open. In those conditions, scientific knowledge was not predominant enough to have some impact on the vision of history that people of those centuries had.

Starting with the sixteenth century, the role and importance of scientific knowledge came into the open, although it was not thoroughly accepted by the dominating intelligentsia of that time. But thanks to the methodology that could be developed and to the increasing success of research in the natural sciences, and also to the industrial use that could be made of some knowledge, science came to be regarded as one of the great achievements of modern humans and more and more as the main source of inspiration for the understanding of the world – at least of the physical world, the world of the natural order. Starting with the Renaissance, science had finally come to be more or less accepted as long as it was dealing only with the natural order, leaving the soul and the life of human beings and their society outside of its realm — that is, in the universe of the higher realities, which have lives either by themselves or through the grace of God and which should never be confused with the natural order. It was clearly understood that the scientific laws could apply to the natural order, where the hard rule of necessity and determinism was the only one that existed. But human beings, it was thought, had inherited either from God, or from the development of their intelligence, or from both, a freedom and a higher destiny that was supposed to put them aside, making them an intermediate being between animals and angels, the king of the creation, the masterpiece of God's creation in this world.

It was a great shock when it first came to be said in the Christian world of the seventeenth and eighteenth centuries that humans were not that superior being that they had been thought to be and that their nature and fate needed to be reconsidered in the light of science and scientific knowledge, without any theological or metaphysical postulate about their superiority. I personally think that this new statement of humankind took place mainly on three occasions of great significance. One was the publication in France of the so-called *Encyclopédie,* which gave rise to the movement of the *encyclopédistes,* the philosophers of the new materialistic approach to the nature and meaning of humankind and, as a consequence, to the meaning of its history. Indeed, the *encyclopédistes* were regarded as the worst threat to religion (the Catholic Church) and to the theology of history that was then still dominant. It was under D'Alembert and Diderot that this vast undertaking took place, which comprised thirty-three volumes that were supposed to be the sum of all the progress that scientific knowledge had made at that time in all the disciplines. People like Voltaire, Montesquieu, Rousseau, and many others were associated with that publication as both contributors and supporters. But summing up the scientific knowledge of the time was really only one aspect of the *Encyclopédie*, the other being the presentation of a vision of the world that was broad enough to take the place of the out-dated religious perspective. It is in this sense that the *Encyclopédie* gave rise to a school of thought, that of the *encyclopédistes,* who were proposing a new vision of humankind and a reinterpretation of its history.

The *Encyclopédie* was published between 1751 and 1766. Some seventy-five years later, a second great event took place in the intellectual life of the Western world, with the publication of Auguste Comte's *Cours de philosophie positive* (1830–1842). It was an important event because this philosopher gave a clear formulation to the new philosophy of history that had been kept mostly latent, although clear enough, in the *Encyclopédie*. Auguste Comte stated his famous "Law of the Three States," according to which the history of knowledge in each discipline was clearly divided into three stages: the theological one, where the foundations of all explanation were to be found in the role and action of gods or spirits or some sort of supernatural beings or forces; the metaphysical stage, a transitory one during which the explanation by supernatural agents was replaced by the recourse to abstractions, ideas, intellectual constructions that were a product of the imagination of the philosophers; and, finally, the positivist stage, where the explanation is looked for by observing the reality as it is, using an adequate methodology, in order to uncover the natural laws that may provide the only true explanation. According to Auguste Comte, all sciences have successively been through these three stages but not necessarily at the same time and at the same tempo. Now, he stated, the time had come for the sciences of humankind to achieve at last their positivist stage; after all, the natural sciences had done so. That is how Auguste Comte finally became the founder of sociology: He coined the word for that new science of humankind, first calling it social physics, the purpose of which was to lay down the foundations of a positivist – that is, a scientific – knowledge of humankind, of its history. Auguste Comte was convinced that the real root of all social problems was ignorance of the scientific laws that govern human society and its history. Just as humankind had gained control of nature when it finally discovered the natural laws, humans would also be able to control their own society and their own history as soon as they became aware of the social laws. Thus Auguste Comte was the founder not only of sociology, but also of what he called a new ethics, which was essentially based on the scientific knowledge of human reality, of its limitations, imperatives, and possibilities. Auguste Comte was therefore the most explicit philosopher of the scientific interpretation of the history of humankind, even though he was neither the only one nor the first one.

But Auguste Comte was probably still more important in that he paved the way to the third event that was to take place in the second half of the nineteenth century, which was the development of evolutionism. At first, evolutionism was not a philosophy but a series of scientific discoveries on the history of living species and on the transmission of acquired biological characteristics. The Austrian botanist Mendel, whose writings were discovered long after he died, the French zoologist Lamarck, and the English biologist Darwin, the latter being probably the best known now, are the three names to be mentioned here of scientists who discovered the main laws of the evolution of living organisms, which provided the key to the history of life over millions and millions of years. Now, for the first time in the Christian civilization, the natural world did not appear as the outcome of a creation that had taken place according to the word of the Bible, but as the outcome of a long evolution that was not made up of mere accidents but that followed specific laws that could now be clearly stated.

It is significant that those men of science did not themselves extend their conclusions to include the realm of human beings. They had been dealing with flowers and plants and animals. But the conclusion was rapidly reached by some other thinkers that humans could not be kept outside that evolution. This was a very important step. Four hundred years before that, Copernicus and Galileo had clearly established that the sun was not revolving around the earth but that the earth was part of the solar system. As we have all learned, Copernicus and Galileo were thus making a drastic change not only in our knowledge of this world, but maybe still more in the image that practically all the preceding generations had had about humankind, its place in the universe, its destiny in this world. It is precisely because Galileo was regarded as a threat to the dominant theological ideology of his time that he was condemned not to publish his discoveries. It was an intellectual and spiritual revolution of the same size that took place in the second half of the nineteenth century with evolutionism. Now, for the first time, it clearly appeared that the evolution of the natural order had not been revolving around the appearance of humans in this world as superior beings of some other nature. Humans were part and members of the natural order; they were one species among the animals, with whom they were related by a common history, and the same rules or laws of evolution applied to them as well.

And not only did the laws of evolution apply to *Homo sapiens* as an animal organism, but they also applied, so it was said, to the human mind and to human societies. Among several others, it is surely the name of the British philosopher Herbert Spencer that must be mentioned here as the thinker who bridged the gap to include human beings, their souls, their history, and their future in the universal processes of evolution. Herbert Spencer was convinced that there was only one great universal law of evolution, which applied altogether to the physical world and to the evolution of human beings and their societies from the most primitive time down to our own time. Spencer's great universal law was based on the observation that the more advanced species – that is, those species that were more mobile, better adapted to movement and change, and that were therefore in a better position to survive – were those characterized by a greater heterogeneity of their parts. According to Spencer, it was therefore possible to specify the age of all beings by the degree of heterogeneity or differentiation that they exhibited. This law was the real explanation, according to Spencer, for the survival of the fittest, which had been observed but which was regarded as a special law of the great general law of evolution. According to Spencer, this law could be applied to humans as individuals, the adult having a much more differentiated mind and psychology than the infant and the young child. Spencer also thought that the same difference could be observed between the so-called civilized human and the primitive, the latter having a rather simplified intellectual view of nature, life, and society. Finally, the same law of evolution also applied to societies, which had been through a long process of evolution, starting with the loosely organized primitive tribes, where a certain form of communism was the norm; which had practically no political authority and still less political structure, very little hierarchy; and where marriage and private property were practically unknown. Compared to those primitive and homogeneous societies, the modern Western industrial society was regarded by Spencer as the other extreme: the complex and differentiated society, made up of a great number of different parts, groups, and associations. But Spencer was convinced that this modern society was only a transition to something else, which he described as a completely individualistic society with practically no political authority, a society that will be differentiated to the point that each individual will have the freedom to be what he or she wants and to behave according to his or her own moral standards, which, Spencer thought, will be more and more generally good without necessarily being the same. It is because of those convictions that Spencer has been the extreme representative of the liberalism of the nineteenth century. Liberals of that time, especially in the United Kingdom, were strongly opposed to any intervention of the state as well as of the church in the lives of individuals because they were convinced that the ideal society would be one in which each member had a mature moral conscience, which would result from general education, higher standards of living, and a greater political consciousness.

This extension of evolutionism to humankind and its history, which was also called social Darwinism, was based on some quite simple postulates. First, there was the postulate that change was necessarily bringing progress because change was necessarily a transition from a more homogenous and a less well-structured stage to a more heterogeneous and therefore better-adapted stage. Long before Spencer, Auguste Comte had divided sociology into what he called the sociology of order – that is, the sociology that studied the social structures – and what he called the sociology of progress, which was the sociological study of history and change. Second, social Darwinism was based on the postulate of unilinear evolution. That is to say, one general rule of evolution and a consequence of the idea of progress was that change was taking place along a straight line that was always pointing in the direction of progress. Consequently, in Spencer's view, the primitive societies were all vestiges of some points along that line. For various reasons, those societies had stopped somewhere along the line of evolution. It was therefore useful to study them, especially in a comparative way, because they provided us with precise knowledge on the successive steps through which the human society has evolved from the beginning of human consciousness to our times. The third postulate is that both long-term evolution and history have a meaning that stems from the pattern of evolution, that can be observed for the past, and that will necessarily be followed in the future. Of course, it is always possible for humans, as it has been in the past for humans and for other living organisms, to resist the line of evolution; it is always possible to counteract or to oppose oneself to the trend of the future. But, as we can learn from the past, those who do that are in danger of being left off somewhere along the line of evolution, while those who follow the right pattern of evolution will be better equipped for the future and will move ahead toward more and more progress.

This conception of human evolution and of the meaning of history has probably been best exposed by Herbert Spencer. But it did not die with Spencer, and it did not end with the nineteenth century. Far from that, it is still very largely shared in the modern world; I would even say that it is now part of the background of our Western culture, among the intellectuals as well as among the population at large. Of course, it is not necessarily expressed in the same terms as those used by Spencer. But the general idea of social Darwinism is still well alive in our minds. Let me give one example of it. I think it is clear enough that the so-called Quiet Revolution that took place in Quebec, starting somewhere in the 1950s and becoming visible mostly in the 1960s, was inspired by an ideology of progress that was based on some more-or-less explicit social Darwinism. Throughout the 1960s it was widely said in Quebec that we, Quebecers, needed to make a certain number of changes in order not to be kept outside of the North American industrial society. It was said time and time again that we were underdeveloped and poor because we had not taken the right steps in the right direction. Education in Quebec was especially regarded as backward, misadapted to the modern world, the vestige of a preindustrial society. Educational reform was therefore one necessary step toward the improvement of our society and a better adaptation to the requirements of the society of tomorrow. It was assumed that if we did not undertake this reform, Quebec and especially the French Canadians in Quebec, were condemned to stay where they were on the line of evolution, leaving to others the advantages that come to those who follow the patterns of evolution and change, the advantages that the industrial and postindustrial societies seem to promise.

More generally, this applies not only to Quebec but to all the emerging nations of the Third World. Whether they use the socialist model, or the capitalist one, or a mixed one that they think will be more adapted to their situation, the emerging nations of the Third World have been very deeply influenced by the social Darwinist ideology, even though they will never refer to that ideology explicitly. But it is surely one remnant of the colonial regime that the emerging nations have been profoundly influenced by their white colonial administrators, whose ideals they now use as models and norms to measure their change and to make plans for the future.

We can therefore say here that some apparently modest scientific discoveries of the eighteenth and nineteenth centuries provided the main elements for the new ideology of change and history that was to compete in the twentieth century with the old theological vision of the world. Indeed, the latter is not necessarily dead; it is alive and still finds expression in many ways. But it has been replaced more or less completely in certain quarters by a very strong and deeply entrenched ideology of change based on a social Darwinist conception of the world, physical, organic, psychological, and social.

But the situation is still more complex due to the presence of a third ideology of great importance: the socialist interpretation of humankind and of history. In a way, we can say that it is the youngest of all three because it took shape only in the first half of the nineteenth century in some European countries, especially England, Germany, and France. But one could also bring a good deal of evidence to prove that the socialist ideology has roots that go back much further in the history of the Western world. I don't think, however, that we should go into that argument here.

Socialism has one characteristic in common with the evolutionist ideology: It is a secular representation of the world and its history. On that ground, both ideologies are in complete opposition to the theological one. Neither of the two has any otherworldly dimension. Still more, as presented and developed by some thinkers, both were and still are, at least to a very large extent, highly critical of the theological ideology. Conversely, representatives of the latter have condemned successively each of the former in vigorous terms. I think that the Roman Catholic Church has been especially vocal in doing so. For instance, I remember that in 1952, when I joined the faculty of Laval University, there was an annual religious ceremony that took place in the chapel of the old seminary of Quebec on December 8 – that is, on the day of the Feast of the Immaculate Conception –

which had been defined as the anniversary of Laval University. During that ceremony, the rector or president of the university, who indeed was a priest or a monseigneur, used to read in front of us and in our name a pledge called the antimodernist pledge, which was a detailed condemnation of all the heresies and fallacies and misconceptions that were not allowed to be taught in a Catholic university. Of course, it was understood that all members of the faculty were Roman Catholics or at least Christians. And I remember that the authorities of the university were proud to say that in the Faculty of Medicine, one highly respected professor was an atheist, which proved that we were rather broadminded!

But it was always mentioned that this professor was a Frenchman and that he was a recognized authority in his field. Moreover, although he did not attend the religious ceremony of the December 8, he was respectful of the Roman Catholic Church and of the sectarian character of Laval University. I don't know exactly when this oath was read for the last time, but I can say that it was still taken quite seriously in 1952. Thereafter, it started to be questioned more and more as a vestige of out-dated positions of the Church, and it was finally discarded. But I must emphasize that my appointment to the faculty and the gradual disappearance of this ritual were mere coincidence! As to the anti-Communist position of the Roman Catholic Church, it is surely too well known to be documented here. While the antipositivist position of the Roman Catholic Church is now less openly asserted, anti-Communism is still predominant. In 1952 an atheist could be tolerated at Laval University. But an openly Marxist historian, or economist, or philosopher would have been unthinkable, surely at Laval and at the University of Montreal, and probably also in all our Canadian universities. But in our universities, at least, the main reason was not only that Marxism threatened the existing social order, but much more that it was a materialist philosophy of life that had been severely condemned by the Vatican and by our bishops.

One reason why the Roman Catholic Church and Christians in general have been so strongly antisocialist and anti-Communist is that socialism, and especially Marxism, is a total philosophy of life, much more so than positivism and social Darwinism. Dialectical materialism, which can be regarded as the core and the most highly generalized expression of socialist thought, covers altogether a representation of the natural world, the position of human beings in the cosmic order, and a main key for the understanding of human history. Just like the universal law of evolution was regarded by Spencer as the final word to explain the world, so it is with dialectical materialism with regard to the socialist outlook on the world. On the other hand, dialectical materialism is not exactly a law, in the positivist sense of the word. It is rather a general epistemological and methodological foundation that is basic altogether to our knowledge of world history and policy making, and it is at the same time the main rule for practical action, both individual and collective. In that sense, dialectical materialism is a totalitarian view of humankind and its history, because it embraces the totality of humankind and offers a definite blueprint for its future.

But paradoxically enough, it is also through the theory of dialectical materialism that socialism has three characteristics in common with the two preceding ideologies. The first one, which is of great importance for our purposes, is that they all share optimistic views on the future of humankind. The theological ideology of history can not be pessimistic about the future since its end is necessarily the kingdom of God. Evolutionist positivism, for its part, is also necessarily optimistic because it is heading toward an ever-increasing progress. As to the socialist view of the future, it forecasts the coming of a new society where alienation and injustice will progressively disappear to the extent that private property, which has been the source of all inequalities, will disappear, and also to the extent that the state, after a period of inflation with the dictatorship of the proletariat, will wither away and finally disappear.

The second characteristic that the three ideologies have in common is a certain form of fatalism. In the case of the theological ideology, humans can resist the will of God, they can oppose the will of God, but in the end the kingdom of God will necessarily triumph, the forces of evil will finally be defeated and with them all the individuals and societies that have lined up with them. In the evolutionist perspective, those individuals and societies that do not recognize or cannot recognize and follow the general laws of evolution will either disappear or be left aside, and there will be groups and collectivities as well as individuals who will progress according to the laws of change. As to the socialist ideology of history, it is based on the conviction that the capitalist society is close to its end, that it will necessarily explode and breakdown. Of course, this inevitable breaking-down of the capitalist society can be postponed or delayed by the action of some groups or by the lack of action of some other groups, but it is sure that it cannot be postponed very long. And a new classless society will finally succeed to the dictatorship of the proletariat.

Finally, along with this fatalism, all three ideologies make some room for the intervention of human beings. The theological ideology calls for the action of individuals of good will, those who have understood the message of God and who struggle in various ways for the kingdom of God. In the evolutionist perspective, human beings must actively seek the knowledge they need in order to understand the great laws of change and to master history as well as nature according to those laws. The socialist ideology holds that humans not only must get the right objective knowledge, but must also get organized and fight to bring about the necessary revolutions that will change the power structure to the advantage of those who have been exploited up to now: that is, the working class and the proletariat.

In Canada, like in all North America, the place where the socialist ideology is best represented is probably our colleges and universities, much more than the working class and the proletariat. I think there are good reasons for this, the main one being probably that socialism, and especially Marxist socialism, is presently the sole coherently critical interpretation of capitalist society and the most promising blueprint for a better world of tomorrow. And in an advanced industrial society like the North American one, some intellectuals and some youth are among those who are the most sensitive to the ideal of justice and to the need for drastic social changes. But at the same time, this means that in our country this ideology is still only very mildly influential, to say the least, compared to the two others. But the same cannot be said of the rest of the world, where the socialist ideology under different forms (Marxist-Leninist, Maoist, Stalinist, non-Marxists, etc.) now has a very large audience and is one of the main factors that will determine the history of the coming decades, if not of the coming centuries.

But I don't want to leave the impression that I believe that the socialist ideology is the only living one or that it is the dominant one. On the contrary, I do believe that all three ideologies have a very profound influence on our modern thinking. To speak only of the Western world, it is altogether still deeply Christian in its way of thinking, profoundly positivist and evolutionist in its conception of the world and of history, and more and more socialist in its representation of the present society and its future. Although quite divergent from one another, and conflicting on some points, these three ideologies represent three aspects of modern humans that are not necessarily well integrated but that co-exist in our personalities and in our collective minds.

I think that what I have just said will now help me to explain in what sense I think that these three representations of history are three forms of what I now call mythical thinking. One thing must be very clear: The word "myth" does not necessarily have a negative meaning; it does not necessarily mean something false or untrue. As far back in the past as we can go, human beings have always used mythologies to explain to themselves where they come from, what they are, where they are going, and not only themselves as individuals but also and maybe still more the society or collectivity to which they belong. It is through these mythologies that human life has had any meaning at all for billions and billions of men and women in all types of societies and cultures and civilizations, under all latitudes, and in a great variety of climates. I do believe that these mythologies are essential to human beings. We are, at least to our knowledge, the only animal that has developed this abstract world of myths and mythologies because we are the only animal that feels the strong need to give some meaning to life, to our presence in this world, and that needs some views on what the future will be for us or our descendants.

Although it may appear somewhat shocking, the three ideologies of history that I have outlined belong to this world of mythical thinking. For the benefit of our intelligence of the world, they put order in the otherwise chaotic past and present, and in the insecure future that lies ahead of us.

But then, the problem that they raise is the following: Is there any truth in these ideologies? Which one is closer to the truth than the others? Is the image of humankind and its history and its future that is provided by these ideologies reliable? And behind these question marks, there is one question that is more fundamental, which we finally cannot escape, and it can be phrased in very simple terms: Has human history any meaning at all? And how can we know that history has some kind of meaning?

PART TWO

Thus far I have provided a very broad overview of the three main philosophies of history that have had and still have an influence on our thinking and our vision of the world: the religious, Judeo-Christian tradition of interpretation of history; the scientific evolutionist and positivist ideology; and the socialist ideologies. I have used the words "myths" and "mythologies," and I have applied them to these three currents of thought. But I have not used these words in a derogatory manner but rather in the anthropological sense, meaning that they are broad representations of the past as well as rather coherent interpretations of the present with some kind of a blueprint for action in the future.

Let me continue by disclosing one of the main sources of inspiration for the reflections that follow. Strangely enough, the author to whom I am alluding or from whom I will borrow his *vision du monde* is not a sociologist, he is not a historian, and he is not a contemporary either. He is a philosopher who lived and wrote in the second half of the nineteenth century and whose work is still partially known: His name is Friedrich Nietzsche. In my opinion, the nineteenth century has been the greatest intellectual century of the Western world, and we still live on the heritage of the great thinkers of that century. Compared to the nineteenth century, the twentieth century is far from being as productive and as creative. I might point out that two out of the three great mythologies that I have presented – namely, the positivist evolutionist one and the socialist one – have found their expression through and have been shaped by an impressive number of thinkers of the nineteenth century. The twentieth century is surely more advanced technically than the nineteenth century, and we have surely achieved a greater control over nature now than then, to the extent that we have spoiled nature like none of the other generations before us. But the horizons of human thought have been extended by thinkers of the nineteenth century many more times than by thinkers of the twentieth century. Our century has yet to give birth to individuals of the stature of Auguste Comte, Karl Marx, Hegel, Darwin, Spencer, and Nietzsche. I would make an exception for Freud and Jung, who created the theory of the unconscious and laid the ground to psychoanalysis in the first decade of the twentieth century. But it is well known now that both Freud and Jung, especially the second, who was more explicit about it, were deeply influenced by Nietzsche, who wrote fascinating pages many years before them on the unconscious in the human being, on the interpretation of dreams, and on the symbolism of dreams.

I must admit that I have come to Nietzsche's works rather late in my life. But I have an excuse for that. Nietzsche's books, which were published at the end of the nineteenth century, were far from being bestsellers. And after his death in 1900, his works were expurgated by his sister before being published again because it had been felt that his thought was too explosive. It is only recently that Nietzsche's works have become more accessible to English- and French-speaking readers.

It is not easy to speak about Nietzsche and his influence. We do not all read the same thing in Nietzsche's works. For my part, I have been especially influenced by the general critical and skeptical approach that is characteristic of Nietzsche's thought and that goes right to the heart of the dogmas that human beings have created all around them and of which they have become prisoners although these dogmas are self-created. Nietzsche called himself the immoralist, by which he meant that he was questioning the recognized and dominant dogmas and ethics that are taken for granted, and in so doing he was recovering the freedom that human beings have lost, because this freedom is based essentially on the understanding that human beings are mainly responsible for their own lives, for their own destiny, and for their own history. In my view, Nietzsche has shaken in a very lucid and radical way the foundations of our beliefs, not only our religious beliefs as is usually thought, but also our scientific and pseudo-scientific beliefs.

For my own purposes, I want to bring forward one main lesson that I learned from Nietzsche. It has become more and more clear to me that human beings have too easily relied upon ends and purposes and objectives that were external to them in order to explain and justify their motivations and their actions. And this is especially true when we come to the interpretations that have been given to explain human history, past, present, and future. Thus in the three great interpretations of history that I have presented, the will of God, progress taken as an absolute, and the historical revolutionary role of the working class have been successively invoked as main agents and goals of history. In each case, therefore, human beings are prevented from being the main agents of their own lives and of their own history.

Behind this critical approach, one of Nietzsche's fundamental contributions to our understanding of human beings is his assertion that human beings have been afraid to recognize their loneliness and the consequences of their loneliness. It is in order to protect themselves against this feeling of loneliness and the panic it creates in them that human beings have had recourse to a certain number of absolute external beings or ideas whom they could say were bearing the responsibility that humans refused to assume. That is why Nietzsche contended that if human beings accepted that the God they had themselves created was now dead or rather that they had killed their own God, they would have gotten rid of the main obstacle to their acceptance of their loneliness as well as of the freedom that comes with this loneliness.

But God is only one figure that human beings have used to protect themselves against their terrifying loneliness. In Nietzsche's views, the idea of progress and all the other similar ideas put forward by science have served the same purposes. And although Nietzsche did not know Marx's works, he was well aware of the socialist tradition of thought, and, in his mind, the role attributed to the working class or to the masses has also served to disguise and to conceal human beings from themselves.

At the same time that Nietzsche was reminding us of the loneliness that is the characteristic of human experience, he was also emphasizing that human beings have more possibilities than they have been told; they are not as powerless as some philosophers and historians have wanted us to think. When human beings are finally freed from all the dogmas and when they have learned to take their own responsibilities and to shape their own destiny, they will realize that they can rely on a variety of inner resources. Standing up by themselves and taking their lives in their own hands, without any illusion of any sort about themselves, human beings will call upon resources in themselves, and it is through this liberating process that humankind can finally achieve its full destiny and its real calling.

Needless to say, Nietzsche has been regarded and denounced as one of the most threatening enemies of Christianity because he surely was the most astute and the most vocal atheist among the contemporary philosophers. His words "God is Dead" have often been taken as one of the main illustrations of the pernicious attacks against religion in our times. But it has never been really underlined how reluctantly Nietzsche, who was the son of a minister and who had been brought up in a Christian family, came to that conclusion and how threatening this statement appeared to him because of all the consequences that it brought with it. Contrary to the image that is often presented, Nietzsche was not offering this conclusion as good news but as the announcement of something like an earthquake, after which human life and the world would never be again the same as they were before. A good part of Nietzsche's works can be read as a tragic meditation on how human beings can go on living without God – that is, without all of what they have invested in the name of God and to His image and without all they have sacrificed to the idea of God. This is perhaps one of the main reasons for the tragic climate that dominates the writings of Nietzsche.

Although it may not have been underlined as much as his anti-Christian and antireligious position, Nietzsche also represented a threat to the other two ideologies, the positivist and the socialist ones. In his sweeping rejection of any a priori absolute and in his struggle to free human beings from all the ghosts that they have created and in favour of whom they have alienated their freedom and responsibilities, Nietzsche reacted strongly against the belief that science had the answer to all the questions and would provide a full blueprint for a better future for humankind. Nietzsche's attacks against positivism were even more convincing since he himself recognized that he had a positivist period in his life, when he was teaching at the University of Basel in Switzerland and in his first works.

As to the socialist ideology, it is clear that Nietzsche never had any socialist temptation because he was too entirely devoted to the development of the human individual against all the social, cultural, and ideological pressures. This respect for humankind, and his personality, led Nietzsche to adopt elitist positions that took the form of an overemphasized view of the historical power that a few enlightened men and especially a few philosophers enjoyed in modern society. This was necessarily to lead Nietzsche to the opposite pole of the current socialist tradition of thinking.

I know for sure that it is more popular these years to be a disciple of Marx than a student of Nietzsche. And I agree that there are good reasons for that. But I do believe that the Western world and the twentieth century owe a great intellectual debt to that outstanding thinker of the nineteenth century. I do know that Nietzsche has been condemned by many people not only for his atheism, but also for having inspired the German Nazi ideology and probably also some other European Fascism. But Nietzsche has been acquitted of this last charge, founded on some parts of Nietzsche's works but leaving aside the complete architecture of Nietzsche's works – which was, by the way, an advanced denunciation of Nazism and Fascism. The hypothetical fascist trends in the work of Nietzsche are not what I have in mind when I say that Nietzsche has deeply influenced our century. What I really mean is that Nietzsche's critical approach to human beings, their beliefs and myths, their philosophy of history, their more or less hypocritical morality, paved the way to the social critique of this second half of the twentieth century and had already announced the so-called counter-culture that runs parallel to the dominant culture of our societies.

In a recent and very enlightening book, the French philosopher and sociologist Henri Lefebvre, who has himself been a Marxist and one of the best interpreters of Marxist philosophy and sociology, has presented the thought of three great German philosophers of the nineteenth century: Hegel, Marx, and Nietzsche. Henri Lefebvre's position is that our Western modern world of thought is altogether Hegelian, Marxian, and Nietzschean, although those three thinkers were often said to be three opponents. It is well known that Karl Marx struggled all his life against Hegel's idealism. On the other hand, Marx died before Nietzsche started to be known, while Nietzsche did not know Marx and was strongly anti-Hegelian. But the fascinating aspect of Henri Lefebvre's book lies precisely in his *rapprochement* of those three thinkers, without ever confusing them. Lefebvre demonstrates that modern society owes different aspects of what it is now to each of those men, the philosophy of the state having been developed by Hegel, the interpretation of conflict and revolution presented by Karl Marx, and the quest for freedom and authenticity having been taught by Nietzsche.

But my intention in bringing Nietzsche in has more to do with the questions I raised at the end of part one than with what I have just said. From Nietzsche, one learns one great lesson about the understanding of history and social change: We are invited by Nietzsche to question the oversimplified interpretations of history that we are too easily tempted to adopt. One does not have to share Nietzsche's atheist position to think that the history of humankind has not been patterned according to the needs or to the ends of the kingdom of God. Similarly, we can hope that change may sometimes mean progress, but we must also know that this is not necessarily the case, and we know now for sure that progress may mean the destruction of humankind and also maybe of the earth. As to the socialist ideology, with which I must admit that I am in sympathy, one must recognize that its predictions have not been realized since there has been no revolution of the working class in any of the capitalist industrial societies and also because the socialist ideology has been implemented in rural countries, where it has finally become another model of industrialization parallel to the capitalist one and finally more and more similar to the latter. To explain this failure, the question has been raised of whether it was in the nature of the socialist regime to be repressive and bureaucratic to a point that has been seldom seen, or whether it is a mere historical accident that the Gulag Archipelago was born and expanded in the country that has been regarded for a long time as the ideal model for all the future socialist nations.

These examples bring me to the conclusion toward which I have been labouring: that it is very difficult to believe that history has some inherent meaning and that it is necessarily oriented toward some future aim. There are too many examples to the contrary. If there is any supreme end to human history, if there is any latent meaning behind social change, I think it is still hidden or concealed and still remains unknown. Here, I think, the relativism of the sociologist meets Nietzsche's questioning of supreme and absolute truths standing up "there," outside human beings, dominating them and at the same time giving meaning to their lives.

Spengler and Sorokin have presented history as a kind of big wheel that is turning very slowly. According to both men, human society goes successively through the same three or four periods (like the recurrence of big epidemics), so we can predict where humankind is going in the coming centuries. But the trouble I have always had with these views, however fascinating they may be, is that they are based solely on the history of the Western world, and mostly on the history of the last 1,500 or 2,000 years. Hence I cannot be fully satisfied with these syntheses of history and these panoramic overviews of our past, present, and future. Even though Sorokin was a sociologist (that was not the case with Spengler), I think that his philosophy of history, as well as Spengler's, was more influenced by his value judgments and his normative expectations than by truly sociological foundations. I do believe that philosophical reflections and ethics now cannot do without the social sciences and the knowledge that these sciences are providing. To me, Nietzsche was that kind of philosopher even before the social sciences started to develop. Nietzsche even liked to call himself a psychologist, rather than a philosopher, which was true in many respects, and I would personally add that he was also one of the forerunners of sociology, although he is not yet recognized at all by contemporary sociology. His philosophical questioning was always inspired by psychological and sociological observations of his own. That is surely one reason why Freud and Jung have read Nietzsche and why Jung especially has explicitly recognized the debt he owed him.

If, following Nietzsche, we turn to the social sciences in order to find inspiration for a more realistic philosophy of history, what kind of knowledge do they provide us that might shed some light on the meaning of history? The answer is probably less simple than the one we get through our own wishes and through the most popular current ideologies. Consequently, the answer is also less interesting for many people because it does not necessarily support the commitment to one clearly defined cause, or side, or ideology.

I think that sociologists must say that there are no clear and definite aims that can be regarded as the alpha and omega of history, besides those that human beings themselves put forward or take for granted and that they try and struggle to implement. This means that if and when some goals that groups of people or societies are pursuing happen to be reached, it is not necessarily because they were already written somewhere in golden letters either by God or by some historical necessity. It is rather because some individuals have strongly believed in those goals, have made them their ideals, and have devoted time and energy and sometimes their lives and the lives of many others to achieving them. Of course, not all goals pursued by individuals or groups of individuals are finally achieved. There are probably many more that are not than there are that are implemented. It is precisely to explain this difference that one might say that the goals that are reached were falling in line with the great laws of history and were bound to succeed, while the others were either coming too late or too early or were just not congruent with the development of history. But what does that mean? I think it is just begging the question since it means that we can judge the historical merits of human wishes, ideals, aspirations, goals, and ends simply by what really happens.

The historical actions of human beings take place through a great number of conditions, factors, constraints that more or less favour the attainment of human goals. Some of these factors are attached to the individual and human action, while others are external to the individual. Those attached to the individual are such things as the level of intelligence, the astuteness, the cleverness that some people put into the implementation of their goals, as well as the amount of work, energy, vitality, enthusiasm, and emotional involvement that some people are willing to put into the pursuit of their ideals. Another series of human factors has to do with the quality of the group of individuals who have joined their forces in order to achieve some common goals. Most of the time, those various human factors seem to be taken for granted by the philosophers of history. But in so doing, they conceal all the voluntaristic elements of history, which, in my view, cannot be explained without the intervention of human beings because this intervention represents the margin of freedom and initiative that is left to us. And by this, I don't mean that psychology has all the answers to the questions raised by history. On the contrary, I believe that the social sciences in general have tended to overemphasize some general laws or some general characteristics that tend to conceal the role played by the convergence of a certain number of factors attached to some of the actors implied in the processes of change. The social sciences have too often buried human grandeur, power, and margin of freedom in emphasizing determinisms.

Finally, we now come to what is usually put first: a series of determinisms or constraints that either contribute to limiting the actions of human beings or favour some orientations rather than some others. These are, for instance, the physical constraints that are related to the natural resources, the climate, the physical geography of the environment; they are also the demographic limitations, which have to do with such things as the density of the population, its dispersion over a more-or-less wide territory, the distribution of the population by age, and so on. There are also some economic determinisms, such things as the type of property that has been traditionally maintained, the state of the technology, the development of the labour force, the conditions of transportation, the amount of capital available, and so forth. Political factors also play the role of constraints or conditioning factors, such as the power structure, the organization of the management of the resources (human and physical), the amount and the quality of the information that those in power receive and can use. Finally, some cultural factors are also at play to condition the orientation of history, such as religious beliefs, the interpretations of history that are currently accepted, the images of human beings and nature that are currently dominant. However, now, even the most physical of these forces are being submitted to some human action that modifies them, not to speak of the economic and political reality that is, to a certain extent, self-made. Hence why do we speak of determinism?

While I am in that vein, let me finally add one last factor that is usually taken for granted, although it should not be: sheer good luck or bad luck, chance, coincidence, which also enter into the fabric of history under the form of some accidental events or circumstances that bring together specific conditions favourable or unfavourable to the orientation of history in one direction rather than in another one. As an example, I think it has been bad luck for socialism that the first country to implement the model of a socialist nation was the USSR. The repressive, authoritarian, and bureaucratic socialist society that was shaped by Stalin was rooted in the traditions of tsarist society, which had not gone through a so-called democratic revolution previous to the socialist revolution.

By now it is probably clear what I have been aiming at with this enumeration of factors that must be taken into account in the interpretation of history: I wanted to underline the fact that no single explanation can be regarded as universally valid, that no general principle seems to lie behind the processes of history. There is no one specific determinism that can be singled out as providing the final and only valid interpretation of what takes place. Actual history is the outcome of a great variety of intermingling and intertwining factors, some of which are external to individuals and some others closely related to human actions. History is therefore the outcome of a mixture of voluntarism, determinisms, and accidents; it is made up of a complex interplay of a great variety of different elements.

Still more, this complexity of the historical process increases with the increasing complexity of societies themselves. The more complex and differentiated societies are, the more difficult it is to apply a simple unilinear model of change to their historical processes. This is especially the case with modern industrial societies. In the smaller primitive or traditional or illiterate societies, the role of some determining factors as well as the influence of some specific individuals or groups were probably much easier to pinpoint. But our complex industrial societies, socialist as well as capitalist, cannot be easily put into some simple formula. In these societies, one can identify at the same time several sources of change, some being complementary while others are contradictory or conflicting. For instance, one can identify a variety of human agents of change who are attempting to influence the history of the societies according to several more-or-less contradictory or conflicting orientations at the same time. It is therefore of the utmost importance to underline the fact that no specific group has the monopoly of influence, that no specific group can be said to be the privileged agent of change in our complex differentiated societies.

I think that this goes enough against some current ideas about change to deserve some explanation. Many things have been said these last years on how history is largely determined by the actions of two groups – namely, the youth and the working class – who have been singled out as the main agents of change and as the two groups that are mostly responsible for the present evolution of society and who will surely shape the future. I personally hold that the influence of those two groups has been highly exaggerated and is far from what some wishful thinking has made it.

With regard to the youth, I think this mistake could be made because there has been a short period of contemporary history, let us say from 1955 to 1970, during which the youth have been very vocal, questioning modern society, protesting against a certain number of things. This has brought some sociologists to believe that the youth will now have in the future the historical role that Karl Marx attributed to the working class. But I do personally think that several observations must lead us to question this viewpoint as being very largely mythological and utopian. Let me present here three observations that seriously limit the actual role of the youth in contemporary history. First, the young have not invented new ideas and new values in these last years. Rather, when we look at it carefully, one must conclude that the youth were expressing ideas that were very largely borrowed from elder people. The youth have taken it upon themselves to diffuse those ideas and to apply some of them, but they did not create them. Those so-called new ideas had already been expressed in many ways, and we can trace them back very clearly to either some schools of Marxist thought, like Marcuse, Althusser, Habermas, or to some schools of social criticism, like C. Wright Mills or Alvin Gouldner, or to some literary works, like those of Jack London, William Faulkner, Steinbeck (before he became reactionary), and many others. One can say that the youth have been more receptive for a while to these ideas and to these authors, most of whom were in turn relating themselves to quite a long tradition of critical thought.

Second, one should not speak of the youth, as if a whole generation was altogether engaged in a movement of protest. As a matter of fact, protest was mostly to be found among a specific class of youth: the student youth. And even then it has always been only a minority among the student youth who were seriously and actively engaged in the movement of protest. The majority of the youth have always been much more fundamentally conformist than has been said and thought for a while and by some social scientists.

Finally, the period of protest by the youth was rather short-lived: It lasted at best about fifteen years – and probably less than that. Since the beginning of the 1970s, the movement of protest among the youth has slowed down and practically died. For the last five or six years, the youth have entered a period of conformism. Even though they may be talking about change, they have developed a clear fear of change. Indeed, they have good reasons for that. The economic recession, the fuel crisis, the inflation, the saturation of the labour force, coupled with the society of consumption that is more dominant than ever, are all factors that have contributed to integrating the youth in the dominant system to the point that they have no more interest in changing things. Because the spirit of the society of consumption is very largely shared by the youth, who have grown up in a period of prosperity and comfort, a strong individualism has developed that has resulted finally in personal aspirations for social mobility and wellbeing, which in fact go against any ideology of social change. On the whole, the youth are much more integrated in the society of today and are much more part of the so-called system than they say and than they are said to be.

I do believe that protesting against the total society and the dominant system requires a good deal of psychological and social maturity. Therefore, those who are seriously protesting are not to be found mostly among the youth, but among elder and more mature people, who have really suffered from the dominant system and who have been severely frustrated by it or who have for one reason or another decided to devote their lives to changing society. And those people know something of the rules of the game, something that the youth ignore.

All this does not mean that the youth have no historical role at all. As has been very well documented by Karl Mannheim, each generation introduces something new just because it has been brought up in a unique historical period and has therefore internalized the traditional culture in a unique way, emphasizing some aspects of it and deemphasizing others. It might happen, as I think it did in the 1960s, that one generation of young may have a more visible influence mainly for two reasons: One is that they are suddenly more numerous for a short while; the second that they have been brought up in a period of more rapid and drastic changes. But this is rather exceptional, and it does not necessarily last very long, as we have witnessed in our own lifetime. The youth can therefore be said to be sometime agents of change, but they are neither the only ones, nor the dominant ones, nor the most influential ones. They surely don't have the monopoly on protest, on new ideas, and on new values.

It is only recently that some historical role has been attributed to the youth. The role attributed to the working class has a much longer tradition insofar as it goes back to the origin of socialist thought – that is, to the beginning of the nineteenth century. In a way, the historical role attributed to the working class has a more respectful and honourable past, and much more has been said and written about it than about the role of the youth. But here again, in my opinion, part of what has been said about the working class is also mythological and utopian. Three observations must also be brought up here, which serve to illustrate the limitations of that mythology. First, if we just remain empirical and factual, one must recognize that the history of the modern revolution is very poor evidence of the role of the working class in bringing about drastic changes. Most of the great modern revolutions, starting with the French and the American ones, up to the Russian and Chinese ones, have not been carried out by workers but by either the small bourgeoisie, or the army, or the peasants. This is surely not because the workers were not frustrated and alienated by the capitalist society. On the contrary, they were alienated to the point that they were unable to organize themselves and to conduct a revolution.

Second, in modern societies, the working class is less and less clearly delineated. It was much more of an entity in the nineteenth century, when socialists could quite clearly identify its boundaries. The working class was then clearly demarcated altogether by its clothing, its housing, its complete lack of education, its geographical location. All those boundaries have been more or less blurred. Moreover, and very significantly, unionism is not limited to the working class any more: white collars are now members of the labour unions in greater number than the workers, and trade unions are now related to the middle class more tightly than to the working class. Still more, it is usually the white-collar workers and middle-class people who represent the radical wings in the labour unions much more than the workers, who are generally more conservative. All the major labour conflicts of Quebec right now involve many more white collars than blue collars, many more teachers and civil servants than industrial workers.

The notion of class consciousness is of prime importance in the socialist doctrine, at least in traditional Marxist thought. Class consciousness is the main dynamic element that brings to the working class its revolutionary mood and impetus, thus making of the social class an agent of social conflict and social change. It is when the working class becomes conscious of its alienation, economic but also political and cultural, and when it becomes aware of its possibilities of action to change things, that it can develop some plans of action, some strategies, and turn from apathy to action. All this makes sense, and it has been supported by empirical sociological research in Europe, in North America, and in South America. But at the same time, what is very clear also is that this class consciousness is not a spontaneous creation and that intellectuals who do not belong to the working class contribute very largely to its emergence. They feed from the outside the class consciousness of the working class with some content, with information and goal orientations. Such has been the case with all the great revolutions of the last centuries, as well as the ones that took place in our century. It therefore means that the working class is potentially an agent of change, though not probably the main revolutionary agent, provided it is inspired by intellectuals who belong to the bourgeoisie and who serve as catalysts and *animateurs* of the actions of the working class.

In short, the working class is not necessarily the main agent of revolutionary change and certainly is not the sole one. Moreover, the notion of class consciousness has often served to hide the fact that some intellectuals play a dominant role in the revolutionary process. Not all intellectuals, indeed. Intellectuals have not, any more than any social groups, the monopoly on protest and change, a good number of them being integrated into a system in which they have vested interests. But following Karl Mannheim here again, I am inclined to think that in the modern world, at least, some groups of intellectuals have had a much more active role in the processes of change than is usually recognized, even by intellectuals themselves. These intellectuals usually have no power, but they have influence and, as writers, teachers, researchers, journalists, *chansonniers*, serve to define the situation, following W.I. Thomas's expression. They usually are not efficient in strategies and in concrete action, but they provide ideas and some abstract scheme of thought that, when implemented by others, may sometimes become explosive. But, mind you, I don't want to replace the mythology of the working class with the mythology of the intelligentsia I just want to illustrate the idea that no group has the monopoly on the engineering of historical change.

Another myth must also be explored here: the idea that protest and action are taking place mostly in the urban setting and that changes spread from the cities to the country. Indeed, we live in a civilization that is largely dominated by the cities, at least demographically and economically speaking, so we take for granted that important things are taking place where we live and that this is where great movements and great agitation take place.

We therefore tend to ignore too easily the protest and the revolts of the rural and peasant populations throughout history and in our own times. For instance, we have too easily built the image of the Canadian peasant, and still more of the Quebec *habitant*, as a quiet and submissive person. But those of us who have lived in the country, who have grown up on a farm, or who have been associated with the rural population, know pretty well that our farmers are protesting almost every day against nature, the sun, the moon, the rain, their parish priests or ministers, the urban world, the tourists, God, the devil, and the governments.

The peasants are permanent protesters, especially those who live in more marginal regions or in the frontier regions. And recently we have witnessed the anger of the rural population in North America, in Canada as well as in Quebec, and in France. Because we are an urbanized population, we keep the memory of what has taken place in our cities, and sometimes only of those protests that have taken place on our campuses. We speak of the great revolts of the students at Berkeley in 1964, or in Paris in May 1968, or in Quebec in October 1968. But were we peasants, instead of urbans, we would claim the great revolutionary moment of October 1974, when farmers went as far as killing a great number of calves, which carries, I think, much more impact than the occupation of some dean's office.

Finally, I am sure that in Ottawa a good number of people will agree with me if I say that civil servants and especially higher civil servants have something to say in social change. This is still more true with the expansion that the state has known over the last decade and with the new roles it has entered. Maybe better than anyone else, Hegel forecasted, at the beginning of the nineteenth century, this expanding development of the state in the modern world.

And Hegel saw it not only as a necessity but also as an ideal, since the state was in his mind the bearer of the spirit of the society, the locus where all the great ideas meet and through which the destiny of the collective mind and body can best be achieved. Many people are today less euphoric about the extended role of the state than Hegel was, and I think that in particular the examples that we have seen in this century of state socialist societies have convinced more and more people who, like me, have sympathies for a socialist society to look for some other form of socialism in which the state would be less omnipotent and omnipresent.

Nonetheless, even taking into account this omnipresence of the state, all the studies dealing with the role of civil servants have made clear that their influence is limited by many constraints, such as the vested interests and the fear of change that are generally to be found among politicians, the power that the more conservative wings among the civil servants generally enjoy, the brakes that are applied by civil servants themselves when orders and directives go down the line or when the information goes up the line, the influence of the pressure groups and of the lobbies that are permanently in action around those in power, and more generally the conservative climate that prevails in our large, complex societies of consumption.

I think I have said enough in support of my view that the making of history is the monopoly of no group and of no specific elite and of no class of citizens in our modern industrial society. Neither the youth, nor the working class, nor the intellectuals, nor the bureaucrats, nor the capitalists are the sole or the main agents of change. The drive to bring about some changes is spread throughout many sectors of society, and it is to be found as a potentiality in a great variety of groups, which are not necessarily pushing in the same direction but sometimes in conflicting directions. Such is the situation because we now live in pluralist societies – that is, in societies that are made up of a growing number of parts, elements, segments that are more or less in a permanent state of possible conflicts or at least that pursue more-or-less conflicting interests. Therefore, this type of society always generates new reasons to protest, which may vary almost indefinitely from one period to another, from one milieu to another. Therefore, one must very seldom expect that all the reasons to protest will suddenly be shared by everyone at the same time. To me, that is probably the main reason why radical revolutions are less and less possible and plausible in our modern complex society. Protest weakens as far as it is multiplied. Therefore, there are fewer chances of change when more groups are looking for some change.

I may also add that the propensity to change has been both enhanced and weakened by the democratization of education in our societies. On the one side, people are becoming more critical of their society as they become more educated. This fact has been illustrated many times by empirical research. Social criticism is more explicit, better structured, and more consciously engaged among those who are more educated. But at the same time, those who are more educated have better defense against the actions of others. Therefore, it is not necessarily because the educated people are more conservative that they may block change, but just because they have their own ideas about what change must be and because there are more and more people who don't wish the same changes.

One may quite easily observe that the propensity to change is often cancelled out in our societies. For example, it happens that great protest movements are neutralized by other similar protest movements that are heading in different directions. One other example is the case of the higher civil servants who quite often serve to interpret the movements of protest in modern societies. By their functions, civil servants must know how to use protest coming from the left and protest coming from the right in order to arrive at a middle-of-the-road solution in which both the right and the left find part of their ideas — that it, at a compromise that satisfies completely no group but that results in a reduction of protest. This kind of action on the part of civil servants is one reason why we can say that modern societies recuperate from all their protest movements. As a matter of fact, modern societies have multiple mechanisms of recuperation and reintegration of protest movements. Therefore, while there always is a significant revolutionary potential in our societies because of the many frustrations that are felt and of the widely spread social criticism, there are fewer and fewer opportunities for drastic social change to take place in our societies. I do believe that revolutionary change was more plausible in nineteenth-century societies than it is today in advanced industrial societies. For that very reason, I think that the original Marxist analysis had more meaning for change in the beginning of the industrial societies than it has now in the stage of advanced industrial societies. In the latter, the complexity of our societies is such that the social system itself has become functionalist and conservative.

I would also dare say that another factor of recuperation of radical change is to be found in the actions of the revolutionary movements themselves. Although it may seem paradoxical, the most radical revolutionary movements are agents of the recuperation of the revolutionary potential in our societies, the reason being that the radical revolutionary movements express objectives and aims of change that are borrowed by the establishment and spread through the mass media of communication. Both the civil servants and the management of private industries are clever enough to find in those objectives their inspiration and terminology for more moderate policies. As I said earlier, it is one of the main functions of bureaucratic technocrats to go after the new ideas, to understand them, and to integrate them into the official policies of middle-of-the-road governments. Therefore, it is less and less possible for radical movements to succeed in the destabilization and the overthrow of the present system. Reformist change is much more often the outcome of these processes than of drastic and revolutionary change.

Of course, what I have just said is probably not pleasant to hear for some people who want to believe in radical change and in its occurrence, and I must say that it does not appear to me to be an ideal situation. One has more success, at least among some groups, when one keeps closer to some popular ideologies of revolution than I presently do. But I do believe that sociology must teach realism and present an honest picture of how things take place, in order to discriminate between reality and wishful thinking.

In conclusion, I think that I must emphasize the fact that if history has any meaning at all, this meaning is to be found in the interplay of an increasing amount of conflicting influence and actions that oppose one another, sometimes complement or supplement one another, but very seldom point altogether in the same direction. And so it is because history does not belong to one group and does not follow one specific law of evolution. For some people, this might be seen as a demobilizing conclusion because they need the security of thinking that what they believe in will necessarily triumph in the end. This is precisely mythological thinking. In reality, history is more complex precisely because it is open to all kinds of influences. The only way to believe in history is to fight for one's own beliefs and options, knowing very well that the impact that they may have in the future or their failure to succeed will not necessarily be related to their intrinsic value but to a lot of work on the part of people who share the same ideas, to the strength or weakness of the opposing groups, to the interplay of some external factors, and finally to plenty of good luck.

GUY ROCHER is a professor in the Department of Sociology at the University of Montreal and a researcher at the university's Centre de recherche en droit public. He was a member of the Royal Commission of Inquiry on Education in the Province of Quebec (Parent Commission); Deputy Minister of Cultural Development and Deputy Minister of Social Development in Quebec; and vice-chairman of the Canada Council for the Arts. In 1957 he was one of the founders of the Association internationale des sociologues de langue française. Dr Rocher is the author or coauthor of fifteen books and numerous articles, conference papers, and lectures.

Guy Rocher is a Companion of the Order of Canada and a member of the Royal Society of Canada, as well as a member of nine Canadian and foreign learned societies in the fields of sociology, sociology of law, law, and bioethics. He was awarded the 1995 Léon Gérin Prize, the 1999 Sir John William Dawson Medal, and has received two honorary doctorates.

14

Language and Human Nature

CHARLES TAYLOR, 1978

Language is a central area of concern in the twentieth century. This is evident on all sides. First, our century has seen the birth and explosive growth of the science of linguistics. And in a sense "explosive" is the right word because, like the other sciences of humankind, linguistics is pursued in a number of mutually irreducible ways, according to mutually contradictory approaches, defended by warring schools. There are structuralists in the Bloomfieldian sense, there are proponents of transformational theories, there are formalists.

These schools and others have made a big impact. They are not just collections of obscure scholars working far from the public gaze. Names like Jacobson and Chomsky are known far outside the bounds of their disciplines.

But what is even more striking is the partial hegemony, if one can put it this way, that linguistics has won over other disciplines. From Saussure and the formalists there has developed the whole formidable array of structuralisms, of which Lévi-Strauss is the pathfinder, which seek to explain a whole range of other things: kinship systems, mythologies, fashion (Barthes), the operations of the unconscious (Lacan), with theories drawn in the first place from the study of language. We find terms like "paradigm," "syntagm," "metaphor," "metonymy" used well beyond their original domains.

And then we have to add that some of the most influential philosophical movements of the century have given language a central place; they have not only been concerned with language as one of the *problems* of philosophy, but have also been *linguistic* in that philosophical understanding is essentially bound up with the understanding of the medium of language.

This is true not only of logical positivism and what is often called "linguistic analysis" in the Anglo-Saxon world, but also of the philosophy of Heidegger, for instance, in a very different way, as well as of the philosophies that have arisen out of structuralism – for example, of Derrida and Lacan.

The concern for language as a medium links up with the twentieth-century concern with meaning. What is it that makes speech meaningful, or indeed that makes meaningful any of the things that have meaning? For this question has been raised not just in connection with language, which is what philosophical theories of meaning have been concerned with. It has also been raised acutely for the arts – for instance, music and painting. It is necessarily posed by the rise of nonrepresentational painting and of music that has stepped outside the seemingly fixed code of the eight-tone scale. The revolutions of the beginning of the century – for instance, of Schönberg and cubism – put these questions on the agenda, and they have been kept on it by all the revolutions we have seen since. They have taught us to ask the question "What is meaning?" in a broader context than simply that of language. They induce us to see language as one segment of that range of meaningful media that human beings can deploy. And this range comes to seem all the more problematical.

On top of this, the range of the meaningful has been further extended dramatically by Freudian psychoanalysis. Now not just speech and art objects, but also slips of the tongue, symptoms, affinities, and tastes, can be "analyzed" – that is, interpreted.

And "interpretation" itself has become a key term. "Hermeneutical" approaches have a wide audience in a number of fields, most strikingly in history and social science.

What emerges from this, I believe, is that the twentieth-century concern for language is a concern about meaning. And I believe that this concern reflects a largely inarticulate sense of ourselves that is very widespread in our century and that I shall try to formulate in two related propositions: (1) that the question of language is somehow strategic for the question of human nature, that *Homo sapiens* is above all the language animal; (2) that language is very puzzling, even enigmatic – and all the more so if we take it in a wide sense to include the whole range of meaningful media, something we seem bound to do once we see language as the defining character of human beings, for human beings are also characterized by the creation of music, art, dance, by the whole range of "symbolic forms," to use Cassirer's phrase. The paradox involved in this is that in an age of great scientific advance, and after spectacular progress in so many fields, human language appears to us much more enigmatic than it did to those of the Enlightenment. But I recognize that this is a controversial point and that my thumbnail sketch of our sense of our situation will be strongly resisted by all those who believe or who want to believe in the competence of the methods of natural science to explain human behaviour. Indeed, the trouble with the above sketch is that it is not neutral in one of the big debates of our civilization, so that some will find it banal and others tendentious.

What I ought to attempt now, therefore, is to make it less sketchy for the first and less implausible for the second. But this is something I find hard to encompass by a direct assault. What I want to do instead is trace the origins and hence the growing shape of our intellectual landscape. In doing this, I hope to cast enough light on it to achieve my ends by indirection, which are to allay at least some doubts and to fill in at least some contour.

This will involve weaving together two themes: First, how did we get here? How did we come to see language as central and meaning as puzzling? This is the historical, diachronic theme. The second theme is problematic: What is the problem of meaning, and why is it puzzling?

A word about each to start.

On the first: Our traditional view of humankind was of a rational animal. That is the definition according to the major philosophical tradition of our civilization, going back to the Greeks. How did we slide to the sense that the secret of human nature was to be found in *Homo sapiens* as a "language animal" (to use Georges Steiner's phrase)?

The answer is that the slide was not all that great. If we go back to the original formula in Aristotle, for instance, that *Homo sapiens* is a rational animal, we find that it reads: *zôon logon echon*, which means "animal possessing *logos*." This "logos" is a word we're already familiar with because it has entered our language in so many ways. It straddles speech and thought because it means, *inter alia,* "word," "thought," "reasoning," "reasoned account," as well as being used for the words deployed in such an account. It incorporates in its range of meanings a sense of the relation of speech and thought.

If we wanted to translate Aristotle's formula directly from the Greek, instead of via the Latin *animal rationale*, and render it "animal possessing *logos*," which means in fact leave it partly untranslated in all its rich polysemy, then we don't have such a leap to make between the traditional formulation of the nature of human beings and the one that I want to claim underlies much twentieth-century thought and sensibility. There is a shift, but it is one within the complex thought/language, the displacement of its centre of gravity. A shift of this kind in our understanding of thought/language would explain the change from the old formula to the new. And in fact, I want to claim, there has been such a shift. This is my historical theme.

On the second problematic theme: What is the problem about meaning? And what is it to find it puzzling – or, for that matter, unpuzzling? What questions are we asking, when we are asking about meaning?

We're not asking about meaning in the sense that we may ask about the meaning of life or in the sense of "meaning" where we speak of a love or a job being meaningful. This is a related sense, but here we are talking about the significance things have for us in virtue of our goals, aspirations, purposes.

The question I'm talking about here comprises the radical questions: How is it that these segments of a medium that we deploy, when we talk, make music, paint, make signals, build symbolic objects, *how is it that these say something?* How is it that we can complete sentences of the form "What this means (to say) is …" whereas we cannot say this of sticks, stones, stars, mountains, forests – in short, of the things we just find in the world?

Or if we object to this way of putting it, because it seems to rule out one of the great traditional ways of understanding the world, as signs made by God, or embodiments of the Ideas – a view we will look at in a minute – we could equally ask: What is it that we see in things when we understand them as signs, which we don't when we fail to apprehend them as such, but just as the furniture of a nonexpressive universe?

There are two sides or dimensions of meaningful objects, which can each be taken up as the guiding thread of the answer. The first is what we could call the "designative": we could explain a sign or word having meaning by pointing to what it designates in a broad sense – that is, what it can be used to refer to in the world and what it can be used to say about that thing. I say, "The book is on the table"; this is meaningful speech, and it is so, because "book" designates a particular kind of object and "table" another, "the" can be used to pick out a particular object in some context of reference, and the whole phrase puts together the two referring expressions in such a way as to assert that the designatum of one is placed on the designatum of the other. On this view, we give the meaning of a sign or a word by pointing to the things or relations that they can be used to refer to or talk about.

The second dimension we could call the "expressive." The sentence "The book is on the table" designates a book and a table in a certain relation, but it can be said to express my thought, or my perception, or my belief that the book is on the table. In a wider sense, it might be said to express my anxiety if there is something particularly fateful about the book's being on the table, or perhaps my relief if the book was lost.

What is meant by "expression" here? I think it means roughly this: Something is expressed when it is embodied in such a way as to be made manifest. And "manifest" must be taken here in a strong sense. Something is manifest when it is directly available for all to see. It is not manifest when there are just signs of its presence, from which we can infer that it's there, such as when I "see" that you're in your office because of your car being parked outside. In this kind of case, there is an implied contrast with another kind of situation, in which I could see you directly.

Now we consider things expressions when they make things manifest in the stronger sense, one which cannot be contrasted with a more direct manner of presentation, one where things would be there before us "in person," as it were.

Take the example of facial expressions. If you have an expressive face, I can see your joy and sorrow in your face. There is no inference here: I see your moods and feelings; they are manifest in the only way they can be manifest in public space. Contrast this with your neighbour, who is very good at hiding his feelings; he has a "poker face." But I happen to know of him (because his mother told me) that whenever he feels very angry a muscle twitches just beside his ear. I observe the muscle, and I see that he is angry.

But the muscle twitching doesn't amount to an angry expression. That's because it's like the case above where I see you're in your office from your car's being outside. In these cases, I infer to something that I am not seeing directly. Expressions, by contrast, make our feelings manifest; they put us in the presence of people's feelings.

Expression makes something manifest in embodying it. Of course, a given expression may reveal what it conveys in a partial, or enigmatic, or fragmentary fashion. But these are all manifestations in the above sense that, however imperfect, we can't contrast them with another, more direct, but nonexpressive mode of presentation. What expression manifests can *only* be manifested in expression.

Now we can see much of what we say in both the designative and the expressive dimension, as we did with the sentence above. In each dimension we relate the sentence to something different: to the objects it is about, in one; and to the thought it expresses, in the other.

Each may seem to offer the more natural approach to the question of meaning in different contexts. In discussing the meaning of a sentence like "The book is on the table," we are more naturally inclined to give an account in designative terms. When we are thinking about a poem, or a piece of music, on the other hand, we more naturally think of its meaning in the expressive dimension. Indeed, with a symphony or a sonata, it is hard to speak of designating. This dimension seems to disappear altogether.

But although each is more natural in a certain context, there seems no reason to see the expressive and the designative as rival modes of explanation wherever they both apply, as in ordinary speech. Rather they seem to answer different questions.

But there is an important dispute in the history of thought over the issue of which of these dimensions is more fundamental in the order of explanation. If "The book is on the table" expresses my thought to this effect, is this because the words concerned have the designative meanings that they have? If this is so, then the fundamental phenomenon is that of designative meaning. This is what we need to understand in order to get to the root of things. The expressive function of words will be dependent on this.

Or is there something about the expressive function that cannot be so understood? Is there a dimension of expressive meaning that is not simply determined by designative meaning? Are the tables even to be turned, and is expressive meaning in some way primary, providing the foundation or framework in which words can have designative meaning in the first place? If this is true, then the fundamental thing in language is expressive meaning.

These two approaches define very different ways of understanding the question "What is meaning?" A long struggle between the two has led up to our present understanding of language. Before turning to look at this history, I'd like to say something about the metaphysical motivations of the two types of theory.

Designative theories, those that make designation fundamental, make meaning of something relatively unpuzzling, unmysterious. That is a great part of their appeal. The meanings of words or sentences is explained by their relation to things or states of affairs in the world. There need be nothing more mysterious about meaning than there is about these things or states of affairs themselves. Of course, there is the relation of meaning itself, between word and thing, whereby one signifies or points to the other. But this can be made to seem unmysterious enough. At the limit, if talk about signifying makes us nervous, we can just think of this as a set of correlations that have been set up between noises we utter and certain world events or states. At the end of this road, we have behaviourist theories, like that of Skinner (followed by Quine, who has in turn been influential for Davidson).

But if we aren't all that metaphysically fastidious, we can simply take the designating relation as primitive and hope to illuminate meaning by tracing the correlations between words and things – or, in more contemporary guise, between sentences and their truth conditions.

By contrast, expressive theories maintain some of the mystery surrounding language. Expressive meaning can't be fully separated from the medium because it is only manifest in it. The meaning of an expression can't be explained by its being related to something else but only by another expression. Consequently, the method of isolating terms and tracing correlations can't work for expressive meaning. Moreover, in our paradigm, expressive objects function as wholes. Take a face or a work of art. We can't break either down into parts and show the whole to be simply a function of the parts if we want to show how it is expressive.

The sense that expression is mysterious can be formulated more exactly. The point is that expressive theories run counter to what is considered one of the fundamental features of scientific thought in the modern age, where designative theories do not. Scientific thought is meant to be objective, and this means it must give an account of the universe not in terms of what we could call subject-related properties – that is, properties that things have in the experience of subjects and that wouldn't exist if subjects of experience didn't exist. The most notorious example of these in seventeenth-century discussion were the secondary properties, and it was an integral part of the great scientific revolution of that time that these were expelled from physics.

Now an expressive account of meaning can't avoid subject-related properties. Expression is the power of a subject, and expressions *manifest* things and hence essentially refer us to subjects for whom these things can be manifest. And as I said above, what expression manifests can only be made manifest in expression, so that expressive meaning can't be accounted for independently of expression. If we make expression fundamental, it seems impossible to explain it in terms of something else; but it is itself a subject-related phenomenon and hence doesn't allow of an objective science.

By contrast, a designative theory accounts for meaning by correlating signs to bits of the world, and these can in principle be identified objectively. It offers the promise of a theory of language that can fit within the canons of modern natural science. It is in this sense that they promise to make language unpuzzling and unmysterious.

On this terrain, expressive theories can't follow.

I turn now to the historical account. If we trace the development of these rival theories of meaning, we can see that the preoccupation with *language* is a modern one. The actual doctrines about language, about words, were rather unimportant and marginal among the ancients. They weren't that concerned about speech; they were concerned about thought.

But then how about the insight implicit in the many-meaninged word *logos*? *Logos* meant word, and the root it came from, *legein*, meant "to say." What underpinned this connection between saying, words, and reason was what one could call a discourse-modelled notion of thought. Thought was seen as like discourse; it revealed things as discourse can do. When we take something that is puzzling and we give an account of it in speech, we lay it out, articulate its different aspects, identify them, and relate them. Because thinking was like discourse, we could use the same word *logos* for both. Plato says that you don't really know something unless you can give an account of it. Otherwise, you have just opinion (*doxa*) and not real knowledge (*epistêmê*). But "give an account" translates as *logon didonai*.

But the striking fact about the preponderant outlook of the ancients, which was bequeathed to the European Middle Ages, was their view about reality. It too was modelled on discourse-thought. In Plato's version, underlying reality are the Ideas. Of course, it is we moderns who are tempted to put this by saying that reality was modelled on discourse-thought. For Plato this was no false projection, and we should better say that our discourse and thought ought to be modelled on reality. Reality itself, the ultimate reality of which empirical things are in a sense copies, was Idea; it articulates itself in its aspects, which necessarily connected together according to its inner logic. It should be the aim of our thought to limp along after this and try to match it.

Now beside this powerful line-up of an *ontic logos*, or discourse-thought, which was followed by a *logos* in the thinking subject, words didn't seem very important. They were the mere external clothing of thought. They couldn't aspire to more, not human words, for clearly they weren't necessary to the *ontic logos*. So language plays a small and marginal role in the theories of the ancients.

But a powerful theory of meaning is in embryo here. The ancient view develops through several stages, notably through neo-Platonism, and then through the thought of the early fathers, which owes so much to neo-Platonism: St. Augustine in the West, and the Greek fathers in the East.

In this amalgam of Christian theology and Greek philosophy, a notion is developed that Plato first adumbrated in the *Timaeus*. God in creating the world gives embodiment to his ideas. The Platonic ideas are the thoughts of God.

And so we get an obvious analogy, which St. Augustine makes explicit. Just as our thought is clothed externally in our words, so is the thought of God, the *Logos* – the *Verbum*, for Augustine – deployed externally in the creation. This is, as it were, God's speech. That is why everything is a sign, if we can see it properly.

So the paradigm and model of our deploying signs is God's creation. But now God's creation is to be understood expressively. His creatures manifest His *logos* in embodying it, and they manifest the *logos* as fully as it can be manifest in the creaturely medium. There can be no more fundamental designative relation because, precisely, everything is a sign. This notion is nonsense on a designative view. For words can only have designative meaning if there is something else, other than words or signs, which they designate. The notion that everything is a sign only makes sense on an expressive view.

So what we have in Augustine and his successors is an expressive theory of meaning embedded in their ontology. The originator of meaning, God, is an expressivist. This sets the framework for the theories of the Middle Ages and the early Renaissance, what one could call the semiological ontologies, which pictured the world as a meaningful order, or a text. This kind of view of the world is dominant right up to the seventeenth century, when it was pulverized in the scientific revolution.

It was a view of this kind that understood the universe in terms of a series of correspondences, linking for instance the lion in the kingdom of animals, the eagle among birds, and the king in his realm, or linking stars in the heavens to the shape of the human frame, or linking certain beasts and plants to certain planets. In all these cases, what is at stake is an expressive relation. These terms are linked because they embody/manifest the same ideas. To view the universe as a meaningful order is to see the world as shaped in each of its domains and levels in order to embody the ideas.

We have here a very powerful expressive theory of meaning, a theory of the divine language. But all this is compatible with the relative unimportance of human words. Indeed, it rather requires their taking marginal status because the real thought, that of God or the Ideas, is quite independent of human expression. The theory of language is still in its infancy.

It was the rebellion against this semiological view of the universe, in nominalism, that began to make *language* important.

Medieval nominalism rejected the discourse-thought model of the real. It denied that there are real essences of things, or universals. True, we think in general terms. But this is not because the world exists in general terms, as it were; on the contrary, everything that exists is a particular. The universal is not a feature of the world but an effect of our language. We apply words to classes of objects, which we thus gather into units; that is what makes general terms.

Now this theory gives language a crucial role. The word is that whereby we group things into classes. It is the new home of the universal, which has been chased out of the real. But in giving language a role, this view propounds a purely designative theory of what this role amounts to. It generates a thoroughly designative theory of meaning.

It does so, first, in rejecting the expressive theory of the cosmos, in refusing to see the things that surround us as embodiments of the Ideas; and, second, in seeing words as acquiring meaning only in being used as names for things. Words mean because they designate something. So we cease to see everything that exists as a sign. The only signs are those that are recognized as such, and they are signs because they signify something.

This theory of language came into its own during the seventeenth-century scientific revolution, which we associate with such names as Descartes, Bacon, and Hobbes. This revolution involved a polemical rejection of the vision of the world as meaningful order and its replacement by a conception of the world as objective process in the sense of "objective" described above. The thoroughly designative theory of meaning was one of its main pillars.

The philosophies of the seventeenth century remade our conceptions of humankind, thought, and knowledge to fit the new dispensation. The very notion of what thought is changes. Once we no longer think of discourse-thought as part of the furniture of the real, then we focus on our subjective thinking as a process in its own right.

It is the process by which we are aware of things. How can this be? Once discourse has lost its ontic status, it is not so much the discursive dimension in thought that seems to account for this but rather its representative dimension. Once we focus on thought as a process going on only in our minds, and we ask how can we know about things in thought, the obvious answer seems to be that thought in some way mirrors, or represents, things.

And so we get the new conception of thought as made up of ideas, of little units of representation, rather like inner ghostly snapshots. This is the famous "way of ideas" inaugurated by Descartes and taken up by his successors, both rationalist and empiricist, and that dominated psychology and epistemology for the next two centuries. As the writers of the Port Royal *Logique* put it: "nous ne pouvons avoir aucune connaissance de ce qui est hors de nous que par l'entremise des idées qui sont en nous" (63). And they conclude from this that these ideas themselves must be the focus of our study. Thought as a kind of inner incorporeal medium becomes of central interest.

But it is through our ideas that we know what is outside. How do we do this? No longer by grasping the forms of the real, for there are none such. Rather knowing things outside means grasping how things are put together. And this means that we put them together in idea as they are in reality.

So the method of thought becomes the famous resolutive-compositive one. We break things in our ideas down into their component elements, and then we put them together in idea as they are in reality. That is what understanding is for Galileo, Descartes, Hobbes. As Hobbes puts it in *de Cive*: "everything is best understood by its constitutive causes. For as in a watch, or some such small engine, the matter, figure and motion of the wheels cannot be well known, except it be taken insunder and viewed in its parts; so as to make a more curious search into the rights of states and duties of subjects, it is necessary, I say, not to take them insunder, but yet that they be so considered as if they were dissolved." This means, of course, that our thought too must be broken down into its component bits. These bits are the ideas of seventeenth- and eighteenth-century epistemology.

So what is thinking? It is assembling ideas, properly the assembling of clear and distinct ideas, and according to the way components of the world are assembled. Thinking is mental discourse, to use Hobbes's term, where this is no longer the articulating and making evident of the ancients but a kind of inner disassembly and reassembly.

But if thinking is mental discourse, what is the role of language? Sometimes it seems, in reading the writings of seventeenth- and eighteenth-century thinkers, that its role is as much negative as positive, that words can mislead us and take our attention away from the ideas. Language is seen by them as the great seducer, tempting us to be satisfied with mere words, instead of focussing on the ideas they designate.

But no one held the view that we should try to do without language altogether. This was evidently impossible. For any relatively complex or long drawn-out thought, we plainly need words; all thinkers concur in this. And indeed, this is not only intuitively evident; it is implicit in their nominalistic starting point. It is through words that we marshal our ideas, that we group them in one way rather than another. Words allow us to deal with things in generalities, and not one by one.

And this is the role that this age assigns to language. It is through words that we marshal our ideas, not painstakingly, one by one, in which case we would not get very far in constructing an understanding of the world and would lose through forgetfulness as fast as we gained through insight; rather we marshal them in groups and classes. This is Hobbes's doctrine when he likens reasoning to reckoning, where we get our global result by casting up a number of partial sums, and not simply by counting one by one. Condillac in the next century has basically the same idea when he says that language gives us "empire sur notre imagination."

From this role of language we can see why words are so dangerous. If we use them to marshal ideas, they must be transparent. We must be able to see clearly what the word designates. Otherwise, where we think we are assembling our ideas to match the real, we will in fact be building castles of illusion or composing absurdities. Our instruments will have taken over, and instead of controlling we shall be controlled.

Language for the theory of these centuries is an instrument of *control* in the assemblage of ideas that is thought or mental discourse. It is an instrument of control in gaining knowledge of the world as objective process. And so it must itself be perfectly transparent; it cannot itself be the locus of mystery – that is, of anything that might be irreducible to objectivity. The meanings of words can only consist in the ideas (or things) they designate. The setting up of a designative connection is what gives a word meaning. We set these up in definitions, and that is why thinkers of this period constantly, almost obsessionally, stress the importance of recurring to definitions, of checking always to see that our words are well defined, that we use them consistently.

The alternative is to lose control, to slip into a kind of slavery, where it is no longer I who make my lexicon, by definitional fiat, but rather it takes shape independently and in doing this shapes my thought. It is an alienation of my freedom as well as the great source of illusion, and that is why the thinkers of this age combatted the cosmos of meaningful order with such determination.

As Locke puts it in *Essay* III (ii, 8): "Every man has so inviolable a liberty to make words stand for what ideas he pleases." Even the great Augustus has no power over my lexicon.

The seventeenth-century revolution, which in a way did so much to establish our modern modes of thought, gave us a thoroughly, polemically, designative theory of meaning. This was challenged in the late eighteenth century by a climate of thought and feeling that is loosely called Romanticism. This term is certainly loose because it is stretched to include many people – Goethe, for instance – who didn't define themselves as Romantics and who weren't Romantics in any exact sense. But it's a handy label, and I want to go on using it here.

One of the founding texts of this expressivist reaction is Herder's *On the Origin of Language* (1772). (Herder himself was not properly speaking a Romantic; but one of the originators of *Sturm und Drang*.)

In an important passage of this work, Herder turns to consider one of the typical origin stories of eighteenth-century designative theory, that of Condillac in his *Essai sur l'origine des counaissances humaines* (part 2, section 1, chapter 1). It is a fable of two children in the desert who come to invent language. We assume certain cries and gestures as natural expressions of feeling. Condillac argues that each, seeing the other, say, cry out in distress, would come to see the cry as a sign of something (e.g., what causes distress) and would come to use it to refer. The children would then have their first word. Their lexicon would then increase slowly, item by item.

Herder rebels against this whole conception. For, as he says, it presupposes just what we want to explain. It takes the relation of signifying for granted, as something the children already grasp or that can uproblematically occur to them ("ils parvinrent insensiblement à faire, avec réflexion, ce qu'ils n'avoient fait que par instinct" [para. 3]). Condillac, says Herder, presupposes "das ganze Ding Sprache schon vor der ersten Seite seines Buches erfunden." His explanation amounts to saying, "Es enstanden Worte, weil Worte da waren, ehe sie da waren."

The problem is that Condillac presupposes that his children already understand what it is for a word to stand for something, what it is therefore to talk about something with a word. But *that* is just the mysterious thing. Anyone can be taught the meaning of a word, or even guess at it, or even invent one, once they have language. But what is this capacity that we have and animals don't to endow sounds with meaning, to grasp them as referring to, as used to talk about things?

Let's look at this. I have the word "triangle" in my lexicon. This means that I can recognize things as triangles, identify them, pick them out as such. I can say, for example, "This is a triangle." But what does this capacity amount to? Let's see by comparing it with an analogous animal capacity. I might train an animal (a rat), to react differentially, say, to go through a door that had a triangle painted on it, as against one that had a circle. So my rat would be in a sense recognizing a triangle.

But there is a crucial difference: The rat in a sense recognizes the triangle because he reacts to it. But the human language-user recognizes that this is a triangle; he recognizes that "triangle" is the right word to use here, that this is the right description. This capacity to recognize that "x" is the right description is essentially invoked in our capacity to use language. Of course, we are not usually reflecting as we talk that the words we use are the appropriate ones, but the implicit claim in speaking language is that they are appropriate, and we can all understand the challenge that someone might make at any point: "Is 'x' the right word?" or "Do you really mean 'x'?" And we would all be able to give some kind of reply.

So only beings who can describe things as "triangles" can be said to recognize them as "triangles," at least in the strong sense. They don't just react to triangles, but recognize them as such. Beings who can do this are conscious of the things they experience in a fuller way. They are more reflectively aware, we might say.

And this is Herder's point. To learn a word, to grasp that "triangle" stands for triangles, is to be capable of this reflective awareness. That's what needs to be explained. To account for language by saying that we learn that the letter a stands for as, the letter b for bs, is to explain nothing. How do we learn what "standing for" involves, what it is to describe things — that is, how de we acquire the reflective awareness of the language user?

Herder uses the term "reflection" (*Besonnenheit*) for this awareness. And his point against Condillac is that this kind of reflection is inseparable from language. It can't precede our learning our first word, which is what Condillac implicitly assumes. This is because only someone capable of using language to describe is capable of picking things out as ..., or recognizing things as ..., in the strong sense.

But this means that language is not just a set of words that designate things; it is the vehicle of this kind of reflective awareness. This reflection is a capacity we only realize in speech. Speaking is not only the expression of this capacity, but also its realization.

But then the expressive dimension of language becomes fundamental again. In order for given words to mean something, to designate their respective objects, we have to be able to speak – that is, give expression to this reflective awareness –

because it's only through this expression, through speech, that this reflective awareness comes about. A being who can't speak can't have it. We only have it, in contrast to animals, in that we talk about things. Expression realizes, and is therefore fundamental.

This is once again an expressive theory. But this time it is an expressive theory of language, rather than an expressive theory of the cosmos. In the traditional view, creation expresses the ideas of God; but these exist before/outside creation. The new expressive theory of human language that we find in Herder is, by contrast, constitutive; that is, reflective consciousness only comes to exist in its expression. The expressive dimension is fundamental to language because it is only in expression that language comes to be.

The theorists of the Romantic period were, of course, very influenced by the earlier expressivism of the cosmos, as we might call it. We could say that in a sense they transposed what belongs to God in this older theory on to human beings. For human beings, like God, embody their ideas and make them manifest. But unlike God, human beings need self-expression in order to make their ideas manifest to themselves. Which is another way of saying that our ideas don't properly exist before their expression in language or some other of the range of media human beings deploy. That is what is meant by saying that language, or expression in general, is constitutive of thought.

In this connection, it is no accident that the Romantic period sees a revolution in our conception of art. The traditional view understood art in terms of mimesis. Art imitates the real. It may select, imitate only the best, or what conforms to the Ideas, but basically what it attempts to do is hold the mirror up to nature. The Romantics gave us a quite different conception, by which, in one formulation, the artist strives to imitate not nature but the author of nature. Art is now seen not as imitation but as creative expression. The work of art doesn't refer beyond itself to what it imitates; rather it manifests something; it is itself the locus in which the meaning becomes manifest. It should be a symbol, rather than an allegory to recur to the distinction that people of that generation often invoked.

As Herder put it: "the artist is become a creator God."

The artist creates in his work, as it were, a miniature universe, a whole that has its goal in itself and doesn't refer beyond to anything else. Novalis makes the comparison with the divine creation in these terms: "artistic creation is thus as much an end in itself as the divine creation of the universe, and one is as original and as grounded on itself as the other: because the two are one, and God reveals himself in the poet as he gives himself corporeal form in the visible universe."

But to return to the theory of language. We see that language is no longer an assemblage of words but the capacity to speak/express/realize the reflective awareness implicit in using words to say something. Learning to use any single word presupposes this general capacity as background. But to have the general capacity is to possess a language, so that it seems that we need the whole of language as the background for the introduction of any of its parts – that is, individual words.

This may seem to pose insuperable obstacles for any account of the acquisition of language; and indeed, Herder, in spite of the title of his work (*Uber den Ursprung der Spractie*), ducks the issue altogether. But it does point to a feature of language that seems undeniable: its holism. One might say that language as a whole is presupposed in any one of its parts.

Herder again is the one who formulated this insight. It is ultimately implicit in the point above that to use a word to describe is to identify something. When I say "this is a triangle," I recognize it as a triangle. But to be able to recognize something as a triangle is to be able to recognize other things as nontriangles. For the notion "triangle" to have a sense for me, there must be something(s) with which it contrasts; I must have some notion of other kinds of figures – that is, be able to recognize other kinds of figures for the kinds they are. "Triangle" has to contrast in any lexicon with other figure terms. Indeed, a word only has the meaning it does in our lexicon because of what it contrasts with. What would "red" mean if we had no other colour terms? How would our colour terms change if some of our present ones dropped out?

But in addition, to recognize something as a triangle is to focus on this property; it is to pick it out by its shape, and not by its size, colour, what it's made of, its smell, aesthetic properties, and so on. Here again some kind of contrast is necessary, a contrast of property dimensions. For to say of something "this is a triangle" is to apply this word as the *right* word, the appropriate descriptive term. But someone couldn't be applying a word as the right word and have no sense whatever of what made it the right word, without even grasping for instance that something was a triangle in virtue of its shape, and not its size or colour.

So it appears that a word like "triangle" couldn't figure in our lexicon alone. It has to be surrounded by a skein of other terms, some that contrast with it and some that situate it, as it were, give its property dimension, not to speak of the wider matrix of language in which the various activities are situated, in which our talk of triangles prefigures measurement, geometry, design creation, and so on.

The word only makes sense in this skein, in what Humboldt (who followed and developed Herder's thoughts on language) called the web (*Gewebe*) of language. In touching one part of language (a word), the whole is present.

(Another very persuasive argument is the famous one in Wittgenstein's Investigations I 258+, dealing with sensation E. If you try to give the name "E" to an inner sensation and avoid saying anything else about it, not even that it is a sensation, then you find yourself just wanting to make an inarticulate noise. For in saying nothing else, you deprive "E" of the status of a word. You can't know what you're saying.)

This expressive doctrine thus presents us with a very different picture of language from the empiricist one. Language is not an assemblage of separable instruments, which lie as it were transparently to hand and which can be used to marshal ideas, this use being something we can fully control and oversee. Rather it is something in the nature of a web and, to complicate the image, is present as a whole in any one of its parts. To speak is to touch a bit of the web, and this is to make the whole resonate. Because the words we use now only have sense through their place in the whole web, we can never in principle have a clear oversight of the implications of what we say at any moment. Our language is always more than we can encompass; it is in a sense inexhaustible. The aspiration to be in no degree at all a prisoner of language, so dear to Hobbes and Locke, is in principle unrealizable.

But at the same time, we need to connect this with another feature of language on this scheme, which Humboldt also brought out to the fore. What is crucial to language is what is realized in speech: the expression/realization of reflection. Language is not, once again, a set of instruments: words that have been attached to meanings. What is essential to language is the activity in which by speaking words we pick things out as something (among other things, as we shall see). The capacity that language represents is realized in speech.

As Humboldt puts it, we have to think of language as speech, and this as activity, not realized work; as *energeia*, not *ergon*.

But if the language capacity comes to be in speech, then it is open to being continuously recreated in speech, continually extended, altered, reshaped. And this is what is constantly happening. Human beings are constantly shaping language, straining the limits of expression, minting new terms, displacing old ones, giving language a changed gamut of meanings.

But this activity has to be seen against the background of the earlier point about language as a whole. The new coinages are never quite autonomous, quite uncontrolled by the rest of language. They can only be introduced and make sense because they already have a place within the web, which must at any moment be taken as given over by far the greater part of its extent. Human speakers resemble the sailors in Neurath's image of the philosopher, who have to remake their ship in the open sea and cannot build it from the base in a dry-dock.

What then does language come to be in this view? A pattern of activity by which we express/realize a certain way of being in the world, that of reflective awareness, but a pattern that can only be deployed against a background that we can never fully dominate – and yet a background that we are never fully dominated by because we are constantly reshaping it. Reshaping it without dominating it, or being able to oversee it, means that we never fully know what we are doing to it; we develop language without knowing fully what we're making it into.

From another angle: The background web is only there in that we speak. But because we can't oversee it, let alone shape it all, our activity in speaking is never entirely under our conscious control. Conscious speech is like the tip of an iceberg. Much of what is going on in shaping our activity is not in our purview. Our deployment of language reposes on much that is preconscious and unconscious.

So the expressive view yields us a much broader and deeper conception of language. It is an utterly different phenomenon than the assemblage of designative terms that empiricism gave us. But the implicit extensions go further. The designative theory sees language as a set of designators, words we use to talk about things. There is an implicit restriction of the activities of language. Language primarily serves to describe the world (although designative terms can also be given extended uses for questioning and giving commands).

The expressive theory opens a new dimension. If language serves to express/ realize a new kind of awareness, then it may make possible not only a new awareness of things, an ability to describe them, but also new ways of feeling, of responding to things. If in expressing our thoughts about things, we can come to have new thoughts, then in expressing our feelings, we can come to have transformed feelings.

This quite transforms Condillac's view of the expressive function of language. He and others conjectured that at the origin of language was the expressive cry, the expression of anger, fear, or some emotion; this later could acquire designative meaning and serve as a word. But the notion here was that expression was of already existing feelings, which were unaltered in being expressed.

The revolutionary idea of expressivism was that the development of new modes of expression enables us to have new feelings, more powerful or more refined, and certainly more self-aware. In being able to express our feelings, we give them a reflective dimension that transforms them. The language user can feel not only anger but indignation, not only love but admiration.

Seen from this angle, language can't be confined to the activity of talking about things. We transform our emotions into human ones not primarily in talking about them but in expressing them. Language also serves to express/realize ways of feeling without talking about them. We often give expression to our feelings in talking about something else. (For example, indignation is expressed in condemnation of the unjust actions, admiration in praise of the remarkable traits.)

From this perspective, we can't draw a boundary around the language of prose in the narrow sense and divide it off from those other symbolic-expressive creations of man: poetry, music, art, dance, and so forth. If we think of language as essentially used to say something *about* something, then prose is indeed in a category of its own. But once one takes language as being expressive in this way – that is, where the expression constitutes what it expresses – then talking *about* is just one of the provinces constituted by language; the constitution of human emotion is another, and in this some uses of prose are akin to some uses of poetry, music, and art.

In the Romantic period, there was a tendency to see this constituting of the human emotions as the most important function of language in a broad sense. Language realizes *Homo sapiens* humanity. Human beings complete themselves in expression. It was natural in such a context to exalt art above other forms of expression, above the development of merely descriptive language, or at least to give it equal weight and dignity. It was then that art began to replace religion for many as the centrally important dimension of human life – which it remains for many today.

But the expressive view not only transformed and extended the conception of the uses of language. It also transformed the conception of the subject of language. If language must be primarily seen as an activity – it is what is constantly created and recreated in speech – then it becomes relevant to note that the primary locus of speech is in conversation. People speak together, to each other. Language is fashioned and grows not principally in monologue but in dialogue, or better, in the life of the speech community.

Hence Herder's notion that the primary locus of a language was the *Volk* who carried it. Humboldt takes up the same insight. Language is shaped by speech and so can only grow up in a speech community. The language I speak, the web that I can never fully dominate and oversee, can never be just *my* language; it is always largely *our* language.

This opens up another field of the constitutive functions of language. Speech also serves to express/constitute different relations in which we may stand to each other: intimate, formal, official, casual, joking, serious, and so on. From this point of view, we can see that it is not just the speech community that shapes and creates language but language that constitutes and sustains the speech community.

If we attempt to gather all this together, we can see that the expressive conception gives a view of language as a range of activities in which we express/realize a certain way of being in the world. And this way of being has many facets. It is not just the reflective awareness by which we recognize things as …, and describe our surroundings, but also that by which we come to have the properly human emotions and constitute our human relations, including those of the language community within which language grows. The range of activity isn't confined to language in the narrow sense but rather encompasses the whole gamut of symbolic expressive capacities in which language, narrowly construed, is seen to take its place. This activity, even as regards the production of normal prose about the world, is one that we can never bring under conscious control or oversight in its entirety; even less can we aspire to such oversight of the whole range.

If we now look back over the route we've been travelling, we see how language has become central to our understanding of human beings. For if we hold on to the intuition that *Homo sapiens* is the rational animal, the animal possessing *logos* or discourse-thought, at least in that we concur that this has something to do with what distinguishes us from other animals; the effect, then, of the expressive doctrine is to make us see the locus of our humanity in the power of expression by which we constitute language in the broadest sense – that is, the range of symbolic forms. For it is these that make thought possible. It is this range of expressions that constitutes what we know as *logos*.

The whole development, through the seventeenth-century designative theory and the Romantic expressive view, has brought language more and more to centre stage in our understanding of human beings: first as an instrument of the typically human capacity of thinking, and then as the indispensable medium without which our typically human capacities, emotions, relations wouldn't be.

If we follow the expressive view, then we have to come to understand this medium and the extraordinary range of activities that constitutes it if we are ever to hope to understand ourselves. What I want to suggest is that we have all in fact become followers of the expressive view – not that we accept the detail of the various Romantic theories, but in that we have all been profoundly marked by this way of understanding thought and language, which has had a major impact on our civilization. I would venture to claim that even those who would want to reject expressive theories as metaphysical rubbish and obfuscatory mystification are nevertheless deeply affected by this outlook.

I will make at least a feeble attempt to defend this outrageous claim below. My point here is that the profound influence of the expressive view in modern culture is what underlies our fascination for language, our making it such a central question of twentieth-century thought and study.

This would also explain why language is more enigmatic to us than to previous ages – admittedly another highly controversial claim. For on the expressive view, language is no longer merely the external clothing of thought, nor a simple instrument that ought in principle to be fully in our control and oversight. It is more like a medium in which we are plunged and that we cannot fully plumb. The difficulty is compounded in that it is not just the medium in virtue of which we can describe the world, but also that in virtue of which we are capable of the human emotions and of standing in specifically human relations to each other.

And flowing from this, the capacity we want to understand is not just that by which we produce prose about the things that surround us, but also those by which we make poetry, music, art, dance, and so on, even in the end those by which we have such a thing as personal style.

This means that the phenomenon of language becomes much broader as well as deeper when we move from a designative to an expressive perspective. We are tempted to ask what this range of capacities has in common. And even if we have been taught by Wittgenstein to resist this temptation, the question cannot but arise of how they hold together as a "package." For this they seem to do. It is not an accident that the only speaking animal is also the one who dances, makes music, paints, and so on. Finding the centre of gravity of this range is a much more difficult and baffling question than tracing how words designate – that is, until we come to see that the latter question leads us back to the former.

But this is what the expressive understanding of language puts on our agenda: that we find this centre of gravity, or in other terms, come to some insight about this extraordinary capacity we have for expression.

Or we can get to the heart of the same issues in another way if we ask what is the characteristic excellence of expression. On the designative view, this was clear. Language was an instrument. It was at its best when it best served its purpose, when the terms designated clearly distinct ideas, and we maintained their definitions clearly before us in our reasoning. On this understanding language was an all-purpose tool of thought. But for the expressivist, it is an activity that constitutes a specific way of being in the world, which Herder referred to as "reflection," but which it is hard to find a word for just because we are so baffled to define what I called its centre of gravity.

Another way of asking what this centre of gravity is is to ask when this way of being is at its best, its fullest – in other words, what constitutes its excellence. When are our expressive powers most fully realized? We can no longer assume that just attaining maximum clarity about the things we describe and explain constitutes perfection.

But to know what it is to realize our expressive powers to the fullest must be to know something about the characteristic perfection of human beings on the premises of the expressive understanding, and so this question must come on our agenda.

Again, the question of what expression is can arise in another way. We try to understand how expression can *arise*, how a new medium of thought or understanding can come to be through expression. And since we can't study the genesis of language in human life, our question takes the form of asking, when we come close now to forging new modes of expression: What happens when we extend our capacity for expression? How does this come about?

For a variety of reasons, many contemporaries have thought it plausible that it is in artistic creation that we come closest to understanding this, to understanding the mystery of original expression; and this is one of the reasons why art is so central to our self-understanding.

But the baffling nature of language extends to more than the nature of expression. It also touches the question "Who expresses?" We saw above that language for the Romantics couldn't be seen as the creation of the individual. And indeed, it is hard to fault them on this. We are all inducted into language by an existing language community. We learn to talk not only in that the words are given to us by our parents and others, but also in that they talk to us and hence give us the status of interlocutors. This is what is involved in the centrally important fact that we are given a name. In being given a name we are made into beings that one addresses, and we are inducted into the community whose speaking continually remakes the language. As interlocutors, we learn to say "I" of ourselves, one of the key stages in our becoming language users.

Language originally comes to us from others, from a community. But how much does it remain an activity essentially bound to a community? Once I learn language can I just continue to use it, even extend it, quite monologically, talking and writing only for myself? Once again, the designative view tends to make us see this as perfectly possible. My lexicon is under *my* control. And common sense tends to side here at first sight with the designative view. Surely, I very often do talk to myself, I can even invent private names for people, and why not also private terms for objects that surround me?

Of course, I can invent private terms. But the question is whether my speech doesn't always remain that of an interlocutor in a speech community in an essential way. We might ask whether my conception of what it makes sense to say, of how things may be perspicuously described, of how things can be illuminatingly classified, of how my feelings can be adequately expressed, whether all these are not profoundly shaped by a potential terrain of intersubjective agreement and full communication. I may break away now from my interlocutors and adopt a quite other mode of expression, but is it not always in view of a fuller, more profound and authentic communication, which provides the criterion for what I now recognize as an adequate expression?

So the question remains open as to whether the subject of speech isn't always in some sense, and on some level, a speech community.

Another related question concerns the place of the subject in expression. It is in a sense the question "What is expressed?" or "What comes to expression?" Of course, our developing language, insofar as it is descriptive language, responds to the shape of things around us. But we have seen that there is another dimension to language: that by which its development shapes our emotions and relations. Expression shapes our human lives. The question is, "What is it that, in coming to expression, so shapes our lives as human?"

For the expressivists of the late eighteenth century and the Romantic period, the answer was quite unproblematical. Expression was self-expression. What comes to full expression are my desires, my aspirations, my moral sentiments. What comes to light in the full development of expressive power is precisely that what was striving for expression all along was the self. This may not have been so in the earlier ages of human history, when individuals were prone to see themselves simply as immersed in a larger cosmos and not also as centres of autonomous will and desire. But as it comes to greater self-clarity, expression comes to be recognized as self-expression.

But the basic expressivist insights might also suggest another account: What comes about through the development of language in the broadest sense is the coming to be of expressive power, the power to make things manifest. It is not unambiguously clear that this ought to be considered as a self-expression/realization. What is made manifest is not exclusively, not even mainly, the self, but a world. Why think here primarily in terms of self-expression?

Now the expressivists of the Romantic period didn't really need to pose this question because in a sense they could accept both answers at once. They could do so because of the notion, common in the Romantic period, of God as a kind of cosmic subject, of which we finite subjects are in a sense emanations. This view, which hovers on the brink of pantheism, allows us to see what we make manifest in our language both as our own and as God's, since God lives in us. We express both ourselves and a larger reality of which we are a part.

With the receding of this too indulgent pantheism (as it must appear to us), we are left with the choice: Is the expression that makes us human essentially a self-expression in that we are mainly responding to our way of feeling/experiencing the world and bringing this to expression? Or are we responding to the reality in which we are set, in which we are included, of course, but which is not reducible to our experience of it?

The commonsense of our society takes perhaps too easily the position of the Romantics, without even the excuse of their pantheistic justification. It assumes that in our paradigm of expressive activities – for instance, in artistic creation – we are expressing ourselves, our feelings and reactions. But this answer is also challenged. Some contemporaries would argue that our most expressive creations, hence those where we are closest to deploying our expressive power at the fullest, are not self-expressions – that they rather have the power to move us because they manifest our expressive power itself and its relation to our world. In this kind of expression, we are responding to the way things are, rather than just exteriorizing our feelings.

Heidegger springs to mind in this connection. Something like this view may lie behind this passage, quoted from *Dichterisch wohnt der Mensch*: "Man behaves as if he were the creator and master of language, whereas on the contrary, it is language which is and remains his sovereign ... For in the proper sense of these terms, it is language which speaks. Man speaks insofar as he replies to language by listening to what it says to him. Language makes us a sign and it is language which first and last conducts us in this way towards the being of a thing."

On this view what we strive to bring to expression is not primarily the self. Expressivism here becomes radically antisubjectivist. And of course, this issue arises from another angle: the one mentioned above about the characteristic excellence of expression and hence of human beings.

These questions are all difficult and deep. I mean by that latter term not only that they touch fundamental questions about ourselves, but that they are baffling and very difficult to formulate, let alone find a clear strategy to investigate. But they are among the questions that the expressive view puts on our agenda. My hypothesis is that we are fascinated and baffled by language in part because we are heirs of this outlook.

But I must face the objection, which must have been urging itself all this time, that surely I can't be claiming that we all accept the main doctrines of the expressive view of language, that there are no more designativists, or even more implausibly, that there are no more proponents of objectifying science? Of course, I agree, that would be absurd. The stock of objectifying science is as high as ever. The virtually inarticulate belief that only an objective account is a truly satisfactory one has invaded the sciences of humankind, has shaped the procedures of widely practiced academic disciplines, like psychology, sociology, political science, much of linguistics. Moreover, one of the underlying motives of an objective account, which we saw with the seventeenth-century designative theory – that it seems to promise control over the domain under study – is as forcefully operative today as then; indeed, more so.

But in spite of this, I want to maintain my claim that the expressivist reasons for bafflement are to some extent shared by all of us. I should like to offer two grounds for this.

The first is that much of the Romantic view of language has come to be generally accepted by both metaphysical camps: objectivists and their opponents. We now see language capacity as residing in the possession of an interconnected lexicon, only one part of which is used at any time. We see that the individual term is defined in relation to the others. Fernand de Saussure made this point at the beginning of the century, and it is now common property.

At the same time we recognize the central importance of speech activity for language. Language as a code (Saussure's *langue*) can be seen as a kind of precipitate of speech (Saussure's *parole*). Speech activity itself is complex: The declarative sentence is not just the result of concatenating words with their attached meanings. It involves doing different things, picking out an object of reference, and saying something about this object. These different functions and their combination in the declarative utterance determine to a significant degree the kind of language we have. But on top of this we also recognize that speech activity goes well beyond the declarative utterance, and includes questions, orders, prayers, and so on.

We are also ready to recognize that this activity involves mechanisms of which we are not fully aware and that we do not fully control. We don't find a thesis like that of Chomsky strange – for example, that our grasp of grammaticality involves the application of transformations of which we are not consciously aware, relating a depth structure to a surface structure. We accept without too much demur that there may well be a "depth structure" to our language activity.

And we are perhaps even ready to agree that the language that is evolved through this speech activity is the language of a community and not just of an individual – in other words, that the crucial speech activities are those of the community. We may not be entirely sure what this means, but we have a sense that in some meaning it contains an important truth.

Of course, this doesn't mean that everyone has become an expressivist. We aren't in any sense forced to abandon the metaphysical stance in favour of objective accounts. But what we now have to do is apply them in a new way. We see language as a whole, as an activity with – potentially at least – a depth structure. The task is now to give an objective account of this depth structure and its operation, which underlies the activity of language we observe. This is now the agenda.

In this the science of language is simply one example of a global shift in the objectivistic sciences of humankind since the eighteenth century. The shift is away from a set of theories in terms of "surface" or observable realities, principally the contents of the mind available to introspection, in favour of theories in terms of "deep" or unobservable mechanisms or structures. The shift is one aspect of the virtually total disappearance of the seventeenth- and eighteenth-century "way of ideas," the attempt to understand the mind in terms of its introspectable contents, the science that came to be called "ideology" at the moment when it had passed its peak.

This was grounded in the view, common to Descartes and his empiricist critics, that the contents of the mind were in principle open to transparent inspection by the subject him or herself. Thinking was, as we saw, "mental discourse," which ought to be entirely self-possessed and self-transparent. This view seems very implausible today, where the importance of unconscious structures and processes in thought seems very plausible – indeed, close to undeniable.

But the scientific goals and norms of the seventeenth and eighteenth centuries easily survived the demise of the "way of ideas." In place of the "surface" psychologies of the past, we now have explanation by-passing consciousness: in some cases, by ignoring the psychological altogether and explaining behaviour in terms of stimulus and response or else in terms of a depth theory that is physiological; in others, by what remains a "psychological" theory but one drawing heavily on mechanisms unavailable to consciousness, such as Freudian psychoanalysis or computer-modelled theories of our intelligent performance. In place of "surface" sociologies, based on the adjustment of conscious interests, or the existence or absence of individual habits of mind, we have theories of social structure, in which individuals are caught up in a dynamic that they do not and perhaps cannot understand, where the explanation is at the level of the social whole and of properties of this whole that are not evident to the participants. These follow the laws or obey the constraints of historical materialism or structural-functionalism.

Now in many of these cases – for example, Freud, Marx, structural-functionalism – the depth structures elaborated obviously owe a lot to earlier Romantic theorizing. But the fact remains that the intent of these theories is to give an objectivistic explanation.

And in this, of course, they are following a lead set by the "hard" sciences of nature, which also have had recourse more and more to unobservable depth structures, even including some that violate our ordinary macroscopic understanding of things.

If we were to try to explain this shift that has gradually taken place over the last two centuries, away from the way of ideas, then undoubtedly the example of the hard sciences, always the paradigms of objectivistic science, is an important factor. But it can't be the only one. Something would have to be said about the change in our condition. Perhaps it is that in modern mass societies we feel less of a sense that the factors that are decisive for our behaviour are under our purview, that what society claims of us is something we give knowingly even if not willingly, than did the educated classes of the earlier epoch. I think something like this is true, but even so, a great deal remains to be explained. Why do we understand ourselves so readily in depth-psychological terms? Something very important about the whole development of modern society is waiting here to be uncovered.

But in any case, the science of language has followed this pattern. We are no longer satisfied with surface accounts of the application of words to ideas. We want an account in terms of depth structure. But many want the same scientific goals to be paramount.

But although the metaphysical goals survive unscathed into the new sciences of depth structure, the fact that so much has been taken on board from the Romantic conception makes it inevitable that something like the same questions arise as those expressivism puts on the agenda. For instance, there is a continuing issue about how to understand the notion of depth structure, as the philosophical debates around Chomsky's work attest. Is depth structure to be understood as the operation of an unconscious capacity – for example, do we know how to make transformations even though we are unaware of doing so? This seems to many unbearably paradoxical. Or should we see depth structures in terms of underlying operations that are analogous to those in machines? But then what is their relation to the intelligent and conscious uses of language? From either direction, some mystery surrounds the status of the language capacity as a whole, which plainly underlies our ability to say specific things on specific occasions. The baffling questions the expressive view gives rise to won't disappear just because we stick to our objectivist metaphysic. Some seem to arise inescapably with the intuition that language involves some global underlying capacity, and not just a set of particulate dispositions to utter certain words in certain circumstances.

This threatens to create something of a dilemma for objectivistic thought and leads to the characteristic gamut of modern would-be scientific theories. At one extreme are those who are highly sensitive to the metaphysical dangers of allowing depth explanations. They would like ideally to develop a behaviourist theory, in which the utterance of certain words is made a function of environmental stimulation. Skinner is the most spectacular protagonist of this view.

But the weakness of this strategy is that the explanatory power of such a theory is very poor, and it even comes close to absurdity at times. And so we gain greatly in plausibility by moving along the spectrum to what we might call "neodesignative" theories of meaning, like that, for example, of Donald Davidson. This theory can be called "neo-designative" because it attempts to give an account of meaning in terms of the truth conditions of sentences. These truth conditions are observable states of affairs in the world; hence once again we have the basic demarche of a theory that tries to explain the meaning of language in terms of the relation of linguistic elements to extralinguistic reality. Only here, the modern theory has profited from our understanding of language as a structured reality, so that the elements so related are not words but declarative sentences.

These theories – another example might be explanations of the function of language on the model of information-processing mechanisms – are more plausible than behaviourism, but they still give no recognition to the expressive dimension. But it is possible to move further along the spectrum to give some recognition to this, while trying to explain it in objectivist terms.

Two examples spring to mind, which however are not concerned with theories of language in the narrow sense but with – in different ways – symbolic expression. These are the views of Marx and Freud.

Freud recognizes symbolic expression in our symptoms as well as in what he calls symbols. But these are explained in terms of desires, which are not themselves desires for symbolic expression nor involve such expression in their proper fufillment. On the contrary, the symbolic proliferation results from their blocking or inhibition. The symptom gives my object of desire in symbolic form because I cannot (will not allow myself to) go after it in reality. Moreover, these desires should ultimately be explicable physiologically – hence Freud's electrical and hydraulic languages.

With Marx, we also have a recognition of symbolic expression in ideological consciousness: Religion, for instance, gives us a distorted expression of the human social condition of its age. With the liberation of classless society, and the victory of scientific over ideological consciousness, such symbolic forms of awareness are swept aside. And from the standpoint of scientific consciousness, the ideological symbolism is fully explicable, again in terms that have nothing to do with a motivation directed to symbolic expression. This rather is seen as a distortion of the reality and hence of the underlying motives, which come to clear self-recognition in scientific consciousness.

This account may be somewhat unfair to Marxism, as it may also be to Freud, in giving an unduly reductive cast to their explanations. But whether we have here portrayed true or vulgar Marxism and Freudianism, the theories obviously have their weaknesses in that they have trouble dealing with the place of expression, of symbolism in normal, undistorted or nonpathological life. When they try to say something in the domain of aesthetics, for instance, Marxism and Freudianism must develop more refined interpretations on pain of sounding philistine and implausibly reductive.

We have examples of such developed – and semiologically sensitive – Marxism and Freudianism in contemporary French structuralism – for example, in different ways, Lacan, Barthes, Althusser. But this structuralism has taken a step further along the spectrum. It allows expression a central place in human life. It understands that *Homo sapiens* is the language animal in that language is more than a tool for human beings but somehow constitutes a way of being that is specifically human. We have to understand the growth of language as bound up with the development of a form of life that it makes possible – so that the question can arise of the characteristic excellence of language, of when expression is at its best.

As a matter of fact, modern structuralism owes quite a bit to the reflections of expressivist philosophers. For instance, Levy-Strauss read Merleau-Ponty with interest. Lacan has been very influenced by Hegel and Heidegger (his Hegel being mediated through Kojeve, who picked Heideggerian themes out of Hegel).

But the intent remains "scientific" – that is, objectivist. In Levy-Strauss's case, for instance, drawing from the work of Marcel Mauss, the basic idea – at least of his early theory – seems to be that language arises in a drive to classify, which in turn must be understood as ultimately aimed at social/moral order. We order our lives through classifications of things forbidden and allowed, enjoined or neutral. The classificatory scheme of our totems, of segments of the universe, is ordered to a classification of partners and actions, which alone makes possible social integration.

This theory sees the expressive function as central, sees it as necessary indeed to the very existence of human society. But it lays claim, too, to objectivity, presumably in that its account of language is functional and reductive. For the function that explains language is not the manifestation of anything but the maintenance of a social order. (In this it shows the Durkheimian roots of so much French social thought.) Once more language is to be explained in terms of something else.

But as we come to this end of the spectrum, the questions that the expressive view brings forward become harder and harder to avoid. With contemporary structuralism, great mysteries surround the status of the underlying structures – for example, their relation to the uses of language in everyday life and their relation to the individual subject. These are comparable to the questions that arise from the expressive view; indeed, in some cases the questions are the same.

I ran through this gamut in order to illustrate the dilemma of modern objectivist theories of language. They can avoid the intrusion of the baffling questions concerning the nature of expression only by espousing narrower and more primitive theories that are either implausible, or that fail to explain an important range of the phenomena of language, or both. Or they can win plausibility and explanatory range but at the cost of opening themselves to these questions.

This is the first ground I would put forward for my claim that we are all affected to some degree by the expressivist reasons for bafflement about language. It concerns the predicament of scientific theorizing about language. My second ground can be put much more tersely. Regardless of scientific considerations, modern students of language remain children of our age and immersed in its culture. And this has been so massively affected by the Romantic-expressivist rebellion that no one can remain untouched by it. This effect is particularly visible in our understanding of art, its nature, and its place in human life. One of the most obtrusive effects is the concern of much contemporary art with the process of its own creation, with the properties of its own medium, with the experimental creation of new media. Expression itself becomes its theme: how it is possible, just what it consists in, and what point it can give to human life. The artist becomes his or her own subject, and/or the process of creation his or her theme.

It is very difficult to live in this civilization and not have the problem of expression obtrude on us, with all its enigmatic force. And that is the reason,

I want to maintain, why we are all so concerned and fascinated with language, so that even the most tough-minded and empiricist philosophies, like logical empiricism, are "linguistic" in cast.

I hope that this historical odyssey has cast light on our contemporary fascination with language. I hope that it has also shown why we find it baffling and has done something to explain the paradox that, with all the advance of science, this central human function seems more mysterious to us than to our eighteenth-century predecessors.

In fact, seen from this historical perspective, the development toward our present understanding of language as both central and enigmatic seems irreversible. We cannot recapture the earlier perspectives from which language could appear more marginal or less problematic. The view of the universe as an order of signs is lost forever, at least in its original form, after the coming of modern science and the modern notion of freedom; and the view of language as a set of designative signs, fully in our control and purview, is lost forever with the seventeenth-century view of the punctual subject, perfectly transparent to him or herself, whose soul contained nothing that he or she couldn't observe. From where we stand, we are constantly forced to the conception of *Homo sapiens* as a language animal, one who is constituted by language.

But I don't hope for agreement on this. Because in our bafflement, we naturally split into two camps. This reflects the pull on us of the contradictory metaphysical demands: for the clarity and control offered by an objective account of ourselves and our world, on one hand, and toward a recognition of the intrinsic, irreducible nature of expression, on the other. There are very few of us who don't feel the force of both these demands. And perhaps just for this reason we divide with polemical fervour into opposing parties: expressors and designators.

The battle between expressors and designators is one front in the global war between the heirs of the Enlightenment and the Romantics, such as we see in the struggle between technocracy and the sense of history or community, instrumental reason versus the intrinsic value of certain forms of life, the domination of nature versus the need for the reconciliation with nature. This general war rages over the battlefronts of language as well. Heidegger is one of the prophets of the stance of "letting things be," one of the great critics of modern technological consciousness; the neodesignators defend a notion of reason as instrumental reason. All this is no accident. It shows only how much rides on this issue.

The issue concerns the nature of humankind, or what it is to be human. And since so much of this turns on what it is to think, to reason, to create, and since all of these point us toward language, we can expect that the study of language will become even more a central concern of our intellectual life. It is in a sense the crucial locus of the theoretical battle we are having with ourselves.

As a civilization, we live with a compromise. In our scientific understanding, we tend to be men of the Enlightenment, and we accept the predominance of Enlightenment – one might say, utilitarian – values in setting the parameters of public policy. Growth, productivity, welfare are of fundamental importance. But it is recognized that – without prejudice to the perhaps ultimately available scientific explanation, which will be reductive – people experience things in expressive terms: Something is "more me"; or I feel fulfilled by this, not by that; or that prospect really "speaks to me." Along with this tolerance of experience goes a parallel in the public domain. The main limits of public policy are set by the requirements of production within the constraints of distribution, and these are meant to be established by scientific means and in a utilitarian spirit. But private experience must be given its expressive fulfillment. There is a "Romantik" of private life, which is meant to fit into a smoothly running consumer society.

However effective this compromise may be politically, it is a rotten one intellectually; it combines the crassest scientism (objectivism) with the most subjectivist forms of expressivism. But I suppose I say it's rotten mainly because I think that both of these are wrong and that they leave out the really fruitful line of enquiry: a contemporary expressivism that tries to go beyond subjectivism in discovering and articulating what is expressed.

But even leaving aside my commitments, it is certain that in the absence of a strong expressivist critique, scientism remains smugly satisfied with its half-baked explanations, and the subjectivist conception of experience veers toward formless sentimentalism. The issue of language goes by default, which means the issue of what it is to be human goes, too.

CHARLES TAYLOR is a Board of Trustees Professor at Northwestern University, where he is jointly appointed to the Law School and the Weinberg College of Arts and Sciences. He is also Emeritus Professor in the Department of Philosophy at McGill University and continues to teach both philosophy and political science there. A Rhodes Scholar, Dr Taylor was the Chichele Professor of political and social theory at Oxford in 1976. He is the author and coauthor of many books, among them his well-known *Patterns of Politics*, as well as numerous articles and papers.

Charles Taylor is a Companion of the Order of Canada, a fellow of both the Royal Society of Canada and the British Academy, a member of the American Academy of Arts and Sciences, and a Grand Officer of l'Ordre national du Québec. He has received a number of prestigious awards, including a Canada Council Molson Prize; two Canada Council Killam Research Fellowships; the 1992 Prix Léon-Gérin; and the 1997 Stuttgart Hegel Prize.

15

The Canadian Constitution:
What Is at Stake in the West?

STANLEY C. ROBERTS, 1979

Claude Ryan chose the title "Choose Quebec and Canada" for his document on Quebec's constitutional future released a month ago. Would it be inappropriate of me to subtitle this paper "Choose the West and Canada"?

Anywhere else but in Quebec it seems to be regarded as heretical to place region above country. Premier Peter Lougheed, the skilled and successful defender of Albertan's rights, opens every address related in any way to federal-provincial affairs with a statement such as: "Make no mistake about it, we are Canadians first and Albertans second!" More and more he finds it necessary to repeat what should be the obvious: that we are Canadians first.

Why? Because when you are west of Winnipeg (and sometimes when you are west of the Lakehead) we, all of us, need reminding that we are part of the Canadian family. Surely it must occur to most, as it does to me, that if it is not in question, why *do* we protest so much? Every time I address this topic of Canadianism, a little Shakespearean voice in the back of my head mumbles "The lady doth protest too much, methinks."

All the nation watches with interest, anticipation, and, sometimes, trepidation the result of the Quebec referendum. We have become totally preoccupied with the question of Quebec's future: Will she vote "yes" in the first referendum, who will win the next provincial election, will there be a second or a third referendum? And when the politicians speak of "national unity" as being or, alternatively, as not being the critical issue in the May 22 federal election – don't we all auto-matically assume that the words "national unity" refer to Quebec's place in Canada? That point is driven home in the West, especially because it is usually followed by a reference to the West's natural resources (read that as the western colony's natural resources) as a Canadian resource to be used by the federal government at times of compelling national interest in the name of national unity.

(Let me consider for a moment the thought expressed in a quotation from Premier Allan Blakeney's speech in Toronto in September 1977: "We in the West find it passing strange that the national interest emerges only when we are talking about Western *resources* or Eastern *benefits*. If oil, why not iron ore and steel? If natural gas, why not copper? If uranium, why not nickel?")

But is the national unity question confined to the Quebec/Canada issue? To Westerners it is not.

I assume that we can agree with the pollsters who say that when the Quebec question is put, sometime in the next twelve months, it will read some version of: "Do you give Premier Levesque and the Government of Quebec a mandate to negotiate for the people of Quebec a new and different relationship with the Government of Canada?" And I assume we can agree that some 50 per cent of the people of Quebec will vote "yes." But it has not occurred to most that if the same question was put to any one of the four Western provinces or two territories, substituting "the people of the West" for "the people of Quebec," the answer likely would be an overwhelming "yes" – 50 to 90 per cent in favour of a new deal depending on which province or northern territory (Manitoba being the least favourable). It is self-evident that in the current inflammatory mood in the West, with four provincial elections, a federal election, a government upheaval in the Yukon, and a new Commissioner of the Northwest Territories, all in a period of twenty months, no responsible leader has asked the question "Are we satisfied with Confederation?" To flirt with the question would be undeniably dangerous!

Meanwhile, politicians across Canada involved in election campaigns are successfully using the adage of old and wise philosophers: "To keep people loyal to yourself, keep them angry at someone else."

How is it that such a mood of discontent has developed in the West? What are the forces at play?

The rationale is of both a historic and contemporary nature. The current concerns have been only an extension of and a failure to redress old wounds. While the problems, the disaffections of the West, are being expressed in new ways and the battles being fought by new methods, the issues change very little. Perhaps that is the greatest frustration of all: The concerns of the West always seem so casually brushed aside by the national government – politicians and bureaucrats alike who tap Westerners on the head and say, "You look pretty well-fed to me!"

The new fury of the Westerner demonstrates itself when it strikes home that Quebec's six million-plus citizens have turned the country on its collective ear and created an enormous attention to their problems by the election of a Péquiste government, while the West's six million-plus citizens (still) can't be heard over the rush and scramble to accommodate Quebec. Sometimes the West's frustration and rage is misconstrued as anti-Quebec in nature. It is not. It is, in most cases, envy of Quebec's political prowess combined with fury at the West's own impotence on the national scene.

There is a great deal of excellent material published on the West's disaffection. It should be read because without understanding the historic facts, it is difficult to grasp the nature and depth of feeling in the West. There are several excellent books on the times of Louis Riel, and on the early days of settlement, gold rush, and railroads into British Columbia. J.R. Mallory's *Social Credit and the Federal Power*, Morton's *The Progressive Party*, and recent collections such as *The Unfinished Revolt*, *The One Prairie Province Conference*, *Canada West Foundation's Review of W.E.O.C.*, and 1977's *The Burden of Canadian Unity* should be read. But most of all, every Canadian should read the history of Canada again, especially Arthur Lower's *Colony to Nation*. If one reads and understands our own really very short history, then the prejudices we hold, the difficulty so prevalent in negotiations *within* Canada, and the absence of the glue, the adhesive, so desperately needed to hold Canada together at this time are all more comprehensible.

Perhaps when we better understand this complex and promising creature called Canada, all Canadians will be better able to resolve the conflicts that divide her.

The political history of Western Canada must be included in any understanding of today's problems. Was the West in any way included in the negotiating, bargaining, and dealing that created the BNA Act and Canada in 1867? No, for obvious reasons. But were Manitoba's interests properly represented when she entered Confederation in 1870? Was British Columbia tricked by the wily John A. Macdonald in 1871? Just how much voice did Alberta and Saskatchewan have in determining their own destinies in 1905, when the territories were arbitrarily divided into two provinces. Two provinces, instead of one strong one, would likely remain divided in objectives and not unite to pose a threat to federal dictates, thought Sir Wilfrid Laurier.

Most of all, I suppose, the National Policy imposed on Canada, including the West, by John A. Macdonald one hundred years ago, when the first railway was being built and the national Parliament decided that the West had to be exploited, has had the most impact of all. The National Policy had three essential parts:

First: an admittedly discriminatory freight rate (i.e., higher per ton mile in the West) to pay the big bills of new rail lines across Canada – an issue that has grown and is still in effect today.

Second: a restrictive trade policy imposing high tariffs on most imported goods ("anyone who asked for a tariff got it," said Lower), which favoured growth of central Canadian secondary industry. It hurt all consumers and hurt Western Canadian chances

of developing an industrial base. (This is still a bone of contention in every part of
the West.)

Third: an immigration policy that would populate all of the West as rapidly as people
from all over the world could be attracted.

Roughly one hundred years after Manitoba and British Columbia entered
Confederation, over ninety years after Macdonald's National Policy pronounce-
ment, and nearly seventy years after Saskatchewan and Alberta became
provinces, the first full-scale meeting between East and West took place. The
date was 1973, the place Calgary, the event the Western Economic Opportunities
Conference (WEOC). The prime minister and his Cabinet came West to meet with
the four premiers and their Cabinets.

This is what the four premiers said then:

- Premier Ed Schreyer (Manitoba): "In part I think [Western alienation] exists because
  many Western Canadians feel that their efforts, their contributions to the development
  of our nation, have encountered too many man-made obstacles, which are visible in
  the national policy."
- Premier Peter Lougheed (Alberta): "It's a feeling of Western Canadians that we have
  a great deal going for us in the West, but we feel frustrated in reaching out for potential
  because we sense such potential is not fully understood or appreciated in Central
  Canada and hence, we are thwarted by federal government policies."
- Premier Allan Blakeney (Saskatchewan): "What we are really asking is that you free
  our hands of the shackles of history which deny us the fulfillment of our destiny. We
  come here determined to break out of the economic framework decreed by Canada's
  national policy of the nineteenth century."
- Premier David Barrett (British Columbia): "Unfortunately, present-day federal government policies still encourage the concentration of the country's business, industry,
  and financial capital in Central Canada. It is now time to alter federal government
  policies which, for one hundred years, have worked against the allocation of financial
  resources to the Western region."

The attitude of Westerners – at the government level and at the business level;
indeed, that of most every worker, farmer, and fisherman in the West – is that
the pledges made at the WEOC in 1973 have not been kept by the federal
government, especially on the two issues seen as those that have kept the West
from developing an industrial base all through this century: freight rates and
pro-Central Canada tariffs.

The WEOC created great expectations but has resulted in an even greater
disillusionment.

The new premiers of the West, those who were not in office at the time of the WEOC, have since expressed their views clearly at first ministers conferences and elsewhere. The economic concerns remain, and both have looked to a new order through Canadian constitutional improvements to ameliorate the Western industrial disadvantage. Speaking in Ottawa in October 1978, Premier Sterling Lyon said, "Constitutions and constitutional arrangements are only a means to the end of maintaining a stable, ordered, prosperous, and free society." Premier Bill Bennett said, "In constitutional terms British Columbia [with over 10 per cent of the Canadian population] is afforded little more weight [in the federal system] than it was given in 1871. That situation must change." Speaking with conviction, and with the kind of confidence one gains from an overwhelming mandate, such as that received from the people of Alberta on 14 March 1979, Premier Lougheed said on that night: "The West's time in Confederation has come." The West cheered.

Paradoxically, it may be the third part of Macdonald's national policy that has had the greatest impact on the West.

We are all a product of our heritage, our roots. None more so than Western Canadians.

Western Canadians are not a homogeneous lot, as everyone knows. But they do have one thing in common from Yukon to the Ontario border: they chose the West. Western Canada is not an extension of Ontario and Quebec, Upper and Lower Canada. Western Canada has its own dynamic: The colloquial expression is "the mosaic of the West." They came from nearly every country in the world to pioneer in Western Canada. Some came by water, some overland, more than one-half entered the Prairies via the United States. A minority came from Ontario and Quebec, and those who did *came* because they felt the West offered more opportunity. Western Canada *is not*, as is so often assumed in Ottawa, a westward extension of Central Canada.

Western Canadians, then, have different roots, different cultures, and different biases. They speak mainly English today, but their forefathers spoke Gaelic, German, Ukrainian, Polish, various Scandinavian tongues, English, and Dutch, and some spoke French. It is not difficult to determine why so few Westerners understand the 1965 discovery of the duality of Canada. "Which duality?" it is asked. It is insensitive for successive federal governments to press what are seen as new concepts of language and culture on six and a half million people spread over 70 per cent of Canada's land mass, all of whom have their own hopes and fears, few of whom have any comprehension of the necessity of the two-language concept or the complexity of the bilingual issue. Never has a Canadian program been worse explained, or implemented in a more ham-handed way, than the bilingual project, or for that matter, the provisions of the Official Languages Act.

Western Canadians historically have developed an "unusual-for-Canada" interest in political action. In the recent past the West has given birth to the Cooperative Commonwealth Federation (CCF) Party, the Social Credit Party, the United Farmers of Alberta and of Manitoba, and the Progressives. Each was a protest movement. Each had a purpose, and each established clearly that there was a mood of discontent in the West and that the traditional Grits and Tories of Upper and Lower Canada had not captured the mood, let alone the needs and ambitions, of this new Canada West.

On the federal scene the Progressives achieved the greatest success and in the 1920s could have been the official opposition in Ottawa if they had so chosen. Instead they chose to use their sixty-five seats to cause the Liberals and/or the Conservatives to recognize their demands. After a few concessions and some trade-offs, the wily Mackenzie King managed to absorb by osmosis the leaders of the party and thereby smother the challenge.

More recently, the West saw one of its own, John Diefenbaker, elected as prime minister. There was joy in the Prairies in particular, for it was known that someone "who understood the problems" ruled Canada with a mighty majority in 1958. Soon the joy turned once again to frustration as the West's own son was rejected within four years. "The Bay Street barons had done him in," it was said.

The voting pattern of Western Canadians has long been out of sync with the rest of Canada. In their perceptive study on Western alienation and political culture to appear soon in *The Canadian Political Process*, David Elton and Roger Gibbins established the regional nature of Western voting patterns, and it is their contention that the core of this refusal to vote in a similar pattern to the rest of Canada is really Western alienation.

Certainly it is evident that Western Canadians have not chosen to vote for the party in power during the past twenty years. Alberta, in particular, has refused to elect a Liberal MP for the last two elections. Other Westerners have been only marginally more friendly to the government. It is not hard to find those who will give odds that the Liberals will be blanked again in Alberta, and will win only a handful of seats in the other three provinces, during the 1979 election.

The result has been a continuing chicken-and-egg situation. Western Canadians refuse to vote for the government. There are few MPs and fewer Western Cabinet ministers on the government side, so the voter becomes even more disaffected with the federal government – and indeed with the party system as it operates in Canada today.

The West's political history would indicate the high probability of a new political action emanating from the West should the Liberals continue to dominate national politics. The strength of the disaffection with recent federal governments and the prevailing mood of refusing to be forced to vote in any one way in order to be legitimately heard in Cabinet and in Parliament are clear indicators that Westerners are looking for a "new deal" in Confederation. The Western Canadian history of being able to spawn powerful political movements in an extremely short time would indicate that there likely will be a new protest in the form of political action in the West if there is not immediate satisfaction with the government to be elected 22 May 1979. The once-powerful Progressive Party was organized in less than a year for the 1921 election. It could happen as quickly again. The new-found prosperity of the West would make it very difficult to co-opt such a force, as the Progressives were co-opted fifty years ago.

The negative or positive action that such a new political movement would have on the Canadian scene would depend largely on the leadership of such a party. Would they contribute to building Canada, or would they help to break it into parts as the péquistes of Quebec would do? There is no way of knowing.

In my view, the probability that any Western Canadian concerted action would be country-building in nature, rather than destructive, depends on the people of Canada and their willingness to see, in the very near future, a new deal for Canada. Such a new deal must include a recognition of the concerns and aspirations of the West. It must also include a forum in which those concerns and aspirations can be addressed in an on-going, dynamic way.

What is at stake for the West in a new Constitution, in a new Confederation? At stake is the long-awaited opportunity for the West to be heard at the centre – to have a federal system in place that will allow for the concerns and aspirations of the West (as well as the concerns and aspirations of the people from the Maritimes and Newfoundland) to be heard, addressed, and, where possible, ameliorated by the government of Canada. The rich, fast-growing, vibrant, aggressive, and abrasive regions known as Canada West do not now have fair or proportionate access to the decision-making processes of the nation. Decisions affecting Canada and the West are made without adequate or necessary input from the West.

The West is once again demanding input in 1979 as they did in 1921 and 1958. This time, however, they have the power of a prosperous economy based on natural resources, plus an increasingly vital and essential contribution to Canada's balance of payments and to the prosperity of the land. This time they will be in a better position to make their demands for a revised federal system become reality. The alternative is not clear. At our dozens of public meetings across every part of the West, it is referred to in a typical Western manner: "Or else!" The statement is almost always some version of: "The time has come for a new deal for the West, or else!"

After all these years the West is not impatient for immediate results. What is demanded is an immediate turnaround in the direction of public policy – some evidence of progress. The West feels, as Oliver Wendell Holmes once wrote: "The great thing in this world is not so much where we stand as in what direction we are moving."

Perhaps in the West lies a better understanding of the fundamental principles of a federal system of government than that which exists elsewhere in Canada. It is not an exaggeration to say that if the West is to become a full partner in Confederation – the federation of Canada – then there must be a renewed commitment to certain basics. Federalism is not an absolute but a relative term. But, as we in Canada sometimes forget, certain basic rules apply. The first of these is that federalism is a process rather than a static pattern of government. Second, federalism is a union of territories, united by one or more common objectives. Third, there are two levels of government; one level of government serves all the people of the federation equitably, and the other level of government serves those in a clearly defined region (a specific territory we call a province) that is a part of the federation. Fourth, both the central and regional units are endowed with certain powers and functions *of which neither can be deprived by the other*. Fifth, every individual in the country is equally a full member of both the central and regional units.

Beyond the broad parameters outlined above, each liberal democratic state in the world today living in a federal system of government has designed its own model. Most Westerners have an acute awareness of this fact. Their concern is that we in Canada have not followed all the basic guidelines to a federal system; nor have we designed a model that will meet and ameliorate the uniquely Canadian problems.

The West's concerns about our federal system have become quite evident and in many cases are beginning to be well articulated. First, the West wants a new constitution providing for a "re-Confederation" that will allow for an on-going review. They want that it not be static but rather be dynamic. The West seeks a process by which old and new problems can be heard and addressed. Second, the West wants a clarification or restating of the nation's purposes and objectives. Do we still have them? What are they? Do they include Western aspirations? Third, there is a genuine concern in the West that the peoples of Canada are not being served equitably by their federal government – and that those nearer the seat of power (read Ottawa) are more equal than others in the outer regions (or, as outer regions are called in government reports, the hinterland). Fourth, there is a well-articulated and genuine concern that the specific powers with which the central and regional (provincial) governments were endowed in the BNA Act, or were assigned by tradition, have become most blurred. It is felt that jurisdictional intrusions from federal into provincial, *and vice versa*, are taking place and that they are inefficient and counterproductive at best, destructive at worst.

Finally, Westerners feel that they are not full participating partners of the central government. In recent times, most Western Canadians have turned to their provincial governments in times of need on any issue, whether designated provincial or federal by law or precedent.

Each of the above concerns is an essay topic if not a thesis title in itself. I will deal only with the last listed in this discussion of the West's stake in a new constitution.

Every Canadian has the right to be fully represented at both levels of government. The very essence of federalism is the concept of allowing each voter access to both governments – each government equal in status but each with different powers and responsibilities and each accountable to those whom they represent.

The Western Canadian has never been equally represented in the national government, where the process of negotiating is carried out and where the building of a country takes place. Where is the West when the very purpose of a federal state is carried out, the negotiation of government policy and practice? It is not fairly represented, often left out entirely.

An exaggeration? Perhaps. But it is a sound example of the reason for the West's disillusionment with the Canadian federal scene. And whether it is wholly fact, partly fact and partly perceived, or wholly perceived matters not. If the West is to remain in Canadian Confederation, there must be a born-again affirmation of the principles of the federal state. Westerners must feel that they are equal partners in Confederation and have an impact on all national decisions commensurate with contribution to the nation.

Canada's governments today have been variously described by eminent political scientists as "four-year dictatorships" and "executive federalisms." Either way the input by Westerners through the electoral process is not equitable, not sufficient, and not satisfactory. Never has a democratically elected government possessed and used more power than does a modern Canadian majority government. Never in modern democracies has a whole section, with the size and *relative* importance that the West has in Canada, had so little input into one nation's policy making. The MP *has* little or no influence under the present system. The Senate does not use its legislative power. The power today lies in the Prime Minister's Office (PMO), the Privy Council Office (PCO), and in the Cabinet. Parliament is run by the executive and/or by professional advisors. Western Canada, with 27 per cent of the population, 70 per cent of the land, and most of the promise of the future, has representation in only one of those units of power – that is, the federal Cabinet, where it has but four of thirty-two MPs, or *12.5 per cent*. Our voice virtually goes unheard in the PMO and PCO.

The principle of the problem described is not a new one in federal systems. The USA, with its two hundred-year-old constitution, addressed the problem of regional representation in Congress and resolved it satisfactorily long ago. Austria, Switzerland, and even Australia, with a British parliamentary system not unlike our own, have all addressed the issue of regional representation. The newest federal system, that of West Germany, a 1949 model, built into its very first constitution a successful model of regional representation in the central government – both at the elected lower chamber and selected upper chamber levels. Other nations have recognized the inequity *and have found ways to overcome it.*

Great Britain is suffering a political crisis of its own, not too unlike the Canadian scene. In his most recent book, *The Dilemma of Democracy,* published in April 1978, Lord Hailsham, a thirty-year member of Parliament and long-time senior member of Cabinet, and one of the most highly respected parliamentarians in the free world, describes the political challenges of Britain. Many are those that we should be addressing in our own federal system. Lord Hailsham calls for such sweeping reforms as a fixed election date (say, the first Monday in June every four years); a reduction in the number of votes of confidence (to reduce the power of the party whip over MPs and to give the MP greater freedom and power in that the defeat of a government bill does not equate with the defeat of a government); and the replacement of the House of Lords with an *elected* second chamber, side-by-side with the House of Commons, with clear and definite powers of regional representation. Lord Hailsham suggests the new, elected upper chamber have specific responsibility as a "brokerage house" for the nation and as a "second-thought" chamber for reducing the virtually unlimited power of executive federalism (he calls it "four-year dictatorship") of any British government with a majority.

Should we not note this parliamentarian's ideas? Perhaps they apply to the Canadian scene today. To charges that his proposals of fixed election dates and an elected Senate abrogate British parliamentary tradition, Hailsham replies simply, "Nonsense!"

Exciting things are happening in Canada. They will only result in positive action if we are open to constructive change. We must seek out our purpose as a nation and express it – then find the means to fulfil it. Seneca said, "When a man does not know what harbour he is making for, no wind is the right wind."

Things are beginning to happen in Canada that will help to identify the harbour – the purpose of the nation. There is a cultural flowering and a new sense of pride in two Canadian societies: Canada West and Quebec. There is a less identifiable but changing attitude to Canada and themselves in the Maritimes. There is a new sense of hope and opportunity in a long-depressed community: Newfoundland. There is recognition that a new order giving the other Canadian communities an opportunity for self-fulfillment is essential to the wellbeing of

Ontario. As John Robarts said recently, "What is good for Ontario is not necessarily good for Canada; but what is good for Canada is most certainly good for Ontario."

We are all concerned about our country, which we love in our own way. We are groping for answers at this critical crossroads.

What we need now are statesmen. W.R. Alger said, "True statesmanship is the art of changing a nation from what it is into what it ought to be." Edmund Burke, always with the last word, said, "The great difference between real statesmen and the pretender is, that the one sees into the future, while the other regards only the present; the one lives by the day, and acts on expedience; the other acts on enduring principles and for immortality."

In Canada, in the West as everywhere, there are real statesmen and there are the pretenders. Unfortunately it is sometimes difficult to differentiate between the two. We regularly elect those who capitalize on current populist issues at the expense of enduring principles.

There are those who contribute to disharmony in our land and there are those who are concerned with developing a much needed new national pride. There are those who would scream the nation's inequities in income and opportunity, inflation and interest rates, tariff and freight rates, rather than pause and help to develop a new system of government – a new federal system for this new Canada – that would address itself to the very problems outlined. How else are the economic problems to be resolved but by wise policy emanating from a democratically elected Parliament, operating under favourable guidelines, and responsive to the Canadian identity?

It is quite possible that the power that leading politicians hold, in the present era of executive federalism, is the very factor that is holding back desirable reforms to our basic system of governance. If this is the case then we must recognize the flaw and recognize the fact that it is probably impossible to bring about changes that threaten the egos of those who now have power.

If this thesis is accepted then we are not necessarily doomed to fail but must proceed to do the next best thing – that is, to pressure the elected politicians, the governments, to bring on those constructive and desirable changes that do not threaten them. They will and must yield to public pressure to improve the degree of democracy, to improve the representation of the regions, to reduce the overwhelming power of executive federalism, and to create a new political climate. The new political model could give to each elected member the opportunity to have and to express opinions, and to not always be dominated by the leaders of the political party that they represent.

I am thinking now of the pressure we can place, and encourage others to place, on those politicians that we know. Let us challenge them to become country builders. Let us inspire them to learn the concerns of each of the disparate regions of this country, to learn the sources of the discords of unity – not only in Quebec, but in the West and wherever they lie – and to be willing to initiate such changes as will bring harmony to our country. Such is the challenge.

Of all of the ideas and concepts that have been touched on in this essay, one stands out as a potential contributor to the successful development of all of the country and the harmony of its people. It is the concept of an *elected* second chamber within the Canadian Parliament.

First, such a chamber would replace the present Senate, thus providing no new level of government or significant additional cost. Second, such a chamber would be designed to genuinely represent the regional interests. It would serve as the Fathers of Confederation intended in 1867: as a regional counterbalance to the rep-by-pop power of the House of Commons. Third, this chamber would have similar powers to those given to (but not often used by) the present Senate – that is, the power to turn back legislation from the House of Commons, the power to introduce legislation but not money bills, and the responsibility to scrutinize the wording of all legislation emanating from the House of Commons. In addition, the new Senate should have an advice-and-consent role on senior government appointments and appointments to national regulatory bodies. Fourth, the hidden agenda of such a chamber should be that of a brokerage house: to hear and negotiate the ever-changing needs and concerns of the peoples in all the parts of Canada – not only those with large populations. Fifth, the members of such a chamber would be elected for a fixed term (say, six years with one-half elected at a time (say, at three years). Sixth – and this is extremely important – the elected members of this second chamber would represent constituencies in regions with common properties (not provinces, but interprovincial or intraprovincial regions). Examples of regions with common concerns, but overlapping provincial boundaries, are everywhere: in the Peace River area of Alberta and British Columbia; in the lakes and forests region of eastern Manitoba and northwestern Ontario; in the eastern Quebec/western New Brunswick community of common interest. Clearly an independent commission would have to be appointed to outline the constituency boundaries.

To charges that this revitalized Senate abrogates the British parliamentary system's basic precepts, Lord Hailsham has said, "Nonsense." Most people in the West agree with Lord Hailsham's view.

Does it threaten the present elected bodies – men, women, legislatures, and parliaments? Not to the extent that other proposals do (e.g., province-wide elected Senate, House of Provinces, Council of Federation). Hopefully it can be accepted as a welcome addition to the present federal system of government, which, by now, virtually all Canadians must recognize is in serious trouble. It should fill the serious vacuum in our political process.

The House of Commons would continue to be the senior chamber. It would be in charge of the purse strings, and it would be the chamber from which the Cabinet would be drawn. In the event of serious disagreement, there would be provision by which the Commons' decision would prevail. Present and future duly elected governments should not feel threatened by such a complementary chamber.

It is hoped that by holding the elections at times other than those of provincial or federal elections, and by electing only one-half of the Senate at a time, senators who are not tied to either provincial or federal party platforms will be elected. By making such senators relatively free of party control, and ineligible for appointment to the Cabinet, it is hoped to avert excessive party control over the majority of senators. Theoretically and, it is to be expected, in practice, the new senators will emerge by-and-large free men and women both in expression and in voting pattern.

By having the Senate members represent constituencies, many of which would overlap provincial boundaries, the premiers of the provinces need not feel threatened. The premiers would still speak for their provinces. They would as well have the assurance that legitimately elected (i.e., not appointed by the prime minister) senators would be presenting the case for regions of their provinces *at the centre*, in the Parliament of Canada.

Finally, some of the present senators who have been fighting so vigilantly against any major surgery to their present home would of course continue to "pull their wagons into a circle." But it is clear that, in the West, certain senators such as Ray Perrault, Ernest Manning, Sid Buckwold, and Duff Roblin would be outstanding candidates for this new and more important function. These men would undoubtedly become, once again, leaders in the process of country-building with the legitimacy of being elected by the people in a constituency and, especially, by serving in a much more highly respected Senate.

(It is conventional wisdom in the West that such individuals as Senators Croll and Forsey would and should be elected to such a chamber by central Canadians.)

How far does such a constitutional change go toward filling the needs of the West in a re-Confederation? It could be one constructive move in the right direction. Westerners believe that their grievances against the insensitivity and inflexibility of the central government are legitimate. Through the power of equal representation in a second chamber, through the power of the airing of aspirations and concerns, and through negotiating with other Canadian regions to help each other meet their needs, the creation of such a chamber is perceived to be a positive action in the process of bringing the West into a full partnership role in Canada. In fact, some creation of this sort is perceived as being essential to the greater process of resolving the problems facing all Canadians.

The alternative, the status quo position of doing nothing until all first ministers agree, is to let the powerful centrifugal forces at play divide Canada further. We must find the will and the forum for negotiation and resolution, rather than continue to pitch Canadian against Canadian. If we fail there will be no opportunity left for those who would be country builders.

STANLEY C. ROBERTS, at the time this paper was written, was the president of the Canada West Foundation, a Western-based think-tank promoting the social, economic, and political uniqueness of Western Canada. Mr Roberts later became president of the Canadian Chamber of Commerce and founder of the Western political movement, which was to coalesce into the Reform Party of Canada. Before becoming president of the Canada West Foundation, Mr Roberts had been a vice-president of Simon Fraser University, a member of the Legislature in Manitoba, a grain executive, and a Manitoba farmer. Mr Roberts died in 1990.

16

Reflections on the Management of Government in the 1980s

MICHAEL J. KIRBY, 1980

The management of government within a democratic society will be the single most complex and important problem confronting all democratic countries in the 1980s. This problem has become Canada's greatest challenge: Canada will face grave difficulties if the issue of improving the management of government is not confronted soon, as no real progress can be made without novel approaches to its solution.

Since I am aware that simply stating the problem is essentially a negative exercise, I would like to propose for consideration several modest suggestions that offer opportunities for constructive change. My proposals are neither radical nor extraordinarily different. But they are refinements that represent an unusual approach to the management-of-government issue. I have called them modest to underscore my awareness of the fact that our whole process of government must be rethought before fundamental changes to it are possible.

I will focus on various aspects of the management-of-government problem:

- The pressures on government to manage efficiently and effectively
- The necessity for government to provide information that will enable citizens to gain an accurate perception of the true nature of the problems society faces
- The development of an environment that will encourage and capitalize on the requirement for increased citizen involvement in government decision-making processes
- The need for government to help citizens have more realistic expectations about what government can do for them

I will begin by concentrating on issues that must be considered when government is deciding how a new policy or program will be implemented – that is to say, on the effectiveness aspects of government. Then I will turn to a discussion of ways in which government can increase the sense of participation of individual citizens in its work and conclude with a discussion as to why there is a need for more public information if citizens are to be properly informed about government and the problems it faces.

HOW PUBLIC SERVICE CAN BE DELIVERED

But it is not by the consolidation, or concentration, of powers, but by their distribution that government is effected.

– Thomas Jefferson

Government has now become the largest and most important institution in society. Moreover, it is perceived as a bad manager, one that has lost touch with the public and is wasteful, ineffective, and inefficient. This has led to widespread alienation among the public and a reduction of trust and confidence in government's ability to solve our problems. Survey after survey confirms the fact that public dissatisfaction with government's performance is pervasive. Yet, at the same time, Canadians continue to have high expectations of government. For example, they want government to continue, even to expand, existing social and economic programs.

One can only surmise from all this that what Canadians want is not less government, but better government. The call is not for government to abandon its principles, but to improve its performance. It would seem that the attack on government is made out of a sense of frustration – more in sorrow than in anger.

It rests not so much on disagreement with government's objectives, but rather on the perception that, to date, the actual achievements have been small in relation to the costs and effort involved. In short, the public believes that big government is not efficient.

In a sense, the public's emphasis on economic efficiency as the paramount criterion for judging the effectiveness of government is far too narrow an approach. Economic efficiency is not the central human value, and clearly there are other (some would say even more important) criteria for deciding whether government is performing well. But like it or not, a major problem government faces is its image, or perception, and central to improving this image and restoring a reasonable measure of public confidence in government is making it appear more efficient. It is my conclusion, therefore, that the issue is not whether services for the public good are to be continued or expanded; it is rather how and by whom these services should be provided.

What does this mean for the role of government in the 1980s? It means, first and foremost, that the ways in which many goods and services are provided may have to be changed. This is not to be construed as support for the common, simplistic argument that more services for the public should be provided by the private sector (even if they are financed by government) because the latter is always more efficient. I do not believe that this is the case.

Moreover, "public" versus "private" is far too simple a dichotomy to represent adequately the spectrum of ways in which services can be delivered. In most cases, there are several different mechanisms we can use for delivering a public service, and each involves the public and private sectors in different ways.

Let me elaborate on a range of possible options. But while I do so, it is important to remember that the possible delivery systems I will be enumerating are not mutually exclusive. For example, most provinces provide electricity through a crown corporation (at least at the wholesale level), but the corporation is a monopoly, and the rates it is allowed to charge are regulated by a provincial public-utilities board. This method of service delivery is therefore a combination of the first and fourth delivery methods I shall mention below.

It is also important to keep in mind a key fact about the public sector, namely that there is a wealth of experience demonstrating that it is easier for a public agency to change the behaviour of a private organization than of another public agency, particularly where the two agencies are departments of the same government. The consequences of this generalization will temper our search for alternative mechanisms for service delivery.

The range of service delivery options begins, then, at one end of the delivery spectrum where a government provides a service using a government agency (be it department or crown corporation) and government employees to deliver the service to citizens. The post office and Air Canada are two examples of this delivery mechanism.

Second, there is the provision for "contracting out" the implementation of a public service from one level of government to another. The best example of this "selling" of services by the federal government is the contracting out of services of the Royal Canadian Mounted Police to various Canadian provinces and municipalities. The amount that the federal government charges for these services has increased steadily over the years; even so, the price charged for this service does not cover the cost of its provision.

Third, there is contracting out from the government to private-sector organizations, both profit and nonprofit. All governments use this form of service provision. Municipalities contract out snowplowing and snow-removal services; some provinces contract out day-care services to nonprofit institutions such as churches and neighbourhood associations. The federal government provides fewer services by way of contracting out than do the other two levels of government, due mainly to the fact that, with the exception of transfer payments, the federal government is not involved in the direct provision of services to individuals to nearly the same extent as are provinces and municipalities. In fact, except for the postal service, the federal government does not directly provide any service to all Canadians, a situation that I believe is one of the causes of the alienation that many Canadians feel toward the federal government.

In contrast, provinces, and particularly municipalities, provide several services to all their residents, including police, fire, and education services. (It must be noted, however, that the federal government does directly provide services to special groups of Canadians through programs such as family allowance, the Canada Pension Plan, and unemployment insurance.)

Fourth, another possible arrangement for delivering public services is an indirect one, where government doesn't pay a private firm to provide the service but rather grants an exclusive right to a firm to sell its services in a particular area. In this case, the government usually regulates the price at which the organization can sell services, and the private-sector organization charges the public directly for them. The operations of private bus firms and many telephone companies are examples of this kind of delivery mechanism.

An interesting twist to this delivery system is provided by worker-owned trash collection companies in San Francisco. Since the companies are worker-owned, along with efficient trash collection goes an entrepreneurial pride in the work. This demonstrates that psychological factors are at least as important as technical factors in providing incentives for efficiency of a given operation.

A variation on the fourth delivery method produces a fifth: franchising. In this case, exclusive right to provide a service is sold by government to the highest bidder in much the same way that commercial franchises are sold. New private radio station licences in Britain and cable television franchises in some cities in the United States are granted this way.

In Canada, for example, exclusive franchises for the use of public airwaves could be sold to the highest bidder for a strictly limited period, at which time they would again be subject to auction to their previous owner or to a new bidder. Since the awarding of commercial broadcast licences is, in effect, a sale of scarce resources, the public deserves every penny it can get in return for the bandwidth given up. One step further along these lines would be to auction off annual taxi permits to the highest bidder. In many cities now, these transferable permits change hands for many thousands of dollars. As a result, the value that is created by the public grant of a semiexclusive "franchise" to operate a taxi, which should rightly accrue to the public that created it, goes instead to the taxi-permit owner. (Of course, this is really true for the owner of the original permit since thereafter the seller of the permit is mainly trying to recover the amount he paid for the permit plus a reasonable rate of return on his investment.)

A sixth delivery mechanism results when government decides to give a subsidy to the producer of a service, thereby enabling the producer to sell that service at a lower cost to the public than would otherwise be the case. Some of our transportation services are financed this way, as are our universities. In fact, all of our universities receive a subsidy (usually amounting to greater than 80 per cent of their total cost) for providing their service.

A seventh institutional mechanism for the delivery of public services is the voucher system. In this case, the subsidy is given to the consumer rather than to the producer of the service. Then the consumer is free to go and purchase the service he or she wants in the marketplace at a cheaper rate than he or she would otherwise have to pay. This delivery mechanism has not been as widely used in Canada as it has been in the United States, where food stamps and medicare cards are used extensively to enable individual citizens to purchase services at less than the going rate.

Supporters of the voucher system have long argued that it is the most efficient delivery mechanism because it relies on competition in the marketplace and leaves the government's role to that of subsidizing individual consumers who, for reasons of public policy, are deemed to be worthy of this government assistance. On the other hand, experience shows that voucher systems have not always been successful. Indeed, in many cases where they have been used, often very ingenious methods have been developed by enterprising entrepreneurs to circumvent some of the intentions of the voucher program. For example, the food stamp program in the United States has been fraught with problems, including the emergence of a black market for food stamps and significant problems in actually getting the stamps to those who qualify for them. Similarly, problems have resulted from the application of the voucher system to education. In one case, restriction of vouchers to the public school system led to collusion amongst schools to standardize offerings. In another case, a variety of noneducational activities were introduced to attract voucher students. To be sure, however, there are also examples of successful uses of this approach, and I expect that voucher systems will become increasingly used in experimental approaches to the delivery of public services in the years ahead.

An eighth approach to the provision of services for the public good is to have these services provided through voluntary associations in which people with similar interests, often living in the same neighbourhood, provide a service for themselves. In this case, the service that results is not formally a "public service" since it is neither directed, provided, nor financed by government. But there are services that most of us would instinctively think of as "public services" that are provided in exactly this way. The best example is firefighting; by far the largest majority of fire departments in Canada are volunteer fire departments.

Finally, a ninth method of service delivery commonly used in Canada is self-service. It is common in small towns and villages for a family to haul its own garbage to the municipal dump.

Clearly, then, there are many different mechanisms for delivering a public service, so that the simplistic dichotomy of "public" versus "private" delivery systems is not really helpful to our understanding of the wide range of possibilities that exist.

What is unfortunate, however, is that when new programs are being designed and implemented, the fact that there are at least nine alternative delivery mechanisms appears to be seldom considered. Too often, to the detriment of both government and the public, it appears that an *assumption* is made that the only logical way to deliver a public service is for government itself to do the job.

Yet each of the delivery mechanisms I described really are different. They differ in the role they assign to government; they differ in the role that is played by the private sector; they differ in the role that the consumer of the service plays; they differ in the degree of consumer choice; they differ in the degree of competition that is possible (and, indeed, that can be encouraged) in the delivery of the service; and they are also subject to different economies of scale, which means that the unit cost of delivering the goods or service will vary with the delivery mechanism that is used.

Of equal, and perhaps even greater importance, these various methods of delivering public services differ in their political characteristics. In some of them, government pays the full cost of providing the service, thus increasing government expenditures and the public attack on the size of government. In others, the service is paid for directly by its users, and the role of government is a regulatory one designed to ensure that users are charged a "fair" price. In still other cases, the service is delivered on a universal basis. No attempt is made to distinguish those who "need" government financial assistance to pay for the services from those who don't because to do so would raise the political difficulty of defining "need" and the bureaucratic difficulty of administering a means test fairly.

Perhaps a simpler way to demonstrate the political characteristics of the delivery mechanisms I have described is to note that each delivery system results in different "winners" and "losers." That is, all nine ways have different redistribution implications. (Of course, the need to revise our redistribution system, both in Canada and the world, is part and parcel of the management-of-government problem.)

Indeed, I suspect that it is precisely because of these implications that alternatives to government-only delivery systems are so frequently rejected by government at the time a decision is made about how a service will be provided. Unfortunately, even if a variety of delivery alternatives are considered before a decision is made, this fact remains secret from the public. Inevitably, the public is left with the impression that the only option considered was the one that would result in government itself delivering the service.

Since each of the nine delivery mechanisms I described differs in a variety of ways, a question arises: Which, if any, is best, and why? Or put another way: How does one pick and choose among the options?

As an aside, it is interesting to note that these self-evident questions seem rarely to be asked, except perhaps by some economists and that new breed of professional known as the "policy analyst." If my thesis is correct, this will all change in the 1980s because one of the major aspects of the management-of-government issue will be to determine how various services should be delivered most effectively and efficiently for the public good. Anyone familiar with designing service systems knows that there is no "one best system" for all circumstances. Decisions about optimal systems design must always be based on the weighing of appropriate variables. In the case of a delivery system for a public service, the variables that determine which system arrangement is most efficient for a given service include factors such as the number of people to be served, their geographic distribution, the precise nature of the service, its reasons for being one of the alternatives, money available, and so on.

Weighing these factors appropriately within the political arena to ensure that the principle of "the greatest good for the greatest number" has been met may prove to be the sternest test for our system of government in the future. But I'll return to this argument; first let me pursue the delivery system problem by presenting an example.

An Example

There is one service – garbage collection – that has been studied extensively in over three hundred North American cities, including several in Canada. If the results of this study are any indication of what can be learned by systematically examining alternative methods of delivery, then a lot of reform is possible. Let me illustrate.

The study (by Professor E.S. Savas) showed that for cities with populations larger than fifty thousand, the cost of garbage collection by municipal employees is 60 to 70 per cent higher than the cost of contracting these services out to the private sector. However, the study also demonstrated that if garbage was contracted out to a single private-sector firm (so that a private monopolist rather than a public monopolist was providing the service), the private-sector service was every bit as inefficient and costly as the service provided by the municipality itself. Thus the study showed that it is the environment that provides the appropriate incentive for efficiency, not merely the fact that the service is provided by the private rather than the public sector. After all, private-sector employees are not inherently more efficient than their public-sector counterparts; their efficiency depends on the circumstances under which they are operating.

In order to achieve a 70 per cent reduction in garbage-collection costs, the study showed that it was necessary for a city to be divided into regions or districts, with the right to collect garbage in a region being awarded on the basis of competitive bidding by a number of private-sector firms. In addition, municipalities with the lowest average garbage collection cost found it useful to have the garbage in one district collected by municipal employees, so that the municipal government would have some feel for the true cost of collecting garbage. In this way, the private sector competitors in other regions would be dissuaded from colluding to raise their bids beyond a level that gave them a reasonable profit.

The study also showed that in the monopoly situation the sanitation-truck crew contains 3.2 workers, while in the competitive environment the average crew on a private garbage truck is 2.1 workers. In other words, there were exactly 50 per cent more people staffing a municipally owned garbage truck than a garbage truck owned by a private firm and operated in a competitive environment. Evidence like this certainly lends credence to the widely held view that governments, because of the monopolistic position they hold, are very different in the way they provide services.

Another story may help to reinforce this conclusion. When Windsor City Council recently sought bids from private firms to assume responsibility for the city's garbage collection, the bids the council received were well below the cost of the service being provided by the municipality's own sanitation department. The City Council announced that it was considering laying off its garbage workers and contracting-out the service. The response of the workers was to rearrange their work schedules and increase their productivity to approximately the same level promised in the bids by the private contractors. In this case, it seems that the threat of privatization – of exposing the service to a competitive environment – was sufficient to bring about the desired improvement in efficiency, at least in the short run.

Garbage collection is not an isolated example of a government service that could probably be provided more efficiently by the private sector on a contract basis. The following list (derived chiefly from government examples in the United

States) demonstrates how extensive the range of applications of contracted-out services can be:

- computer services (Orange County, California)
- lawyers to serve as public defenders (Phoenix, Arizona)
- fire protection (notably Scottsdale, Arizona)
- bus shelters (Houston, Texas, and elsewhere)
- school custodians (New York, New York)
- hospital administration (Butte, Montana)
- parking meter operations (Milwaukee, Wisconsin)
- window washing in public buildings (Milwaukee, Wisconsin)
- security for public buildings (Houston, Texas)
- paramedical services (Hawthorne, California)
- vehicle and fleet maintenance (Gainesville, Florida)

Vending machine services in public schools and urban transit systems are a couple of other service areas where contracting-out is widespread. In each of these cases, better or equivalent services at reduced or similar costs were the objective of the exercise, and while the success of such an approach has been difficult to quantify on a national scale, particular instances of success are prevalent.

I have gone into detail with this example not because garbage collection is a major issue in the nation's capital (although I know people elsewhere in Canada believe garbage to be one of Ottawa's biggest problems), nor because the results of this study can be easily extrapolated to other services (for they can't), but because I think this study underscores my point: There is a variety of different ways in which a government service can be provided more efficiently and effectively, and these alternative service-delivery mechanisms should be explored when government is deciding on the way in which a new or, indeed, an existing service will be delivered.

Government must come to recognize that just because something should be financed as a public service, it need not automatically be provided by public employees working for public agencies. In saying this, let me emphasize again that the decision as to whether or not government should contract-out in a specific situation is only partly a matter of economics; government has to take into account a wide variety of political and noneconomic factors in making its decision about how a particular service will be provided. Such factors associated with this are the attitude of public service unions over the threatened loss of jobs that contracting-out represents; the additional temptations to corruption that the contract process will induce; and how the contractor's suitability in "humanistic" terms can be evaluated.

Make no mistake, contracting out will work in some cases and fail in others. It is dependent on specific conditions of the service involved, how skillful government contract management is, the availability of competent organizations to fill the contract, and the nature of the area being served – all of which are not, ultimately, subject to simple economic analysis.

A MORE REVENUE-DEPENDENT PUBLIC SECTOR

The importance of considering alternative mechanisms for delivering and financing public services is examined in some depth in a forthcoming Institute for Research on Public Policy publication on ways to make the public sector more "revenue dependent." This report proposes specific ways for increasing economic efficiency in service delivery by making government departments more dependent on revenue they generate through the sale of services than on revenue they receive through appropriations. The proposals in the report are applicable only to the more economically oriented government services – for example, they do not apply to the services of the departments of defence, external affairs, or the so-called central agencies, and they do not apply to cash transfer programs – and they call for a vastly more extended use of the "user-pay" concept.

The essential principles of a more revenue-dependent public sector are the following:

1 The principle of full costing: All costs incurred in providing a particular public service should be included in the operational budget for the service. In other words, public sector operations should be fully costed.
2 The principle of revenue dependency: All services that have the potential to be marketed should be identified, measured, and fully costed so that they may be priced and sold to customers on a cash transaction basis. Revenue received from such sales would be used by the supplying department or agency to fund its ongoing operations, the size of the increase or decrease depending on consumer services.
3 The principle of direct competition: Direct competition between public- and private-sector producers of a service should be fostered by eliminating the impediments created through governmental funding, regulation, and administrative practices.
4 The principle of consumer subsidization: To the extent that subsidization is required to equalize social and regional patterns, such funding should be provided directly to the consumers of the service rather than to the producers of the service.

The essence of the case for revenue dependency is that the pricing and selling of public services would provide for major increases in efficiency in their production, more competition among suppliers, and thus better levels of service in their delivery and greater public choice in their selection of how and by whom the service would be provided. Because, under revenue dependency, these developments would be the only means of a department ensuring operational survival in the face of competition from the private sector, the survivors would be the most economically efficient suppliers. This means that such a system would make government managers subject to the strong economic incentives that now exist only in the competitive world, and this would make at least part of government decision making subject to the same kind of discipline that governs decision-making processes in the competitive private sector. In other words, revenue dependency would apply the lessons learned from the garbage-collection example to a range of services that are now provided by government.

It must be emphasized that the principle of revenue dependency in the public sector is not new. Indeed, in the Canadian context, it dates back at least as far as the major recommendations of the Glassco Commission, which in 1962 clearly recognized that the full-costing principle was essential both to improved resource allocation decisions and to effective cost-control measures within and across government programs. More recently, the full-costing concept has received further support from the Standing Committee on National Finance, from the Auditor General, and in the Report of the Royal Commission on Financial Management and Accountability.

There are, of course, those who object to moving public-sector management in this direction because of ideological considerations. They argue that the revenue-dependent approach to the delivery of public services works only if the consumers of the service have sufficient resources to be able to purchase it. Moreover, they would insist that, particularly if it is an essential service, revenue dependency can be introduced only after appropriate incomes policies are in place. But since we have shown a marked inability to come to terms with the incomes-policy problem, they will argue that revenue-dependent service delivery is not viable at this time.

This might be a valid criticism if one were to try to apply the principle of revenue to all government services, for we know that this cannot be done. It is my view, however, that we should begin to move in this direction by structuring experiments that would allow us to test the revenue-dependent approach and, in the process, create a more competitive environment for at least some public services. As always, the problem is to determine where, when, and for what services such experiments might best be tried. Two that appear to be ripe candidates are the transportation and communications sectors.

We can, rather than speculating, focus on one area of the federal government where revenue dependency has been tried: the Supply Administration of the Department of Supply and Services (DSS). Since the introduction of revenue

dependency in 1973, major increases in the workload of the Supply Administration have been handled with only a modest increase in personnel, with overall
"rates" charged by the Supply Administration declining on a continuing basis.
Moreover, "profit" in the form of funds generated for the Consolidated Revenue
Fund and occasional rebates to customers have amounted to over $15 million
over the past five years.

Similarly, the application of revenue-dependency principles to Information
Canada when it was taken over by the DSS at the start of the 1976–77 fiscal year
has been impressive. For example, if we ignore the claim that the quality of
service has been substantially reduced (and this is debatable), significant savings
have been achieved in the distribution and sales of Government of Canada
publications. In addition, the exposition division of Information Canada, which
was operating at a $2 million loss in 1976, is now operating at essentially a
break-even position.

I recognize that it would be foolhardy to conclude on the basis of two
examples that the application of the revenue-dependency principle to other
government services would achieve similar savings when applied. Yet, until proof
to the contrary is available, I cannot dismiss this assumption out of hand.

There is, however, one public service (financed almost exclusively through
government funds) that, based on my personal experience, I believe might well
profit from the application of revenue dependency, and that is universities. In making
this declaration, I know I am opening a hornet's nest, but it may be long overdue.

One of the best exponents of the principle of converting the relationship between
a university and its student body to a buyer-seller relationship is Professor E.G.
West of the Department of Economics of Carleton University. In a book entitled
Education and the State, written more than ten years ago, Dr West argues for a
voucher system in which students who are eligible to go to university would
receive from the government a voucher that would cover the estimated cost (less
the current level of student fees) of providing that student with an education in
a specified program and of a given quality. These vouchers would be used by
the student to pay for his or her education at the institution of his or her choice.
The value of a voucher would be equal to the *average* cost of educating a
university student in a particular program. Thus the more efficiently run universities would continue to flourish, while those with above-average costs would
decline unless they became more efficient.

This approach to the financing of higher education was also recommended
by the Graham Royal Commission in Nova Scotia in 1973 and has been advocated by other notable writers on the provision of public services, including
Milton Friedman, Richard Bird, and Christopher Jeneke. In every case, the
authors advocate the voucher system as the only means of returning some
semblance of managerial efficiency to universities, which have in recent years

so decentralized their decision-making processes that efficient management has become virtually impossible.

In fact, within the universities with which I am familiar, there appears to be no *effective* mechanism for setting priorities or assessing costs. Moreover, despite the fact that universities are financed largely from public funds, the "public interest" is not often considered when new programs are designed and existing programs evaluated.

We are, in fact, in a situation in which institutions of higher learning are responsible for their own self-regulation, with few, if any, regulatory agencies willing or empowered to constrain their actions. This, in my view, has generated a host of social and economic problems that cannot long be left unattended. Consider, for example, the number of competing physical education programs that have been started at universities in the Maritimes in recent years. Then consider the difficulties tenure and unionization are posing for university administrators who try to reduce the size of some departments in order to have more faculty members in other departments that have greater student enrolment. Since the principle of self-regulation is being challenged in many areas of society (e.g., for lawyers and doctors), it seems inevitable that universities will soon be subjected to the same challenge.

I realize, of course, that it would not be easy to apply the revenue-dependency principle to universities. There are complex problems involved in assessing (among other things) how quality is to be maintained in a competitive education market; in making certain that universities continue to keep programs (such as classics) that are an essential component of a university even though they attract relatively few students; in deciding how research is to be financed or its value assessed; and in developing and maintaining strong regional institutions. But surely these problems are similar to those that will confront government whenever it tries to move a public service from the status quo to a new method of service delivery. The fact that it is difficult to do is no excuse for not trying.

THE POLITICAL EFFECTIVENESS OF THE INDIVIDUAL: THE PROBLEM OF ALIENATION

Applause, mingled with boos and hisses, is about all the average voter is able or willing to contribute to public life.

– Elmer Davis

I have referred to the complexity of the management-of-government problem as having two components. One is the pressure for government to become more efficient in the way it operates. The other is the increasing demand for citizen involvement in government decision-making processes. Even if government became very efficient and were seen to be so by the general public, the most disturbing aspect of popular attitudes to government would remain: alienation. This alienation is manifested mainly in two ways: (1) the public lacks faith in government's willingness to be responsible to the populace's demands; and (2) individuals perceive that they have suffered a significant decline in personal political effectiveness in recent years. Together these attitudes represent formidable barriers to the effective functioning of government.

Surveys taken at regular intervals in Canada since the end of the Second World War have shown a continued reduction in an individual's perception of his or her personal political effectiveness. These results apply to all education and income levels, all regions of the country, and supporters of all political parties. Canadians no longer believe that they, as individuals, can have any impact on government. They also believe that big government is not interested in solving their problems but rather is only interested in perpetuating itself and in taking care of its own employees, be they bureaucrats or politicians. How aptly George Reedy captured this mood: "Power breeds isolation. Isolation leads to the capricious use of power. In turn, the capricious use of power breaks down the normal channels of communication between the leader and the people he leads. This ultimately means the deterioration of power and with it the capacity to sustain unity in our society. This is the problem we face today."

In a survey taken in 1979, 64 per cent of Canadians said they believed that the federal government had only a poor or fair understanding of their problems and concerns, while 60 per cent believed that members of Parliament were putting their personal interests over those of the voters. Moreover, less than 25 per cent of the people who thought that government *could* do a lot about inflation – the problem the public was most concerned about at the time the survey was taken – considered it very likely that government *would* do something effective about it. In addition, the survey made clear that part of this feeling was related to considerable public mistrust of the intentions or motivations of those in government, both politicians and bureaucrats.

The impact of this current mood on our political system is already evident. Many of the problems that we now see in the political life of Canada – increasing regional and provincial antagonism; the flourishing of groups that try to exercise special veto power to stop certain legislation (or local development projects) or to get special benefits for themselves; the rise of large, single-issue voting blocks; and the perceived decline in the effectiveness of political parties as a means of getting an input into government decision-making processes – are all manifestations of this change in our attitude toward government leaders and government processes.

Perhaps the most serious consequence of this change in public attitudes is the impact it has had on the state of political parties. Political parties have always been essential to the workings of democratic government and represent the only coherent structure for elucidating and enunciating priorities within our political system. They *are* the means whereby an important component of political communication takes place.

For most of Canadian history, political parties served as a vehicle enabling public participation in the governmental process; if you wanted to have a voice, you joined (or started) a party. But this is no longer the case. Parties are in significant decline. The factors that have caused a decline in popular regard for parties need a paper of their own for proper consideration. I can best summarize them here by noting that modern campaigning techniques, which have accommodated themselves to the rise of centralized broadcast media, have also centralized the handling of party-political issues and introduced the era of personality politics and unprecedented financial expenditures. These developments may be beneficial so far as winning elections is concerned, particularly if your party has enough money to "package" the "appropriate" candidate using a "proper" strategy. But they impose the penalty that parties have largely ceased to be effective channels for communication between citizens and their government.

This phenomenon, along with the changes in public attitudes I have previously described, has led to a new (and what I believe to be a profoundly disturbing) change within our political system: the rapid development of what has come to be called "the special-interest state." Voters, firmly believing that governments will only respond to significant pressure far greater than can be exerted by the individual, have banded together to advance their special and particular concerns. They are seldom concerned with the impact of their demands on the other segments of society or on society as a whole. The result, as Dr Alex Corry, a former principal of Queen's University, pointed out in a keynote address to an Institute for Research on Public Policy (IRPP) conference in 1979, is that: "The emissaries of special interests fill the ante chambers of government and get as much space and time in the media as they can. None of them wastes time in taking their troubles to the Lord in prayer; they seek at once solace and assuagement from government. Even hearing their demands is a mounting burden and distraction as governments struggle for coherent policy ... this kind of activity is a main source of rising faction among us."

Clearly, then, another aspect of the challenge of the management of government in the 1980s is how to get effective public input into government processes so that we can reduce the "rising faction among us" and restore some sense of "nationhood" and common purpose among us.

SOME POSSIBLE STEPS

In order to climb a hill one must first put one foot in front of the other.

– Anonymous

If participation is to be of any use, those who invite it must believe in it. They must truly believe that anyone, including the individual in the street, has a contribution to make. I stress this point because far too often those in authority (and here I am not just talking about governments) simply pay lip service to participation because they are not, in truth, at all in favour of participatory procedures. Since the demand for public participation is linked with the distrust of authority, particularly centralized authority, the problem will be compounded if those in authority do not take seriously any participatory mechanisms they launch.

This, of course, raises the question of audience. To whom should participatory procedures be aimed? In some pertinent research on this point, Eric Ashley has shown that the spread of opinion on an issue can be regarded as lying on a bell-shaped distribution curve. In the middle is the uncommitted – indeed, indifferent – majority of citizens. At the extremes are those who strongly oppose or strongly support the proposal being considered. Those between the ends of the distribution and the middle can be classified as being inclined against or toward the issue but willing to reserve their final judgment; that is to say, they are prepared to reconsider their opinion after hearing facts and arguments.

Nothing is likely to change the minds of the hardcore extremists, and nothing short of a major crisis is likely to stir the emotions or the minds of the indifferent majority. Therefore, despite the risk of being labelled a crass cynic, as a matter of practical politics, I believe it is best to design machinery for participation that concentrates upon the bands of open-minded opponents and proponents. Again to quote Ashley: "We can make some assumptions about these people. They will have followed discussions in the media about the issue. Many of them are 'joiners' and belong to groups already identified with views about the issue. They will take the trouble to come to hearings and, if given the opportunity, to prepare themselves beforehand. In any case, I think authorities have the right to say, bluntly, that if willingness to participate justifies inclusion in the decision-making process, then apathy justifies exclusion from the process."

Since we are entering relatively uncharted waters as we look for participatory mechanisms that will begin to ameliorate the alienation problem, let me first suggest that government needs to continue the use of advisory committees, task forces, commissions of inquiry, and royal commissions. These devices, though not new, were used more extensively in the 1960s and 1970s than ever before and have proven useful to governments because they give interested citizens an opportunity to make their views on major issues known before public-policy decisions are made. Indeed, to date, few better techniques have been tried for actively encouraging greater citizen involvement in government's deliberations.

There are those who would argue that it has been these government efforts at encouraging greater citizen participation that have spawned the rise of special-interest groups and single-issue voting blocs. I disagree with this thesis. There is, was, and remains an eagerness on the part of the public to participate in governmental processes. This has been amply demonstrated by the degree of interest, even among citizens who are not normally interested in public affairs, in becoming involved in such diverse issues as the Mackenzie Valley Pipeline Inquiry, the National Unity Task Force, the Parliamentary Committee on Immigration, and, at the provincial level, Ontario's Porter Commission on Electric Power Planning.

These efforts at public involvement have had varying degrees of success in terms of getting input from those who would be affected by the issue being studied. In fact, the only one that can be said to have been completely successful in this regard is the Berger Inquiry on the Mackenzie Valley Pipeline. Its problem, however, was cost, both in terms of dollars spent by participants in the inquiry (including the federal government) and in terms of the time needed to reach a decision on whether or not the pipeline should be built. Any assessment as to the value of such exercises in public participation must weigh these two essentially nonquantifiable costs.

To return to an earlier theme, though it can be stated as a truism that solutions to the alienation problem will require imaginative experimentation, one element in the process that is required does not need any special imagination, and that is the need for special-interest groups, government officials, politicians, and the public at large to approach an issue with an open mind. No experiment will be effective unless trust and cooperation are forthcoming and become the cohesive ingredient within the participatory process. The difficulty is that on this issue we are facing a chicken-and-egg problem: Trust and cooperation can only be built up if government is seen to be serious about being more open and seeking more citizen participation; yet to be effective, a more open, participatory government requires at the outset an attitude of trust and cooperation on the part of the general public.

A second element in the process of improving citizen participation rests on helping citizens to understand how government actually works. For example, in the matter of advisory committees it is important for the public to understand that no matter how thorough or successful an advisory committee is in its work, its role is purely one of advice. Government may not follow that advice.

Indeed, if there has been one continuing sore point in the use of various forms of advisory committees to date, it has been that most nongovernmental people involved in them have assumed that their advice would be followed. Whenever this has not happened, significant political difficulties for government have resulted. This has led many politicians to conclude that advisory committees should not be created again, an action that further alienates the public from their government.

Despite these pitfalls, and because there are no better alternatives on the horizon, I believe governments should persevere with the public-inquiry and task-force approach, as its potential for constructive interchange between citizens and their government has not yet been explored fully.

A different aspect of the problem of alienation as it relates to participation by the public relates to the adversarial and legalistic nature of government procedures. Ways must be developed that appear to be less formal than they are now. This is particularly important given the technological and complex nature of many public issues and the increasing role that experts must play in their solution. Experts are distrusted not because their expertise is doubted, but because the public distrusts their values.

The extensive use of experts, and the fact that many technological issues have no absolute right or wrong, makes it essential that participatory procedures become less adversarial and more inquisitorial than they are now. Procedures need to be developed whose aim is to reach a consensus, not to win a conflict.

As an example of this type of procedure, consider the process that was devised by the San Diego Gas and Electric Company. The company had to put up a new power plant to meet the needs of Southern California. They began by inviting all the environmental and planning organizations in the area to a seminar. At the seminar they explained why there had to be a new power plant and the reasons for selecting the general location for the plant.

They then proposed that those attending the seminar should elect an environmental advisory committee to examine alternative sites and take part in the decision process for settling where the final site should be. It was emphasized that members of the committee would have to do a lot of work, prepare a written report on the project, and make recommendations by a specific date. The company offered to defray all expenses involved in the project and then withdrew from the meeting. The citizens discussed the proposal, accepted it, and elected a working committee of volunteers.

The committee began its deliberations by meeting once a week. In the end it was meeting two or three times a week. The committee educated itself through hearings at which experts of its choice gave evidence. A series of public hearings in the neighbourhoods of the alternative sites was also arranged so that anyone who wished could air views and ask questions.

After some months of this intensive activity, the committee of volunteers really understood the complexities of the matter but had not lost its identity as a representative of the public. Fortunately for the experiment, there is a happy ending. The committee made a recommendation that was accepted by the company.

Of course, this process took time and irritated some of the experts, who wanted to get on with the job. But for anyone who believes (as I do) that the process of decision making in our kind of society is as important as the decision itself – that is, that *means* are in fact as important as *ends* to our society – then this was an important and imaginative experiment.

Since restoring faith in government must be our primary goal, a second method of helping to do this is to decentralize the way in which federal government programs are implemented. Surveys have consistently shown that Canadians feel that the federal government in Ottawa is too remote, too out of touch with local factors that should be taken into account when certain types of national policies are being implemented. Much of this discontent might be eliminated if the public clearly saw that decisions as to the application of some federal government policies were being made by people familiar with local conditions.

I realize, of course, that there are many arguments that can be made against this proposal. For one thing, decentralized decision-making systems are harder to manage than the centralized processes we have now in Ottawa; for another, both political and bureaucratic problems are created when so-called national policies (such as environmental regulations) are applied differently across the country. Yet precisely because of the vastness of Canada and its enormous regional variation, some public policies must be applied with varying emphasis in different regions of our nation.

I realize full well that what I am suggesting is very difficult to do in practice. Some policies must be national in scope and character, but some others need not be. Surely it is important that the federal government be seen to be sensitive to regional variation and to be trying to find the best ways of applying its policies, even if this creates administrative difficulties.

In calling for greater decentralization of administrative decision making, let me stress, however, that I am not suggesting that the federal government should give up any of its current areas of jurisdiction. We are already so decentralized that Dave Broadfoot's remark that "Canada is a collection of ten provinces with strong governments loosely connected by fear" is becoming more truth than jest. What I am saying is that the way this jurisdiction is exercised should be decentralized. This will permit a more useful assessment of the relative importance of differing views within, as well as among, regions.

A third area of major change in government in the 1980s must involve the removal of mystery from government operations. The interested citizen must get a better insight and understanding into why government makes the decisions it does. Only then will the public begin to understand the factors that led to a particular decision being made and only then will the misperception that all decisions are "political" begin to disappear.

An example of how this approach can help was described by Alex Corry in the speech I quoted earlier. In response to student demands for more involvement in university decision-making bodies at Queen's University, students were appointed to them. Corry, then principal at Queen's, described what happened as follows: "Having got access to the inner circles, students found senior officers and members of the teaching staff making decisions with thought and care. They

learned there were reasons for doing this and not doing that, which had never
occurred to them. They found almost none of the skullduggery they suspected."
I'm sure they were disappointed, but that is not my point. My point is that they
ceased complaining about the quality of decision making because they understood
it better.

It is trite to say that there is no substitute for increasing effective communication between the government and the governed; everyone would agree with
that. What is not as well understood is that there is enormous bureaucratic as
well as political pressure to keep government closed, to avoid public scrutiny.
I would be the last to support public access to *all* government information, but
surely the time has come when we must resist pressures that do not support fuller
public disclosure than we have now. No one can doubt that a more open
government would enable citizens to make better judgments about the actions
of government. Such openness would help to eliminate the suspicion of many
Canadians that decisions that affect their daily lives are actually being made not
by their representatives in the Legislature or by ministers, but by nameless,
faceless, unelected bureaucrats who are not truly held accountable by anyone.

In making these suggestions for ways of increasing citizen input into public-
policy decision-making processes, I would be remiss if I failed to note that I
think it would be a serious mistake for Canada to copy some of the approaches
to increased public involvement that have been tried in the United States. In the
USA, many public-policy decision-making processes have virtually ground to a
halt because of the length of regulatory hearings and the number of governmental
decisions that can be appealed to the courts. For example, the decision by the
United States government to allow the Concorde to land at Kennedy Airport in
New York was appealed through several layers of the court system, so that the
final decision was made by judges, not by politicians.

I regard such a situation as completely incompatible with the notion of
responsible parliamentary government, and I hope that the desire of some
special-interest groups in Canada to move in this direction is resisted.

INFORMATION, COMMUNICATION, AND THE MEDIA

The purpose of public relations in its best sense is to inform and to keep minds open: the
purpose of propaganda in the bad sense is to misinform and to keep minds closed.

– J.W. Hill

A more open government requires that information be made available to interested citizens in a form that they can understand and use. This is not a simple
task to accomplish, for it means that government must be prepared to go to

considerable lengths to explain to the public what are often highly technical issues in as simple a language as possible. To reach such a goal, governments must be prepared to invest significant sums of money even though (as in the quality-of-education argument) they will be unable to measure the effectiveness of these expenditures until years later.

Clearly, if we do not increase the amount and quality of public information about government, those in the electorate who seek more facts will be frustrated. This will exacerbate emotional attacks on the public service, act to increase the dominance of personality issues in politics, and make more effective operation of government almost an impossibility.

There can be no meaningful public participation unless the technical aspects of public-policy issues can be understood. This places a considerable burden on government because of the difficulty of finding the expertise needed to translate into simple language the technical aspects of a government document. In fact, the talent needed to do this sort of translation is as professional as the talent needed by the experts who develop these documents in the first place. Moreover such translation talent is in very short supply.

The need to have the technical aspects of public-policy issues understood by the public also places a burden on the media. They, too, must make a determined effort to get the message across. But, although the media are a part of the solution, they are also a part of the problem.

To date, the media seem to want to focus on personalities and conflict rather than on information that is, relatively speaking, dull. The media seem determined to turn every issue into one of conflict. To do so, sometimes they even seem to be trying to generate the conflict itself. Yet, to make more open government work, the media must be effective in communicating the increased information that is available. Attempts at more open government will fail if the media fail to fulfil their responsibility to communicate the facts about a given problem to the general public simply, fairly, and without trying to embellish them with unnecessary or irrelevant personality and conflict issues.

It must be pointed out, however, that even improved clarity in communication will not solve all the problems associated with the technical aspects of many issues. There will inevitably remain the problem of whether experts can mean-ingfully quantify data within a commonly accepted value system.

For example, cost-benefit techniques have been used in evaluating alternate road-construction projects, and in so doing a value has had to be assigned to the cost of a fatal accident. A recent report comparing how this value had been used in road-transport studies in different countries showed that the cost of a fatal accident was valued at $125,000 in Britain, $175,000 in Canada, and $200,000 in the United States. (Obviously an Englishman is worth much less than a

Canadian, who in turn is worth less than an American.) Examples like this show how arbitrary much of the data developed by experts really is.

But quantifying the unquantifiable is not the only issue raised by the use of technocratic approaches in policy analysis. Another, much more difficult problem is raised by the psychological nature of our reaction to certain statistics. Despite the fact that in assessing the risk of a proposed project, we should be concerned with the frequency of an accident occurring, as well as with the severity of the accident if it does occur, most people insist on focusing on the severity issue alone.

An example is our difference in attitude toward highway fatalities and toward the risk of a serious accident in a nuclear power station. Suppose you told Americans that risks from nuclear power ought to be acceptable because only once in ten years or so would there be a major disaster, and then it would cause some half-million deaths: They would be appalled. Yet they do not react negatively to the linear extrapolation, over ten years, of the annual death rate on the roads of the USA, which also happens to be a half-million.

In defiance of all data, the complexity of many modern issues causes people to persist in quite irrational perceptions of many risks and benefits. Thus, in a paper on "Images of Disaster," Paul Slovic and others show how the perceived risk of handguns, automobiles, and nuclear power are rated about equal (which they are not) and are considered to be more dangerous than smoking, mountain climbing, and motorbike riding (again which is not the case).

I use these examples not as an argument for or against a particular point of view, but as an illustration of the fact that making more information available to the public, and discussing it extensively through the media and in a nonadversarial forum, will not completely stop all conflict between citizens and their government. What will happen, however, is that more open government will reduce alienation and help to create a situation in which citizens and the government share a common perception of the problems their society faces.

Any discussion of ways to increase information flow between government and the governed would be incomplete without some comment on the role of public-opinion polls as a way of consulting the public. Many people hold the view that government should act on the basis of public-opinion polls. This view is illustrated by the remark a friend of mine made when he said, "A recent public-opinion poll indicated that environmental concerns were third highest of the concerns listed by Canadians, ahead of national unity and behind inflation and unemployment. Why is it that the expectations of the public are not always translated into effective pollution-control policies?"

This quotation exhibits for me two fundamental misunderstandings that are common to many people. First, it shows that many members of the general public are susceptible to the belief that public-opinion polls contain absolute truth about the kind of trade-offs that the general public wants made among alternatives. But they do not.

Take the poll cited by my friend concerning the environment and unemployment. Based on the results he noted, one could argue (albeit equally falsely) that since the poll showed unemployment to be an issue of greater concern to Canadians than the environment, then the jobs-versus-environment trade-off should *always* be resolved in favour of jobs. This is clearly not what the public always wants done.

The second misunderstanding that is reflected in the comment made to me involves the basic nature of a responsible parliamentary system of government. In our system, there does not *necessarily* have to be a direct connection between public opinion on an issue and the Legislature's response to it in the form of legislative action. Perhaps the clearest example of this in recent years is the capital punishment issue. Even though an overwhelming majority of the electorate favoured the retention of capital punishment, MPS exercised their own judgment in a "free" vote and voted to abolish it.

THE END AS BEGINNING: CONCLUSION

I have tried here to suggest that the answer to the problem I posed at the start of this paper – namely how can government meet the public's desire that it be made more efficient and effective, while at the same time enabling the public to get a better understanding of major issues and to have more input into their solutions – requires two separate sets of new policies.

The first is managerially oriented. It requires a thorough reexamination of the means by which public services are now provided so that, wherever possible, existing delivery mechanisms are changed to take advantage of the efficiencies inherent in the market-like competitive environment. This need not mean that the services should necessarily be provided by the private sector. It means only that regardless of who provides them, clear economic-incentive systems and competitive forces should be used to ensure that they are provided as efficiently as possible.

The second set of policies must be aimed at reducing the feeling of alienation that many Canadians have for their government by increasing their understanding of public issues and the options available for solving them. We must find new, innovative ways to include the public in the decision-making process before decisions are made. No progress will be made in improving the current attitude toward government until this happens.

In a recent book, *The Trouble with Nowadays*, Cleveland Amory succinctly describes the problem we must overcome: "Please note that I have called this chapter '"Your" Government.' For all I know – and I don't know you from Adam – it isn't yours. You may feel exactly the same way I do – in which case I apologize. But one thing I do know – and that is that it isn't my government. It might as well be a foreign government. I don't see why they don't run a foreign flag up the flagpole and be done with it."

In essence I have argued that, to start to change this attitude, what governments and private sector organizations, including special-interest groups, must provide is leadership: leadership in developing new ways in which government is managed; and leadership in creating new forms of involvement for people in the work of government.

Effective leadership is, without doubt, the greatest challenge facing those who will manage our society in the 1980s. The failure to meet this challenge will have dire consequences. As Robert Maynard Hutchins long ago warned us: "The death of democracy is not likely to be an assassination from ambush. It will be a slow extinction from apathy, indifference, and undernourishment."

What I have tried to argue here was summarized by D'Arcy McGee in a speech here in Ottawa on 14 October 1862, when he said: "Retrenchment is the immediate duty – the duty of the day and the hour – but government must lead as well as save, it must march as well as fortify, it must originate plans for the future, as well as correct the errors of the past."

I'm not cynical enough to close by arguing that "plus ça change, plus c'est la même chose," but I am realistic enough to recognize that McGee's admonition contains the essence of what must be done if we are to attack the problem of the management of government in the 1980s successfully.

MICHAEL KIRBY was appointed to the Canadian Senate by Prime Minister Trudeau in 1984. He is currently chair of the Standing Senate Committee on Social Affairs, Science, and Technology, which recently released its final report on the Canadian health care system, *The Health of Canadians: The Federal Role*, popularly known as the Kirby report. He is also active in business and serves on the boards of several companies. Over the course of his political and public-service career, Senator Kirby has been assistant principal secretary to Prime Minister Trudeau; president of the Institute for Research on Public Policy; secretary to the Cabinet for federal-provincial relations; and deputy clerk of the Privy Council. In these latter two capacities, he was deeply involved in the negotiations that led to the patriation of the Canadian Constitution and the inclusion of the Charter of Rights in the Constitution.

Senator Kirby received an honorary Doctor of Laws from Dalhousie University in Halifax in 1997.

17

Bureaucrats and Reformers: A Remediable Dissonance?

JOHN MEISEL, 1983

Alan B. Plaunt was, with Graham Spry, the cofounder of the Canadian Broadcasting League, that singularly successful force that paved the way for the establishment of public broadcasting in Canada. He was also the league's first secretary. When a publicly owned broadcasting company was created in 1936, he became a key member of its board, from which, however, he resigned because of a disagreement about its management a year or so before his untimely death at thirty-seven.

Plaunt, therefore, played three major roles: He was, first, a tireless reformer and, second, a man deeply involved in the administrative processes of the Canadian Broadcasting Corporation during its formative years. Since the CBC at that time performed regulatory functions, he was also, third, a regulator. While he was never, strictly speaking, an official, his close involvement and concern with the administration of the CBC have led me to identify in Plaunt the embodiment of three essential roles in government that provide the theme of this paper.

It is not, I think, far-fetched to see a fairly close relationship between the functions of reform, administration, and regulation although the inclusion of the latter may provoke a flicker of some eyebrows. Since this is, I admit, a somewhat eccentric or idiosyncratic view, I had better explain.

Classical democratic theory makes a simple distinction between law making, law implementation, and law adjudication. The legislature, the executive, and the judiciary were seen to be performing these roles. But life was never quite so simple, even in the laissez-faire days of the nineteenth century, which gave rise to both the theory and practice of liberal democracy. Greater realism and the overwhelming aggrandizement of the roles of government and its terrifying complexity combined to make obsolete the tripartite division of governmental functions. On the input side, to use David Easton's terminology,[1] the mechanisms for expressing what seem, at any given time, people's needs and wants consist of a great deal more than just legislatures.

These assemblies have in fact increasingly come in for scathing criticism and accusations of inadequacy.[2]

The process of law making cannot be understood without relating it to the roles and operations of political parties and the electoral process, to opinion formation, and to the ubiquitous and far-reaching activities of organized interests, pressure groups, and lobbyists. Furthermore, law making and law application have become a continuous and indivisible process. Legislatures can at best produce only extremely general expressions of what they want done, and this assumes that laws do, in fact, reflect the wishes of parliaments and not simply those of the executives. The real substance of policy emerges from the manner in which the laws are carried and filled out, applied, interpreted, and enforced by civil servants and administrative and regulatory tribunals, many of which are in the hands of officials rather than judges. The sheer number and complexity of the rules needed to ensure an orderly and well-managed modern society are so immense that only vast armies of specialists and experts can produce them.

Parliaments have, indeed, recognized that, quite apart from the number of decisions needed, their own inadequate knowledge not only of the relevant facts, but often of public perceptions, prevents them from engaging in detailed law-making. It is in part for this reason that they have delegated some of their responsibilities to regulatory agencies. These in turn accumulate detailed knowledge and expertise. At the same time, they often hold public hearings at which interested parties can express their wishes and points of view. The desires of various publics can therefore be taken into account in delegated legislation. Regulatory agencies, like government departments, are of course ultimately responsible to Parliament, but in neither case is it easy to develop adequate means for effective accountability.

At any rate, from this perspective, it is clear that the major burden of government administration has come to rest on the shoulders of a gigantic and immensely

---

1 David Easton, *The Political System* (New York: Alfred A. Knopf, 1953).
2 R.J. Jackson and M.M. Atkinson, *The Canadian Legislative System* (Toronto: MacMillan of Canada, 1974); W.A.W. Neilson and J.C. MacPherson, eds, *The Legislative Process in Canada* (Montreal: Institute for Research on Public Policy, 1978); J. Meisel, "New Challenge to Parliament: Arguing Over Wine Lists on the Titanic?" *Journal of Canadian Studies* 14, no. 2 (Summer 1979); P.M. Pitfield, "Bureaucracy and Parliament," unpublished speech, Ottawa, 25 February 1983.

powerful bureaucracy. While this does, of course, pose innumerable problems, there is nothing wrong with it, provided that the bureaucrat performs his or her work effectively and responsibly. To do this, an amazingly elaborate and complex mass of rules, procedures, folkways, and formal structures have evolved, which, together, comprise the bureaucratic phenomenon.[3]

Although innovation is not incompatible with bureaucratic decision-making, sweeping reforms and radical departures are not common in it. Reformers are, on the whole, rare birds in the public-service aviary. The bureaucratic style stresses stability, predictable continuity, and caution, rather than exciting experimentation or the daring exploration of novelty. This is compatible with accepted theory of liberal-democratic government.

In a democratic state, bureaucracies are entrusted with the efficient translation into policies and administrative procedures of the goals set by their political masters. If they become policy makers in their own right, which of course they do from time to time, there is a danger that politicians, instead of aggregating the interests of their constituents and responding to the requirements of the public, become the captives of their officials. While this does happen from time to time and has even been known to produce felicitous results, it is more likely that government outputs will, under these conditions, increasingly reflect only the interests of the administrative state, thus alienating the people from their government.

Whatever the influence of bureaucracies, they are not as a rule motivated by an irresistible urge to champion reform. On the contrary, they normally tend to perpetuate the status quo. Bold innovation, while of course not unknown even in large-scale formal organizations, more typically emanates from a quite different quarter of society: the disenchanted, those smarting under prevailing conditions, and particularly perhaps individuals fired by the dream of a new society or a new way of attacking a lingering or urgent problem. Reformers, hellbent on eradicating shortcomings and instituting novel solutions to plaguing problems, thus provide the motive force for substantive, genuine change, as distinct from the illusory innovation of administrative tinkering. Bernard Shaw came close to encapsulating perfectly the place of the reformer in the scheme of things when he compared reasonable and unreasonable people. "The reasonable man adapts himself to the world; the unreasonable one persists in trying to adapt the world to himself. Therefore all progress depends on the unreasonable man," Shaw concluded.

---

3 In borrowing Michel Crozier's phrase, I do not, of course, wish to suggest that the particular model he described in his classic book is the only one I have in mind. The work of Max Weber and hundreds of more recent scholars illustrates the universal phenomenon of bureaucratic behaviour.

A well-functioning political system manages to make effective use of both reforming zeal and bureaucratic commonsense and stability. The ideal liberal-democratic model is one in which a variety of interests, including those of reformers, are sifted, assigned priority, and finally translated by political parties and pluralist politics into policy. In a number of key areas, the need to ensure complete independence from political pressure, to consult interested parties, to utilize quasi-judicial procedures and to apply specialized knowledge has led to the creation, as we already noted, of independent regulatory agencies. These are composed of independent members who make decisions with the help of their own bureaucracies. They, in a sense, and within the closely circumscribed confines of their jurisdiction, combine the roles of legislatures and bureaucracies and complement the work of these institutions. By creating delegated legislation after public consultation, they provide a means of linking expert and public opinion to the process of bureaucratic decision making. Ideally, regulatory agencies should respond both to the need for reform and to the requirements of administrative consistency.

The presence of reformers, the existence of competent public services, and the independent decision making of regulatory agencies are important elements in a society wishing to benefit from a political system combining responsiveness to human needs, innovation, and orderly and predictable administrative procedures.

Alan Plaunt made a remarkable contribution to Canada by ensuring that its political process dealt effectively with a matter of capital importance: the establishment of a viable public broadcasting system. His role as a reformer, and after the creation of the CBC as a member of its Board of Governors, focuses our attention on the need for, and the difficulties of combining, the reforming and administrative functions in the modern state. For the sake of brevity we can think of the required relationship as that between the reformer and the bureaucrat. I will consider here what has been happening to this relationship in Canada and draw some conclusions that might be helpful in the future.

In juxtaposing the reformer and the bureaucrat I am of course resorting to a rhetorical device and to drastic oversimplification. It is surely not necessary to explain what I mean by bureaucrat, bureaucracy, and bureaucratic style, except to indicate that I attach no pejorative significance to these terms and to note that they refer to phenomena inevitable in large-scale organizations. A word needs to be said, however, about my reformer. By drawing on Alan Plaunt as a prototype I endow the word with a special content. Reform, change, and innovation are related notions although each has a distinct meaning. The first, reform, usually refers to some improvement, but it does, of course, raise the question of the criteria used in evaluating any change. The ayatollah's reform may be the shah's abomination. While flexibility and change are generally accorded approbation in my comments, and are sometimes seen as challenging bureau-cracy, they are not necessarily to be linked to reform. The latter, in my lexicon, relates to change that is deemed by reasonable judgment to be in the public interest. The difference between Plaunt and Spry, on the one side, and a great many activists exerting political pressure on the other, is that the former's cause was related to a general good and not to private gain.

Consider what Brooke Claxton, a companion warrior of Plaunt's, said of him while introducing the first Plaunt lecture: "The secret of Alan Plaunt's success was that he sought nothing for himself. What he wanted was in the interest of the country. He made no speeches; gave few interviews; circulated no photo-graphs; but wherever he went he lit a spark which became fanned into a flame of unselfish action."

The reformer, in the present context, is therefore someone who champions the public, rather than a particular, interest. The two are not necessarily mutually exclusive, of course, but my reformer pursues the common weal for its own sake, without any regard for personal or private gain. The public interest is served, in my view, when policies favour the establishment or maintenance of a caring society in which the basic necessities of life are accessible to all citizens and in which government enhances rather than stifles the attainment of conditions enabling both individuals and collectivities to lead creative lives.

Among the many factors that have altered the relationship between reformers and bureaucrats since Plaunt's day, five seem to me to be of particular relevance and interest. There are others, of course, but let me at least make a beginning by considering the consequences and problems related to:

- The attenuation of public zeal for general, community-wide causes
- The institutionalization of reform
- A reorientation in the priorities of bureaucrats
- The still-growing complexity of government
- The increasing role of regulation

ATTENUATION OF ZEAL FOR PUBLIC CAUSES

Pluralism in the Western world has to some extent run amok. There is no interest, regardless of how small, narrow, or antisocial it may seem, that is not furthered by some organized movement, usually composed of a nucleus of those who stand to benefit from it and a wider circle of sympathizers. This is not the place in which to evaluate this development, but we must note one of its major conse-quences for democratic decision making: The emergence of single-cause orga-nizations and pressure groups has made it more difficult to mount campaigns for the general public good and has hindered the efforts of political parties and politicians to aggregate existing interests into broad, acceptable policies. Powerful veto groups increasingly succeed in blocking governmental initiatives that might be of overall benefit but that offend certain narrow, particular interests. The single-issue phenomenon and the concomitant, all-enveloping specialization requires the breaking-down of most problems into their component parts, leading to fragmentation and to difficulties in putting Humpty Dumpty together again. It is easier – and often more financially rewarding – to placate the more focused pressure groups than to accommodate the more diffused and universal interests.[4]

A striking example comes to mind: Although the Canadian Broadcasting League (the former Radio League) still exists (and I salute and support Graham Spry's efforts to assure its viability), its voice appears to be almost drowned out by the insistent and constant drumming of organizations pursuing much narrower (and lucrative) goals than public broadcasting. Compare the resources and clout of the Broadcast League with those of the broadcasters' associations, the cable associations, the Alliance of Canadian Cinema, Television and Radio Artists (ACTRA), or the American Association of Musicians. While some such organizations may support public broadcasting, it is usually a subsidiary interest that often plays second fiddle to more immediate concerns of their members.

Alan Plaunt and Graham Spry would have had a much harder time today in making their ideas prevail and not only because public broadcasting is now established and hence has made its enemies. The main reason is that in the face of an increasing stampede of narrow, organized interests clamouring for attention, efforts such as theirs to promote the general public good are only rarely heard – and only seldom successful.

INSTITUTIONALIZATION OF REFORM

The context in which reformers operate has become much more difficult. Not only has the number of specific interests seeking to be heard multiplied immeasurably, but the way in which individuals and groups seeking change go about promoting their business has also altered greatly. With so many players trying to influence policies and their application, the process of promoting one's ideas is now much more competitive, specialized, and expensive. Dealing with the government is a major industry, particularly in Ottawa, attracting numerous lawyers, one-time civil servants and politicians, and increasingly all manner of other specialists who peddle persuasion and their orienteering skills in the

---

4 Mancur Olson, *The Logic of Collective Action* (Cambridge, Mass.: Harvard University Press, 1965).

corridors of power. The individual reformer, working alone or with a small group of like-minded souls, without an administrative and consulting infrastructure, is an endangered species in the process of becoming extinct.

Charles Addams made the point perfectly in a *New Yorker* cartoon not long ago. Departing from his usual macabre preoccupations, he provided a modern cityscape displaying the usual skyscrapers, a neoclassical building, and an attractive parkette. There are also three monuments. In each case, a small cluster of men and women stand on a sizeable pedestal, looking pensive. Some are clutching papers or a briefcase. A man and a youngster stroll past one of these sculptures, gazing in admiration at the figures towering above them. The caption says it all: "There are no great men, my boy, only great committees."

The professionalization of reform has taken place and requires anyone wishing to wield influence to be as concerned with the *art* of persuasion as with the *substance* of the desired change. There is therefore likely to be a dispersal of energies and zeal between the policy objective and the procedures required to attain it.

A mammoth structure like a modern government is almost impervious to being moved by a single individual driven largely by zeal and passion in his or her armoury. A reformer who aims to succeed must work within an organization that provides expertise in putting across a point of view and in packaging it. This sometimes causes the wrappers to discolour the contents.

There are other consequences. Reform itself is becoming bureaucratized. Associations dedicated to bringing about change assume the characteristics of all organizations: Differences of view or in emphasis may develop between the elected members (volunteers) and the staffs (professionals). Organizations also have a natural propensity to grow, to seek aggrandizement, and to strengthen the bureaucratic element. The stronger the organization becomes, the more likely that its cause will be expressed with managerial efficiency rather than with the passionate conviction of the believer.

The administrative scaffolding of the organization imperceptibly acquires its own goals, watering down or completely submerging the original, basic purpose of its formation. The central drive for and purpose of a desired change may therefore be set aside in favour of a demand emanating from the organizational structure itself. At the risk of treading on territory from which prudence, if I had more of it, would keep me, I would like to cite one example that not only concerns the Canadian Radio-Television and Telecommunications Commission (CRTC), but is also before the Supreme Court. The illustration is irresistible because it shows that even so small and seemingly simple an organization as the Canadian Broadcasting League is subject to the processes I am describing. Without prejudice and without in any way commenting on the substance of the case, I would like to draw attention to the fact that the Canadian Broadcasting League has challenged the CRTC's jurisdiction over cable rates. When the Federal Court of Appeal upheld the commission in 1982, the Canadian Broadcasting League appealed the decision to the Supreme Court. Why? How could the cause of public broadcasting benefit from a legal challenge to the regulator's jurisdiction over cable rates? I would not have been surprised had the Canadian Cable Television Association initiated these proceedings. But I am at a loss to see the relation between them and what I take to be the organization Alan Plaunt and Graham Spry founded to espouse the cause of public and good broadcasting.

One of the reasons for the staff or consultants of an interest group assuming a dominant, organization-oriented – rather than a "movement-oriented" – stance is that a bureaucracy, being concerned with organizational survival, develops particular skills in assuring it. It must always justify its existence and its claims for resources by being busy. A critical aspect in this context relates to the financial underpinnings of the enterprise. Since the 1960s, when participatory democracy caught many people's imagination, public funds have been available for various organizations espousing diverse causes. This has meant that a number of groups attempting to influence government are, in fact, dependent on its grants. In some instances, public officials have been instrumental in establishing groups that then use the taxpayers' money to persuade government to adopt favourable policies. This procedure, and the financing of interest groups out of the Consolidated Revenue Fund, may be appropriate and desirable elements in the democratic process. But whatever their merits, they have institutionalized reform in a manner that makes it a totally alien process from that exemplified by Alan Plaunt. The logic and imperatives of impersonal, bureaucratized organizations have replaced the individual commitment of strong personalities. I find it difficult to believe that the character and worth of governmental decisions are not affected by this qualitative change in the means of championing reform.

REORIENTATION IN PRIORITIES OF BUREAUCRATS

It is not only reform movements and voluntary associations that have undergone change and become bureaucratized. Bureaucracy itself has experienced a number of nearly cataclysmic metamorphoses. The subject has received extensive treatment since, curiously, public servants almost seem to rival the media in the degree to which they display professional navel gazing. Several royal commissions, massive numbers of internal documents, and an impressive array of academic studies[5] have traced and plumbed the transformations of our public services. Major shifts have occurred in the emphasis placed on such fundamental features as patronage, the merit system, scientific management, representativeness, and accountability, to name only a few. At the heart of most of the issues lies the problem of reconciling the effective and efficient "professional" performance of administration with the political goals of governments and of the populations they serve.

The amusing British television series *Yes, Minister* has done much to popularize some of the factors impinging on this problem. Among the wide range of changes brought about to achieve the appropriate relationship between a capable public service and a well-briefed, smoothly running, and effective cabinet, one is particularly relevant to our current concern. Despite its importance, it has received little or no attention.

Among the innovations proposed by the Glassco Commission was the idea that deputy ministers be rotated from department to department. There is much to be said for this practice, which was tried during the Pearson years and applied with considerable zest by Mr Trudeau. I believe that only six deputy ministers out of thirty-two now hold the same post they occupied when the present government was elected to office in 1980. Like most changes, this one had not only its anticipated but also its unanticipated consequences. Among the latter was a fundamental change in the job orientation not only of deputy ministers, but ultimately also of public servants generally.

The uprooting of deputies has led to a new psychological mindset in which they and their juniors increasingly come to see themselves as experts in policy making and management as such and hence not related to any one policy sector. Where previously civil servants expected to devote their entire working lives to a particular aspect of public policy, they now expect to roam over many fields in the course of their careers. They are less specialists in the substance of any one area than experts in the general art of policy analysis and in the folkways of bureaucracy. "Have tools! Will travel!" In contrast to their predecessors, public servants have therefore become less oriented to certain policy areas and more concerned with their own advancement in the invitingly open and ever-more rewarding hierarchy of the governmental priesthood. Policy focus has been replaced by career focus.

---

5 For useful recent guides, see J.E. Hodgetts, "Implicit Values in the Administration of Public Affairs," *Canadian Public Administration* 25, no. 4 (Winter 1982): 471–83, and A. Paul Pross, "From System to Serendipity: The Practice and Study of Public Policy in the Trudeau Years," ibid., 520–44.

The old slogan of the scientific management school that administration is administration is administration (regardless of what is being administered) has therefore really come into its own. It is perhaps significant, in this context, as J.E. Hodgetts has observed, that the upper echelons of the public service have recently been designated as senior management. "If values can be inferred from the titles we attach to official functions (as I believe they can), then the growing preference for the term management as opposed to administration demonstrates the durability of the values espoused by the scientific management movement."[6]

In the past, the deeply rooted, permanent attachment of an official to one ministry may have led to a narrowness of view, affinity for well-established policies and procedures, and the danger of becoming captive to a particular interest or sector. It also, however, often engendered a passionate commitment to a cause. The kind of commitment, in fact, that characterized the old-fashioned reformer. And while Emerson no doubt overstated the case when he said that "there is no strong performance without a little fanaticism in the performer," the absence of a total commitment is not without consequence. Today's peripatetic official, more or less in transit from one rung in the hierarchy to another, may be intensely keen on an immediate problem but is unlikely to consider that the work at hand requires the total and sustained dedication of his very being. Among the consequences, which are not necessarily all harmful, is the relative decline in a preoccupation with the real substance of issues and what is behind them in favour of a more instrumental approach.

The rapid circulation of members of our bureaucratic elite sometimes leads to another questionable consequence. Expecting that he or she has only a short time in which to make his or her mark in any one job, the upwardly mobile official may avoid attacking major issues of substance. These usually take a very long time to master and to cope with. It is much easier and quicker to devise some spectacular administrative or procedural innovation. The boldness of the conception will reflect well on its originator, but its real consequences, if any, will not be known until long after he or she has risen to greater heights in another assignment. Genuine policy reform may, in the meantime, languish.

GOVERNMENT COMPLEXITY

The relative influence of what I have loosely termed reformers and bureaucrats and the relationship between them have also been altered by the growing complexity of government. This too is a subject on which numerous observers

---

6 J.E. Hodgetts, "Implicit Values in the Administration of Public Affairs," *Canadian Public Administration* 25, no. 4 (Winter 1982): 477–78.

have lavished their attention. In the context of this paper, the most important manifestation of this phenomenon is the increase in the numbers of actors involved in the policy process and particularly the key role played by the so-called central agencies.[7]

Alan Plaunt's and Graham Spry's successful efforts toward the creation of the CBC would probably have been quite inadequate today. Their systematic attempts to inform and mobilize the public, and particularly the politically alert members of it, are a timeless tactic. But their attempts to "educate" members of the government would require nowadays an infinitely greater effort. There is so much more of government, and it is so much more complex: For every key decision maker then, there are now probably fifty. The difference is not only in numbers, but also in the multiplicity of power centres to be assailed. Whereas formerly the prime minister, a handful of colleagues, and a couple of officials would have been "sufficient" targets, today two or three related ministries, the Treasury Board, the Privy Council Office, a couple of coordinating ministries of state, the Department of Finance, and a couple of Cabinet committees would, among others, need to be tackled.

The division of labour achieved through Cabinet committees and the existence of several central agencies have changed the roles once fulfilled by normal government departments and by plenary meetings of the Cabinet. A multiplicity of decision-making sites exists, ensuring that a broad consensus is struck within the government, that the left hand knows what its right mate is doing, and that all relevant aspects and power bases are taken into account. The disadvantage is that a certain emasculation of ideas often occurs in the process and that a great many bold proposals are toned down to accommodate the various interests. There are exceptions, of course, and the system does have many positive features as well. But it tends to discourage daring reform in favour of the prudent judgments of sound guardians of their particular domains. Under these circumstances, it is easy to overlook the useful fact that falling flat on your face is still moving forward.

Another critical change making for greater complexity is related to Canada's new federalism. Despite the provincialist tendencies of the Judicial Committee of the Privy Council in Westminster, Ottawa was unmistakably the governmental centrepiece in Plaunt's day. Since then the country's federal system has undergone a fundamental transformation. There are few areas, including even such key matters as its own budget, that can be dealt with unilaterally by the central government without consulting or noting provincial interests. The relative

---

7 For a useful overview, see R.J. Van Loon, "Kaleidoscope in Grey: The Policy Process in Ottawa," in M.S. Whittington and G. Williams, eds, *Canadian Politics in the 1980s* (Toronto: Methuen, 1981), 292–312.

increase in the power, competence, and ambition of provincial governments has therefore also multiplied the number of decision-making sites in Canada and has significantly enlarged the number of actors involved in formulating and applying any major policy. In a complex world where everything seems to be related to everything else, even clear constitutional boundaries often give way to practical, informal arrangements cutting across jurisdictional lines.

Anyone wishing to affect public policy must not only take on Ottawa's massive and diffused policy machine, but may also have to contend with several provincial power centres. Innovation and reform – normally resisted under the best of circumstances – become even more problematic in a federal state displaying strong centrifugal tendencies.

THE INCREASING ROLE OF REGULATION

Alan Plaunt, as we noted, was also briefly a regulator, but that honourable profession played only a minor role in his life and that of his contemporaries. Regulation, in the present sense, was unknown then. It was not until the Second World War and its political and economic aftermath that the modern regulatory state came into being.

By injecting yet another level of decision making into the governmental process, regulatory agencies clearly complicate the task of persons wishing to turn the government around. The tendencies of many regulatory agencies to pursue careful, quasi-judicial procedures, to work closely and for long periods of time with certain problems and industries, and to make day-to-day decisions within the framework of regulations having universal applicability predispose them to a certain conservatism. On the other hand, their independence of the government of the day; their frequent reliance on public consultation; the openness of some of them to representations from general interests and to supporting public intervenors; their composition, reflecting in most cases diverse regions of the country; and particularly their statutory obligation to defend the public interest as defined by Parliament endow them with qualities that could make them receptive to new ideas and reform.

On the basis of what is admittedly a highly impressionistic judgment unfettered by serious research, I conclude that, on balance, regulatory agencies have reflected the bureaucratic style much more readily than that of the reformer. One reason for this is, of course, that many innovations put before them serve the narrow interests of particular applicants at the cost of the public weal. But other reasons, related to their structure, composition, and modus operandi are at least equally responsible.

Whatever the reasons, I am convinced that regulatory agencies have the potential to influence the resolution of the tension inherent between reformers and bureaucrats. Whether they can realize this potential will depend in part on what changes, if any, are made with respect to how they will operate in the future. Regulation has recently been the subject of inquiry by the Lambert Commission, the Economic Council of Canada, the Law Reform Commission, two parliamentary committees, and the Privy Council Office, and I believe that a document dealing with regulatory reform is soon to be put before the Cabinet.[8]

Decisions will have to be made with respect to a number of key matters. One of these concerns independence: independence of the regulatory agencies from the government and their ministerial link with Parliament; independence from the industries they regulate, from the central agencies, particularly the Treasury Board under the terms of the Financial Administration Act; and independence from potentially impinging new policies when these are inconsistent with their statutory mandates.

While the autonomy of the regulatory process in these matters must be maintained and perhaps strengthened, means must also be found to ensure that it functions in congruence with broader governmental objectives and policies. Under appropriate safeguards, Cabinet directives are a useful device in this context, as is the prudent and carefully circumscribed availability of appeals to the governor-in-council. Procedures and particularly their openness are also relevant, as is the capacity and willingness of Parliament to assure the accountability of regulatory agencies. Most important of all is the necessity to fill vacancies on the regulatory bodies promptly and with exemplary nominees. The fact that these and related issues have received so much attention and continue to be examined does not imply that the past performance in most of the relevant areas has been found wanting. Although improvement, as in all human endeavour, is of course possible and even desirable, the record is by no means discouraging. In reviewing current practices, and in contemplating change, the presence of reforming and bureaucratic tendencies in society should be kept in mind. It will be desirable to devise structures and practices geared to bringing them into fruitful harmony.

---

8 *Final Report of the Royal Commission on Financial Management and Accountability* (Lambert Commission), March 1979; *Reforming Regulation: Report of the Economic Council of Canada on the Regulation Reference,* 1981; *Independent Administrative Agencies,* Law Reform Commission Working Paper 25, 1980; *Fourth Report of the Standing Joint Committee of the Senate and the House of Commons on Regulations and Other Statutory Instruments,* July 1980; *Report of the Special Committee on Regulatory Reform* (Peterson Task Force), December 1980.

CONCLUSION

This fusion of reform and bureaucracy brings me to the conclusion of my argument. In pitting Alan Plaunt's world of the inspired, public-spirited reformer against the changes that have affected government since his time, I have set up a somewhat oversimplified dichotomy between the reformer and the bureaucrat. I have argued that the role of the reformer has shrunk and that the role of the latter has grown. I have also suggested that the regulatory process could become particularly well-suited to the effective combination of the respective styles of both reformers and bureaucrats.

While I hold to these positions, I must confess to being guilty of a tiny bit of expositional mischief. My two basic notions – the reformer and the bureaucrat – are ideal types in the Weberian sense. They do not in fact exist but are focal points of two clusters of related tendencies. Alan Plaunt and Graham Spry come close to embodying the quintessence of the reformer; I will refrain from naming a prototype of the bureaucrat. My reticence here is understandable but actually unnecessary. Invidious comparisons between our two ideal types are out of place. Seeking public-spirited change and administering in an orderly fashion are not mutually exclusive activities. Each has its own dominant traits, but these are not pure or exclusive. A reformer can have some characteristics of the bureaucrat, and the latter can be a reformer. A perfect overlap is rare, and we are justified in recognizing the two separate types.

Furthermore, both the reformer and the bureaucrat are essential to society. A world made up of only the former would be chaotic; one composed of only the latter would be static and dull. If an underlying tone has crept into my comments denoting a preference for the reformer, it is because, as I have indicated, I believe that changes since Plaunt's day have inhibited the survival of his type while favouring the cloning of the bureaucrat. We are, if my analysis is correct, in greater need of reformers than of bureaucrats not because the first are more essential but merely because they are in short supply.

If this imbalance is to be redressed, two developments will be required. First, we must encourage a large number of citizens to become engaged in seeking reform and in keeping up their spirit despite the many obstacles they are bound to encounter. Second, more reformers will have to be coaxed into bureaucracies and means devised to enable them to maintain their zeal once inside.

These are not easily reached goals. Yet they are not impossible. Significant numbers of people seriously pursuing a public good, rather than a private gain, will only emerge as the result of a fairly fundamental change in societal attitudes. Some will argue that the time does not appear propitious for this. This decade so far has not been notorious for a sense of civic duty, a public philosophy, or a magnanimous desire to improve the world. We continue, with a vengeance, the tradition of "I'm alright, Jack!" and the "me generation." But times change. Consider the differences in the dominant values of young people in the 1960s, the 1970s, and now the 1980s. And although the Alan Plaunts are less in evidence than one would wish, the breed has not yet vanished totally. Ralph Nader, Terry Fox, Stratford's Tom Patterson, and Graham Spry cannot be written off. It is not unthinkable that a spirit of altruism, public concern, and civility might once again become fashionable. It would be congruent with the currently heightened concern for nuclear disarmament and environmental protection. It is, of course, the ideas and actions of a few generous and far-sighted individuals, the formal and informal educational process, the media, popular culture, and that mysterious affinity propagating the tenets of underground culture that would be the source of a revitalized sense of reform. Despite – or perhaps because of – the current retreat in some quarters from a welfare society, a change toward a reform-oriented value system is by no means unthinkable.

Insofar as bureaucracies are concerned, one is tempted to conclude that only cataclysmic changes in the whole system could achieve the desired end. A few years ago, in contemplating the problems confronting Parliament, Robert Stanfield concluded that the only solution was to reduce the scope of governmental activities.[9] The same medicine might well be prescribed in our case, for smaller, simpler government would certainly facilitate the task of reformers. But, alas, it is most improbable that this solution can be realized. Mr Stanfield's approach nevertheless directs our attention to the fact that a full illumination of our problem may have to be sought not only in the bureaucracy or in the nature of reform, but also in the general relationship between officials and politicians and particularly between departments and their ministers. One may, indeed, look further still and consider the relations between ministers and their Cabinet colleagues and the critical role of the prime minister him or herself.

Pending this massive extension in the scope of our problem, however, it will be prudent and realistic to stick to our original and simpler perspective and to seek more modest means of redress. A suitable equilibrium between bureaucratic and reformist tendencies is likely to prevail when the public service devises procedures that reward public-interest-oriented innovation and that impede the manifestation of an administration-for-the-sake-of-administration mentality.

Institutional inducements will be needed to leaven the inevitable characteristics of large-scale organizations with elements stressing altruistic reform. This

---

9 "The Present State of the Legislative Process in Canada: Myths and Realities," in W.A.W. Neilson and J.C. MacPherson, eds, *The Legislative Process in Canada* (Montreal: Institute for Research on Public Policy, 1978), 39–50.

will not be easy. The tendency of all organizations is to perpetuate procedures and work ways that serve the organization itself and to rationalize them by a rhetoric invoking the public interest. Nevertheless, our central agencies, notably the Privy Council Office, Treasury Board, and the Public Service Commission, have in the past been immensely fertile in devising organizational and procedural practices reflecting current goals. They have been aware in the past of the need to "de-bureaucratize" the bureaucracy and to make government responsive to broad policy innovation and to the requirements of altruistic reform. I have no doubt that if they attached sufficient importance to the matter, they could come up with new schemes ensuring the attraction and encouragement of the reforming element in terms both of recruitment and of operating procedures.

Some efforts to deal with matters related to the central issue underlying my concern were actually made in the decade starting in the late 1960s, albeit from a perspective that differed substantially from my own. I refer to the experiments tried by some central agencies and departments with so-called strategic planning. These were designed to create an administrative process that was rational, coordinated, and highly sensitive to actual and future public needs. These initiatives did not, however, live up to expectations, nor did they resolve the difficulties that result from the lack of congruence between the reforming and bureaucratic styles. They were important essays at innovation, however, and a new and searching look, in the context of the present discussion, at what can be learned from them would be extremely useful. "The longest journey begins with a single step," goes the Chinese proverb, and the quest for the institutional inducements I have just called for could well start with this review of our experience with strategic planning.

Since this paper is offered under the aegis of Carleton University, which is making a major contribution to the description, analysis, and evaluation of the governmental process, it is appropriate to note that I believe that there is room, in relation to the present discussion, for considerable improvement in the manner in which the government benefits from the resources inherent in Canada's academic community.

There is a great deal of interaction, of course, which has benefited both sides. The principal contact is through the participation of university people in government projects under contract or by academic involvement in royal commissions and similar inquiries. While this interaction could fruitfully be extended and improved, it is not the area that causes the greatest concern. What must give pause is the fact that apart from the contractual arrangements, inquiries, and the occasional joint participation in seminars or conferences, there is inadequate contact between government officials and what we might term independent intellectual life in the universities.

We tend to shy away in Canada from admitting that class differences exist among us and that significant consequences flow from divisions rooted in disparities in our educations, occupations, incomes, and self-perceptions. We also turn a blind eye to the presence of an intelligentsia. Consequently, we overlook the fact that much of the mandarinate and many of our academics constitute an extremely important element of what, for lack of a better term, we can call the country's intellectual class. But although their educational backgrounds are often similar, as are many of their tools of the trade, there is relatively little communion between them except in relation to the very specific areas noted earlier. What is lacking is a mutual enrichment in relation to general preoccupations of a philosophical, social, or cultural nature. A quick glance at the circulation patterns and particularly the readership of Canada's English academic quarterlies, particularly those of a general nature, like the *Dalhousie Review* or the *Queen's Quarterly*, indicates that there are more solitudes in this country than the two portrayed by Hugh McLennan.

The reasons for this state of affairs are not far to seek. They relate primarily to the nearly crushing burden of work of many senior public servants, to a certain opaqueness in some academic writing, and to the occasional presence on both sides of a somewhat narrow, self-absorbed, and partial perspective. But whatever the causes, the consequences affect the manner in which bureaucrats and reformers interact. For much of the underlying impetus for reform and its rationale comes from ideas nurtured and developed in the universities even though they may at first appear to be very far indeed from policy concerns. The potential contribution of both reformers and bureaucrats would be enhanced by a greater exchange of their respective concerns and thoughts.

There are many ways to meet the needs I have identified in this paper. Our past record shows that we have the capacity to respond to the challenge. Even under the conditions I have described as inadequate, great innovative thrusts have occurred. Without necessarily approving the substance of each policy, we must acknowledge that a system is not impervious to initiating change when it can generate major new departures and redirection in such areas as language policy, the envelope system, energy policy, or constitutional change. But for each of these innovations, we must also acknowledge numerous instances of blockages and inaction. The latter are in part to be attributed to the paucity of reformers, as well as to the growing number of impediments standing in their way. I cannot conclude this paper better than by saying that it is a measure of the man that Alan Plaunt's life has directed us toward identifying some of the reasons for our shortcomings and that it has inspired us to seek their redress.

JOHN MEISEL is the Sir Edward Peacock Professor of Political Science Emeritus and Senior Research Fellow in the Centre for the Study of Public Opinion at Queen's University. He has been a pioneer in Canada of research on electoral behaviour, political parties, and the relationship between politics and leisure culture, particularly the arts. Dr Meisel is also a past chairman of the Canadian Radio-Television and Telecommunications Commission (CRTC), past president of the Social Science Research Council of Canada, and has served on a number of royal commissions.

Dr Meisel is an Officer of the Order of Canada and a Fellow and past president of the Royal Society of Canada. He has been awarded the Centennial, Queen Elizabeth II Jubilee, and 125th Anniversary of Canada commemorative medals; the Northern Telecom International Canadian Studies Award of Excellence; the John Orr and Agnes Benidickson awards; and the Montreal Medal. He held a Killam Award from the Canada Council for five years and has honorary doctorates from six Canadian universities.

18

The World Economy: Marking Time

SYLVIA OSTRY, 1984

In 1983 the world economy began to emerge from the most serious recession in the postwar era. For the industrialized market economies as a whole – the countries of the Organization for Economic Cooperation and Development (OECD) – this is the second year of that recovery. But even the most casual observer senses that the longer-term outlook is fraught with uncertainty. The prevailing mood is one of *attentisme:* marking time. This paper will trace the provenance of the great recession, the nature of the recovery, and the legacy of unresolved economic problems that are the source of the gathering cloud of uncertainty shrouding the window to the future.

Let me begin, then, with the sources of the recent recession. The most convenient point at which to start the story is with the second oil shock of 1979–80 (OPEC II). In truth, however, the roots of our present problems lie far deeper. Perhaps the hardiest of these roots is a legacy of the 1970s: the legacy of inflationary expectations. The accelerating inflation of that decade was in fact launched in the 1960s by the fateful decision of the US to finance the war in Vietnam and the New Society by vastly expansionary policies. The inflationary expectations thus ignited were confirmed and ratcheted up by matching expansionary policies in most OECD countries at the outset of the 1970s, the breakdown of the Bretton-Woods system of fixed exchange rates in 1973, and the massive supply shocks of commodity and oil prices that soon followed. The OECD economies had not made anywhere near a full adjustment to those shocks or to the quickening pace of technological change and the steady, ongoing shift of industrialization to a number of Third World countries when the fall of the Shah of Iran precipitated OPEC II.

The second oil shock posed an enormously difficult dilemma for OECD member governments. A policy response was needed to prevent the external price pulse from embedding itself in the underlying domestic rate of inflation and ratcheting up, once again, the inherited deep-rooted inflationary expectations. In a medical analogy, there was a need to contain the infection of oil and energy price rises from spreading to all prices through a wage-price carrier. At the same time, however, it was well understood that the oil shock itself would cause a recession by reducing OECD incomes and demand. Policies directed at containing inflation would inevitably intensify these recessionary pressures.

In the event, governments uniformly tightened their fiscal and monetary policies, opting for the first horn of the dilemma. This decision was not made lightly. Ministers of the OECD meeting in the spring of 1980 fully recognized the risk of this course but assessed the risks of rekindling inflation as being immeasurably greater. This judgment was strongly influenced by the vivid memory of the inflationary explosion and sharp profit squeeze that followed the first shock, when some countries tried to escape a recession by expansionary policies, and by the deeply disquieting fact that when that shock had passed the underlying inflation rate in the OECD area stood at nearly 9 per cent, higher than in any year since the Korean War. There was no other option than to fight inflation first.

The inflation-first policy was deemed essential for another, equally compelling reason. It was fully recognized that dealing with the oil shock was not the only problem to be faced. Indeed, the impact of the two shocks served in some sense to throw into sharp relief many rigidities stored up from past policies, rigidities that might have been exposed more slowly and less painfully under other circumstances but that were problems to be tackled sooner or later if the OECD economies were to adapt to a world of higher energy prices, to the competitive challenge of the "new Japans," and to the information-technology revolution. The precondition judged essential for achieving sustainable growth and improved adaptability was the unwinding of inflation and inflationary expectations. Given this precondition, there was a strong, though by no means unanimous, view that a spontaneous, or what came to be called a self-levitating, recovery would ensue after a difficult – though, as many hoped, relatively brief – transition.

This inflation-first policy was, in the event, rather successful in its own terms. Inflation after OPEC II peaked at a lower level and subsided much more rapidly than after the first shock. In part, this was due to more modest wage behaviour, especially in the three largest economies – the US, Japan, and Germany – as well as in the UK and many of the smaller European countries, because workers understood that a real income transfer to OPEC had taken place and couldn't be recouped. (Canadian inflation, it should be noted, proved more stubborn and was reduced only after a much longer lag.)

It should be underlined, however, that a major factor in the better inflation performance in the OECD area as a whole was the surprisingly dramatic fall in nonoil commodity prices, which may have accounted for as much as 40 per cent of the deceleration in consumer prices for the area as a whole between 1979 and 1982. (This unexpectedly rapid descent was not an unmixed blessing since it is, at least in part, transitory and has its counterpart in weakening many heavily indebted Third World economies. But more of that later.)

Another striking success of the strategy was that those OECD economies that took the full brunt of the oil-price increase adapted impressively fast to high-cost energy. For the area as a whole, oil efficiency of production improved dramatically, oil use per unit of GNP fell by over 20 per cent from its 1979 level as other fuels were substituted for this high-cost energy source, and even energy intensity fell by about 10 per cent as conservation was spurred by higher costs.

Both improved energy efficiency and the recession led to a softening of oil prices and a further reduction in inflation. Again, not an unmixed blessing, as OPEC demand for OECD goods began to decline, adding further to recessionary pressures, especially in Europe.

So the policy scores high on inflation and energy adaptiveness. But as we know the self-levitating recovery didn't happen. Instead of a brief transition to renewed growth, the industrialized countries suffered the worst recession since the Second World War. Growth slowed throughout the area while unemployment rose grimly and steadily. Signs of severe financial strain became evident as company balance sheets sharply deteriorated. Bankruptcies in every OECD country reached record levels. The debt position of many Second and Third World countries became increasingly precarious as interest rates rose, the dollar rose, commodity prices plummeted, and export markets shrank. Protectionist pressures were fanned by rising unemployment and exchange rate distortions, especially the overvalued dollar and the undervalued yen. These pressures were not entirely resisted as creeping protectionism slowly began to erode the world trading system.

Why were the results of the synchronized policy response to OPEC II so different from those expected when the decision to coordinate an inflation-first strategy was undertaken in the spring of 1980? It is important to stress that the outcome was unexpected in two respects. First, inflation fell faster than antici-pated. Forecasters were all caught by surprise, especially by the plunge in commodity prices as well as by the behaviour of exchange rates, and specifically by the dramatic rise in the dollar, which was a major factor in the excellent inflationary performance of the US. Second, output fell faster and unemployment rose more than expected. Another way of saying this is that the value of GNP, or what is called nominal GNP (the combination of prices and output), was far weaker for a much more prolonged period than expected or intended.

The complete answer to the question "Why was nominal GNP far weaker than expected or intended?" – or, if one prefers, "What caused the great recession of the early 1980s?" – will be hotly debated by economists for years to come. My own view was developed when I was at the OECD in the acutely uncomfortable position of forecasting, from the end of 1980, the most elusive recovery in history. This discomfort was somewhat eased by the fact that we were not alone in repeatedly announcing the imminent arrival of the hide-and-seek recovery. We were in the same boat as every national and international forecaster. Indeed, since the OECD publishes projections only twice a year, we made fewer errors than those who forecast more frequently!

Trying to understand forecasting errors could perhaps be termed economic autopsy and should serve the same purpose as does its medical counterpart to doctors. But the science of economic autopsy is in its infancy and the diagnosis to be derived from it correspondingly tentative. Be that as it may, it seems an inescapable conclusion that in good part the disinflation was so much faster and greater than intended because the extent and nature of both real and financial linkages among the OECD economies and between the OECD and the rest of the world were by no means fully understood and had been seriously underestimated. When there is a synchronization of policy among the industrialized countries, the effects are far more powerful than any individual country, even the largest, will foresee.

There is, in other words, far greater interdependence within the world economy than we, at present, can fully comprehend. Further, this interdependence is manifested not only by increased trade and financial links, as well as by a growing integration of production (as in the case of the automobile and aircraft industries), but also by the complex interrelationship among the major forces shaping the present and foreseeable world economic system: debt affecting trade and vice versa; exchange rates affecting trade and vice versa; exchange rates affecting debt and vice versa.

The difficulty of anticipating the consequences of the post-OPEC II policy response was also exacerbated by the uncertainty of the cumulative impact of a prolonged period of unprecedented monetary tightness. We had entered, by the end of 1980, a terra incognita as interest rates in the United States reached record levels and other countries tightened policy defensively to stave off further depreciation-induced inflation. Here, too, however, is an example of a degree of interdependence unthinkable in an earlier period. The vast expansion of international financial markets in the 1970s, itself in large degree a consequence of the inflation and the oil shocks of that decade, heightened and strengthened the transmission of financial impulses from the United States even though its relative economic size has shrunk since the early postwar years.

I shall return to the issue of interdependence later in this paper, as it has important policy implications, both domestic and international. For now, let me turn from the recession to the recovery that, as I have already mentioned, began at the beginning of 1983.

The major forces that led to the recovery were: the disinflationary process itself, which stimulated consumer spending and a turnaround in inventories; the easing of monetary policy initiated in the United States suddenly in the late summer of 1982 and then matched by most other OECD countries; and the expansionary thrust of US fiscal policy with its present and prospective budget deficits. The pace and nature of the upturn, however, differed markedly among the major "blocks" of the OECD – North America, Europe, and Japan – and were also affected by development in the non-OECD world and by "systemic" factors such as the global debt problem and creeping protectionism.

Thus, for the area as a whole, growth in 1983 was just over 2 per cent. For the US and Canada, however, the rate was between 3 and 3.1 per cent, in contrast to an average for Europe of 1 per cent. Japan, the only major OECD economy where activity has been maintained since the second oil shock, continued grow-ing at over 3 per cent, above the OECD average but well below Japan's own historical standards. While some modest convergence of growth rates is forecast for this year, the US economy is still likely to far outstrip the rest of the OECD economies in the vigour of its growth.

This divergence was amplified when one considered the unemployment pic-ture. In North America the growth pick-up has led to some diminution of the jobless rate – more dramatically in the US (from an end-of-1982 peak of nearly 11 per cent to under 8 per cent at present) than in Canada. In sharp contrast, European unemployment rates have continued their steady rise and by the end of 1983 had climbed another full point (two million persons) above their 1982 level, reaching approximately 18 million, a rate more than triple that in 1973. A further rise is projected for the current year, 1984, when the rate is expected to reach nearly 12 per cent. Of this total, in many European countries, between one-third and one-half are long-term, hardcore unemployed who have been without work for a year or longer (the comparable figures for Canada and the United States are under 10 per cent). Finally, while Japanese unemployment edged upward (from 2.5 to 2.75 per cent between 1982 and 1983), it is strikingly low by international standards and forecast to decline.

The pattern of divergence did not apply on the inflation front. The rapid decel-eration is now over although wide differences in rates among member countries remain. Moderate wages and productivity gains are now the essential sources of further disinflationary momentum and, indeed, of successful consolidation of the progress already made. This reasonably optimistic outlook on inflation rests, however, on the assumption of no change in exchange rates. A marked fall in the US dollar would not only increase US inflation, but also, if American interest rates rose, threaten the sustainability of recovery for the OECD countries as a whole. Finally, there remains in all countries of the OECD a fundamental but unanswered question: Are inflationary expectations simply quiescent or finally quelled?

To summarize, it seems that the elusive recovery is on its way, reasonably so in North America and Japan, barely so in Europe. The big bang in disinflation is over, but – for the present – the gains appear, by and large, successfully consolidated. There are major risks and uncertainty in this outlook, which over the near term centre on the likely course of US interest rates and the dollar. And there persists, in the longer term, the question about inflationary expectations.

But, returning to the recovery, why the pattern of divergence? In point of fact, the differentiated pace and nature of growth among the major industrialized countries of the OECD reflects differences both in the dynamic forces initiating the recovery and in the underlying "construct" or "configuration" of the economy. Let me illustrate what I mean.

In the US the proximate force propelling the recovery was the easing of monetary policy in the late summer of 1982, when, faced by the de facto default of Mexico, the chairman of the Federal Reserve Board of the US, Mr Paul Volcker, moved to prevent a world financial crisis. The subsequent steep decline in nominal interest rates and the dazzling stock-market rally fuelled a consumer boom that marked the end of the recession. Another very important force was the highly stimulative fiscal policy of the Reagan administration, especially the tax cuts of 1981, which both increased consumer demand and greatly enhanced company profit flows.

So one could say that the US recovery was a classic, old-fashioned, policy-led turnaround. But, in truth, it was more complex than that. Although nominal interest rates had fallen, real interest rates (that is, corrected for inflation) remained, as they do today, at record high levels. An important causal factor for these rates is the alarming prospective fiscal deficit in the US. These interest rates, in turn, were an important factor in attracting massive flows of capital from around the world, thus pushing up the American dollar. The overvalued American dollar, as well as the quickening of the American recovery, sucked in imports and depressed exports, producing an unprecedented deficit in trade, fanning protectionist pressures, and acting as a strong negative factor on growth. Despite this, the vigorous growth of the US economy has exceeded expectations and continues to bedevil forecasters. One is forced to conclude that other influences are at play: Prominent among these is what I have termed (for want of a better word) the "configuration" of the economy – an underlying bullishness, confidence, flexibility, and dynamism.

It's not unlike what Keynes called "animal spirits," the vital ingredient of growth. He went on to observe: "It is the return of confidence ... which is so insusceptible to control in an economy of individualistic capitalism."[1] The difference in the pace of the Canadian and the American growth rate that may now be emerging could give us reason to ponder Keynes's words.

Turning from the US to Europe, one faces almost a mirror image. While the situation varies somewhat from country to country, the dominant factor initiating the recovery has been a decline in household savings as a result of the fall in inflation, not a strong or, on its own, a sustainable dynamic force. The US trade deficit and overvalued dollar – a negative for the Americans – is a plus for Europe (as it is for us). The easing of US monetary policy allowed European governments to follow suit. But in marked contrast to the US, European fiscal policy is tight and tightening as governments strive to reduce their deficits, and this acts, at least in the short term, as a strong negative factor. Finally, and perhaps most important, there is an equally marked contrast with the US in the underlying configuration of the economy. This latter difference may perhaps best be described by the term "Eurosclerosis," with its symptoms of hardening of the economic arteries in product and labour markets, a disease stemming largely from government action and inaction over a period of many years that impairs the essential flexibility and adaptability of the economy. European governments are well aware of their problems and are now visibly beginning to tackle them.

But Eurosclerosis developed over a long time, and there is no miracle, overnight cure.[2] Unfortunately, slow growth may well cause further hardening of the economic arteries, so what is seen as a vital element in the cure – cutting fiscal deficits – may, for a time, worsen the disease. Nor is the patient improved by the cold winds of uncertainty blowing across the Atlantic – uncertainty about interest rates, the value of the dollar, the threat of increased protectionism in the US in an election year. If the European disease is Eurosclerosis, the American disease might be called "fiscal catatonia." They don't go well together. Nor is

---

1 John Maynard Keynes, *The General Theory of Employment Interest and Money* (London: 1936), 317.
2 Parenthetically, it may be noted that in seeking to reduce the role of government in their economies and encouraging more active markets, the Europeans are beginning to transform what I have termed their "social market economies" that so differentiated them from the more individualistic and pluralist American market economy. Does economic interdependence create a strong pull to matching basic configurations of economies? For a fuller description of the social market economy, see Sylvia Ostry and Val Koromzay, "The United States and Europe: Coping with Change," *OECD Observer*, May 1982.

there any assurance that, over the longer run, the American disease will not inflict serious damage on the American body economic.

Finally, to complete the profile of the recovery, a look at Japan. Japan, as I have said, maintained positive growth throughout the world recession although at a rate far below her historical experience. It did so, indeed, largely by strong exports in 1980 and 1981, meanwhile exhibiting an astonishing capacity to adapt to the oil-price rise and to structural changes in production and demand. With inflation now below the rate of the 1960s – about 11 per cent – and very low unemployment, the main problem for the Japanese is growing protectionism. From the end of 1981, export volumes began to taper off. How much of this was due to the general weakening of world trade and how much to the voluntary export restraints negotiated with the US, Canada, and Europe for cars and a wide range of other products is hard to gauge. But given the greatly enhanced competitiveness of Japanese exports due to the rapid development of new products, the substantial depreciation of the yen during 1982 (and again in 1983 vis-à-vis the dollar), and the extreme modesty of wage developments, it seems likely that protectionism of one kind or another has played a role.

If export restraint continues, Japan will have to shift increasingly to domestic growth. As the yen strengthens, there will be more room to manœuvre in easing monetary policy, and insistent US pressure on Japan to open up her financial markets is intended to hasten the internationalization of the yen (another example, by the way, of how interdependence feeds on itself, creating the demand for more linkage). On the other hand, there is limited room on the fiscal side. The Japanese deficit is large and threatens to grow in coming years as expenditure on social security, especially pensions for an aging population, mounts. While the fiscal situation is not nearly so immediately threatening as in the US, partly because of the very high household savings rate in Japan, the Japanese economic predicament is real and promises to increase over time.

But there is a deeper dilemma inherent in the present situation, a dilemma that seriously adds to strains within the OECD countries as a whole. The prolif-eration of so-called neoprotectionist measures against Japan over the past few years will have a pernicious effect on the structural adaptability of the importing countries. Mounting protectionism has, moreover, led to higher export prices for Japanese products, as Japanese producers have responded to these restraints both by moving upstream in products and, because of floor-price mechanisms, by increasing profit margins – thus possibly accelerating technological change (through increased research and development) and stimulating further "target-ing." Thus the vicious circle widens. Because the Japanese have adapted so quickly to the voluntary restrictions, the value of Japanese exports in these sectors has been affected far less than the volume. Yet some of the present weakness in domestic investment is no doubt related to the present trading environment and to fears of further protectionism, which are impeding the desired shift in growth from external to domestic demand. Moreover, it is partly fear of protectionism that has stimulated the marked increase in Japanese direct investment abroad (another step, by the way, in the inexorable growth of inter-dependence of the world economy). While this is a welcome development, there is growing concern about a competitive scramble for such investment, which could induce further distortions in the multilateral trading system.

In the account thus far of the nature and pace of the present recovery of the OECD economies, I have stressed factors largely internal to the industrialized world. In quantitative terms these intra-OECD forces are of overwhelmingly greater significance than any plausible range of developments in economies outside the OECD. Yet interdependence, while stronger among the advanced industrial nations, does now, and will increasingly, embrace other parts of the world economy. This is most vividly illustrated, at the present time, by the debt problems of the Third World.

Although there was some highly imprudent lending and borrowing, especially toward the end of the 1970s – and certainly domestic policies in some of the developing countries left much to be desired – as I have already suggested the origins of the debt problem must be traced to the dramatically changed environment after the second oil crisis. What this means is that the impact of OECD policy and performance on the world is extremely powerful. Nonetheless, the linkages do operate in both directions. The impact of the developing countries now and for the foreseeable future will be a brake on the growth of OECD countries as their capacity to import from us is reduced by the need to use a good portion of their export receipts to service their immense debt, now esti-mated at over $800 billion, of which over half is Latin American. It almost goes without saying that servicing this debt cannot proceed unless our markets remain open to their exports.

Of equal or greater importance than the trade linkage is the financial linkage since it is the banks of the industrialized countries that are heavily exposed to the debt of less developed countries and since it is this exposure that represents the threat to the stability of the international financial system.

The response to this threat has been a case-by-case rescheduling (and provi-sion of new funds) managed by the International Monetary Fund and involving the debtor countries, the central banks of the industrialized countries, and the commercial bank creditors. In 1983 there were thirty-three such reschedulings. To qualify, countries are required to undertake a number of policy changes, in effect a difficult retrenchment process – the so-called conditionality required by the fund. So far this approach has worked well, and a major financial crisis has been averted. But there is growing realization that the process of reaching a sustainable situation will be very lengthy, and there are signs of serious political and social strain in several of the debtor countries, especially as they come to understand that they are paying more in interest than they are receiving in net new financing. Some evolution of the case-by-case approach may be required – likely a lowering of interest rates and a stretching-out of repayment periods – but no such program has yet been enunciated. (It's worth noting that the highly complex eleventh-hour deal over Argentina's debt involved lower interest rates than 1983's reschedulings.) But it seems fair to say that the potential for a shock to financial-market confidence remains (especially if US interest rates rise), and this adds yet another major element of uncertainty in the present economic outlook. The characterization of *attentisme,* or marking time, is especially appropriate to the international debt situations.

Finally – and this brings me full circle – there can be no question of a longer-term solution to the global debt problem or to the more pervasive systemic strains in the absence of durable, more balanced growth in the OECD countries.

Let me then confront that problem – how to achieve sustained and balanced growth – in more specific policy terms. I have argued that one reason for the divergence within the OECD countries lies in the deep-seated structural dimensions of the different economies – their basic "configuration." By definition, what I have termed the "configuration" of the economies will be difficult to change and can be changed only slowly. (Again, the thrust of change will, I suggest, be in the direction of further linkage and thus stronger interdependence most likely involving a greater reliance on market mechanisms.) But I have also argued that the present set of policies, or policy mix, at the macro level (monetary and fiscal policy) is exacerbating the divergence. There is a story current in Europe that is apt here. A man was driving down a highway at top speed, weaving from side to side, narrowly missing lorries in both directions. Finally, the police caught up with him, forced him to stop, and ordered him out of the car. The officer said, "I don't need to administer a Breathalyzer test, you're obviously disgustingly drunk." "Thank heaven," said the man, "I thought the steering mechanism had gone!" Macro policy is the steering mechanism.

But better macro policy in each country may not be sufficient. The fallout from the current mix of US policy (the overvalued dollar and the high real interest rates), which may or may not wreak permanent damage on the American economy, has a major impact, for both good and ill, on the rest of the world. The slower growth of Europe, by creating strains both within the community and between Europe and the rest of the OECD countries, will ultimately affect the performance of both the US and Japan. What is needed, then, to ensure balanced and sustainable growth in an interdependent world is policy coordination among the major economies. Such coordination would require a much more explicit acknowledgement of the extent and nature of economic and financial linkage within the OECD area. It would, moreover, effectively limit the scope for independent domestic economic management. And there's the rub. In practice, of course, the process of domestic policy making reflects domestic preoccupations, and what is regarded as an erosion of domestic sovereignty is deeply resented or, where a country is powerful enough, simply ignored. Yet we will, I suspect, be forced to recognize that the "loss of sovereignty" involved in coordinating macro-economic policies is largely illusory.

We are trapped in a time warp between the policy orbit of the nation-state appropriate to the postwar past of American hegemony and more limited international linkage and the more cooperative forms of leadership and responsibility required for the interdependent world economy of today and the global economy of tomorrow. These issues are being widely discussed, and there is growing understanding of the dilemma of interdependence. But, thus far, there has been little action. We're still marking time.

SYLVIA OSTRY is Distinguished Research Fellow at the Centre for International Studies at the University of Toronto. Her numerous posts in the public and private sectors include being a director of Power Corporation, an expert advisor to the Commission on Transnational Corporations of the United Nations, and a member of the Group of Thirty in Washington. Dr Ostry's many positions in the federal government include chief statistician, chairman of the Economic Council of Canada, deputy minister of International Trade and of Consumer and Corporate Affairs, ambassador for multilateral trade negotiations, and the prime minister's personal representative for the Economic Summit. She also served as head of the Economics and Statistics Department of the Organization for Economic Cooperation and Development in Paris. Dr Ostry was chancellor of Waterloo University and has written numerous books and articles on various aspects of the international economy.

Her work has been recognized with nineteen honorary degrees. Dr Ostry is a Companion of the Order of Canada and a Fellow of the Royal Society of Canada and has received the Outstanding Achievement Award of the Government of Canada.

19

The More Thou Searchest, the More Thou Shalt Marvel: The Role of Canadian Science

LARKIN KERWIN, 1985

When he died at the young age of thirty-seven in 1941, Alan Plaunt had already exerted a powerful influence on the national life of Canada for the rest of the twentieth century and beyond. Our very culture has flourished and expanded because of his determination and influence. He did it with science.

Mr Plaunt's background was in the lumber business, as was that of my own father. This is the sort of business that promotes a special love of Canada; Alan Plaunt recognized that the vastness from east to west that is ours needed strong ties to oppose the divisive effects of the shorter north-south attractions. He found these ties in technology and urged, insisted, and lobbied until what was to become the Canadian Broadcasting Corporation–Radio Canada was implemented by the government.

Plaunt realized that the application of scientific principles could have a tremendous impact on all other spheres of human activity. Today, his intentions are being furthered by electronics, solid-state physics, lasers, fibre optics, satellites, and computers. Modern communication has become the outstanding feature of this century and has made possible such varied activities as improved rescue at sea, improved northern medicine, and space exploration.

The means by which Alan Plaunt achieved his nationalistic goal was science and its application for good. Let me therefore consider Canadian science: its beauty and wonder, its delicacy and power, its potential for good and its potential for evil.

I will avoid the pointless debate about whether "Canadian" science exists. Certainly there are Canadian scientists whose contributions have greatly affected Canada. They have influenced the international community as well, participating in the global exchange of ideas and technologies that make up the dynamic century in which we live. Canadian scientists and their work comprise the subject of my discourse.

I will mention the following points:

- The beauty of Canadian science
- The technology that has emerged from it
- The contributions of Canadian inventors
- The current state of Canadian science and technology
- And the promise of the future

There is great beauty in science: Its practitioners find themselves caught up in spiritual and intellectual experiences that leave them in awe before the infinite and almighty. Gerhard Herzberg, our distinguished Canadian Nobel Prize scientist, is also a fine classical singer who has performed in concert. He speaks of the pleasure he experiences when performing beautiful but complex arias. He states that the experience is similar, if not as intense, to that of mathematically reconstructing a molecular band spectrum. Certainly an atomic scientist, contemplating with understanding Herzberg's magnificent spectrum of atomic hydrogen, gets the same thrilling sensation as in looking at Andromeda on a clear night and realizing that one's gaze has pierced the galaxy.

Canadian scientists have contributed immensely to the beauty and marvel that are science's legacies to humanity. For the most part, these are twentieth-century contributions, but there are some heart-warming precursors of earlier decades.

One precursor was John McLennan, born in Ingersoll, Ontario, during Confederation year: 1867. He began his research at about the time of the discovery of radioactivity by Becquerel and immediately recognized its fundamental importance. Working at the University of Toronto, McLennan opened up the new field of physics to a whole generation of scientists. He was a generalist and achieved equal competence in spectroscopy and low-temperature research.

An almost precise contemporary of McLennan's was Ernest Rutherford, who worked at McGill University and also conducted research in radioactivity. Rutherford was able to explain the many sequences that cause the radioactive families of elements to cascade in leaps and bounds of alpha, beta, and gamma particles from their lofty uranic ancestors to the calm serenity and stability of the lead and thallium descendants. The modern chemistry student, who retravels this path, never fails to be stimulated by the orchestration achieved by nature in this quantum world, where energy and mass intertransform with gay abandon.

However, Rutherford is best known for his model of the atom. Before his time the atom was considered to be something like a small dense sphere containing a mixture of electricity and matter – rather dull lumps of reality. Through a series of relatively simple experiments, Rutherford gave us a radically different, wonderful picture. Each atom, of which everything in the universe, including ourselves, is composed, is a miniature of the solar system. It is made of a dominating central body containing a very dense mass and positive charge. This mass is surrounded by orbiting planets of negative charge called electrons, which circle, swoop, and emit and absorb light and other radiations. The atom is largely empty – relatively emptier than the solar system itself. This vision was later elaborated on by Bohr and the quantum mechanicists to approach the models that are preferred today. Rutherford lifted the curtain on a completely new and dramatic presentation of nature.

Wilder Penfield made a different type of contribution to Canadian science. He is remembered as a great neurosurgeon who applied his art and science to the relief of suffering. Penfield was fascinated by the workings of the human brain; he launched numerous research projects on its structure and functioning. His work on cerebral localization and dedicated functions won him international distinction. The strokes that Penfield added to the canvas of the physiological picture of the brain were master strokes, indeed.

I have often reflected on one of the beautiful thought-questions that Richard Feynman wrote of in one of his books. He considers what takes place on the seashore when he looks at waves, where molecules of water join by the untold trillions to produce the marvellous swellings and crashings that we watch with fascination. The light reflected from the drops and surfaces crosses the air into our eyes and stimulates electrical signals on the retina, which are brought by the optic nerve to the brain, where their energy rearranges some of the molecular energy levels in the cerebral network.

From the work of Penfield and others, we know a great deal now of the configuration and role of these structures. We know that phosphorous atoms are an important component in them. But we also know from studies with radioactive tracers that there is constant changing of the atoms in these structures, and on the average they remain there only a couple of weeks, to be replaced by other phosphorous atoms. And so, a few months later, we think of the seashore, and we remember the waves. The memory comes from patterns that were impressed on the brain cell molecules months before and that now return the proper signals to our consciousness. The same thing happens when we remember a face. But what is remembering? The phosphorous atoms that received the impressions are gone – new atoms that were not present at the seashore have replaced them. What is remembering? Is it the abstract geometry of the atoms' positions? This is a precious and moving thought, an example of how science rescues the spirituality of human beings from their materialistic detractors.

I mentioned Gerhard Herzberg. He is one of the main composers who fashioned the symphony of light from the model atoms proposed by Rutherford,

Bohr, and the quantum mechanicists. There is probably no variety of light, from the infra-red to the ultra-violet, that he has not examined, fitted into place, and harmonized with great theories. Herzberg's set of books on the various spectra are a superb and lasting legacy. The simplicity and lucidity of his explanations rival some of the best literary poetry. The sweep of Herzberg's discoveries ranges from the electrical servants in the silicon chips of pocket computers to newly discovered organic molecules in intergalactic space. He has added new dimensions to the wonder of the world.

A truly contemporary person is Saran Narang. This biotechnologist has addressed himself to the wonderful spiral structures that constitute basic biological elements, such as genes. Painstakingly probing their structure and arrangement, Narang has discovered much about the nature of their elements and the mechanisms of their construction. The magic helix, as some have called the biospiral, is revealed in marvellous detail by Narang's probings. He has discovered ways in which the spiral may be disassembled, with certain key elements being removed to be replaced by others, to give the spiral new, perhaps more desirable, characteristics. This leads to the purposeful alteration of gene-like structures – genetic engineering – which holds great promise in biotechnological applications. Speaking with Saran Narang, one gets caught up in the passion and adventure of a great intellectual experience.

Another contemporary shining star of Canadian science is Ursula Martius-Franklin. She works in materials research and applies many technologies to examine and characterize various materials. Dr Franklin has learned how these materials change with time in themselves and because of changes in the technological environment. This has led to the measurement of the age of materials using a variety of techniques, from work on radioactive content to the most modern of surface techniques. She has been a leading figure in the development of a new science: archaometry, the measuring of the old. This field is enriching the work of archaeologists, paleontologists, and historians, in addition to its intellectual appeal. Hearing Dr Martius-Franklin's discourse is a privilege.

There are myriad Canadian scientists whose basic work justifies the idea that discovering the intimate, detailed nature of the universe is essential to the triple *raison d'être* of humanity: theology, the fine arts, and science. Lingering on the contributions of people like Pierre Dansereau, Leo Marion, Keith Ingold, Tak Wah Mak, and so many others would be stimulating. But there are other aspects to Canadian science.

One will recognize that much of the work of Canadian scientists had practical effects: that of Rutherford led to the development of nuclear energy; Narang's work led to the synthesis of the insulin molecule; Dansereau's to the protection of the environment; Penfield's to new successes in brain surgery. The application of science by engineering and other disciplines has led to such improvements in the quality of life that many justify the promotion of science on this basis alone. This is an unbalanced view of science although it has considerable merit.

Canadian engineers and applied scientists have also produced work of intellectual brilliance. In addition, we must remember that the economic return of applied science is the basis of modern economies. Canada has made world-class contributions to this practical side of science.

One of these is air travel. Because of Canada's geography, and the sparseness of the population, it is small aircraft that have held our engineering attention. From bush-craft to those intended for short intercity flights, well-adapted aircraft have poured from the design boards of Canadian aeronautical and mechanical engineers. Their very names evoke Canada: the Beaver, the Otter, the Caribou, the Buffalo, all of which have been great international successes. The contemporary STOL Dash aircraft and the intercontinental Challenger represent adaptations to extreme and specialized requirements. Another Canadian name, the Arrow, might have changed the course of our aerospace industry and economy had it been permitted to survive.

For similar geographic and population reasons, the engineering of communication has risen to great heights in Canada. The telephone was invented in this country by Bell, as was the AM radio by Fessenden. For generations these two technologies were the backbone of the most avant-garde systems in the world. Our leading position is being maintained: Systems developed by Canadians through organizations like Bell-Northern have achieved world prominence. Canada was the first country to use space satellites for commercial communication; our space industry is sought by other countries to design and build similar systems for them. Microwave, laser, and optical fiber technologies are some of the others Canadian engineers are working on to improve our quality of life.

The mention of space satellites recalls another field in which Canadian engineering excels: the design and construction of space systems. The best known is Canadarm, the most complicated robot ever constructed, which performs flawlessly time after time in one of the most hostile environments ever chanced by human beings.

In chemical engineering, the clever application of science is illustrated by the recent development of biodegradable plastics at the University of Toronto. These may soon be added to mulch for agricultural purposes and could solve one of the most ominous urban problems: the multiplying use of cheap, convenient plastics, which threatens to become an ecological disaster. Industrial development of this biodegradable material is promising.

Canadian engineers must be recognized for their great civil works as well, performed under harsh, challenging conditions. The Rideau Canal in the Ottawa region is one example; the great railways built across the Prairies and over the

Rocky Mountains and the St Lawrence Seaway are others. Canadian engineers have dug coal four miles out under the Atlantic Ocean; they have constructed the mightiest dams in the world in northern Quebec to harness the hydro energy of river systems larger than most European countries; they have transported electrical energy across thousands of kilometres at voltages unsurpassed anywhere in the world on this scale. Canadians built the world's largest free-standing structure and the world's most efficient and safest nuclear reactors. Of the world's nuclear electricity generating plants, six of the ten most dependable are Canadian Candus, including the top four.

One of our least appreciated success stories, but certainly not the least important, is that of Canada's consulting/engineering firms. These are among the largest and most successful in the world. Some of them employ thousands of engineers. They have contracts in the Middle East, South America, South-East Asia, and Africa. They carry out major projects like the development of whole cities, highway networks, hospitals, and school systems, as well as bridges, dams, dikes, and airfields. Some of Canada's most impressive technological monuments are in far-away developing countries.

A particular class of applied science contributions is provided by inventors. Some inventors base their work on basic science considerations; others are inspired by an unfulfilled need or a happy flash of insight. Canadian inventions include CAD/CAM systems, the roller painter, the snowmobile, Pablum, standard time, pantyhose, kerosene, the Laser sailboat, and the marvellous cobalt radiation therapy unit. There are thousands more; the story of Canadian inventiveness is a topic that deserves its own dissertation.

As I discuss the merits of Canadian science and technology, I imagine that some might wonder, "What about Hiroshima? Napalm? The neutron bomb? Chemical pollution, acid rain, and radiation risks? Are they not part of science and technology?" The answer is, "No, they are part of human nature." This is a point worth considering because it causes well-meaning people to suggest research and development should be curtailed or even, in some cases, forbidden.

The question of ethics in scientific research has been a prominent subject of news coverage over the past few years. The fact is that the ethical responsibilities of scientists are no different from those of other citizens.

The pursuit of fundamental knowledge, which is basic to science, is a good, moral act in itself. There are no areas in which basic research should be avoided on ethical grounds. However, scientists have an obligation to carry out their research in an ethical way: they may not rob grocery stores to finance their work; they may not interfere with other people's rights in carrying out investigations; they must report their work objectively and honestly; they may not cheat, waste resources, or plagiarize.

A scientist is subjected to the same constraints in applying science to practical ends as is any citizen. Research must be applied to good, moral purposes; it must not be applied to evil. This is the general ethical choice that confronts all human activity.

However, a scientist has the additional responsibility that comes with being a specialist: explaining science to the public, advising of its usefulness and benefits, and warning of its dangers and disadvantages. This is the responsibility of any specialist.

Canadian scientists are highly regarded throughout the world for their ethical standards and are recognized for their defense of free investigation and the free circulation of scientists. Canada's use of science, as in the case of nuclear energy, has been for peaceful, humanitarian purposes, such as the generation of electricity and cancer treatment.

Like most industrial nations, the development of science and technology has tremendous economic impact in Canada.

In 1881, when McLennan and Rutherford were teenagers, Canada's population was 4.3 million, of which 44 per cent (1.37 million) were employed; 662,000 of these jobs were in agriculture.

In 1984 there were only 509,000 jobs in Canada's agricultural sector. During the last century, then, over 150,000 agricultural jobs have been lost, mostly because of advances in technology put in motion by people like McLennan and Rutherford.

Canada's population in 1984 was 25 million. Of these, not 44 per cent but about 60 per cent of the working population was employed: 11.36 million. Therefore, in spite of the threat to employment in agriculture that technology was thought to pose at the turn of the century, over 10 million jobs have been created, mainly because of technological growth. These jobs are highly productive; hence the gross national product and standard of living are relatively higher in 1985 than a century ago. Science has been put to good use in Canada: We have a healthier, better educated, more productive people because it has been applied wisely.

However, this isn't cause for complacency. Canada's place among the twenty-five or thirty advanced industrial nations with high standards of living has been eroding during the last generation. Most of these countries, making greater use of scientific research and development than we, have outstripped our productivity. Canada's economy is faltering; our standard of living is slipping.

Let's consider for a moment why we're in such bad shape. The reasons aren't as mysterious as they might seem. They may be summed up in the following way: We consume more than we produce; we import more than we export of value-added commodities. We are in debt. We have become poor.

We massively export agricultural and forestry products, as well as natural gas and some oil. At the same time, we voraciously import manufactured products, and our adverse balance of trade in technology products from 1978 to 1982 was about $8 billion. In 1980 we imported 75 per cent of the transportation equipment we use, 75 per cent of the machinery we use, 75 per cent of the scientific and professional equipment we use. Our manufacturing industry cannot fulfil the country's needs. The newer the technology, the more we need to import to maintain our quality of life. In 1984 we imported over $4 billion in computers, despite the fact that our high-technology companies produce state-of-the-art equipment. We exported only $1 billion in office machines and equipment, including computers, in 1984.

Canadian science is qualitatively excellent; we simply don't do enough. Canada spends only half as much per capita as her industrial competitors on research and development, 1.2 per cent of her GNP compared with about 2.5 per cent for other advanced countries. This factor of two is felt everywhere. There is only half as much equipment in Canadian universities as in other countries; there is half as much in the National Research Council and other national laboratories; there is half as much money going to industrial research, half as much to standards, half as much to medical research. Our GNP is relatively high, but our priorities differ from other countries on how to spend it. This has contributed to our present deficit and other economic difficulties.

The problem is deeply rooted in Canada's history and geography. In colonial times the economy was based on the export of raw materials, once thought to be inexhaustible. Much of our export profile reflects this philosophy. Later, when manufacturing became an important part of the economy, it was initiated in many cases by foreign companies, which are now multinationals. Canadian production has followed established patterns, rather than daring to innovate. In the age of technology, this characteristic serves us ill. Innovation requires many components: scientific research and development, market surveys, brilliant design capability, venture capital, patent and licensing protection, marketing skills, and an incentive-oriented income tax system. Each and every one of these areas leaves much room for improvement in Canada.

These questions have been analyzed and discussed at length over the past decade. Efforts are being made to correct the errors, from the revising of patent laws to awarding prizes for brilliant design. The past six federal ministers of state for science and technology have advanced as policy the increase in the percentage of the GNP spent on research and development. The target is presently set at 2.5 per cent to correct the factor that I mentioned.

I believe Canada can achieve this important goal if political will can bring itself to modify traditional priorities. In doing so, we shall achieve a healthy economy to which strong scientific and technological activity will contribute. The quantity of Canadian science will then be commensurate with its quality.

What will characterize Canada's future science picture? The film is developing rapidly; the emerging photograph is fascinating. We need only look to the sky for our first clue: the future promise of space technology. In 1984 export sales from Canada's space-related products and services exceeded $200 million. Our commitment to the American space station will allow us to continue to excel in the production of space technology products.

The space station, planned for launch in the early 1990s, will be a self-contained world. It will have space laboratories, observatories, and manufacturing facilities. There will be a maintenance and storage depot, a servicing station for orbital platforms and satellites, and living quarters for astronauts. It will serve as an evolutionary research facility. In the zero gravity of space, scientists will be able to produce new and rare drugs, grow living cells, and create new materials we cannot create on Earth.

The space station is a cooperative effort involving many countries of the free world. Canada is developing several options for participation: first, a robotic servicer and an integrated servicing and test facility for satellite repair, a key function in outer space; second, providing solar arrays that would be the primary source of power to the astronaut-tended platforms or auxiliary power for the station; third, implementing a remote-sensing facility based on RADARSAT.

Canada would supply specialized equipment and would be a part-time user of the space station for scientific research, remote sensing, and industrial testing.

Over 3,000 Canadians now earn their living in space work; over 200 Canadian space scientists study the earth, its atmosphere, outer space, and astronomy. The space station will open our window to the universe in ways human beings never dreamed possible until now.

Canada is also taking part in the future dream of biotechnology, an exciting field that promises substantial rewards in fundamental knowledge, as well as commercial success. Biotechnology gives us a greater understanding of biological systems and has broad-based applications to industrial, agricultural, and health-care-related problems.

Canada's computer expertise is used by our country's biotechnologists in such esoteric fields as protein engineering. Dr Michael Smith of the University of British Columbia and Dr Michael James of the University of Alberta are working with computers to design proteins. Their work could lead to the synthesis of hormones, anti-inflammatory and anti-rejection drugs, and many other products.

Canadian biotechnologists are also working on plant-strain development, pulp and paper applications, mineral leaching, and metal recovery, to mention just a few of the fascinating areas.

The National Research Council (NRC), for its part, will open a research laboratory of the future in March 1986: the Biotechnology Institute. Working together with industry, scientists at the institute will explore such vital problems as pharmaceuticals to develop new ways of synthesizing costly drugs and vaccines.

Moreover, scientists throughout the world have begun researching the next generation of computers – artificial intelligence – which will allow computers to "think." Dr Alex Szabo, an NRC physicist, has developed and patented techniques relating to artificial intelligence that could revolutionize the computer industry. Dr Szabo has designed an optical memory, by which tiny holes are burned in crystal, to greatly increase computer memory capacity. His process relies on the basic physical principles of the electromagnetic spectrum and atomic absorption and emission. For the first time, we can envisage a density of computer memory equal to that of the human brain. This optical memory will provide the storage capacity needed for the complex process of reasoning; computers of the future will have the ability to learn from experience as humans do. Crystal memory may be Canada's answer to achieving this end.

Now, if we look at the other side of the coin, we see that Canada is making progress not only in teaching computers to learn, but also in using computers to help humans learn. What I'm referring to is known as CAL: Computer-Assisted Learning. Canada is a world leader in the development of CAL programs, called Coursewear. These allow computers to teach humans many tasks in a variety of ways, such as by simulating real-life situations or by simplifying them to make difficult concepts understandable. The key aspect is the computer's programmed ability to respond to and interact with the user.

CAL is a new industry with a significant employment generation potential; it has a major role to play in enabling the fuller participation of the individual in a society of an increasingly technical nature. Computer-assisted learning might well represent Canada's best high-technology growth opportunity, creating jobs and providing a flexible training and retraining capability.

Jack Brahan, a research engineer at the NRC, heads a team of scientists who work in cooperation with industry to design tailor-made programs suited for a variety of tasks. For instance, Hydro-Quebec, the Canadian Forces, and the Public Service Commission are among the groups already applying Coursewear to staff training. Seven Ontario community colleges have also recently begun to install Coursewear learning stations to assist instructional design students in video-disc production techniques. The Coursewear stations include microcomputers that run the computer language, called NATAL, and a graphics display terminal that allows human-computer interaction. Canadian research teams develop the program material, which is provided to the students on discs.

The appearance of the microcomputers was advantageous to CAL; it significantly reduced the cost of hardware needed to support it. CAL technology continues to evolve, and other technologies such as video-discs and voice synthesis are opening up even greater avenues for the usefulness of CAL, allowing the long-dreamed of possibility of humans speaking with computers to be realized.

I have thus mentioned three fields where Canadian science may expect to flourish during the decades ahead. First, space: A few intelligent creatures, evolving for millions of years on a small planet of an ordinary star, are now daring to step away from home, to explore their planet's neighbourhood. Gazing further out, beyond the solar system, beyond the galaxy, to the farthest reaches of space and time, human beings are enriching their knowledge of our ultimate beginnings, purposes, and destinies.

Second, biotechnology, which will lead us inward to the smallest elements of human consistence: the structures and processes deep within our physiology that have enabled us to survive millions of years of evolution and to understand its nature. To the best of our knowledge, we are the only creatures of the universe that consider and question the cosmos, that encompass detailed ideas of a galaxy in elemental brain structures that are 10^{30} times smaller.

Third, computers, which will aid us in much of this work. During the greater part of the nineteenth and twentieth centuries, the human race applied science to multiply its muscle. Now, science is multiplying its brain.

There are numerous other examples I could mention, including those involving quantum optics, materials science, off-shore engineering, bioagriculture, or Arctic engineering. All of these provide difficult but fascinating work. And they hold great promise: in jobs, a higher quality of living, and the important role of achieving world peace. We have made tremendous progress since the time that McLennan and Rutherford toiled, and we can do it again.

For many people the National Research Council's building at 100 Sussex Drive represents the focal point of Canadian scientific excellence. There, high above the portal, one finds engraved these wonderful words:

Great is Truth, and Mighty Above all Things,
It Endureth and is Always Strong;
It Liveth and Conquereth for Evermore.
The More Thou Searchest, the More Thou Shalt Marvel.

(Esdras, I, II)

To understand is to marvel. To marvel with understanding is to achieve the highest of intellectual states, to justify the triple *raison d'être* mentioned above: to be sensitive to theology, to aesthetics, and to science.

It is true that our concern with these truly human matters is distracted and diverted by the material and socioeconomic problems that are our lot. However, our society's efforts are directed to solving these problems, and unless we are adamant pessimists we must believe that these efforts will succeed. In our planning and programs, then, we may envisage, at least as ideal objectives, a world in which there will be no wars, no poverty, no exploitation, no crime, no illness, no frustrations.

And if we do so succeed – what then? Is that the end of it?

No. There will still be theology, aesthetics, and science. There will still be sculpture and geology, poetry and mathematics, music and physics, painting and chemistry, archangels and astronomy. That is really what Canadian science is all about, and I sense that it is also what Alan B. Plaunt was all about.

LARKIN KERWIN was the first president of the Canadian Space Agency. A distinguished physicist and educator, he enjoyed a successful teaching career at the University of Laval before becoming the school's first lay rector. Following his term, he was appointed president of the National Research Council of Canada. He completed two terms at the council and then took up his new post at the Canadian Space Agency, where he remained until his retirement.

Dr Kerwin has received many prestigious awards in recognition of his contribution to the advancement of science in Canada. He is past president of the Royal Society of Canada and the Canadian Academy of Engineering Canada, as well as having been active throughout his career in numerous scientific organizations. He is a Companion of the Order of Canada, an Officer of l'Ordre national du Québec, an Officer of the Légion d'honneur de France, and a member of the Académie des Grands Quebécois. Dr Kerwin has also been awarded fifteen honorary degrees from Canadian universities.

20

Opportunities for Canadian Growth: Canada-United States Trade

PETER LOUGHEED, 1986

Perhaps once in each decade in Canada we face a major policy decision – a crossroads if you like. Without question one could rate equally the issue of Canada-United States trade with the last major one in our country, which was the issue of the federal system of Canada, the nature of federalism as reflected in our constitution, and how it had evolved. That was not just a constitutional debate; it was much more – a debate about Canada and how we were going to develop as a nation. And the conclusion, as we recall without going into the matter too extensively, was a reaffirmation by Canadians that they wanted a federal system, that they wanted strong provinces, and that they wanted a system not directed from the centre but with an appropriate balance between the federal government and the provinces. And our "made-in-Canada" constitution was a reaffirmation, therefore, of our federal system. I was privileged and honoured to play a part in it.

We face a new issue today in terms of a current major policy decision: how best to preserve and perhaps improve the standard of living and the job prospects for young Canadians in every part of the country. In the fall of 1982 the former Liberal federal government set up a very important Royal Commission on Economic Union and Development Prospects for Canada, known as the Macdonald Royal Commission. That royal commission concluded its report in the summer of 1985 by stating: "We must venture into untried ways that will demand open-mindedness, courage, innovation, and determination." And further, the commission report concluded, "We must concentrate our efforts on obtaining secure access to the American market on which continental economic forces have made us increasingly dependent."

So I chose this key issue, the most important economic policy decision, perhaps, of this generation, as the subject of this paper. Not just because it is so important, but also because I believe that there is a window of opportunity and that it will not remain open long. Time is not on Canada's side. And also because I had a small personal part in initiating the Canadian debate at the First Ministers' Conference in Regina in February of 1985. But also because, as a private citizen, it would not seem inappropriate for me to become involved again in the public arena on certain issues of the day without in any way being in conflict with the government of the province of Alberta that I have served these past fourteen years. I also believe, as a matter of debate, that the naysayers, or the other point of view, have had centre stage in this debate now for many weeks and that perhaps it is time for a strong proponent to have an opportunity to present some different views.

First of all, what is being proposed exactly? It is not, as Prime Minister Mulroney said on 26 September 1985, a negotiation of a custom union or of a common market or of any other economic arrangement that would affect our own Canadian independence or our relations with the rest of the world outside of the United States. As the prime minister stated in his statement of 26 September 1985, "We seek to negotiate with the United States the broadest possible package of mutually beneficial reductions in tariff and non-tariff barriers." However, there is a fair amount of confusion about what is really being proposed. I found the proposal best expressed in the Macdonald Royal Commission report itself on pages 374 and 375:

Commissioners review of the various elements of what would be involved in developing an effective new framework for Canada-US free trade leads us to conclude that a successful agreement would include the following arrangements:
- It would establish a free-trade area rather than a customs union or common market.
- It should be a broad agreement, covering substantially all trade between the two countries, rather than a collection of sectoral agreements.
- Some sectors could be excluded from the agreement's coverage.
- It should be consistent with Canada's continued participation in GATT.
- It should apply to tariffs, contingency protection, and other forms of non-tariff barriers.
- The elimination of tariffs should be phased in over a period of several years. In recognition of the relatively greater affect on the Canadian economy, the phase-in period of the elimination of the Canadian tariff should be longer than that for the United States.
- Non-tariff barriers should be neutralized or reduced by means of common procedures and controlled by codes of conduct; these codes should provide for decision-making and implementation by a joint tribunal.

- It should provide for agreed measures of transitional adjustment assistance and safeguard.
- It should include effective dispute-settlement procedures whereby national politicians jointly arrive at final decisions; compulsory arbitration by a neutral panel should be stipulated as a procedure of last resort.
- It needs to be guaranteed by national laws, and it should provide adequate room to involve provincial and state interests.

It is important to understand the nature of the proposal to determine whether it is beneficial or not for Canada today. My term is a *comprehensive trade agreement* with the United States that provides Canada with assured market access for our products and services to the United States.

I believe it would be useful to sketch the key events leading up to this current major decision for the Canadian people.

During 1977–79 this country was part of, and in the midst of, the process of the last round of General Agreement on Tariffs and Trade (GATT) negotiations in Geneva, Switzerland, called the Tokyo Round. In 1977–79 the provinces were seeking consultation and involvement in that last round. During that period as well, the premiers in their 1977 conference noted that, contrary to what appeared to be the then-prevailing view of the federal government, there should be a two-pronged effort in Canadian trade initiatives both with a multilateral approach through GATT as well as on a bilateral basis with the United States.

In April 1979 the Tokyo Round concluded. I believe strongly, and I know there are those who disagree, that Canada did not do very well in the end result. We did not do very well because we are not part of a trading block like the European Economic Community, nor did we have the leverage of countries like the United States and Japan. Nor did we have the empathy of lesser-developed countries and various other groups throughout the world. We were on the outside of the key discussions when the final deal was concluded. There were some benefits for Canada in the Tokyo Round but not nearly enough, particularly in some sectors.

In 1980 Ronald Reagan sought election as president in the United States, and one of his early commitments was to improving relations with their continental neighbours of Mexico and Canada.

In 1983 the Macdonald Royal Commission held public hearings and discussed, in endless meetings throughout this country, the future of the Canadian economy – where the opportunities might be, where the job prospects might be. At the same time, the Ontario Economic Council produced the report by Messrs Harris and Cox, to the effect that within Ontario there would be higher real incomes for Canadian labour and lower prices for many imported and domestically produced goods in the event that we had a comprehensive trade arrangement with the United States.

In 1984 the United States, for a multitude of reasons, including, perhaps, an overvalued United States dollar, began to develop a deficit position on merchandise trade of a substantial nature. This large increase in imports together with a reduction in exports caused protectionist bills to spring up in all corners of the United States House of Representatives and Senate. I visited the United States during this time and observed this mood of growing protectionism in their Congress.

During 1984 we had an election of a new federal government in Canada with a large majority committed to new trading relationships with the United States. On 29 January 1985 the federal government set forth three options for securing and enhancing Canadian access and export markets. On 15 February we held the First Ministers' Conference in Regina, Saskatchewan. I took the position, as strongly as I could, that there was not such an option as a status quo and that a window of opportunity existed. On March 17 Prime Minister Mulroney and President Reagan met and started the ball rolling from the Quebec City Summit. In the spring of 1985 a very highly reputable organization in this country, the C.D. Howe Institute, led by Professor Lipsey, produced an excellent document delving extensively into the benefits and the costs of a comprehensive trade arrangement with the United States.

Then in July 1985 the Macdonald Royal Commission reported. Perhaps I can offer (now that I'm not in public life) a few insights that I could not properly express when I was an elected public person. I had a lead in the spring of 1985 as to what they might propose. I am not going to divulge the precise source, but I was most surprised. When the Macdonald Royal Commission was set up, I was critical of both the nature of its mandate and the people chosen. I did not believe it had a broad enough spectrum of interest and philosophy. Oh was I wrong! I was wrong, and I can say that now because I was so pleased with the end result. I did not expect at all that the Macdonald Royal Commission report would have as its number one recommendation for major economic policy a comprehensive trade arrangement with the United States. The report has had an important impact upon the country because, in political terms, it emanated from a group that most observers would not have expected its majority would have so recommended.

In August of 1985 I attended my last conference, as a provincial premier, in Newfoundland. A very spirited debate ensued between David Peterson, who had become the new premier of Ontario, and myself, which is part of the Canadian process. Yet what was interesting was that although we did not mince words and were most candid with each other, when it was over, we could both sit down together and have dinner as friends.

On 26 September 1985 came Prime Minister Mulroney's statement that committed the federal government to proceeding with these crucial negotiations. That fall the federal government appointed a chief negotiator. In Halifax in late November the premiers met with the prime minister to discuss the process of provincial involvement. During the following winter we heard the counterarguments by the various groups who oppose this initiative. In March 1986, we had the start of the sixty-day approval process in the US Senate. We believe the response there will be affirmative and a reaffirmation of the recent summit discussion in Washington between President Reagan and Prime Minister Mulroney. So, ahead of us, we have the final response of the United States Congress and the need to resolve the process of provincial involvement. The negotiating teams should get underway in the summer of 1986.

Let me turn next to the question of provincial participation. It is not an easy matter. The provincial interests, by the nature of the subject, are very much on the table. There are diverse interests in this country. There will be trade-offs at the conclusion of the negotiations, and they will be crucial. There has to be a process of provincial involvement in the deal making. Consultation is not enough – not just because of the lack of trust that arose out of the previous GATT negotiations, but by the very nature of the federal system. On the other hand, you can only have one negotiating team at the table speaking for Canada. So how do we involve the provinces? It seems to me that we will have to come up with a completely new and innovative process that will allow only one negotiating team at the table but, at the same time, will ensure that when the deal making occurs, and those words are very carefully chosen, the deal will have provincial involvement, not just provincial consultation.

The process of provincial involvement obviously must be resolved before serious negotiations get underway with the United States. If I were the United States negotiator, (at the outset) I would ask of the Canadian negotiators, "Do you speak for Canada and its provinces in your federal system or do you not?" That has to be resolved and soon. On the other hand, I believe it is essential that interprovincial trade barriers between the provinces must be dissolved concurrently with the negotiations with the United States. It is a good time to have this happen. I support in our Constitution the mobility provisions of the Charter, and I support the elimination of these interprovincial trade barriers. It should occur concurrently with the other process.

Our perspective for these negotiations has to keep in focus certain fundamental facts. Among the developed countries of the Organization for Economic Cooperation and Development (OECD), Canada is second after West Germany in the percentage of our gross national product dependent upon external trade. Canada is a trading nation, and approximately three-quarters of our trade is with the United States. It involves autos and trucks, forest products, oil and gas and petroleum products, and many other products. We are a trading nation; our prosperity depends upon our success in trade. The United States has a significant trade deficit. It is being ameliorated somewhat by the relative reduction in the value of the US dollar. However, with Japan, their trade deficit remains large. It is important to understand the difference between the deficit of the United States in their trade with Japan as compared to their trade with Canada. With Japan the United States exports a significant portion of raw products (coal, agriculture products, etc.), and they buy from the Japanese, to a very large degree, finished products. With Canada it is a very different trading relationship – this largest trading relationship in the world.

To illustrate the magnitude of the communication problem, the Canadian premiers were all invited to Idaho in August 1985 to meet with the US governors. The day before we arrived, the governors involved the Japanese ambassador in a trade discussion. Seven US governors referred to Japan as their biggest customer, when it is obviously Canada. That illustrates the magnitude of the communication problem even within senior government circles in the US.

With Canada the trading relationship is much different, as one would expect. Canada imports mainly machinery and finished goods from the United States. This has a very significant bearing on the surprisingly large number of American jobs that are involved with the exports of goods to Canada.

A word should be said about the next round of GATT negotiations. It will get underway probably in September 1986. There are many variables involved, including the European unemployment situation and the European Economic Community agriculture policy. Canada will be negotiating in Geneva concurrently with the separate negotiation for a comprehensive trade arrangement with the United States. Keep in mind one change that has occurred. In 1985, for the first time, aside from the United States, our largest external trade was with the Pacific Rim countries rather than with Europe.

We, as a country, have extensive natural resources. Those resources need to be upgraded by processing before shipment – such as a resource of natural gas becoming a value-added petrochemical product. Canadians must recognize how involved we are personally in commodity prices and that our resources in some important cases are depleting.

Next, I would like to turn to the benefits, as I see them, for Canada of a comprehensive bilateral trade treaty with the US. Yes, a "treaty." I am of the view that this process will only really work in the long term, if it does come to successful conclusion, provided it is reflected in an actual treaty signed between Canada and the United States. The key benefit is assured access. We need a *treaty* with the administration approved by Congress.

What are the benefits? First, the manufacturing sector centred in Ontario will become more competitive by encouraging a process of restructuring and rationalization of Canadian industry to service a total North American market and then, from that base, will be better able to penetrate overseas markets. The resulting economies of scale, product quality and specialization, and technology enhancement, within a North America market, will subsequently make us more competitive overseas.

The second significant benefit would be a substantial increase in the security of our most important external market – a condition essential for growth and for new investment given the relatively small domestic Canadian market. There are key areas, such as steel, petrochemicals, and telecommunications, that are particularly significant. There are decisions about to be made in Canada by major successful Canadian organizations interested in market expansion into the United States. The decision is a fundamental one. Where should the new plant be located? Should it be located here in Canada beside our existing plants, where we would have the benefits of working together and where we can efficiently put together many of the production elements? Or should the plant be located in the United States, where our market potential lies? In my opinion, if assured access to the United States is not established, many of these decisions will sadly be made on the basis that it is not worth the risk and that plant expansion should take place in the United States. Remember, we cannot control the flow of capital across borders.

The third benefit in improving our access to the United States market is that it would allow certain Canadian industries, which are now essentially shut out of the market, to grow and invest with renewed confidence. This includes areas such as urban transportation and processing of red meats.

Then, there is a very important benefit often overlooked: The end result for the consumer across Canada should be increased product selection at lower product prices.

Now, there obviously are offsetting costs. There will also be areas that require adjustment. The sector adjustments required are going to have to happen, in many cases, in any event. But the sector adjustments have to be cushioned by the introduction of appropriate transitional adjustment assistance.

Specific barriers could be reduced by a comprehensive trade agreement. In many ways Canadian companies' access to the United States market can now be frustrated by their use of trade remedy laws. The ease with which imports in Canada are swept away by the United States in measures not aimed at Canada but at others; the continual threat of unilateral changes in the rules of the game; the lack of access to the US procurement market due to "buy America" provisions at the federal and state levels in the United States; the large number of US tariffs that continue to limit access to that market; and the inadequacy of current mechanisms to resolve disputes: All of these should be front and centre as key parts of our objectives for an agreement.

I want to do a brief overview of the country from a regional and provincial basis as to the probable benefits arising from successfully concluding such a trade deal.

It is my view that the principal beneficiary of a comprehensive trade arrangement with the United States would be the manufacturing centre in Ontario, which involves steel, processed foods, telecommunications, urban transportation, and many other areas. The country as a whole will also be economically stronger; thus the domestic market in the other regions in Canada will grow and the demand for Canadian manufacturing products will increase.

In Quebec hydroelectric exports to the United States have to be crucial. Yes, they may occur in any event. But in terms of investment and growth potential, an assured access by way of a treaty with the US is certainly positive to Quebec. It is true that the textile industry is having difficult times, but the problems come from outside North America. I was delighted to read the comments by Mr Nigard the other day about how we simply have to compete in the clothing marketplace and how we, in fact, can compete.

In Atlantic Canada we are cut off periodically at the whim of Congress from exporting our fish, which involves the livelihood of so many people. There are also agriculture products such as potatoes involved, as well as the gas and oil potential of Nova Scotia and Newfoundland that would benefit.

In Manitoba there is hydro potential as well as gains from being the manufacturing centre of Western Canada. Of course, agriculture would benefit, as Manitoba learned in 1985 when, at the whim of four states in the US, their entire business completely dissipated within a matter of days. For Saskatchewan primarily agriculture products and potash would benefit. Obviously, for British Columbia forest products and the thousands of jobs in that province depend upon market access.

For Alberta I do not believe there is a problem for oil and gas access to the United States; they need our oil and our natural gas. But Alberta would have a beneficial return in terms of processed red meats, specialty agriculture products, and obviously petrochemicals.

There is also a benefit, in my opinion, for such a move to strengthen Canadian unity. With prosperity goes confidence. With a new trade relationship such as this should go prosperity. (The breakdown of provincial barriers that will be required is also good for Canada and reduces our regionalism.) We will become competitive in the world, not just continue to function within a shrinking, protective domestic market. However, if this effort is frustrated here in Canada, then the attitude of the outer regions of Canada toward those groups opposing a deal will seriously strain national unity.

Why would the United States be interested? Their citizens are not now even aware that the debate is underway. There is a very small group of longer-term thinkers in the United States government and in Congress who are upset with Japan and the European Economic Community. One of the reasons for them to want to move ahead with this initiative is to show, by example, that free trade can be mutually beneficial. Then there is the even longer view that a prosperous Canada is good for the United States.

My major concern is that the support must be not only significant in the United States, but quite strong. Because – and this may be the most fundamental point – for this deal to work it has to, on the face of it, be a *better deal* for Canada than for the United States. On the face of it, the adjustment period for the small country has to be longer. In the tariff reductions, the phase-out, all of the provisions that will have a time frame, Canada has to get the major break. We are the smaller country. This is not an easy political sell in the United States, but it is still possible. If it is approached in the right way, the Americans can take some pride in having that attitude toward the final negotiations. It won't be easy. They have been so imbued with their "buy America" approach that this will require a new perspective. But even so, my conclusion is that we have little to lose by trying to secure these markets even if we do not succeed and a lot to lose by procrastinating and missing this window of opportunity, by failing to seize upon the supporting attitude of the current United States president.

Let me conclude. It was put forth in the spring of 1985 that Canada had three options. I do not think options exist. The sectoral option really is not in the cards: the idea that we could chose a few areas, the United States could chose a few other areas, and this would establish some limited trade arrangement. I do not think this will fly. That is certainly what the senators told me on my last official visit to Washington. Alternatively, we can maintain the status quo. In my opinion this is the weakest point of the counterargument. There is no status quo; we are into a period of intensive volatility in world trade matters, and changes are occurring rapidly: the development of certain countries such as Brazil, India, and Korea, as well as the development within the United States itself, with their economic vitality. Trade patterns are changing dramatically. There is no such thing as the status quo.

The United States is certainly not passive in trade matters. Just ask a farmer in this country about the impact of the US Farm Security Bill. The US are fighting the European Economic Community's common agriculture policy on a dollar basis, and it is impossible for the Australians, the Argentines, and the Canadians to compete in such a league.

What happens to Canada if we drift? We will become less and less competitive in the real world. For example, the United States takes up an issue like softwood lumber. They say that our fees in British Columbia for stumpage are a subsidy and that this is unfair competition. They argue the matter, at substantial expense, through the process of the International Trade Commission. The International Trade Commission concludes that there is no such subsidy, that the case is invalid. Within eighteen months Congressman Sam Gibbons puts a bill forward and says, "I don't care what the International Trade Commission says; it is, in fact, a subsidy, and let's close off the border to Canadian softwood lumber." That is the nature of the world of trade we are living with in North America today. There is no status quo. It is now very difficult for Washington to exempt Canada from a trade bill. There is no status quo – just volatility and greater risk.

So, in my judgment, we are at a crossroads. I do not minimize the risks. I do not suggest for a moment that there will not be dislocations. If we get to the point that the deal is not going to be good enough, then the Canadian negotiators will let us know we could not get a good enough deal. But I think it is wrong not to press for it during this window of opportunity – and to try hard! Because I believe that Canada, as a nation, simply cannot look at job prospects for our young people now and in the next decade ahead without facing the reality that our prosperity comes from external trade. We have to become not just good traders, but the best traders. We have to have assured access to the biggest market in the world. We must take the view expressed by entrepreneurs – small, large, and intermediate, all across this country – who almost overwhelmingly say, "We can compete." I cast my vote with them. I do not cast it without appropriate recognition of the risks in this new and different world. But I do not believe as Canadians that we can sit still and drift. So let's get on with the negotiation; let's continue with the debate. But let's see if we can make a good deal that can mean jobs and opportunities for our country in the decades ahead.

PETER LOUGHEED is a partner in the Calgary law firm of Bennett, Jones, and Vercheres, chairman of the Quorum group of companies, and a director of numerous public, private, and not-for-profit companies. He currently serves as a member of the Trilateral Commission, as a member of the Canada-Japan Forum, and as an advisor to the government of the Northwest Territories. From 1971 to 1985 Mr Lougheed was the Premier of Alberta. Since 1985 he has served in various capacities in the public and private sectors, including as co-chair of the Canadian Alliance for Trade and Job Opportunities and as honorary chairman of the Fifteenth Olympic Winter Games Organizing Committee. He was the chancellor of Queen's University from 1996 to 2002.

Mr Lougheed is a Companion of the Order of Canada and has received honorary degrees from five Canadian universities. Among his many awards, he has received the B'nai Brith Canada Award of Merit and the Legal Humanitarian of the Year Award.

21

Abandoning the Greatest
Asset That We Have

MEL HURTIG, 1988

Many years ago, when my hair was black and I was twenty-three years of age, I made the decision to open a book store. It was a kind of existential decision. I didn't know anything at all about a book store, but I knew I didn't particularly care to work at something I didn't want to do. And I was working then at something I didn't want to do, and I decided to open a book store, and everybody said that was an insane idea.

Believe it or not, at that time Edmonton did not have a single book store. There was a store that was selling luggage and stationery and books as well. The Bay department store did not a bad job of books, but I wanted to open the first full-time book store in Edmonton.

I had just gotten married, and I had the lovely sum total of $500 saved up, and I thought, well, this will be a snap. I mean, it's such a good idea and it's such an obvious thing to do. I'll go to the bank and tell them I want $10,000. A very nice gentleman in a three-piece suit, named Mr McDermott, said to me, "Hurtig, there's no way we're going to give you $10,000. We'll give $3,500 if your father signs the note." And my father said, to the idea of a book store in Edmonton, "Are you kidding?"

Anyway, we eventually managed to open this tiny, little store that would be about the size of one's living room. And I had so few books in the store when we opened that we had to turn them face out on the shelves to make the shelves look full. The first day we were to open, we unpacked books until two o'clock in the morning. At nine o'clock we were back there with big signs in the window saying the store was going to open. And nine o'clock came, five after nine, ten after nine, quarter after nine, twenty after nine, and nothing happened; no customers came in. So I asked my wife to go and get some change even though we didn't really need any. And she went out, and about ten customers came in, and we did $435 worth of business the first day. And I was really impressed because I had $500, and $435 was a lot of money.

Now, I'm recounting this story because one of the customers we had was a lady who used to come into the store and walk very quickly in quite a brusque manner; she meant business. And she would go immediately to the art section or immediately to the gardening section or to whatever section, and then, if we didn't have the book, she'd come to the counter, and she wanted us to order it, and she wanted us to get the book very quickly.

And she was a wonderful customer. She was one of the real reasons that my store became somewhat successful and that we were able to expand. In fact, for many years, we had the largest book store in Canada. She was one of the two or three best customers we ever had. A very nice lady. No monkey business. Very straight and to the point.

One day she phoned me, and she said, "Mel, how would you like to serve on the board of the Edmonton Art Gallery?" And I said, "I don't know anything about art," and she said, "That's okay, nobody else on the board knows anything about art either." And I subsequently learned that this is not an uncommon characteristic of some art galleries. So I served on the board.

The Edmonton Art Gallery at that time was located in an old three-storey house. We had very little money. I remember we actually had a meeting where we debated for half an hour as to whether we could afford to replace the weatherstripping under the front door.

One day, a man named Bill Morrow phoned me. He later became Mr Justice William Morrow of the Northwest Territories. He was a lawyer at that time in Edmonton. He said, "Mel, I have a client, and I have to see you about this particular lady. I can't tell you anything more, but this lady is very ill and she is going to leave the Edmonton Art Gallery some money." And I said, "That's wonderful, I mean I'm sorry to hear the lady is ill, but how much money?" And he said, "I can't tell you."

But, in any event, word got around before the next board meeting. By this time I had become the president of the Edmonton Art Gallery, for God knows what reason, and I announced that we expected to get a bequest. The rumour was we were going to get about $10,000. And it was just like twenty-five Christmases put together. Everybody was just absolutely overjoyed. The lady died about a week later and left us $875,000. And we used that money to build a new art gallery.

Now the lady who was my customer, she and I then had a disagreement. She wanted to put the new Edmonton Art Gallery out in the West End at the site of the provincial museum, and I wanted it downtown. I remember one Sunday morning taking a man, named Bill Sinclair, who became the Chief Justice of Alberta, and another chap down and showing them the site where I thought we should put the art gallery. And it was an old house of ill repute, and there were drunks lying out on the street on a Sunday morning. And they said, "You want to put the art gallery here?" And I said, "Yes."

I prevailed, and the board agreed with me although the lady in question thought it should be out in the West End. During the course of our disagreement, she asked me to come to her home. When I walked in the front door, I immediately saw this most magnificent painting. It really struck me at the time. This lady had a wonderful collection of Emily Carrs and A.Y. Jacksons and MacDonalds and Milnes – you name it. She had this fantastic collection.

I learned later, much later, that she was the patron of A.Y. Jackson and the patron of many other well-known Canadian painters. And the more I got to know about her afterward, the more I realized that this was some remarkable human being. We spent some time talking, but she disagreed with me about the location of the gallery. And, subsequently, after she passed away she left her collection to the National Gallery, to the Victoria Art Gallery, and to her daughter, and not to the Edmonton Art Gallery.

But the more I got to know of her, the more I realized, my goodness, I wish I had gotten to know her a little bit better. I just this last week found out that she was a very close friend of the Gordon family. The late Walter Gordon was one of my closest friends, and she was a very close friend of Liz Gordon. Now, the lady in question was Bobby Dyde, Bobby Plaunt, Dorothy Plaunt, who was the wife of Alan Plaunt, who died at the age of thirty-seven of cancer. And her only daughter, Frances, was born six weeks after Alan Plaunt died. Frances worked in my book store for a year.

Last year my daughter (one of four daughters), who a few years earlier had been totally unpolitical, graduated in political science from Carleton University. She praises Carleton and Blair Neatby and many others for changing her life. She has become a wonderful, bright young lady who intends to move back to Ottawa in the near future. One of my favourite stories is that one day, without knowing that she was in the class, Mitchell Sharp came to Peyton Lyon's class and began his talk by saying, "I never thought there would be a day when I agreed with anything that Mel Hurtig said," but he went on to talk about the free-trade agreement, which is the subject at hand.

I am going to start off with two anecdotes. The first story occurred in March of 1985, and it concerns a twenty-seven-year-old nurse who came to my home in Edmonton. She worked at the famous UCLA bone marrow clinic in Los

Angeles. She sat in my living room and said, "You know, Mel, every week I see parents crying in the hospital room with their children because the hospital bill collector is hounding them for money that they are unable to pay." Every child in the bone marrow unit had a stationary bicycle for exercise purposes, and every child was charged $75 a day for the stationary bicycle. A couple of aspirins cost a dollar, a shot of Demerol cost $180, blood transfusions between $300 to $500 each, isolation rooms (and many of the children needed to have isolation rooms) were $1,200 a day or $36,000 a month. And Janie said to me, "Every week I see children not admitted to that hospital, who should be in that hospital, because their parents can't pay the bills." The same young lady had her first child last year, who developed a slight kidney complication requiring hospitalization for two days. The cost of having her first child ran up to $12,800 in Los Angeles.

The second anecdote concerns a speech I was asked to give in Montreal in 1986. One day my secretary, Rhonda, said, "They want you to go to the Four Seasons Hotel in Montreal. Pierre Berton will be the moderator. You will debate a guy named John Crispo from the University of Toronto. They want to know if you'd be interested." I said, "Well, what's the name of the organization?" And Rhonda said, "They won't tell me." And I said, "What do you mean they won't tell you?" And she said, "They won't tell me. It's a public relations firm that's setting it up, and they won't tell me the name of the sponsoring organization." And I said, "Well, that's ridiculous, Rhonda, just tell them to forget it."

Two days later they phoned back and said, "If Mr Hurtig were to agree to the debate, what would he charge?" And I said, "What is the name of the organization, Rhonda?" And she said, "They won't tell me the name of the organization." I said, "Well, look, Rhonda, just tell them five times whatever I've ever charged anybody in the past. We'll see what happens." A week later, they phoned back and accepted my fee. They told me the sponsor was the Grocery Products Manufacturers of Canada. I said I would go.

I knew that the Grocery Products Manufacturers of Canada is an important and powerful lobby group. They're very Canadian. They're made up of good Canadian companies, like Coca-Cola, Pepsi-Cola, Nescafe, Nabisco, General Food, General Mills, and other good, solid Canadian companies. So I agreed to go but asked to see what they'd been sending to Ottawa. I wanted to know what they'd been advocating, vis-à-vis the free-trade agreement. They were kind enough to send it to me.

I had been saying, since early 1985, that one of the problems that would inevitably result from this agreement would be that the "level playing field" would extend far beyond what we had anticipated. Down the road there'd be a group of people from the Business Council on National Issues (BCNI) and the C.D. Howe Institute and the Conference Board and other places, gathered around

24 Sussex with cognacs in hand after dinner – and they'd be saying, "you know, (Michael, Brian, Pat, whoever), you wanted us to play on a level playing field, and that was a pretty good idea. But look, if we're going to have a level playing field, what we better do is we better have the same taxes as the Americans. You know, how can we compete eyeball to eyeball on a level playing field and pay higher taxes?

"And, you know, Brian and Michael, you better forget about doing anything significant about the environment because if we do something significant about the environment and the Americans don't, how can we compete eyeball to eyeball on a level playing field? And, you know, those so-called right-to-work states, the twenty-one states in the United States, they have the anti-trade-union laws. We better have that kind of law here in Canada, too. Because, if we don't, and you know the competition laws and the anti-trust laws they have down in the States, we better have the same kind of competition and anti-trust laws as well. Because, otherwise, how can we compete on a level playing field?

"And the tax rates are too high here and we better start looking at the social programs. We better start looking at the idea of privatizing the medicare system because we cannot compete eyeball to eyeball on a level playing field."

I have been saying, for about a year and three-quarters, all across the country, that the inevitable results of this so-called trade agreement, which goes well beyond a normal trade arrangement, will have enormous political, social, economic, and cultural ramifications.

So the Grocery Products Manufacturers of Canada sent me the stuff they had been sending to Ottawa. And here it was in writing. Exactly what I had been saying. Number one, we believe there should be a free-trade agreement between Canada and the United States. Number two, it should be a comprehensive agreement. Number three, we believe that our industry should be part of that agreement. Number four, we've got to get rid of our marketing boards. And, number five, we shouldn't be obligated to buy the contents of our food packaging (the agricultural products) from Canada. We better be able to buy them from the United States, where they're considerably cheaper. The material also said that we Canadians cannot afford our costly social programs. They went on at great length to explain why that was the case. And I used this example in 1985 and 1986 and eventually, growing tired of it, went on to other things.

On 12 March 1988 the *Toronto Star* published a column titled "Executives Urge Close Policy Links With The United States":

Canada's economic policies must closely follow US policies if Canadian companies are going to thrive under free trade, corporate executives say. "It is just plain dumb to lead us into an open trading relationship with the US while we are shackled with a regulatory and tax environment that is negative here in Canada," says David Beatty, President of Weston Foods Limited. The federal government should realign its policies to support, instead of handicap, firms forced to compete in free trade's more open environment, he said in a speech on the proposed Canada/US trade agreement. Beatty said, "Ottawa's failure to link Canada's systems to US policies will discourage investment and spark an exodus of production, plants and jobs to the United States. If governments don't help but hinder it's no longer grin-and-bear-it but relocate that will be the cry of the Canadian manufacturer," he said in a speech delivered at the Conference Board of Canada meeting this week. Other executives present agreed in their presentations to the privately funded think tank. "We know there must be new investment but the uncertainties for investing in this country are too substantial," says Larry Baganta, the president of a giant automotive-parts maker. "Another chief concern is Canada's apparently insatiable appetite for costly social programs," he added.

But, if you look at all the nations of the Organization for Economic Cooperation and Development (OECD) and at where Canada sits in comparison, Canada's pretty well right smack in the middle in social spending. Of course, the United States is at the lower end. But compared to many other developed nations in the world and industrialized nations in the world, we are not high per capita social spenders. But no, "We have an insatiable desire for social programs. Services such as a national daycare program, indexed pensions, universal medicare, and others may be laudable but they add to the cost of doing business in Canada. And these are not costs incurred by many of our international competitors."

When I first heard some of my colleagues back in 1985 talk about the threat to Canada's social programs, I must admit I was very skeptical. I didn't talk about it very much myself. But increasingly, after having the opportunity to look at what is actually in the agreement, and, increasingly, as I began to look at what the motivations are of the people who have sponsored this agreement, of the Business Council on National Issues, and the C.D. Howe Institute, and some of the others, it has become more and more relevant.

The first couple of years when I travelled across Canada and talked about the likely ramifications of the agreement for Canadian sovereignty, for the ability of Canadians to determine their own future, for the investment potential and the energy potential, people kept saying, "How does Mr Hurtig know all that stuff?" "How can he talk about something when we don't have a document yet?"

The answer is interesting. People from the Ontario and Manitoba governments – good, loyal civil servants – and occasionally people from Washington were keeping me informed on a pretty regular basis about what was actually happening around those tables. And the more I heard, the more apprehensive I became. Having now studied the actual agreement, and having spent an awful lot of time talking long-distance with people – various attorney generals, departments, lawyers, and trade specialists – I can say that if I was apprehensive in 1985 when we founded the Council of Canadians, I never in my darkest dreams, never in my worst worries, never in my worst nightmares believed that any group of Canadians could sign such an enormously bad agreement – that they could abandon so much Canadian integrity, so much Canadian sovereignty, so much of the ability of Canadians to determine their own future.

During that first year and a half, many times after I gave a speech, somebody in the audience would stand up and say, "Mr Hurtig, if you're right, why are they doing this?" And I was obliged to come up with some answers, such as, well, it's ideological, or they really do believe the cranked-out stuff from the C.D. Howe Institute and from the Economic Council of Canada, the economic models, the econometric studies. Some pretty lame answers of that kind. I now have a totally different perception, which I'll discuss in my conclusion.

Marjorie Cohen, the economist from the Ontario Institute for Studies in Education (OISE), recently said about health care, "The trade agreement negotiated with the United States will put our Canadian health care system in grave danger. This is not rhetoric or scaremongering. It is based on a tough analysis of the long-term implications of the deal. Not only will it jeopardize the health care system, it will undermine the wages and working conditions of health care workers, the great majority of whom are women."

I wish to leave that topic. Most people are only familiar with what the government tells them – the pamphlets, the brochures, and the speeches they're giving. And it's one of the terribly sad things that is happening in this country. There's only one word for the answers the government is giving about what is actually in the agreement: dishonest. Misleading and dishonest. Misleading very often by omission.

I want to switch over to the question of investment. I received a letter from Michael Wilson, dated 1 December 1987, in response to a letter I had written him concerning whether the government had ever attempted to measure the net benefit of direct foreign investment in Canada. And I received this response from him: "My view is that the pendulum has swung too far in recent years in the direction of restricting or inhibiting foreign investment in Canada to the point where potential foreign investors felt unwelcome in this country. I am pleased to say that Canada is now projecting a more positive image at home, as well as abroad, as a place for foreigners to invest."

In January 1988, the 1985 Corporations and Labour Unions Return Act report was published. It's always hopelessly late. Here are some figures from that time when we were hostile to foreign capital, when we were closed to business, when we had received a reputation for being anti-other-countries, when Brian went down to New York on one of his first major speaking engagements after becoming prime minister. He said, "We've been hostile to foreign capital in the past, but from now on we're going to be open for business."

Here are the figures: The profits made by non-Canadians in the mineral/fuels industry were 67.6 per cent of all profits; in the mining industry, 67.5 per cent; in the food processing and packaging industry, 53.4 per cent; tobacco products, 99.9 per cent; rubber products, 84.2 per cent; textile mills, 45.1 per cent; paper and allied industries, 39.3 per cent; machinery industry, 62.7 per cent; transportation equipment industry, 94.4 per cent; electric products, 66.6 per cent; nonmetallic mineral products, 71.4 per cent; petroleum and coal products, 46.7 per cent; chemicals and chemical products, 87.1 per cent. When we were hostile to foreign capital, before Brian declared us open for business, 44.1 per cent of all taxable income in Canada went to non-Canadians.

There isn't a state or country in the world that has a figure remotely similar to that. And I can say that in 1986 and 1987, since Brian declared us open for business, we have had an all-time record growth of foreign direct investment in Canada. And now that we are "open for business," I can provide an educated guess that today close to 50 per cent of all taxable income in Canada is going to non-residents and that this number is increasing by a profound amount every single day.

Since Brian Mulroney became the prime minister of Canada, about 2,400 Canadian companies have been taken over in about $52 billion worth of takeovers. And the new investment capital that came in at the same time was not $52 billion but rather $3 billion. We are not open for business; Canada is clearly up for sale.

We had an all-time current account deficit in 1986, an all-time record directly related to the amount of foreign ownership and investment in Canada. In 1987 we had another brand-new all-time current account deficit, and in 1988 we will have another all-time current account deficit.

Then there's the list I've used before and add to every week. We've said goodbye to the Ritz-Carleton Hotel; goodbye to DeHavilland Aircraft; goodbye to Mitel; goodbye to the West Kootenay Power and Light Company in southeast British Columbia and its four hydroelectric dams, which control the water and electricity of the Kootenays and the Okanagan Valley – the first ever hydroelectric facility in the 120-year history of our country to be sold to nonresidents, sold to people 2,000 miles away in Kansas with no experience managing hydroelectric facilities.

Goodbye to BC Forest Products, Canada's second-largest forest company; Star Oil and Gas; Westburne International; Lake Ontario Cement; Hiram, Walker, Gooderham and Worts; AES Data; the Bank of British Columbia, the first ever Schedule A bank in the 120-year history of Canada taken over by non-Canadians;

half of Husky Oil; Bow Valley; Dome Petroleum, with fifteen million acres of oil and gas properties and $4 billion worth of Canadian taxpayers' money invested in it; Crown Forest Industries; Bowerings; Maple Leaf Mills Ltd; the Keg Restaurants; twenty-three Woodwards Food Stores in Western Canada taken over by Safeway; the Toronto Argonauts and the Quebec Nordics sold from one foreign owner to another; Cadillac Fairview with the Eaton Centre, 50 per cent of the Toronto Dominion Centre, a third of the Pacific Centre, and the Montreal Trust Building in Montreal, $50-million-plus income-producing properties.

Here's one page out of twelve from the latest Investment Canada Report: a petroleum company in Alberta; a mining company in the Queen Charlotte Islands; the Peco Oil and Gas fields in Alberta; a rock quarry in Nova Scotia; a mineral exploration property with headquarters in Toronto; Hazelnut Foods of Weston, Ontario; Manning Biscuits and Primo Foods of Weston; Stafford Foods; a bottling company in Saint John, New Brunswick; other bottling companies in Sudbury, Uxbridge, and St John's, Newfoundland, and another in Trois Rivières, all taken over by Coca-Cola; a paper and plastics goods manufacturer in Toronto; a manufacturer of paper cups in Toronto; a plastic packaging company in Nova Scotia; a trucking and storage company in Downsview; a producer of elastic yarn in Montreal; a carpet manufacturer in Nova Scotia; a men's and ladies' slacks manufacturer in Toronto; a store fixture company in Quebec; a pulp company in Castlegar. The list goes on and on and on.

It is possible to argue the benefits of free trade in terms of classical economics as it is taught in universities across Canada. It is possible to argue that foreign investment can bring some benefits. There is no question. I've always said that foreign investment is a little bit like a martini. There's nothing wrong with a really good martini before dinner in front of the fireplace. But if you have two, you have a bit of a problem, and if you have three, you have a serious problem. It is absolutely impossible to argue simultaneously that you can have free trade operating by the classical theories of free trade while viewing the incredible takeover of Canada, mostly by American companies.

About 82 per cent of foreign direct investment in Canada is American, and it's increasing almost every day. In yesterday's *Financial Post*, the headline was "Free Trade Could Release Flood of Takeovers in Canada." And of course it will. France has one-eighth of the foreign direct investment that we do. Italy has one-fifth. Of all the OECD countries, Canada has five times as much foreign direct investment on a per capita basis, which is increasing dramatically every day.

Laurier said the twentieth century was supposed to belong to Canada, and I say if this agreement goes through, not even Canada is going to belong to Canada. My simple question: Is our idea of a country a place where we, our children, and our grandchildren are meant to be tenants in our own country?

Because this is not my concept of what a country is all about. And if Brian Mulroney gets his way and if the Business Council on National Issues gets their way and if this trade agreement is signed, then Canada is up for sale, and Canada will quickly be bought up.

About a month ago I received a telephone call from a gentleman who said, "I know the Council of Canadians is short of money and we want to help. We're going to give you a modest donation." It was Wallace McCain of McCain Food Products. He said, "We have just figured out that we can move our production from Florenceville eighteen miles into Maine after the trade agreement, and we can make millions of dollars extra profit after this trade agreement. And we will drop our employment in New Brunswick by roughly 95 per cent."

In Alabama there is no minimum wage; in Arizona there is no minimum wage; in Florida there is no minimum wage; in Iowa there is no minimum wage; in Louisiana and Mississippi and South Carolina and Tennessee there is no minimum wage. In Texas, the third most populous state in the United States, the minimum wage is $1.40 an hour; in Wyoming it's $1.60; in Nebraska it's $1.60; in Kansas it's $1.60. The state of Washington has just raised the minimum wage to $2.30 an hour. Alberta has the lowest minimum wage in Canada at $3.80 an hour, and they're in the process of planning an increase.

David Peterson phoned me about a month ago. He said, "Quick, Mel, without thinking about it, tell me right away your main objections to the trade agreement. Is it sovereignty, is it culture, is it Canadian identity, is it our ability to decide our own future, what is it?" And I said, "David, it's none of those things. It's not one of those things. My main concern is jobs, the Canadian standard of living, and the ability of Canadians to live a decent life."

In the last ten years, the gross national product of Canada has increased by about 48 per cent. In the last ten years, the gross national product of the states along the Canadian border have increased by only 28 per cent. More and more American companies in New York and other border states transferred their production down to those states with no decent minimum wage laws, to the *maquiladoras* in Mexico, where the wages are 65 cents an hour, or $4.50 a day, or to Puerto Rico. They transferred to the twenty-one so-called right-to-work states, which are really anti-trade-union states with the lowest incomes in terms of personal income per capita, nine of which have no minimum wage.

Thirty-seven per cent of Canadian workers are unionized versus 17 per cent in the United States, which is pretty close to being the lowest, if not the lowest, in the industrialized world. There are no proper pay equity schemes; there is no pregnancy leave for women; there are no decent unemployment insurance and pension plans or workmen's compensation plans. What we have developed in Canada, under good Conservative governments, under good Liberal governments, under the impact of NDP and Cooperative Commonwealth Federation (CCF) thinking, is a better system of doing things – a better and more compassionate way of treating people, a better way of distributing income.

So what will happen after the trade agreement? Where will the jobs go? Eric Kierans says, "The incentive to let productive capacity in Canada run down is going to be irresistible." Gordon Sparks, the chairman of the Department of Economics, Queen's University, "Canadian firms will locate their new product facilities in the United States where they can still service the Canadian market." Richard Zuckerman, the president of a textile company in Montreal that employs 528 people, wrote to me recently and said, "It's going to be a lot easier to serve the Canadian market from the United States rather than the other way around. We're going to lose our manufacturing and industrial base in Canada."

Ed Stewart, the vice president of Labatt's, said recently, "The logical business step will be to put operations in the largest population centres. It would be much more efficient to be located in Michigan or New York than to stay in Toronto." And Marjorie Nichol, writing in the *Ottawa Citizen* and the *Vancouver Sun*, said:

Oregon and Washington, with triple British Columbia's population and lower production costs, drool at the prospects of wrestling industry from Southern California. The idea that Vancouver would become a new industrial giant on the West Coast defies all logic. If there were no tariffs or other barriers to trade, why would an industry locate in Vancouver when it could be settled in Seattle where it has similar human and natural resources but a larger local market, a more central locale to serve the coastal free trade region and a $2 an hour minimum wage?

Tom Stanfield in Nova Scotia, from the famous Stanfield Company, said, "We'd wind up doing what our competitors have been doing. Moving our production to Mexico, the Caribbean basin, Korea, Taiwan, China, whatever. Ninety per cent of our jobs in Nova Scotia will go. We'll leave a distribution warehouse in Truro."

And Northern Telecom, the shining example we so often use, has lowered employment in the past year in Canada by 2 per cent while increasing employment in the southern United States by 46 per cent. In a recent bid on a major American contract, they promised they would have no Canadian content if they won.

A Department of Regional Industrial Expansion study – marked confidential – crossed my desk in 1987, and it said, "In most cases, the capacity of US plants is so great that a 10 per cent increase in a production run to satisfy Canadian demand would not be difficult at all."

The president of Campbell's Soups of Canada Ltd, in a private discussion with Simon Reisman in Winnipeg, said, "Look, under this agreement, it's pretty simple. What we will simply do is we will close our production here in Canada, and we will supply the entire Canadian market with one-hour Sunday night production from our factory in Chicago."

There's a closed down, state-of-the-art Miller brewery in Trenton, Ohio, that can easily look after all of Ontario's beer-drinking requirements for a year, with no new capital investment, at prices a third lower than existing prices in Canada. A new Coors brewery in Colorado can look after three-quarters of the beer-drinking capacity of all of Canada. A General Electric small appliance plant in Tennessee has an existing overcapacity that can service all the small appliance needs in Canada for a year.

American industry at the present time is operating well below capacity. A 10 per cent expansion of US production will simply swamp the Canadian market. Anyone with any business experience knows that the most profitable aspect of any business is always, without fail, the tail end of production runs. That's where you make most of your profit.

Frank Stronach, the president of Magna, said recently in a speech in Saskatoon, "Magna during the past five years has invested a billion dollars in new plants and machinery, 70 per cent in Canada and 30 per cent in the United States. Under the free-trade agreement it will be exactly the reverse. It will be 70 per cent in the United States and 30 per cent in Canada." Bill Loewen, the president of Comcheq Ltd, asks, "Why isn't Winnipeg the size of Fargo or Bismarck?" Why is Winnipeg the size that it is? Why do we have that kind of investment there? Or, why is Saskatoon bigger than a lot of the other places?

The point is that under this trade agreement – and I've never used the following figure ever before; I just had one of my researchers dig it up yesterday, and it's an incredible figure – less than one-half of 1 per cent of all the corporations in Canada, Canadian and foreign, make 71 per cent of all the profits made in Canada. Essentially, it's these very people who are pushing this agreement, who are behind the so-called free-trade agreement, which is, in very important ways, an agreement about how they want to profoundly change Canada. How they want to bypass government at the federal level, at the provincial level, and even at the municipal level. And, how behaving in the traditional way of the transnational corporation, they really don't want anybody to interfere with their decisions about how they operate in the future.

In the period 1978 to 1985 inclusive, the most recent years for which reliable figures are available, Canadian-controlled companies produced 876,000 new jobs in Canada. During that same period of time, American-controlled companies in Canada produced 1,400 new jobs. And other foreign corporations in Canada actually decreased their employment by 12,800 jobs in Canada.

In the goods-producing sector of the Canadian economy, in the period 1978 to 1985, Canadians increased their employment by 102,600 jobs. American-controlled companies in the goods-producing sector actually decreased their employment by 61,000 jobs in Canada. Other foreign-controlled companies decreased their employment by 25,400 jobs in Canada. And here's the statistic I like best of all: For every billion dollars in profits made in Canada during this period of time, Canadian corporations created 5,765 new jobs. For every billion dollars in profits, American corporations created the grand total of 17 new jobs.

Perhaps we should feel sorry for the American corporations because maybe they weren't doing that well in Canada during this period of time. On the contrary, in 1978 American corporations had profits of $8.3 billion, which they had more than doubled to $16.9 billion by 1985. Foreign corporations, while decreasing employment in Canada, actually doubled their profits from $9.9 billion to $19.8 billion during this same period of time.

And lastly, who was it that actually created jobs for Canadians? Was it the Business Council on National Issues? Was it the 135-odd companies, mostly big transnational corporations, who are funding much of the activity supporting free trade? The answer is no. The companies that want this trade deal have every intention of locating their new production in the United States and not in Canada. In the period 1978 to 1985, small Canadian-owned companies with little or no export propensity of any kind, with fewer than twenty employees, created 819,600 new jobs, while large firms in Canada with 100 or more employees actually decreased their employment in Canada by 31,900 jobs.

I have seen a confidential study by the Bank of Nova Scotia, for internal circulation to senior officers only, dated 8 October 1987, after the preliminary trade agreement was signed. This was an update of another document. Why does a bank go to the trouble of producing a massive document on the so-called trade agreement? Why? They do it to give to their credit officers across Canada. Don't lend any more money to those fruit growers in the Okanagan Valley. Don't lend any more money to those grape growers in the Niagara Peninsula. Don't lend any more money to those shoe manufacturers outside of Montreal, those textile companies. Don't lend any more money to those Western wall-board companies in Drayton Valley, and so on.

This confidential report outlines the risk factor involved in each of the major sectors of the Canadian economy. The resources sector, for example, is rated at +4. Well, everybody knows the name of the game is for Canada to continue to be hewers of wood and drawers of unemployment insurance and to pump the natural resources out of Canada just as quickly as we can. So, it's a +4. However, the resource sector of the Canadian economy employs only 5.1 per cent of all Canadian employees.

The manufacturing sector is a −1; the agricultural sector, −1. The services sector of the Canadian economy − and there is no other nation in the world that has a greater percentage of its workforce employed in the service sector of the economy than Canada (70 per cent), highest among all the OECD nations – is rated a –2. All the new jobs in Canada have virtually been created in the service sector of the economy. So 81 per cent of all jobs in Canada are expected by this confidential document to suffer a negative impact. And the service sector of the economy, which employs 70 per cent of Canadians, is expected to suffer a very serious negative impact. A few sentences later it says, "the settlement mechanism agreed to is considerably less than a binding or guaranteed arrangement."

Then there is the matter of energy. As an Albertan, I can't believe what we've done about energy. I don't believe that one in 10,000 people walking through the Sparks Street Mall, or one in 10,000 people walking down Yonge Street or Bloor Street, or Jasper Avenue, or Granville Street, or Barrington Street, across this country, understands this colossal, incredible sellout in energy. There is no other country in the world that would have tolerated signing this kind of agreement, dreamed of abandoning control over its energy and other resources. If Alberta, which produces between 83 and 86 per cent of all Canadian hydrocarbons, decides its own needs are not being looked after properly, then Ontario can do without, Manitoba can do without, Saskatchewan can do without, British Columbia can do without, but not the Americans. We will still, if we want to cut back production, have to continue sharing production with the Americans on roughly a 40 per cent pro rata basis whether or not we Canadians are running short.

There is no other country in the world that would have agreed to sign an energy deal in which you can't charge people who live outside your country higher prices. There is no other country in the world that would have abandoned the control over the pricing of its energy supplies, abandoned the control that it had under the General Agreement on Tariffs and Trade (GATT) of so many things in relation to processing and upgrading resources. There is no other country in the world that would have said energy is just something we export. Every other country in the world recognizes that energy is used as an industrial tool. It can be used to produce petrochemicals or agricultural chemicals or to attract industry, sometimes by giving preferential energy rates.

We can't do that anymore under this agreement. And Mr Bourassa is in for one hell of a surprise. The *Globe and Mail* and the *Financial Post*, without doing any research on the subject, have been trumpeting the fact that, boy, we're able to take hydro power and sell it to the United States at three times the price we're getting in Quebec. And Don Getty says, yah, we will still be able to offer energy rebates in the province of Alberta, and we'll still be able to use energy as a tool. Both of these people are in for a big surprise. Everyone I have talked to in Washington says, "No way." The minute that agreement is signed, the Americans will say there will be no more lower energy prices for Canada than the United

States. You want to charge Americans higher prices? No problem whatsoever. Then you have to charge Canadians higher prices as well.

Sovereignty is really what the agreement is all about, and the sharing of goods. How many Canadians realize we have just agreed to share our aluminum even if we begin to run short, our copper, our lead, our nickel, our zinc, our oil, our natural gas, our sulphur, our softwood lumber, our chemicals, our pulp and paper, even if we Canadians run short? Not one in 10,000.

As to the provinces, there will be a massive change in provincial jurisdiction. I won't get into that here, but I will discuss the whole question of national unity, of East/West, of having a country, of having national programs across the country. Richard Simeon said, "We Canadians, under this agreement, run the risk of reducing the capacity to build national support across regions for common national purposes. The reduction in the relative imports of economic linkages within Canada would make the eventual separation of Quebec more feasible. It becomes much more difficult to think coherently about an economic entity called Canada."

Raymond Garneau recently said:

What will become of East/West economic flows in the Conservative perspective of laissez-faire? What will remain of Canada tomorrow as a political entity? What political bond will be strong enough to withstand the economic pressures of market forces favouring North/South flows? Will deregulation result in the American giants controlling an ever-increasing part of our economy? Canadians who live in Quebec and who have fought for Canadian unity are wondering whether they have fought only to see the Conservatives put forward an economic policy whereby the regions of Canada shall see their future as being almost exclusively in the South.

What happens to the East/West when Alberta builds its export highway to the south as they're planning to, with the possibility of a railway to link with the Port of Seattle? What will happen to East/West transportation, to the TransCanada Highway, to our railways? What will happen to the St Lawrence Seaway when the expanding, giant Cargill grain company decides that under this trade agreement they're going to start to ship Canadian grain down the Mississippi River? What will happen to Vancouver, Prince Rupert, Churchill, Thunder Bay? What will happen in the monopolies section of the agreement? What will happen to our ability as Canadians to develop new national programs? The fundamental basis of this agreement is more North/South and forget about East/West.

Incredibly, just the other day, the *Toronto Star* published a statement by Donald Campbell of the Department of External Affairs, who oversaw these agreements. I looked at that statement and wondered whether anybody realized what he had just said. Donald Campbell, an assistant deputy minister in External Affairs, praised the trade agreement, contending that it will lead to more sustainable growth than any other single initiative. One particular area that would be affected is regional development policy. He said, "Regions of Canada may be influenced by gradually stronger North/South economic orientation as they become part of the North American as much as the Canadian economic region." And, of course, they will.

Joe Ghiz said recently in a speech, "Can you imagine any other government saying that to evolve new national regional development programs they will have to go the capital city in another country and talk to congressmen and senators and get their permission under the trade agreement?" That's what we're going to have to do to develop new regional programs.

I'll end with some quotations. Farley Mowat said, "This is one more spike in the coffin of this country. One more victory for those who would sell us out." Pierre Berton, "We're selling the very soul of our country." David Suzuki, "I'm horrified by the dimensions of this sellout." Edgar Benson, Canada's former minister of finance, "Under this deal Canada has given the Americans the right to control us on all fronts." Frank Miller, the former Conservative premier of Ontario, "I have serious nagging concerns about how much sovereignty Canada will lose." Robert Stanfield, the former leader of the Conservative Party of Canada, "If I felt I had a choice this would certainly not be it. We wouldn't have put so many eggs in one basket." Jean-Luc Pepin, the former federal minister of transport, "Those who support the agreement must accept that it will put an end to the political structure of Canada as we know it."

And there's the wonderful quotation by William Randolph Hearst, the editor of the Hearst newspapers in the United States, "The momentous move toward unifying the two countries economically is very gratifying. For more than a decade my pop urged in his newspapers that Canada become part of the United States. North America should be one country. Brian Mulroney is one of the most pro-American Prime Ministers in Canada's history." John Halstead, the former Canadian ambassador to NATO said, "What is at stake is the ability of Canada to act as a coherent political entity." Mitchell Sharp, "The price that we Canadians will pay will be a progressive erosion of Canadian independence and identity." Jean Chretien, "Canada has given away all of its bargaining chips. What is left is for the United States to try to force us to recognize that medicare is an unacceptable subsidy, that regional development grants are unacceptable subsidies, that cheap petrochemical feed stock plants in Alberta are unacceptable subsidies."

Robert Reich, the leading Harvard University political economist, "Canada has been sold a big bag of goods. The agreement is not worth the paper that it is written on." David Peterson, the premier of Ontario, "Under this agreement our access to the US markets would not be appreciably more secure than it was the day that negotiations got underway." Joe Ghiz, the premier of Prince Edward Island, "What is at stake is nothing less than the kind of country that we will leave to our children. I cannot accept this surrender of my country. This is a framework for the accelerated disappearance of Canada." And George Grant, the great Conservative philosopher, "The agreement will destroy Canada's social programs and hurt innocent and ordinary people in this country." Bruce Wilkinson, one of the great economists in this country, "What is really involved for Canada is whether the Canadian economic, political, and social model is going to retain its own identity or increasingly reflect the American society. It will certainly move Canada closer to political integration."

And my last quotation, my favourite, is by Eric Kierans: "What will future generations have to say about us when they learn that they do not own the land on which they stand. We have reduced our status as a nation to that of an American colony. I am filled with disgust that the Government of Canada should seek and accept such an agreement. If an American president had ever thought of giving up one-hundredth of the political jurisdiction that we have thrown on the table he would have been impeached instantly."

And, in conclusion, I now believe something I didn't believe a year ago. I believe there is a hidden agenda as part of all of this: deregulation. The intention is to weaken the power of the elected representatives of the people in Canada and to weaken the federal and provincial and municipal levels of government in Canada and to bypass them. I truly believe that our country is at a crossroads. I know there have been many important debates in the past in Canada – the conscription debate, the patriation debate, the famous reciprocity debate, and many others – but I truly believe, having studied the agreement closely and consulted with as many people as a I could, that if Brian Mulroney gets his way and this deal is implemented and left in place for just a very short period of time, there will not be a Canada a generation from now.

To use Frank Underhill's famous expression, what will be left will at best be "a geographic expression instead of a country." I think the future of our country is at stake. The very destiny of our country is at stake in the next few weeks and months. I don't mean a couple of years from now. In the short period of time from now until the next federal election, we must do everything we possibly can to defeat this government that will sell out our country once and for all in perpetuity. I don't care who Canadians vote for as long as they make sure this trade agreement is defeated.

To the people of Canada, to the people in the New Democratic and Liberal Parties, and to the true Conservatives who remember the history of the Conservative Party of Canada, who remember the policies and platforms of John A. MacDonald and Robert Borden and John Diefenbaker, I say very simply that we

Canadians are damn lucky to live in this country. We've got lots of problems. We haven't treated our Native people properly; we haven't solved youth unemployment and other problems. But there are a lot of wonderful things that we Canadians can do together.

By signing this agreement we abandon the greatest asset that we Canadians have: our ability to determine our own future. And I say let's not do that. Let's get together with good Conservatives, good socialists, good Liberals, and good people from all political perspectives to build a better country. We are already the envy of the world.

Last August I was sitting on a plateau, about 4,500 feet high in Yoho National Park at Lake O'Hara, looking down on three different levels of magnificent lakes with an equally magnificent waterfall cascading down the mountain to my left. I spent the day up there hiking, and when I came back to the lodge afterward, I met people from Korea, Japan, Austria, and Norway. At dinner they asked me, "Do you Canadians know how lucky you are to live in this country? How blessed you are?" I said, "I think most Canadians do, but sometimes we have to be reminded."

Let us not give up our ability to make this an even better place for human beings to live. And let us join together. I'll end by saying, let us join together and make sure that the heritage of John A. Macdonald, Walter Gordon, John Diefenbaker, and Tommy Douglas does not go down the drain without, at least, one hell of a big fight.

MEL HURTIG is an author and publisher who has spent the past twenty-five years speaking across Canada about economic, social, political, and cultural matters. He is a founding member and past national chairman of the Committee for an Independent Canada and the founder and former chairman of the Council of Canadians. Mel Hurtig has been chairman of the board of the Canadian Booksellers Association, and Hurtig Publishers has produced many titles that have won numerous awards and prizes, including the Governor General's award. In 1980 Mr Hurtig launched the largest and most ambitious project in the history of Canadian publishing: *The Canadian Encyclopedia*.

Mr Hurtig has himself received numerous awards, including Officer of the Order of Canada, honorary doctor of law degrees from six Canadian universities, the Lester B. Pearson Man of the Year Peace Award, the Speaker of the Year Award, The Royal Society of Canada's Centenary Medal, and several publishing industry awards, including, on two occasions, the Canadian Book Publisher of the Year Award.

22

Some Personal Reflections on Canadian Foreign Policy

ALLAN GOTLIEB, 1989

It is not inaccurate to say that, on the whole, the subject of Canadian foreign policy is a neglected subject. When I look at the stream of Canadian periodical literature, newspaper articles, commentary, popular and less popular books, the topic of Canadian foreign policy is rarely the focus of attention or serious debate. There is, of course, the refrain of "do something," which is heard from time to time when a serious world problem gets momentary attention on our national screen. And there are sporadic expressions of concern or anger about our allegedly towing the American line on some issue or other or our unwillingness to speak out more vigorously in favour of peace or disarmament or other international goals.

But the unpleasant truth of the matter is that the Canadian people do not appear to be deeply interested in Canadian foreign policy and our media possibly even less so.

When one of the most distinguished authorities on Canadian foreign policy died not too long ago, a man who spent his lifetime writing and thinking about Canadian foreign policy, and indeed making and molding it – I am referring to John Holmes – the obituary notices in our prosperous and popular dailies gave only the most perfunctory account of his life and work. There was nothing in print or elsewhere to indicate the formative role he had played in the making of the foreign policy of this country in the critical years of the 1950s, when, with Lester Pearson, he occupied so large a place in our history of the period. Nor what was so quintessentially Canadian about his approach to the world. No man brought to Canadian diplomacy the qualities of Canadianness in finer balance. Instead we got a short recital of tombstone data and no more.

I mention this point only to illustrate our national tendency toward indifference to the story of our Canadian foreign policy, to those who have made it, to what it is really all about, and what makes it Canadian. To be great, a nation must have a sense of what it is and where it is in the world. It cannot take its past for granted, nor should it ignore its accomplishments.

Most important, a nation should endeavour to grasp the deeper forces and factors that make its foreign policy what it is. Without these insights, we will as a nation most assuredly fail to understand ourselves or even the issues of the present day, nor will we fulfil our greater potential to play a constructive role on the world stage.

I am being critical here not of Canadian scholarship in respect of foreign policy, because I believe it to be significant and growing in range of interest, but of the lack of public attention to the whole subject.

The task of increasing awareness is not an easy one. Television, the principal mode by which we receive information in the broadest sense of the term, is inimical to nuances. The implications of this are ominous when we consider that, in the phrase of Dr Kissinger, foreign policy consists of a thousand nuances. But I believe our media, both those parts of it which are publicly supported and those whose purpose is profit, have an obligation, as a part of their Canadianness and of their role in society, to try to go beyond the surface and the superficial and the most immediate. They have an obligation to contribute, in their pages and images, to an understanding of our past and present in the community of nations and to help us understand our potential role in the future.

One may say this is all very well, but it won't happen, that it is just an idle wish. I don't believe Canadians should leave it at that. If we do, Canadian foreign policy will become a hermetic field, sealed from the rest of the country, the preserve of the professors, the practitioners, and the few.

In other societies with which I am familiar, great contributions to understanding foreign policy, whether in the form of criticism, analysis, advocacy, or even praise, are a daily occurrence in the media. And the quality of the criticism is often high, on a level to be found at the best universities.

Hence Canadians must not be indifferent to the indifference of those who have the means and the responsibility to promote our national heritage.

When John Holmes was still an active senior officer – that was some thirty-two years ago – I joined the Department of External Affairs at the bottom of the diplomatic ladder. Holmes was then one of a handful of assistant undersecretaries occupying offices on what was known as "Killers' Row" in the east block, when Lester Pearson was still secretary of state for External Affairs.

And what a bustling, tumultuous place it was. Obviously, not all of the three hundred or so officers were of equal talent. But there was still a sense of explosive energy about the place that continues to impress one after so many years. Norman Robertson, Escott Reid, Arnold Smith, Jules Leger, Marcel Cadieux, Chester Ronning, John Holmes, George Ignatieff, Robert Ford, and Charles Ritchie were all still in their prime and overcharging the expanding telecommunications system with ideas, criticism, attacks, counterattacks, and altogether much controversy.

This was, I suppose, close to the end of what can correctly be described as the golden age of Canadian diplomacy, when history, circumstances, and talent all came together to enable Canada to play so impressive a role on the world stage. While still at Oxford, I recall Stuart Hampshire telling me I was joining the best foreign service in the world. Soon after my arrival in Ottawa, I remember how impressed I was to read the brilliant telegraphic accounts of Arnold Smith's conversations with Khrushchev and later of John Starnes's with Nasser.

The most striking aspects of our foreign policy were, aside from the energy that animated it, its globalism, its creativity, its multilateralist impulse, and its resistance to the rigidities of thought and policy formation that were characteristic of the Cold War.

From Colombo-plan building on the Indian subcontinent and peacekeeping in Vietnam to alliance building in Europe and peacemaking in the Middle East, from institution building in the UN and Commonwealth to development programs in Africa, the global features of our foreign policy were astonishing. This is especially so when one considers that Canadian independence in foreign policy was only a few decades old. Moreover, our national interest in no way dictated, required, or even suggested such a role. Equally astonishing was the degree of creativity that was injected into so many of these undertakings.

Multilateralism went hand in hand with our globalist imperative. The Canadians were motivated, I believe, primarily by a desire to bring the US and Western Europe together in the pursuit of collective security. We wanted to prevent the Americans from doing what they had done a generation earlier: pick up their chips and withdraw from the world game. And we wanted a strong international organization for peace and security so as to avoid a repetition of the sorry story of the League of Nations, conscious also, as we were, of our own sorry role in it.

Our aggressive pursuit of multilateralism was not motivated by a desire to limit US influence or by an attempt to create countervailing forces against American power. In some instances that may have been the case, but I can think of only one: Canada's initiative to get the UN, at the time of the Law of the Sea conferences, to endorse wider coastal jurisdiction for fisheries and then for other areas, such as archipelagic waters, so as to create general support for legal regimes that, at the time, the US opposed. But in general our multilateralism was not motivated in any conscious way by a rationale that was based on the national interest.

Of course, the global foreign policy that we were constructing did accord, in the large sense, with our national interest and, in particular, with the overriding one of avoiding another world war. But it was not based on the national interest in the sense that it could be differentiated from the national interest of all other countries.

Another feature of our international style of diplomacy at the time was, as I mentioned, the ability of our foreign-service practitioners to withstand some of the rigidities of Cold War thinking. I am here advocating no revisionist philosophy. There were reasons for the Cold War. And we now know how appalling, how aberrational and murderous, was the behaviour of the Soviet leader at the time that the Cold War began.

But even in those dark hours many of our diplomats retained considerable intellectual freedom. How clearly I recall Norman Robertson, in the late 1950s, advocating the recognition of East Germany and its admission to the UN – this at a time when the Hallstein Doctrine was in its ascendancy. Or Arnold Smith telling me that he personally agreed with much of the Soviet position rather than with the Western one on the political desirability of defining aggression.

How does one explain the nature and characteristics of Canadian foreign policy at the time? First, our important military role during World War Two gave us a new-found confidence in the task of building the peace. Such were the ravages of war that Canada emerged, after the US and UK, as one of the few vigorous nations, with its economy strengthened.

Second, in an era when most Third World nations had not yet reached independence, Canada was well placed, in a world community of some fifty nations, to establish middle-power leadership in dealing with great-power conflicts.

Third, our sense of being a small, young nation, newly emerged from colonial status, and our domestic experience in seeking to balance interests over a physically huge land mass with a small and linguistically divided and dispersed population, made it possible for us to understand the sensitivities of smaller and weaker powers everywhere. These in turn saw Canada as a strong, influential, and sympathetic Western country.

Finally, the personnel of the Department of External Affairs were an elite group and were widely recruited from among the ablest in the land. Most were mature when they joined the service; hence they brought with them considerable intellectual capital and wartime idealism, which they drew upon and which inspired them through their active years.

For Canada, this was a glorious era, and Canadians were very proud of their achievements on the world stage. Indeed, our successes, and the respect we gained from others for them, became a positive factor in the building of our nationhood. We came to believe, or at least half-believe, that we had a special vocation for making peace and helping solve the problems of the world. The Danes were talented for making furniture, the Swiss made watches, the Germans made cameras, the French made wine, and the Canadians made peace. The regard with which we were held on the international stage, culminating in the Suez affair, when we moved in opposition to our two mother countries, flowed back into our own land and helped increase our regard for ourselves.

But the seeds of serious problems in both our foreign policy and style of diplomacy were planted during this period.

As the international community greatly expanded, with the block in UN membership being overcome through the initiatives of Paul Martin and External Affairs, our own UN broker-type role necessarily diminished. And as the world became progressively more gripped by the transforming nuclear arms race, the ability of non-nuclear powers to affect the course of events shrank.

Because of the harmony of Canada's interests with those of our friends and others in the early postwar period, our foreign policy and our practitioners did not need to be greatly concerned with, or seek to promote, the national interest in the narrower – but very vital – sense of the term. When international circumstances changed, Canadian diplomats were not all that well equipped to deal with the new and very different challenges of the 1960s and 1970s, challenges directed to the sovereignty, the unity, and the economic health of the nation. Deep fissures formed in the internal cohesion of the department, and our multilateral efforts seem to have become over-energetic at times.

I will illustrate my comments about our diplomacy and the national interest by relating some of my earlier experiences. When I joined the Department of External Affairs, there were, if I recall correctly, only two officers working in the US section, or unit – and they dealt with bridges and fish. This had been true for many years. In our Legal Division the summer I arrived, the number was down to three or four, although "full strength" was slightly higher than that. Others, such as the Economic Division, would deal with US problems, but, aside from the Defence Division, these were only one component of their activity. Some years later US affairs was elevated to a division in the Bureau of Western Hemispheric Affairs. Not until the late 1970s was the US Bureau formed as an independent geographic bureau on a par with Europe and Africa and the Middle East – I'm happy to say it happened on my watch.

In the 1980s, after integration and other institutional changes, the US Bureau became a branch, headed by its own senior assistant deputy minister, who was assisted by two other assistant deputy ministers, with four director-generals, seven directors, and a staff of well over a hundred formed into many bureaus, divisions, and whatever.

The two-person unit was transformed, in a single generation, into the largest and most voracious political branch of the department.

I do not wish to suggest that, back in the 1950s, the department was perverse in its allocation of personnel. There were reasons for it. It is difficult to believe, but Canada was engaged in relatively few major economic disputes with the US in this period. Ambassador to Washington Arnold Henney states in his memoirs, *Render Unto Caesar,* that in 1959, when he was briefing John Diefenbaker, there were no serious economic conflicts with the US.

Nor did we have problems of national unity to cope with, nor the machinations of foreign powers, nor were we then grappling too deeply with environmental issues, nor did we believe we needed to.

But beyond all these factors that made a preoccupation with the national interest unnecessary, there was another: The culture of the foreign ministry was oriented toward the political function. Here was where the action was and – need I say? – the glory.

One of the strongest memories I have of my early days was my assignment to the General Assembly in 1958 as adviser to the Canadian delegate to the Sixth (Legal) Committee. At issue was whether the UN should try to convene a second Law of the Sea conference to resolve the issue of the breadth of the territorial sea and fishing zone. The extension of our coastal limits was a major national objective of the new Conservative government. Yet the committee was being manned, on the Canadian side, by one political appointee and one adviser – myself – with less than two years experience.

A few days after I arrived, I stepped into the General Assembly room, where the First (Political) Committee was sitting, discussing disarmament, with John Holmes in the Canadian chair.

There was an enormous crowd of Canadian advisers around him, bustling, jumping up and down, passing papers. I was struck by the animation, the sense of excitement that prevailed. I was equally struck by the enormous difference from the Canadian presence in my bread-and-butter committee.

I had come into the room for a purpose. John Holmes was the senior departmental officer in the delegation. I directed to him a handwritten note recommending that a senior officer of our Department of Fisheries, Mr S.V. Ozere, be allowed to join our delegation for a week to help brief our representative, Senator Thorvaldson, and other delegates, of which there were many, interested in the Canadian position on the territorial sea and fishing zones.

The answer to my question "Do you agree with my recommendation?" came back from his desk at the conference table. It was a simple "No."

It took me a while to understand that the reason was that it did not appear all too seemly, in the eyes of the senior Canadian officials, to have a domestic adviser lobbying other countries on a domestically inspired issue.

The 1960s and 1970s were to bring with them some very major foreign policy challenges for Canada: the explosion of our trade with the US; the overflow of American investment into the country; the beginnings of US protectionism; vigorous counterresponse to some of our measures to limit US influence; conflicts over environmental issues, sovereignty, and pollution in the Arctic; and ownership of cultural industries, to name a few concerning our closest neighbour.

Serious domestic conflict with Quebec also arose and was played out, unfortunately, on the international field. As Quebec sought special international status and the exercise of treaty-making powers in foreign affairs, and with foreign agents mixing into our internal affairs in Quebec, New Brunswick, and Manitoba, Ottawa plunged headlong into a triangular, transatlantic conflict. Indeed, we were faced with a series of international crises in the late 1960s as the separatist drive to international status and independence grew more and more intense. It reached its culminating point in Lester Pearson declaring President de Gaulle's behaviour in Quebec "unacceptable" and in the subsequent suspension of diplomatic ties with Gabon, which was, then, operating under direct French influence.

Our foreign policy had to respond to these new and disparate challenges, and respond it did. Most dramatically, Marcel Cadieux, formerly departmental legal adviser, became undersecretary and led the long, arduous battle against separatist manœuvres on the international plane and against foreign involvement here until Pierre Trudeau became prime minister.

Stringent countermeasures against US economic influence also began to be taken, not all that successfully, during the 1970s. Canada assumed a leadership role in environmental efforts globally, although with mixed results with regard to the US. Indeed, on the environmental and maritime fronts, a number of our goals remain less than fully realized to this day.

The balance sheet shows that Canadian diplomacy was responding to these new and serious challenges of the time. But not without controversy, doubt, and internal strife.

The White Paper on Foreign Policy for Canadians, published in 1970 by the Trudeau government, was much criticized for making the national interest the basis for our foreign policy. This was seen by many of the, by then, "older school" to be a betrayal of what Canadian diplomacy and foreign policy were all about. But, of course, Trudeau was right.

What seems to me curious today is that the articulation of such a fundamental premise of nationhood should have been so controversial. It is all the more curious given the emphasis on international goals in the various papers. But the most curious aspect of the White Paper is that it did not deal specifically with our relations with the US. It was as if to say there is foreign policy and there is the US. But, notwithstanding the great deal that was traditional in the document, the foreign service was very reserved about its underlying concepts.

The concern about making the national interest the focus of our foreign policy was aggravated by a growing malaise about our foreign policy generally. As I mentioned earlier, Canada's nationhood and our sense of national identity had been strengthened by our diplomatic achievements in designing the architecture of the postwar world order. In the 1960s and the 1970s, the expectations of the Canadian public for a continued series of sterling successes and initiatives was high. Mr Diefenbaker realized this. Howard Green realized this: He pleaded with foreign service officers for new initiatives; each of us was asked to contribute an idea. Paul Martin also realized this. He was, like his predecessors, relentless in his efforts to establish a Canadian presence on the international scene.

Both Green and Martin achieved some measure of success. But not sufficiently for Canadian public opinion, which saw no glories or achievements notable enough to make us all feel proud. And the public sensed, I believe, a sort of overreaching, a quality of trying too hard. So our very successes of the brilliant postwar period carried with them the seeds of subsequent malaise in the Canadian psyche, a sort of profound national disappointment that our international role was not more stellar.

The Canadian desire to return to the golden days when our foreign achievements strengthened our nationhood culminated in the public response to the timely Trudeau peace initiative of 1983. At that time the Canadian media, and the Canadian public, went overboard; they seemed to lose all sense of balance and proportion about the significance of the undertaking.

At any rate, the 1940s and 1950s left us with something of a foreign policy malaise in the 1960s and 1970s. This malaise was, if anything, aggravated by brave attempts on the part of the Trudeau government to lead the Canadian public and media to understand the nature of Canadian foreign policy in an era of limited growth, increasing international competition, environmental challenge, and internal conflict.

The national malaise about our foreign policy was, I think, strongly reflected in the inner councils of External Affairs. The overriding urge of the majority of the officers was to try to continue the traditions of the earlier days, without sufficient recognition of the growing significance of the bread-and-butter issues, national unity, perceived challenges to sovereignty, and other emerging problems.

These contradictions and uncertainties were, I think, largely to be resolved in the 1980s, and it is to these significant developments that I now turn.

The quest for national unity and strengthened nationhood came to dominate our foreign policy in the last twenty years and dominate it overwhelmingly. Thanks largely to the gifted and courageous leadership of the senior francophone in the department, and after some resistance, the Canadian diplomatic service, the organization of affairs at headquarters, diplomatic representation abroad, and the composition of international delegations all came to reflect the constitutional and linguistic character of Canada. The foreign challenges to our unity, after time and strenuous effort, were overcome.

Soon the major focus of the national interest turned south, to defining our relationship with the United States. Canadian foreign policy began to grapple increasingly and in time overwhelmingly with the greatest challenge to our national interest: how best to coexist with our powerful neighbour to the south. After a long series of policy initiatives running through the Third Option, the Foreign Investment Review Agency (FIRA), restrictive sectoral ownership laws, the National Energy Policy (NEP), the Liberal's sectoral free-trade initiative, and other efforts, a culminating point was reached in Prime Minister Mulroney's comprehensive free-trade initiative.

The free-trade initiative, which I cannot stress too strongly was a Canadian idea and proposal, has to be seen in this light – that is to say, in the light of a continuum of major national efforts to address how Canada could make itself less vulnerable to the future laws and policies and economic pressures of the superpower to the south.

Canadians, in the historic election of 1988, chose the path of free trade and institution building with the US. Canada decided to see the US not primarily as a threat from which we must have protection, but as our comparative advantage in the world. The improved and more secure access we have achieved has become a part of our international comparative advantage.

As I see the event, and I realize that we are perhaps too close to see it clearly, the adoption of the Free Trade Agreement exorcises a strong negative factor in the Canadian psyche: a fear of the US and its influence, which in turn conceals a fear of coming to terms with our own potential and even of our greatness.

In opting to see the US relationship as a positive asset that needs to be preserved and enhanced, we have, I believe, liberated ourselves and our foreign policy from overwhelming American preoccupations – and even obsessions. Perhaps we are now liberated, so to speak, to get on with other challenges on the international plane and to our larger role.

Trade and economic disputes, which were minor in the 1940s and 1950s, which grew in the 1960s, which came to dominate our foreign policies in the 1970s and our national life in the 1980s, will of course, continue. But the objective, bilateral institutions should settle and defuse them. Serious economic disputes will, of course, remain and arise in future. But I believe they will not so dominate our energies and our international efforts as to deprive us of the will to pursue new and broader goals.

I don't wish to exaggerate the significance of the changed North American environment. After all, Congress is still Congress, and they are an unruly bunch with an excess of international power, not always accompanied by a parallel sense of responsibility. But the raw power of the pressure groups and their Congressional Knights are now subject to new constraints and new transnational processes. Hence, I am confident in predicting a more serene relationship and better conditions for focusing our talents and energies on other pressing global concerns. And there are enough of these: international indebtedness, poverty in the Third World, respect for human rights everywhere, nuclear and conventional disarmament, and our role in Europe and the Far East.

Some of the ambivalences and ambiguities affecting the Canadian diplomatic service are also at a point of resolution. The integration of the trade service and trade policy functions into a single department, along with the immigration functions, was a long needed institutional reform. When foreign service officers must respond to Canadian economic needs so directly, there can be no arguing about the role of the diplomat.

The promotion of the national interest now sits at the very heart of the greatly expanded and increasingly relevant institution. Its capacities and skills are now thoroughly central to our national interest. Its members can no longer think of themselves (a few, not many, did) as detached practitioners of international affairs divorced from the arts of the salesperson and advocate. The resolution of our decades-long debate about our relations with the US in favour of an open economic approach will, in time, lead members of our service, of whom there are some, away from the type of thinking that recognizes a Canadian position on an international matter as valid and legitimate only if it differs from the US position.

When we look at Canadian foreign policy in the years ahead, we can see that we are now well positioned to devote increased effort to the global scene and global goals. With our principal economic relationship now well defined by treaty and with an acid-rain accord in the offing, Canada can now, with greater vigour and use of resources, pursue new international goals.

In doing so, it is important, I would maintain, to avoid thinking of ourselves as a "middle power." The term gained currency in Canada, and indeed became a favourite of politicians and press, because it seemed modest and suggested that we belong comfortably in a large group of states that never has to risk the danger of being out-of-step. Being a middle power was thought to be appropriate for Canada and a guarantee of respectability. If we were condemning the Soviet Union, or knocking Uncle Sam, or criticizing Iraq, Iran, or Israel, or taking a stand on any number of controversial issues, Canadian politicians, and especially the diplomats, always wanted to be in good company. The position was, perhaps, not always as important as the group we were in.

But two things have happened to limit the usefulness of this rather shallow approach to foreign policy. One is that Canada is no longer a middle power. With the seventh largest economy in the non-Communist world, as a member of the Economic Summit Seven, as a leading member and architect of the modem Commonwealth and La Francophonie, with enough natural wealth to make us a natural resource superpower, as the home of many of the world's major and most aggressive multinationals, and, by some accounts, as one of the two largest foreign investors in the US, we are seen by other nations, more accurately, as a major power.

We need not fear taking international stands alone, or in the company of the few – that is to say, to be ahead of the pack or not running with it at all. We do not need to be in "good company" in taking any initiative or stance if we believe we are acting in our just interests. Multilateralism is a vital tool of international diplomacy – the world would be unthinkable without it – but we need not be overly concerned with middle-power politics.

A second factor bearing on the notion of being in "good company" is that we can no longer look at most of the Western European states as members of the company. The members of the European Community have long been forging a process through which they express, with one voice, a common foreign policy. Beyond that, and beyond the Unified Market of 1992, which will assuredly come about, the Europeans are forming a new supranationality, a European nation, the United States of Europe.

L'Europe des patries is dead, and at the forefront of those who have slain the dragon are, paradoxically, the French. This means that we cannot look to individual European nations to link up with in our middle-power collective. The Danes, the Spaniards, the Irish, not to mention the Germans, Italians, British, all now speak on the international stage with, in most instances, a single voice. A recent example was the recall of all European Community ambassadors from Iran following the Rushdie affair.

More and more, I submit, Canada will need to become accustomed to being outside of any grouping of the middle although we can certainly be leaders of the middle and will often, of course, vote with them. If we think of ourselves as a major power, as a major player, we will be more disposed, I believe, to act without the comfort-blanket of good company. Need one say it? The majority is not always right. Perhaps also the notion that we need not be minor players on the world scene will awaken a greater interest in our public and media and a larger intellectual commitment to understanding our foreign policy.

What is happening in Europe is perhaps one of the two or three most important political developments occurring in the world today. It is impossible to exaggerate the economic significance of the creation of the Western world's largest single market, nor the political significance of the emergence of a new European nation. These developments will occur, and the only uncertainty will be the answers to the following questions: What is Europe? Where from a political and economic standpoint does it end on its eastern glacis? Will we see the Europeanization of Germany's *ostpolitick*, as most think likely, or will we see the Germanization of European *ostpolitick*? What are the implications for German reunification and for the West in what may emerge as the first revision of the European political framework since Yalta?

All of these questions pose fundamental foreign policy challenges to Canada.

One cannot underestimate the unique historical significance of the European experience today. Our interests in that arena and in what is happening in the USSR and Eastern Europe, including the emergence of political pluralism, are surely as great, if not greater, than our interests in the period after 1945. For, in time, all the same basic issues will arise: the role and future of the military alliances, the future of Germany, the implications for defence strategies and weapons development, and so on.

To me, this suggests that Europe should become a principal focus of thought and analysis for our leaders and our most gifted practitioners and policy makers.

This need not take from attention to important regional issues, but we should understand that they are not the main act on the broad geopolitical stage. Europe shares main stage with Moscow, where epoch-making developments are occurring, as the Soviet leadership, under the leadership of one of the most remarkable individuals of our era, Michael Gorbachev, is de-legitimating, one after another, the Soviet leaders since Lenin.

No one, no expert or authority in any country, predicted that in the space of a few years Gorbachev would, in effect, have achieved *glasnost*. But *perestroika* is another matter. *Perestroika* means decentralization of economic decision making, and for this to occur there must be decentralization of political decision making. And this, in turn, means delegation to the ethnically dominated components of the USSR, in most of which major nationalist manifestations have already occurred. The danger of balkanization is clear.

Of course, no one can predict the future course of the USSR any more than we were able to predict the past course of events. But whether the Soviet Union is going to succeed in these grand domestic strategies, as we all hope; or, as some think, fail and fall into decline to some form of Ottomanization; or, as is perhaps possible, enter into a long period, possibly decades, of instability, the challenge to Western countries to define their policies will be equally great.

When the Soviet Union was locked into the long winter of sclerosis, we needed no new policies. Now we could, if we wished, allow ourselves to be simply bystanders in respect of what is happening in Moscow and the capitals of Eastern Europe. But it is not in the Canadian tradition to do so.

We are approaching what may well be the most significant reordering of political realities in Western and Eastern Europe and in East-West relations in a half-century or more. Canadians need to be far more cognizant of the magnitude of these events, develop our own creative ideas, and use our access and standing in international capitals – not least, Washington – to seek to encourage positively their future course.

We should clearly distance ourselves from some of the critics to the south and elsewhere who see the formation of a new European nation, and the final termination of the European civil war, as a zero-sum economy game and a grand protectionist ploy.

It has been said that the Soviet Union has *glasnost* and no *perestroika,* whereas China has no *glasnost* but does have *perestroika.* Perhaps a quarter of the economy of China is now privatized. With the ascendancy of Japan to global economic and financial primacy and its increasing domination of Far Eastern economies, and with the emergence of dynamic new Asian economies, our economic and trading relations with the major powers of the Far East take on exceptional importance.

As the United States seeks to examine the framework for its economic and trade relations with Japan, it becomes more pressing for us to do so. In the Pacific region, it may be premature to expect new forms of international political or economic association to emerge soon, but I believe this is an idea of long-term importance whose time may come soon. As a large Pacific nation with experience in institution building, Canada might be at the forefront of those exploring it.

Looking to another continent closer to home, we may have thought – we presumably have – that not joining the Organization of American States (OAS) was good for us. But was it good for the OAS or for political dispute settlement in Latin America? It is worth examining our somewhat half-hearted approach to Latin America and assessing the opportunities for new or reinvigorated regional political institutions.

Finally, as we look to the immediate south, it would be in Canada's interests to explore the possibility of new institutions to deal with nontrade disputes with the US. The force of pressure groups and special interests in modern democracies has grown so much and become so intense in the past two decades that pure political dispute settlement has become exceptionally difficult, almost impossible.

No democratic government seems prepared to incur the political wrath and ill will of local or other special-interest groups, whether they be potato farmers or lobster or herring fishermen or whatever, by agreeing to the position of the other side or by subordinating the local interest in favour of the national or the foreign relationship.

In short, conflicts of public policies affecting competing special interests on each side of the border are not soluble, in most instances, by negotiation. This is so whether the dispute relates to a resource, the environment, fisheries, boundary waters, or whatever. Objective bilateral dispute settlement is an idea whose time has come.

Moreover, now that Canada has reinstituted its acceptance of the World Court's compulsory jurisdiction, and pioneered in the modalities of its use, it would be timely to pursue ideas for strengthening procedures for judicial settlement of disputes in a multilateral format.

I make these particular suggestions as examples of opportunities and challenges for Canadian foreign policy in the years ahead. They are far from being the only subjects of priority concern: A more comprehensive list would include human rights, Third World indebtedness, the Middle East and other regional issues, the protection of the environment, an international verification capability for disarmament measures, and so on.

The epochal changes in East-West relations add great new pressures for a solution to regional issues. I believe it is true to say that the next decade may be the most significant one in the second half of this century and may produce the most far-reaching political changes. It is essential, therefore, that our government put its best minds, thinkers, and experts to a consideration of their significance for us.

Much emphasis has been given in the past two decades, and needed to be given, to the trade, national unity, and economic themes that dominated our agenda. Our diplomacy must recognize the continuing importance of these basic dimensions of our interests. But it is now time, I believe, to place new and increased emphasis on the broader, geopolitical skills of the sort with which Canadian diplomacy was so richly endowed in earlier years.

A half-century later, as the old order changes, we need the best and the brightest, the most learned and the most imaginative, to help guide us and plan our diplomacy. As intellectual capital was gathered across the nation some fifty years ago, perhaps it is again time for our capable cadres of diplomats to be enriched by knowledgeable people from different walks of national life who, having in their professional careers already acquired new capital from thinking, could add new perspectives on our foreign policy.

The main requirement, I believe, and it seems to me to be one of some urgency, is to re-establish in the heart of our diplomatic life a sharper and deeper focus on the broader political dimensions of international relations. Now is the time to widen our angle of vision.

If we re-establish the centrality of our foreign policy concerns, and if we enrich our cadres with new injections of intellectual capital, and if our governments give it the right priority, and if the public cares enough, we may yet witness another golden age of Canadian diplomacy.

ALLAN GOTLIEB is a senior consultant in the law firm of Stikeman Elliott. Formerly the Canadian ambassador to the United States and chairman of the Canada Council, Mr Gotlieb is also a director of several major corporations and has held a number of senior government posts. He is chairman of the Donner

Canadian Foundation; Canadian chairman and North American vice-chairman of the Trilateral Commission; and a member of the boards of the Canadian Institute for Advanced Research and of the governing council of the International Institute for Strategic Studies in London, England. A Rhodes Scholar who has written widely on international law and diplomacy, Mr Gotlieb was the 1989 W.L. Mackenzie King Visiting Professor at Harvard University.

Allan Gotlieb is a Companion of the Order of Canada and has received other such prestigious awards as the 1983 Outstanding Achievement Award from the Government of Canada, the Vinerian Prize from Oxford, and the Deak Prize from the Society of International Law.

23

Le Canada est-il viable ?
Il lui faudrait des prophètes...

LISE BISSONNETTE, 1991

En ces temps que l'on dit troublés, vous vous attendiez peut-être à ce que la directrice du *Devoir* soit fidèle à la tradition de ce journal, et vous entretienne des dernier développements de la querelle entre le Québec et le Canada. Jeune journaliste, j'ai eu parfois à remplacer mon directeur, M. Claude Ryan, qui s'adressait régulièrement à des auditoires comme celui-ci. Il ne prenait pas le temps de faire ce rhétorique et allait toujours, dès l'abord, à l'essentiel de ce qu'était pour lui la description des deux grands courants qui se disputaient l'adhésion de la société québécoise. « D'un côté la voie canadienne, » expliquait-il, « et de l'autre, la voie québécoise. » Il reprenait l'histoire de ce dilemme depuis la Confédération et incitait le Canada aux accommodements nécessaires pour faire triompher la voie canadienne, qui lui semblait raisonnable, sans que jamais il condamne vraiment l'autre.

Aujourd'hui, M. Ryan est ministre du gouvernement québécois et il a signé, il y a quinze jours, le rapport dit Bélanger-Campeau, du noms des co-présidents de la Commission sur l'avenir politique et constitutionnel du Québec. Et le discours est toujours le même, une hallucinante répétition. Il n'y a que deux voies pour le Québec, dit le rapport. Ce sont le fédéralisme renouvelé et la souveraineté. Si le Canada ne veut pas que le Québec choisisse le souveraineté, il peut toujours lui présenter des offres de renouvellement de la fédération. Le seul élément nouveau, par rapport aux anciens textes comme ceux de M. Ryan, c'est la stratégie. Autrefois, il n'était pas question de s'engager dans des négociations à l'extérieur des voies habituelles du dialogue et de la procédure traditionnelle d'amendement à la constitution. Aujourd'hui, la menace a largement remplacé le dialogue, et le

Québec refuse de reprendre les négociations à onze, qui ont lamentablement failli l'année dernière. Il utilise plutôt l'ultimatum : s'il n'y a pas d'accord, il tiendra un referendum sur la souveraineté au plus tard en 1992.

Au plan stratégique, donc, on bouge. Au plan intellectuel, l'enlisement est toujours le même. C'est un phénomène éprouvant, corrosif, déprimant. Je relisais, il y a quelques jours, des textes des années soixante, parus dans le célèbre revue *Cité Libre,* et repris dans une anthologie tout juste publiée aux Éditions Stanké. Le débat entre les nationalistes, qu'on n'appelait pas encore souverainistes, et les fédéralistes, qui occupaient toujours avec arrogance le haut du pavé, était vif, passionné, producteur de ferment intellectuel. Peut-être était-ce que le combat n'avait pas encore gagné la classe politique où ses protagonistes allaient le porter avec le passage de Pierre Trudeau et de Gérard Pelletier au gouvernement fédéral. Peut-être était-ce tout simplement que le débat était jeune, que les automatismes des répliques mutuelles n'étaient pas encore maîtrisés. Quoi qu'il en soit, ce duel respirait le plaisir. Ce n'est plus le cas. Je ne connais guère plus de gens au Québec, même chez les plus engagés politiquement, qui trouvent encore stimulant d'expliquer ou défendre leur thèse. Tout a été dit, semble-t-il, et reprendre ces descriptions relève du pire pensum.

Je ne les reprendrai pas. La guerre des absolus est terminée. L'on sait aujourd'hui qu'il n'y aura de solution confédérale que si le Canada consent au Québec un espace suffisant d'autonomie, et qu'il n'y aura pas de souveraineté sans liens d'interdépendance avec le Canada. Personne ne sait encore quelle forme ce compromis inévitable prendra, ni par quels tourments il faudra passer pour y arriver, ni les coûts que nous aurons tous à assumer. Quant au fond du débat sur les mérites respectifs des deux options, il y a perdu son sens justement parce que la solution sera un entre-deux. Sauf chez certains attardés des anciennes joutes intellectuelles, personne ne saurait prétendre avoir le monopole de la vertu.

Le débat, en somme, a perdu sa virginité. Un peu comme en Europe, où les textes visionnaires de Jean Monnet, le père de l'union européenne, ne servent plus qu'à ornementer les réceptions officielles. Nous sommes entrés dans l'ère du design industriel des sociétés. Un jeu de briques, de tuyaux, de passerelles où chacun cherche à se tailler la niche la plus confortable, avec la vue la plus belle. Toutes nos discussions sont stratégiques, et toutes nos solutions sont mécaniques.

Voyez le rapport Allaire, du Parti Libéral du Québec, ou celui de la Commission Bélanger-Campeau, dont je parlais ci-haut. Ils vont peut-être faire débloquer la crise, parce qu'ils proposent, pour l'essentiel, un échéancier, un débat référendaire, des moyens d'amener la population à trancher. Ce sont des rapports instrumentaux. Il en va de même pour la commission mixte sur la formule d'amendement de la constitution, le comité Beaudoin-Edwards. Elle porte sur les moyens. J'ose à peine évoquer la commission Spicer, cette fumisterie qui prétend chercher le sens même que les citoyens donnent au débat, et qui est devenue un vaste laboratoire de manipulation des émotions publiques à l'aide de gadgets techniques.

Les prochains dix-huit mois seront à l'image des dernières semaines. Nous nous passionnerons pour cet énorme jeu d'échecs. Il ressemblera au suspense qui a entouré les derniers moments des accords du lac Meech. Les meilleurs stratèges gagneront. C'est un jeu nécessaire, remarquez, qui commandera notre vigilance et la plus grande rigueur d'analyse, puisqu'il y va de changements institutionnels importants, qui auront un effet sur la vie des citoyens. Mais admettons qu'il ne présente plus guère de défi intellectuel. Je me surprends, de plus en plus, à le commenter sans conviction.

Je définirai ici brièvement ma position, comme point de référence. La logique de l'impossibilité d'un projet canadien satisfaisant au plan politique, me fait souhaiter un maximum de souveraineté pour le Québec, dans un arrangement plus sain et plus égalitaire avec le Canada. Je suis prête à défendre le sens de cette option. Je voie le gouvernement fédéral envahir le milieu de l'éducation, de la culture, s'apprêter à imposer des normes pan-canadiennes dans les services sociaux et de santé, tout cela sous la poussé d'une opinion canadienne dont je comprends les angoisses. Je ne veux pas de ce contrôle grandissant du gouvernement central canadien sur les institutions québécoises, qui se sont développées selon leur logique propre, leur dynamisme propre, et qui n'ont besoin ni de cet envahissement, ni de cette tutelle éventuellement. Je comprends le projet « national » que chérissent tant de mes amis du Canada anglais, qui mettent leurs espoirs dans un état fort, distinct de son voisin américain, capable de porter en entier un grand projet de société. Mais je ne peux le partager. Au *Devoir* et ailleurs, je défendrai donc les solutions qui m'apparaîtront garantir la plus grande autonomie au Québec, et des arrangements mutuels raisonnables avec le Canada. Je sais que ce ne sera ni simple, ni bref, ni indolore. Et je n'aurai d'autre comme choix que de m'intéresser à la stratégie et à la mécanique.

Mais le défi intellectuel se situera ailleurs. Qu'on le veuille ou non, que nos deux sociétés soient vaguement séparées ou vaguement unies, elles devront tout de même s'interpénétrer, ou du moins se comprendre. Je suis fascinée par ces à-côtés du débat qui n'ont presque pas bougé depuis un quart de siècle, ou du moins depuis que la Commission royale sur le bilinguisme et le biculturalisme, la commission Laurendeau-Dunton, a tenté d'expliquer une société à l'autre et a exposé, ad nauseam, l'ampleur de nos inguérissables malentendus. Tout se passe comme si la guerre constitutionnelle avait paralysé une part de notre intelligence.

Encore une fois, je compare le Canada à l'Europe, où les discussions entre nations ont donné lieu à un immense brassage d'idées sur la question des nationalités, des identités, du passage commun au troisième millénaire. Les préjugés, les résistances, le racisme même ne sont pas absents des débats européens, mais ils sont sans cesse battus en brèche par les transformations politiques. Le mouvement politique et économique les laisses derrière. On l'a vu dans le cas de la réunification de l'Allemagne, et dans le refonte des constitutions des pays de l'Est. Je ne dis pas que les guerres entre ethnies sont terminées, ni que l'Européen moyen ne pense pas le pire de ses voisins. Mais tout cela ne semble pas inhiber la capacité de changer, et profondément, et rapidement, les institutions qui doivent l'être.

Au Canada, au contraire, c'est le débat sur les institutions qui nourrit les stéréotypes. C'est là, me semble-t-il, l'un de ses effets les plus pervers. Au lieu de mener au changement, il fige les vieilles conceptions que nous nous faisons de nous-mêmes et des autres, jusqu'à ce que ces préjugés, qui sont le plus souvent des mythes, empêchent à leur tour tout mouvement.

On n'en finirait pas de débusquer toutes les fausses perceptions qui ont cours, et qui ne sont pas loin de relever du terrorisme intellectuel pour bloquer toute perspective de règlement. Je suis tout particulièrement frappée par la perception mutuellement négative que nous entretenons à propos de nos deux nationalismes, canadien et québécois. Dans les deux cas, nous avons probablement affaire à des mouvements dynamiques, porteurs de progrès et de projets originaux. Par example, dans la mesure où il ne relève pas de l'anti-américanisme primaire, le nationalisme canadien a certainement été le moteur intellectuel de l'affirmation, au nord du 49ᵉ parallèle, d'un pays nord-américain attaché à ses institutions distinctes et capable, quoi qu'on en dise chez les féroces adversaires du gouvernement actuel, de mener une politique interne et internationale relativement autonomes. Au Québec, ce nationalisme canadien est presque universellement perçu comme une pesanteur historique, ainsi qu'une réaction de défense contre la diversité, notamment celle qu'impose la présence du Québec. En cette fin de vingtième siècle, on n'est pas loin de percevoir le nationalisme canadien comme une simple version contemporaine de la vieille proposition de Lord Durham.

À l'inverse, on ne peut nier que le nationalisme québécois, depuis la Révolution tranquille, a été dans l'ensemble une immense force de progrès économique, social, politique, et qu'il le demeure. Dans la mesure où on ne cesse de souhaiter à tous les peuples de la terre qu'ils prennent en main leur propre développement, c'est exactement ce que le Québec a fait et continue de faire, même si sa classe entrepreneuriale semble désormais plus active à cet égard, que ses classes technocratique et intellectuelle. Pourtant ce nationalisme vigoureux – et je me promène suffisamment à travers le Canada pour pouvoir en témoigner – est encore perçu, et peut-être plus que jamais, comme un relent de tribalisme du dix-neuvième siècle, une force de résistance au mouvement mondial d'osmose entre les peuples.

Afin de parler plus concrètement, prenons le débat de 1988 sur le libre-échange, qui se poursuit encore, et qui va reprendre maintenant que les pourparlers s'engagent à inclure le Mexique dans la libéralisation du commerce nord-américain. Comme une bonne partie de l'élite canadienne-anglaise s'opposait à une telle ouverture des frontières avec les États-Unis, et que la proposition fédérale a rencontré beaucoup de résistance hors Québec, il est fréquent d'entendre dire, dans les cercles intellectuels québécois, que le nationalisme canadien est protectionniste, frileux, nostalgique et sans audace. Qu'il ne reconnaît pas les nouvelles réalités du village planétaire, qu'il veut protéger artificiellement des institutions culturelles qui ne survivraient pas autrement – comme Radio-Canada par exemple – et qu'il boude le meilleur de ce que l'Amérique libérale à offrir. Tout cela alors que le reste du monde, y compris les toutes nouvelles démocraties, reprend le flambeau des valeurs de liberté qui ont fleuri de ce côté de l'Atlantique.

Prenons ensuite le débat sur la loi 178, la législation linguistique qui a amendé la célèbre loi 101 au Québec, en passant outre à un jugement de la Cour suprême qui donnait le feu vert à l'affichage commercial dans les deux langues. La population québécoise francophone a alors largement manifesté son appui à la loi 101, et ses élites ont retrouvé, pour l'occasion, une part de leur militantisme des années soixante-dix. On en a conclu, au Canada anglais, que le nationalisme québécois est toujours protectionniste, frileux, nostalgiques et sans audace, qu'il n'ose pas se colleter au village planétaire et qu'il refuse la coexistence multilingue à laquelle l'Europe, par exemple, adhère de façon innovatrice.

Chacun, donc, impute à l'autre la résistance réactionnaire. Et chacun se définit par contraste *la* force de mouvement, le porteur des lumières. Un échantillon extra-ordinaire de cette sorte de pensée manichéenne, qui invente la stéréotype selon les besoins, se trouve dans le récent article de Rick Salutin dans la dernière livraison du magazine *Saturday Night*, une publication que j'adore pour la perspective anthropologique qu'elle fournit sur le Canada, et ceci souvent inconsciemment. Pour M. Salutin, qui n'y va pas de main morte, le Québec contemporain a délaissé son nationalisme de gauche des années soixante, celui pour lequel il avait personnellement de l'amitié et peut-être un brin de sympathie agissante. Il serait plutôt passé à un neo-nationalisme de droite qui soumet la société aux entrepreneurs, et qui embrasse le libre-échange pour participer à la mesquinerie de l'univers que l'Amérique a hérité de Ronald Reagan. Pendant ce temps, dit-il, le Canada pour sa part abandonne son vieux fond colonial et conservateur, et choisit plutôt la compassion et l'ouverture. L'Ontario, symbole même de l'immuabilité, ne vient-elle pas de faire confiance au Nouveau Parti démocratique tandis que d'autres provinces s'apprêtent à en faire autant?

Bien sûr, on pourrait démolir cet échafaudage simplement en soufflant dessus. Le nationalisme progressiste que M. Salutin a rencontré au Québec il y a quinze ans était plus fermé et plus frileux que celui des jeunes Québécois d'aujourd'hui N'importe quelle comparaison de discours ou les archive des mouvements indépendantistes, le montrerait éloquemment. Quant à la conversion canadienne au socialisme, nous porterons jugement alors que les électeurs ontariens l'auront ratifiée majoritairement, ce qui était loin d'être le cas aux dernières élections provinciales. Il faut sûrement lire ce courant en même temps que celui de la montée du Reform Party partout ailleurs dans l'Ouest. Rien, dans cette contradiction, n'est jamais aussi simple que les stéréotypes, anciens ou nouveau, permettent de la croire.

(J'ajouterai que si M. Salutin se lançait dans le même type d'exercice en essayant cette fois de départager les Noirs des Blancs, plutôt que les Québécois des Canadiens, on aurait vite fait de le conspuer chez la gauche qu'il fréquente et de lui indiquer qu'il est sur la pente du racisme. Une pente douce, mais une pente dangereuse tout de même. C'est pourquoi il faut toujours se méfier des caractérisations collectives, même quand elles sont tentantes aux fins de discussion politique. Et j'admets qu'en nous accrochant à la notion de « société distincte, » à des fins politiques aussi, nous nous somme rendus vulnérables à ce genre d'accident.)

Outre le fait qu'elles me répugnent, ces discussions semblent aussi brouiller les pistes pour l'avenir. C'est ainsi qu'en collant à une caractérisation négative, on peut se permettre de prédire qu'un Québec souverain, par exemple, ne respecterait sûrement pas les droits des minorités aussi bien que le Canada et que, tout imbu de ses intérêts collectifs, il traiterait plus légèrement les libertés individuelles. Rarement a-t-on vu d'accusations plus gratuites, venant de gens qui ont tout de même, pour la plupart, soutenu la violation des libertés fondamentales par la Loi fédérale des mesures de guerre, en octobre 1970 !

Personne ne peut prédire comment évoluera une collectivité, et ce encore moins dans les sociétés démocratiques comme la nôtre, où nul ne peut imposer de système de valeurs. On ne peut certainement pas projeter tout simplement le présent dans le futur, sans s'adonner à un déterminisme primaire. Ce qui est intéressant, et possible, c'est d'essayer plutôt de déceler les courants souterrains qui annoncent la transformation des valeurs. Sur ce plan, ce ne sont ni les résultats d'élections, ni les déclarations de l'*establishment* politique ou intellectuel du jour qui fournissent les meilleurs indices. Partout au monde, c'est l'univers de la création qui devance la société, la conteste, initie les ruptures, et c'est lui qui annonce les tendances, toujours diverses, qui agiteront plus tard une société.

Je ne tenterai pas ici de décoder ce que seront les valeurs des Canadiens au tournant du prochain millénaire. Je ne suis pas assez branchée sur l'ensemble du milieu culturel canadien pour me livrer à cet exercice périlleux. Mais je souhaiterais que plusieurs de mes collègues le fassent, au Canada, et nous livrent un portrait plus nuancé des courants qui se préparent à monter au pays. Quelques échos, tout au plus, me font croire qu'on met actuellement en cause les milieux littéraires, le vieux mythe intégrateur de la «survie,» celui que définissait Margaret Atwood, pour s'éclater dans des visions beaucoup plus audacieuses et libérantes, qui ne renieront peut-être plus très longtemps l'américanité profonde du Canada. Ou peut-être est-ce que le vieux folklore de la diversité et du multiculturalisme est en train de se réinterpréter et d'amener une confrontation des cultures plutôt qu'une coexistence indifférente.

Mais je n'irai pas plus loin sans risquer de tomber, à mon tour, dans le tourisme intellectuel dont je déplore la pratique trop poussée envers le Québec. Je tenterai tout simplement d'ouvrir une fenêtre sur les valeurs que brassent les milieux québécois de création, ceux qui forgent les ruptures dont nous avons besoin pour évoluer et qui nous disent peut-être à quoi nous ressemblerons demain.

Le Québec des années soixante, celui de la Révolution tranquille, nul ne pouvait le prévoir, même au milieu des années cinquante, si on s'en tenait au discours de surface. C'était encore une société massivement cléricale, qui paraissait soumise, attachée à ses institutions autoritaires, repliée sur ses valeurs familiales. Rétroactivement, on peut pourtant retrouver, dans les milieux de l'art et de la création, et plus largement dans les milieux intellectuels contestataires, toutes les nouvelles valeurs qui en ont fait, à la vitesse de l'éclair, une société largement laïque, matérialiste, boulimique de changement, de consommation urbaine et de satisfaction individuelle.

Dans un ouvrage remarquable intitulé *L'entrée dans la modernité* (Éditions Saint-Martin, 1986), le sociologue Marcel Fournier propose justement d'aller au delà de l'observation du virage idéologique qui s'opérait au Québec au milieu du siècle, de la vague constatation de la popularité croissante du progressisme qui s'opposait au conservatisme ambiant. En s'attachant aux œuvres des individus qui ont été porteurs de changement, il retrouve en filigrane les valeurs mêmes qui seront beaucoup plus tard les grands credos de la Révolution tranquille. Ce à quoi on assistait, dit-il, c'est la modification «du rapport à la réalité.» L'engouement pour l'empirisme, la fascination pour la technique et la méthode apparaissent en milieu universitaire avec la première génération de chercheurs scientifiques professionnels et se répendra petit à petit dans les nouvelles facultés de sciences sociales, où la préoccupation humaniste des fondateurs cède bientôt aux tenants du fonctionnalisme, qui ne jurent plus que par les instruments à développer pour agir sur l'univers politique. Le lettré dominait jusque là l'univers intellectuel; il est remplacé par le savant, le naturaliste, le producteur de connaissances objectives. Partout, on commence à récuser les doctrines pour ne plus jurer, dans tous les domaines, que par les enquêtes sur le terrain, par la vérification objective. C'est par là qu'il faut passer pour comprendre pourquoi, dix ou quinze ans plus tard, le Québec se modernisera en devenant une immense technocratie. Après avoir été l'idée centrale de l'avant-garde intellectuelle qui combattait la noirceur du duplessisme, la foi en l'instrument allait devenir le credo de la nouvelle classe dominante, ces intellectuels et commis de l'État en croissance qu'on allait appeler les « nouveaux clercs. »

Il en va de même dans le domaine des arts, de la création proprement dite. Là aussi, et plus encore, le changement du rapport à la réalité annonce le futur. L'automatisme, le mouvement qu'anime Borduas et qui culmine en 1949 avec le célèbre manifeste du *Refus global*, a été conspué jusque dans le *Devoir*. Mais il n'y a pas de meilleure source pour comprendre ce qui méduse souvent les historiens, la rapidité avec laquelle le Québec abandonnera tout l'appareil doctrinaire religieux qui a encadré la société presque jusqu'au milieu des années soixante et qui était pourtant disparu en 1970. Borduas et son groupe, c'est évidemment une revendication de liberté totale, mais c'est aussi un discours sur la méthode, et cette méthode, c'est la libération des forces intérieures comme mode de connaissance du monde. Quand ma génération est arrivée à maturité, à la toute fin des années soixante, rien ne décrivait mieux la jeunesse québécoise active ou militante que le refus profond de toute rationalité imposée de source externe. On nous aurait dit que Paul-Émile Borduas était notre maître et nous aurions été étonnés. Pour la plupart, nous ne savions même pas qui il était. « Le Canada français moderne commence avec lui, » écrivait Pierre Vadeboncœur dans *La ligne du risque*, un essai capital paru une vingtaine d'année après le *Refus global*.

Certes, l'exercice de détection des valeurs structurantes d'une société est plus facile quand on le fait à rebours, quand on sait quels créateurs, quels milieux de pensée, quels contestataires ont réussi à mener des courants jusqu'à leur terme, jusqu'à une domination à leur tour. Mais on peut au moins faire quelques hypothèses sur le changement de rapport à la réalité qu'on peut observer dans les milieux actuels d'avant-garde intellectuelle ou artistique. Et si ces courants se développent pour devenir des fleuves, le Québec de l'an 2000 ne ressemblera pas à celui qu'on prédit aujourd'hui en projetant trop simplement le présent dans le futur. J'oserai formuler quelques hypothèses, quelque pistes sans plus.

Ceux qui mettent en cause les valeurs dominantes, à l'université – et ils ne sont pas encore très nombreux – font preuve d'une remarquable imperméabilité à l'idéologie sous toutes ses formes, et tendent à poser les problèmes contemporains en termes de choix moraux, qu'il faut bien distinguer de choix moralisants. Les militantistes intellectuels, même les plus nobles comme on en trouve dans les mouvements pacifistes ou écologistes, commencent à faire l'objet d'un contestation qui confine au mépris. On dit beaucoup, c'est la mode à Paris en tout cas, que nous assistons déjà à la fin des idéologies. Je crois plutôt que nous y sommes toujours, elles sont simplement plus multiples et s'annulent l'une l'autre, comme on vient de le voir dans le débat autour de la guerre du Golfe.

Que sera un monde où les idéologies seront vraiment battues en brèche ? J'ai de la difficulté à l'imaginer. Mais on peut penser que cela aura un effet sur la conduite des affaires politiques, et notamment sur la nationalisme comme système de pensée. Cela ne veut pas dire qu'il disparaîtra, mais qu'une autre génération pourrait le subordonner à des impératifs sociaux plus larges. Évidemment, ce serait encore plus plausible dans un Québec devenu indépendant.

Je suis cependant encore plus fascinée par ce que j'observe dans les milieux artistiques, dont je suis plus proche encore. Au moins deux phénomènes sont en train de bouleverser l'univers connu. L'un est le métissage qui s'opère à la fois par la rencontre et l'osmose, en milieu urbain, de diverses traditions culturelles. Mais plus profondément ce métissage s'impose à l'individu-artiste en soi, dans sa propre réflexion. À la différence de Borduas, il repart à la recherche de principes externes pour contester le temps présent, le lieu présent. Ce n'est plus un refus, c'est un quête, celle d'un ailleurs, de toutes les étrangetés qu'on veut s'approprier. Le théâtre, la littérature, la musique, les arts plastiques disent tous des choses qui prennent racine dans l'ici et le maintenant. L'autre phénomène est le refus du collectif. La rage est individuelle, intime, feutrée, pleine de murmures plutôt que de grandes paroles.

J'ose à peine évoquer le Québec éclaté, moins parleur, que ces avant-gardes semblent annoncer. Son énergie me semble désormais plus physique qu'intellectuelle et c'est peut-être nécessaire pour absorber tous les chocs externes que cette société semble vouloir attirer. Chose certaine, je ne vois pas comment on pourrait prédire de repli, de fermeture, d'obsession de frontière pour le Québec de la nouvelle génération, celle qui fera ou héritera d'un pays plus autonome, sinon souverain, en Amérique du Nord.

De cette réflexion, je ne tire pas beaucoup de leçons pratiques pour résoudre le petit drame canadien dont nous faisons, tous ensemble, un grand drame. Je constate simplement qu'un peu plus d'attention aux valeurs souterraines, qui seront bientôt des valeurs montantes, aurait peut-être permis d'éviter quelques uns de nos pires malentendus d'il y a plus de vingt ans, alors que le débat constitutionnel a repris au beau milieu de la Révolution tranquille. La lecture que l'on faisait alors du Québec, ailleurs au Canada, était fondée sur des projections des années cinquante, sur la peur d'un nationalisme de droite, sur Maurice Duplessis, qui n'avait plus grand chose à voir avec celui des générations qui accédaient au pouvoir. J'irais même jusqu'à dire que le Canada n'a pas su profiter, au tout début des années soixante, d'une période de grâce où les nouvelles valeurs technocratiques, laïques, et empiriques, transcendaient le nationalisme chez bien des individus qui venaient de triompher de l'obscurantisme et qui regardaient l'ancien nationalisme avec méfiance. Faute de voir ce changement et de donner au nouveau dynamisme québécois l'espace dont il avait besoin pour se développer à l'intérieur du Canada, comme il le réclamait à l'époque, on a fait de la résistance jusqu'à ce que renaisse, au sein des groupes de progrès, un nationalisme plus éclairé, mieux outillé, mieux articulé qui atteint aujourd'hui les dimensions d'un mouvement de masse.

Ce n'est pas pour rien qu'instinctivement, quand on critique le leadership politique contemporain, on se plaint de l'absence de gens de vision. C'est un manque que l'on cherche à combler par l'utopie, comme fut le cas quand le Canada confondit les obsessions de Pierre Trudeau avec une vision d'avenir. La vision, c'est la capacité de lire une société, de voir s'esquisser les tendances porteuses de développement et d'articuler des solutions réalistes en même temps qu'inspirantes. C'est beaucoup demander à la classe politique, qui se débat comme elle peut dans la crise, que de mener parallèlement une telle réflexion. Mais on pourrait l'attendre de la classe intellectuelle, dont c'est le métier et le devoir, envers et contre tout, de tenter d'être prophète en son propre pays.

C'est pourquoi je vous remercie vivement d'avoir accueilli mon début de réflexion sur ce vaste sujet, et de vouloir la partager dans la discussion qui va suivre.

LISE BISSONNETTE has served as president and CEO of La grande bibliothèque du Québec since 1998. She spent many years at the influential Montreal daily newspaper *Le Devoir* as a journalist, editor, and editor-in-chief. After leaving the paper, she wrote as an independent journalist, columnist, and consultant for both French- and English-language media in Canada. In 1991 Ms Bissonnette returned to *Le Devoir* as publisher. She is the author of four works of fiction, published in both English and French, and two collections of essays.

Lise Bissonnette was inducted into the Canadian Journalism Hall of Fame, is an Officer of l'Ordre national du Québec, and has been named a member of l'Ordre de la Pléiade (of La Francophonie) and of the Légion d'honneur de France. She is the recipient of several awards, including a lifetime achievement award from the Académie des lettres du Québec and five honorary doctorates from universities in Canada and the United States.

24

The Survival of Canada through Broadcasting

BERNARD OSTRY, 1992

Remembering the example of Alan Plaunt, who in his short, unselfish, and useful life accomplished more than most gifted persons can achieve in a normal lifespan, we may remind ourselves that the dangers to our country that Alan Plaunt confronted so effectively have again become grave and threatening. Not only dangers to the polity and economy, though they too are at risk, but of the multiplying threats to our cultural and national integrity posed by the babel not just from outside our borders, but from outer space. I don't want to sound like a science fictioneer howling and boding in the latter days of the second millennium, but there are dangers in the uncontrollable advance of communications technology. Though they may not seem material and concrete, they're nonetheless real. But where there is danger there is opportunity, and this is part of the lesson of Alan Plaunt's life.

Consider what Canada was like when Plaunt returned from Oxford and his travels in 1929. The bubble of prosperity had burst; it was a time of depression, shock, poverty. That alone would make the period worth examining, in many ways so like our own. The most striking thing is young Plaunt's scale of priorities.

He came of an Ottawa timber dynasty; he was well heeled, a scion of wealth and privilege. According to Michael Nolan's study, *Foundations*, Alan seemed to his family a little on the pink side, if not what Oxford contemporaries would have called a Bollinger Bolshie. Like many of his call and generation he was a nationalist, but he also felt deeply for victims of the Depression and seems to have been remarkably free of any sort of bigotry. And perhaps this social conscience was the most striking thing about him at the threshold of his career.

He could not have seemed particularly promising. At University College, Toronto, he had scored Cs; at Christ Church College, Oxford, he'd graduated with third-class honours. But at both universities, as at his secondary schools, he had made many friends who would go on to positions of influence in business, politics, labour, and the public service. Our generation imagines that it invented networking, but I doubt if Canada has ever seen an exercise of that kind more far-reaching and effective than the campaign put on by Graham Spry and Alan Plaunt in the early days of the Canadian Radio League.

Alan Plaunt also showed an early interest in Canadian culture, in the arts: The Group of Seven and the poetry of F.R. Scott and Dorothy Livesay were among his enthusiasms. Some thought him anti-British – Oxford sometimes had that effect on Canadians. Among Plaunt's close friends were several Rhodes Scholars: D.A. (Sandy) Skelton, Stephen Cartwright, and A.E. (Dal) Grauer. All were well connected, as Rhodes Scholars tend to be. The most important Rhodes Scholar in Plaunt's life was to be Graham Spry, with whom as I said he was to join in forming the Canadian Radio League, their brilliantly successful lobby and agitation for national and public broadcasting in Canada. Spry was a Westerner as well as a nationalist, with a prairie man's boldness to seek radical solutions. And like Plaunt, he came to know everybody.

It is remarkable how much our historic development owes to a few visionary persons. We can think of our modern Canadian story as having three stages. The first was that of the CPR, of the railway confederation that linked the far-flung colonies of British North America and set them on the path to nationhood. The vision of Sir John A. Macdonald, D'Arcy McGee, and a handful of others brought it about. The second stage was that of radio, where Plaunt and Spry showed the way to cultural development and national integrity and to the subtle, but essential connections between them. And the third is the present age, when our Siamese twins of communications technologies – now cultural communications – and the political community we call Canada venture out into the world from our home base. The first stage is familiar to us. I shall speak about the second stage before considering how we are faring and what we should be doing in the third stage.

To return to the point raised earlier about Plaunt's priorities. His first interest, after graduating, was in international affairs. In 1929 he attended a conference in Kyoto on the effects of industrialization on Asian countries. After that Plaunt took the Trans-Siberian Express to Moscow and had a look at the new Soviet Union, then of great interest to minds troubled by the Great Depression. He might have gone into leftist politics, as later did Graham Spry and F.R. Scott, another Rhodes Scholar. Instead, Plaunt took up a cultural and national cause: the quest for public broadcasting.

Radio broadcasting had been developing throughout the 1920s in ways more or less haphazard. As Frank Peers tells us in his history *The Politics of Canadian Broadcasting, 1920–1951,* "From the beginning, Canadians listened to American stations more than to their own." Americans had been quick to see openings for profit. Yet their leaders recognized the dangers. In 1922 Secretary of Commerce Herbert Hoover said it was "inconceivable that we should allow so great a possibility for service ... to be drowned in advertising chatter." In 1929 President Roosevelt hoped that Canada would not let broadcasting develop haphazardly, but would learn from the American experience "and establish a system that would serve the community, and that radio be organized from the beginning on a basis of public service." Despite these American views from on high, nothing was done.

There was little commercial competition from the Canadian side. Private stations at first did not expect to profit from broadcasting.

The Radio Telegraph Act of 1913 gave Ottawa responsibility for issuing licenses but not the power to control content. When, therefore, in 1928 Canadian religious broadcasters began savaging and bad-mouthing each other, the public uproar forced the government to think again. After a debate in the Commons, in which the sole member to raise the spectre of American control was J.S. Woodsworth, Prime Minister King took the usual course. He appointed a royal commission; it was imperative to remove this contentious matter from the political arena.

Two of the three commissioners were men who might have been suspected of a bias toward commercial broadcasting: Sir John Aird, president of the Canadian Bank of Commerce, and Dr Augustin Frigon, an electrical engineer and educator whose experience with public bodies had left him with unfavourable impressions of their competence. The third, Charles Bowman, editor of the *Ottawa Citizen*, was on record as favouring public broadcasting. After hearing briefs and witnesses, the commissioners were struck by the extent of anxiety in the country about American dominance of the air. They were also impressed by the British public broadcasting system, the BBC under John Reith, when compared with the American alternative.

The Aird report, submitted in September 1929, observed that the commission had found unanimity on one proposition: that Canadian radio listeners wanted Canadian broadcasting. Canadians and their country "could be adequately served only by some form of public ownership, operation and control behind which is the national power and prestige of the whole public of the Dominion of Canada."

The report was clear and decisive. In October 1930 Alan Plaunt and Graham Spry formed the Canadian Radio League and began organizing opinion in favour of implementing the report. Plaunt was now twenty-six; Spry was thirty. Their success in lobbying and focusing opinion on a vital national issue demonstrates that one does not have to be a venerable old party to get things done. Energy and dedication, backed by vigorous networking, were to carry the issue. Graham Spry, as secretary of the Association of Canadian Clubs, was well known to business and civic leaders across the country. Plaunt, too, had extraordinary access to the panjandrums of business, academe, and politics; he was also at ease with union bosses, workers, and farmers. Both young men came of mixed British and French stock. Plaunt had the additional advantage of private means. Both took to the task of agitation with something like glee.

A design by Quebec, backed by Ontario, to assert jurisdiction over broadcasting was forestalled when the Federal Radio Act of 1927 was upheld by the Supreme Court. Quebec's appeal to the judicial committee of the Imperial Privy Council was quashed in 1932. The arguments that finally laid down the law had been framed by Brooke Claxton, a Radio League activist, with Plaunt's help.

While these proceedings were underway, debate raged throughout Canada on the issue of public versus commercial broadcasting. In effect it was the same debate that has been continuing ever since.

Opposition to the Aird proposals was organized by the Canadian Broadcasting Association and by American interests. But in hindsight the most striking thing about the agitation is the massive grassroots support the league received. Not that Plaunt and Spry were kicking down an open door; without their efforts the fight for public broadcasting might have been lost. Powerful interests were arrayed against it. Even more remarkable is that, at a time when governments as well as citizens were broke, two deeply conservative prime ministers could be made to see and act upon the need to respond to a cultural concern.

The Conservative government of R.B. Bennett introduced the Canadian Radio Broadcasting Act of 1932, a decisive step toward national broadcasting. But it was a halting step. Instead of setting up a semi-independent crown corporation, the act created the Canadian Broadcasting Commission, essentially an organ of government. Radio was still under the authority of the minister of marine, still at sea as it were, and if the commissioners had a problem I suppose they could tell it to the marines.

The first chairman of the new commission was Hector Charlesworth, editor of *Saturday Night* magazine, a drama critic who had been converted at the eleventh hour from his long opposition to public broadcasting, publishing his recantation at the same moment that he asked for the job!

The commission's broadcasts in French to Western Canada set off an uproar. It was understandable that where almost no one understood French and no other Canadian programs were available, there would be discontent. In any case the commission began programming separately in the two languages – French voices for Quebec and the isolated pockets of French speakers scattered across the other provinces, English for the rest of Canada – a practice continued by its successor, the Canadian Broadcasting Corporation. Thus the institution designed to unite the country deepened its divisions.

It's no wonder many came to believe that the concepts of Quebec sovereignty and independence were hatched in federal broadcasting institutions and that the CBC would become Rene Levesque's forcing-bed and soapbox.

It's worth thinking about the implications. One point is immediately clear. The awakening of Quebec from its long colonial sleep was primarily a cultural arousal. The other implication is that since all our cultural institutions have had to function in a similar dualism, associate sovereignty for Quebec in cultural matters was reinforced early in our history. It may also be hazarded that this cultural sovereignty could have been safeguarded and developed only within a democratic political confederation.

Since the Conservatives showed no intention of reforming their broadcasting structure, the Radio League went to work among the Liberal opposition. Brooke Claxton helped Plaunt prepare a twenty-four-page memorandum on Canadian broadcasting reorganization, which Plaunt discussed with C.D. Howe when the Liberals returned to power in 1935.

Plaunt's memo stressed the need for political independence, for a board of governors as a buffer to protect the executive, and for a single chief executive in charge of operation. In a passage originally drafted by Graham Spry (who had left the Radio League to help found the Cooperative Commonwealth Federation [CCF]) the memo suggested that broadcasting could supply something all other media had failed to generate: "a glowing spirit of nationality."

A few days after agreeing with Plaunt's proposal, Howe was backing off. He was entertaining proposals from private broadcasters that the government concern itself only with regulation, leaving broadcasting to the commercial interests. They were raising an objection that would be heard often in the years to come: that it was not fair to be regulated by their competitor.

The original intention of the broadcasting legislation, however, was that private and public broadcasters would all be part of the same national system and subject to the same direction. In such a system private and public broadcasters would not be competitors but complementary services. But since the CBC, unlike the Canadian Broadcasting Commission, was selling advertising, it was hard for private broadcasters intent on profit to call it anything but a competitor.

In the event, the Canadian Broadcasting Act of 1936 was close to the draft originally proposed by Plaunt and Claxton. Peers tells us, "In July 1936, it looked almost as if there was a consensus on what the Canadian broadcasting system should be."

The dangers to a public system come from two quarters: first, from the commercial interests hampered by it; second, from political interference. The newly constituted CBC coped well with the commercial threat. Plaunt was one of the governors, and the new chairman, Leonard Brockington, a feisty and eloquent Welshman, was of one mind with him on principles. The general manager was Gladstone Murray, who had learned his trade and developed his backbone at the BBC under the redoubtable Lord Reith. As for the political threat, when C.D. Howe tried to bring the fledgling CBC under his control, he was effectively balked by Brockington, whose vigorous defence of turf was matched by clear formulations of principle.

Here is Brockington on nationalization: "If radio in Canada had not been nationalized the great American chains would have dominated Canada." And here he is on independence: "We are not part of the government of Canada. We are not civil servants ... We alone are responsible for policy." On the greater issue of the nation and its necessary links with culture, here is Brockington in 1939: "The maintenance of the national position needs vigilance and determination. Without public control and progressive public development, sustaining educational and cultural features cannot be extensively broadcast. Without public control listeners in isolated and less populous parts of the country cannot enjoy the privileges which have hitherto been reserved for some of the great centres of population."

I dwell on these early years of radio to show that the principles of public broadcasting have not changed and, despite our very different technical environment, are as relevant today as they were on the eve of the Second World War. Brockington expressed them as well as anyone could. Free of equivocation, he presents a clear vision with the voice of common sense. The key ideas are freedom of opinion, accessibility, cultural development and its connection with the emerging nation, and independence from party-political and plutocratic control alike.

Before we fast-forward to the present age of rapidly changing technology, we should notice that Brockington's departure from the CBC in October 1939 coincided with the onset of Alan Plaunt's fatal illness, from which he was to die in 1941 at the age of thirty-seven. The departing chairman (unaware of Plaunt's illness) recommended the young man as his successor: "If I were to assess the contribution made by individuals to national radio, I would place his constant and untiring effort easily first." It was not long, however, before Plaunt resigned. On the eve of war he had had differences with Gladstone Murray.

Younger Canadians would do well to consider the enduring contribution to public broadcasting made by Alan Plaunt in his young life. It was not, however, his youth that made Plaunt's achievement extraordinary. Mozart, we recall, took a cynical view of people who expressed amazement at the young prodigy's performance. None of them, he said, could do what he did even if they lived to be ninety!

In the years between the end of the Second World War and the launching of television broadcasting, the CBC made a contribution to Canadian culture and self-awareness that was unmatched by that of any other public agency of the crown. The stage series under Andrew Allan gave many writers experience and steady work; performing artists of all kinds began to earn a modest living. The program CBC *Anthology* took the place of a national literary journal; it gave many authors now internationally known early exposure. In city apartments, in small towns, in scattered farms and camps, in cars and trucks, CBC Radio quickly became a comfort to be relied on and enjoyed at all levels. At times it could bring the whole country into one community of listeners – for example, *Hockey Night in Canada* and above all the *National News*. Broadcasters like Lorne Greene, Norman de Poe, Matthew Halton, and Brockington himself became national figures during the Second World War.

In music, too, CBC Radio played a vital part in developing and nurturing talent at the production end and appreciation at the listening end.

The pursuit of excellence discovered a body of talent and a boldness of conception that carried over to the television age. The first eighteen plays broadcast by *General Motors Theatre* included fifteen by Canadians. From 1953 to 1962, when it was replaced by *Bonanza,* the show featured Canadian writers, producers, and performers.

What we have discussed so far has been the second, or radio, stage of our Canadian story. We have now to look to the third stage, in which we engage with the whole world from our home base. We have seen the synergy of holding to national goals with a strong broadcasting system dedicated to cultural development and how the clear vision and strong advocacy of a few Canadians showed us the way forward. We have finally to consider how the principles and policies enunciated by the leaders of this movement can be embodied in our future advances as we seek to establish our own visible address in the global village.

The original aims of Canadian broadcasting were largely defeated as the flood of slick American programming overwhelmed homegrown production not only because more money had been spent on it than Canadians could afford, but because it had already recovered its costs plus a profit in the US and could be offered at prices Canadian producers could not refuse. Canada, in this third stage, had obligingly built a gleaming delivery system for American culture and entertainment.

This process was given a name by other nations suffering in similar ways. The name is "Canadianization." We were, and are, not proud to have our country become, literally, a byword for cultural defeat.

Fast-forward. We are again in a severe recession, again in hard times. The homeless camp in our urban streets; the armies of unemployed line up for handouts. Social services are almost overwhelmed. Though the hunger and poverty are not so severe as they were in the Great Depression, though the safety net of social security breaks the fall of many victims, this time it seems more difficult than ever before to confront the stresses and dangers together as a united, dignified, and relatively independent country. A central doctrine of American culture has invaded the minds of Canadians and our political leaders: the ideology of the bottom line. In the Great Depression, when so many were starving, somehow the money and grassroots support was found for Canadian cultural development and its most effective medium: public broadcasting.

Above all, in the early days of public broadcasting in Canada, the principles at stake seemed clearly understood and vigorously acted upon.

This time the country is in disarray and disunity, obsessed with constitutional and political questions. We seem unable to get it together. Yet increasingly it becomes obvious that these problems and difficulties are largely cultural.

Can we look at the whole matter in a more hopeful way? As Walt Kelly's famous cartoon character Pogo sees it: "We are confronted by overwhelming possibilities." Pogo also has said, "From here on down it's uphill all the way."

The communications technology that for years we hoped to control by regulation has now left the earth altogether. First the satellites made possible the transnational mega-corporations and sky channels, which are beyond the reach of any sort of control. Now direct broadcast satellites from space can beam at us whatever they like, which inevitably will be news and entertainment with an American accent. What every nation now has to confront is the subversion for profit of television – the socially most useful technology for disseminating information, education, and culture in democracies – on the false premise that it is for freedom.

The television networks, as everyone knows, are no longer as profitable as they once were and are losing audiences at a great rate. One recent survey shows that most of us no longer watch TV the way we used to; the audience for videos is now bigger than that for cable. Advertisers are worried. But there is a plus side to it. What it means is that the individual viewer is finally taking an active interest in what he or she sees. When we remember that a video has to be rented and returned – in other words it involves active effort – we have some idea of the degree to which viewers are disillusioned with the so-called wasteland of the idiot box.

There is also a plus side to these new technologies, like direct broadcast satellites, tied to digital compression, fibre optics, and revitalized telephone and computer networks. We, too, can and should get into that particular act, using it for purposes that all can agree on, the defence of Canada through cultural development, that we may survive as a state and as a national community by conserving our cultural integrity and distinctiveness. There was a time, not so long ago, when such engineering was developed and exploited first by the public sector. The demand for cultural sovereignty, to be masters in the house of our spirit, reflects anxieties that are now all but universal. All national cultures tend to show a certain built-in defensiveness in the forms of conservatism and xenophobia. It may be that racial bigotries and jokes are part of this defensiveness, a kind of fence building or marking of psychic territory. The paradox of culture is that like a great tree: It is rooted and nourished in a particular soil yet spreads its branches into the universal air, from which it also draws nutrients. But trade and communications are now almost universal, the great corporations are transnational, and the signals of news and commerce are lightning flashes from the stratosphere. In our new world such lightning can strike and kill one's own tree.

Those lightnings and comets at present strike in the form of denatured productions from multinational broadcasters whose object is to sell goods and services. There is nothing wrong with that – it's part of life – but it has to be balanced by less self-interested communication.

We have to understand that these seemingly immaterial matters are as real as the ground we walk upon. The Irish poet W.B. Yeats put it like this:

Civilization is hooped together, brought
Under a rule, under the semblance of peace
By manifold illusion; but man's life is thought

There must be room for that life of thought, as for the images of which we construct our community and society and for the knowledge and discovery and imagination that amount to civilization. We need to be able to find that life of thought within our own culture. We should not allow ourselves to be distracted by the chatter of advertising.

There are urgent reasons why we and the governments we elect should rediscover the principles of public broadcasting. There is a crisis in education, a crisis in literacy, a crisis in training for jobs. Public broadcasting is the most powerful medium to deliver effective remedies. There is a cultural crisis. Public broadcasting can once more lead a cultural renewal, a multicultural regeneration. There is a crisis of nationalism. Public broadcasting can display the rituals by which we create and share our identities. There can be no isolation of culture or nation. The two are one.

There's no safe place, no Himalayan refuge or Shangri-la, where a culture can immure itself in cloistered and fugitive virtue. We have seen in the Soviet bloc how the ruthless idealism that sought to create heaven made for itself a hell on earth. In a single generation, as we saw, Shangri-la became Albania, a country whose citizens abandoned it in despair; Utopia became Vietnam, casting its children on the waters.

It seems that whatever we do in cultural development we should, and indeed must, do together with other cultures, other nations. In a time when the costs of transnational communication are as high as the satellites themselves, we Canadians not only can do what the sky barons and skypans and skycoons have done – collaborate with other nations on a massive scale – but can outdo them in imaginative uses of the new technologies. Only by joining and trying to lead the crowd, the satellite set, can we assure our solitude, our unique way of becoming what we are and what we ought to be. That is what Plaunt and his devoted colleagues did in more difficult times two generations ago.

Deep in our collective memories is the notion that plurality of languages and cultures is nothing less than babel, a divine curse on human pride. Yet when we look at the biological world, what we see is an extraordinary multiplication of living forms, of genera and species and mutants pullulating and seething and adapting to myriad ecological niches. It seems a cruel and a wasteful world, the food chain in which species preys on species, devours its own young and its own mates. Yet without this miraculous propensity of life to differentiate into infinite variety, it could never have evolved or have generated the creatures that survive in every sort of environment. Even on the glaciers of high mountains one finds the humble algae and their predators. Even in the ocean abyss, where the sun never penetrates, life has found the way, taking its energy from the earth's own internal fires. Without differentiation the earth would be naked and sterile. We could do without the black fly, we could do without the mosquito and the gypsy moth caterpillar, but we're stuck with them, and maybe for the best.

It is not so different with human cultures. Variety of cultures is the most striking fact in ethnology. Never static, cultures grow and change, adapting to new environments and technologies.

The tendency of systems, of machines, of rationality is toward uniformity and a kind of static order. The tendency of cultures is to grow and differentiate and boil over. In a world whose communications increasingly dissolve borders and differences, it is vital that room should be made for national and local cultures to survive and develop. It is natural that Quebecers would be deeply occupied with this problem.

There's a relation between culture and communication, as there is between political economy and communication. But human society is not merely a creation of communication. James A. Carey in his book *A Cultural Approach to Communication* suggests that a narrow view of communication as transmission or transportation is a legacy of nineteenth-century imperialism. Instead of seeing communication as transmission, Carey offers what he calls a ritual view, a process through which a shared culture is created, modified, and transformed. Here, as I've suggested, is a human use for television.

In Parliament the Standing Committee on Communications and Culture has submitted its first report. And in all modesty I can't help noticing that it's recommendations and arguments are more or less those that I offered myself in my book *The Cultural Connection,* written in the mid-1970s. After fifteen years a committee of eight members of Parliament finally agrees with me. Not bad at all for an aging mandarin.

So it's natural that I should be happy with the report in almost every respect. The title is "The Ties That Bind." The committee concludes that "Culture and communications are fundamental investments that will help to achieve renewal of our sense of pride and unity as a nation. We sincerely believe that, in both resolving the constitutional crisis which now confronts us and fulfilling the distinctive constitutional promise that lies before us, culture and communications will truly prove to be the ties that bind."

It's promising that the difficulties with Quebec nationalism have at last been recognized as cultural ones. And as I suggested earlier, the CBC long ago began the task of developing cultural sovereignty in both Canadian language groups and still offers the best hope for continuing the work. But even if Quebec chooses political independence, it will still have to collaborate to conserve and develop its culture – not only with English-speaking Canada, but with other countries facing similar challenges.

The committee is also to be commended for not being content with pious verbiage, long the curse of any deliberation on culture. Recommendation No. 5 reads: "As an investment in the future of our Canadian society and in support of the growth potential of cultural industries, both domestically and internationally, the Government of Canada target an increase in its current budget investments in culture and communications in the order of 5 per cent annually over the next five years." No. 6 asks "That the Government of Canada initiate a comprehensive strategy of incentives to encourage and motivate high levels of philanthropy and voluntarism in support of cultural activities in Canada." Other recommendations are to strengthen the Canada Council, compensate artists, improve Canadian film distribution, provide the CBC with a stable and predictable five-year funding program revolving annually, and take measures to haul Radio-Canada International out of the slough of despond.

All this is admirable and a step forward in clarity and courage. In the matter of public broadcasting it brings us almost to the original principles on which our Canadian broadcasting system is founded: freedom of opinion, accessibility, cultural development and its connection with the emerging nation, and independence from party-political and plutocratic control alike.

My only cavil, as usual, is that the recommendations don't go quite far enough. They don't take account of the heavy expense that is going to be imposed by the need to compete with the sky barons and the challenge of Direct Broadcasting Satellites, and the consequent need to collaborate with other countries in similar straits. And by the way, when it comes to collaboration, we should certainly not go into a huddle with the neighbourhood strongboy and try to work out a bilateral deal, in which we would surely be worsted. That is not the table on which to place culture. We should go where others share our anxieties and aspirations.

One more thing. If we are to survive at all, we are going to have to treat the matter as seriously as we would a material threat to our security. We are going to have to spend the kind of money we would not grudge if some enemy were bombarding our cities. There is no cultural defence against direct satellite broadcasts. The only defence is to attack, as it were, by putting up our own satellites in alliance with friends and fellow broadcasters and by generating our own excellent productions.

More than ever before, our survival depends on being able to compete with our trade partners in education, information, research, and cultural development. At present we are losing our competitive edge. Singapore, for example, a tiny country that only yesterday was Third World, spends four times as much as we do per capita on education. They are also spending very heavily on culture, with the excuse that it will be good for tourism – but here they are missing the point. They spend a lot more per capita than we do on research and development, which is, of course, another example of the competition we are facing in the global market.

But I have to say that the Standing Committee on Communications and Culture has given an excellent example of how the dangers and difficulties may be seized as opportunities. At last a group of parliamentarians have understood the kind of world we're living in, the poet's world of shadows, of manifold illusion, which nevertheless is real and palpable, a world where ideas and images, values and aspirations are as potent as substantial things. Only by developing the mind and imagination of Canadians can we survive with influence over our life and community. Only by that influence can we come together, even if only in the old way we know so well, the way of agreeing to differ, of live and let live.

Only one thing remains. We have to act. The chairpersons of the standing committee – Conservative, Liberal, nationalist – have work before them. Bud Bird, Sheila Finestone, and Jean-Pierre Hogue have to rise from their chairs and get on the road across Canada with their NDP committee colleagues. First they have to talk to their caucuses, to teach them, if necessary, the ABCs of survival in the information age, to secure their enthusiastic support for strong action. In the provinces they have to win support from the governments and drum up grassroots support for cultural development through public broadcasting the way Alan Plaunt and Graham Spry did in the 1930s.

There is work, above all, for the Government of Canada. We have seen that in this age no one can go it alone: Canada must go to the arenas where we have friends and collaborators. First to the Organization for Economic Cooperation and Development (OECD), a body that includes the Europeans as well as the US and Japan, because we need a lot more first-rate analysis of cultural and broadcasting issues, and the OECD has the human and financial resources to provide it. Next, to signatories of the General Agreement on Tariffs and Trade (GATT), among whom we have so many friends, to make strong representations that the cultural and service matters be tabled and agreements reached that will guarantee everyone a place at the cultural feast. And finally to the United Nations Educational, Scientific, and Cultural Organization (UNESCO), where Canada chairs the powerful executive committee. There is urgent need to discuss and agree on measures to develop and distribute the images of our cultures. Here again, the Government of Canada should instruct our representatives that the matter is urgent, not just something to be put on a list and dropped in exchange for free importation of canaries. We need world services fully funded by international institutions governed by universally agreed rules.

I am calling for action backed by faith. In conclusion, let me tell a story. There's a Hassidic tale of a rabbi to whom God showed the burning pit, full of fire and hideous demons, stinking of brimstone and smoke. God told the rabbi to jump in, and such was his faith (the story says) that when he was launched in mid-air, the demons turned into beautiful angels, the stench of brimstone became a sweet perfume of roses, the fire turned into delicate air that let him down gently on a grassy bank. You'd never get *me* to jump, yet I see the point of the story, which is that if you believe that good must prevail, maybe it will. Maybe we *will* survive.

BERNARD OSTRY has had a long and distinguished public service career in the areas of culture and communications, including serving in Ottawa as chief consultant to the Canadian Radio and Television Commission; assistant undersecretary of state, deputy minister of communications, and CEO of the National Museums of Canada Corporation; then in Ontario as deputy minister of industry, industry and trade, citizenship and culture, and chairman and CEO of TVOntario. He is the author or coauthor of four books, served as chair of the Board of Directors of the Marshall McLuhan Centre on Global Communications from 1990 to 1999, and remains associated with a number of boards, including serving as chair of the Advisory Circle of the Writers' Trust of Canada, as a member of the Board of Governors of the Shaw Festival, which he formerly chaired, and as the vice-chair of the Board of Directors of the National Ballet School of Canada.

Mr Ostry is an Officer of the Order of Canada. He has received the 125th Anniversary of Canadian Confederation Commemorative Medal and honorary degrees from three Canadian universities.

Appendix

Introductory remarks made by the Honourable Brooke Claxton, member of the Board of Governors of Carleton University, on the evening of the first Alan B. Plaunt Lecture, 30 January 1958

These lectures have been established as a memorial of Alan B. Plaunt: His life was cut short by illness in September 1941 when he was thirty-seven years of age. For all his adult years, he devoted a large part of his talents, his energy, and his private means to his concept of what Canada was and his vision of what it might become. More than almost anyone else, he had to do with the birth of the Canadian Broadcasting Corporation and the formation of its character as a great source of information and entertainment serving the Canadian people in the cause of national unity and understanding.

But Alan Plaunt would be the last person to make such a claim. What he would like is that other young Canadians might be inspired by faith in Canada to a brave adventure against great odds and, by persistence and persuasion, to win a worthy fight for his native land.

Alan Plaunt was born here in Ottawa in 1904. More than a hundred years ago, Xavier Plante, Alan's great-grandfather, came from the Island of Orleans to settle in Renfrew. There he married Janet McLean, and story has it that she spoke only Gaelic, whereas her husband spoke only French. Alan was the son of François Xavier Plaunt and Mary Butterworth, whose forebears had come to Ottawa from Nova Scotia. Alan was educated at Ottawa public schools and St Andrew's College,

Aurora, as well as at University College, Toronto, where he took his BA in 1927. From there he went to Christ Church, Oxford, receiving his BA in honours history in 1929.

Many Canadians returning to Canada from service or study abroad see their country with a fresh vision of its greatness and a new recognition of the immensity of its opportunities. Alan Plaunt came home from Oxford with a broader understanding of his country and a real sense of dedication. He intended to "do something about it."

Soon after his return to Ottawa in 1929, he met Graham Spry, who was then secretary of the Association of Canadian Clubs, itself at the time a forceful factor in the creation of national sentiment. A royal commission with Sir John Aird, president of the Canadian Bank of Commerce, as chairman had reported in favour of such a system in 1929. Graham Spry and Alan Plaunt took the lead in organizing the Canadian Radio League, which they set up to secure the implementation of the Aird report. They believed this to be in the interest of a united country – in fact, essential – if Canada was to survive against the invasion of the unremitting sound waves that kept rolling in across the border.

Following the establishment of the Radio League in 1930, the government of the day was approached and its interest aroused. The federal government's jurisdiction over broadcasting having been questioned by several provinces, the constitutional question came before the Supreme Court and the Privy Council in London in 1931. I represented the league at both these hearings. Once the jurisdiction of the federal government had been confirmed, the government set up a parliamentary committee. By this time, the Radio League had won the support of many national organizations, and its representations were backed by mobilized public opinion along nonpolitical lines to a greater degree than any movement known to me since Confederation. The league was represented at the meetings of the parliamentary committee. The bill to set up the Canadian Radio Broadcasting Commission passed Parliament without a dissenting voice.

When Spry entered actively into politics in 1934, Alan Plaunt took his place as chairman of the Radio League and carried on the fight to get Canadian broadcasting set up on sound national lines. With the change of government in 1935, a new parliamentary committee had been set up. The league renewed and pressed its representations, and in 1936 the new government introduced a new bill to set up the Canadian Broadcasting Corporation along the lines persistently advocated by the Canadian Radio League.

The part taken by the league was recognized when Spry, Plaunt, and I came to have a good deal to do with drafting the act setting up the CBC and its bylaws and regulations. Alan Plaunt had earned his place as one of the original governors of the Canadian Broadcasting Corporation. To its work he gave almost his whole time, and he had a major influence in shaping the CBC as a great instrument of public service.

His work in radio was paralleled in numerous other activities. Always interested in painting, writing, and international affairs, he helped a number of young workers in these fields. Very few people realized how much he was doing. He was also one of those who, through the 1920s and 1930s, worked through numerous agencies to gain for Canada recognition of the place gained originally by the Canadian Corps. The story of the twenty years between 1919 and 1939 in the fight to make Canada a nation must someday be told.

From 1932 to 1934 Alan Plaunt and Graham Spry owned and published the *Farmers' Sun*, a farm weekly that had been established by Goldwin Smith in the 1890s. During the same period, he was connected with the New Canada Movement, enlisting young men and women in rural areas in an active campaign for a more enlightened interest in problems affecting farm living and public life. Through this, a number of progressive young Canadians learned their lesson in public service as first steps to the prominence they have since achieved.

Alan Plaunt had the enduring fibre and fabric of character as well as the warm heart of friendship. In 1940 he resigned from the Canadian Broadcasting Corporation because he felt that it was slipping from its brave new beginnings. The report of the parliamentary committee in 1942 vindicated his action and helped to set the CBC back on the course he had charted five years before. Alan Plaunt had died in September 1941.

Upon Alan's death, L.W. Brockington, QC, who was the original chairman of the Board of Governors of the Canadian Broadcasting Corporation, gave the press a statement from which the following is taken:

I consider it one of the great privileges of my life to have been associated with him in public service and private friendship. No man I have ever known was more anxious to do something for his country. He returned to Canada from Oxford with a determination to serve his fellow citizens. In his opinion, no field of public endeavour presented larger opportunity for quiet, useful labour than the development of broadcasting as a public service ... When the history of national broadcasting is written, Alan Plaunt's name will be honoured above all others ... The building of the chain of radio stations which the Canadian people today take for granted was his work.

The achievement of Alan Plaunt, Graham Spry, and the others associated with them in bringing into being the CBC and a nationwide system of public service broadcasting was one of the most remarkable accomplishments ever to take place in our country. They had to cure ignorance, overcome apathy, arouse support, and meet and master interested, organized, and unfair opposition.

It is not easy to explain the reasons for this success. Partly it was due to the climate of the country, the sense of manifest growth and unfolding development that was stirring Canadians in every aspect of public service and private life. The pulse of Canadian national sentiment beat steady and strong. Spry and Plaunt showed how broadcasting could be a great bond of national strength and unity. The secret of Alan Plaunt's success was that he sought nothing for himself. What he wanted was in the interest of his country. He made no speeches, gave few interviews, circulated no photographs, but wherever he went, he lit a spark that became fanned into a flame of unselfish action.

The Alan B. Plaunt Lectures were established in his memory by his widow, now Mrs H.A. Dyde of Edmonton. It is particularly appropriate that the lectures should be given at Carleton University, which is rooted in the Ottawa Valley. But Carleton is also located in the nation's capital and has the outlook and the opportunities that result from that fact. Carleton is the kind of young and forward-looking institution to which Alan would have given all possible help.

One can think of no more fitting memorial to Alan Plaunt's life and work as a young Canadian for his country than a lectureship at Carleton University for these same purposes for which Alan Plaunt had worked so hard and with such remarkable success.